# AMERICAN ORCHESTRAL MUSIC

## a performance catalog

by

## RICHARD KOSHGARIAN

The Scarecrow Press, Inc.
Metuchen, N.J., & London
1992

British Library Cataloguing-in-Publication data available

Library of Congress Cataloging-in-Publication Data

Koshgarian, Richard, 1955-
    American orchestral music : a performance catalog / by Richard
Koshgarian.
        p.    cm.
    Includes bibliographical references.
    ISBN 0-8108-2632-1 (acid-free paper)
    1. Orchestral music--Bibliography.   2. Music--United States--
Bibliography.   I. Title.
ML128.05k67  1992
016.784'0973--dc20                                          92-35275

To my wife, Bridget, whose support, assistance and ideas were a constant source of inspiration.

# TABLE OF CONTENTS

## PREFACE

Throughout the latter half of this century, American orchestras have placed increasing emphasis on performing compositions written by American composers. This emphasis has created a demand for a comprehensive performance catalog of American orchestral compositions. It is the purpose of this catalog to provide conductors, music directors, managers, and orchestra librarians with a practical and accessible source to meet that demand.

The catalog represents American composers who were born within the last 100 years. The repertoire listed consists of works for orchestra, concertos, orchestral works with chorus, orchestral works with vocal solo(s), and chamber orchestral works. As the project progressed, I realized that defining "orchestral music" was not a simple task, mainly due to the continually changing state of both the orchestra and its music in the latter part of this century (more than several composers informed me that the computer is the orchestra of today. This presented a stimulating issue over which to ponder, but I eventually acquiesced to the "accepted tradition" of orchestral music in the final compilation).

Operas, staged works, film scores and ballets are generally not included, unless the composer personally sanctioned a concert performance of such a work.

My original intent was to include only those works that are published. After direct contact with over 700 composers, however, I realized that this would be a serious error, because a substantial number of them maintain direct control over the performance rights of their orchestral works. In the final analysis, I realized that excluding unpublished works would be prejudicial and would undermine the purpose of this project.

Finally, I must acknowledge that the catalog is by no means exhaustive, and that its imminent obsolescence is testimony to the remarkable productivity of American composers, both past and present.

## GUIDE TO USING THE CATALOG

This catalog provides basic information about each work listed: title, date of composition, duration, instrumentation, and where the performance materials are published. It is organized alphabetically by composer, and chronologically within each composer's listing. In cases where more than one work was composed in a given year, the works are listed either by opus number or alphabetically.

The instrumentations listed follow the standard format for orchestral compositions: soloists; chorus; woodwinds; brass; percussion; harp; keyboard instruments; miscellaneous instruments (i.e., guitar, accordion, banjo, etc.); strings; electronic equipment. If the instrumentation of a work cannot be adapted to the format, it is given by listing individual instruments.

Combinations of abbreviations that are listed on page xi are used to indicate instruments of the orchestra with compound names. Thus *cbsn* denotes *contrabassoon*, *b tpt* indicates *bass trumpet*, and *ca* indicates *contra alto* or *contralto*. When a registral abbreviation (s, a, t, bar, b) appears before the instrumentation, it refers to a vocal part. When it appears after the listing of the woodwind section, it will refer to saxophones.

*Sample Entry*

solo s (or t); satb cho; 3=3*3+3; 4331;     15'
timp+3, hp, pf/cel, str (12-10-8-6-4)        GS

The above work is scored for solo soprano or tenor voice (the composer has indicated that either voice would suffice), four-part chorus consisting of sopranos, altos, tenors and basses, 3 flutists (with both piccolo and alto flute needed), 3 oboists (with English horn needed), 3 clarinettists (with piccolo clarinet in E-flat needed), 3 bassoons, 4 French horns, 3 trumpets, 3 trombones, 1 tuba, 1 timpanist, plus 3 additional percussionists, 1 harp, 1 keyboard player doubling on piano and celesta, and a string section of 12 first violins, 10 second violins, 8 violas, 6 cellos, and 4 double basses. In instances where the composer has not made a distinction between first and second violins, only four numbers are used. If there is no indication for number of strings, discretion is left to the conductor.

It is important to note that the symbols used to indicate auxiliary instruments mean only that the particular instrument is needed, and may be used by itself or in a doubling capacity. Whenever more than one of an auxiliary instrument is needed, a parenthetical indication immediately follows the number of players needed. Hence 3(2picc) means that 3 flute players are needed, two of whom are required to play piccolo.

Durations are listed to the right of the title of the work. If the duration for a work was unavailable, the "NA" code (not available) is used. When the duration is indeterminate, the "var" code (variable) is used.

The capital letter publisher code following the instrumentation denotes who publishes the performance materials. Appendix E lists these abbreviations with the publishers' names and addresses. Compositions followed by the "MS" code (manuscript) may be obtained directly from the composer. Addresses and telephone numbers of composers are listed in Appendix F.

# LIST OF ABBREVIATIONS

| | | | |
|---|---|---|---|
| a | alto | mar | marimba |
| acc | accordion | mez | mezzo-soprano |
| amp | amplified | MS | manuscript |
| | | | |
| b | bass | NA | not available |
| bar | baritone | narr | narrator |
| bd | bass drum | | |
| bj | banjo | ob | oboe |
| br | brass | ob d'am | oboe d'amore |
| bsn | bassoon | opt | optional |
| | | orch | orchestra |
| c | contra | orch'd | orchestrated |
| cel | celesta | org | organ |
| cho | choir/chorus | | |
| cl | clarinet | perc | percussion |
| cnt | cornet | pf | piano |
| | | picc | piccolo |
| db | double bass | | |
| dmst | drumset | qnt | quintet |
| | | qt | quartet |
| eh | English horn | | |
| elec | electric | rec | recorder |
| ens | ensemble | rev | revised |
| euph | euphonium | | |
| | | s | soprano |
| fl | flute | sax | saxophone |
| flu hn | flugel horn | str | strings |
| | | synth | synthesizer |
| glock | glockenspiel | | |
| gtr | guitar | t | tenor |
| | | tba | tuba |
| hca | harmonica | tbn | trombone |
| hklph | heckelphone | timp | timpani |
| hn | French horn | tpt | trumpet |
| hp | harp | | |
| hpsd | harpsichord | uke | ukelele |
| | | unis | unison |
| instr | instruments | | |
| | | v | voice |
| kybd | keyboard | var | variable |
| | | vc | violoncello |
| mand | mandolin | vib | vibraphone |

| vla | viola |
| vln | violin |
| vv | voices |
| ww | woodwind(s) |
| xyl | xylophone |

# LIST OF SYMBOLS

\*       use of primary auxiliary instruments in
        woodwind section
        (piccolo, English horn, bass clarinet,
        contrabassoon)

+       use of secondary auxiliary instruments in
        woodwind section
        (alto flute, piccolo clarinet in E-flat)

=       both primary and secondary auxiliary
        instruments are in use

/       performer doubling between instruments

## ACKNOWLEDGMENTS

From the beginning of this project, there have been many people who were of tremendous help. I wish to express my deepest gratitude to Eero Richmond and Jerome Kitzke (American Music Center), Pat McCarty (Carl Fischer, Inc.), Marcia Goldberg (Magnamusic Baton), Judith Ilika and Tom Broido (Theodore Presser), Deborah Long (American Composers Alliance), and Emily Goode (Broadcast Music, Inc.). Their assistance was simply invaluable.

I also wish to thank Raul Ronson (Seesaw Music) and Bruce Taub (C.F. Peters) for the patience and consideration with which they answered countless inquiries.

Lastly, I must offer my sincerest admiration, respect and gratitude to the hundreds of composers who took an active interest in the project and tolerated my requests for information with support and understanding. In the most literal sense, without them, this project truly would not have been possible.

CATALOG:

ALPHABETICAL LISTING

BY COMPOSER

ADAM, CLAUS    (1917-1983)

Concerto for Cello and Orchestra (1973)        23'
    solo vc; 2*2*2*1; 0100; timp+1, str         GS

Concerto Variations (1976)                      22'
    2222; 2221; timp+3, pf, cel, str            MG


ADAMS, JOHN    (1947-    )

Christian Zeal and Activity (1973)              10'
    narr (on tape); 1011; 0000; hp, str         BH
    N.B.  The narrator tape is to be prepared
    by the performing organization.

Shaker Loops (1978)                             28'
    str                                         AMP

Common Tones in Simple Time (1979)              19'
    3*232; 2200; 2perc, 2pf, str                AMP

Harmonium (1981)                                35'
    satb cho (divisi); 4*33*3*;                 AMP
    44(picc tpt in D)31; timp+4, hp,
    pf/synth, cel, str

Grand Pianola Music (1981-1982)                 30'
    soli 2pf; 3 amp fem vv; 2*22*2; 2221;       AMP
    3perc, str

Harmonielehre (1984-1985)                       40'
    4*3*4*4*; 4432; timp+4, 2hp, pf,            AMP
    cel, str

The Chairman Dances - Foxtrot for
    Orchestra (1985)                            12'
    2*22*2; 4221; timp+3, hp, pf, str           AMP

Short Ride in a Fast Machine (1986)             4'
    4*3*44*; 4431; timp+3, 2synth(opt), str     BH

Tromba lontana (1986)                           4'
    4*220; 4200; 3perc, hp, pf, str             BH

Nixon in China - Arias (1987)

    1. News is a kind of mystery - solo bar    7'
    2. Mr. Premier, Distinguished Guests -
       solo bar                           3'
    3. This is prophetic! - solo s          9'
    4. I am old and I cannot sleep - solo bar  5'

    orch:  2*2*3=0; satb sax; 0330; perc,    BH
    2 elec pf, Yamaha HX synth, str

Fearful Symmetries (1988)                 27'
    2*2*3*1; s,2a,bar sax; 2330; timp,     BH
    synth (Yamaha HX-1 Electone);
    sampler (Roland S-50), str

Eros Piano (1989)                       15'
    solo pf; 2*22*2; 2000; perc,        BH
    synth(opt), str

The Wound Dresser (1989)               19'
    solo bar; 2*22*2; 21*00; timp,       BH
    synth (Yamaha HX-1 Electone with
    opt pedals), str (6-6-4-4-2)


         ADAMS, LESLIE  (1932-    )

A Kiss in Xanadu (1954; rev 1973)      40'
    3*222; 4230; timp+1, hp, pf, cel, str   AA

Piano Concerto (1968)               24'
    solo pf; 23*12; 4231; timp+1, cel, str  ACA

Ode to Life (1977)                  12'
    2222; 4331; timp+3, cel, str      ACA

Meadow Lark - from "Dunbar Songs" (1980)  5'
    solo s (or t); 2222; 4331; perc, str   ACA

Dunbar Songs (1981)                15'
    solo s (or t); 1111; 2000; timp+1,   ACA
    hp, str

Symphony No. 1 (1982)              56'
    3*3*3*3*; 4331; timp+3, hp, cel str   ACA

Prelude to Blake (1985)             6'
    3*222; 4231; timp+1, hp, str     ACA

Righteous Man - cantata (1985)                     25'
   ssaattbb cho; 0121; 2000; timp+1, hp, str   AA

Five Millay Songs (1987)                           15'
   solo mez (or bar); 1111; 2000; timp+1,      ACA
   hp, str

Six Songs on Texts of African - American
   Poets (1987)                                    17'
   solo mez (or bar); 1111; 2000; timp+1,      ACA
   hp, str

Hymn to Freedom (1989)                             10'
   soli s, t, bar; 102*1; a sax; 0121;         ACA
   perc, pf, str


        ADLER, SAMUEL  (1928-      )

Symphony No. 1 (1953)                              27'
   3*3*23*; 4331; timp, hp, str                TP

Toccata for Orchestra (1954)                       12'
   3*3*3*3*; 4331; timp+3, pf, str             AMP

The Feast of Lights (1955)                          4'
   satb cho; 2*222; 2221; timp+1, hp, str      GS

Summer Stock - A Short, Merry
   Overture (1955)                                  5'
   2222; 2230; timp+1, str                     GS

Symphony No. 2 (1957)                              29'
   3*3*3*3*; 4331; timp+1, pf, str             TP

Jubilee - A Fanfare for Orchestra (1958)            8'
   3*3*3*3*; 4331; timp, pf, str               AMP

Rhapsody for Violin and Orchestra (1961)           17'
   solo vln; 3*3*3*3*; 4331; timp+2, str       OXF

Song and Dance for Viola and
   Orchestra (1961)                                13'
   solo vla; 3*222; 2220; timp+2, str          OXF

Vision of Isaiah (1962)                            15'
   satb cho; 2222; 2220; timp+3, str           MS

B'Shaaray - Tefilah (1963)                                60'
    solo b; satb cho; 3*3*3*3*; 4331;                     MS
    timp+2, org, str

Requiescat in Pace (1963)                                 14'
    3*3*3*3*; 4330; timp+1, hp, str                       OXF

The Binding - oratorio (1967)                             55'
    soli 2s, a, t, b; satb cho; 3*3*3*3*;                 OXF
    4331; timp+3; hp, str

Symphony No. 4 "Geometrics" (1967)                        27'
    4*3*3*3*; 4331; timp+3, pf, str                       OXF

City by the Lake (A Portrait of
    Rochester, NY) (1968)                                  7'
    3*222; 2231; timp+1, hp, str                          GS

Lament (1968)                                              5'
    solo bar; 1111; 1100; perc, str                       LDW

A Whole Bunch of Fun - cantata (1969)                     20'
    solo mez (or bar); 3 choruses (2-pt,                  OXF
    3-pt, 4-pt); 3*3*3*3*; 4231; timp+2, str

Concerto for Organ and Orchestra (1970)                   15'
    solo org; 3*3*3*3*; 4331; timp+3, hp, str             CF

Concerto for Orchestra (1971)                             20'
    3*3*3*3*; 4331; timp+4, str                           BH

Sinfonietta for Orchestra (1971)                           7'
    1111; 1111; timp+1, str                               MS

Elegy (1972)                                               8'
    str                                                   TP

Symphony No. 5 "We are the Echoes" (1975)                 22'
    solo mez; 3*3*3*3*; 4331; timp+3, pf, str             BH

Concertino No. 2 (1976)                                   12'
    str                                                   LDW

Concerto for Flute and Orchestra (1977)                   20'
    solo fl; 3*3*3*3*; 4331; timp+3, str                  MS

A Falling of Saints (1977)                                25'
    soli t, bar; satb cho; 3*3*3*3*; 4331;               TCM
    timp+2, hp, str

Joi, Amor and Cortezia - "Seven Dances of
   Joy, Love and Courtliness" for Chamber
   Orchestra (1982)                                    17'
   2*2*22; 2000; 2perc, str                            GS

Concerto for Piano and Orchestra (1983)               22'
   solo pf; 3*222; 4331; timp+1, str                  GS

In Just Spring (1984)                                 8'
   3*3*3*3*; 4331; timp+3, hp, str                    TP

Concerto for Saxophone Quartet and
   Orchestra (1985)                                   22'
   solo sax qt; 3*222; 4331; timp+3, str              MS

Judah's Song of Praise (1985)                         5'
   satb cho; 2222; 0000; perc, str                    GS

Symphony No. 6 (1985)                                 22'
   3*3*3*3*; 4331; timp+3, pf, str                    TP

High Flight (1986)                                    NA
   satb cho; 2020; 0200; perc, str                    GS

Choose Life (1987)                                    35'
   soli mez, t; satb cho; 3*3*3*3*; 4331;             GS
   timp+3, pf, str

Beyond the Land (1988)                                28'
   3*3*3*3*; 4331; timp+3, pf, str                    GAL

The Fixed Desire of the Human Heart (1988)            9'
   3*222; 2220; timp+2, str                           GAL

Any Human to Another - cantata (1989)                 16'
   satb cho; pf, str                                  MS

A Song of Hanukkah (NA)                               4'
   satb cho; 2*222; 2220; timp+1, hp, str             GS

Wisdom Cometh with the Years (NA)                     8'
   satb cho; 1111; 0310; timp, str                    PS


         ADOLPHE, BRUCE   (1955-    )

Out of the Whirlwind (1981)                           25'
   soli mez, t; 3*3*4=3*; 2220; 2perc, hp,            GAL
   pf, db

A Dream of My Parents Dancing (1983)            12'
   1111; 2100; pf, str                          ACA

Night Journey (1986)                            15'
   2220; 4220; perc, hp, str                    ACA

Three Pieces for Kids and Orchestra (1989)      12'
   children's cho; solo fl; 2222; 2211;         ACA
   timp+1 str
   OR:  2222; 2200; str
   N.B.  The individual movements ("Dances",
   "The Virtuoso", and "Variations") are
   available separately from the publisher.


          ADOLPHUS, MILTON   (1913-1988)

Interlude, op. 96 (1953)                          8'
   solo vc; 1121; 1000; str                     ACA

Bitter Suite, op. 98 (1955)                      10'
   0140; 0000; str                              ACA

United Nations Suite, op. 106 (1961)             22'
   222*2*; 2220; timp, str                      ACA


          AITKEN, HUGH   (1924-    )

Aspen Concerto (1978)                             7'
   solo vln; str                                 TP

Rameau Remembered (1980)                         20'
   solo fl; 1201; 0000; str                      TP

In Praise of Ockeghem (1981)                     17'
   str                                          ECS

Concerto for Violin and Orchestra (1984)         21'
   solo vln; 3*3*3*3*; 4231; timp+2, hp, str    TP

Cantata VI (1986)                                20'
   solo bar; 2222; 2000; str                    OXF

Happy Birthday Overture (1988)                    8'
   4*4*4*4*; 6441; timp+3, hp, pf/cel, str      MS

Cantata IX (1989)                                15'
   solo s; 2222; 2200; str                      OXF

ALBERT, STEPHEN    (1941-    )

Bacchae:  A Ceremony in Music (1968)              18'
   solo b; satb cho; 3*3*3=3*; 2a,t,bar sax;      GS
   4332; perc, hp, pf, cel, elec gtr,
   b gtr, str

Wolf Time (1969)                                  20'
   solo s; soli amp fl, amp cl; 1110; 0000;       GS
   6perc, hp, pf, elec hpsd (or synth/kybd
   computer), elec gtr, b gtr, str

Voices Within (1975)                              16'
   3*3*3=3*; a sax; 4331; timp+3, hp, pf, str CF

Riverrun:  Symphony in Four Movements
   (1983-1984)                                    45'
   3=3*3=3*; 4331; timp+2, 2hp, pf, str           GS

Treestone (1983-1984)                             45'
   soli s, t; 1=01*0; 1100; perc, hp, pf,         GS
   str (2-1-1-1)

Flower of the Mountain (1985)                     16'
   solo s; 2222; 2200; perc, hp, pf, str          GS

In Concordiam: Concerto for Violin and
   Orchestra (1986)                               18'
   solo vln; 2=2*2*2*; 2200; timp+3; str          GS

Into Eclipse (1986)                               30'
   solo t; 1*01+0; 1100; perc, hp, pf, str        GS
   OR:  2222*; 4231; perc, hp, pf/cel, str

Anthem of Processionals (1988)                    16'
   3*3*3*2*; 4331; timp+2, hp, pf, str            GS

Distant Hills Coming Nigh (1989)                  25'
   soli s, t; 1111; 1000; pf, str (2-1-1-1)       GS

Concerto for Cello (1990)                         20'
   solo vc; 2222; 2200; perc, hp, pf, str         GS


      ALBRIGHT, WILLIAM    (1944-    )

Masculine/Feminine
   (Part I of "Alliance") (1967)                  10'
   3*3*3*3*; 4331; perc, pf, cel, org, str        JOB

Alliance (1970)                                        30'
  3*3*3*3*; 4331; perc, pf, cel, org, str             JOB

Night Procession (1972)                                12'
  1221; 2000; perc, pf, str                            MS

Gothic Suite (1973)                                    16'
  org, 1-2perc, str                                    UE

Bacchanal (1981)                                       15'
  solo org; 3*3*3*3*; 4431; timp+3, hp,               CFP
  cel, str

Chasm (1985-1989)                                      13'
  3*3*3*3*; 4431; timp+3, hp, pf/cel, str             CFP

Concerto for Harpsichord and Strings (1991)           25'
  solo hpsd; str                                      CFP


            ALEXANDER, ELIZABETH  (1962-1988)

So Many Corners (1987)                                 15'
  solo s; 2*2*3=2; 2200; timp+1, hp, pf,              NOA
  cel, str


            ALEXANDER, JOSEF  (1910-    )

Dialogues Spirituels (1945)                            13'
  satb cho; 3*3*3*3*; 4331; timp+2, hp,               MS
  org, str

Symphony No. 1 (1948)                                  25'
  3*3*3*3*; 4331; timp+3, hp, str                      MS

Dithyrambe (1949)                                      16'
  3*3*3*3*; 4331; timp+3, 2hp, str                     MS

Epitaphs (1953)                                        23'
  3*3*3*3*; 4331; timp+1, pf, str                      CF

Symphony No. 2 (1954)                                  23'
  3*3*3*3*; 4331; timp+3, pf, str                      CF

Canticle of the Night (1955)                           12'
  solo mez (or bar); 3*3*23*; 4331 timp+4,            MS
  hp, str

Concertino for Trumpet and Strings (1959)       8'
    solo tpt; str                               SHA

Symphony No. 3 (1961)                          22'
    3*3*3*3*; 4331; timp+4, hp, str             MS

Duo Concertante (1965)                         25'
    soli tbn, perc; str                         MS

Quiet Music for Strings (1965)                 20'
    str                                         MS

Symphony No. 4 (1968)                          32'
    3*3*3*3*; 4331; timp+3, hp, pf, str         BTN

Salute to the Whole World (1976)               28'
    narr; 3*3*3*3*; 4331; timp+3, hp, str       MS


        ALEXANDER, WILLIAM  (1927-    )

Episodes (In a Winter's Journey) (1983)        12'
    3*23*2; 4331; timp+2, str                   CCP

Music for Two Trumpets and Strings (1984)      10'
    soli 2tpt; str                              MS

Salpinx (1987)                                 10'
    1111; 1000; str                             CCP

Suite for Small Orchestra (1987)               10'
    1111; 1000; str                             CCP

Discourses - Suite for Orchestra (1990)        18'
    2*23*2; 4231; timp+3, str                   MS

Portraits of Friends (1990)                    17'
    2*121; 2110; str                            MS


        ALLANBROOK, DOUGLAS  (1921-    )

Four Orchestral Landscapes
    (Symphony No. 3) (1967)                     24'
    3*3*3*3*; 4331; timp+4, 2hp, cel, str       BH

Symphony No. 5 (1977)                          20'
    solo br qnt; 3*222; 0000; timp+2, str       BH

Serenade (1982)                                      30'
  3*3*3*2; 2100; timp, pf, str                       BH


        AMES, WILLIAM   (1901-      )

Symphony No. 1 (1933)                                20'
  2222; 2221; perc, str                              ACA

Nocturne and Scherzo (1942)                          5'
  soli 2pf; str (no db)                              ACA

Symphony II (1943)                                   30'
  3*3*3*3*; 4331; perc, str                          ACA

Concerto for Piano and Orchestra (1947)             25'
  solo pf; 3*3*3*2; 4330; timp+1, str                ACA

Rhapsody (1947)                                      15'
  solo vln; 3*3*3*3; 4321; timp, str                 ACA

Granite and Cypress (1948)                           20'
  satb cho; 23*04*; 4331; timp+1, hp, str            ACA

Rhapsody II (1950)                                   8'
  3*3*3*3*; 4331; timp+1, str                        ACA

Song for Orchestra (1951)                            4'
  23*3*2; 4330; timp, hp, str                        ACA

Concerto for Clarinet (1956)                         25'
  solo cl; 1111; 1110; timp, str                     ACA

Prologue (1957)                                      15'
  solo timp; str                                     ACA

Prologue (1957)                                      20'
  fl; hn; timp, str                                  ACA

Prelude (1962)                                       2'
  str                                                ACA

Equinox (1967)                                       25'
  3*3*3*3*; 4331; timp+1, str                        ACA

Excursion (1969)                                     20'
  2120; 2231; timp+1, str                            ACA

High Mountain Lake (1970)                            15'
  2*000; 0000; timp, xyl, str                        ACA

Night Noises (1970)                                  20'
  3*3*3*3*; 4331; timp+8, str                    ACA

Suite for Timpani and Strings (1974)                 20'
  solo timp; str                                 ACA

Morning (1976)                                       20'
  2222; 4220; timp+1, str                        ACA

Excursion II (1979)                                  12'
  2222; 2200; timp, str                          ACA


      AMIRKHANIAN, CHARLES  (1945-    )

Egusquiza to Falsetto (1979)                         14'
  4 vv; 1111; 0000; 5perc, str (1-1-1-1),        APP
  tape

His Anxious Hours (Somnisoniferences of
  Johannes Brahms) (1986-1987)                     24'
  vocalist(s); winds, brass and strings;          APP
  perc, pf/kybd, tape (8-60 players)
  N.B.  The work is performed without conductor.


      AMLIN, MARTIN  (1953-    )

Quotations from the "Rubaiyat" (1977)                15'
  solo s; 3*3*00; 2100; 2perc, hp, cel, str      MS

Shadowdance (1982)                                   10'
  3*222; 2120; 2perc, hp, str                    MS


      AMRAM, DAVID  (1930-    )

Autobiography (1959)                                  8'
  str                                            CFP

Shakespearean Concerto (1959)                        22'
  0100; 2000; str                                CFP

The American Bell (1962)                             45'
  narr; 1111; 2111; str                          CFP

A Year in Our Land (1964)                            25'
  soli s, a, t, bar; satb cho; 2222; 2220;       CFP
  timp+2, pf, str

Concerto for Horn and Orchestra (1965)                    12'
   solo hn; 3*3*3*3*; 4331; timp+4, hp,                CFP
   pf, str

Let Us Remember (1965)                                    20'
   solo vv; satb cho; 2222; 4220;                      CFP
   timp+1, str

Three Songs for America (1969)                            9'
   11*1*1; 1000; str (2-1-1-1)                         CFP

Elegy (1970)                                              12'
   solo vln; 22*2*2*; 4331; timp+3, hp, str            CFP

Triple Concerto (1970)                                    25'
   soli: 1111; a,bar sax; 2211; perc, pf, db           CFP
   orch: 2*2*2*2*; 2220; timp+5, hp, cel, str

Concerto for Bassoon and Orchestra (1971)                 22'
   solo bsn; 3*3*3*2; 4331; timp+1, hp, pf,            CFP
   cel, str

Concerto for Violin and Orchestra (1972)                  22'
   solo vln; 3*3*3*3*; 4331; timp+3, str               CFP

The Trail of Beauty (1976)                                25'
   solo mez; solo ob; 21*22; 4231; timp+1,             CFP
   hp, str

En Memoria de Chano Pozo (1977)                           10'
   soli jazz trio:  fl, pf, b gtr; 2222;               CFP
   4231; 4perc, str

Ode to Lord Buckley (1980)                                18'
   solo a sax; 2222; 2221; timp+1, str                 CFP

Honor Song (Song for Sitting Bull) (1983)                 25'
   solo vc; 3*3*3*2; 2220; 4perc, str                  CFP

Across the Wide Missouri (1984)                           10'
   2*2*22; 4231; timp+3, hp, str                       CFP

Fox Hunt (1984)                                           2'
   2222; 4321; 4perc, str                              CFP

Travels (1985)                                            15'
   solo tpt; 2*2*22; 4220; timp+3, str                 CFP

American Dance Suite (1988)                               20'
   2*2*2*2; 2211; 3perc, str                           CFP

Songs for the Soul (Shiray Neshama) (NA)      NA
   2*2*22; 4221; 3perc, str                   CFP


ANDERSON, BETH   (1950-   )

Revelation (1981)                             12'
   1111; 2211; timp+1, hp, str                ACA

Revel (1984)                                  8'
   1111; 2211; perc, hp, str                  ACA


ANDERSON, RUTH   (1928-   )

Fugue (1948)                                  7'
   str                                        ACA

Prelude and Rondo (1956)                      14'
   fl; str                                    ACA

Two Pieces (1957)                             10'
   str                                        ACA

Two Movements (1958)                          6'
   str                                        ACA


ANDERSON, THOMAS JEFFERSON   (1928-   )

Introduction and Allegro (1959)               10'
   2222; 4231; timp+1, str                    ACA

New Dances (1960)                             17'
   2222; 4231; timp+1, pf, str                ACA

Classical Symphony (1961)                     15'
   2222; 4231; timp+1, pf, str                ACA

Six Pieces for Clarinet and Chamber
   Orchestra (1962)                           13'
   solo cl; 2221; 1111; timp+1, hp, str       ACA

Symphony in Three Movements (1964)            15'
   2222; 4231; timp+2, str                    ACA

Squares - An Essay for Orchestra (1965)       10'
   3*222; 4331; timp+2, str                   ACA

Chamber Symphony (1968)                                    14'
    1111; 1110; timp+1, pf, str                           ACA

Intervals - Set VIII (1970-1971)                          42'
    3*3*3*3*; a,t sax; 4331; timp+3, hp, pf,              ACA
    cel, str

In Memoriam - Malcolm X (1974)                            10'
    solo mez; 3*3*3*3*; 4331; timp+3, hp, str             ACA

Horizons '76 (1975)                                       50'
    solo s; 3*3*3*3*; a,t sax; 4331; timp+3,              ACA
    hp, pf/cel, str

Messages - A Creole Fantasy (1979)                        14'
    3*3*3*3*; 4331; timp+3, hp, pf, cel, str              CF

Spirituals (1979)                                         35'
    solo t; solo jazz qt; narr; children's                ACA
    cho; satb cho; 2222; 2200; timp, str

Chamber Concerto (Remembrances) (1988)                    14'
    1011; 1110; dmst, hp, pf, str                         ACA


                ANTHEIL, GEORGE  (1900-1959)

Heroes of Today (1945)                                     7'
    4*3*3*3*; 4331; 4perc, str                            AP

Over the Plains (1945)                                     8'
    3*23*2; 4331; timp+1, hp, str                         GS

Symphony No. 4  "Tragic" (1945-1946)                      25'
    3*3*3*3*; 4331; timp+4, hp, pf, str                   BH

Concerto for Violin and Orchestra (1946)                  27'
    solo vln; 2222; 4220; 3perc, str                      AP

Spectre of the Rose Waltz (1946-1947)                     18'
    213*2; 3221; 3perc, 2pf, str                          AP

Autumn Song, An Andante for Orchestra (1947)              7'
    3*3*3*3*; 4331; timp+2, pf, str                       AP

Symphony No. 5  "Joyous" (1947-1948)                      21'
    3*3*3*3*; 4331; timp+5, pf, str                       AP

McKonkey's Ferry Overture (1948)                           8'
    4*3*3*3*; 4331; timp+1, hp, str                       GS

Serenade (1948) 12'
   str                                                      GS

Serenade II (1949) 18'
   2110; 2110; perc, pf, str             AP

Symphony No. 6 "After Delacroix" (1954) 20'
   3\*3\*3\*3\*; 4331; perc, pf, str         GS

Capitol of the World - Suite in Three
   Movements (1955) 14'
   2222; 4331; timp+1, hp, str        GS

Cabeza de Vaca (1955-1956) 52'
   satb cho; 113\*0; 2220; timp+3, pf,    SHA
   hpsd, str

ANTONIOU, THEODORE (1935-    )

Piano Concerto, op. 16b (1962) 11'
   solo pf; perc, str                 BAR
   N.B. Much divisi in all string parts.

Meli (Sappho), op. 17 (1962) 10'
   solo mez (or bar); 1\*011; 0110; 2perc,    BAR
   gtr, str

Antithesis, op. 18a (1962) 18'
   solo str qt; 1011; 0100; perc, hp, str    BAR

Jeux, op. 22 (1963) 13'
   solo vc; str                       BAR

Micrographies, op. 24 (1964) 15'
   3\*3\*3\*3\*; 6331; timp+5, hp, pf, cel, str    BAR

Kontakion (Romanos the Melode) (1965) 12'
   soli 2s, 2a, t, b; str           BAR

Violin Concerto, op. 28 (1965) 20'
   solo vln; 1111; 1111; 3perc, hp, cel, str   BAR

Op Overture (1966) 15'
   112\*0; 2221; 3perc, 2pf, str, 3 groups of   BAR
   loudspeakers

Kinesis ABCD, op. 31 (1966)                           15'
    two string orchestras                             BAR
    1:   3-3-3-2-1
    2:   3-3-3-2-1

Klima tis apoussias
    (Climate of Absence) (1968)                       10'
    satb cho; 1111; 0000; perc, pf,                   BAR
    str (solo or sect)

Events I (1968-1969)                                  20'
    soli vln, pf; 2*222; 4231; 3perc, hp,             BAR
    hpsd, str

Events II (1969)                                      15'
    4*4*4*4*; 6441; 5perc, hp, pf, str,               BAR
    elec instr

Events III (1969)                                     12'
    1111; 0000; 2perc, pf, str, elec tape,            BAR
    slides

Nenikakamen (1971)                                    40'
    soli mez, bar; narr; satb cho; 33*3*3*;           BAR
    4331; 4perc, hp, pf, str

Protest II (Mixed-Media) (1971)                       15'
    112*0; 1121; perc, amp pf, elec org,              BAR
    str (2-1-0-1)

Chorochronos II (1973)                                17'
    solo bar; narr; 2+12*1; 1110; 2perc, hp,          BAR
    pf/elec org, str (solo or sect)

Die Weisse Rose (1974-1975)                           22'
    solo bar; 2narr; children's cho;                  BAR
    satb cho; 4+3*3*3*; 6442; timp+4, hp,
    pf/Hammond org, str

Fluxus I (1974-1975)                                  16'
    4=3*3*3*; 6441; 4perc, hp,                        BAR
    pf/cel/elec org; str

Fluxus II (1975)                                      18'
    solo pf; 1+1*1*1; 1110; perc,                     BAR
    str (solo or sect)

Circle of Accusation - ballet (1975)                  25'
    2=12*0; 2221; 2perc, pf/elec org,                 BAR
    str (no vln, vla)

Double Concerto (1977)                                    16'
   soli 2perc; 1*12*1; 2211; hp, pf,                BAR
   str (solo or sect)

Circle of Thanatos and Genesis - cantata
   (1977-1978)                                       20'
   solo t; narr; satb cho; 2=23*2; 4231;              BAR
   4perc, hp, pf, str

The GBYSO Music (1982)                                    16'
   3*3*3*3*; 4331; 4perc, hp, pf, str                MG

Prometheus (Aeshylus) - cantata (1983)                    27'
   solo bar; narr; satb cho; 3*3*3*3*; 4331;          MG
   4perc, hp, pf/org, str

Skolion (1986)                                            15'
   3*3*3*3; 4331; 3perc, hp, pf, str                 MG

Paean (1989)                                               9'
   4*4*4*4*; 6431; timp+4, hp, pf, str               MG

Stimmung Der Abwesenheit (NA)                             10'
   med v; 1111: 0000; perc, pf, str                 BAR


APPLEBAUM, ALLYSON BROWN   (1955-    )

Symphony in Two Movements (1988)                          25'
   3*3*3*3*; 4331; timp+2, hp, pf/cel, str           MMB


APPLEBAUM, EDWARD   (1937-    )

The Frieze of Life (1973-1982)                            75'
   soli s, a, t, b; satb cho (16 vv);                MMB
   1=1*1=1; 202(b tpt)0; perc, hp,
   pf/cel/hpsd, str
   N.B. Paintings of Edvard Munch are projected
   onto a screen located behind the performers.

Symphony No. 1 (1980)                                     15'
   4(3picc)4*4=4*; s sax; 5331; timp+2,               HNS
   hp, cel, str

Concert Aria (1981)                                       12'
   solo vc; 2*12=1; s/a/bar sax; 2210;               MMB
   perc, hp, str

Symphony No. 2 (1983)                                        17'
   3=3*3*3*; 4441; timp+3, hp, pf/cel, str                  MMB

Concerto for Viola and Orchestra (1984)                     15'
   solo vla; 2*3*3*3*; 2120; str (0-0-3-1)                  MMB

Piano Concerto - Dreams and Voyages (1985)                  19'
   solo pf; 3*3*3*3*; 4331; timp+3, hp, str                 MMB

The Princess in the Garden (1985)                            6'
   str                                                      MMB

Night Waltz - Guitar Concerto (1987)                        14'
   solo gtr; 2*2*2*2*; 4221; 3perc, hp,                     MMB
   pf/cel, str

The Song of the Sparrows (1987; rev 1991)                   35'
   soli s, t, b; narr; satb cho;                            MMB
   children's cho; 3=3*3*3*; 2rec; 4331;
   timp+5, hp, pf/cel/hpsd(amp), str

Waltz in Two (1989)                                         12'
   narr; 2*22=2; 4221; timp+2, hp, str                     MMB

Symphony No. 3 (1990)                                       18'
   3=3*3*3*; 4331; timp+2, hp, pf/cel, str                 MMB

Landscape of Dreams (Concerto for Violin
   and Orchestra) (1991)                                    16'
   solo vln; 2*22*2*; 4220; timp+2, hp, str                MMB

Variations for Orchestra (NA)                               18'
   3*3*3*4*; 6441; hp, cel, str                            MMB


                APPLETON, JON   (1939-    )

After "Nude Descending a Staircase" (1965)                  13'
   2222; 2240; perc, str                                    MS

The American Songs (1966)                                   12'
   2222; 2240; str                                          MS


                ARGENTO, DOMINICK   (1927-    )

Divertimento for Piano and
   String Orchestra (1955)                                  17'
   solo pf; str                                             BH

Ode to the West Wind (1956)                                28'
  solo s; 3*3*3*3*; 4331; timp+2, hp, str            BH

The Resurrection of Don Juan - suite (1956)                22'
  2*222; 4221; timp+2, hp, str                       BH

Overture - The Boor (1957)                                 6'
  112*1; 2100; perc, pf, str                         BH

Songs About Spring (1960)                                  12'
  solo s; 2202; 2110; timp+2, hp, cel, str           BH

Royal Invitation Suite (Homage to the Queen               23'
  of Tonga) (1964)                                    BH
  1202; 2000; str

Variations for Orchestra
  (The Mask of Night) (1965)                          28'
  solo s; 2*22*2; 4331; timp+3, hp, str               BH

Bravo Mozart!: An Imaginary Biography (1969) 30'
  2*12*0; 1220; 3perc, pf, cel, str                  BH

A Ring of Time - Preludes and Pageants for
  Orchestra and Bells (1972)                          28'
  4*4*4=4*; 4331; timp+2, hp, pf, cel, str            BH

In Praise of Music - Seven Songs for
  Orchestra (1977)                                    30'
  3=3*3*3*; 4331; timp+3, hp, pf/cel, str             BH

Fire Variations - Eight Variations and
  Finale on a Blacksmith's Worksong (1981)            20'
  3*3*3*3; 4331; timp+2, hp, pf/cel, str              BH

Casa Guidi (1983)                                          20'
  solo mez; 3=3*3*2; 4331; timp+2, hp,                BH
  pf, mand, str

Capriccio for Clarinet and Orchestra
  "Rossini in Paris" (1985)                           21'
  solo cl; 3*3*3*3*; 4331; timp+3, hp, str            BH

Le Tombeau d'Edgar Allan Poe (1985)                        16'
  solo s (or t); 3*3*3*3*; 4331; timp+3,              BH
  hp, str
  N.B.  The soloist performs offstage.

Te Deum (1987)                                                40'
    satb cho; 2*2*2*2; 4331; timp+2, hp,                      BH
    cel, str

From the Album of Allegra Harper (NA)                        9'
    2222; 3210; perc, hp(opt), pf, str                       BH


                ARMER, ELINOR   (1939-      )

Pearl (1986)                                                 14'
    2*2*4=2; 4231; 3perc, hp, pf/cel, str                    MS

The Great Instrument of the Geggerets (1988)  16'
    narr; 2*22*2*; 2211; timp+2, pf, str                     MMB


                ATKINSON, CONDIT   (1928-      )

A Musical Trip to the Zoo (1983)                             17'
    narr; 2*2*2*2; 4331; timp+2, str,                        ECS
    film slides

Alexander Evergreen (1984)                                   9'
    narr; 2*2*3*2; 4331; timp+2, hp, str                     ECS

The Dinosaur's Tale (1987)                                   22'
    narr; 2*2*3*2; 4331; timp+3, hp, str                     ECS

A Musical Trick or Treat (1989)                              18'
    3*222; 4331; timp+3, hp, str                             ECS


                AUSTIN, JOHN   (1934-      )

Prelude, Fugue and Chorale (1969)                            14'
    23*3*3*; 2231; str                                       ACA

Triple Play (1976)                                           7'
    2222; 2220; timp, str                                    ACA

The Moon Wears a Wax Moustache (1978)                        14'
    solo s; satb cho; 2222; 2441; 2perc, str   ACA

Requiem (1981)                                               50'
    soli s, a, t, b; 1=1*1*1*; a sax;                        ACA
    111(b tbn)0; perc, str (2-1-1-0)

Eight Changes on "Amazing Grace" (1988)                      12'
    satb cho; 22*22; 2221; timp, str                         ACA

AUSTIN, LARRY (1930-   )

The Ordinary of the Mass (1959)                     30'
    satb cho; 1111; 2000; str                       ACA

Improvisations for Orchestra and
    Jazz Soloists (1961)                            15'
    soli cl, a sax, t sax, bar sax, tpt,            MJQ
    dmst, db; 2=22=2; 4331; timp+4, pf/cel, str

Open Style for Orchestra with
    Piano Soloist (1965)                            7'
    solo pf; 3*23*2; 4331; 4perc, str               MJQ

Phantasmagoria:  Fantasies on Ives'
    "Universe Symphony" (1977; rev 1981)            22'
    narr; 3=3*4*3*; 4441; 4perc, hp, pf/cel,        ACA
    dig synth, str, tape

Sinfonia Concertante:  A Mozartean
    Episode (1986)                                  17'
    1111; 1100; timp, hp, pf, str, tape             ACA
    N.B. Computer music narrative on tape.


AVERITT, WILLIAM (1948-   )

Elegy for Flute, Percussion and
    Strings (1977)                                  15'
    solo fl; 4perc, str                             DRN

Gentle, Into That Night (1988)                      12'
    2*22*2; 4331; timp+2, hp, str                   MMB

Inventions (1991)                                   17'
    2*222; 4230; 3perc, str                         MS

Palmer House Dream Dances (1991)                    15'
    2*2*2*2; 4331; timp+2, str                      MS


AVSHALOMOV, AARON (1894-1965)

Concerto in G for Piano and
    Orchestra (1935)                                32'
    solo pf; 3*222; 4231; 3perc, hp,                ACA
    cel, str

Concerto in D for Violin and
  Orchestra (1936)                                          30'
  solo vln; 2221; 2200; timp+1, hp,                        ACA
  cel, str

Symphony No. 1 in C minor (1939)                           36'
  3*3*22; 4331; timp+4, hp, pf, str                       ACA

Feng-Huang - ballet (1945)                                 80'
  soli 3vv; satb cho; 2111; 2000; timp+1,                 ACA
  hp, cel, str

Concerto for Flute and Orchestra (1946)                    15'
  solo fl; 1222; 2231; timp+1, hp, str                   ACA

Symphony No. 2 in E Minor (1949)                           34'
  3*3*3*3*; 4331; timp+4, hp, pf, cel, str               ACA

Symphony No. 3 in B Minor (1953)                           26'
  3*3*3*3*; 4331; timp+1, hp, pf/cel, str                ACA


      AVSHALOMOV, JACOB DAVID   (1919-     )

The Taking of T'ung Kuan (1943)                             8'
  3*23*2; 4331; timp+3, str                              ACA

Slow Dance (1945)                                           6'
  1121; 2100; timp+1, hp, pf, str                        MER

Sinfonietta (1946)                                         17'
  2*2*3*1; 2210; timp+1, pf, str                         ACA

Evocations (1947)                                          17'
  solo cl; fl/picc; 3perc, pf, str                       ACA

How Long, O Lord (1948)                                    15'
  solo a; satb cho; 2222; 2211; timp+1, str              MS

Cues from the Little Clay Cart (1953)                      12'
  2*22*0; 0000; 2perc, hp, bj, str                       ACA

Phases of the Great Land (1958)                            16'
  22*22; 4331; perc, pf, mand, str                       HG

Symphony "The Oregon" (1962)                               27'
  3*3*3*3*; 4331; hp, str                                ACA

City Upon a Hill (1964)                             22'
   narr; satb cho; 2222; 4231; 3perc,              ACA
   liberty bell, str

Thirteen Clocks (1973)                              23'
   2narr; 3*222; 4330; perc, hp, str                ACA

Raptures for Orchestra on Madrigals of
   Gesualdo (1975)                                  22'
   5-pt madrigal cho; 2223*; 4230; str              ACA

Open Sesame! (1985)                                 20'
   2222; 4330; perc, pf, str                        ACA

Glorious Th' Assembled Fires (1990)                 37'
   solo boy s; satb cho; 3*3*3*3*; 4231;            ACA
   4perc, str

BABBITT, MILTON    (1916-    )

From Three Theatrical Songs
  (orch'd by G. Schuller) (1946)        NA
  solo v; 2*121; 2111; perc, dmst,    AMP
  pf/cel, str

Composition for Twelve Instruments (1948)   7'
  1111; 1100; cel, str (1-1-1-1)       AMP

Relata I (1965)                   18'
  3*3*3*3*; 4431; mar, vib, xyl, hp,   AMP
  pf, cel, str

Correspondences (1967)            11'
  str, tape                  AMP

Relata II (1968)                 19'
  3*3*3*3*; 4431; perc, hp, pf, str   AMP

Ars Combinatoria (1981)           19'
  2*2*2*2*; 2211; 3perc, hp, pf, cel, str  CFP

Concerto for Piano and Orchestra (1985)   20'
  solo pf; 2*2*3=2*; 3231; perc, hp, str  CFP

The Crowded Air (1987)            10'
  1111; 0000; mar, pf, gtr, str (1-1-1-1)  CFP

Transfigured Notes (1990)         19'
  str                     CFP


BABIN, VICTOR    (1908-1972)

Capriccio (1949)                 12'
  3*3*3*3*; 4331; timp, hp, str     BH

Concerto No. 2 for Two Pianos (1956)    24'
  soli 2pf; 2*222*; 4231; timp+3, str   BH


BACH, JAN    (1937-    )

Toccata for Orchestra (1959)        10'
  3*444; 4331; timp+3, str       MS

Burgundy Variations (1968)                                    17'
   3*3*3*2; 4331; timp+3, str                  ECS

Spectra (1971)                                                60'
   soli black s, white bar; satb cho;          MS
   3*3*3*3*; s sax; 4331; 5perc, kybds,
   hp, str, tape, slide projections

The Oregon Trail (1975)                                       20'
   soli t, bar; satb cho; 3*23*2; 4331;         MS
   4perc, str

Piano Concerto (1975)                                         35'
   solo pf; 3*3*22; 4331; timp+2, hp,           ECS
   pf, str, tape

The Happy Prince (1978)                                       35'
   narr; 1*1*11; 2220; timp+3, hp, str          ECS

Gala Fanfare (1979)                                           3'
   3*222; 4231; timp+3, hp, str                ECS

Sprint (1982)                                                 13'
   3*3*3*2; 4331; timp+3, hp, pf, str          ECS

Concerto for Horn and Orchestra (1983)                        35'
   solo hn; 223*3*; 4331; timp+3, hp, str      ECS

Alla breve (1984)                                             5'
   3*222; 4331; timp+3, hp, str                MS

Escapade (1984)                                               12'
   3*3*3*2; 4331; timp+3, hp, str              MS

Dompes and Jompes (1986)                                      25'
   str                                         ECS

Harp Concerto (1986)                                          25'
   solo hp; 1111; 2110; timp+2, str            MS

Estampie (1988)                                               12'
   3*3*3*2; 4331; 5perc, hp, pf, str           MS

Euphonium Concerto (1990)                                     20'
   solo euph; 3*23*2; 3331; timp+3, pf, str    MS

BACON, ERNST   (1898-1990)

Symphony No. 1 (1931)                                              36'
   3*3*3*3*; a,t sax; 4431; timp+3, hp,                      FLE
   pf, cel, str

Symphony No. 2 (1937)                                              26'
   2(2picc)2*22*; 4331; timp+2, hp, cel, str              FLE

Ford's Theater (1946)                                             20'
   22*3(bar sax)3; 4331; perc, hp, cel, str                AMP

From Emily's Diary (1947)                                         20'
   sa cho; 1111; 1000; perc, pf, str                        GS

From These States (1951)                                          15'
   2222; 3331; perc, str                                    AMP

Fables (1953)                                                     23'
   narr; 1121; 2000; perc, pf, str                          FLE

Great River (Symphony No. 3) (1956)                               30'
   narr; 2222; 4331; 2perc, hp, pf, str                     FLE

Concerto Grosso (1957)                                            19'
   str                                                      FLE

Elegy (1957)                                                       9'
   solo ob; str                                             FLE

Erie Waters - suite (1961)                                        14'
   2222; 4331; perc, str                                    FLE

Riolama (Ten Places for Piano and
   Orchestra) (1963)                                        25'
   solo pf; 2222; 4331; perc, str                           FLE

Requiem "The Last Invocation" (1968-1971)                         60'
   soli s, b; satb cho; 2222; 3331;                         FLE
   perc, pf, str


BAKER, CLAUDE   (1948-    )

The Glass Bead Game (1982-1983)                                   23'
   3*3*3*3*; 4431; timp+3, hp, pf, cel,                     MMB
   str (11-11-8-8-6)

Three Pieces for Five Timpani and
   Five Roto-Toms (1989)                    11'
   solo timp; 3(2picc)33*3; 4331; timp+3,   MMB
   hp, pf, str

Shadows:  Four Dirge-Nocturnes for
   Orchestra (1990)                        17'
   3(2picc)33*3; 4331; timp+3, hp, pf,   MMB
   cel, str


BAKER, DAVID  (1931-    )

Kosbro (1973)                           13'
   3*3*3*3*; 4331; timp+2, pf, str     AMP

Le Chat qui pêche (1974)              34'
   solo s; solo jazz qt:  a/t sax, pf/elec   MMB
   pf, db/b gtr, dmst; 3*3*3*3*; 4331;
   timp+1, hp, str

Two Improvisations (1974)             8'
   solo jazz combo:  pf, db, drums;    AMP
   3*3*3*3*; 4331; timp, pf, str

Concerto for Cello and Chamber
   Orchestra (1975)                      15'
   solo vc; 1111; 2000; timp+1, hp,    AMP
   str (no celli)

Concerto for Two Pianos, Jazz Band,
   Percussion and Strings (1976)         23'
   soli 2pf; jazz band; 5perc, str     MMB

Concerto for Clarinet and Orchestra (1985)  22'
   solo cl; 3*3*3*3*; 4331; timp+2, str   MMB

Concerto for Trumpet, Jazz Band and String  21'
   Orchestra (1987)                      MMB
   solo tpt; jazz band:  2a,2t,bar sax,
   5tpt, 4tbn, tba, pf, db, dmst; str

Homage:  Bartok, Bird, Duke  (1988)      16'
   1111; 0211; 2perc, 2hp, str        MMB

Life Cycles (1988)                      20'
   solo t; solo hn; str              MMB

Alabama Landscape (1990)             21'
   solo bar; 3*3*3*3*; 3331; 2perc, str   MMB

Concert Piece for Viola and Orchestra (1990)   17'
    solo vla; 3*3*3*3*; 3331; 2perc, str       MMB

Concert Piece for Trombone and
    Strings (1991)                             18'
    solo tbn; str                              MMB


                BAKSA, ROBERT  (1938-    )

Meditation for Orchestra (1956)                7'
    3122; 4030; str                            CLE

Chamber Concerto No. 1 (1961; rev 1985)        20'
    1111; 0000; str                            CLE

Sinfonia for Strings (1964; rev 1985)          19'
    str                                        CLE

Chamber Concerto for Oboe and Strings (1972)   17'
    solo ob; str                               CLE

Overture to "Aria da Capo" (1978)              9'
    1*1*1*2; 2110; 2perc, hp, str              CLE

Concerto for Harpsichord and Strings (1984)    18'
    solo hpsd; str                             CLE

Sonnet for Strings (1984)                      11'
    str                                        CLE


                BALADA, LEONARDO  (1933-    )

Musica Tranquila (1960)                         6'
    str                                        BTN

Piano Concerto (1964)                          21'
    solo pf; 223*2; 3331; timp+3, str          BTN

Guitar Concerto (1965)                         21'
    solo gtr; 2122; 2200; 2perc, str           BTN

Guernica (1966)                                12'
    2222; 2221; 4perc, str                     BTN

Sinfonia en Negro:  Homage to Martin
    Luther King (1968)                         19'
    2222; 2321; 3perc, pf, str                 BTN

Maria Sabina - cantata (1969)                              35'
   narr; satb cho; 2222; 2321; 4perc,                     BTN
   pf/org/accord, str

Bandoneon Concerto (1970)                                  18'
   solo bandoneon; 0000; 2220; 2perc, str                 BTN

Sinfonia Concertanta "Persistencias" (1972)               22'
   solo gtr; 2*222; 2230; perc, pf, str                   GS

Steel Symphony (1972)                                      18'
   3*223*; 4431; timp+4, pf, str                          BEL

Auroris (1973)                                             14'
   3*3*3*2; 4331; timp+3, hp, pf, str                     TP

Ponce de León (1973)                                       24'
   narr; 3*223*; 4331; timp+3, pf, str                    BEL

No-Res (1974)                                              40'
   narr; satb cho; 2*23*3*; 4331; timp+4,                 GS
   pf, hpsd/prep pf, elec org/acc, str, tape

Homage to Casals (1975)                                    9'
   2*2*22; 3331; timp+3, hp, pf, str                      GS

Homage to Sarasate (1975)                                  8'
   2*22*2; 3331; timp+3, hp, pf, str                      GS

Concerto for Four Guitars and
   Orchestra (1976)                                       22'
   soli 4gtr; 2112; 2200; perc, pf, str                   GS

Three Anecdotes - Concertino for Percussion               8'
   and Chamber Orchestra (1977)                           GS
   solo perc; 1*11*1; 1100; str

Sardana: Dance of Catalonia (1979)                        15'
   3*3*4=2; 4331; 4perc, hp, pf, cel, str                 GS

Quasi un pasodoble (1981)                                  13'
   3*223*; 4331; 3perc, hp, pf/cel, str                   GS

Concerto for Violin and Orchestra (1982)                  20'
   solo vln; 2*22*2; 2220; timp+1, str                    GS

Alegrias (1987)                                            7'
   solo fl; str                                           BTM

Fantasias Sonoras (1987)                      14'
  3*222; 4331; timp+1, hp, pf, str       BTM

Zapata:  Images for Orchestra (1987)          18'
  2222; 3331; timp+1, hp, str            BTM

Columbus:  Images for Orchestra (1991)        20'
  2222; 3331; timp+1, hp, str            BTM

Divertimentos (1991)                          15'
  str                                    BTM


     BALAZS, FREDERIC  (1920-    )

An American Symphony (1945)                    30'
  3*3*3*2; 4331; timp+1, str             ACA

An Evening Song (1953)                         8'
  satb cho; hp, str                      ACA

Kentuckia (1953)                               13'
  str                                    ACA

Symphony on a Plain-Chant Fragment (1954)      16'
  3*3*3*3*; 4331; timp+3, hp, str        ACA

Kentuckia (1956)                               14'
  solo vc (or solo vln); 2222; 4231;     ACA
  timp+1, hp, str

Pueblo Bonito (1956)                           30'
  narr; unis cho; 11*1*0; 1100; perc,    ACA
  hp, pf, str

The Trail (1957)                               6'
  2222; 4331; hp, str                    ACA

Two Dances after David (1957)                  15'
  solo fl; 4*23*1; 0000; timp, hp, str   ACA

Song for Pablito (1960)                        6'
  2222; 4231; perc, str                  ACA

Statement of Faith (1961)                      12'
  2222; 4231; timp+1, hp, str            ACA

Concerto - In Memoriam (1962)                  25'
  solo vc; 2222; 4231; timp+1, str       ACA

Symphonic Metamorphosis on "B-G" (1964)          20'
   solo cl; 2222; 4231; timp+1, hp, cel, str    ACA

Passacaglia (1968)                               15'
   3*223*; 4331; timp+1, hp, cel, str           ACA

Concerto for Orchestra and Voices (1977)         28'
   soli 4vv; ssaa cho; 2222; 4231; 5perc,       ACA
   hp, str

Concerto for String Quartet and
   Orchestra (1988)                             40'
   solo str qt; 3*3*3*3*; 4331; timp+4,          ACA
   hp, pf/cel, str

Two Pieces for Orchestra (1988)                  15'
   3*3*3*3*; 4331; timp+4, hp, pf/cel, str       ACA

Variations on Five Notes (1988)                  20'
   3*3*3*3*; 4331; timp+4, hp, pf/cel, str       ACA
   N.B.  There are solos for the principal
   strings.

Angels (1989)                                    41'
   solo boy s; narr; 1111; 1110; hp, pf/cel,     ACA
   b gtr(opt), str


      BALES, RICHARD  (1915-    )

Ozymandia (1945)                                 5'
   solo mez; 1121; 2000; str                     PS

Primavera (1947)                                 5'
   1121; 2210; timp+1, str                       FLE

Episode from a Lincoln Ballet (1947)             14'
   narr; 1121; 2210; timp+1, pf, str             FLE

The Confederacy (1953)                           40'
   soli s, bar; narr; satb cho; 2222; 2211;      MS
   timp+1, hp, pf, str

The Republic (1955)                              80'
   soli s, bar; narr; satb cho; 1121; 2210;      MS
   timp+1, hpsd, str

The Union (1956)                                 50'
   soli s, bar; narr; satb cho; 1121; 2210;      MS
   timp+1, hp, str

National Gallery Suite No. 3 (1957)                 18'
    narr; 11*21; 2210; timp+1, str                  FLE

St. Paul's Communion Service (1959)                 10'
    0202; 2200; timp, str                           MS

National Gallery Suite No. 4 (1965)                 22'
    1121; 2210; timp+1, hp, str                     FLE


            BALLARD, LOUIS W.  (1931-      )

Newakis - ballet (1962)                             30'
    1121; 2110; timp+1, str                         NSW

Fantasy Aborigine No. 1 "Sipapu" (1963)             15'
    2222; 4220; timp+2, str                         MS

The Gods Will Hear (1964)                           15'
    satb cho; 3*3*3*3*; 4331; timp+3, hp, str       BOU

Scenes from Indian Life (1964)                       5'
    2222; 4220; timp+2, str                         BOU

Koshare - ballet (1965)                             31'
    2222; 4220; timp+3, str                         NSW

The Four Moons (1967)                               30'
    2222; 4220; timp+3, str                         NSW

Why the Duck has a Short Tail (1969)                20'
    narr; 2222; 4231; timp+4, hp, pf, str           BOU

Portrait of Will Rogers (1972)                      25'
    narr; satb cho; 2332; 4231; timp+4,             NSW
    hp(pf), str

Devil's Promenade (1973)                            15'
    2222; 4331; timp+6, hp, cel, str                BEL

Incident at Wounded Knee (1974)                     16'
    1112; 2000; perc(opt), str                      BEL

Ishi "America's Last Civilized Man" (1975)          15'
    2222; 4210; timp+2, str                         NSW

Fantasy Aborigine No. 2 "Tsiyako" (1976)            13'
    str                                             NSW

Fantasy Aborigine No. 4 "Xactce'oyan -
  Companion of Talking God" (1982)                 25'
  2222; 4231; timp+4, hp, cel, str                 NSW

Fantasy Aborigine No. 5 "Naniwaya" (1988)          15'
  4*4*4*4*; 6442; 2timp+4, hp, cel, str            NSW

Live on, Heart of My Nation (1990)                 25'
  soli s, a, t, b; narr; satb cho; 1111;           NSW
  0000; perc, str


        BALLOU, ESTHER  (1915-1973)

Beguine (1950)                                      4'
  2222; 4331; timp, hp, str                        ACA

Prelude and Allegro (1951)                          7'
  pf, str                                          ACA

Adagio (1952)                                       4'
  solo bsn; str                                    ACA

Concertino for Oboe and Strings (1953)            12'
  solo ob; str                                     ACA

In Memoriam (1960)                                 5'
  solo ob; str                                     ACA

Concerto for Piano and Orchestra (1964)           35'
  solo pf; 2222; 4221; 2perc, pf, cel, str        ACA

Concerto for Guitar and Orchestra (1966)          12'
  solo gtr; 1111; 1110; str                        ACA

Konzertstück (1969)                                10'
  solo vla; 2222; 4330; timp+1, str               ACA


        BARAB, SEYMOUR  (1921-    )

Child's Garden of Verses (1952)                    35'
  0111; 0100; str                                  BH

Concerto for Horn and String Orchestra (1955) 12'
  solo hn; str                                     BH

Six Tennyson Songs (1956)                          10'
  solo s; hp, str                                  BH

Tales of Rhyme and Reason (1967)                    90'
   1.  Always Arguing                               15'
   2.  Bigger and Better                            15'
   3.  Braggarty Rabbit                             15'
   4.  A Kiss from Alice                            15'
   5.  The Lordly Lion                              15'
   6.  What Will the Neighbours Say?                15'

   narr; 1121; 2110; perc, hp, str, dancers    BH
   N.B.  Individual movements are available
   for performance.

G.A.G.E., A Christmas Story (1981)                  20'
   narr; 2222; 2220; 2perc, hp, pf, str        GS

Concerto Grosso (1982)                             20'
   str                                         GS


      BARATI, GEORGE   (1913-    )

Chamber Concerto (1952)                            23'
   soli fl, ob, cl, bsn; str                   CFP

Tribute (1952)                                     7'
   3*222; 4230; timp+1, str                    ACA

Concerto for Cello and Orchestra (1957)            26'
   solo vc; 2222; 2220; timp+2, str            CFP

Configuration for Large Orchestra (1957)           13'
   3*3*3*3*; 4331; timp+3, hp, str             PS

The Dragon and the Phoenix (1960)                  14'
   2*2*22; 4231; timp+2, hp, cel, str          CFP

Polarization (1965)                                16'
   2222; 4331; timp+1, hp, cel, str            CFP

The Waters of Kane:  Festival Ode (1966)           10'
   satb cho; 3*222; 4231; timp+3, str          ACA

Vaudeville for Orchestra (1967)                    6'
   3*222; 4331; timp+1, hp, str                ACA

Festival Hula (1968)                               12'
   2222; 4231; perc, hp, cel, str              ACA

Symphony (1968)                                    25'
   2222; 4331; timp+2, hp, cel, str            CFP

Baroque Quartet Concerto (1969)                15'
   soli fl, ob, db, hpsd; 0011; 2110;        ACA
   timp+2, str

Piano Concerto (1973)                          23'
   solo pf; 2222; 2230; timp+1, str           ACA

Concerto for Guitar (1976; rev 1982)           20'
   solo gtr; 1010; 1000; timp+2, str          ACA

Branches of Time (1981)                        22'
   soli 2pf; 2222; 2220; timp+2, str          ACA

Confluence (1982)                              12'
   3*3*3*3*; 4331; timp+3, hp, pf/cel, str    ACA

The Ugly Duckling - suite (1982)               20'
   narr; 213*1; a,t,bar sax; 1231;            ACA
   timp+2, str

Violin Concerto (1986)                         23'
   solo vln; 2222; 4230; timp+2, hp, str      ACA


## BARBER, SAMUEL (1910-1981)

Overture to The School for Scandal (1931)      8'
   3*3*3*2; 4331; timp+1, hp, cel, str        GS

Music for a Scene from Shelley, op. 7 (1933)   8'
   3*3*3*3*; 4331; timp+2, hp, str            GS

Symphony No. 1 in One Movement, op. 9 (1936)   19'
   3*3*3*3*; 4331; timp+2, hp, str            GS

Adagio for Strings, op. 11 (1936)              11'
   str                                        GS

First Essay, op. 12 (1937)                     8'
   2222; 4331; timp, pf, str                  GS

Concerto for Violin and Orchestra,
   op. 14 (1939)                              22'
   solo vln; 2222; 2200; timp, pf, str        GS

Second Essay, op. 17 (1942)                    10'
   3*3*22; 4331; timp+2, str                  GS

Symphony No. 2, op. 19 (1944)                  27'
   3*3*4=3*; 4331; timp+2, pf, str            GS

Capricorn Concerto, op. 21 (1944)                14'
    soli fl, ob, tpt; str                        GS

Concerto for Cello and Orchestra,
    op. 22 (1945)                                26'
    solo vc; 2222; 2300; timp+1, str             GS

Medea - ballet suite, op. 23  (1947)             20'
    2222; 2221; timp+1, hp, pf, str              GS

Knoxville:  Summer of 1915, op. 24 (1947)        16'
    solo s; 2*111; 2100; perc, hp, str           GS

Souvenirs - suite, op. 28 (1952)                 17'
    2222; 4330; timp+1, hp, cel, str             GS

Medea's Meditation and Dance of Vengeance,
    op. 23a (1953)                               14'
    3*3*4=3*; 4331; timp+2, hp, pf, str          GS

Prayers of Kierkegaard, op. 30 (1954)            18'
    solo s; satb cho; 3*3*3*2; 4331; timp+1,     GS
    hp, pf, str
    OR:  112*1; 2110; timp+1, org, str

Vanessa, op. 32 - selections (1958; rev 1978)
    1.  Anatol's Aria:  solo t                   4'
    2.  Do Not Utter A Word:  solo s             4'
    3.  Must Winter Come So Soon:  solo mez       4'
    4.  Intermezzo                               4'

    3*3*3*2; 4331; timp+1, hp, str               GS

Toccata festiva, op. 36 (1960)                   14'
    3*3*3*2; 4331; timp+1, str                   GS

Die Natali, op. 37 (1960)                        16'
    3*3*3*2; 4331; timp+1, hp, str               GS

Concerto for Piano and Orchestra,
    op. 38 (1962)                                26'
    solo pf; 3*3*3*2; 4330; timp+1, hp, str      GS

Andromache's Farewell, op. 39 (1962)             12'
    solo s; 3*3*3*2; 4331; timp+1, hp, str       GS

Two Scenes from "Antony and Cleopatra",
    op. 40 (1963)                                16'
    solo s; 3*3*3*3*; 4331; timp+1, 2hp,         GS
    pf, str

Night Flight, op. 19a (1964)                                    8'
   3*3*4=2; 4331; perc, pf, str                  GS

The Lovers, op. 43 (1971)                                       31'
   solo bar; satb cho; 4*3*3*2; 4331;            GS
   timp+1, hp, pf, cel, str

Fadograph of a Yestern Scene, op. 44 (1971)                    7'
   3*3*3*2; 4331; timp+1, 1-2hp; pf,             GS
   cel, str

Third Essay, op. 47 (1978)                                      14'
   3*3*4=1; 4331; euph; timp, 2hp, pf, str       GS

Canzonetta, op. 48
   (orch'd by C. Turner) (1978)                  8'
   solo ob; str                                  GS


## BARKIN, ELAINE (1932-    )

Plus ça change (1971)                                           12'
   3perc, str                                     ACA


## BARNES, LARRY

Solar Winds (1973)                                             10'
   3*3*3*3*; 3331; timp+3, 2pf, str               MS

Concerto for Piano and Orchestra (1979)                        14'
   solo pf; 3*3*3*3*; 4441; timp+3,              MS
   str, tape

Morning Gigue (1991)                                            5'
   3*3*3*2; 2221; timp+2, str                    MS


## BARTLES, ALFRED (1930-    )

Music for Symphonic Orchestra and Jazz                         NA
   Ensemble, op. 4 (1966)                        MJQ
   jazz ens: 2a,2t,bar sax; 4tpt,
   4tbn; rhythm section
   orch: 3*3*3*3*; 4321; 2perc, hp, str

## BASSETT, LESLIE (1923- )

Five Movements (1961)     25'
3*3*3*3*; 4331; timp+3, pf, str     ACA

Variations for Orchestra (1963)     23'
2222; 4231; timp+3, hp, pf, cel, str     CFP

Colloquy (1969)     10'
3*3*3*3*; 4431; timp+3, hp, pf/cel, str     CFP

Celebration: In Praise of Earth (1970)     10'
narr (amp); satb cho; 2*2*22; 3221;     CFP
4perc, hp, pf/cel, str

Forces (1972)     12'
2*2*3*2; 3221; 4perc, str     CFP

Echoes from an Invisible World (1975)     15'
2222; 4431; timp+4, hp, pf, cel, str     CFP

Concerto for Two Pianos and Orchestra (1976)     15'
soli 2pf; 3*23*2; 4231; 4perc, str     CFP

Concerto Lyrico (1983)     15'
solo tbn; 3*23*2; 4231; 4perc, hp,     CFP
pf/cel, str

From a Source Evolving (1985)     13'
3*3*3*3*; 4331; 4perc, hp, pf, str     CFP

Concerto for Orchestra (1991)     20'
3*3*3*3*; 4331; 4perc, hp, pf/cel, str     CFP


## BAUER, MARION (1887-1955)

Symphony No. 1 (1947-1950)     17'
3*3*4=2; 4331; timp+1, 2hp, str     MER


## BAUER, ROSS (1951- )

Sospenso (1987)     9'
str     ACA

Neon (1988)     9'
3*3*3*3*; 4331; timp+3, hp, pf/cel, str     ACA

## BAVICCHI, JOHN  (1922-    )

Tobal, op. 5 (1952)                                          11'
  223*2; 4330; timp+2, str                                  BKJ

Four Songs for Contralto and Chamber
  Orchestra, op. 6 (1952)                                   14'
  solo ca; 212*0; 2000; str                                 FLE

Concerto for Clarinet and String
  Orchestra, op. 11 (1954)                                  20'
  solo cl; str                                              OXF

Suite No. 1, op. 19 (1955)                                  23'
  3*3*3*3*; 4331; timp, str                                 OXF

Farewell and Hail, op. 28 (1957)                            11'
  solo s; tpt, str                                          BKJ

A Concert Overture, op. 29 (1957)                            8'
  3*221; 4330; timp+1, str                                  OXF

Fantasy, op. 36 (1959)                                      10'
  solo hp; 1111; 1000; str                                  BKJ

Concertante, op. 44 (1961)                                  15'
  1001; 0000; str                                           BKJ

Three Psalms, op. 50 (1963)                                 13'
  soli s, a, t, b; satb cho; 2tpt; str                      BKJ

Fantasia on Korean Folk Tunes, op. 53 (1966)  8'
  213*1; 2231; timp+1, str                                  BKJ

Caroline's Dance, op. 67 (1974-1975)                         5'
  2222; 4230; timp+3, str                                   BKJ

Mont Blanc - overture, op. 72 (1976-1977)                   10'
  2121; 2230; timp+3, str                                   OXF

Music for Small Orchestra, op. 81 (1981)                     8'
  2222; 2200; timp, str                                     BKJ

Fusions for Trombone and Orchestra,
  op. 92 (1984-1985)                                        12'
  solo tbn; 3*222; 4431; timp+1, str                        BKJ

There is Sweet Music Here, op. 93 (1985)                    15'
  solo s; 2222; 2210; timp, str                             BKJ

Pyramid, op. 95 (1986)                                7'
   3*222; 4231; timp+1, str                       BKJ

Canto I, op. 96 (1987)                               11'
   str                                               BKJ

Sherbrook West, op. 99 (1988)                         8'
   3*23*2; 4230; timp+1, str                       BKJ

Songs of Remembrance, op. 100 (1988-1990)            50'
   soli s, a, t, b; satb cho; 3*23*2; 4331;        BKJ
   timp+1, str


          BAZELON, IRWIN   (1922-      )

Concert Overture (1951-1952)                         10'
   3*3*3*2; 4331; timp+1, pf, str                  EWM

Short Symphony
   "Testament to a Big City" (1961)                14'
   4*24=2; 2321; timp+4, pf, cel, str              BH

Symphony No. 1 (1962)                                30'
   3*3*3*2; 4331; timp+3, pf, str                  MS

Symphony concertante (1963)                          20'
   soli cl, tpt, mar; 3*23*2; 4331; timp+4,        TP
   prep pf, str

Overture to Shakespeare's
   "Taming of the Shrew" (1964)                    10'
   1*111; 2210; timp+1, pf, str                    MS

Dramatic Movement (1964-1965)                        12'
   4*3*4=3*; 4331; timp+1, pf, str                 MS

Symphony No. 4 (1964-1965)                           30'
   4*3*4*3*; 4331; timp+4, pf, cel, str            MS

Excursion (1965)                                     15'
   3*3*3*3*; 4331; timp+4, pf, str                 MS

Symphony No. 5 (1967)                                28'
   4*3*4=3*; 4331; timp+4, pf, str                 BH

Symphony No. 6 (1969)                                24'
   3*24=33; 4331; timp+5, pf, acc, str, tape       MS

A Quiet Piece for a Violent Time (1975)            10'
    3=12*1; 3221; 3perc, hp, str                   BH

Spirits of the Night (1976)                        18'
    3*3*4=3*; 4331; timp+4, pf, str                TP

De-tonations (1978)                                18'
    solo br qnt; 3*24=3*; 3221; timp+4, str        TP

Junctures (1979)                                   17'
    solo s; 3*24=3*; 4331; timp+4, pf, str         TP

Symphony No. 7  "Ballet for Orchestra" (1980)  18'
    3*24=3*; 4331; timp+4, amp pf, str             TP

Memories of a Winter Childhood (1981)              17'
    5*23*3*; 4331; timp+4, hp, pf, cel, str        TP

Spires (1981)                                      18'
    solo tpt; 3*3*3*3*; 2220; perc, pf, str        TP

Tides (1982)                                       17'
    solo cl; 2=12*1; a sax; 3220; 2perc, hp,       TP
    str (0-6-4-2)

For Tuba with Strings Attached (1982)              12'
    solo tba; str                                  TP

Trajectories (Concerto for Piano
    with Orchestra) (1985)                         20'
    solo pf; 3*23*3*; 4321; timp+5, str            TP

Motivations for Trombone and Orchestra (1986)  12'
    solo tbn; 3*23*3*; 4321; timp+4, pf, str       TP

Symphony No. 8 for Strings (1986)                  25'
    str                                            TP

Fourscore and 2 (1987)                             25'
    soli 4perc; 3*3*3*3*; 4331; timp, pf, str      TP

Symphony No. 8½ (1988)                             12'
    3*23*2; 2221; timp+3, pf, str                  TP


            BEALE, JAMES  (1924-     )

Symphony for Chamber Orchestra (1950)              22'
    2*222; 2000; timp, str                         ACA

Divertimento (1954)                                11'
   3*1*21; 2220; timp+2, pf, str                  ACA

Concerto for Violoncello and
   Orchestra (1956)                               14'
   solo vc; 2132; 4231; timp, str                 ACA
   N.B. The concerto bears the subtitle
   "Lyric Piece for Violoncello and Orchestra"

Cressay Symphony (Symphony No. 2) (1961)           22'
   3*3*3(s sax, b cl)3*; 4331; timp+3,             ACA
   hp, str

Music for Soprano and Orchestra (1965)             15'
   solo s; 22*3*2; 2231; 3perc, str                ACA

Suite for Strings (1981)                           20'
   str                                            ACA

Ballade for Viola and Strings (1989)               9'
   solo vla; str                                  ACA


       BEASER, ROBERT  (1954-    )

Symphony (1977)                                    30'
   solo s; 3=3*2=2; 4231; timp+1, hp,             EAM
   pf, str

The Seven Deadly Sins (1984)                       20'
   solo t (or bar); 2*22(a sax, b cl)2;            EAM
   4231; timp+3, hp, pf, str

Song of the Bells (1987)                           13'
   solo fl; 1*2*22; 3100; timp+2, hp,             EAM
   pf, str

Piano Concerto (1988)                              20'
   solo pf; 3*332; 4331; timp+1, hp, str          EAM


       BECK, JEREMY  (1960-    )

Innis Fodhla (1982)                                10'
   2*222; 2210; 3perc, str                         AMG

Overture (1984)                                    6'
   2222; 2110; 2perc, pf, str                      AMG

Piano Concerto No. 1 (1984)                        20'
   solo pf; 2222; 2110; 2perc, str               AMG

Sinclair Listens (1986)                             5'
   3*23*2; 2331; 4perc, hp, str                 AMG

Ballade (1987)                                      8'
   solo pf; 1011; 1110; perc, str               AMG

Requiem for the Twentieth-Century
   (Part I) (1989)                              18'
   satb cho; 2*222; 4331; timp+2, hp, str       AMG

State of the Union (1991)                          12'
   3*23*2; 4331; timp+3, hp, pf, str            AMG


      BECKER, JOHN   (1886-1961)

Symphony No. 1 (Etude Primitive) (1922)            20'
   3*3*24*; 4231; timp+3, pf, str               ACA

Cossak Sketches (1924)                              9'
   2121; 2221; timp+2, hp, str                  ACA

Out of the Cradle Endlessly Rocking (1929)         20'
   soli vv; narr; satb cho; 2222; 4200;         ACA
   timp, str

Concerto Arabesque (1930)                          15'
   solo pf; 1112; 1100; str                     ACA

Soundpiece No. 1 (1932)                            12'
   solo pf; str                                 ACA

Concerto for Horn and Orchestra (1933)             18'
   solo hn; 2222; 0200; timp, str               ACA

Concerto for Viola and Orchestra (1937)            20'
   solo vla; 2222; 2200; timp, str (no vla)     ACA

Satirico (Piano Concerto No. 2) (1938)             15'
   solo pf; 2222; 4221; 2perc, str              ACA

Prelude to Shakespeare (1939)                      10'
   2222; 2230; timp, str                        ACA

Rain Down Death (1939)                             30'
   1111; 1100; timp+1, pf, str                  ACA

Symphony No. 5 (Homage to Mozart) (1942)        15'
    1100; 2200; str                              ACA

Victory March (1942)                            6'
    3*223*; 4231; timp+4, pf, str               ACA

Symphony No. 6 (Out of Bondage) (1942)          30'
    narr; satb cho; 23*22; 2231; timp+2, str    ACA

Violin Concerto (1948)                          15'
    solo vln; 2223; 4231; timp+1, str           ACA


              BECKLER, S. R.   (1923-    )

Symphony No. 1 in B minor, op. 4 (1948)         NA
    2222; 4331; timp+2, str                     MS

Twelve Variations on a Welsh Hymn,
    op. 7a (1950)                               NA
    2222; 4331; timp+2, str                     MS

Symphony No. 2 in C Major, op. 11 (1951)        NA
    2222; 4331; timp+2, str                     MS

Playing in the Paintbox, op. 14 (1952)          15'
    2222; 4331; timp+2, str                     MS

Symphony No. 3 - In Memoriam, op. 16 (1953)     14'
    2222; 4331; timp+2, str                     MS

Varied Distortions of "The O.G.M.",
    op. 15b (1955)                              15'
    2222; 4331; timp+2, str                     MS

Symphony No. 4 in D minor, op. 33 (1956)        25'
    2222; 4331; timp+2, str                     MS

Festival Overture, op. 39b (1957)               14'
    2222; 4331; timp+2, str                     MS

Symphony No. 5, op. 50 (1961-1977)              15'
    2222; 4331; timp+2, pf, str                 MS

Dirge, op. 20, No. 2b (1966)                    20'
    2222; 4331; timp+2, str                     MS

The Seven Ages of Man, op. 83 (1972)            18'
   3*3*3*3*; 4331; timp+3, str                  MS

Fanfare, op. 93, No. 1 (1977)                   2'
   2222; 4331; timp+2, str                      MS

Concerto for Orchestra, op. 96 (1981-1985)      13'
   3*3*3*3*; 4331; timp+3, hp, pf, str          MS


         BEELER, C. ALAN  (1939-    )

Sinfonia for Strings (1962)                     6'
   str                                          MS

Cinematic Scene - A Train on Eads
   Bridge (1963)                                4'
   1111; 2110; perc, str (2-1-1-0)              MS

Quintessence I and II (1965-1966)               10'
   3*222; 4221; 2perc, str                      MS

Homage to Roger Sessions (1986)                 5'
   2222; 4231; timp+1, str                      MS

A Mad Song (1986)                               6'
   2222; 2231; timp+1, wind machine, str        MS


         BEERMAN, BURTON  (1943-    )

Moments 1977 (1978)                             21'
   2222; 2220; perc, str                        ACA

Mourning Songs (1990-1991)                      11'
   2222; 2110; perc, str                        ACA


         BEESON, JACK  (1921-    )

Two Concert Arias from "The Elephant" (1953)    8'
   solo s; 2*222; 3210; timp+1, hp, str         MS

Hymns and Dances from "The Sweet Bye
   and Bye" (1958)                              15'
   3*3*3=3*; 4331; timp+2, hp, pf(4-hands),     BH
   cel, str

Symphony No. 1 in A (1959)                       20'
   2*2*2*2; 4230; timp+3, hp, cel, str          BH

Transformations (1959)                                   10'
  3*3*3*3*; 4331; timp+2, hp, str                     BH


BEGLARIAN, GRANT (1927-    )

Twelve Hungarian Songs (1957)                            25'
  2-part cho; 2222; 4231; timp+1, str                MS

Nurse's Song (1960)                                       7'
  ssa cho; 2222; 4230; timp, str                     MS

Sinfonia for Orchestra (1961)                            17'
  2222; 4230; timp+1, str                            MS

Diversions (1972)                                        14'
  soli vla, vc; 2222; 4230; timp+1, str             EBM

Sinfonia for Strings (1974)                              13'
  str                                                EBM

To Manitou (1976)                                        23'
  1100; 1000; str                                   EBM

Partita for Orchestra (1986)                             16'
  2222; 4231; timp+1, str                            MS

Divertimento for Orchestra (NA)                          20'
  2222; 4230; timp+1, str                           EBM


BELL, ELIZABETH (1928-    )

Symphony No. 1 (1971)                                    20'
  3*3*3*3*; 4331; timp+3, str                        ACA

Concerto for Orchestra (1976)                            10'
  2222; 4231; perc, str                              ACA

Rituals for Orchestra (1988)                             10'
  3*3*3*3*; 4331; timp+4, str                        ACA


BELL, LARRY THOMAS (1952-    )

Continuum for Orchestra (1971)                            8'
  2*2*2*2*; 1211; 2perc, hp, pf, str                ACA

The Idea of Order at Key West (1981)                  21'
   solo s; solo vln; 4perc,                           ACA
   str (9-8-7-6-5 desks)

Sacred Symphonies (1985)                              25'
   1111; 1100; 2perc, hp, pf, str                     CRP

Concerto for Piano and Orchestra (1989)              25'
   solo pf; 1111; 1110; str (2-1-1-1)                 CRP


               BENJAMIN, THOMAS   (1940-    )

Violin Concerto (1966)                                25'
   solo vln; 2222; 2200; timp+1, str                  MS

Concerto for Piano and Orchestra (1967)              20'
   solo pf; 2222; 2221; timp+2, str                   MS

Sinfonia (Symphony No. 1) (1971)                      30'
   2*22*2; 4221; timp+2, str                          MS

Epode:  for Oboe and String Orchestra (1972)  12'
   solo ob; str                                       MS

Invariants (1974)                                      9'
   3*222; 4321; timp+5, hp, str                       MS

The Righteous Nation (1975)                           45'
   soli s, t; narr; satb cho; 2*222;                  MS
   4331; timp+3, str

Unto the Hills (1982)                                 12'
   solo vln; satb cho; str                            MS

Viola Concerto (1983)                                 25'
   solo vla; 2*22*2; 4321; timp+3, pf, str            MS

Symphony No. 2 (1989)                                 18'
   1111; 1100; 2perc, pf, str                         MS


           BENNETT, ROBERT RUSSELL   (1894-1981)

Suite of Old American Dances (1949)                   15'
   2*2*3*2; 4331; timp+5, str                         TP

Overture to the Mississippi (1950)                     9'
   2*2*3*2; 4331; timp+3, hp, bj, str                 TP

Concerto for Violin, Piano and
   Orchestra (1958-1959)                        24'
   soli vln, pf; 2222; 4230; timp, str         TP

A Commemoration Symphony (1959)                  24'
   satb cho; 3*3*3*2; 4331; timp+1, hp, str    TP

Carol Cantata I, II, III, IV (1979)              12'
   satb cho; 2222; 4330; timp+1, hp, str       GS

The Easter Story (1979)                          30'
   satb cho; 23*3*2; 4331; timp+1, str         GS


     BENSON, WARREN  (1924-   )

Psalm XXIV (1957)                                11'
   ssaa cho; str                               CF

Concerto for Horn and Orchestra (1972)           21'
   solo hn; 2222; 4331; timp+3, pf, str        CF

The Man with the Blue Guitar (1980)              14'
   2222; 4331; timp+3, hp, pf, str             TP

Beyond Winter:  Sweet Aftershowers (1981)        14'
   str                                         TP

Concertino for Flute, Percussion and
   Strings (1983)                              20'
   solo fl; perc, str                          CF

Aeolian Song (NA)                                5'
   solo a sax; 2*111; 1000; perc, str          MCA


     BERG, CHRISTOPHER  (1949-   )

Mass (1978)                                      20'
   solo s; satb cho; 03*02; 4220; timp,        MS
   hp, cel, str

Not waving but drowning (1979)                   18'
   solo mez; 1111; 1110; perc, hp, pf/cel,     PS
   str (4-4-2-2-1)

Four Songs on Poems of Vladimir
   Nabokov (1991)                              15'
   solo s; 2*2*2=2; 4231; perc, hp,            MS
   pf/cel, str

BERGER, ARTHUR   (1912-      )

| | |
|---|---|
| Serenade concertante (1945; rev 1951) | 9' |
|   soli fl, ob, cl, bsn, vln; 0000; | CFP |
|   2100; str | |

| | |
|---|---|
| Three Pieces for String Orchestra | |
|   (1945; rev 1982) | 10' |
|   str | CFP |

| | |
|---|---|
| Ideas of Order (1952) | 12' |
|   3*23*2; 4220; timp+1, hp, str | CFP |

| | |
|---|---|
| Polyphony (1956) | 14' |
|   2222; 4220; timp+2, hp, cel, str | BOE |

| | |
|---|---|
| Chamber Concerto (1960; rev 1978) | 12' |
|   2121; 1100; perc, hp, pf, cel, str | BOE |

BERGER, JEAN   (1909-      )

| | |
|---|---|
| Creole Overture (1949) | 5' |
|   3*121; 2221; timp+2, pf, str | BRO |

| | |
|---|---|
| Short Symphony (1952) | 15' |
|   2222; 2330; timp+1, str | BRO |

| | |
|---|---|
| Short Overture (1958) | 6' |
|   str | BRO |

| | |
|---|---|
| Divertissement (1970) | 12' |
|   str | GS |

| | |
|---|---|
| Concert Piece (1972) | 15' |
|   soli 2fl; str | BRO |

| | |
|---|---|
| Diversion for Strings (1977) | 14' |
|   str | EAM |

BERGSMA, WILLIAM   (1921-      )

| | |
|---|---|
| Music on a Quiet Theme (1946) | 8' |
|   2*2*22; 4231; timp+1, str | ECS |

| | |
|---|---|
| The Fortunate Islands (1947; rev 1956) | 19' |
|   str | CF |

Symphony No. 1 (1949)                                      25'
   3*3*3*2; 4331; timp+1, str                          CF

A Carol on Twelfth Night (1954)                           8'
   1*222; 4231; timp+1, hp, str                        GAL

March with Trumpets (1957)                                6'
   3*222; 4331; timp+2, str                            ECS

Chameleon Variations (1960)                               13'
   3*22*2; 4331; timp+2, hp, pf, str                   GAL

In Celebration (1963)                                     12'
   3*23*2; 4231; timp+1, pf, str                       GAL

Documentary I "Portrait of a City" (1963)                17'
   2*2*2*2; 4231; timp+2, str                          GAL

Confrontation (Job) (1963; rev 1966)                      27'
   satb cho; 2*02*1; a sax; 2221; timp+4,               GAL
   pf, str (0-0-10-8)

Serenade "To Await the Moon" (1965)                       13'
   2*22*2; 2000; perc, hp, str                         GAL

Concerto for Violin and Orchestra (1966)                 21'
   solo vln; 2*21*2; 2200; perc, hp, str               GAL

Documentary II "Billie's World" (1968)                   10'
   3*23*2; 4331; timp+1, pf, str                       GAL

Changes (1971)                                            9'
   solo ww qnt; timp+1, hp, str                        GAL

In Space:  Four Play; Catalina  (1973)                   18'
   solo s; 112*1; 1001; timp+2, pf, str                ECS

Symphony No. 2 "Voyages" (1976)                          25'
   solo vv; satb cho; 2*22*2; 4231;                    GAL
   timp+2, pf, str

Sweet was the Song the Virgin Sang:
   Tristan Revisited (1978)                             27'
   solo vla; 2*23*2; 4231; timp+2, hp, str              GAL

In Campo Aperto (1981)                                    18'
   solo ob; 2bsn; str                                   ECS

BERLIN, DAVID   (1943-    )

Variants for Orchestra (1974)                          15'
   2222; 3330; timp+1, str                             FLE

Structures (1975)                                      10'
   1111; 1120; timp+2, str                             FLE

Menagerie (1979)                                       10'
   112*1; 1110; perc, str (1-1-1-1)                    FLE

Metamorphism (1980)                                    13'
   1*111; 1110; 2perc, str                            FLE

Concerto for Clarinet, Tuba and
   Orchestra (1983)                                    15'
   soli cl, tba; 2222; 2210; perc, str                FLE


BERNSTEIN, LEONARD   (1918-1990)

Jeremiah Symphony (Symphony No. 1) (1943)    23'
   solo mez; 3*3*3*3*; 4331; timp+1, pf, str   WBM

Fancy Free - ballet (1944)                             24'
   2*222; 4331; timp+2-3, pf, str                      BH

On the Town - Three Dance Episodes (1945)    9'
   1*13=0; 2330; timp+2, pf, str                       BH

Facsimile - choreographic essay (1946)       21'
   2*22+2; 4231; timp+2, pf, str                       BH

Symphony No. 2 "Age of Anxiety" (1949)       30'
   solo pf; 3*3*3*3*; 4331; timp+4,             GS
   hp, pf, str

Serenade:  after Plato (1954)                          33'
   solo vln; 5perc, hp, str                            BH

On the Waterfront - Symphonic Suite (1955)   23'
   3*24=3*; a sax; 4331; timp+4, hp, pf, str   BH

Candide (1956; rev 1982)                               BH
   1.   Overture                                       4'
       3*24=3*; 4321; timp+2, hp, str

   2.   Glitter and Be Gay                             6'
       solo s; 2*1*2*1; 2200; timp+2,
       hp, str

3.   Suite                                              50'
       solo vv; satb cho; 2*1*2=1; 2221;
       timp+2, hp, str

West Side Story:  Overture
   (arr Peress) (1957)                                   5'
   2222; 4331; timp+1, hp, pf, str                       GS

West Side Story - Selections (1957)        GS
   N.B. Violas are tacet in all selection
   numbers.

   1.   Overture
          2*031*; 2320; perc, pf, gtr, str

   2.   Prologue
          2*03=1; a,t,bar,bs sax; 2320; perc, pf,
          gtr, str

   3.   Jet Song
          solo bar; satb cho; 103*2; s,a,t,bar sax;
          2320; perc, pf, gtr, str

   4.   Something's Coming
          solo t; 304*1; 2330; perc, pf, gtr, str

   5.   Dance Sequence
          2*13*1; a,t,bar,bs sax; 2320; perc, pf,
          gtr str

   6.   Maria
          solo t; 1121; 2320; perc, pf, gtr, str

   7.   Balcony Scene (Tonight)
          soli s, t; 113*1; 2320; perc, pf, cel, str

   8.   America
          fem cho; 2*13=1; 2320; perc, pf, gtr, str

   9.   Cool
          male cho; 2*03*1; a,t,bar,bs sax; 2320;
          perc, pf, gtr, str

   10.   One Hand, One Heart
          soli s, t; 113*1; 1210; perc, pf, gtr, str

   11.   Tonight
          soli qnt; satb cho; 112*1; 2320; perc, pf,
          cel, str

   12.   I Feel Pretty
            solo s; 1011; 2320; perc, pf, str

   13.   Ballet Sequence
            2*1*3=1; 2320; perc, pf, str

   14.   Gee Officer Krupke
            male cho; 2*021; 2320; perc, pf, gtr, str

   15.   A Boy Like That
            soli s, a; 102*1; 2320; perc, pf, gtr, str

   16.   Somewhere
            soli s, t; 112*1; 2320; perc, pf, gtr, str

   17.   Finale
            soli s, t; 2021; 2320; perc, gtr, str

West Side Story - Symphonic Dances (1960)          22'
   3*3*4=3*; a sax; 4331; timp+4, hp,             BH
   pf, str

Symphony No. 3 "Kaddish" (1963; rev 1977)          40'
   solo s; narr; satb cho; boys cho;              BH
   4=3*4=3*; a sax; 4431; timp+2, hp, pf, str

Chichester Psalms (1965)                           19'
   solo boy s; satb cho; 0000; 0330;              BH
   timp+1, 2hp, str

Two Meditations (1971)                             7'
   perc, hp, pf, org, str                         BH

Dybbuk:  Suite No. 1 (1974)                        30'
   soli bar, b; 3*3*4=3*; 4331; timp+3,           BH
   hp, pf, str

Dybbuk:  Suite No. 2 (1974)                        20'
   3*3*4=3*; 4331; timp+3, hp, pf, str            BH

Take Care of This House (1976)                     4'
   solo v; 113*1; 2221; timp+1, hp,               BH
   pf, gtr, str

Slava! - overture (1977)                           4'
   3*3*4=3*; s sax; 4331; 5perc, pf,              BH
   elec gtr, str

Songfest (1977)                                      40'
    soli s, mez, a, t, bar, b; 3*3*4=3*;             BH
    4331; timp+5, hp, pf/cel/elec pf,
    Fender b gtr, str

Three Meditations (1977)                             19'
    solo vc; perc, hp, pf, cel, org, str             BH

Divertimento (1980)                                  15'
    3*3*4=3*; 4331; timp+5, hp, pf, str              BH

A Musical Toast (1980)                                2'
    4*3*4=3*; 4331; timp+5, hp, pf, str              BH

Arias and Barcarolles (1988)                         29'
    soli mez, bar; 2perc, str                        BH

Concerto for Orchestra
    (Jubilee Games) (1988)                           30'
    solo bar; 4=3*4=3*; a sax; 4331;                 BH
    timp+5, hp, pf, mand, str, tape


            BESTOR, CHARLES  (1924-    )

Overture to a Romantic Comedy (1982)                 12'
    2*222; 4321; timp+3-4, str                       GS

In Memoriam Bill Evans (1989)                         9'
    2*222; 4221; timp+2, str                         TMP

Variations for Orchestra (1991)                      10'
    2*222; 2220; 1-2perc, str                        TMP


            BEVERSDORF, THOMAS  (1924-1981)

Reflections (1947)                                   NA
    2*222; 2220; timp+1, hp, str                     FLE

Suite for Clarinet, Violoncello and
    Strings (1947)                                   NA
    soli cl, vc; str                                 FLE

Concerto Grosso (1950)                               12'
    solo ob; 1111; 1111; timp, hp, str               FLE

Symphony No. 2 (1950)                                NA
    3*3*3*3*; 4331; timp+1, hp, pf, str              FLE

New Frontiers (1952)                NA
   3*3*3+3*; 4331; timp+2, hp, str     FLE

Ode for Orchestra (1952)            NA
   3*3*3*3*; 4331; timp+1, hp, str     FLE


## BEZANSON, PHILIP (1916-1975)

Rondo Prelude (1954)               8'
   3*23*3*; 4331; timp+2, str       ACA

Songs of Innocence (1959)          14'
   1111; 2000; str (4-2-2-1 desks)    ACA

Capriccio concertante (1967)       16'
   223*2; 2230; timp+1, str        ACA

Concertino for Oboe and Strings (1968)    7'
   solo ob; str                    ACA

Sinfonia concertante (1971)        14'
   2111; 1211; timp+1, pf, str      ACA

Memory (1975)                     7'
   satb cho; 4hn; str (4-2-2-1)     ACA


## BIANCHI, FREDERICK (1954-    )

Rauschenberg Variations (1987)      10'
   23*3+2; 4331; timp+3, hp, pf, str   NOA


## BIGGS, JOHN (1932-    )

Concerto for Oboe and String Orchestra (1958) 18'
   solo ob; str                    CST

Triple Concerto (1961)             19'
   soli hn, tpt, tbn; str          CST

Symphony No. 1 (1964)            27'
   2222; 4221; timp+1, str        CST

Concerto for Viola, Woodwinds and
   Percussion (1966)             23'
   solo vla; 2022; 0000; perc      CST

Variations on a Theme of Shostakovich (1977)     21'
    solo pf; 2222; 4221; 3perc, str                 CST

Songs of Laughter, Love and Tears (1985)         20'
    solo t; str                                     CST

Concerto for Orchestra (1988)                    20'
    2*2*22; 4331; timp+3, hp, str                   CST

Concerto for Violin and Classical
    Orchestra (1988)                             24'
    solo vln; 2222; 2200; timp, str                 CST

Symphony No. 2 (1991)                            23'
    2222; 4331; 3perc, hp, str                      CST


            BINGHAM, SETH   (1882-1972)

Concerto for Organ, Brass, Percussion
    and Strings, op. 46 (1946)                   21'
    solo org; 0000; 0220; timp+1, str               TP

Connecticut Suite, op. 56 (1953)                 15'
    tpt, tbn(opt), org, str                         TP


            BINKERD, GORDON   (1916-      )

Sun Singers (1952)                               10'
    3*3*3*3*; 4331; timp+1, hp, str                 BH

Symphony No. 1 (1955)                            23'
    3*3*3*3*; 4331; timp+4, hp, str                 BH

Symphony No. 2 (1957)                            27'
    3*3*3*3*; 3331; str                             BH

Symphony No. 3 (1959)                            13'
    3*222; 3331; timp, str                          BH

Movement for Orchestra (1972)                    11'
    2222; 2200; timp, str                           BH

A Part of Heaven (1972)                          16'
    solo vln; 3*3*3*2; 2220; timp, hp, str          BH

Five Transcriptions for String
    Orchestra (1974)                             18'
    str                                             BH

On the King's Highway - cantata (1979)          17'
   children's cho; 2222; 2200; timp, pf, str    BH

Two Meditations for Strings (1981)               5'
   str                                          BH


      BINNEY, OLIVER   (1928-    )

Haiku Cycle (1964)                              10'
   solo fl; str                                 IR

Three Poems for English Horn and
   Strings (1965)                                8'
   solo eh; str                                 IR

Sonnet for Violin (1966)                        12'
   solo vln; timp, str                          IR

Chorale for String Orchestra and
   Five Horns (1967)                            20'
   5hn; str                                     ACA


      BISCARDI, CHESTER   (1948-    )

At the Still Point (1977)                       15'
   3*222; 2221; timp+3, 2pf, str               MER
   N.B. The orchestra is divided into four
   groups - highs, lows, center, and
   trio (soli fl, pf, vln)

Eurydice (1978)                                 12'
   sa cho; 3*010; 2020; pf, str (4-0-4-0)      ACA

Concerto for Piano and Orchestra (1983)         20'
   solo pf; 2*2*2*2; 4221; timp+4, hp, str     MER

Tight-Rope (1985)                               89'
   9 singers; 1*11*1; a sax; 2110; 3perc,      MER
   hp, pf, str (3-3-3-2-2, min)


      BLACKWOOD, EASLEY   (1933-    )

Symphony No. 1, op. 3 (1958)                    29'
   4*3*4=4*; 6431; timp+1, cel, str            ELK

Symphony No. 2, op. 9 (1961)                    24'
   3*3*3*3*; 4431; timp+1, hp, str              GS

Concerto for Clarinet and Orchestra,
   op. 13 (1964)                                                   15'
    solo cl; 4*4*02; 3330; str                                   GS

Symphony No. 3, op. 14 (1965)                                      15'
   2121; 2000; str                                                 GS

Symphonic Fantasy, op. 17 (1965)                                   11'
   3*3*3*3*; 4331; timp+1, str                                     GS

Concerto for Oboe and String Orchestra,
   op. 19 (1965)                                                   15'
    solo ob; str                                                 GS

Concerto for Violin and Orchestra,
   op. 21 (1967)                                                   15'
    solo vln; 0200; 2000; str                                    GS

Concerto for Flute and String Orchestra,
   op. 23 (1968)                                                   14'
    solo fl; str                                                 GS

Concerto for Piano and Orchestra,
   op. 24 (1970)                                                   23'
    solo pf; 3*23*3*; 3220; timp+1, str                          GS

Symphony No. 4, op. 27 (1973)                                      33'
   6*4=4+5*; 854(cb tbn)1; timp+2, str                              GS

Symphony No. 5, op. 34 (1978)                                      23'
   33*3*3*; 4331; timp+2, str                                      BE


      BLANK, ALLAN   (1925-      )

Meditation for Orchestra (1967)                                    3'
   223*2; 4330; timp, hp, cel, str                                 TP

Music for Orchestra (1967)                                         8'
   3*3*4=3*; 4331; timp+4, hp, pf, cel, str              MER

Six Miniatures and a Fantasia (1972)                               15'
   3=3*3*3*; 4331; timp+4, hp, cel, str                            CF

American Folio (1974)                                              12'
   satb cho; 23*00; 2211; perc, str                               AMP

Six Significant Landscapes (1974)                                  18'
   1=12*1; 1110; hp, mand, str (1-1-1-1)                           ACA

Concertino (1984)                                        15'
   solo bsn; str                                       ACA

Utterances (1984)                                        12'
   soli s, a, t, b; 1020; 1110; 2perc,               ACA
   pf, str

Concertino (1987)                                        10'
   str                                               ACA

Overture for a Happy Occasion (1987)                     5'
   3*23*2; 4341; timp+4, pf/cel, str                 ACA

Concerto for Clarinet and String
   Orchestra (1990)                                  18'
   solo cl; str                                      ACA


      BLICKHAN, TIMOTHY  (1945-    )

Five Songs for Soprano and
   Strings (1980-1982)                               11'
   solo s; 3perc, hp(or pf), str                     MS

Dialectics for Orchestra (1983-1984)                     10'
   2222; 4331; 4perc, org, str                       MS


      BLITZSTEIN, MARC  (1905-1964)

The Airborne Symphony (1946)                             50'
   soli t, bar; narr; ttbb cho; 3*3*4=3*;            TP
   4331; perc, hp, pf, cel, str

Native Land - suite (1946)                               30'
   1*1*2(t sax)1; 0210; perc, pf/acc, str            TP

The Guests - suite (1948)                                20'
   2*2*2*2; 4220; perc, hp, pf, cel, str             TP

This is the Garden (1957)                                NA
   satb cho; 2*2*2+2; 2210; perc, pf,                TP
   hca, str

Lear; A Study (1958)                                     26'
   3*3*4+3*; 4531; timp+1, hp, str                   TP

BLOCH, ERNEST (1880-1959)

Concerto symphonique (1947-1948)                          38'
  3*3*3*3*; 4331; timp+3, cel, str                     BH

Scherzo fantastique (1948)                                9'
  3*3*3*3*; 4331; timp+1, hp, str                      GS

Concertino (1950)                                         8'
  soli fl, vla; str                                    GS

Suite hebraique (1951)                                    12'
  2222; 4300; timp+1, hp, str                          GS

Concerto Grosso No. 2 (1952)                              8'
  solo str qt; str                                     GS

In memoriam (1952)                                        3'
  2222; 2200; timp, str                                BRO

Sinfonia breve (1952)                                     18'
  3*3*3*3*; 4321; timp+1, hp, str                      GS

Symphony for Trombone and Orchestra (1954)                17'
  solo tbn; 3*3*3*3*; 4331; timp+2,                    BRO
  hp, cel, str

Symphony in E-flat (1954-1955)                            24'
  3*3*3*3*; 4331; timp+1, str                          GS

Proclamation (1955)                                       6'
  solo tpt; 2222; 4200; timp+1, str                    BRO

Suite modale (1956)                                       12'
  solo fl; str                                         BRO

Two Last Poems (1958)                                     13'
  solo fl; 23*22; 4200; timp+1, hp, str                BRO


BLUMENFELD, HOWARD (1923-    )

Elegy for the Nightingale (1954)                          15'
  solo bar; satb cho; 3*3*3*3*; 4230;                  MMB
  timp+2, str

Dramatic Symphony from "Amphitryon 4" (1962)              22'
  solo mez, bar; satb cho; 2*121*; 3220;               MCA
  timp+3, hp, cel, str

Miniature Overture (1962)                                   5'
   2*121*; 3220; timp+3, hp, cel, str          MMB

Song of Innocence (1975)                                   25'
   soli mez, t; satb cho; 2121; 4111;            MMB
   perc, str

Starfires (1975)                                           20'
   soli mez, t; 0000; 3111; timp+3, cel,         MMB
   str (0-1-1-1)

Scenes from Rimbaud (1988)                                 19'
   3=3*3=3*; 4331; timp+4, hp, pf, cel, str      MMB

#### BODA, JOHN  (1922-    )

Sinfonia (1959)                                            25'
   2222; 4331; timp+1, str                        TP

#### BOHMLER, CRAIG  (1956-    )

Celebre - Sonata for Flute and Chamber
   Orchestra (1988)                              17'
   solo fl; 1*1*11; 2111; timp+1, hp, str        MMB

#### BOHRNSTEDT, WAYNE  (1923-    )

Essay for Orchestra (1947)                                 22'
   3*3*3*3*; 4431; timp+1, hp, str                MS

Ballad for LaCrosse (1948)                                 12'
   satb cho; 2222; 2231; timp+3, str              MS

Essay on an Original Air (1949)                             8'
   2222; 4231; timp+2, hp, pf, str                MS

Idyll (1949)                                                6'
   hp, str                                        MS

Romantic Overture (1950)                                    7'
   2222; 4331; timp+3, pf, str                    MS

Symphony No. 1 (1951; rev 1955)                            21'
   3*222; 4331; timp+3, pf, str                   MS

Concerto for Trumpet and Orchestra (1952)                 13'
   solo tpt; 1111; 1000; timp, str                MS

Festival Overture (1956)                          6'
  2*222; 4331; timp+3, pf, str            MS

Concerto for Piano and Orchestra (1957)          20'
  solo pf; 2222; 4331; timp+2, str        MS

Dance Suite (1958)                               12'
  222(a sax)2; 4331; timp+3, str          MS

Concertino for Timpani, Xylophone and
Orchestra (1959)                                 10'
  soli timp, xyl; 2222; 4220; str         MS

Concertino for Trombone and Strings (1960)       10'
  solo tbn; str                           MS

Tetrachord Suite (1961)                           9'
  2222; 4231; timp+2, pf, str             MS

A Little Piece for a Great Hall (1971)            6'
  3*222; 4231; 3perc, hp, str             MS

Variations for a Celebration (1987)              15'
  3*3*3*3*; 4331; timp+4, hp, str         MS

Concerto for Viola and Orchestra (1989)          23'
  solo vla; 2222; 4200; timp+1, str       MS

Concerto for Two Horns and Orchestra (1991)      18'
  soli 2hns; 2222; 4200; str              MS


      BOLCOM, WILLIAM  (1938-    )

Songs of Innocence and Experience
(1956-1981)                                      160'
  soli s, mez, ca, t, bar, b, boy s;      EBM
  country, rock, folk singers
  (5 to 10 soloists); satb cho; madrigal cho;
  children's cho; 3*3*3*3*; a,t sax; 6553;
  7perc, hp, elec pf, cel, org, hca, gtr,
  b gtr, 2 elec vln, str

Symphony No. 1 (1957)                            20'
  2222; 2200; timp+1, pf, str             MS

Concertante for Violin, Flute, Oboe
and Orchestra (1961)                             18'
  soli vln, fl, ob; 113*2; 2100; hp, str   EBM

Concerto Serenade for Violin and String
   Orchestra (1964)     18'
   solo vln; str     EBM

Symphony No. 2 (Oracles) (1964)     16'
   2221*; 4231; 4perc, hp, pf/cel, str     MS

Commedia (for "Almost" 18th Century
   Orchestra) (1971)     10'
   1*21+2; 2000; pf, str     EBM
   N.B. There are solos for 2 violins and 1 cello.

Summer Divertimento (1973)     25'
   3*011; 0100; perc, pf, hpsd, str (3-2-2-2) EBM

Open House (1975)     35'
   solo t; 1212; 2000; perc, pf, str     EBM

Concerto for Piano and Orchestra (1976)     28'
   solo pf; 4*4*4=4*; 4432; timp+1, hp, str     EBM

Humoresk (1979)     12'
   solo org; 2222; 4231; timp+1, pf, str     EBM

Symphony No. 3 (1979)     35'
   1=21=2; 2000; pf/elec pf/cel,     EBM
   str (6-4-4-3-1)

Ragomania - A Classical Festival
   Overture (1982)     10'
   3*3*3*3*; 4331; timp+1, hp, pf, gtr, str     EBM

Concerto in D for Violin and
   Orchestra (1984)     20'
   solo vln; 2222; 2221; timp+2, hp, pf,     EBM
   cel, str

Fantasia Concertante for Viola, Cello and
   Orchestra (1985)     15'
   soli vla, vc; 3*3*3*3*; 4000; timp+1, str     EBM

Fourth Symphony (1986)     35'
   solo mez (or bar); 3*3*3=3*; 4441;     EBM
   timp+1, hp, pf, str

Seattle Slew - dance suite (1986)     24'
   3*3*3*3; 43(flu hn)31; timp+1, hp, pf str     EBM

Spring Concertino (1986-1987)     10'
   solo ob; 21*22; 1000; hp, str     EBM

Fifth Symphony (1989)                                        24'
    3*3*3*3*; 4331; timp+4, hp, str                          EBM

MCMXC, Tanglewood (1990)                                      5'
    3*3*3*3*; 4331; timp+3, pf/cel, str                      EBM

Concerto for Clarinet and Orchestra (1990)                  25'
    solo cl; 3*323; 4341; timp+3, hp,                       EBM
    pf/cel, str


        BOND, VICTORIA  (1945-      )

Recitative for English Horn and
    Strings (1970)                                            5'
    solo eh; str                                            SEE

Two Orchestral Interludes (1970)                             4'
    1121; 2111; 2perc, hp, pf, str (0-4-4-2)                MS

Elegy (1971)                                                 2'
    1111; 2220; timp+1, str                                 MS

Four Fragments for Orchestra (1972)                          6'
    timp+2, pf, str                                         MS

Sonata for Orchestra (1972)                                  5'
    2*222; 2221; timp+1, hp, str                            SEE

C-A-G-E-D for String Orchestra (1974)                       11'
    str                                                     SEE

Equinox - suite (1977)                                      30'
    2222; 2210; timp+1, hp, pf, str                         SEE

Concertino:  Variations on an American
    Folksong (1981)                                         10'
    1*21+2; 2000; timp+1, str                               MS

Great Galloping Gottschalk (1981)                          20'
    3*2*22; 4331; timp+2, hp, pf, str                       TP

Journal 1981 (1981)                                          7'
    1212; 2200; timp+1, str                                 MS

The Frog Prince (1983-1984)                                 24'
    narr; 222*2; 4331; perc, str                            GS

What's the Point of Counterpoint? (1984-1985) 24'
    narr; 2*2*2*2; 4331; timp+3, hp, str                    MS

Ringing (1986)                                        4'
   3*2*32*; 4331; timp+1, str            MS

Black Light (1988)                                   20'
   solo pf; 3*222; a,t sax; 4331; perc, str   MS


     BOONE, CHARLES  (1939-    )

The Edge of the Land (1968)                          14'
   2*222; 4221; 2perc, hp, pf,           SAL
   Hammond org, str

Chinese Texts (1971)                                 15'
   solo s; 2222; 3221; 3perc, pf, str    SAL

First Landscape (1971)                               15'
   4*4*4*4*; 4431; perc, pf, str         SAL

Second Landscape (1973)                              14'
   1111*; 0200; 2perc, pf, str (2-1-1-2)  SAL
   N.B.  May also be performed with multiple
   strings.

String Piece (1978)                                  12'
   str (4-3-2-2-1, desks)                SAL


     BORISHANSKY, ELLIOT  (1930-    )

Music for Orchestra (1958)                           12'
   3*3*3*3*; 4230; timp+1, str           TP

In Commemoration (1981)                               3'
   str                                   ACA


     BORROFF, EDITH  (1925-    )

Concerto for Marimba and Orchestra (1981)            12'
   solo mar; 2222; 2200; perc, str       ACA


     BOTTJE, WILL GAY  (1925-    )

Concerto for Flute, Trumpet and
   Strings (1955)                        22'
   soli fl, tpt; timp+1, hp, cel, str    ACA

Concerto for Piano and Orchestra (1955)            20'
    solo pf; 2222; 4221; perc, str                      ACA

Concertino for Piccolo and Orchestra (1956)   10'
    solo picc; 2222; 3220; perc, str                    ACA

Symphony No. 5 (1959)                              15'
    3*222; 4331; timp+1, str                            ACA

Wayward Pilgrim (1961)                             50'
    solo s; satb cho; 2121; 2110; perc,                 ACA
    pf, str

Rhapsodic Variations (1962)                        12'
    solo vla; pf, str                                   ACA

Ballad Singer (1963)                               8'
    213*1; 3331; timp+1, str                            ACA

Tangents (Symphony No. 7) (1970)                   20'
    3*3*3*3*; 4331; 3perc, pf, str, tape                ACA

Chiaroscuros (1975)                                15'
    4*24=2; a sax; 4331; perc, pf, str                  ACA

Concerto for Tuba (1977)                           16'
    solo tba; 3*23*2; 4330; timp+1, str                 ACA

Mutations (1977)                                   16'
    2121; 2110; 2perc, str                              ACA

Concerto for Oboe, Bassoon and
    Chamber Orchestra (1981)                       16'
    soli ob, bsn; 2*02*0; 2110; timp+1, str             ACA

Songs from the Land between Rivers (1981)     39'
    satb cho; 3*23*2; 4331; 4perc, str                  ACA

Commentaries (1983)                                17'
    solo gtr; 1121; 1100; perc, str                     ACA

Sounds from the West Shore (1983)                  16'
    3*222; 4221; timp+3, str                            ACA

Concerto for Oboe, Violin and Small
    Orchestra (1984)                               19'
    soli ob, vln; 2202; 0110; 2perc, hp, str            ACA

Concerto for Two Flutes and Orchestra (1986)  19'
    soli 2fl; 2111; 2110; hp, str                       ACA

BOURLAND, ROGER  (1952-     )

Clarinet Rhapsody (1979)                          9'
   solo cl; 2*202; 2000; perc, str              MG


BOWMAN, CARL  (1913-     )

Ballad (1947)                                     6'
   solo hn; 2121; 0210; timp, str               AMC

Commentary (1954)                                8'
   solo tbn; str                                AMC

Fantasy on a Carol Tune (1960)                   3'
   213*1; 3321; str                             AMC

Triptych (Symphony)                             22'

   1. Symphonic Statement (1958)               10'
        str                                     AMC

   2. Primavera (1963)                          5'
        3*24*2; 4331; euph; timp+1, db          AMC

   3. Theater Piece (1983)                      7'
        3*24*2; 4331; euph; timp+1, str         AMC


BOYKAN, MARTIN  (1931-     )

Concerto for Thirteen Players (1972)            25'
   1021; 1110; hp, pf, str (1-1-1-1)            BOE

Symphony (1989)                                 25'
   solo bar; 3*3*3=3*; 4331; timp+1, hp, str   ANM


BRADSHAW, SAMUEL  (1937-     )

Five Movements for Orchestra (1975)             27'
   3*3*3*2; 4331; timp+1, hp, pf, str          AMC

Symphony in Three Movements (1977)              26'
   3*3*3*2; 4331; timp+1, hp, pf/cel, str      AMC

BRANDT, WILLIAM E.   (1920-      )

The Enchanted Garden - suite (1947)                    6'
  2*222; 2200; timp, pf, str                         MS

Sinfonietta II (1948)                                 18'
  3*222; 4200; timp, str                              MS

Symphony No. 1 (1950)                                 22'
  3*222; 4231; timp+2, hp, str                        MS

Suite for Small Orchestra (1950)                      28'
  2*222; 2200; timp. pf, str                          MS

Music for the Decalogue (NA)                          28'
  narr; 3*222; 4331; timp+3, pf, str                  MS


BRANT, HENRY   (1913-      )

  N.B. An asterisk before the title of a
composition denotes that spatial separation
is required.

Dedication in Memory of FDR (1945)                     7'
  2222; 4231; timp+1, str                             CF

The 1930's - Symphony in B-flat (1945)                21'
  3*3*3*3*; 4331; timp+3, str                         CF

Concerto for Clarinet and Orchestra (1946)            14'
  solo cl; 1122; 2210; timp+1, pf, str                CF

*Antiphony I (1953; rev 1968)                         11'
  opt vv; 3330; s,a,t,bar sax; 5330;                  CF
  timp+1, str
  N.B. Four assistant conductors are needed,
in addition to the principal conductor.

Stresses (1954)                                        7'
  hp, pf/cel, str                                     CF

Labyrinth I (1955)                                    13'
  soli 2s, 2a (opt); str                              CF

On the Nature of Things
  (After Lucretia) (1956)                             14'
  1101; 1000; glock, hp, unis str (no db)             CF

*Mythical Beasts (1958)                                          12'
    solo mez; 1111; 2110; perc, pf,                             CF
    str (2-1-1-1)

*Atlantis (1960)                                                 20'
    solo mez; narr; satb cho; 3*3*23*; 4330;                    CF
    timp+4, hp, pf, org, str
    band:  2*130; a,t,bar sax; 1331; 2euph; 4perc

*Fire in Cities (1961)                                           6'
    cho I:  men (or women); cho II:  sab;                       CF
    0220; timp+6, 4pf, org, unis str

*Voyage Four (1963)                                             45'
    solo s; 3*3*13*; 4331; timp+3, hp, hpsd,                    CF
    2org, mand, str

Odyssey - Why Not? (1965)                                       18'
    solo fl; 1222; 2220; timp+2, hp, pf, str                    CF

*Kingdom Come (1967)                                            21'
    solo fem v; 6*3*6=3*; 2a,t,bar sax; 4663;                   CF
    euph; timp+5, 2hp, org obbl, str

*Nomads/Triple Concerto (1974)                                  18'
    solo bar; soli babone (tbn with bsn bocal                   CF
    and reed), steel drums; 3*(3picc)333;
    4431; timp+4, str

*Homage to Ives (1975)                                          20'
    solo bar; 3*3*3*3*; 4331; timp+1, hp, str                   CF

*Spatial Concerto
    (Questions from Genesis) (1976)                             22'
    solo pf; ssaa cho; 3*3*3*3*; 4331;                          CF
    timp+3, hp, str

*Antiphonal Responses - Triple Concerto for
    Three Bassoons with Orchestra, Isolated
    Musicians and Piano Obbligato (1978)                        18'
    soli 3bsn; 3*3*3*3*; 4331; timp+4, hp,                      CF
    pf, str

*Curriculum II (Spatial Tone Poem) (1978)                       14'
    1212; 1110; timp, hp, pf, str                               CF

Saraband (1978)                                                 2'
    solo vln (or vla); str                                      CF

*Secret Calendar (1980)                                  60'
  3*3*3*3*; s,a sax; 2222; timp+2, pf,          CF
  hpsd, org, gtr, bj, str

*Meteor Farm (1982)                                      60'
  soli 2s; 3*23*2; 4000; str                     CF
  satb cho 1:  with 2a,t sax
  satb cho 2:  with 3fl(3picc)
  br cho:  3tpt, 3tbn
  2 perc groups of 4 players each
  jazz band:  2a,2t,bar sax; 3tpt, 3tbn, tba
  Javanese gamelan orch
  West African drum ensemble
  South Indian trio

*Desert Forests/Spatial Panoramas (1983)                 15'
  3*3*4*3*; 5331; timp+4, hp, cel, str            CF

*Litany of Tides (1983)                                  23'
  soli 4s, vln; 3*3*3*3*; 5332; timp+3,           CF
  2pf, hp, mand, str

*Western Springs (1984)                                  55'
  satb cho I & II                                 CF
  orch 1:  2222; 2220; timp+2, pf, str
  orch 2:  2222; 2220; timp+2, pf, str
  jazz combo 1:  s,a,t,bar sax; tpt, tbn,
  4perc, org
  jazz combo 2:  s,a,t,bar sax; tpt, tbn,
  4perc, org

*Prisoners of the Mind (1990)                            28'
  orch 1: 13*13*; 0031; timp+2, hp, pf, str   CF
  orch 2: 203=0; 0001; timp+2, hp, pf, str
  br cho 1: 4200
  br cho 2: 4200
  2 steel drum bands of 7 drums each
  two symphonic bands, each consisting of:
  8fl(3picc), 1ob, 10cl(e-flat, 2b cl), 1bsn;
  2a,t,bar sax; 1663; 2euph; perc

*The Old Italians Dying (1991)                           17'
  narr; 3*3*3*3*; 5331; timp+3, hp. pf, str   CF


     BREHM, ALVIN   (1925-    )

Hephaestus Overture (1966)                               10'
  3*223*; 4331; timp+1, str                       EBM

Concerto for Tuba and Orchestra (1982)            22'
   solo tba; 222*2; 4330; timp+1, hp,            GS
   pf/cel, str


     BRESNICK, MARTIN   (1946-      )

Ocean of Storms (1969-1970)                       13'
   3*22*2; 4331; 2perc, pf, str                  BB

Wir weben, wir weben (1976-1978)                  24'
   str (6-6-3-3-1)                               CMM

One (1986)                                        10'
   2*2*2*2; 2220; vib, str                       CMM


     BRINGS, ALLEN   (1934-      )

A Cradle Song (1954; orch'd 1959)                  2'
   solo med v; 2222; 2220; hp, str               MMA

Never Seek to Tell thy Love
   (1954; orch'd 1959)                            3'
   solo med v; 2222; 2220; hp, str               MMA

Song (1956)                                        5'
   solo med v; 2222; 2220; hp, str               MMA

Concerto for Orchestra (1957; rev 1978)           16'
   2222; 2210; timp+1, str                       MMA

Symphony (1964; rev 1984)                         24'
   3*222; 4230; timp+3, hp, pf/cel, str          MMA

Concerto da Camera No. 1 (1974)                   11'
   solo pf; 1111; 1110; timp+1, str              SEE

Concerto da Camera No. 3 (1976)                   10'
   solo fl; str                                  SEE

Three Songs (1976)                                12'
   solo med v; 2222; 2220; timp+1, hp, str       SEE

A Herrick Suite (1977)                             4'
   1.  To Primroses filled with                  MMA
      Morning Dew
      satb cho; 2222; 2000; str
   2. To Music, to becalm his fever
      satb cho; 2222; 2000; str

Two Pieces for Orchestra (1977)                            11'
  3*3*3*3*; 4331; timp+4, hp, str                 SEE

Scherzi musicali (1987)                                     8'
  2*222; 2210; timp+1, str                        MMA

Three Holy Sonnets (1988)                                  10'
  satb cho; 2222; 4231; timp+2, str               MMA

Sinfonia da Camera (1990)                                  18'
  1111; 1110; timp+1, str (2-1-1-1)               MMA

Serenade for Orchestra (1991)                              9'
  2222; 2200; timp+1, str                         MMA


     BRITAIN, RADIE   (1899-     )

Jewels of Lake Tahoe (1945)                                5'
  2112; 2221; timp+1, str                         FLE

Red Clay (1946)                                            7'
  3*223*; 4331; timp+2, str                       HMP

Serenata Sorrentina (1946)                                 3'
  2112; 2220; timp+1, str                         HMP

Umpqua Forest (1946)                                       8'
  3*223*; 4321; timp+2, str                       HMP

Paint Horse and Saddle (1947)                              7'
  2222; 4331; timp+2, str                         HMP

Chicken in the Rough (1951)                                4'
  2121; 2221; timp+1, str                         HMP

Cactus Rhapsody (1953)                                     8'
  2222; 4221; timp+2, str                         FLE

The Earth Does Not Wish For Beauty (1953)                 12'
  satb cho; 2222; 4330; perc, str                 HMP

Angel Chimes (1954)                                        3'
  1111; 1100; perc, cel(or pf), str               HMP

Solar Joy (1955)                                           4'
  3*222; 4331; timp+2, str                        HMP

Cowboy Rhapsody (1956)                                    13'
  3*222; 4331; timp+2, str                        FLE

Minha Terra (1958)                                              4'
    2222; 3221; timp+1, str                                    HMP

This is the Place (1958)                                       5'
    2222; 4331; timp+2, str                                    HMP

Nisan (1961)                                                   8'
    ssaa cho; str                                              HMP

Cosmic Mist Symphony (1962)                                   24'
    3*222; 4331; timp+4, str                                   FLE

Kambu (1963)                                                   8'
    2222; 4331; timp+1, str                                    HMP

Little per cent (1963)                                         4'
    2222; 4331; timp+1, str                                    HMP

Brothers of the Clouds (1964)                                 10'
    ttbb cho; 2222; 4331; perc, str                            HMP

Les Fameux Douze (1965)                                       5'
    1111; 0011; str                                            HMP

Pyramids of Giza (1973)                                       8'
    1111; 1100; perc, str                                      HMP

The Builders (1978)                                           4'
    satb cho; 2221; 2200; timp+1, str                          HMP

Anwar Sadat (In Memory) (1982)                                8'
    2222; 3331; perc, str                                      FLE

Mother (A Melody of Love) (1982)                              9'
    solo v; narr; 2222; 2220; timp, hp, str    HMP

Earth of God (1984)                                           9'
    str                                                        FLE

Sam Houston (1987)                                           18'
    2222; 4331; timp+2, str                                    HMP

Texas (1987)                                                 18'
    2222; 4331; timp+1, str                                    FLE


            BROOKS, RICHARD  (1942-    )

Chorale Variations (1980)                                    15'
    soli 2hn, str qnt; str                                     ACA

Symphony (1981)                                    20'
   3*222; 4331; 3perc, str                         ACA

Seascape:  Overture to Moby Dick (1987)            7'
   3*3*4=3*; 4331; timp+3, str                     ACA


      BROOKS, WILLIAM   (1943-    )

Dancing on Your Grave (1989-1990)                  18'
   1=02=1*; t sax; 11(flu hn)11(euph);             SMI
   3perc, hp, pf, str (4-3-2-2-2)


      BROWN, EARLE   (1926-    )

Folio (1952)                                       var

   1.  November 1952 (Synergy)                   var
      any number of any instruments            AMP

   2.  December 1952                             var
      any number of any instruments            UE

   3.  Trio for Five Dancers                     var
      any number of any instruments            UE

Four Systems (1954)                                var
   any number of any instruments                  AMP
   N.B.  This work may also be included
   in "Folio".

Indices (1954)                                     29'
   1000; 1100; 2 perc, 2vib, marimbula,           MS
   glock, pf, 2 amp gtr, str (2-0-2-2)
   N.B.  Percussion requirements are as follows;
   3 gongs, 2 brake drums, 5 cowbells,
   3 Chinese drums.

Pentathis (1957-1958)                              var
   101*0; 0220; hp, pf, str (1-1-1-0)             MS

Available Forms I (1961)                           var
   112=0; 1110; 2perc, hp, pf, str                AMP
   N.B.  Duration is between 12' and 15'.

Available Forms II (1962)                              var
   orch 1:  2*2*1*1; 3221; 2perc, hp, gtr,            AMP
   str (8-7-6-5-4)
   orch 2:  2+122*; 3221; 2perc, hp, pf/cel,
   str (8-7-6-5-4)
   N.B.  Requires two conductors for performance.
   Duration ranges from 15' to 20'.

Novara (1962)                                         11'
   101*0; 0100; pf, str (2-1-1-0)                     UE

From Here (1963)                                      10'
   satb cho (4-4-4-4); 1131; 1111; 2perc,            UE
   hp, pf, amp gtr, str

Modules I (1966)                                      var
   212*1; 2221; str                                   UE

Modules II (1966)                                     var
   12*12*; 2220; str                                  UE

Event:  Synergy II (1967-1968)                        var
   2*3*4=2; 0000; str (4-2-2-1)                       UE

Modules III (1969)                                    var
   2121; 1210; perc, xyl, mat, vib, hp,              UE
   pf, str
   N.B.  Any two of the "Modules" may be performed
   simultaneously by a double orchestra with two
   conductors.

One to Five (1969)                                    var
   any number of any instruments                      MS

New Piece (1971)                                      var
   any number of any instruments                      MS
   (minimum of 20)

New Piece:  Loops (1972)                              var
   large satb cho; 2122; 2222; 2perc, 2hp,           UE
   2pf, str
   N.B.  Duration ranges from 15' to 20'.

Sign Sounds (1972)                                    17'
   1021; 0110; 4perc, hp, pf, cel,                   UE
   str (2-1-1-1)

Time Spans (1972)                                     12'
   3+2*43; 4442; 2vib, 2mar, 2hp, 2pf, str           UE

Centering (1973)                                      20'
   solo vln; 1011; 1110; pf, str (1-1-1-0)      UE

Cross Sections and Color Fields (1975)                19'
   4*23*2; s sax; 4332; 6perc, 2hp, pf,          UE
   cel, str

Sounder Rounds (1983)                                 15'
   2+3*3*2*; 4321; vib, mar, xyl, glock, hp,     MS
   pf, str (16-14-10-8-6, all divisi a 2)

For P.B. (1985)                                        8'
   minimum players:  pf, 2vln, 2vc, db            MS
   N.B.  The string parts may be increased.

Hear We Go Again (1991)                               var
   101*0; 0000; perc, pf, vln, vc                 MS
   N.B.  Instrumentation may be doubled or tripled.


     BROWN, J.E.   (1937-     )

Intermezzo (1962)                                      7'
   str                                            MS

Fontaine, Je ne boirai pas de ton eau (1966)  8'
   solo s; 1111; 1110; hp, str                   ACA

Fragments (1966)                                       6'
   1111; 1110; hp, str (no db)                   ACA

Fixed Ideas (1974)                                    10'
   2022; 2220; 2perc, str                        ACA

Notturno (1985)                                        6'
   2222; 2110; hp, str                           ACA

Symphony for Chamber Orchestra (1988)                 16'
   2222; 2110; timp, hp, str                     ACA


     BROWNE, PHILIP  (1933-     )

Prelude and Scherzo for Orchestra (1960)               9'
   23*3*2; 4331; timp+1, str                      MS

Serenade for Orchestra (1973)                          8'
   23*3*2; 4331; timp+1, str                     EAM

Concerto for Strings (1976)                              8'
   str                                     EAM


     BRUBECK, DAVID  (1920-    )

The Light in the Wilderness (1968)                       30'
   solo bar; ssaattbb cho; 3*3*3*3*; 4331;   SHA
   perc, hpsd, org, str

Fugal Fanfare (1970)                                     10'
   3*3*3*3*; 4331; timp+3, str               SHA

Truth is Fallen (1971)                                   31'
   soli s; jazz combo; 3*3*3*3*; 4331;       SHA
   2perc, hpsd, org, str

La Fiesta de la Posada (1975)                            35'
   soli s, a, t, b; satb cho; children's cho; SHA
   3*3*3*3*; 4331; timp+2, hp, hpsd, gtr, str

Beloved Son (1978)                                       36'
   solo bar; ssaattbb cho; 23*3*3*; 4331;    SHA
   timp+1, hpsd, str

Brandenburg Gate: Revisited (NA)                         12'
   112*1; 2000; str                          SHA

Cathy's Waltz (NA)                                       7'
   solo jazz combo; 23*22; 4331; timp+2, str SHA

In Your Own Sweet Way (NA)                               7'
   solo jazz combo; str                      SHA

Out of the Way of People (NA)                            5'
   solo jazz combo; 3*3*3*2*; 4331;          SHA
   2perc, str

Summersong (NA)                                          9'
   solo jazz combo; 23*3*1; 4331; 2perc, str SHA


     BRUBECK, HOWARD  (1916-    )

The Devil's Disciple - Overture (1954)                   10'
   2*2*22; 4230; timp+2, pf, str             DRY

Four Dialogues (1956)                                    23'
   solo jazz combo; 2*2*22; 4331;            DRY
   timp+2, str

Symphonic Movement on a Theme of Robert
    Kurka (1958)                                    9'
    2*2*22; 4331; timp+2, str                       DRY

The Gardens of Versailles (1960)                   18'
    2*222; 2220; timp+1, str                        DRY


                BRÜN, HERBERT   (1918-     )

Concertino for Orchestra, op. 2 (1947)             NA
    3*3*22; 2110; str                               SMI

Overture, op. 8 (1949)                             10'
    3*3*22; 4331; 2perc, str                        SMI

Mobile for Orchestra (1958)                        13'
    4(picc,b fl)3*4=3*; 436(3b tbn)3; timp,         SMI
    str (8-5-4-3 players)


            BRUNELLI, LOUIS JEAN   (1925-     )

Essay for Cyrano (1971)                            21'
    3*3*3*3*; 4331; timp+1, hp, str                 BH

Two Gentlemen from Verona (NA)                      9'
    2*2*22; 2220; timp, hp, str                     TP


            BRUNSWICK, MARK   (1902-1971)

Symphony in B-flat (1945)                          18'
    3*222; 2220; timp, str                          ACA

Eros and Death (A Choral Symphony) (1954)          45'
    satb cho; 3*3*3*5*; 6441; timp+1, hp,           ACA
    pf, str

Air with Toccata (1967)                             6'
    str                                             ACA


            BUBALO, RUDOLPH   (1928-     )

Strata (1974)                                      11'
    2222; 2210; 3perc, hp, pf, str                  MS

Spacescape (1975)                                     12'
   3*3*3*3*; 4331; 5perc, pf,                         GAL
   str (12-12-10-10-8)

Seven Rays (1976)                                     18'
   3*23*2; 4331; 3perc, hp, pf, str                   MS

Trajectories (1979)                                   20'
   3*3*3*3*; a,t,bar sax; 4331; 5perc, hp,            MS
   pf, elec pf, str (12-12-10-10-8), tape

Adagio and Allegro (1983)                             15'
   solo cl; 2222; 2210; 2perc, pf,                    MS
   str (12-10-8-6-4)

Symmetricality (1983)                                 16'
   solo pf; 2222; 2210; 2perc,                        MS
   str (12-10-8-6-4)

Concertino for Orchestra (1985)                       12'
   3*3*3*3*; 4331; 5perc, hp, pf, str                 MS

Offset I (1985)                                       17'
   1121; 2110; 2perc, 3synth, str                     MS

The Sound of Isness (1986)                            16'
   1111; 1110; perc, 2synth, str                      MS

Concerto for Cello for Orchestra (1991)               20'
   solo vc; 223*2; 2111; perc, 2synth, str            MS


              BUCCI, MARK  (1924-    )

Concerto for a Singing Instrument (1966)              NA
   solo any melodic inst; hp, cel, str                GS

Little Bird (NA)                                       2'
   solo med v; 1111; 1000; hp, str                    MCA


              BURTON, ELDIN  (1913-    )

Nocturne:  A Piece for Clara (1945)                    4'
   soli ww qnt; str                                   ACA

Ballade (1949)                                        13'
   2222; 4331; timp, str                              ACA

BURTON, STEPHEN   (1943-      )

Ode to a Nightingale (1963)                          23'
    solo s; fl, hp, str                              SCH

Sinfonia for Large Orchestra (1968)                  18'
    4=4*12; 5440; timp, hp, pf, str                  BB

Dithyramb (1972)                                     12'
    3*3*3*3*; 4331; timp+4, hp, pf, str              SAL

Stravinskiana:   Concerto for Flute
    and Orchestra (1975)                             20'
    solo fl; 0000; 4221; timp+1, hp,                 MS
    pf/cel, str

Symphony No. 2 "Ariel" (1975)                        45'
    solo bar; 4=4*3*2; 5440; timp+2, hp,             SAL
    pf, str

Song of the Tulpehocken (1976)                       50'
    solo t; 3*3*3*3*; 4230; timp+4, hp, str          SAL

Variations on a Theme of Mahler (1982)               20'
    3*3*3*3*; 4331; timp+3, hp, pf, str              DYD

Fanfare for Peace (1983)                             15'
    3*3*3*3*; 4331; timp+3, hp, pf, str              DYD

Pied Piper Overture (1983)                           15'
    3*3*3*3*; 4331; timp+4, hp, pf, cel, str         DYD

I Have a Dream (1987)                                25'
    solo s; narr; satb cho; 3*3*3*3*; 4331;          DYD
    timp+4, hp, str

CAGE, JOHN   (1912-1992)

The Seasons - Ballet I (1947)                         15'
  2*2*2=2; 2220; timp+1, hp, pf/cel, str       CFP

Concerto for Prepared Piano (1950-1951)               19'
  solo prep pf; 1*2*21; 1121; 4perc, hp,       CFP
  pf/cel, str

Concerto for Piano and Orchestra (1957-1958)   var
  solo pf; 1=011; bar sax; 0111;               CFP
  str (3-2-0-1)
  N.B. May be performed in whole or in part,
  in any duration, with any number of the
  above performers.

Atlas Eclipticalis (1961)                             var
  3*3*3*3*; 5333; 3timp+9, 3hp, str            CFP
  N.B. 86 parts to be used in whole or in
  part, any number, any combination.

Cheap Imitation (1969; orch'd 1972)                   var
  Version for 24:   3=2*2*1; a sax; 1111;      CFP
  2perc, hp, pf, cel, gtr, str (2-1-1-1)

  Version for 59:   6=4*4*2; 2a sax; 2222;
  timp+4, 2hp, pf, cel, gtr, str (12-4-4-3)

  Version for 95:   9=6*6*3; 3a sax; 3333;
  timp+4, 3hp, pf, cel, gtr, str (24-9-9-3)

Et cetera (1973)                                      30'
  1111; 1101; 6perc, 2pf, str (2-1-1-1),       CFP
  tape

Score and 23 Parts (1974)                             28'
  for any combination of 23 instr and/or       CFP
  vv and tape

Apartment House 1776 (1976)                           var
  soli 4vv (live or rec); any number and       CFP
  combination of instruments

Quartets I-VIII (1976)                                  40'
   Version for 24:  1212; 2000;                      CFP
     str (5-4-3-3-1)

   Version for 41: 2222; 2200;
     str (8-7-6-5-3)

   Version for 93:  34*4=3; 6431;
     str (18-15-12-11-9)

Renga (1976)                                            35'
   78 parts for any instruments and/or voices CFP

Dance Four Orchestras (1981)                            18'
   3*3*3*3*; 4331; timp+3, hp, pf,                CFP
   str (8-8-6-5-3)

Thirty Pieces for Five Orchestras (1982)               30'
   3=333; 556(2t,2b,2cb)0; timp+2, pf, str         CFP

A Collection of Rocks (1984)                            20'
   ssaattb cho; 2222; a,t,bar sax; 2230;          CFP
   str (no vla, db)

Ryoanji (1984-1985)                                    var
   any 20 instruments                             CFP

Et cetera 2/4 Orchestras (1986)                        30'
   3=3*3*2*; 4331; 3perc, hp, pf,                 CFP
   str (12-12-8-6-4), tape

Europeras I/II (1987)                                  var
   soloists; 3(2picc)3(2eh)3*2; 2231;             CFP
   timp+1, str (2-1-1-1), tape

101 (1989)                                             var
   4=4*4*4*; 6431; timp+4, hp, pf,                CFP
   str (18-16-11-11-8)

Twenty-Three (1989)                                    23'
   str (13-5-5-0)                                 CFP


       CALABRO, LOUIS  (1926-      )

Symphony No. 1 in One Movement (1956)                  20'
   3*3*3*2; 4331; timp+1, str                     ELK

Symphony No. 2 (1957)                                        20'
   str                                                         ELK

Ten Short Pieces (1961)                                       8'
   str                                                         ELK

Symphony No. 3 in One Movement (1962)                        17'
   3*3*3*3*; 4331; timp+2, cel, str                          ELK

Voyage (1975)                                                NA
   solo mez; narr; satb cho; 3*222; 4331;                    AMC
   timp+3, hp, pf, cel, str

Cantilena (NA)                                                6'
   solo s; str                                               ELK


     CALDWELL, JAMES  (1957-    )

Sinfonia Concertate in Stilo Moderno (1982)                 12'
   1111; 1110; str                                           MS


     CALLAWAY, ANN  (1949-    )

Concerto for Bass Clarinet (1989)                           16'
   solo b cl; 1121; 2110; 2perc, cel, str                    ACA


     CALTABIANO, RONALD  (1959-    )

Medea (1982)                                                 18'
   solo s; 1*12*1; 1100; str (1-1-1-1)                        MER

Concerto for Alto Saxophone and
   Orchestra (1983)                                          22'
   solo a sax; 2*2*2=2; 4221; 4perc, str                     MER

Poplars (1985)                                               15'
   3*3*3*3; 4331; timp+3, str                                MER

Northwest! (1988)                                            12'
   2*2*2*2; 4221; timp+2, str                                MER

Concertini (1991)                                            16'
   1*111; 2110; perc, pf, str                                MER

CAMPO, FRANK    (1927-      )

Alpine Holiday Overture (1955)                              15'
  3*3*3*3*; 4331; 4perc, str                      FLE

Concerto for Bassoon and Strings (1966)                    15'
  solo bsn; str                                   MS

Variations for Orchestra (1978)                            20'
  4*3*4=3*; 4331; 5perc, str                      FLE

Alba (1979)                                                11'
  1111; 1000; 2perc, pf, str (2-2-2-1)            MS

Concerto for Trumpet and Orchestra (1982)                  18'
  solo tpt; 3*3*3*2; 4230; 4perc, str            MS

Serenade for Chamber Orchestra (1983)                      18'
  2222; 2110; perc, pf, str                       MS

Luce bianca (1986)                                         20'
  3*3*3*3*; 4441; 4perc, str                      MS

Concerto for Piano and Winds (1989)                        17'
  solo pf; 3*23*2; 2231; 3perc                    MS


CANNING, THOMAS    (1911-1989)

Meditation for Strings (1957)                               4'
  str                                             ACA

O God, Our Lord, Thy Holy Word (1959)                       5'
  satb cho; 0000; 2220; str                       ACA

Meditation on "Hyfrydol" (1960)                             5'
  solo ob; str                                    ACA

Anthem (on the tune "Hyfrydol") (1964)                      5'
  solo s; satb cho; 0000; 0330; str               ACA

Fantasy on a Hymn by Justin Morgan (NA)                    10'
  soli 2str qt; str                               CF


CARL, ROBERT    (1954-      )

The Distant Shore (1981)                                    9'
  2111; 1110; 2perc, hp, str                      ACA

Images of Birth (1987)                                        16'
  2222; 4330; perc, hp, pf/cel, str                         ACA

The Stars' Harmony/The Night's
  Pleasure (1989)                                             8'
  3*33+3*; 4331; 3perc, hp, pf/cel, str                   ACA

A Wide Open Field (1990)                                      13'
  solo elec vc; 2*11*1; 21(offstage)1(bs)0;       ACA
  3perc, hp, pf/cel, str (6-6-5-4-3 players)


     CARLSEN, PHILIP  (1951-     )

Polter te Creso (1973)                                         8'
  14-pt cho; 13*21; 1110; str                             ACA

Palette (1978)                                                 8'
  1111; 1110; perc, hp, pf, str                          ACA

Fair Seed-Time (1980; rev 1985)                              17'
  solo t; 2222; 2110; perc, pf, str                      ACA

Four Journeys in Maine (1989)                                16'
  solo s; 2*22(a sax, b cl)2; 1110;                      ACA
  perc, str


     CARLSON, DAVID  (1952-     )

Variations for Chamber Orchestra (1978)                       9'
  1111; 2111; timp+1, hp, cel, str                        TP

Cello Concerto (1979)                                        24'
  solo vc; 2*2*2=2*; 3000; timp+1, hp,                    TP
  cel, str

Rhapsodies (1986)                                            14'
  2*111; 2110; timp+1, hp, pf/cel, str                    TP

Lilacs (Epitaph) for String Orchestra (1988)                 10'
  str                                                      TP

Violin Concerto (1988)                                       30'
  solo vln; 2=222; 2200; timp+1, hp,                      TP
  cel, str

Twilight Night (1989)                                         7'
  3*233*; 4331; timp+1, hp, cel, str                      TP

Notturno (1990)                                      20'
    satb cho; 3*2*22; 4221; timp+1, hp,             TP
    cel, str


          CARLSON, MARK    (1952-      )

Mass:  Christ in Majesty (1987)                      15'
    satb cho; 1111; 1220; 2perc, org, str           ECS

A Wreath of Anthems (1990)                           25'
    solo vv; satb cho; 2111; 1211; 2perc,           ECS
    cel, str


          CARTER, ELIOT   (1908-      )

Tarantella (1936)                                    8'
    ttbb cho; 3*23*3*; 4331; timp+2, str            AMP

Symphony No. 1 (1942; rev 1954)                      25'
    222+2; 2210; timp, str                          AMP

The Harmony of Morning (1944)                        9'
    ssaa cho; 1111; 1000; pf, str                   AMP

Holiday Overture (1944; rev 1961)                    10'
    3*3*3*3*; 4331; timp+1, pf, str                 AMP

The Harmony of Morning (1945)                        9'
    ssaa cho; 1111; 1000; pf, str                   AMP

Musicians Wrestle Everywhere (1945)                  3'
    satb cho; str                                   MRC

Suite - The Minotaur (1947)                          25'
    2*2*2*2; 4220; timp+1, pf, str                  AMP

Voyage (1947; orch'd 1975)                           8'
    solo mez (or bar); 2121; 1000; vib,             AMP
    hp, pf, str

Elegy (1952)                                         NA
    str                                             PS

Variations for Orchestra (1954-1955)                 24'
    2*222; 4231; timp+1, hp, str                    AMP

Double Concerto for Harpsichord and
   Piano (1961)                                              23'
     soli hpsd, pf; 1*11*1; 2110; 4perc,            AMP
   str (1-1-1-1)

Concerto for Piano and Orchestra (1964-1965)   25'
   solo pf; 3*3*3*3*; 4331; 2perc, str            AMP

Concerto for Orchestra (1968-1969)             23'
   3*3*3=3*; 4331; timp+8, hp, pf, str            AMP

A Symphony of Three Orchestras (1976)          17'
   orch 1:  0000; 3231; timp,                     AMP
     str (8-0-4-3-2)
   orch 2:  003=0; 0000; 3perc,
     str (2-0-0-3-1)
   orch 3:  3*3*03*; 2000; perc,
     str (8-0-4-0-2)

In Sleep, In Thunder (1981)                    20'
   solo t; 1=1*1*1; 1110; perc, pf,               BH
   str (2-1-1-1)

Penthode (1985)                                18'
   1=1*2=1; 1211; 3perc, hp, pf,                  BH
   str (2-1-1-1)

A Celebration of Some 100x150 Notes (1986)     3'
   3*3*3*3*; 4331; timp+1, pf/cel, str            BH
   N.B.  Movement I of "Three Occasions for
   Orchestra."

Three Occasions for Orchestra (1986-1989)      16'
   1.  A Celebration of 100x150 Notes             BH
   2.  Remembrance
   3.  Anniversary

   3(2picc)3*3*3*; 4331; timp+2, pf/cel, str

Oboe Concerto (1987)                           25'
   solo ob; concertino:  4vla, 1perc             BH
   orch:  1=01*0; 1010; perc, str

Remembrance (Paul Fromm) (1988)                7'
   3*3*3*3*; 4331; timp+1, pf/cel, str            BH
   N.B.  Movement II of "Three Occasions for
   Orchestra".

Anniversary (1989)                                              6'
    3*3*3*3*; 4331; timp+2, pf/cel, str                        BH
    N.B.   Movement III of "Three Occasions for
    Orchestra".

Violin Concerto (1990)                                         28'
    solo vln; 3*3*3=3*; 4331; 2perc, str                       BH


          CASTALDO, JOSEPH   (1927-      )

Flight (1955)                                                  30'
    4*444; 4431; timp+3, hp, cel, str                          PS

Askesis (1969)                                                 17'
    1110; 1110; 2perc, pf, str                                 PS
    N.B.   All players double on percussion
    instruments.

Lacrimosa I (1976)                                            15'
    str                                                        PS

Lacrimosa II (1977)                                          18'
    str (6-6-4-4-2 players)                                    PS

Cello Concerto (1984)                                        23'
    solo vc; 3*222; 2220; 2perc, hp, str                      KAL

Concerto for Viola and Orchestra (1988)                     23'
    solo vla; 3*233; 4221; timp+4, hp,                        MS
    pf, cel, str

Ancient Liturgy (1991)                                       35'
    narr; satb cho; 2perc, pf, str                            MS


          CAZDEN, NORMAN   (1914-1980)

Symphony, op. 49 (1948)                                      26'
    3*3*3*3*; 4331; timp, pf, str                             MCA

Three Ballads, op. 52 (1949)                                12'
    1121; 2220; timp, str                                     ACA

Woodland Valley Sketches, op. 73 (1958)                     10'
    3*13*1; 2110; perc, str                                   MCA

Adventure, op. 85 (1963)                                    13'
    soli 2fl, 2cl, 2vln; 0000; 0110;                         MCA
    timp, str

The Tempest - incidental music (1963)                  23'
   3*13*1; 2s,a rec; 2220; timp+1,                      MCA
   thundersheet, str

Chamber Concerto for Clarinet and String
   Orchestra, op. 94 (1965)                            14'
   solo cl; str                                        MCA

Concerto for Viola and Orchestra,
   op. 103 (1972)                                      22'
   solo vla; 3*222; 2230; timp+1, hp, str              MCA


     CHADABE, JOEL  (1938-      )

Many Mornings, Many Moods (1988)                       20'
   solo perc; full orch (instr flexible),             MS
   electronics


     CHANCE, NANCY LAIRD  (1931-     )

Liturgy (1979)                                         18'
   23*3*3*; 4321; 4perc, hp, cel, str                  GS

Odysseus (1984)                                        25'
   solo bar; 3*3*3*3*; 4331; 5perc, hp, str            TP
   N.B. May also be performed without
   baritone solo.

Elegy (1986)                                            9'
   str                                                 MMB

In Paradisum (1987)                                    13'
   solo s; satb cho; 3*3*3*3*; 4331;                   MMB
   5perc, hp, str

Planesthai (1991)                                      13'
   1111; 1111; 2perc, hp, pf, str                     MMB


     CHEETHAM, JOHN  (1939-     )

Amalgam (1973)                                         15'
   2222; 4331; timp+4, str                             MS

Three Binghams (1985)                                  10'
   str                                                 SHA

Propheta Lucis (Prophet of Light) (1989)          25'
    satb cho; 3*3*3*2; 4331; timp+4, hp, str      MS

Variations on a Gregorian Theme (1989)            15'
    3*3*3*2; 4331; timp+4, hp, str                LDW


        CHENOWETH, GERALD  (1943-     )

Cracks/Reforms/Bursts (1979)                      10'
    2222; 4331; 3perc, str                        ACA


        CHIHARA, PAUL   (1938-     )

Forest Music (1971)                               10'
    3*003*; 4331; timp+3, str                     CFP

Grass (1972)                                      20'
    solo db (amp); 2*101; 2031; timp+4,           CFP
    str, tape(opt)

Windsong (1972)                                   16'
    solo vc; 2222; 3230; timp+1, str              CFP

Ceremony III (1973)                               11'
    1201; 2000; timp+4, str                       CFP

Ceremony IV (1973)                                9'
    3*32*3; t sax; 6441; timp+3, hp, str          CFP

Shinju (Lover's Suicide) (1973-1974)              40'
    2+202*; 3330; timp+3, hp, pf, str             CFP

Concerto for Guitar and Orchestra (1975)          16'
    solo gtr; 1101; 0100; str                     GS

Symphony No. 1 "Symphony in
    Celebration" (1975)                           20'
    3*3*23*; t sax; 6441; 3perc, 2hp, str         CFP

Mistletoe Bride - ballet (1978)                   31'
    2*222; 4231; timp+2, hp, pf/cel,              CFP
    str, tape

Concerto for String Quartet and
    Orchestra (1980)                              19'
    solo str qt; 0000; 4231; timp+1, hca, str     GS

The Tempest - ballet (1980)                              120'
   2*222*; 4231; timp+3, hp, pf/cel,                      CFP
   str, tape

Saxophone Concerto (1981)                                 18'
   solo alto sax/tenor sax/E-flat sopranino               CFP
   sax; 2*222; 4331; timp+2, hp, str

Symphony No. 2 "Birds of Sorrow" (1981)                   18'
   3*2*22*; 4431; timp+3, hp, cel, str                    CFP


              CHILDS, BARNEY (1926-    )

Concerto for English Horn, Strings, Harp
   and Percussion (1955)                                  15'
   solo eh; 3perc, hp, str                                ACA

Second Symphony (1956)                                    18'
   2222; 4221; 3perc, str                                 ACA

Music for Piano and Strings (1965)                        var
   pf, str                                                CF

Concerto for Clarinet and Orchestra (1970)               17'
   solo cl; 12(hklph)1(a sax)1; 4331; euph;               ACA
   timp+5, hp, str

Concerto for Timpani and Orchestra (1989)                14'
   solo timp; 223*2; t sax; 4331; 3perc, str             MS


              CHOU, WEN-CHUNG (1923-    )

Landscapes (1949)                                          8'
   2200; 2020; timp+1, hp, str                            CFP

All in the Spring Wind (1952-1953)                        8'
   2222*; 2221; timp+3, hp, pf/cel, str                   CFP

And the Fallen Petals (1956)                             10'
   223*2; 4231; timp+1, hp, cel, str                      CFP


              CLAFLIN, ALAN AVERY (1898-1979)

Fishhouse Punch (1945)                                    5'
   3*3*3*3*; 4331; timp+1, hp, str                        ACA

Teen Scenes (1954-1955)                          22'
    str                                          ACA

Four Pieces for Orchestra
    (Symphony No. 3) (1956)                      21'
    3*3*3*3*; 4331; perc, hp, str                ACA

Concerto Giocoso (Piano Concerto) (1957)         17'
    solo pf; 3*3*22; 4331; timp+1, hp, str       ACA

Pop Concert Concerto (1957)                      17'
    solo pf; 3*3*22; 4331; timp+1, hp, str       ACA

Seven Meditations for Holy Week (1957)           39'
    223*2; 2200; str                             ACA


        CLAPP, PHILIP GREELEY   (1888-1954)

A Hill Rhapsody (1945; rev 1947)                 NA
    3*3*3*3*; 4231; timp+2, 2hp, cel, str        FLE


        CLARKE, HENRY LELAND   (1907-    )

Gloria (1950)                                    5'
    satb cho; solo vln; 3*222; 4231;             ACA
    timp+1, str
    N.B.   In the five official languages of the
    United Nations.

Monograph for Orchestra (1952)                   9'
    3*222; 2231; timp+1, str                     ACA

Primavera (1953)                                 3'
    ssa cho; str                                 ACA

Saraband for the Golden Goose (1957)             4'
    1111; 1110; str                              ACA

Lyric Sonata (1960)                              12'
    str                                          ACA

Points West (1960; orch'd 1970)                  15'
    2222; a,t,bar sax; 4330; timp+1, str         ACA

Encounter for Viola and Orchestra (1961)         15'
    solo vla; 3*222; 4231; timp+1, str           ACA

Variegation (1961)                                8'
  3*222; 4231; timp+2, hp, pf, str             ACA


    COHEN, STEVE  (1954-    )

Symphony in One Movement (1979)                   18'
  3*3*3*3*; 4331; timp+4, hp, pf, str            MS

Adagio for Alto Saxophone and Chamber
  Orchestra (1985)                                7'
  solo a sax; 2*1*2*1; 2220; timp, str           MS


    COHN, ARTHUR  (1910-    )

Histrionics, op. 32 (1945)                        28'
  str                                            BEL

Quintuple Concerto for Five Ancient
  Instruments and Orchestra, op. 31 (1945)       52'
  soli pardessus de viola, viola d'amore,        BEL
  viola da gamba, bassa viola, hpsd;
  3*3*3*3*; 4331; timp+6, hp, str

Four Symphonic Documents, op. 30 (1945)           32'
  4=4=4*4*; 4331; timp+6, anvil, hp,             BEL
  cel, str

Kaddish for Orchestra (1964)                       7'
  3*3*22; 4331; anvil, str                       BEL


    COHN, JAMES  (1928-    )

Sinfonietta in F, op. 6 (1946)                    13'
  1*121; 2000; timp/perc, str                    FLE

Concertino, op. 8 (1946)                          22'
  solo pf; 2*222; 2000; timp+1, str              FLE

Symphony No. 1 in E-flat, op. 11 (1947)           17'
  1*122*; a,bar sax; 2121; timp+1, str           FLE

Symphony No. 2 in F, op. 13 (1949)                23'
  2*2*3*2*; a sax; 2121; timp+1, str             FLE

Israfel, op. 24 (1954)                             3'
  solo t; str                                    XLNT

Music for Strings, op. 14a (1955)                15'
   str                                            FLE

Symphony No. 3 in G, op. 27 (1955)              21'
   1*111; a sax; 1110; timp+1, str              BH

Symphony No. 4 in A, op. 29 (1956)              16'
   1*111; a sax; 1110; timp+2, str              BH

Homage, op. 31 (1959)                            7'
   1*111; a sax; 1110; timp+1, str              FLE

Symphony No. 5 in B-flat, op. 32 (1959)         23'
   1*111; a sax; 1110; timp+2, str              BH

Variations on "The Wayfaring Stranger",
   op. 34 (1960)                                11'
   1*111; a sax; 1110; timp+1, str              BH

Enchanted Journey, op. 35 (1961)                19'
   1*111; a sax; 1110; timp+2, hp, str          XLNT

Prometheus - overture, op. 37 (1962)             6'
   1*111; a sax; 1110; timp+1, str              XLNT

Symphony No. 6 in B, op. 43 (1965)              19'
   1*111; a sax; 1110; timp+1, str              XLNT

Concerto in A for Concertina and Strings,
   op. 44 (1966)                                15'
   solo concertina; str                         FLE

Symphony No. 7 in D, op. 45 (1967)              20'
   1*111; a sax; 1110; timp+1, str              XLNT

Variations on "John Henry", op. 46a (1968)       4'
   2*122; a sax; 3331; timp+2, str              CF

The Little Circus, op. 51 (1974)                 6'
   1*021*; 2211; perc, str                      BH

Nine Miniatures for Orchestra, op.25a (1975)    14'
   0111; 01(flu hn)00; str                      XLNT

Symphony No. 8 in C, op. 54 (1978)              16'
   1*111; a sax; 1110; timp+1, str              XLNT

March-Caprice, op.58 (1982)                      4'
   solo bsn; str                                XLNT

Concerto for Clarinet and String
   Orchestra, op. 62 (1986)                13'
   solo cl; str                             XLNT

Mount Gretna Suite, op. 69 (1991)           17'
   1011; 0000; pf, str                      XLNT


     COKER, WILSON  (1928-1982)

Symphony No. 1 (1958)                        16'
   3*3*3*2; 4231; timp+1, str               TP

Overture Giocoso (1962)                      8'
   3*3*3*3*; 4431; timp+1, str              TP

Paean (1966)                                 12'
   satb cho; 3*3*3*2; 4431; timp+1, str     TP

Lyric Statement (1967)                       9'
   23*3*2; 4331; timp+4, str                TP

Declarative Essay (1974)                     7'
   23*3*2; 4331; timp+3, hp, str            TP


     COLGRASS, MICHAEL  (1932-    )

Seventeen (1960)                             8'
   3*3*3*3*; 4331; timp+3, str              CF

Divertimento (1961)                          8'
   8perc, pf, str                           CF

Rhapsodic Fantasy (1965)                     8'
   solo perc; 2=111; 1110; timp+5, hp,      MCA
   cel, str
   N.B.  Solo part requires 15 chromatic
   roto-toms.

As Quiet As (1966)                           14'
   3*3*3*3*; 4331; timp+3, 2hp, pf, cel,    MCA
   hpsd, str

Sea Shadow (1966)                            10'
   1111; 1110; perc, hp, str                CF

The Earth's a Baked Apple (1969)             11'
   satb cho; 2*031; 4431; timp+1, hp,       MCA
   cel, str

Auras (1973)                                                13'
    solo hp; 2222; 2220; 3perc, pf/cel, str               CF

Image of Man (1974)                                        22'
    solo vv; satb cho; 2222; 4331; 4perc,                 CF
    elec pf/cel, str

Concertmasters for Three Violins and
    Orchestra (1975)                                       22'
    soli 3vln; 2222; 4331; 4perc, 2hp,                    CF
    hpsd/cel, str

Theatre of the Universe (1975)                             17'
    soli s, mez, t, bar, b; satb cho;                     CF
    3*3*3*3*; 4331; 4perc, 2hp, pf/cel, str

Best Wishes USA (1976)                                     29'
    soli s, mez, t, bar; ssaattbb cho; 2222;              CF
    a sax; 4331; timp+4, elec pf/cel, acc,
    gtr/bj, uke, hca, jazz db, str

Letter from Mozart (1976)                                  16'
    2222; 2221; timp+4, hp, pf/cel, str                   CF
    N.B. Requires two conductors.

Déjà Vu for Percussion Quartet and
    Orchestra (1977)                                       18'
    solo perc qt; 3*03*3*; 4331; 2hp,                     CF
    pf/cel, str

Delta (1979)                                               18'
    soli vln, cl, perc; 2222; 2220;                       CF
    str (10-8-6-5-4)

Memento for Two Pianos and Orchestra (1982)   17'
    soli 2pf; 3*13*3*; 4330; 4perc, hp,                   CF
    cel, str

Demon (1983)                                               11'
    solo amp pf; 203*1; a sax; 4331;                      CF
    timp+3, str, tape, 3 radios

Chaconne for Viola and Orchestra (1984)                    30'
    solo vla; 3*23*1; 4331; timp+4, hp,                   CF
    pf/cel, str

The Schubert Birds (1989)                                  18'
    2222; 2200; timp+1, str                               CF

Snow Walker (1990)                                      21'
   solo org; 2222; 2221; timp+1, hp, pf, str    CF


        CONE, EDWARD  (1917-     )

Elegy for Orchestra (1953)                              12'
   2222; 4221; timp, str                                MS

Symphony (1953)                                         40'
   3*3*3*3*; 4330; timp+2, hp, pf, cel, str     MS

Nocturne and Rondo for Piano and
   Orchestra (1957)                                     15'
   solo pf; 23*22; 4231; timp+1, str                    MS

Concerto for Violin and Small
   Orchestra (1959)                                     25'
   solo vln; 2222; 2220; timp, hp, cel, str     MS

Music for Strings (1964)                                10'
   str                                                  EBM

Variations for Orchestra (1968)                         10'
   3*3*3*3*; 4331; timp+2, hp, cel,             MS
   bells, str

Cadenzas (1979)                                         12'
   soli ob, vln; str                                    MS


        CONSOLI, MARC-ANTONIO  (1941-     )

Profiles (1973)                                         20'
   3*23*3*; a,t,bar sax; 5331; timp+3,          ACA
   hp, pf, cel, str

Music for Chambers (1974)                               14'
   1010; 1110; xyl, vib, hp, str (2-1-1-0)      ACA

Odefonia (1976)                                         23'
   2*2*2*2; 2210; timp+1, str (0-0-4-2)         MG

Naked Masks (Three Frescoes from a
   Dream) (1980)                                        20'
   2222; 4221; timp+3, hp, pf, str              ACA

The Last Unicorn (1981)                                 16'
   3*3*3*3*; 4331; timp+3, hp, str              NOA

Afterimages (1982)                                            22'
   3*3*3*3*; 4331; timp+3, hp, str                        MG

Musiculi (Le Quattro stagioni) (1985-1986)                    21'
   12 fem vv; 3*33*3*; 4331; timp+1, 2hp,                 NOA
   pf, cel, str

Cello Concerto (1988)                                         22'
   solo vc;  1120; 1110; perc, hp, pf, str               RIN

Greek Lyrics (1988)                                           14'
   satb cho; pf, str                                     RIN

## CONSTANTINIDES, DINOS  (1929-      )

"Diukos Suite" for Orchestra (1961)                           20'
   3*3*3*3*; 4331; 2perc, hp, str                        MS

Concerto for Violin, Cello, Piano and
   Orchestra (1967)                                      18'
   soli vln, vc, pf; 23*3*2; 4331;                       SEE
   timp+1, str

Symphony No. 1 (1967)                                         12'
   23*3*3*; 4331; 3perc, str                             SEE

Composition for String Orchestra (1968)                       8'
   str                                                   SEE

Designs for Strings (1971)                                    5'
   str                                                   SEE

Four Songs on Poems by Sapphos (1971)                        5'
   solo v; 3*23*2; 4331; timp+2, str                     SEE

Dedications for Orchestra (1974)                             9'
   3*23*2; 4331; timp+1, hp, str                         SEE

Kaleidoscope (1974)                                          25'
   solo v; 2121; 1110; perc, hp, pf, str                 SEE

Antithesis (1975)                                           10'
   solo t; narr; 2000; 0030; perc, hp,                   SEE
   pf, str

Concertino for Euphonium (or Tuba) and
   Orchestra (1980)                                      8'
   solo euph (or tba); 2222; 4321;                       MS
   2perc, str

Mountains of Epirus (1980)                                    8'
   solo vln; 3*222; 4331; 2perc, str                        MS

New Orleans Divertimento (1982)                              24'
   0000; 1110; perc, hp, str                                MS

Hymn to the Human Spirit (1983)                             12'
   solo t; 2222; 4220; 2perc, str                           MS

Symphony No. 2 (1983)                                       23'
   3*3*3*3*; 4331; 3perc, hp, synth, str                    MS

Walls of Time (1986)                                        14'
   soli s, a; ssaattbb cho; 23*3*3*; 4331;                  MS
   3perc, str

Grecian Variations (1987)                                   20'
   solo vla; str                                            MS

Concerto for Orchestra (1988)                               18'
   23*3*3*; 4331; 3perc, str                                MS

Homage (1988)                                               15'
   solo fl; str                                             MS

Midnight Song (1988)                                        10'
   solo s; 1111; 1110; perc, str                            MS
   N.B. This work has been arranged for
   solo alto sax under the title "Midnight
   Fantasy II."

Patterns for Violin and String
   Orchestra (1989)                                          8'
   solo vln; str                                            MS

Transformations for Oboe and String
   Orchestra (1989)                                         14'
   solo ob; str                                             MS

China II - Beijing (1990)                                    8'
   str                                                      MS

Suite No. 2 for Orchestra (1990)                            12'
   2222; 4331; 3perc, str                                   MS

Anniversary Celebration (1991)                              20'
   solo gtr; str                                            MS

China I - Shanghai (Songs of
    Departure) (1991)                              15'
    solo s; bsn; str                              MS


        CONTE, DAVID    (1955-      )

Invocation and Dance (1987)                       14'
    ttbb cho; 2perc, hp, pf (4-hands), str        ECS

Hymn to the Nativity (1988)                       10'
    solo s; ttbb cho; 12*00; 2000; perc,          ECS
    hp, str


        COOLIDGE, PEGGY STUART    (1913-1981)

An Evening in New Orleans - suite (1965)          17'
    3*2*3*2*; 4220; timp+3, hp, str               PS

Rhapsody for Harp and Orchestra (1965)            9'
    solo hp; 3221; 4320 (or 2210);                PS
    timp+2, str

Spirituals in Sunshine and Shadow (1969)          14'
    3*222; 4331; timp+2, hp, str                  PS

Pioneer Dances (1970)                             12'
    3*222; 4331; timp+3, hp, str                  PS
    OR:    1121; 1210; timp+3, str.

New England Autumn (1971)                         12'
    2*2*2*2; 2210; timp+3, hp, str                PS

The Voice (1981)                                  14'
    3*23*2; 4331; timp+3, hp, str                 PS


        COOPER, PAUL    (1926-      )

Symphony No. 1 "Concertant" (1966)                15'
    solo str qt; 1111; 1110; timp+1, hp,          HC
    cel, str

Concerto No. 1 for Violin and
    Orchestra (1967)                              15'
    solo vln; 3*3*3*3*; 4331; timp+1, hp,         HC
    pf, cel, str

Credo (1970)                                                    30'
    ssaattbb cho; 3\*3\*3\*2; 4231; perc, hp,             HC
    pf/cel, str

Symphony No. 3 "Lamentation" (1971)                            20'
    str                                                      HC

Cantigas (1972)                                                34'
    satb cho; unis men's cho; 1111; 0000;          HC
    perc, hp, pf/cel, str

Symphony No. 4 "Landscape" (1973-1975)                        21'
    soli fl, tpt, vla; 23\*3\*2; 4231; perc,         HC
    hp, pf/cel, str

A Shenandoah for Ives' Birthday (1974)                         8'
    soli fl, tpt, vla; 23\*3\*2; 4231; timp+3,       HC
    hp, pf/cel, str

Descants (1975)                                               14'
    solo vla; 1111; 1110; timp+1, pf/cel, str   HC

Concerto for Violoncello and Orchestra
    (1976-1978)                                              21'
    solo vc; 3+3\*3\*2; 4231; timp+1, 2hp,           HC
    pf, cel, str

Homage (1976)                                                  5'
    33\*3\*2; 4331; timp+1, hp, pf/cel, str         HC

Refrains (1976)                                               30'
    soli s, bar; satb cho; 23\*3\*2; 4331;          HC
    timp+3, hp, pf/cel, str

Variants (1978)                                               15'
    223\*2; 4331; timp+3, pf/cel, str               HC

Coram Morte (1979)                                            21'
    solo mez; 1+1\*1\*0; 0000; 2perc, pf,           HC
    cel, str

Concerto for Flute and Orchestra (1980-1981)   17'
    solo fl; 01\*1\*1\*; 1110; timp+1,              HC
    pf/cel, str

Concerto for Organ and Orchestra (1982)        18'
    solo org; 2222; 2220; timp+1, cel, str       HC

Concerto No. 2 for Violin and
   Orchestra (1982)                                  27'
   solo vln; 23*22; 2200; perc, hp, str             HC

Symphony No. 5 (1983)                                18'
   3*3*3*3*; 4431; 3perc, hp, str                   HC

Voyagers (1983)                                      21'
   satb cho; 23*3*2; 4431; timp+3, hp,              HC
   pf/cel, str

Concerto for Orchestra (1984)                        14'
   1111; 1110; perc, hp, cel, str                   HC

Love Songs and Dances:  Concertante
   (1986-1987)                                       14'
   1=1*1*1; 1110; perc, hp, str (4-3-2-2-1)         HC

Double Concerto for Violin, Viola and
   Orchestra (1987)                                  19'
   soli vln, vla; 2222; 2200; timp+2,               HC
   hp, cel, str

Symphony No. 6 "In Memoriam" (1987)                  26'
   3+3*3*3*; 4431; 2perc, hp, pf, cel, str          HC


         COPE, DAVID  (1941-      )

Tragic Overture (1960)                                4'
   timp, str                                        SEE

Contrasts (1966)                                      7'
   2220; 4231; timp+1, hp, str                      SEE

Music for Brass, Strings and
   Percussion (1967)                                 11'
   0000; 4222; timp+1, str                          SEE

Streams (1973)                                       14'
   3*121; 4331; 3perc, pf, str                      SEE

Concerto for Tenor Saxophone and
   Orchestra (1976)                                  12'
   solo t sax; 2222; 4330; 2perc, str               BRO

Threshold and Visions (1977)                         32'
   1111; 2120; 2perc, hp, pf, org, str              BRO

Concert for Piano and Orchestra (1980)               29'
    solo pf; 1112*; 2120; perc, hp, org, str         MS

Afterlife (1982)                                     29'
    2222; 4230; perc, hp, str                        MS

Cradle Falling (1985)                                NA
    solo s; 1111; 1010; 2perc, hp, 2pf,              MS
    str (1-1-2-1)


    COPLAND, AARON   (1900-1991)

Cortège Macabre (1923)                               8'
    3343; 4531; timp+3, 2hp, pf, cel, str            BH

Symphony for Organ and Orchestra (1924)              25'
    solo org; 3*3*3*3*; 4331; timp+4,                BH
    2hp, cel(opt), str

Dance Symphony (1925)                                18'
    3*3*2=3*; 45(2 cnt)31; timp+3, 2hp, pf,          BH
    cel, str

Music for the Theatre (1925)                         22'
    1*1*1+1; 0210; perc, pf, str                     BH

Piano Concerto (1926)                                18'
    solo pf; 3*3*4=3*; a sax (s sax); 4331;          BH
    timp+5, cel, str

Symphony No. 1
    (from Symphony for Organ) (1928)                 19'
    3(2picc)3*3*3*; a sax; 8531; timp+5, 2hp,        BH
    pf, cel, str

Two Pieces (1928)                                    11'
    str                                              BH

Symphonic Ode (1929; rev 1955)                       19'
    4(2picc)4*4=4*; 8431; timp+4, 2hp,               BH
    pf, str

Short Symphony (Symphony No. 2) (1933)               15'
    3=3*3*3*; 4200; pf, str                          BH
    N.B.  An optional heckelphone part
    is available.

Statements for Orchestra (1934)                      19'
    3*3*3*3*; 4331; timp+4, str                      BH

El Salón México (1936)                              12'
  3*3*4=3*; 4331; timp+2, pf, str          BH
  N.B.  E-flat clarinet, bass clarinet, and
  contrabassoon parts are optional.

Prairie Journal (1937)                              12'
  2*24(a,t sax, b cl)1; 2321; timp+2,       BH
  pf, pf/cel, str

Billy the Kid (1938)                                35'
  3*222; 4331; timp+5, hp, pf, str          BH

An Outdoor Overture (1938)                          10'
  3*222; 4230; timp+3, pf, cel(opt), str    BH

Our Town - film score (1940)                        11'
  32*3*2; 3321; perc, str                   BH

Quiet City (1940)                                   10'
  tpt, eh, str                              BH

John Henry (1940; rev 1952)                         4'
  2*222; 2210; timp+1, pf(opt), str         BH

Danzon Cubano (1942)                                6'
  3*3*3*3*; 4331; timp+5, pf, str           BH

Four Dance Episodes (from "Rodeo") (1942)           18'
  3(2picc)3*3*2; 4331; timp+2, hp,          BH
  pf/cel, str

Lincoln Portrait (1942)                             14'
  narr; 2*3*3*3*; 4331; timp+4, hp,         BH
  cel(opt), str
  N.B.  English horn, bass clarinet, and
  contrabassoon parts are optional.

Music from the Movies (1942)                        16'
  1*111; 1210; timp+1, pf, str             BH

Rodeo - ballet (1942)                               24'
  3(2picc)3*3*2; 4331; timp+2, hp,          BH
  pf/cel, str

Letter from Home (1944; rev 1962)                   6'
  223*2; 2220; timp+2, hp(opt),             BH
  pf(opt), str

Appalachian Spring (1945)                           33'
  2*222; 2220; timp+2, hp, pf, str          BH

Symphony No. 3 (1946)                                              38'
    4*3*3+3*; 4431; timp+5, 2hp, pf, cel, str   BH

Concerto for Clarinet and Orchestra
   (1947-1948)                                       17'
    solo cl; hp, pf, str                         BH

The Red Pony - suite (1948)                                       24'
    2*2*4=2; 4331; timp+2, hp, pf/cel, str       BH

Preamble for a Solemn Occasion (1949)                             6'
    narr; 3*3*3*3*; 4331; hp, str                BH

Old American Songs - Set 1 & 2 (1952)                             BH

    Set 1: solo mez (or bar); 1*121; 1110;      13'
    hp, str
    Set 2: solo mez (or bar); 1*121; 2110;      12'
    hp, str

Canticle of Freedom (1955)                                        13'
    satb cho; 3*2*22; 4331; timp+4, hp, str     BH

The Tender Land (1956)                                            BH

   1. Orchestral Suite                               21'
      3*2*2*2; 4331; timp+2, hp, pf, cel, str

   2. The Promise of Living                          5'
      satb cho; 22*22; 2220; timp+2, hp,
      pf/cel, str

   3. Stomp your foot                                3'
      satb cho; 2*2*22; 2220; timp+2, hp,
      pf/cel, str

Orchestral Variations (1957)                                      14'
    2*2*2*2; 4231; timp+2, hp, str               BH

Eight Poems of Emily Dickinson (1958-1970)                        20'
    solo mez (or bar); 1111; 1111; hp, str       BH

Dance Panels (1959)                                               26'
    2=121; 2210; 2perc, str                      BH

Connotations for Orchestra (1962)                                 20'
    4*3*4=3*; 6441; timp+5, pf/cel, str          BH

Down a Country Lane (1964)                                        3'
    2121; 2110; str                              BH

Music for a Great City (1964)                      24'
   3=3*3*3*; 4330; timp+5, hp, pf/cel, str      BH

Inscape (1967)                                     13'
   3*3*3*2; 4331; timp+4, hp, pf/cel, str        BH

Happy Anniversary (1969)                            1'
   3*232; 4331; perc, str                        BH

Three Latin American Sketches (1972)               10'
   1111; 0100; 2perc, 2pf, str                   BH

Proclamation (1982)                                 2'
   3*222; 4331; timp+1, pf, str                  BH

Jubilee Variations (1984)                           3'
   3*3*3*3*; 4331; timp+2, pf, str               BH


     CORBETT, SIDNEY  (1960-    )

Ghost Reveille (1987)                              13'
   3=3*3*3*; 4331; 4perc, hp, pf/cel,            NOA
   str (18-6-6-4)
   N.B.  The violins are divided into three
   sections of 6 players each.


     CORDERO, ROQUE  (1917-    )

Symphony No. 1 (1945)                              30'
   3*23*2; 4331; timp+1, str                     PS

Movimiento Sinfónico (1946)                        16'
   str                                           PS

Panamanian Overture No. 2 (1946)                   12'
   3*23*2; 4330; timp+1, str                     PS

Ocho Miniaturas (1948)                             11'
   1111; 1110; str                               PS

Introduccion y Allegro Burlesco (1950)             18'
   3*3*3*2; 4331; timp, str                      MS

Adagio Tragico (1953)                               9'
   str                                           PS

Symphony No. 2 (1956)                              24'
   3*3*3*3*; 4231; timp+1, str                   PS

Funeral Message (1961)                                       9'
   solo cl; str                                             PS

Concerto for Violin (1962)                                  29'
   solo vln; 3*23*2; 3231; timp+1, str                     PS

Symphony No. 3 (1965)                                       16'
   3*23*3*; 4231; timp+1, str                              PS

Elegy (1973)                                                 8'
   str                                                     PS

Five Brief Messages for Orchestra (1973)                    15'
   33*3*2; 4231; timp+1, pf, str                           PS

Momentum Jubilo (1973)                                       2'
   0000; 3331; timp+2, str                                 PS

Six Mobiles for Orchestra (1975)                            20'
   3*3*3*3*; 4331; timp+6, hp, str                         PS

Cantata para la Paz (1979)                                  35'
   solo bar; satb cho; 3*3*3*3*; 4231;                     PS
   timp+4, str

Obertura de Salutacion (1980)                                9'
   3*3*3*2; 4331; timp+1, str                              MS

Symphony No. 4 ("Panamanian") (1986)                        35'
   3*3*3*2; 4331; timp+3, str                              PS


     CORIGLIANO, JOHN   (1938-    )

A Dylan Thomas Trilogy (1961-1976)                          GS

   1. Fern Hill (1961)                                     16'
      satb cho; 2222; 4220; timp+2, hp,
      pf, str

   2. Poem on October (1970)                               16'
      solo t; satb cho; 1110; 0000; hpsd, str

   3. Poem on his Birthday (1976)                          30'
      solo bar; satb cho; 2*22*2; 4220;
      timp+3, hp, pf, str

The Cloister (1965)                                         13'
   solo mez; 2222; 2200; timp+1, str                       GS

Elegy (1965)                                           8'
    2*222; 2110; timp+1, pf, str                      GS

Tournaments Overture (1967)                           12'
    3*3*3*3*; 4331; timp+3, hp, pf, str               GS

Concerto for Piano and Orchestra (1968)               30'
    solo pf; 23*3*2; 4331; perc, hp, str              GS

Creations:  Two Scenes from "Genesis" (1972)          24'
    narr; 2*2*2*1; 2110; timp+1, hp, pf, str          GS

Gazebo Dances (1973)                                  16'
    2*222; 4331; timp+3, pf, str                      GS

A Williamsburg Sampler (1974)                         11'
    2101; 0000; hpsd(or hp), str                      GS

Aria (1975)                                            6'
    solo ob; str                                      GS

Concerto for Oboe and Orchestra (1975)                26'
    solo ob; 3*122; 2110; timp+2, hp,                 GS
    pf/cel, str

Voyage (1976)                                          7'
    str                                               GS

Concerto for Clarinet and Orchestra (1977)            29'
    solo cl; 4*1*3*4*; 6431; timp+3, hp,              GS
    pf, str

Soliloquy for Clarinet and Orchestra (1977)            9'
    solo cl; 3*2*1*3*; 1231; hp, pf, str              GS

Concerto for Flute and Orchestra (1981)               35'
    solo fl/picc/tin whistle;                         GS
    233(A-flat cl)3*; 4331; timp+6, hp,
    pf, cel, str
    N.B. Also requires a children's group.

Promenade Overture (1981)                              8'
    3*223*; 4431; timp+4, hp, str                     GS

Three Hallucinations (1981)                           14'
    3*333; 4331; 6perc, hp, 2pf, org, str             GS

Summer Fanfare (1982)                                  9'
    3*333; 6(2 opt)6(3 opt)31; timp+4,                GS
    hp, pf, str

Fantasia on an Ostinato (1986)                           14'
  3*333*; 4431; timp+4, hp, pf, str                   GS

Campane di Ravello (1987)                                 3'
  4*4*4*3*; 4431; timp+6, hp, pf, str                 GS

Symphony No. 1 (1989)                                    35'
  4*3*4=4*; 6542; timp+5, hp, pf, str                 GS


      CORTES, RAMIRO, JR.   (1938-1984)

Sinfonia Sacra (1954; rev 1959)                          25'
  3*3*3*2; 4231; timp+1, str                          ELK

The Eternal Return:  Introduction and
  Rondo (1963)                                        11'
  23*3*2; 4221; timp, str                             ELK

Yerma:  Symphonic Portrait of a Woman (NA)               12'
  3*3*4*3*; 4331; timp+1, cel, str                    ELK


      CORTESE, GLEN   (1960-    )

Canso D'Amare (1987)                                      16'
  solo s; 1*2*11; 211(b tbn)0; timp+2,                NOA
  pf/hpsd, str


      CORY, ELEANOR   (1943-    )

Tapestry (1983)                                          15'
  3*3*3*2; 4331; 3perc, str                           ACA


      COTEL, MORRIS   (1943-    )

Symphonic Pentad (1964)                                  30'
  solo s; 3*3*3*3*; 4431; timp+1, hp,                 MMP
  pf, str

Concerto for Piano and Orchestra (1968)                  15'
  solo pf; 0030; a,t,bar sax; 03(3cnt)00;             MMP
  3perc, str (4-4-4-0-0 desks)

Variations on a Theme by Haydn (1973)                     8'
  2202; 2200; timp+1, str                             MMP

Harmony of the World (1975)                              12'
    str (10-10-8-8-6 desks)                             MMP


            COTTON, JEFFREY  (1957-      )

Fantasia (1987)                                          14'
    3*3*33; 4331; timp+3, hp, cel, str                  NOA


            COWELL, HENRY  (1897-1965)

Some Music (1914-1922)                                   7'
    44*4*4*; 5331; timp+1, pf, str                      AMP

Ensemble (1924; rev 1956)                               10'
    str                                                 AMP

Concerto for Piano and Orchestra (1928)                 23'
    solo pf; 3*4*3*3*; 4431; timp+1, str                AMP

Sinfonietta (1928)                                      14'
    1111; 1110; str (2-2-1-1-1)                         AMP

Polyphonica (1930)                                       4'
    1111; 1110; str                                     AMP

Synchrony (1930)                                        12'
    3*3*3*3*; 4331; timp+1, str                         CFP

Celtic Set (1938)                                       14'
    2222; 2211; timp+1, str                             AMP

Symphonic Set (1938-1939)                               14'
    223*2; 2210; timp+1, str                            BH

Old American Country Set (1939)                         12'
    2222; 2211; perc, bj, str                           AMP

Vox Humana (1939)                                       NA
    3*3*3*2; 4331; timp+1, hp, str                      FLE

Ancient Desert Drone (1940)                              5'
    3*3*3*3*; 4331; perc, hp, str                       AMP

Four Irish Tales (1940)                                 13'
    solo pf; 3*3*3*3*; 4331; timp+1, str                AMP

Pastorale and Fiddler's Delight (1940)                   6'
    3*3*3*3*; 4331; perc, str                           AMP

Symphony No. 3 (Gaelic) (1942)                        23'
    33*4*3*; 2a,t,bar sax; 4332; perc, str           AMP

American Pipers (1943)                                 4'
    3*3*3*3*; 4321; timp+1, str                      AMP

United Music (1943)                                    9'
    3*3*3*2; 4331; perc, hp, str                     AMP

Hymn and Fuguing Tune No. 2 (1944)                     7'
    str                                              AMP

Hymn and Fuguing Tune No. 3 (1944)                     7'
    2222; 4221; timp+3, str                          AMP
    N.B.  Two of the horn parts are optional.

Little Concerto (1945)                                12'
    solo pf; 3*333; 4331; timp+1, str                AMP

Big Sing (1945)                                       11'
    23*3*3*; 4331; timp+1, str                       CFP

Hymn and Fuguing Tune No. 5 (1946)                     7'
    str                                              AMP

Symphony No. 4 (Short Symphony) (1946)                19'
    3*3*3*3*; 4331; timp+2, hp, str                  AMP

Saturday Night at the Firehouse (1948)                 4'
    2121; 2200; perc, hp(opt), str                   AMP

Overture for Large Orchestra (1949)                   10'
    3*3*4*2; 4331; timp+2, pf, str                    PS

Symphony No. 5 (1950)                                 28'
    3*3*3*3*; 4331; 2perc, pf, str                   AMP

Hymn, Chorale and Fuguing Tune No. 8 (1951)            8'
    str                                              AMP

Air for Violin and String Orchestra (1952)             4'
    solo vln; str                                    CFP

Fiddler's Jig (1952)                                   2'
    solo vln; str                                    AMP

Rondo for Orchestra (1952)                             7'
    33*33; 4331; timp, str                           AMP

Symphony No. 6 (1952)                                         23'
  3\*3\*3\*3\*; 4331; timp+1, str                         CFP

Symphony No. 7 (1952)                                         24'
  21\*2\*1; 2110; timp+2, pf, str                        AMP

Symphony No. 9 (1953)                                         22'
  2222; 2220; timp+1, hp, pf, str                       AMP

Symphony No. 10 (1953)                                        23'
  22\*2\*2; 2200; timp, str                             AMP

Symphony No. 11:  Seven Rituals of
  Music (1953)                                          21'
  2222; 4331; timp+3, hp(opt), pf/cel, str             AMP

Ballad for String Orchestra (1954)                           4'
  str                                                   AMP

Hymn and Fuguing Tune No. 10 (1955)                          8'
  solo ob; str                                          AMP

...if He please (1955)                                       20'
  6-pt fem cho; 6-pt male cho; 3-pt boy                CFP
  cho; 2222; 2321; timp+1, hp(or pf), str

Symphony No. 12 (1955-1956)                                  15'
  3\*2\*32; 4321; timp+2, pf, cel, str                 AMP

Lines from the Dead Sea Scrolls (1956)                       10'
  tttbbb cho; 2222; 2220; timp, str                    AMP

Symphony No. 13 "Madras" (1956-1958)                         20'
  2222; 2000; timp+3, hp, cel, str                     CFP
  N.B. This work requires 5 tabla and a
  jalatarang in the percussion section.

Variations for Orchestra (1956; rev 1959)                    21'
  3\*3\*3\*3\*; 4331; timp+3, pf, str                   AMP

Music for Orchestra (1957)                                   10'
  3\*3\*3\*3\*; 4331; timp+2, cel, str                  AMP

Ongaku (1957)                                                14'
  22\*22; 2200; timp+1, hp, cel, str                   AMP

Persian Set (1957)                                           15'
  solo Persian drum(or tam-tam); 2\*010;               CFP
  0000; pf, gtr, mand, str

Concerto for Percussion and Orchestra (1958)  19'
    soli timp+4; 2222; 2231; timp, hp,    CFP
    pf/cel, str

Antiphony for Divided Orchestra (1959)  12'
    orch 1:  1111; 1110; str    CFP
    orch 2:  1111; 1111; str

Symphony No. 14 (1959-1960)  25'
    3*3*3*2; 4331; timp+3, pf, cel, str    AMP

Concerto Brevis for Accordion and
    Orchestra (1960)  13'
    solo acc; 2222; 4221; timp+1, str    MMC

Edson Hymns and Fuguing Tunes (1960)  10'
    satb cho; 2222; 4221; timp, str    AMP

Symphony No. 15 "Thesis" (1960)  23'
    3*3*3*2; 4331; timp+2, str    AMP

Variations on Thirds for Two Violas and
    String Orchestra (1960)  12'
    soli 2vla; str    CFP

Chiascuro (1961)  11'
    3*3*3*3*; 4331; timp+2, str    AMP

Duo Concertante for Flute, Harp and
    Orchestra (1961)  14'
    soli fl, hp; 3*3*3*3*; 4331; timp+2,    AMP
    pf/cel, str

Concerto for Harmonica (1962)  18'
    solo hca; 2*110; 0100; perc, str    CFP

Concerto No. 1 for Koto and Orchestra (1962)  24'
    solo koto; 2*222; 2220; timp+2, hp, str    AMP

Symphony No. 16 "Icelandic" (1962)  16'
    2222; 2221; timp+2, hp, str    AMP

Air and Scherzo for Alto Saxophone and
    Small Orchestra (1963)  8'
    solo a sax; 2121; 0000; str    AMP

Concerto Grosso (1963)  24'
    soli fl, ob, cl, hp, vc; str    AMP

The Creator - oratorio (1963)                           25'
    soli s, a, t, b; satb cho; 3*3*3*3*;                 CFP
    4331; timp+4, str

Symphony No. 17 "Lancaster" (1963)                      22'
    2222; 4221; timp+2, str                             AMP

Hymn and Fuguing Tune No. 16 (1964)                      6'
    2222; 2331; str                                     CFP

Symphony No. 18 (1964)                                  26'
    3*3*3*3*; 4331; timp+2, str                         CFP

The Tender and the Wild:  Song and
    Dance (1964)                                         7'
    3*3*3*3*; 4331; timp+2, str                         AMP

Carol (1965)                                             9'
    2222; 2200; hp(or pf), str                          AMP

Concerto No. 2 for Koto and Orchestra (1965)  20'
    solo koto; 2111; 1100; timp+1, str                  CFP

Symphony No. 19 (1965)                                   8'
    3*3*3*3*; 4331; timp+3, pf, str                     AMP

Twilight in Texas (1965)                                 8'
    3*3*3*3*; 4331; timp+2, str                         CFP


        CRAWFORD, JOHN   (1931-      )

In Praise of Music (1952)                                5'
    1111; 2000; str                                     ACA

Magnificat (1956)                                        8'
    satb cho; str                                       ECS

Metracollage (1973)                                      8'
    2222; 4231; timp+2, str                             MS


        CRESTON, PAUL   (1906-1985)

Two Choric Dances, op. 17a (1938)                       12'
    1111; 1000; timp+1, pf, str                         GS
    OR:   3*222; 4231; timp+1, pf, str

Symphony No. 1, op. 20 (1940)                                20'
   3*222; 4231; timp, str                     GS

Concertino for Marimba and Orchestra,
   op. 21 (1940)                               15'
   solo mar; 2110; 2000; timp, str             GS

Prelude and Dance, op. 25 (1941)                             7'
   1121; 2110; timp+1, pf, str                 GS

Concerto for Alto Saxophone and Orchestra,
   op. 26 (1941)                               16'
   solo a sax; 3*222; 4231; timp, str          GS

A Rumor, op. 27 (1941)                                       5'
   1121; 2210; str                             GS

Pastorale and Tarantella, op. 28 (1941)                     10'
   3*222; 4231; timp+1, pf, str                GS

Dance Variations, op. 30 (1941-1942)                         6'
   solo s; 3*222; 4231; timp+3, str            GS

Fantasy for Piano and Orchestra,
   op. 32 (1942)                                8'
   solo pf; 2222; 4220; timp+1, str            GS

Chant of 1942, op. 33 (1943)                                10'
   3*222; 4231; timp+1, pf, str                GS
   OR:  2222; 2200; timp+1, pf, str

Frontiers, op. 34 (1943)                                    10'
   3*3*3*3*; 4331; timp+1, pf, str             GS

Symphony No. 2, op. 35 (1944)                               24'
   4*3*3*3*; 4331; timp+3, pf, str             GS

Psalm XXIII, op. 37 (1945)                                   3'
   solo s; satb cho; 2222; 4231; timp,         GS
   hp, str

Poem, op. 39 (1945)                                         15'
   solo hp; 3*222; 4231; timp+1, str           GS

Homage, op. 41 (1946)                                        8'
   str                                         SHA

Fantasy for Trombone and Orchestra,
   op. 42 (1947)                               10'
   solo tbn; 2222; 4231; timp, str             GS

Concerto for Piano and Orchestra,
    op. 43 (1949)                                        20'
    solo pf; 4*222; 4231; timp, pf, str                 SHA

Missa Solemnis, op. 44 (1949)                           20'
    satb (or ttbb) cho; 2222; 2220; hp, str             BEL

Symphony No. 3, op. 48 (1950)                           28'
    4*3*3*3*; 4331; timp, hp, str                       SHA

Concerto for Two Pianos and Orchestra,
    op. 50 (1951)                                        27'
    soli 2pf; 3*222; 4231; timp, str                    FC

Symphony No. 4, op. 52 (1951)                           24'
    3*222; 4231; timp, str                              GS

Walt Whitman, op. 53 (1952)                             12'
    4*3*4*3*; 4331; timp+1, hp, cel, str                FC

Invocation and Dance, op. 58 (1953)                     12'
    4*3*3*3*; 4331; timp+1, pf, str                     GS

Dance Overture, op. 62 (1954)                           12'
    3*3*23*; 4331; timp+1, str                          SHA

Symphony No. 5, op. 64 (1955)                           27'
    4*3*4=3*; 4331; timp+1, str                         FC

Concerto No. 1 for Violin and Orchestra,
    op. 65 (1956)                                        23'
    solo vln; 3*222; 4231; timp, str                    FC

Lydian Ode, op. 67 (1956)                               12'
    3*222; 4231; timp, str                              FC

Toccata, op. 68 (1957)                                  10'
    4*3*4=3*; 4331; timp+1, str                         GS

Pre-classic Suite, op. 71 (1957)                        10'
    3*3*3*3*; 2200; str                                 FC

Concerto for Accordion and Orchestra,
    op. 75 (1958)                                        20'
    solo acc; 2222; 4231; timp, str                     FC

Janus, op. 77 (1959)                                    12'
    4*3*3*3*; 4331; timp+1, pf, str                     FC

Concerto No. 2 for Violin and Orchestra,
   op. 78 (1959)                      20'
   solo vln; 3*222; 4231; timp, str   FC

Isaiah's Prophecy, op. 80 (1962)      30'
   soli s, a, t, b: satb cho; 3*222; 2220;  FC
   timp+1, hp, str

Corinthians XIII, op. 82 (1963)     14'
   4*3*4*3*; 4331; timp+6, hp, pf/cel, str  FC

Nocturne, op. 83 (1963)           9'
   solo s (or t); 1111; 1000; pf; str  BEL

Fantasy for Accordion and Orchestra,
   op. 85 (1965)                    7'
   solo acc; 2121; 2210; timp+2, str  TP

Choreografic Suite, op. 86 (1965)   25'
   1111; 2210; perc, pf, str     BEL

Introit (Hommage à Pierre Monteux),
   op. 87 (1966)                    3'
   2222; 2221; timp, hp, str    GS

Pavane Variations, op. 86 (1966)   14'
   3*3*3*3*; 4331; timp+1, pf, str  GS
   OR:  2222; 2200; timp+1, pf, str

Chthonic Ode, op. 90 (1966)      20'
   3*3*3*3*; 4331; euph; timp+1, pf, cel, str GS

Sadhana, op. 117 (1981)          20'
   solo vc; 2222; 2220; timp+1, hp, str  GS

Symphony No. 6 ("Organ Symphony"),
   op. 118 (1982)               25'
   solo org; 2222; 2220; perc, str  GS


      CROCKETT, DONALD  (1951-    )

Lyrikos (1979)                 21'
   solo t; 2+22*2; 2210; 2hp, str  PS

Vox in Rama (1983)           25'
   soli s, a, t, b; satb cho; 2*2*2*2; 2200;  MMB
   2perc, str

Melting Voices (1986)                                          13'
   3*3*3=3; 4331; 2perc, hp, pf/cel, str           MMB

The Tenth Muse (1986)                                          30'
   solo s; 2=2*2*2; 2210; timp+1, str               MMB

The Sun and Moon Dance and Blow
   Trumpets (1987)                                   4'
   333+3; 4331; 2perc, hp, pf, str                  MMB

Still Life with Bell (1990)                                    15'
   1*01*1; 1110; perc, pf, str (2-1-1-1)            MMB

Wedge (1990)                                                   10'
   33*3*3; 4331; timp+3, hp, pf, str               MMB


     CRUMB, GEORGE   (1929-      )

Variazioni (1959)                                             25'
   3*3*4=3*; 4331; 5perc, hp, cel, mand, str       CFP

Echoes of Time and the River
   (Echoes II) (1967)                               18'
   3*32+0; 3330; timp+4, hp, pf, pf/cel, str       BEL

Star Child (1977)                                             33'
   solo s; children's cho; male speaking           CFP
   cho; bell ringers; 4*4*4=4*; 6731; 8perc,
   org, str

A Haunted Landscape (1984)                                    18'
   3*3*3*3*; 4331; timp+4, 2hp, pf, str            CFP


     CSONKA, PAUL   (1905-      )

Fantastic Variations (1945)                                   20'
   3*3*3*3*; 4331; timp+4, hp, pf, cel, str        PS

Cuban Concerto No. 1 (1946)                                    8'
   solo pf; 2222; 4231; timp+4, hp, cel, str       PS

Cuban Concerto No. 2 (1950)                                   11'
   solo vln; 2222; 4231; timp+4, hp,               PS
   2pf, str

Santa Lucia Variations (1950)                                 17'
   3*222; 4231; timp+2, hp, pf, cel, str           UE

Concertino for Oboe and Bassoon (1951)                12'
   soli ob, bsn; 2121; 2200; 3perc, pf, str      PS

Serenata for Violoncello and
   Orchestra (1953)                                  12'
   solo vc; 2222; 2200; timp, pf, acc,               PS
   2gtr, str

Ten Symphonic Etudes (1953)                           20'
   3*3*3*3*; 4431; timp+3, hp, cel, str             PS

Prisma Sinfonico (1954)                                6'
   2222; 2210; timp, str                            PS

Symphonietta (1957)                                   16'
   str                                              PS


      CUMMINGS, CONRAD   (1948-    )

Morning Music (1973)                                   8'
   1*11+1; 1110; 2perc, pf, str (2-1-1-1)          BEL

Composition for Orchestra (1977)                      15'
   3(3 picc)222; 4331; timp+3, pf, str             BEL

Dénouement (1991)                                      8'
   3*3*3*3*; 4331; timp+3, pf, str                 CUM


      CUNNINGHAM, ARTHUR   (1928-    )

Adagio (1954)                                          5'
   solo ob; str                                    MS

Night Lights (1955)                                    5'
   2221; 3330; timp+2, str                         MS

Dialogue for Piano and Orchestra
   (1966; rev 1989)                                  5'
   solo pf; 2221; 2220; timp+1, str                TP

Prometheus (1966)                                     30'
   solo low v; 3*222; 2221; timp+1, str            TP

Theatre Piece (1966)                                   8'
   2222; 3330; timp+2, str                         MS

Concentrics (1968)                                    28'
   2221; 3311; perc, str                           TP

Dim du mim (Twilight) (1969)                          8'
    solo eh; 2021; 2221; perc, str                   TP

Lullaby for a Jazz Baby (1969; rev 1972)             6'
    solo tpt; 223*1; 2220; perc, hp, str             TP

The Walton Statement (1971)                          15'
    solo db; 2221; 3330; timp+1, str                 TP

Litany for the Flower Children (1972)                15'
    satb cho; 223*0; 2220; perc, dmst, str           TP

Night Song (1973)                                    60'
    satb cho; 2220; 3330; timp+2, pf, gtr,           TP
    b gtr, str

Pataditas (1973)                                     5'
    solo pf; 223*1; 3330; timp+1, str                TP

The Prince (1973)                                    25'
    solo b-bar; 3*222; 2221; timp+2, str             TP

Sun Bird (1974)                                      15'
    solo ca; solo gtr; 2121; 0000;                   TP
    timp+3, str

Rooster Rhapsody (1975)                              8'
    narr; solo rock qt; 3*3*3*3*; 3330;              TP
    timp+2, str, group of people making
    sound effects

Night Bird (1978)                                    10'
    solo jazz qnt; 223*0; 3330; timp+2, str          TP

Sun Catcher (1991)                                   14'
    soli s, a, t, b; satb cho; 223*0; 3330;          MS
    timp+4, str


            CUNNINGHAM, MICHAEL   (1937-      )

Dialogue for Orchestra and Wind Trio,
    op. 11a (1959)                                   7'
    soli fl, cl, bsn; 23*11; 4431;                   SEE
    timp+1, str

Counter Currents, op. 16a (1960)                     6'
    3*3*3*3*; 4331; timp+1, hp cel, str              SEE
    N.B.  Also arranged for string orchestra.

Ballet in Jazz Style (Post-Meriddean)
   (1964-1967)                                          15'
   1020; a sax; 0100; perc, str                          MS

Concerto for Trumpet, op. 23a (1967)                     15'
   solo tpt; 4*13*1; 0000; perc, str                    SEE

Piano Concerto, op. 26 (1968)                            20'
   solo pf; 3*3*3*2; 4331; timp+1, str                  SEE

Free Designs, op. 45 (1971)                              15'
   3*222; 4331; perc, hp, pf, str                       SEE

Irish Symphony, op. 48 (1972)                            12'
   str                                                  SEE

Symphonic Arias: Night (1974-1976)                       20'
   soli s, ca, t, b; satb cho; 223*2; 4431;             MS
   timp+1, hp, pf, cel, str

Figg and Bean Overture
   (Potpourri Overture) (1975)                           2'
   1010; 1000; str                                      SEE

Aedon (1976)                                              9'
   1*111; 2000; str, tape                               SEE

Time Frame, op. 90a (1980)                                9'
   a fl(or cl), fl, bs fl/cl; vib,                      SEE
   hpsd(or pf), str

Trans Actions, op. 90b (1980)                             8'
   2222; 4221; hp, cel, str                             SEE

Islands, op. 99 (1983)                                    5'
   3*3*3*2; 4331; timp+1, hp, str                       SEE

Venus and Adonis, op. 141 (1989)                         10'
   323*2; 4331; timp+1, hp, pf/cel, str                 MS


      CURTIS, MARVIN    (1951-     )

Testament (1987)                                         10'
   narr; satb cho; 3*3*3*3*; 4331;                      MFM
   timp+3, str

A Stanislaus Overture (1989)                              4'
   3*3*3*3*; 4331; timp+3, str                          MS

CURTIS-SMITH, CURTIS   (1941-      )

Xanthie:  Winter Pieces (1974)                      30'
    1111; 2000; pf, str                             MS

Bells (Belle du jour) (1974-1975)                   18'
    solo pf; 3*33*3*; 4430; timp+2, str             SAL

GAS! (Great American Symphony) (1982)               22'
    3*3*4=3; a sax; 4431; timp+4, pf, mand,         TP
    bj, elec gtr, b gtr, str

Songs and Cantillations (1983)                      20'
    solo gtr; 2222; 4220; timp+2, str               MS

Chaconne á son goût (1984-1985)                     14'
    3*3*3*3*; 4331; timp+3, pf, str                 MS

Celebration (1986)                                   6'
    2222; 4220; timp+2, str (7-6-5-4-2 desks)       MS

Float wild birds, sleeping:  Haiku
    Settings (1988)                                 20'
    3=233; 4230; timp+3, hp, pf/cel, str            MS

CUSHING, CHARLES   (1905-      )

Divertimento (1947)                                 15'
    str                                             MMB

Cereus (1960)                                        8'
    3*3*3*2; 4230; timp+1, hp, cel, str             SHA

CUSTER, ARTHUR   (1923-      )

Passacaglia for Small Orchestra
    (1958; rev 1963)                                10'
    1*1*1*1; a sax; 2111; timp+1, str               ACA

Concert Piece for Orchestra (1959)                  10'
    2*22*2; 4231; timp+3, str                       ACA

Symphony No. 1 (Sinfonia de Madrid) (1961)          20'
    2222; 4231; timp+4, str                         ACA

Five Dialogues (1962)                               16'
    solo vc; 2222; 2221; timp+1, pf, str            ACA

Songs of the Seasons (1964)                            18'
   solo s; 1*11(a sax)1; 2100; timp, str              ACA

Found Objects II - Rhapsodality
   Brass! (1969)                                       12'
   3*23*3*; a sax; 4331; timp+4, hp, str               ACA

Doubles (1972)                                         18'
   solo vln; 2=11*2*; 2120; perc, hp, str             ACA

DAHL, INGOLF   (1912-1970)

Symphony Concertante (1952)                          27'
    soli 2cl; 3*202; 2221; perc, hp, str            EAM

The Tower of St. Barbara (1954)                      23'
    2222; 4331; timp+2, hp, str                     SHA

Aria sinfonica (1965)                                17'
    3*3*3*3*; 4331; timp+2, str                     EAM

Quodlibet on American Folktunes (1965)               6'
    323*2; 4331(opt); timp+2, pf(opt), str          CFP

Variations on a Theme by C.P.E. Bach (1967)          14'
    str                                             EAM

Elegy Concerto
    (1970 - completed by D. Michalsky)              14'
    solo vln; 0200; 2000; str                       EAM


DANIELPOUR, RICHARD   (1956-    )

Concerto for Piano and Orchestra (1982)              27'
    solo pf; 23*3*3*; 4331; timp+1, str             CFP

Prologue and Prayer (1982)                           18'
    satb cho; str                                   AMP

Symphony No. 2 "Visions" (1986)                      36'
    soli s, t; 22*3*2; 4331; timp+2,                AMP
    hp, pf, str

Elegy (1987)                                         17'
    223*2; 2220; timp+3, hp, str                    AMP

First Light (1988)                                   13'
    21*22; 4220; timp+2, hp, pf,                    AMP
    str (12-12-10-8-6)
    OR:  11*11; 2110; timp+2, hp, pf,
    str (6-6-4-4-2)

Journey without Distance
  (Symphony No. 3) (1990)        28'
  satb cho(opt); 3*2*2*2*; 4331;     AMP
  timp+3, hp, str

Metamorphosis (1990)             24'
  solo pf; 2*2*2*2; 2220; timp+3, hp,   AMP
  amp pf/cel, str

### DAUGHERTY, MICHAEL (1954-    )

Snap! (1987)                  7'
  1*12*0; 1110; 3perc, synth, str (2-1-1-1)   PS

Firecracker (1988)           15'
  solo ob; 1*02*1; 0020; synth,      PS
  str (4-2-2-1)

Mxyzptlk (1988)              7'
  soli 2fl/picc; 0222; 2110; 2perc,   PS
  synth, str

Oh Lois! (1989)              5'
  2*222; 4330; timp+2, kybd/synth, str   PS

Strut (1989)                 6'
  str                     PS

Lex (1990)                   8'
  solo elec vln; 2222; 4330; timp+4,   PS
  synth, str

Flamingo (1991)              8'
  2*111; 111(b tbn)0; 2perc, str     PS

### DAVIDOVSKY, MARIO (1934-    )

Concertino (1954)            18'
  perc, str               MS

Suite Sinfonica Para El Payaso (1955)   40'
  3*3*4=3*; 4331; perc, pf, str     MS

Serie Sinfonica (1959)         17'
  2222; 4331; perc, str        MS

Contrastes (1960)            15'
  str, electronic sounds       MS

Planos (1961)                                          12'
   3*3*3*3*; 4331; perc, str                           MS

Inflexions (1965)                                       7'
   2010; 0110; 4perc, pf/cel, str (1-1-1-0)           EBM

Transientes (1972)                                     10'
   3022; 4231; perc, pf, str                          EBM

Pennplay (1973)                                        11'
   2=02=0; 1111; 2perc, pf, str (2-1-1-1)             CFP

Synchronisms No, 7 (1973)                              10'
   3=03*2*; 4331; timp+4, pf, str, tape               EBM

Divertimento (1984)                                    17'
   solo vc; 2=2*2*2*; 4221; 2perc, pf, str            CFP

Concertante (1989)                                     18'
   solo str qt; 4=2*3(2b cl)3; 4331; 3perc,           CFP
   hp, pf, str


            DAVIS, ALLAN   (1922-      )

Festival Concerto (1974)                               20'
   solo cl; 2202; 2000; timp+1, str                   OXF

Divertimento (NA)                                      25'
   1111; 2200; str                                    OXF


            DAVIS, ANTHONY   (1951-      )

Still Waters (1982)                                    17'
   2111; 2010; timp+4, hp, pf, str                    GS

Wayang V (1985)                                        25'
   2*12*1; 2120; timp+4, str                          GS

Malcolm's "Prison Aria" (1986)                          5'
   solo bar; 2*12(a,t sax)2*; 2120;                   GS
   timp+3, pf, str

Maps (Violin Concerto) (1988)                          25'
   solo vln; timp+5, hp, str                          GS

Notes from the Underground (1988)                      25'
   2*222; 2221; 3perc, pf, str                        GS

DAVIS, CURTIS   (1928-1986)

Four Sonnets (1975)                                             15'
   solo s; 2222; 4331; timp+3, hp, str                        MMB

Recollections for Large Orchestra (NA)                         14'
   3*3*3*3*; 4331; timp+3, hp, str                          PS


DAVIS, WILLIAM MAC   (1953-    )

Symphony in Three Movements (1981)                             20'
   3*23*2; 4231; timp, str                                 MS

The City of Light (1989)                                       30'
   soli s, t, bar; narr; satb cho; 3*23*2;                 MS
   4331; timp+3, hp, pf, str

Festival Fanfare on "Foundation" (1990)                        3'
   3*222; 4331; timp+3, str                                MS


DELLO JOIO, NORMAN   (1913-    )

Magnificat (1942)                                              16'
   3*020; 4100; perc, pf, str                              CF

To a Lone Sentry (1943)                                        12'
   1*010; 4131; timp, str                                  GS

Concert Music (1944)                                           21'
   3*3*3*3*; 4331; 2perc, str                              CF

Concerto for Harp and Orchestra (1945)                         20'
   solo hp; 1121; 2000; timp+1, str                        CF

Ricercari (1946)                                               20'
   solo pf; 3*222; 4331; timp+1, str                       CF

Variations, Chaconne and Finale (1947)                         21'
   3*3*3*3*; 4331; timp+2, str                             CF

Serenade (1947-1948)                                           16'
   3*3*3*2; 4330; timp+2, hp, pf/cel, str                  CF

Concertante (1949)                                             17'
   solo cl; 2222; 2200; timp+2, str                        CF

New York Profiles (1949)                                       20'
   2222; 2200; timp+1, str                                 CF

A Psalm of David (1950)                                  25'
    satb cho; 0000; 4431; timp+2, str                   CF
    OR: 223*2; 4331; timp+2, str (no satb cho)

Epigraph for Orchestra (1951)                            7'
    3*23*2; 4331; timp+1, hp, str                       CF

The Triumph of St. Joan - symphony (1951)               27'
    23*22; 4231; timp+2, str                            CF

Song of Affirmation - cantata (1953)                    42'
    solo s; narr; satb cho; 3*222; 4331;                CF
    timp+2, str

Lamentation of Saul (1954)                              20'
    solo bar; 3*3*3*2; 4331; timp+2, hp,                CF
    pf, str

Meditations on Ecclesiastes (1956)                      22'
    str                                                 CF

Air Power (1956-1957)                                   39'
    2222; 4331; timp+2, str                             CF

A Ballad of the Seven Lively Arts (1957)                10'
    solo pf; 2222; 3231; timp+1, str                    CF

On Stage - suite (1959)                                 15'
    23*22; 4231; timp+1, pf, str                        GS

Fantasy and Variations (1961)                           22'
    solo pf; 3*23*2; 4331; timp, cel, str               CF

Antiphonal Fantasy on a Theme of
    Vincenzo Albrici (1965)                             17'
    0000; 4431; org, str                                EBM

Air (1967)                                               7'
    str                                                 BRO

Five Images for Orchestra (1967)                         7'
    3*23*2; 4231; timp+1, str                           EBM

Homage to Haydn (1968-1969)                              8'
    3*3*3*3*; 4331; timp+1, str                         EBM

Evocations (1970)                                       32'
    satb cho; 3*3*3*3*; 4331; timp+3, str               EBM

Choreography (1972)                                      9'
   str                                                      EBM

Lyric Fantasies (1973)                                   17'
   solo vla; str                                            GS

Mass in Honor of the Eucharist (1975)                    24'
   solo cantor; satb cho; 0000; 4331;                       GS
   org, str

Colonial Variants:  Thirteen Profiles of
   the Original Colonies (1976)                           26'
   3*3*3*3*; 4331; timp+2, hp, str                        GS

Southern Echoes (1976)                                   16'
   23*3*0; 4331; 2perc, str                               GS

Songs of Remembrance (1977)                              20'
   solo bar; 3*3*3*3*; 4331; timp+1, hp, str   GS

Arietta (1978)                                           3'
   str                                                      EBM

As of a Dream! - masque (1978)                           30'
   soli s, a, t; satb cho; 1*1*1*1; 3221;                 GS
   perc, pf, str

Three Hymns without Words (1980)                         14'
   satb cho; 2222; 4231; timp+1, str                      GS

Ballabili (1981)                                         23'
   3*3*3*2; 4331; timp+2, hp, str                         GS

East Hampton Sketches (1983)                             10'
   str                                                      GS

Lyric Dances (1986)                                      11'
   1110; 1100; str                                         GS


     DEL TREDICI, DAVID  (1937-    )

Szygy (1966)                                             24'
   solo s; solo hn; 2(2picc, a fl)2*2*2*;                  BH
   1200; 2perc,str (2-2-1-1)

The Last Gospel (1967)                              13'
    solo amp s; satb cho; rock group: s sax,    BH
    s sax/t sax, 2elec gtr; 3*4(2eh)04(2cbn);
    0110; str (2-1-1-1)
    OR:  3(2picc)3*4=3*; 4431; timp+5, str

Pop-pourri (1968; rev 1973)                         28'
    solo amp s; solo mez or countertenor(opt); BH
    satb cho (opt); rock group: s sax,
    s sax/t sax, elec gtr, b gtr;
    2(2picc)2*2*2*; 0220; 3perc, str

An Alice Symphony - In Two Parts (1969)             41'

    I.  Illustrated Alice                           17'
        solo amp s; folk group: s sax/a sax,    BH
        a sax/s sax/t sax, mand, t bj, acc;
        2*222*; 4221; timp+5, str

    II. In Wonderland                               24'
        solo amp s; folk group: 2s sax,         BH
        mand, t bj, acc; 2(2picc)2*2=2*;
        4221; timp+4, str

The Lobster Quadrille (1969; rev 1974)              13'
    solo amp s (or t); folk group: 2s sax,      BH
    mand, t bj, acc; 2(2picc)2*2=2*; 4221;
    4perc, str

Adventures Underground (1971)                       23'
    solo amp s; folk group:  2s sax, mand,      BH
    t bj, acc; 2*22+2; 4222; timp+5, 2hp,
    cel, str

Vintage Alice:  Fantascene on a Mad
    Tea Party (1972)                                28'
    solo amp s; folk group:  2s sax, mand,      BH
    t bj, acc; 1*11+1; 2110; timp+1, str

Final Alice (1976)                                  64'
    solo amp s (or narr); folk group: 2s sax,   BH
    mand, t bj, acc; 4(3picc)4*4=4*; 6441;
    timp+7, 2hp, cel, str

*DEL TREDICI*                                             133

Child Alice - In Two Parts (1980-1981)        137'

    I. In Memory of a Summer Day                    63'
       solo amp s; 3(2picc)3*2=3*; 4431;           BH
       5perc, 2hp, cel, str

   II. All in the Golden Afternoon                  35'
       solo amp s; 3(2picc)3*4=3*; 4431;           BH
       timp+5, 2hp, cel, str

       Happy Voices                                 21'
       3(2picc)3*4=3*; 4431; timp+5, 2hp,          BH
       cel, str

       Quaint Events                                25'
       solo amp s; 3(2picc)3*4=3*; 4431;           BH
       timp+5, 2hp, cel, str

March to Tonality (1983-1985)                      22'
    4(2picc)3*4=3*; 4431; timp+4, str              BH

The Last Gospel (1984 version)                     13'
    3*3*3*3*; 4431; timp+5, str                    BH

Tattoo (1986)                                      20'
    speaking cho; 4=3*4=3*; 4432; timp+6,          BH
    hp, cel, str

Acrostic Song (1987)                                4'
    1010; 1000; perc, pf, str                      BH

Steps (1990)                                       31'
    4*3*4=3*; 4441; timp+5, hp, cel, str           BH


        DE MARS, JAMES

Spirit Horses (1986)                               15'
    navajo flute; perc, str                        MS

The Prophet (1987)                                 22'
    satb cho; 1111; 1220; perc, str                MS

Tito's Say (1989)                                  26'
    satb cho; 0000; 0330; pf, str                  MS

Two World Symphony (1989)                          30'
    solo s; soli cedar flute, African drums;       MS
    1010; a,bar sax; 1000; 2perc,
    pf, str (no vla)

Two World Overture (1991)                          13'
    solo s; 3*3*3*3*; 4331; 3perc, hp,            MS
    pf, str

Ventura and Clemente (1991)                        12'
    3*3*3*3*; 4331; 3perc, hp, str                MS


        DEMBSKI, STEPHEN  (1949-    )

Of Mere Being (1975; rev 1983)                      8'
    solo s; 3*3*3*3*; 43(2flu hn)31; vib/xyl,    CBM
    hp, pf/cel, str

Spectra (1985)                                     15'
    1111; 1100; perc, str                         CBM

Refraction/Retracja (1986)                          5'
    1111; 1211; perc, str                         CBM


        DIAMOND, DAVID LEO  (1915-    )

Concert Piece for Large Orchestra (1939)           11'
    2222; 2320; timp+2, pf, str                   PS

Symphony No. 1 (1940-1941)                         21'
    3*3*3*3*; 4331; timp+1, str                   PS

Symphony No. 2 (1942)                              34'
    3*3*3*3*; 4331; timp+3, str                   PS

Symphony No. 3 (1945)                              26'
    3*3*3*3*; 4431; timp+4, hp, pf, str           PS

Symphony No. 4 (1945)                              20'
    4(2 picc)4*4*4; 6431; timp+2, 2hp,            GS
    pf, str

Music for Shakespeare's "Romeo and Juliet"
    (1947; rev 1950)                               8'
    2*2*2*2; 2210; timp+2, hp, str                BH

The Enormous Room (1948)                           11'
    3*3*3*3*; 4331; timp+3, hp, str               PS

Timon of Athens (1949)                              9'
    2222; 4231; timp+1, pf, str                   TP

Concerto for Piano and Orchestra (1949-1950)  22'
   solo pf; 3*3*3*2; 4231; timp+3, str  PS

The Martyr (1950)  10'
   ttbb cho; 234+3; 43(picc tpt)31; timp+1,  PS
   pf, str

Symphony No. 5 (1951; rev 1964)  17'
   3*3*4=3*; 4431; timp+3, pf, org, str  PS

Symphony No. 6 (1951-1954)  25'
   3*3*4+3; 4331; timp+2, pf, str  BRO

Sinfonia concertante (1954-1956)  23'
   2211; 1331; timp+5, hp, pf, str  PS

The World of Paul Klee (1957)  12'
   3*3*3*2; 4330; timp+5, hp, pf/cel, str  PS

Symphony No. 7 (1959)  24'
   3*3*4=3*; 4431; timp+5, hp, pf, str  PS

Symphony No. 8 (1960)  28'
   3*3*4=3*; 4331; timp+5, hp, pf, str  PS

This Sacred Ground (1962)  15'
   satb cho; children cho; 3*3*3*3*; 4331;  PS
   timp+5, hp, str

Elegies (1962-1963)  17'
   soli fl, eh; str  BRO

Concertino for Piano and Orchestra (1964)  12'
   solo pf; 2*2*2*2; 2210; timp+3, str  PS

To Music: A Choral Symphony (1967)  34'
   soli t, bar; satb cho; 3*3*4=3*; 6431;  PS
   timp+4, hp, pf, str

Concerto No. 3 for Violin and Orchestra
   (1967-1968)  23'
   solo vln; 3*3*3*2; 4221; timp+3, pf, str  PS

Music for Chamber Orchestra (1969)  17'
   2=1*1+1; 2110; timp+4, hp, pf, str  PS

Overture No. 2 "A Buoyant Music" (1970)  5'
   3*3*4+3; 4331; timp+1, hp, pf, cel, str  PS

A Secular Cantata (1976)                          40'
    soli t, bar; satb cho;                        GS
    1*1*1(picc cl in D)1; 2210; timp+1, pf,
    org, str

Kaddish (1990)                                    12'
    solo vc; 3*3*3*3*; 4431; timp+3, hp, str     GS


        DICKERSON, ROGER  (1934-    )

A Musical Service for Louis
    (Armstrong) (1972)                            15'
    satb cho(opt); 3*3*3*2; 4431; timp+3,        PS
    hp, pf, str

Orpheus an' his Slide Trombone (1975)             16'
    narr; 3*3*3*3*; 4341; timp+4, hp, pf, str    PS

New Orleans Concerto (1976)                       22'
    solo pf; 3*3*3*2; 4331; timp+3, str          PS


        DI DOMENICA, ROBERT  (1927-    )

Symphony (1961)                                   17'
    3*222; 4331; timp+1, str                     EBM

Concerto for Violin and Chamber
    Orchestra (1962)                              18'
    solo vln; 1111; 1000; str (2-1-1-1)          MJQ

Concerto for Woodwind Quintet, Timpani
    and Strings (1964)                            20'
    solo ww qnt; timp, str                       EBM

Music for Flute and String Orchestra (1967)      8'
    solo fl; str                                  EBM

The Holy Colophon (1980)                          20'
    soli s, t; satb cho; 3*4*4*4*; 4331;         MG
    timp+2, hp, 2pf, cel, str

Concerto No. 2 for Piano and
    Orchestra (1982)                              30'
    solo pf; 2*222; 2231; timp+1, hp,            MG
    cel, str

Dream Journeys (1984)                             10'
    3*3*3*3*; 4331; timp+3, 2hp, str             MG

Variations and Soliloquies (1988)                       24'
  3*3*3*3*; 4331; timp+3, 2hp, str            MG


    DIEMENTE, EDWARD  (1923-    )

Three Scenes from Pinocchio (1966)                      10'
  3*24=1; 4230; timp+1, pf, str                MS

Murmurs (1975)                                          13'
  3*222; 4330; timp+2, str                     MS

Wheels (1978)                                           15'
  2*111; 1110; 3perc, str (2-1-1-1)            MS

Scenes from Miro (1980)                                 21'
  1111; 1110; timp+1, str (6-6-4-3-2)          MS

Credo (1982)                                            45'
  solo s; satb cho; 3*23*2; 4330;              MS
  timp+5, str

Violin Concerto (1984)                                  26'
  solo vln; 3*23*2; 4330; timp+5, str          MS

Italian Serenade (1985)                                 8'
  str                                          MS

Elegy for String Orchestra (1990)                       4'
  str                                          MS

Paganini Pops (1990)                                    18'
  3*222; 4330; timp+2, str                     MS


    DIEMER, EMMA LOU  (1927-    )

Symphony No. 1 (1952)                                   15'
  2222; 4331; timp+2, str                      MS

Concerto for Piano and Orchestra (1953)                 15'
  solo pf; 2222; 4331; timp+2, str             MS

Suite for Orchestra (1954)                              20'
  2222; 4231; timp+1, hp, pf, str              SEE

Concerto for Harpsichord and
  Orchestra (1958)                             12'
  solo hpsd; 2222; 4320; timp+2, str           SEE

Pavane (1959)                                          8'
  str                                              CF

Symphony No. 2
  (American Indian Themes) (1959)                 15'
  3*3*3*3*; 4331; timp+2, pf, cel, str             SEE

Youth Overture (1959)                                  4'
  3*222; 4331; timp+3, str                        BEL

Rondo Concertante (1960)                               5'
  3*222; 4331; timp+3, pf, str                    BH

Festival Overture (1961)                               7'
  3*222; 4331; timp+3, pf, str                    SEE

Symphony No. 3 (Symphonie antique) (1961)              12'
  2222; 4331; timp+2, str                         BEL

To Him all Glory Give (1962)                           5'
  satb cho; 2222; 4331; timp+2, str               ELK

1962 Overture (1962)                                   5'
  3*222; 4331; timp+5, str                        MS

Concerto for Flute and Orchestra (1963)               24'
  solo fl; 3*33*3*; 4331; timp+3, hp,             PS
  pf/cel, str

Fairfax Festival Overture (1967)                       8'
  2222; 4231; timp+1, hp, pf, str                 SEE

Anniversary Choruses (1970)                           15'
  satb cho; 2222; 4331; timp+2, str               CF

Four Poems by Alice Meynell (1976)                    15'
  solo s (or t); 2*000; 0000; 4perc, hp,          CF
  pf, hpsd, str

Concert Piece for Organ and Orchestra (1977)          10'
  solo org; 2222; 4331; timp+2, str               SEE

Concerto for Trumpet and Orchestra (1983)             15'
  solo tpt; 2222; 4331; timp+2, str               MS

Concerto for Violin and Orchestra (1983)              15'
  solo vln; 2222; 4331; timp+2, str               MS
  N.B.   This work is a revision of the
  "Concerto for Trumpet."

Invocation (1985)                                      7'
  satb cho; 2222; 4331; timp+2,                CF
  pf(or org), str

Suite of Homages (1985)                                18'
  2222; 4331; timp+2, pf, str                  CF

Serenade for String Orchestra (1988)                   10'
  str                                          SEE

Concerto in One Movement for Marimba
  and Orchestra (1991)                         18'
  solo mar; 2*222; 2210; timp+2,               MS
  pf/cel. str


     DLUGOSZEWSKI, LUCIA  (1934-    )

Fire Fragile Flight (1973-1974)                        12'
  1111; 1120; 2perc, hp, pf, str               MG

Abyss and Caress (1974-1975)                           35'
  solo tpt; 2210; 1020; pf, str                MG

Strange Tenderness of Naked Leaping (1978)             25'
  2*000; 0200; str                             MG

Startle Transparent Terrible Freedom (1981)            25'
  3*3*3*3*; 4331; timp+3-4, hp, pf, str        MG

Radical Quidditas Dew Tear Duende (1991)               23'
  3*3*3*3*; 4331; timp+3. hp, pf, str          MG


     DODGE, CHARLES  (1942-    )

Rota (1966)                                            14'
  3*3*33*; 4231; timp+5, pf. str               ACA

Palinode (1976)                                        17'
  2222; 4231; 2perc, str, computer tape        ACA
  playback


     DOLLARHIDE, THEODORE  (1948-    )

A Fantasy of Ivory Thoughts and Shallow
  Whispers (1972)                              10'
  2222; 2001; str                              ACA

Movements (1973)                                    15'
   3*23*2; 4331; 4perc, pf(w/asst), str        ACA

Other Dreams, Other Dreamers (1976)                 10'
   3=3*3*3; 4331; 4perc, 2hp, pf, cel, str      MMB

Pluriels - for two orchestras (1979)                9'
   orch 1:  2*2*2*2*; 3221; str                 MMB
   orch 2:  2*2*2*2*; 3221; str
   N.B.  The work also requires 5perc, 2hp,
   pf, cel.


DONATO, ANTHONY  (1909-1990)

Mission San Jose de Aguaya (1945)                   5'
   2222; 0000; str                              FLE

Prairie Schooner Overture (1947)                 .. 6'
   2222; 4330; timp+2, hp, str                  FLE

Suite for Strings (1948)                            11'
   str                                          PS

The Plains (1953)                                   6'
   2222; 4330; timp+2, hp, str                  FLE

Episode for Orchestra (1954)                        12'
   3*3*3*3*; 4331; timp+3, str                  PS

Solitude in the City (1954)                         24'
   narr; 3*3*3*3*; 4331; timp+3, str            FLE

Sinfonietta No. 2 (1959)                            14'
   2222; 2210; timp+2, hp, str                  EBM

Serenade for Small Orchestra (1962)                 13'
   1111; 1110; timp+1, hp, str                  FLE


DONOVAN, RICHARD  (1891-1970)

Suite (1945)                                        17'
   solo ob; str                                 ACA

New England Chronicle (1947)                        10'
   3*3*3*3*; 4331; timp+1, str                  FLE

Passacaglia on Vermont Folk Tunes (1949)            13'
   2*222; 4231; timp+1, str                     ACA

Epos (1963)                                                   11'
   3*3*3*3; 4331; timp+2, str                                ACA


         DOPPMANN, WILLIAM  (1933-    )

Counterpoints (1987)                                         17'
   solo pf; 2perc, str (8-5-4-2-1)                           MG


         DOUGLAS, SAMUEL  (1943-    )

Pachyderm (1985)                                            25'
   2222; 2110; timp+3, pf/cel, str                          MS

Concerto for Double Bass and
   Orchestra (1989)                                         20'
   solo db; 1111; 1000; perc, pf, cel, str                  MS


         DOWNEY, JOHN  (1927-    )

La joie de la paix (1955)                                   10'
   3*3*3*2; 4221; timp+3, str                                MS

Chant to Michelangelo (1958)                               13'
   3*23*2; 4431; timp+2, str                                 MS

Concerto for Harp and Chamber
   Orchestra (1964)                                         20'
   solo hp; 1111; 1110; 4perc, str                          MS

Jingalodeon (1968)                                         12'
   2202; 4231; timp+1, str                                  EDB

Prospectations III - II - I (1970)                         25'
   orch 1:  3*3*3*3*; 4331; timp+3, str                     MS
   orch 2:  3*3*3*3*; 4331; timp+3, str
   orch 3:  str
   N.B.  Requires three conductors for
   performance.

Symphonic Modules V (1972)                                 46'
   4=3*4=3*; 6431; timp+5, hp, cel, str                     TP
   N.B.  Percussion requires oriental dragon
   drum and sel-rod chimes.  There are two
   orchestral suites derived from this work
   that are also available from the publisher.

The Edge of Space (1978)                        18'
    solo bsn; 23*3*2; 2221; 4perc, hp,         TP
    elec gtr, str

Declamations (1985)                             16'
    3*3*3*3*; 4331; 3perc, str                  TP

Discourse (1986)                                18'
    solo ob; hpsd, str                          CFP

Concerto for Double Bass and Orchestra
    (1987; rev 1989)                            30'
    solo db; 3*3*3*3*; 4231; timp+1, hp,        TP
    cel, str

Meni Odnakoro (1990)                            8'
    solo b; 223*3*; 4231; timp+2, str           MS


        DRESHER, PAUL

Reaction (1984)                                 26'
    2*12*2*; 2221; 2perc, pf/cel, str           MMX

Cornucopia (1990)                               16'
    2*2*2=2; 3100; perc, pf, str                MMX


        DREW, JAMES   (1929-    )

October Lights (1969)                           10'
    3*010; 2321; perc, 2pf, str                 TP

Symphony No. 2 (1971)                           20'
    satb cho; 3*1*32; 2211; 4perc, hp,          TP
    pf, str

West Indian Lights (1973)                       25'
    3*23*2; 4431; perc, hp, pf, cel, str        TP

Symphonies (1981)                               25'
    4*121; 2321; perc, str                      TP

Donaldson:  Steeples, Whistles and
    Fog (1987)                                  18'
    2*132*; 4331; timp+3, hp, pf, cel, str      TP

DRUCKMAN, JACOB   (1928-      )

The Sound of Time (1965)                                  12'
   solo s; 1*22*2; 2100; timp+1, pf, str           BH

Windows (1972)                                           21'
   3*3*3*3*; 4331; timp+3, hp, pf, str             BH

Incenters (1973)                                        13'
   soli hn, tpt, tbn; 3*3*3*2; 3021; 5perc,        BH
   hp, pf/elec org, str
   OR:   1111; 0000; 3perc, pf/elec org, str

Lamia (1974; rev 1975)                                  24'
   solo s; 3*23*2; 4331; timp+3, hp, pf,           BH
   elec org, str
   N.B.   Two conductors are required for
   performance.

Mirage (1976)                                           24'
   3*3*3*2; 4331; timp+4, hp, pf,                  BH
   elec org, str

Chiaroscuro (1977)                                      16'
   3*3*3*2; 4331; timp+3, hp, pf, elec pf,         BH
   elec org, str

Concerto for Viola and Orchestra (1978)                 22'
   solo vla; 3=2*3*2; 4331; 4perc, hp,             BH
   pf, str

Aureole (1979)                                          12'
   3+3*3*2; 4331; timp+3, hp, pf, str              BH

Prism (1980)                                            22'
   3=3*3*2; 4331; timp+3, hp, pf,                  BH
   elec hpsd, str

Vox Humana (1983)                                       31'
   soli s, mez, t, bar; 3=3*3*3*; 4331;            BH
   3 perc, hp, pf, str

That Quickening Pulse (1988)                             7'
   3=3*3*2; 4331; timp+3, hp, pf, str              BH

Brangle (1989)                                          20'
   3=3*3*2; 4331; timp+3, hp, pf, str              BH

Nor Spell nor Charm (1990)                              15'
   1+22*2; 2000; pf/synth, str                     BH

Shog (1991)                                              20'
    3=3*3=2; 4331; timp+5, hp, pf, str                  BH


            DUBENSKY, ARCADY  (1890-1966)

Concerto grosso (1949)                                  12'
    soli 3 tbn, tba; 2222; 0000; timp+1,                FC
    hp, str

Trombone Concerto (1953)                                20'
    solo tbn; 2222; 4231; timp, hp, str                 FC


            DUCKWORTH, WILLIAM  (1943-    )

When in Eternal Lines to Time
    Thou Grow'st (1974)                                 15'
    2222; 4231; perc, str                               FLE


            DUKELSKY, VLADIMIR (1903-1969)

Symphony No. 1 (1928)                                   18'
    3*3*3*3*; 4431; timp+3, pf, str                     BH

Symphony No. 2 (1929)                                   17'
    4*4*4*3*; 4331; timp, pf, str                       BH

Epitaph (On the death of Diaghilev) (1932)              10'
    solo s; satb cho; 3*3*3*3*; 2211; timp+2,           BH
    pf, 2gtr, str

Concerto for Violoncello and
    Orchestra (1946)                                    28'
    solo vc; 3*3*3*3*; 3011; timp+1, hp, str            CF

Ode to the Milky Way (1946)                             10'
    3*3*3*3*; 4331; timp+1, hp, pf, str                 BEL

Symphony No. 3 (1947)                                   45'
    3*3*3*3*; 4331; timp+3, pf, cel, str                CF

Variations on an Old Russian Chant (1958)               10'
    solo ob; str                                        BRO

Souvenir de Monte Carlo (1960)                          15'
    2*2*11; 1111; timp+1, pf, cel, str                  BRO

### DUTTON, BRENT   (1950-      )

Songs for Orchestra (1969)                                     10'
  2022; 4331; 8perc, str                               MS

Symphony No. 2 (1971-1972)                                     25'
  223*2; 4331; perc, str                               SEE

Images for Strings (1973)                                      15'
  str                                                  MS

Quebec, Spring (1974)                                           5'
  str                                                  MS

Symphony No. 4 (1978)                                          25'
  223*2; 4331; 3perc, str                              MS

Black Moon (1988)                                             14'
  3*23*2; 4331; 4perc, str                             MS

Krakow, Summer (1988)                                         14'
  str                                                  MS

Symphony No. 6 (1988)                                         60'
  3*23*2; 4331; 3perc, str                             MS

The Traveller (1988)                                           8'
  3*23*2; 0000; str                                    MS


### DZUBAY, DAVID   (1964-      )

Siren Song (1987)                                              8'
  3=3*3*3*; 4331; timp+4, hp, pf, cel, str            MMB

Snake Alley (1989)                                            10'
  3=3*3*3*; 4331; timp+3, hp, pf/cel, str            MMB

Tantalus (1990)                                                6'
  str                                                 MMB

EATON, JOHN C.  (1935-      )

Song Cycle on "Holy Sonnets" of John
   Donne (1957)                                    21'
   solo s; 2222; 4331; timp+1, hp, str          SHA

Tertullian Overture (1958)                      10'
   2222; 4220; timp, str                        SHA

Adagio and Allegro (1960)                       8'
   1100; 0000; str                              SHA

Concert Piece for Syn-ket and Symphony
   Orchestra (1968)                             13'
   solo syn-ket; 3*3*4*4*; 4331; timp+2, str    SHA

Ajax (1972)                                     11'
   2222; 1100; 3hp, 2pf, str (2-1-1-1)          SHA
   N.B. May be performed with a full
   complement of strings.

Symphony No. 2 (1981)                           25'
   333*3*; 4431; timp+1, 2pf,                   AMP
   musical saw, str

Remembering Rome (Symphony for String
   Orchestra) (1986)                            18'
   str                                          AMP

Songs of Despair (1986)                         22'
   solo mez; 1*1*1*1; 1111; 2perc, hp,          AMP
   pf, str

The Cry of Clytaemnestra:
   Aria and Scena (NA)                          17'
   solo mez; 1111; 1000; timp+2, 2pf,           SHA
   str (4-2-2-1),tape, offstage
   steirhorn (or reasonable substitute)

Danton and Robespierre - selections (NA)        14'
   soli coloratura, mez, bar, b;                SHA
   satb cho(opt); 4*4*6=6*; 6442; timp+4,
   3hp, 2pf, str, elec performer

"Herakles" (NA)

    1. Three Arias from Act I                         35'
        soli s, t, bar; 4*4*6=5*; 8441;               SHA
        timp+2, 6hp(or 2hp), str

    2. Aria from Act II                               14'
        solo mez; 4*4*6=5*; 8441; timp+2,             SHA
        6hp(or 2hp), str

    3. Aria and Scena from Act II                     23'
        soli mez, t; 4*4*6=5*; 8441; timp+2,          SHA
        6hp(or 2hp), str

The Lion and Androcles:  Wild Animal
    Parade (NA)                                        6'
    2222; 2230; timp+2, synth, str                    SHA

The Reverend Jim Jones (NA)

    1. Mad Scene from Act III                          9'
        solo bar; 3*3*4*4*; 4331; timp+2,             SHA
        2hp, str, elec performers

    2. Aria from Act III                               4'
        solo s; 3*3*4*4*; 4331; timp+2, 2hp,          SHA
        str, elec performers

The Tempest (NA)

    1. Opening Storm                                  11'
        male cho; 3*3*4*4*; 4331; timp+2,             SHA
        3hp, 2pf, str, 3elec performers
        N.B.  Also requires onstage Renaissance
        ensemble of recorders(or flutes),
        shawm(or oboe), lute(or hpsd) and onstage
        jazz group of a sax, elec gtr, b gtr, dmst.

    2. Songs of Ariel                                  8'
        solo mez; 3*3*4*4*; 4331; timp+2,             SHA
        3hp, 2pf, str, 3elec performers
        N.B.  Also requires onstage Renaissance
        ensemble of recorders(or flutes),
        shawm(or oboe), lute(or hpsd) and onstage
        jazz group of a sax, elec gtr, b gtr, dmst.
        (May be performed with Renaissance
        ensemble only.)

   3. Prospero Arias:  The Renunciation of
      Powers and Final Aria                         13'
      solo bar; 3*3*4*4*; 4331; timp+2,            SHA
      3hp, 2pf, str, 3elec performers
      N.B.  Also requires onstage Renaissance
      ensemble of recorders(or flutes),
      shawm(or oboe), lute(or hpsd) and onstage
      jazz group of a sax, elec gtr, b gtr, dmst.


           EBERHARD, DENNIS  (1943-     )

Marginals (1976)                                    15'
   4tbn; 3 str orch                                 MG

Ephrata (1980-1981)                                 13'
   soli 4perc; 3*3*3+3*; 4331; hp,                  MG
   pf/cel, str

The Bells of Elsinore (1988)                         9'
   3*3*3*3*; 4331; timp+3, 2hp, cel, str            MG

Berceuse (1989)                                     11'
   solo cl; hp, str                                 MG


           EDWARDS, GEORGE   (1943-     )

Giro (1974)                                         17'
   4*3*3*2; 2230; str                               BOE

Moneta's Mourn (1983)                               17'
   223*2; 4230; timp+1, hp, str                     ACA

Heraclitean Fire (1987)                              7'
   solo str qt; str                                 ACA


           EFFINGER, CECIL   (1912-1990)

Little Symphony No. 1, op. 31 (1945)                12'
   2121; 2100; str                                  CF

Suite, op. 32 (1945)                                14'
   solo vc; 1*222; 2200; str                        ARC

Symphony No. 2, op. 34 (1946)                       17'
   3*3*4*2; 4331; timp+2, str                       ARC

Symphony No. 1, op. 40 (1947)     20'
   3*3*3*3*; 4331; timp+2, str    ARC

Concerto for Piano and Chamber Orchestra,
   op. 44 (1948)    15'
   solo pf; 1111; 1100; str    ARC

Pastorale, op. 45, No. 2 (1949)    5'
   solo ob; str    ARC

Lyric Overture, op. 49 (1949)    7'
   3*222; 4330; timp, str    ARC

Symphony No. 4 (for Chorus and Orchestra),
   op. 54 (1952)    29'
   satb cho; 3*3*3*3*; 4331; timp+1, str    CF

The St. Luke Christmas Story,
   op. 56, No. 1 (1953)    35'
   solo s, a, t, b; satb cho; 0200; 0200;    GS
   timp, org, str

Symphony No. 3, op. 50, No. 1 (1954)    21'
   3*222; 4331; timp+4, str    ARC

Symphonie concertante, op. 57, No. 2 (1954)    19'
   soli hp, pf; 1*121; 2220; timp, str    ARC

Tone Poem on a Square Dance,
   op. 58, No. 1 (1955)    13'
   3*3*3*3*; 4331; timp+3, str    ARC

Evensong, op. 59 (1956)    10'
   2*222; 4330; timp+2, str    ARC

The Invisible Fire, op. 61 (1957)    57'
   soli s, a, t, b; satb cho; 3*222; 4331;    TP
   timp+1, str

Little Symphony No. 2, op. 52, No. 1 (1958)    12'
   3*222; 2210; str    CF

Symphony No. 5 (Icelandic), op. 62 (1958)    20'
   3*222; 4331; timp+1, str    CF

Trio Concertante, op. 71, No. 1 (1964)    18'
   soli hn, tpt, tbn; 1*111; 1110; timp+1,    ARC
   hp, str

Landscape I, op. 74 (1966)                                    7'
   0000; 4331; str                                          ARC

Paul of Tarsus, op. 79 (1968)                               40'
   solo bar; satb cho; org, str                            GS

Let Your Mind Wander Over America,
   op. 80 (1969)                                            8'
   satb cho; 3*31*2; 2a,t,bar sax; 4331;                    GS
   euph; timp+1, str

The Long Dimension, op. 83 (1970)                           30'
   solo bar; satb cho; 2*121; 2100;                        ARC
   perc, str

Cantata for Easter, op. 85, No. 1 (1971)                    20'
   satb cho; str                                           GS

Concerto for Violin and Chamber Orchestra,
   op. 82 (1972)                                           30'
   solo vln; 2222; 1110; 2perc, pf, str                    ARC

Quiet Evening, op. 86, No. 2 (1972)                         10'
   fl; mar, str                                            ARC

Capriccio, op. 91 (1975)                                    14'
   3*3*3*3*; 4331; timp+3, hp, cel, str                    ARC

Fanfare 1980 (1980)                                          7'
   2*202; 4321; perc, str                                  ARC

Toccata for Chamber Orchestra, op. 98 (1980)                14'
   2111; 2100; str (4-4-2-2-2)                             ARC

Landscape II, op. 113 (1983)                                14'
   3*3*3*3*; 4331; timp+2, str                             ARC

Sonnet at Dusk, op. 115 (1984)                               8'
   satb cho; str                                           ARC

Landscape III, op. 120 (1987)                               15'
   2*222; 4331; timp+2, str                                ARC


      EHLE, ROBERT C.  (1940-      )

A Space Symphony (1961)                                     29'
   3*3*3*3*; 4331; timp+1, str                             AMC

Folk Song Suite (1964)                                       8'
    str                                                      AMC

Soundpiece (1965)                                            10'
    3*3*3*3*; 5341; timp, hp, cel, str                       CF

Bay Psaulmes - 1640 (1970)                                   20'
    satb cho; 3*3*3*3*; 4331; timp+3,                        FLE
    hp, pf/cel, str

Ritual Conflicts (1972)                                      6'
    large orch; tape                                         MS
    N.B.  The number and size of the
    orchestra are variable.

Biomass and Strange Particles (Symphony for
    Synthesizer and Orchestra) (1980)                        10'
    3*3*3*3*; 4331; synth, str                               FLE

Earth Garden Symphony (1983-1984)                            20'
    3*3*3*3*; 4331; timp+4, hp, cel, str                     AMC

Rebus for Orchestra (1989)                                   45'
    3*3*3*3*; 4331; timp+2, str                              AMC


            EKIZIAN, MICHELLE  (1956-      )

Birthday Chords (A Variation on the song
    "Happy Birthday")                                        1'
    2222; 4231; timp+3, str                                  ACA

The Exiled Heart (1986)                                      15'
    3*3*3=3*; 4231; timp+3, str                              GS

Prologue:  Pulse (1986)                                      2'
    3*3*3=3*; 4231; timp+3, str                              GS
    N.B.  Taken from "The Exiled Heart."

Morning of Light (1988)                                      23'
    solo mez;  2*2*2=2*; 4231; timp+3, str                   ACA

Two Roethke Songs (1988-1989)                                10'
    solo mez; 2*2*2=2*; 4231; timp+3, str                    ACA
    N.B.  These songs are the Vocal
    Epilogues to "Morning of Light" and
    "Beyond the Reach of the Stars."

Beyond the Reach of Wind and Fire (1989)                     25'
    solo mez; 2*2*2+2; 4231; timp+3, str                     ACA

Saber Dance (1991)                                    12'
   3*3*3=3*; 4331; timp+3, str                        ACA


      EL-DABH, HALIM  (1921-    )

Symphony No. 1 (1951)                                 15'
   3*3*3*2; 4331; timp+1, str                         CFP

Symphony No. 2 (1952)                                 20'
   3*3*3*2; 4331; timp+1, str                         CFP

Symphony No. 3 (1956)                                 25'
   3*3*3*2; 4331; 2perc, str                          CFP

Clytemnestra - ballet suite (1958)                    20'
   2222; 2220; perc, hp, pf, str                      CFP

Agamemnon - ballet suite (1959)                       20'
   2222; 4331; perc, hp, pf, str                      CFP

Bacchanalia (1959)                                     5'
   1111; 1110; timp, hp, str                          CFP

Fantasia - Tahmeel (1959)                              7'
   timp, str                                          CFP

Iphigenia - ballet suite (1959)                       12'
   2222; 2220; perc, hp, pf, str                      CFP

Music of the Pharaohs (Three Parts) (1960)            24'

   1. Lament of the Pharaohs                           8'
      soli s, bar; ssaa cho; 1*020; 4200;             CFP
      2perc, 2hp, str

   2. Pyramid (Rock to the Sky)                        8'
      ttbb cho; 21*32; 4340; timp+1,                  CFP
      2hp, str

   3. Gloria Aton                                      8'
      satb cho; 2200; 4340; perc,                     CFP
      str (no vln, vla)

Saladin (Citadelle) (1960)                            22'
   3*23*2; 4340; perc, 2hp, str                       CFP

The Ghost (1964)                                      20'
   solo s; 0110; 1100; str                            CFP

Tahmeela (1965)                                          9'
  1*1*11; 1110; timp+1, str                             CFP

Lucifer - ballet suite (1976)                          30'
  1*1*11; 1111; timp+1, hp, pf, str                    CFP

Unity at the Cross Road (1979)                          8'
  3*222; 2220; timp+3, str                             CFP

Ramesses the Great (Symphony No. 9) (1987)             20'
  4=3*4=3*; 4431; 4perc, hp, str                       CFP


              ELISHA, HAIM  (1935-    )

Dance Suite (1970)                                     20'
  3*222; 4430; timp, hp, str                            MS

Ten Variations for Orchestra (1975)                    12'
  3*23*3*; 4330; perc, pf, str                         BRO

Concerto for Flute and String
  Orchestra (1979)                                     17'
  solo fl; str                                         IMI

Concerto for Timpani and Orchestra (1988)              15'
  solo timp; 2221; 0200; str                            MS


         ELLINGTON, EDWARD K. "DUKE"  (1899-1974)

Black, Brown and Beige (1943)                          38'
  3*3*3(b cl, a sax)3*; 4331; timp+2,                   GS
  dmst, hp, db, str

Harlem (1950)                                          18'
  2*22*2; 2a,2t,bar sax; 4331; timp+2,                  GS
  dmst, hp, str

New World A Comin' (1960)                              10'
  solo pf; 2*23*2; 4431; timp+1, hp, str                GS

Night Creature (1962)                                  17'
  222*2; 2a,2t,bar sax; 4431; timp+2,                   GS
  hp, str

ELWELL, HERBERT   (1898-1974)

Lincoln:  Requiem Aeternam (1946)                     20'
    solo bar; satb cho; 2222; 2200;                   AMP
    timp+1, str

Ode for Orchestra (1950)                              10'
    3*3*3*2; 4231; timp+1, cel, str                   BH


ENTSMINGER, DEEN   (1950-    )

The Happy Prince - cantata (1979)                     28'
    soli s, a, b; satb cho; 3*121; 4221;              MS
    timp+2, hp, str

Suite No. 1 for String Orchestra (1982)               12'
    str                                               MS


EPSTEIN, DAVID   (1930-    )

Movement for Orchestra (1952)                         10'
    2222; 4230; timp, str                             CF

Symphony No. 1 (1958)                                 30'
    223*2; 4330; timp, str                            CF

Four Songs (1960)                                     13'
    solo s; hn; str                                   CF

Sonority Variations (1967)                            15'
    3*3*3*2; 4331; timp+1, hp, pf/cel, str            MCA

Ventures (1970)                                       13'
    3*3*3*3*; 4331; timp+4, pf, str                   CF

Night Voices (1974)                                   13'
    narr; children's cho(opt); 2222; 2221;            CF
    timp+3, hp, str


EPSTEIN, PAUL   (1938-    )

Variations for String Orchestra (1987)                15'
    str (divisi)                                      FLE

ERB, DONALD   (1927-      )

Chamber Concerto (1958)                                      11'
   solo pf; str                                             MER

Bakersfield Pieces (1962)                                    10'
   3*222; 4331; timp+1, pf, str                           MER

Cummings Cycle (1963)                                        8'
   satb cho; 3*222; 4331; timp+2, pf,                     MER
   cel, str

Symphony of Overtures (1964)                                 16'
   3*23*3*; 4331; timp+3, hp, pf, str                     GAL

Concerto for Percussionist and
   Orchestra (1966)                                       10'
   solo perc; 3*23*3*; 4331; timp+2, hp,                  MER
   pf, str

Christmas Music (1967)                                       7'
   3*222; 2210; 2perc, hp, pf, cel,                       MER
   hpsd, str

The Seventh Trumpet (1969)                                   16'
   3*3*3*3*; 4331; timp+3, hp, pf/cel, str                MER

Klangfarbenfunk I (1970)                                     16'
   solo rock group; 223*3*; 2211; timp+1,                 MER
   amp hp, str, tape

Autumn Music (1973)                                          20'
   3*222; 4231; timp+1, hp, str, tape                     MER

Treasures of the Snow (1973)                                 10'
   3*23*2; 4331; timp+2, str                             MER

New England's Prospect (1974)                                30'
   narr; sssaaatttbbb cho; children's cho;               MER
   3*23*3*; a sax; 4331; timp+1, hp,
   pf/cel, 16hca, str

Music for a Festive Occasion (1975)                          7'
   3*23*3*; 4331; timp+3, pf/cel, str, tape              MER

Concerto for Trombone and Orchestra (1976)                  17'
   solo tbn; 3*23*3*; 4331; timp+3,                       MER
   pf/cel, str

Concerto for Violoncello and
    Orchestra (1976)                                          13'
    solo vc; 3*23*3*; 4331; timp+2,                           MER
    pf/cel, str

Concerto for Keyboards and Orchestra (1978)    16'
    solo pf/elec pf/cel; 3*23*3*; 4331;                      MER
    timp+1, hp, str

Concerto for Trumpet and Orchestra (1980)      15'
    solo tpt; 3*23*3*; 4331; timp+1, hp,                    MER
    pf/elec pf, str

Sonnaries for Orchestra (1981)                            15'
    3*23*3*; 4331; timp+3, hp, str                          MER

Prismatic Variations (1983)                               15'
    3*3*3*3*; 4331; timp+3, hp,                             MER
    pf/elec pf, str
    N.B. Approximately 100 children are needed
    in the audience.

Concerto for Clarinet and Orchestra (1984)     14'
    solo cl; 2*232*; 2220; timp+2, hp,                      MER
    pf, str

Concerto for Contrabassoon and
    Orchestra (1984)                                         13'
    solo cbsn; 3*23*2; 4331; timp+3, hp,                    MER
    pf/elec pf, pf, str

Concerto for Orchestra (1985)                             20'
    3*3*3*3*; 4331; timp+3, hp, pf/elec                    MER
    pf, cel, str

Dreamtime (1985)                                          10'
    3*23*3*; 4331; timp+3, hp, pf, str                     MER
    N.B. Also requires 4perc and 4tbn,
    positioned in the audience.

Concerto for Brass and Orchestra (1986)        20'
    3=3*3*3*; 4331; timp+3, hp,                             MER
    pf/elec pf, str

Solstice (1988)                                           12'
    2*2*2*2*; 2200; timp+1, synth, str                     MER

Ritual Observances (1991)                                 28'
    3*3*4*3*; 4331; timp+3, hp, pf, cel, str   MER

ERICKSON, ROBERT   (1917-    )

Fantasy for Cello and Orchestra (1953)          15'
  solo vc; 223*2; 4231; timp+1, str              SMI

Variations (1957)                               14'
  3*24=3*; 4331; timp+1, hp, pf, str             MER

Chamber Concerto (1959)                         20'
  112*1; 1110; 2perc, hp, pf, pf/hpsd,           TP
  str (1-1-1-1)

Garden (1977)                                   NA
  solo vln; 1111; 1110; perc,                    SMI
  cel/elec org, str

Auroras (1982)                                  20'
  3*3*3*2; 4331; 4perc, hp, pf, cel,             SMI
  str (3-3-2-3-4)

Corona (1986)                                   NA
  4=4*4*4*; 6441; 2timp+1,hp, pf/cel, str        SMI


ETLER, ALVIN   (1913-1973)

Passacaglia and Fugue (1947)                     9'
  3*3*3*3*; 4331; timp, str                      AMP

Symphony No. 1 (1951)                           25'
  3*23*3*; 4331; timp+2, str                     AMP

Dramatic Overture (1956)                         8'
  2222; 4331; timp, str                          AMP

Concerto in One Movement for Orchestra (1957) 12'
  4+4*4+4; 4331; timp+3, str                     AMP

Concerto for String Quartet and String
  Orchestra (1957)                              18'
  solo str qt; str                               AMP

Elegy (1959)                                     6'
  1122; 2000; str                                AMP

Concerto for Wind Quintet and
  Orchestra (1960)                              20'
  solo ww qnt; 0000; 4440; timp+1, 2hp, str      AMP

Triptych (1961)                                          16'
    2*2*2*2*; 2220; timp+3, str                          AMP

Concerto for Brass Quintet, Percussion and
    String Orchestra (1967)                              17'
    solo br qnt; 3-6perc, str                            PLY

Convivialities (1967)                                    11'
    3*2*3*3*; 4331; 4perc; str                           PLY


            EVETT, ROBERT  (1922-1975)

Concertino (1952)                                        12'
    23*3*3*; 4331; timp+1, str                           ACA

Concerto for Small Orchestra (1952)                      20'
    2222; 1110; timp, str                                ACA

Concerto No. 1 for Violoncello (1954)                    20'
    solo vc; 1111; 1000; str                             ACA

Concerto for Piano and Orchestra (1957)                  18'
    solo pf; 1111; 1100; timp, str                       ACA

Symphony No. 1 (1960)                                    22'
    2222; 4331; timp+1, str                              ACA

Concerto for Harpsichord and Orchestra (1961) 20'
    solo hpsd; tpt; timp+1, cel, str (no db)      CFP

Anniversary Concerto:  75 (1963)                         25'
    3*3*3*3*; 4331; timp+6, hp, cel, str                 ACA

Lauds:  In Honor of St. Ignatius (1964)                  30'
    ttbb cho; 2222; 4331; timp+1, hpsd, str       ACA

Symphony No. 3 (1965)                                    23'
    2222; 4331; timp+1, str                              ACA

Vespers (1967)                                           20'
    satb cho; bells, str                                 ACA

Concerto No. 2 for Violoncello (1971)                    20'
    solo vc; 2222; 4330; 3perc, str                      ACA

The Windhover (1971)                                     15'
    solo bsn; 2120; 4320; timp+1, str                    ACA

Monadnock (1975)                                         5'
    satb cho; 23*3*3*; 2120; 2perc, str                  ACA

FAITH, RICHARD   (1926-    )

Elegy (1976)                                    9'
   23*22; 4231; timp, str                      GS


FALARO, ANTHONY   (1938-    )

Cosmoi (1967)                                   12'
   for 56-part string orch                      CF

Suite for Strings (1971)                        11'
   str                                          CF


FARBERMAN, HAROLD   (1929-    )

Concerto for Bassoon and Strings (1956)         11'
   solo bsn; str                                BRO

Symphony for Percussion and Strings (1957)      18'
   7perc, str                                   BRO

Concerto for Timpani and Orchestra (1958)       14'
   solo timp; 3*23*2; 2321; 2perc, str          DSH

Impressions for Oboe (1960)                     14'
   solo ob; 2perc, str                          DSH

Suite from "The Great American
   Cowboy" (1968)                               14'
   2222; 4331; timp+3, bjo, str                 DSH

If Music Be... (1969)                           21'
   solo rock group (b gtr, kybd, dmst);         DSH
   3*23*2; a,t sax; 4331; timp+2, hp, cel,
   gtr, str, film, audience participation
   N.B.  Requires four conductors for performance.

Initiation Ballet (1971)                        6'
   solo jazz qt (a sax, tpt, db, dmst);         DSH
   3*24=0; 4332; timp+6, pf, elec gtr,
   str (no db)

Reflected Realities - for Violin and
   Orchestra (1974)                                        29'
   solo vln; 223*3*; a sax; 4231; timp+4,                 DSH
   hp, pf, b gtr, str

Concerto for Violin and Orchestra (1976)                    20'
   solo vln; 3*3*3*3*; 4331; timp+4, hp,                  DSH
   pf, gtr, str

War Cry on a Prayer Feather (1976)                          25'
   soli s, bar; 3*3*3*3*; 4331; timp+5, hp,              DSH
   prep pf, acc, mand, str

The (You Name It!) March (1981)                              5'
   2*222; 4431; timp+3, str                              DSH

Shapings (1984)                                             10'
   solo eh; 2perc, str                                   DSH

Double Concerto for Single Trumpet (NA)                     15'
   solo tpt; narr; 3*3*3*3*; 4331;                       BRO
   timp+3, str

Paramount Concerto (NA)                                     14'
   solo pf; 2222; 4331; timp+4, hp, str                  DSH

There's Us, There's Them...Together? (NA)                   15'
   solo jazz combo (elec org, db, dmst);                 DSH
   223*2; 4331; timp+1, str


## FELCIANO, RICHARD  (1930-    )

The Captives (1965)                                         10'
   satb cho; 3*23*2; a sax; 4331; timp+1,               ECS
   hp, pf, str

Mutations (1966)                                            15'
   3*3*3*3*; 4331; timp+3, hp, pf, str                   ECS

Galactic Rounds (1972)                                     10'
   3*3*3*3*; 4441; timp+1, hp, pf, str                   ECS

Orchestra (1980)                                           20'
   3*3*3*3*; 4331; timp+4, hp, pf, cel, str             ECS

Concerto for Organ and Orchestra (1986)                    20'
   solo org; 3*3*3*3*; 4331; timp+4, hp,                 MS
   pf, cel, str

FELDMAN, MORTON  (1926-1987)

N.B.  An asterisk before a title denotes that
      the score is in graphic notation.

*Intersection I (1951)                                    var
   winds; brass; str                                      CFP

*Marginal Intersection (1951)                             var
   winds; brass; perc, pf, str,                           CFP
   2 oscillators

Structures (1960-1962)                                    11'
   3+3*3*2; 4331; perc, hp, cel, str                      CFP

First Principles (1966-1967)                              18'
   1000; 1012; 2perc, hp, pf(4-hands),                    CFP
   str (2-0-3-2)

In Search of an Orchestration (1967)                      8'
   3*3*3*3*; 23(b tpt)31; perc, hp, pf, cel,              UE
   str (no vln or vla)

On Time and the Instrumental Factor (1969)                8'
   4=3*3*3*; 23(b tpt)31; hp, cel,                        UE
   bells, str

Chorus and Orchestra I (1971)                             15'
   solo s; satb cho; 3=3*3*2; 2221; 4perc,                UE
   hp, pf/cel, str

The Viola in my Life IV (1971)                            20'
   solo vla; 23*3*2; 2221; 2perc, hp, pf,                 UE
   cel, str

Cello and Orchestra (1972)                                20'
   solo vc; 3=3*4*3*; 24(b tpt)31; perc,                  UE
   hp, str

Chorus and Orchestra II (1972)                            22'
   satb cho; 2=2*3*2*; 2220; hp, pf/cel, str  UE

Voice and Instruments (1972)                              15'
   solo s; 2*12*1; 1110; timp, hp,                        UE
   pf/cel, str

String Quartet and Orchestra (1973)                       21'
   solo str qt; 4=3*4(s sax, a sax, b cl)3*;  UE
   2221; 2perc, hp, pf, cel, str

Piano and Orchestra (1975)                              21'
    solo pf; 4(picc, 2a fl)4*4*4*; 2331;        UE
    2perc, hp, pf/cel, str

Elemental Procedures (1976)                             20'
    solo s; satb cho; 4*4*4*4*; 2331; perc,     UE
    hp, pf/cel, cel, str

Oboe and Orchestra (1976)                               18'
    solo ob; 4*4*4*4*; 3331; 3perc, hp,         UE
    pf/cel, str

Orchestra (1976)                                        18'
    4*4*4*4*; 2331; 4perc, hp, pf,              UE
    pf/cel, str

Flute and Orchestra (1977-1978)                         35'
    solo fl; 3*4*4*4*; 3341; 6perc, hp,         UE
    pf, cel, str

Violin and Orchestra (1979)                             60'
    solo vln; 4*4*4=4*; 3341; 4perc, 2hp,       UE
    2pf, str

The Turfan Fragments (1980)                             17'
    2222; 2220; str (0-6-4-4)                   UE

Coptic Light (1986)                                     30'
    4*4*4*4*; 4441; timp+4, 2hp, 2pf,           UE
    str (18-16-12-12-10)


## FENNELLY, BRIAN  (1937-    )

In Wilderness is the Preservation of
    the World (1975)                            16'
    2222; 4331; timp+2, hp, str                 ACA

Concert Piece for Trumpet and
    Orchestra (1976)                            8'
    solo tpt; 1111; 2000; perc, cel, str        ACA

Quintuplo (1977-1978)                                   14'
    solo br qnt; 23*3*2; 4231; timp+2, str      MG

Empirical Rag (1980)                                    5'
    2222; 2221; timp+2, str                     ACA

Scintilla prisca (1980)                                 15'
    solo vc; 2222; 2000; 2perc, hp, str         ACA

Tropes and Echoes (1981)                                15'
   solo cl; 11*1*1; 1110; 2perc, pf, str        ACA

Concerto for Alto Saxophone (1984)                      30'
   solo a sax; str                              MS

Fantasy Variations (1985)                               22'
   3*3*3*3*; 4331; 3perc, hp, str               ACA

Thoreau Fantasy No. 2 (1985)                            20'
   2222; 4331; timp+4, pf, str                  ACA

Lunar Halos (1990)                                      13'
   solo db; 2=2*2*2; 2200; 2perc, str           ACA


     FENNER, BURT   (1929-     )

Chamber Symphony (1958)                                 20'
   1111; 2000; timp, str                        MS

Symphony No. 2 (1961)                                   25'
   2222; 4331; timp+1, str                      FLE

Variations for String Quartet and
   Orchestra (1962)                             15'
   solo str qt; 2222; 4200; timp, str           FLE

An Exsufflation (1970)                                  18'
   2222; 4331; timp+1, str                      FLE

Untitled: Orchestra with Synthesizer (1973)             var
   2222; 4331; timp+2, synth, str               MS

Symphony No. 3 (1975)                                   24'
   2222; 4331; timp+2, pf, str                  FLE

Suite for Strings (1976)                                25'
   str                                          FLE


     FERNEYHOUGH, BRIAN   (1943-     )

Epicycle (1968)                                         15'
   20 solo strings                              CFP

La Terre est un Homme (1977-1979)                       15'
   4(2picc)4(2eh)4=4*; 4432; timp+4, 2hp,       CFP
   pf, cel, hpsd, cymbalom,
   amp acoustical gtr, str

Carceri d'Invenzione II (1984)                    14'
    solo fl; 12*2=1; 2000; str                    CFP


            FERRITO, JOHN  (1934-    )

Omaggio a Berio e Fellini, op. 11 (1970)          15'
    3*3*3*3*; 4331; timp+3, hp, pf, str           ACA

Variations, op. 16 (1977)                         13'
    4(2picc)3*23*; 4331; timp+4, hp, str          ACA

Concerto for Violoncello and Orchestra,
    op. 17 (1979)                                 23'
    solo vc; 3*222; 4331; timp+2, str             ACA

Celebrations, op. 19 (1983)                        9'
    3*222; 4331; timp+3, hp, str                  ACA


            FETLER, PAUL  (1920-    )

A Comedy Overture (1953)                           7'
    2222; 2230; timp+1, str                       CF

Gothic Variations (1953)                          12'
    2222; 4331; timp+1, str                       MS

Symphony No. 3 (1954)                             20'
    2*222; 4331; timp+4, str                      AMP

Contrasts (1958)                                  22'
    3*3*3*3*; 4331; timp+2, pf, str               TP

Of Earth's Image - cantata (1958)                 19'
    solo s; satb cho; 3*222; 4331;                MS
    timp+5, str

Soundings (Symphony in Five
    Movements) (1962)                             21'
    3*3*3*3*; 4331; timp+5, pf, cel, str          MS

Cantus Tristis (1964)                             11'
    3*3*3*3*; 4331; timp+2, str                   MS

Symphony No. 4 (1968)                             22'
    3*3*3*3*; 4331; timp+2, str                   MS

This Was the Way - cantata (1969)                 25'
    solo s; satb cho; 2222; 4331; str             MS

Concerto for Violin and Orchestra (1971)          24'
   solo vln; 1*202; 2000; timp+2, cel str          GS

Three Poems by Walt Whitman (1975)                18'
   narr; 3*3*3*3*; 4331; timp+4,                   GS
   pf/toy pf/cel, str

Celebration (1976)                                24'
   3*3*3*3*; 4331; timp+1, cel, str               EAM

Three Impressions (1977)                          25'
   solo gtr; 2020; 2000; perc, cel, str           EAM

Violin Concerto No. 2 (1981)                      35'
   solo vln; 3*3*3*3*; 4331; timp+2, str          MS

Piano Concerto No. 1 (1984)                       25'
   solo pf; 2222; 2100; timp, str                 MS

Capriccio (1985)                                   9'
   2222; 2000; str                                MS

"Three Excursions" (Concerto for Piano and
   Orchestra) (1988)                              18'
   soli timp+3, pf; 3*3*3*3*; 4331; str            MS


FINE, IRVING  (1914-1962)

Toccata concertante (1947)                        11'
   3*3*3*3*; 4231; timp+2, pf, str                GS

Notturno (1950-1951)                              15'
   hp, str (6-4-3-3-1)                             BH

Serious Song:  A Lament (1955)                    10'
   str                                             BH

Blue Towers (1959)                                 3'
   3*222; 2a,t sax; 4331; timp+4, str              BH

Diversions for Orchestra (1959-1960)               9'
   22*22; 2a,t,bar sax; 4331; timp+4,              BH
   pf, str

Symphony (1962)                                   24'
   3*3*3*3*; 4331; timp+8, hp, pf, cel, str        GS

Partita for Orchestra
  (arr Spiegelmann) (1970)                      15'
  3*222; 4331; timp+2, str                      BH


               FINE, VIVIAN   (1913-     )

Meeting for Equal Rights - 1966 (1976)          NA
  soli mez, bar; narr; satb cho; 2222;          MS
  2220; timp+1, str

Romantic Ode (1976)                             13'
  soli vln, vla, vc; str                        MG

Drama for Orchestra (1982)                      NA
  4*4*4*3*; 6431; 3perc, hp, cel, str           MS


               FINK, MYRON   (1932-     )

Concerto No. 1 for Piano and
  Orchestra (1972)                              30'
  solo pf; 2222; 4231; timp+1, str              MS

Ann Rutledge - Epitaph from "Spoon River
  Anthology" (1976)                             17'
  solo s; pf, str                               MS

Scherzo for Orchestra (1979)                    10'
  2*222; 4231; timp, str                        MS

Suite from "Chinchilla" (1985)                  15'
  2222; s,t sax; 4231; timp+2, str              MS

Concerto for Violin and Orchestra (1986)        25'
  solo vln; 222*2; 4231; timp, str              MS

Symphony No. 1 (1987)                           54'
  3*3*3*3*; 4331; timp, str                     MS

Symphony No. 2 (1989)                           35'
  2222; 4231; timp, str                         MS

Concerto No. 2 for Piano and
  Orchestra (1990)                              25'
  solo pf; 2*222; 2220; timp, str               MS

FINKO, DAVID  (1936-    )

Concerto for Viola, Doublebass and
   Orchestra (1975)                                          22'
   soli vla, db; 3021; 2110; 2perc, str                    TP

Violin Concerto (NA)                                           20'
   solo vln; 2020; 2110; 2perc, str                        TP


FINNEY, ROSS LEE  (1906-    )

Violin Concerto No. 1 (1933; rev 1952)                         35'
   solo vln; 2222; 4231; timp+1, hp, str                   CFP

Piano Concerto No. 1 (1948)                                    15'
   solo pf; 2*222; 4221; timp+1, str                       CFP

Variations for Orchestra (1957)                                12'
   3*3*4*3*; 4331; timp+1, hp, cel, str                    CFP

Symphony No. 2 (1958)                                          21'
   3*3*4*3*; 4331; timp+1, 2hp, pf, str                    CFP

Symphony No. 3 (1960)                                          22'
   3*3*3*3*; 4331; timp+1, 2hp, pf, cel, str               CFP

Earthrise Trilogy (1962)                                       24'
                                                       CFP

   1. Still are New Worlds
      narr; satb cho; 3*3*3*3*; 4231;
      timp+2, hp, cel, tape

   2. The Martyr's Elegy
      solo s (or t); satb cho; 3*3*3*3*;
      4331; timp+2, hp, str

   3. Earthrise
      soli a, t; satb cho; taped voice;
      3*3*3*3*; 4331; timp+2, pf, cel, str

Three Pieces (1962)                                            10'
   1111; 1000; timp+2, cel, str, tape                      CFP

Concerto for Percussion and Orchestra (1965)   15'
   soli 4perc; 3*3*3*3*; 4331; timp+2,                     CFP
   hp, cel, str

Nun's Priest's Tale (1965)                                35'
   soli s, bar, b; narr; folk singer (with      CFP
   elec gtr); cho: 4 fem, 4 male; 1*111;
   2221; timp+2, str (3-3-2-2-2)

Symphonie concertante (1967)                              26'
   3*3*3*3*; 4231; timp+2, hp, cel, str          CFP

Piano Concerto No. 2 (1968)                               20'
   solo pf; 3*3*3*3*; 4231; timp+2, hp,          CFP
   cel, str

Landscapes Remembered (1971)                              14'
   1=010; 0110; perc, hp, pf, str                CFP

Spaces (1971)                                             20'
   3*3*3*3*; 4331; timp+2, hp, cel, str          CFP

Symphony No. 4 (1972)                                     21'
   3*3*3*3*; 4331; timp+3, hp, pf, cel, str      CFP

Violin Concerto No. 2 (1973)                              15'
   solo vln; 3*3*3*3*; 4331; timp+2, hp,         CFP
   pf, str

Narrative (1976)                                          14'
   solo vc; 1*130; 2210; str (2-1-0-1)           CFP

Concerto for Strings (1977)                               17'
   str (3-3-2-5-2)                               CFP
   N.B.  Strings may be doubled.

Bleheris (1987)                                           15'
   soli a, t; 2*2*2*2*; 4231; timp+2, hp, str CFP

Computer Marriage (1991)                                  NA
   soli 2s, mez, a, t, bar, b; 3narr;            CFP
   2*12*1; 02*21; perc, hp, pf/cel, str


      FISCHER, IRWIN  (1903-1977)

Marco Polo - fantasy overture (1932)                      15'
   3*222; 4331; timp+1, cel, str                 ACA

A Sea Bird (1933)                                         3'
   3*222; 4231; timp+1, str                      ACA

Rhapsody on French Folk Tunes (1934)                      8'
   2222; 4331; timp+2, hp, cel, str              ACA

Piano Concerto in E minor (1935)                           17'
    solo pf; 2222; 4230; timp+1, hp, str             ACA

Sketches from Childhood (1937)                              8'
    2222; 2230; perc, hp, str                        ACA

Ariadne Abandoned (1938)                                    5'
    2222; 4231; timp, hp, str                        ACA

Chorale Fantasy (1938)                                     15'
    solo org; 3*222; 4321; timp, str                 ACA

Lament (1939)                                               5'
    solo vc; 3*222; 4331; timp, str                  ACA

Variations on an Original Theme (1941)                     11'
    2222; 4331; timp, str                            ACA

Symphony No. 1 (1942)                                      20'
    2222; 4231; timp, str                            ACA

The Pearly Bouquet (1943)                                  12'
    solo cel; str                                    ACA

Piece Heroique (1945)                                       8'
    23*22; 4331; timp, org(opt); str                 ACA

Idyll (1949)                                               11'
    solo vln; 2222; 4230; timp+1, str                ACA

Variations on an Original Theme (1950)                     11'
    2222; 4331; timp, str                            ACA

Legend (1956)                                               6'
    3*222; 4331; timp+1, str                         ACA

Mountain Tune Trilogy (1957)                               11'
    2222; 4331; timp+1, hp, str                      ACA

Fantasie with Fugue, Plain and
    Accompanied (1958)                               10'
    solo vln; 1110; 0000; hp, str                    ACA

Poem (1959)                                                 6'
    solo vln; 3*3*22; 4230; timp, str                ACA

Short Symphony (1960)                                      14'
    3*222; 4331; timp+1, str                         ACA

Passacaglia and Fugue (1961)                          13'
  3*3*3*3*; 4331; str                                  ACA

Overture on an Exuberant Tone Row (1964)           8'
  3*222; 4331; timp+1, str                            ACA

Concerto giocoso (1971)                              16'
  solo cl; 3*212; 2220; timp+2, str                   ACA

Orchestral Adventures of a Little Tune (1974) 15'
  narr; 1111; 1110; perc, str                         ACA

Symphonic Adventures of a Little Tune (1975) 35'
  narr; 3*3*3*2; 4231; 3perc, str                     ACA

Statement (1976)                                     15'
  solo s; satb cho; 0000; 4331; timp+1, str ACA


      FITELBERG, JERZY   (1903-1951)

Symphony for Strings (1946)                          29'
  str                                                   PS

Concertino for Trombone, Piano and
  Strings (1947)                                      12'
  soli tbn, pf; str                                   EBM


      FLAGELLO, NICOLAS   (1928-        )

Piano Concerto No. 1, op. 7 (1950)                  26'
  solo pf; 2222; 4230; timp+1, str                     TP

Suite for Amber (1951)                              15'
  2221; 2210; timp+2, pf, str                         VPF

Symphonic Aria, op. 9 (1951)                         5'
  4*3*3*3*; 4321; timp+1, hp, str                      TP

Overture giocosa, op. 10 (1952)                      5'
  3*3*3*3*; 4332; timp+1, str                          TP

Concerto Antoniano for Flute and Orchestra,
  op. 11 (1953)                                       26'
  solo fl; 0222; 2110; timp+2, hp, str                VPF

The Land, op. 15 (1954)                              24'
  solo bar; 1111; 1000; timp+1, pf,                   VPF
  cel, str

Theme, Variations and Fugue, op. 17 (1955)     27'
   3*3*3*3*; 4331; timp+3, hp, pf, cel,      TP
   org(opt); str

L'Infinito (1956)                               2'
   solo bar; 1111; 1000; pf, cel, str         VPF

Piano Concerto No. 2, op. 18 (1956)            24'
   solo pf; 2222; 4230; timp+1, str           TP

Processional (1957)                             5'
   2222; 4322; timp+1, str                    TP

Adoration (from "The Judgment of
   St. Francis") (1959)                        4'
   hp, str                                    TP

Concerto for String Orchestra, op. 27 (1959)   24'
   str                                        VPF

Tristis est anima mea, op. 29 (1959)            9'
   satb cho; 3*3*3*3*; 4331; timp+3,          TP
   pf/cel, str

Capriccio for Violoncello and Orchestra,
   op. 35 (1962)                              16'
   solo vc; 2*2*20; 2210; timp+1, hp,         VPF
   cel, str

Contemplazioni, op. 42 (1964)                  23'
   solo s (or t); 2*2*22; 2210; timp+4,       VPF
   hp, str

Island in the Moon (1964)                      16'
   solo s (or t); 2*222; 2000; timp+1, hp,    VPF
   pf/cel, str

Goldoni Overture (1967)                         6'
   3*222; 4221; timp+1, hp, pf, cel, str      TP

Te Deum for All Mankind, op. 55 (1967)         12'
   satb cho; 3*23*2; 4331; timp+2, hp,        CF
   org, str

Symphony No. 1, op. 57 (1968)                  33'
   3*3*3*3*; 4331; timp+1, hp, pf, cel, str   TP

Serenata, op. 58 (1968)                        16'
   1111; 2000; hp, str                        VPF

Passion of Martin Luther King, op. 59 (1968)   40'
    solo bar; satb cho; 3*3*22; 4331; timp+1,   TP
    hp, cel, str

Symphony No. 2, op. 63 (1970)                   17'
    3*3*3*3*; 4331; timp+1, hp, pf, cel, str    VPF

    N.B. This is a partial listing.  Inquiries
         regarding these and other works by Mr.
         Flagello may be directed to Mr. Walter
         Simmons at VPF Music.


            FLAHERTY, TOM  (1950-    )

Flute Concerto (1987)                           16'
    solo fl; 2222; 2000; hp, pf, str            MG


            FLANAGAN, WILLIAM  (1923-1969)

Divertimento (1948)                             16'
    2222; 2200; timp, str                       BEL

A Concert Ode (1951)                            16'
    3*3*23*; 4331; timp, hp, pf, str            PS

The Weeping Pleiades (1953)                     19'
    solo bar; solo vln; 1010; 0000; pf, str     PS

Another August (1966)                           10'
    solo s; 1222; 2200; timp, pf, hpsd, str     CFP


            FLETCHER, GRANT  (1913-    )

Symphony No. 1 (1950)                           25'
    2222; 2200; timp, str                       FLE

Two Orchestral Pieces (1956)                    13'
    2222; 2210; timp, str                       FLE


            FLOYD, CARLISLE  (1926-    )

Susannah - Selections (1954)                    BH

    1. Orchestra Suite                          19'
        2222; 4231; timp+1, hp, str

2. Blitch's Prayer of Repentance                    5'
   solo bar; 2222; 4231; timp+1, str

3. I'm a lonely man, Susannah                       3'
   solo bar; 2222; 4231; timp+1, str

4. It's about the way people is made                4'
   solo t; 2222; 4231; timp+1, str

5. Jay-Bird Song                                    3'
   soli s, t; 2222; 4231; timp+1, str

6. The Trees on the Mountains                       7'
   solo s; 2222; 4231; timp+1, str

Pilgrimmage (1956)                                  20'
   solo bar; 2222; 0220; timp+1, hp,            BH
   cel, str

Wuthering Heights - suite (1957-1958)               22'
   2222; 4231; timp+1, hp, str                  BH

The Mystery (1960)                                  17'
   solo s; 2222; 4220; timp+2, hp, cel, str     BH

Introduction, Aria and Dance (1967)                 16'
   23*3*2; 4331; timp+1, hp, str                TP

In Celebration (1971)                               10'
   23*22; 4221; timp+2, hp, str                 TP

Citizen of Paradise (1984)                          34'
   solo mez; 22*22; 2110; timp+2,               BH
   pf/cel, str

Flourishes (1987)                                   4'
   3*23*2; 4331; timp+1, str                    BH

Of Mice and Men:  Two Interludes (NA)               NA
   2222; 4221; timp+1, hp, cel, str             BEL


            FOLEY, DANIEL   (1952-      )

Glasperlenspiel (NA)                                12'
   3*222; 4231; timp+2, str                     PS

FOSS, LUKAS  (1922-      )

The Prairie - symphonic excerpts (1943)          15'
    3*222; 4331; timp+2, hp, pf, str              GS

The Prairie - cantata (1944)                     50'
    soli s, a, t, b; satb cho; 1*1*1*1*;          GS
    1310; timp+1, pf, str

Symphony No. 1 (1944)                            32'
    3*3*3*3*; 4330; timp+1, hp, pf, str           GS

Ode (1945; rev 1958)                             10'
    3*3*3*3*; 4331; timp+1, hp, pf, str           CF

Song of Anguish (1945)                           19'
    solo bar; 3*23*3*; 4331; timp+3, hp,          CF
    pf/cel, str

Pantomime (after "Gift of the Magi") (1946)      16'
    3*222; 4331; timp+2, hp, pf, cel, str         HAR

Song of Songs (1946)                             23'
    solo s; 3*3*3*3*; 2320; timp+4, hp, str       CF

Concerto for Oboe and Orchestra (1948)           15'
    solo ob; 1011; 1110; str                      PS

Recordare (1948)                                 13'
    3*3*4=3*; 4331; timp+4, hp, pf, cel, str      PS

Elegy for Clarinet and Orchestra (1949)          8'
    solo cl; 2212; 2210; timp+2, str              GS

Piano Concerto No. 2 (1949; rev 1953)            34'
    solo pf; 3*23*3*; t sax; 4311; timp+2, str    CF

A Parable of Death (1952)                        17'
    solo t; narr; satb cho; 2*222; 2210;          CF
    timp+2, pf, org, str

Psalms (1955-1956)                               13'
    satb cho; 1*021*; 2110; timp+4, hp, 2pf,      CF
    org, str

Symphony of Chorales (1956-1958)                 31'
    3*23*3*; 4331; timp+3, hp, pf,                CF
    mand(opt), str

Time Cycle (1959-1960)                                                22'
   solo s; 2020; 2210; timp+3, hp, str                                CF

Baroque Variations (1967)                                            25'
   3*3*3(E-flat sopranino sax)1; 3311;                                CF
   timp+3, elec pf, cel, hpsd, elec org,
   elec gtr, str (6-12 players)

Cello Concerto (1967)                                                28'
   solo vc; 0000; 2120; 3perc, pf, org,                               CF
   piano strings, str

Geod (1969)                                                          var
   2*1*3*3*; 4230; hp, pf, org, str                                   CF
   N.B.  Requires one principal conductor and
   four assistant conductors.  Eleven or twelve
   folk instruments are also required
   (determined by country in which performance
   is given).

Concerto for Piano and Orchestra (1973)                              24'
   solo pf; 3*222; 2230; timp+1, str                                  GS

Fanfare (1973)                                                       10'
   2222; 0330; perc, pf org, str                                      SAL
   N.B.  Three folk instruments are also
   required - guirnata, kaval and zurnā.

Concerto for Solo Percussion and
   Orchestra (1974)                                                   30'
   solo perc; 1*111; 1221; 3perc, pf, org,                            SAL
   elec gtr, str
   OR:  1*111; 1221; str (5-2-2-1)

Symphony of Rossi
   ("Suite Salomon Rossi") (1975)                                     9'
   1(picc, s rec)2*02; 0220; timp, hp, str                            SAL

Folksong for Orchestra (1975-1976)                                   15'
   3(2picc)3*3*3*; 5331; timp, dmst, xyl,                             GS
 ▪ hp, pf, solo db, str (div a 3)
   N.B. The winds and brass are divided into
   three groups of four players each.

American Cantata (1976)                                              32'
   soli s, t; male and fem narr with                                 BH
   megaphones; boys' voice (live or taped);
   ssaattbb cho; 1*1*1*1*; 0220; 2perc,
   pf/cel, elec org, elec gtr/mand,
   elec gtr/b gtr, 2bj, acc, hca, str

Quintets for Orchestra (1979)                          17'
    1. 203*0 (winds)                                   PEM
    2. 03*02 (winds)
    3. 2120 and 1210 (both are brass)
    4. org, str
    5. timp/perc, elec org

Night Music for John Lennon (1979-1980)                15'
    solo br qnt; 1111; 1110; perc, pf,                 PEM
    elec gtr, str

Exeunt (1982)                                          17'
    2*222; 4231; timp+3, hp, pf,                       PEM
    elec gtr, str

Orpheus and Euridice (1983)                            24'
    soli 2vln; 0200; 0000; 2chimes, 2hp,               SAL
    pf strings, str

Measure for Measure (1984)                             10'
    solo t; 1*2*02; 0220; timp, hp, str                GS

Renaissance Concerto (1985-1986)                       20'
    solo fl; 1*111; 1210; timp+2, hp,                  PEM
    hpsd(opt), str (vln I: 2-14; vln II: 2-12;
    vla: 2-10; vc: 2-8; db: 1-6)

Three American Pieces (1986)                           14'
    solo fl (or vln); 1011; 1110; 2perc,               CF
    pf, str

Griffelkin Suite (1986)                                25'
    2*22*2; 2221; timp+1, str                         CF

With Music Strong (1987)                               28'
    satb cho; 3*3*3*3*; 4331; timp+3, hp,              CF
    pf, str

Concerto No. 2 for Clarinet (1988)                     20'
    solo cl; 1110; 1110; 2perc, pf, str                CF

Elegy for Anne Frank (1989)                            5'
    opt winds:  2cl or 2bsn; 2tpt or 1-2 hn;           CF
    2tbn or tbn or tba; low drum, pf obbl, str
    N.B.  The winds may be implemented as noted
    above, or in combination.

Guitar Concerto (American Landscapes) (1989)           26'
    solo gtr; large or small orch (instr var)          CF

FOUNTAIN, PRIMOUS, III (1949-    )

| | |
|---|---|
| Manifestation (1969)<br>3*222; 4531; timp+1, pf, str | 15'<br>MG |
| Ritual Dance of the Amaks (1973)<br>3*3*4=2; 4330; timp+1, pf, str | 25'<br>MG |
| Exiled (1974)<br>4=3*3*2; 4331; timp, hp, pf, str | 13'<br>MG |

FOX, FREDERICK (1931-    )

| | |
|---|---|
| Bec-10 (1968)<br>1111; 0110; perc, str | 15'<br>SEE |
| Concerto for Violin and Orchestra (1971)<br>solo vln; 3*23*2; 4331; 3perc, str | 22'<br>SEE |
| Matrix (1972)<br>solo vc; str | 15'<br>SEE |
| Ternion - Concerto for Oboe and<br>Orchestra (1973)<br>solo ob; 3*001; 2330; timp+3, str | 15'<br>SEE |
| Variables No. 5 (1974)<br>3*3*3*2; 4331; timp+4, str | 19'<br>SEE |
| Beyond Winterlock (1977)<br>3*23*2; 4331; 4perc, pf, str | 19'<br>SEE |
| Night Ceremonies (1979)<br>3*3*3*3*; 4331; timp+3, hp, pf, str | 25'<br>MMB |
| Tracings (1981)<br>3*3*3*3*; 4331; timp+3, hp, pf, str | 22'<br>MMB |
| Januaries (1984)<br>3*3*3*3*; 4331; timp+3, hp, cel, str | 21'<br>MMB |
| Now and Then (1985)<br>1111; 1000; perc, pf, str (4-2-1-1) | 16'<br>MMB |
| In the Elsewhere (1986)<br>3*3*3*3*; 4331; timp+3, hp, pf, str | 26'<br>MMB |
| Nightscenes for Strings and Percussion (1988)<br>5perc, hp, pf, cel, str | 18'<br>MMB |

FRACKENPOHL, ARTHUR   (1924-      )

Concertino for Clarinet and Orchestra (1948)   7'
    solo cl; 2202; 2210; timp+1, hp, str          FLE

Divertimento in F for Chamber
    Orchestra (1952)                             13'
    1010; 1110; str                              FLE

Arioso for Flute and Strings (1953)             4'
    solo fl; str                                 FLE

Allegro Scherzando (1957)                        6'
    2222; 4331; timp+1, str                      EBM

A Jubilant Overture (1957)                       8'
    2222; 4331; timp+4, str                      CF

Overture in D (1957)                             8'
    2222; 4331; timp+1, str                      TP

Symphony No. 2 (1960)                           21'
    str                                          CF

Largo and Allegro (1962)                         8'
    solo hn; str                                 GS

Concertino for Trumpet and Strings (1970)        9'
    solo tpt; str                                GS

Little Suite (NA)                                4'
    1121; a,t sax; 2221; timp+2, str             ELK

The Natural Superiority of Men (NA)             13'
    ssa cho; 2121; 0000; pf, str                 CF

Rondo Marziale (NA)                              5'
    3*23*3*; 4331; timp+1, str                   SHA


FRANCO, JOHAN   (1908-      )

Sinfonia (1932)                                  8'
    1111; a sax; 1110; timp+1, str               ACA

Symphony No. 1 (1933)                           20'
    3*3*22; a sax; 2221; timp+2, pf, str         ACA

Peripetie - symphonic poem (1935)               12'
    4*4*4*4*; 2321; timp+1, pf, cel, str         ACA

Concerto Lirico No. 1 (1937) 15'
   solo vln; 1121; 0110; timp+1, str   ACA

Serenade Concertante (1938) 12'
   solo pf; 1111; 1110; timp+1, str   ACA

Symphony No. 2 "George Washington" (1939) 20'
   2222; 4331; timp+1, pf, str   ACA

Symphony No. 3 "Concertante" (1940) 15'
   2222; 3330; timp+2, str   ACA

Baconiana (1942) 4'
   3*23*2; 2320; timp+1, str   ACA

Prophecy (1943) 4'
   1111; 1100; str   ACA

Suite (1945) 15'
   str   ACA

Clodagh (1946) 6'
   1222; 2220; timp+1, str   ACA

Fantasy for Violoncello and Orchestra (1951) 10'
   solo vc; 223*2; 3330; perc, str   ACA

Nocturne (1953) 8'
   223*2; 2211; timp+1, hp, cel, str   ACA

The Stars Look Down
   (Christmas Oratorio) (1957) 60'
   solo 5vv; satbb cho; boys cho; 2222;   ACA
   3320; timp, hp, str

Symphony No. 5 (1958) 25'
   2222; 2221; timp+1, hp, cel, str   ACA

Concerto Lirico No. 2 (1962) 20'
   solo vc; 2222; 2311; timp+1, hp, str   ACA

Concerto Lirico No. 3 (1967) 20'
   solo pf; 1211; 1111; 2perc, str   ACA

Supplication, Revelation and Triumph (1967) 15'
   2222; 4321; timp+2, hp, str   ACA

Concerto Lirico No. 4 (1970) 20'
   solo perc; 1111; 1110; str   ACA

Concerto Lirico No. 5 (1971)                                20'
    solo gtr; 1111; 2110; perc, hp, str                     ACA

Concerto Lirico No. 6 (1974)                                18'
    solo fl; 01*11; 2110; timp+1, hp, str                   ACA


### FRANK, ANDREW   (1946-      )

Symphony for Full String Orchestra (1978)                  12'
    str                                                     MOB

Variations for Chamber Orchestra (1980)                    12'
    1212; 2000; perc, pf, str                              MOB

Sinfonia Concertante (1986)                                20'
    soli vln, vla; 2222; 2210; 2perc, hp, str   MG

Paraphonia (1988)                                          17'
    1111; 1110; perc, pf, str (1-1-1-1)                    ACA

Brightness Falls from the Air (1990)                       20'
    3*3*3*3*; 4331; timp+3, hp, pf, str                    MS


### FRAZELLE, KENNETH   (1955-      )

Playing the "Miraculous Game" (1987)                       14'
    3*2*22; 2220; timp+1, str                              PS

Blue Ridge Airs II (1991)                                  21'
    solo fl; 3*3*3*2; 4230; timp+2, str         MS
    N.B.  Two Appalachian lap dulcimers and
    two large gourd rattles are required in
    the percussion section.

Elegy for Strings (1991)                                   11'
    str                                                     MS


### FREDRICKSON, THOMAS   (1935-      )

Sinfonia Concertante (1958)                                14'
    223*2; 4331; timp+1, str                               MS

"Illinois" Variations (1967)                                9'
    33*3*2; 4331; timp+1, pf, str                          MS

Sinfonia II (1973)                                         16'
    33*3*2; 4331; timp+1, hp, pf, cel, str                 MS

Reflections (1980)                                      10'
   str                                    MS


FREED, ARNOLD  (1926-     )

The Zodiac:  A Masque (1960)                            38'
  narr; satb cho; 2222; 4331; timp+1,         AMC
  pf, str

Alleluia (1969)                                         9'
  2222; 4231; timp+1, str                      BH


FREUND, DONALD  (1947-     )

Adagio (1967)                                           4'
  2*2*22; 4000; timp, str                      MS

Piano Concerto (1970)                                   23'
  solo pf; 3*3*3*2; 4331; timp+2, hp, str      SEE

Canzona for Orchestra (1971)                            10'
  2222; 2210; hp, pf, str                      SEE

Cello Concerto (1979)                                   19'
  solo vc; 3*23*2; s sax; 4331; timp+2, str    MS

Passion with Tropes (1983)                              170'
  satb cho; chant choir; pop singers;         MS
  various chamber groups; jazz ensemble;
  3=13*1; a sax; 3221; 2perc, pf, str,
  actors

Passion Music - oratorio from "Passion with
  Tropes" (1983)                               45'
  soli s, mez, t, b; satb cho; 3=13*1;        MS
  a sax; 3321; 2perc, pf, str

A Sermon of Jonne Donne (from "Passion with
  Tropes") (1983)                              4'
  narr; 3=13*1; a sax; 3221; 2perc, pf, str   MS

Sinfonietta (1989)                                      18'
  3*23*2; a sax; 4331; timp+2, pf, str        MS

Gold (from Poem Symphonies) (1990)                      5'
  str                                          MS

FRIEDMAN, JOEL PHILLIP  (1960-     )

Concerto (In the Form of Variations) for
   Viola and Orchestra (1988)                              21'
   solo vla; 2*22*2; 2221; timp+2, hp,            MMB
   pf, str


FROHNE, VINCENT  (1936-     )

Adam's Chains, op. 21 (1964)                                21'
   solo s; 3*2*3*2; 4331; timp+3, hp, pf,          BB
   cel, str

Antimony, op. 25 (1966)                                     20'
                                              AMC

   1. Ordine I:  3*2*4*2; 4331; timp+1, hp,
      pf, cel, vc, db

   2. Ordine II:  str

   3. Counterpoise:  3*2*4*2; 4331; timp+1,
      hp, pf, cel


FULEIHAN, ANIS  (1900-1970)

Mediterranean (1925)                                       13'
   3*3*4=3*; 4331; timp+2, hp, str                 PS

Preface to a Child's Storybook (1932)                       8'
   3*3*3*3*; 4231; timp+1, hp, str                 PS

Invocation to Isis (1933)                                   7'
   3*3*3*3*; 4231; timp+2, str                     PS

Symphony No. 1 (1936)                                      23'
   3*3*3*3*; 4331; timp+1, str                     BH

Fiesta (1939)                                               6'
   3*3*3*3*; 4331; timp+2, str                     PS

Suite Concertante (1940)                                   15'
   solo fl; str                                    BH

Symphonie Concertante (1940)                               25'
   solo str qt; 3*3*3*2; 4231; timp, str           PS

Three Cyprus Serenades (1942)                              13'
   3*3*3=3*; 4331; timp+2, cel, str                PS

Fantasy for Theremin (1944)                                16'
   solo theremin; 23*22; 4331; timp, str        PS

Rhapsody for Cello and String
   Orchestra (1946)                                    18'
   solo vc; str                                        FLE

Symphony No. 2 (1962)                                      25'
   3*3*3=3*; 4331; timp+2, str                  BH

Concertino for Bassoon and Orchestra (1965)   9'
   solo bsn; 2221; 2200; timp, str              BH

Concerto for Violin (NA)                                   20'
   solo vln; 2222; 4331; timp, str              PS

Divertimento (NA)                                          9'
   0211; 1100; str                                    PS


FUSSELL, CHARLES   (1938-      )

Sweelinck Liedvariationen, "Mein Junges
   Leben" (1964)                                       11'
   soli vln, vla, vc; 2*2*11; 1110; timp,       GS
   mar, hp, mand, str

Poems for Chamber Orchestra and Voices (1965)  14'
   soli 2s, 2a, 2t, 2b; 2*111; 2210; 3perc,    GS
   hp, pf/cel, str (2-2-2-2)

Symphony No. 2 (1967)                                      46'
   solo s; 3*3*3*3*; 4331; timp+5, 2pf, str     GS

Aria of the Blessed Virgin (1968)                    7'
   12*00; 0100; hpsd, mand, str                 GS

Northern Lights - Two Portraits for Chamber
   Orchestra (1977-1979)                             15'
   soli 4vln; 2fl, timp, str                    MS

Landscapes (Symphony No. 3) (1978-1981)          30'
   satb cho; 3*3*3*3*; 4331; timp+4, hp,        MS
   pf, cel, str

GABURO, KENNETH   (1926-      )

Three Interludes for String Orchestra (1948)    10'
   str                                             MS

Concertante for Piano and Orchestra (1949)      25'
   solo pf; 3*3*3*3*; 4331; timp+5, hp,         MS
   pf, cel, str

On a Quiet Theme (1950)                          9'
   1*1*12*; 2110; timp+1, str                  TP

Elegy for Small Orchestra (1959)                15'
   2110; 0230; str                             TP

Antiphony IX
   (---a Dot is no mere thing---) (1984)        30'
   2222; 4331; timp+7, hp, 2pf, str            MS
   N.B.   Spatial separation is required.


GANNON, LEE   (1960-     )

The Sunday Comics (1980)                         11'
   1111; 0000; str                             MS

Free From Season's Passing (1988)                4'
   2222; 2200; timp+2, hp, str                 MS

Prickly Heat (1990)                              5'
   1111; 1100; perc, str                       MS

On the Surface (1991)                            14'
   2222; 4221; timp+2, pf, str                 MS


GARLICK, ANTONY   (1927-     )

Mardi Gras (1972)                                7'
   3*222; 4231; 3perc, str                     SEE

Canto - A Symphonic Poem (1973)                  15'
   3*222; 2221; timp+2, str                    SEE

Danza Barbara (1974)                             7'
   3*23*2; 4331; timp+1, str                   SEE

Pasticcio (1977)                                               10'
   3*222; 4331; perc, pf, str                   SEE

Symphony No. 1 (1977)                                          20'
   3*222; 4331; timp+1, str                      SEE

Symphony No. 2 (1979)                                          25'
   3*222; 4331; timp+1, str                      SEE

Symphony No. 3 (1979)                                          25'
   3*23*2; 4331; timp+1, str                     SEE

Symphony No. 4 (1980)                                          25'
   223*2; 4331; timp+1, str                      SEE

Symphony No. 5 (1981)                                          27'
   223*2; 4331; timp+1, str                      SEE

Symphony No. 6 (1982)                                          27'
   3*222; 4331; timp+1, str                      SEE


### GELLER, TIMOTHY JACKSON  (1954-    )

Where Silence Reigns (1987)                                   25'
   solo bar; 3=02*0; 1110; 2perc, hp,            MG
   pf/cel, 2 wine glasses, str (2-1-1-1)


### GELT, ANDREW  (1951-    )

Lamento for Strings, op. 22 (1973)                             7'
   str                                           MS

Symphony No. 1, op. 34 (1977)                                 23'
   3*224; 4331; timp+1, pf/org/hpsd, str         MS
   N.B.  Eight offstage trumpets are
   also required.

Tempus Fugit, op. 34a (1977)                                   7'
   2222; 4331; str                               MS


### GEORGE, EARL  (1924-    )

Adagietto (1946)                                               7'
   2222; 4231; timp+1, str                       FLE

Introduction and Allegro (1946)                                8'
   3*222; 4331; timp+1, str                      CF

Concerto for Strings (1948)                          11'
  str                                            FLE

Abraham Lincoln Walks at Midnight (1949)             5'
  2*222; 4231; timp+2, pf, str                    FLE

A Thanksgiving Overture (1949)                       5'
  2*222; 4231; timp+2, pf, str                    BH

A Currier and Ives Set (1953)                        11'
  1121; 2210; perc, pf, str                       FLE

Concerto for Piano and Orchestra (1958)             20'
  solo pf; 2222; 4231; 2perc, str                 OXF

Introduction, Variations and Finale (1959)          13'
  2*221; 4331; timp+3, pf, str                    FLE

Concerto for Violin and Orchestra (NA)              23'
  solo vln; 3*3*3*3*; 4331; timp+3, hp, str  FLE


    GEORGE, THOM RITTER  (1942-      )

Concerto for Bass Trombone and
  Orchestra (1964)                               10'
    solo b tbn; 3*222; 4331; timp+3, str  ACC

Concerto for Flute and Orchestra (1966)             8'
  solo fl; 0200; 2000; str                        ACC

Sinfonietta (1967)                                  20'
  3*23*3*; 4331; timp+3, hp, pf/cel, str          MS

Bal a Bougival:
  Overture after Renoir (1968)                   8'
  3*3*3+3*; 4331; timp+3, hp, pf, str             MS

Celebration Overture (1970)                         4'
  3*222; 4231; timp+3, str                        MS

Ballade for Orchestra (1972)                        8'
  3*222; 4231; timp+3, str                        MS

First Rhapsody for Orchestra (1974)                 10'
  3*23*2; 4331; timp+4, str                       MS

The Soul of Wit:  Comic Overture (1974)             3'
  3*3*3*3*; 4331; timp+5, pf, str                 MS

The People, Yes (1976)                                        47'
   solo mez, t, bar; satb cho; 3*3*3*3*;        MS
   4331; timp+4, hp, pf/cel, str

Four Games (1977)                                            20'
   1111; 2110; timp/perc, hp, pf, str           MS

Erica (1979)                                                 19'
   1=111; 2000; 2perc, hp, pf/cel, str          MS

Piano Concerto No. 2 (1979)                                  27'
   solo pf; 3*222; 4331; timp+3, str            MS

Olympic Overture (1983)                                       3'
   3*222; 4331; timp+3, str                     MS

Concertino for Tuba (1984)                                    8'
   solo tba; str                                MS

Suite for Strings (1984)                                     12'
   str                                          MS

Laude (Festive Overture) (1986)                               6'
   3*23*3*; 4331; timp+4, hp, str               MS

Third Suite in D (1988)                                      19'
   1*111; 2110; timp/perc, hp, pf, str          MS

Prelude and Toccata (1989)                                    5'
   str                                          MS


     GERSCHEFSKI, EDWIN    (1909-    )

Half Moon Mountain, op. 33 (1947-1948)                       18'
   solo bar; ssa cho(or satb); 2222; 4331;      AMP
   timp+1, str

The Lord's Controversy with His People,
   op. 34, No. 1 (1949)                          12'
   solo bar; ssa cho; 1111; 2110;               ACA
   timp+1, hp, str

There is a Man on the Cross,
   op. 34, No. 2 (1950)                           5'
   solo ca; satb cho; 2222; 4231;               ACA
   timp+1, str

Concerto for Violin and Orchestra,
   op. 35 (1951-1952)                                    33'
   solo vln; 3*222; 4231; perc, str                  ACA

Salutation of the Dawn, op. 37 (1952)                11'
   satb cho; 3*220; 4331; perc, str                  ACA

Toccata and Fugue, after Bach, op. 40 (1952)  9'
   3*222; 4231; timp+1, hp, str                      ACA

Nocturne, op. 42, No. 2c (1953)                       6'
   23*22; 4330; hp, str                              ACA

Classic Overture, op. 4a (1963)                       5'
   2222; 2200; timp, str                             ACA

Classic Symphony, op. 4f (1963)                      20'
   str                                               ACA

Celebration, op. 51 (1964)                           18'
   solo vln; 2222; 4231; timp, pf, str               ACA

Letter from BMI, op. 83 (1981)                       12'
   satb cho; 2020; 2000; 2perc, pf, str              ACA

Nocturne for Cello and Orchestra,
   op. 42, No. 2 (1991)                               6'
   solo vc; 23*22; 4330; timp+1, hp, str             ACA


#### GHEZZO, DINU   (1940-      )

Thalla (1975)                                        14'
   solo pf; 1111; a sax; 2210; str (2-1-1-1)   SEE

Seven Short Pieces (1978)                            13'
   1111; 1110; perc, str (1-1-1-1)                   SEE

Celebrations (1979)                                  21'
   2111; 1010; perc, str (1-1-1-1)                   SEE

Echoes of Romania (1990)                             10'
   str                                               SEE


#### GIANNINI, VITTORIO  (1903-1966)

Concerto for Trumpet and Orchestra (1945)     16'
   solo tpt; 2222; 4221; timp+2, hp,                  GS
   cel, str

Concerto Grosso (1946)                                         13'
  solo str qt; str                                  BRO

Frescobaldiana (1948)                                         15'
  3*3*3*3*; 4331; timp+1, str                       FC

Symphony No. 1 "Sinfonia" (1950)                              21'
  3*3*3*3*; 4322; timp+1, hp, str                   FC

Canticle of Christmas (1951)                                  23'
  solo bar; satb cho; 3*3*3*3*; 4331;               RIC
  timp+1, str

Divertimento No. 1 (1953)                                     14'
  2222; 2210; timp+1, hp, str                       FC

Prelude and Fugue (1955)                                      10'
  str                                               FC

Symphony No. 2 (1955)                                         22'
  3*222; 4331; timp+1, str                          BRO

Canticle of the Martyrs (1956)                               21'
  satb cho; 3*222; 4331; timp+1, str               FC

Suite "Love's Labour Lost" (1958)                            25'
  2111; 2110; perc, hp, str                         FC

The Medead (1960)                                            39'
  solo s; 2222; 4221; timp+1, hp, str              FC

Symphony No. 4 (1960)                                        30'
  3*3*3*3*; 4331; timp+1, hp, str                   FC

Divertimento No. 2 (1961)                                    15'
  2222; 2210; timp+1, hp, str                       FC

Antigone (1962)                                              28'
  solo s; 3*3*3*3*; 4322; timp+1, hp, str          FC

Psalm CXXX (1963)                                            20'
  3*3*23*; 4331; timp+1, hp, str                    FC

Divertimento No. 3 (1964)                                    15'
  2020; 0110; timp+1, pf, str                       FC

Symphony No. 5 (1965)                                        23'
  3*3*3*3*; 4231; timp, str                         FC

GIBBONS, MARK EDWARD  (1960-    )

Stories of Passion (1987)                               11'
    solo s; 23*3*2; a sax; 4230; timp+3,            NOA
    hp, pf, cel, str


GIDEON, MIRIAM  (1906-    )

Symphonia Brevis - Two Movements for
    Orchestra (1953)                                  9'
    2222; 4220; timp, str                           ACA

Adon Olom (1954)                                       6'
    satb cho; 0100; 0100; str                       ACA

Lyric Piece (1956)                                     6'
    str                                             ACA

Songs of Youth and Madness (1977)                     16'
    solo s (or t); 1111; 1100; timp+1, str          MOB


GILLIS, DON  (1912-1978)

Symphony No. 1 (1939)                                 27'
    2*2*3*2; 3331; timp+1, str                      BG

Symphony No. 2 "A Symphony of Faith" (1941)          37'
    2*2*3*2; 3331; timp+4, hp, str                  BG

Symphony No. 3
    "A Symphony for Free Men" (1942)                 25'
    2*2*3*2; 3331; timp+5, hp, str                  BG

Symphony No. 4 "The Pioneers" (1944)                 32'
    2*2*3*2; 3331; timp+5, hp, cel, str             BG

Short Overture to An Unwritten Opera (1945)           4'
    223*2; 3331; timp+2, hp, str                    BH

Symphony No. 5 "In Memoriam" (1945)                  31'
    2*2*3*2; 3331; timp+5, hp, str                  BG

This is our America (1945)                            16'
    solo bar; satb cho; 223*1; 3321; 3perc,         TP
    pf, cel, org, str

To an Unknown Soldier - tone poem (1945)             10'
    2*2*3*2; 3331; timp+4, hp, str                  BG

Three Sketches for Strings (1945)                    9'
    str                                              BH

Rhapsody for Harp (1946)                            14'
    solo hp; 2*2*3*2; 3331; timp+3, hp, str         BG

Symphony No. 5½ (1946)                              14'
    2*2*3*2; 3331; timp+5, pf, str                   BH

Symphony No. 6 (1948)                               25'
    22*3*2; 3331; timp+5, hp, str                   BEL

The Alamo (1949)                                    13'
    223*2; 3331; timp+3, hp, str                    CRE

Intermission:  Ten Minutes (1949)                    8'
    3*23*2; 3331; timp+3, str                        TP

The Man Who Invented Music (1949)                   14'
    narr; 3*3*3*2; 3331; timp+3, pf, cel, str       TP

Symphony No. 7 (1949)                               25'
    22*3*2; 3331; timp+1, hp, str                    TP

Symphony No. 8 (1949)                               18'
    2*2*3*2; 3331; timp+5, cel, str                 BEL

Alice in Orchestralia (1950)                        22'
    narr; 3*3*3*2; 3331; timp+7, hp,                BEL
    pf, cel, str

Thomas Wolfe, American (1950)                       20'
    223*2; 3331; timp+2, hp, str                     BG

Tulsa:  A Symphonic Portrait in Oil (1950)          10'
    3*23*2; 3331; timp+6, pf, str                    TP

Shindig - ballet (1951)                             22'
    223*2; 3331; timp+2, hp, pf, str                 TP

Atlanta Suite (1952)                                36'
    3*3*3*2; 3331; timp+4, hp, pf, cel, str         BEL

From an Evening in Autumn (1955)                     4'
    str                                              TP

Retrospection - Poem for Violin and
    Orchestra (1955)                                 6'
    solo vln; perc, hp, pf, cel, str                BEL

Adoration at Eventide (1956)                              4'
   str                                                      TP

Concerto No. 1 for Piano and
   Orchestra (1956)                                       15'
   solo pf; 223*1; 4332; perc, str                        BG

Mandarin Dance (1956)                                     3'
   223*2; 3331; timp+1, pf, str                           BEL

Scherzino for Strings (1956)                              3'
   str                                                      TP

Temple Dance from "Twinkle Toes" (1956)                   5'
   223*2; 3331; timp+1, pf, str                           BEL

Vim, Vigor and Velocity from
   "Twinkle Toes" (1956)                                  4'
   3*23*2; 3331; timp+1, pf, str                          BEL

Four Scenes from Yesterday (1957)                         16'
   1110; 0000; timp+5, hp, pf/cel, str                    BH

The Coming of the King (1958)                             26'
   narr; satb cho; 223*1; 3000; perc, hp,                 TP
   pf, cel, str

Soliloquy for Strings (1958)                              4'
   str                                                      CRE

Strictly for Strads (1958)                                5'
   str                                                      CRE

Amarillo (1962)                                           18'
   22*3*2; 3331; 3perc, pf, cel, str                      BG

Paul Bunyan (1964)                                        7'
   2202; 2200; perc, pf, str                              BG

Concerto No. 2 for Piano and
   Orchestra (1967)                                       38'
   solo pf; 223*1; 4332; perc, str                        BG

Rhapsody for Trumpet and Orchestra (1970)                 18'
   solo tpt; 2222; 4331; perc, hp,                        BG
   pf/cel, str

Symphony X (1972)                                         19'
   223*2; 3331; 4perc, pf, str                            BH

GIMBEL, ALLEN  (1956-     )

Symphony (1979)                                               30'
    2222; 4331; perc, str                                     MS

The Four Temperaments (1991)                                  15'
    3*222; 4321; perc, pf, str                                MS


GIUFFRE, JAMES  (1921-     )

Mobiles (1956)                                                21'
    solo cl; str                                              MJQ

Threshold (1963)                                              10'
    soli vib, pf, db, dmst; 2111; 2000; str        MJQ

Hex (1965)                                                    5'
    2202; a,t sax; 2421; timp+2, gtr, str          MJQ

Symphonic Movement (1969)                                     15'
    3*3*3*3*; 4331; 3perc, hp, cel, str            MG

Mirrors for Jazz Trio and Orchestra (1975)     20'
    soli cl/fl/b fl/s sax/t sax, dmst, db;         MG
    0000; 2220; str

Piece for Clarinet and
    String Orchestra (1978)                                   18'
    solo cl; str                                              MJQ


GLANVILLE-HICKS, PEGGY  (1912-     )

    N.B. Only those works composed 1952-1959.

Letters from Morocco (1952)                                   16'
    solo t; 1101; 0100; 3perc, hp, str             CFP

Sinfonia da Pacifica (1953)                                   12'
    1111; 1110; timp+3, str                                   AMP

Etruscan Concerto (1956)                                      16'
    solo pf; 1111; 1100; 4perc, str                CFP

Concerto Romantico (1957)                                     21'
    solo vla; 11*1*0; 1100; timp+1, hp, str        CFP

Masque of the Wild Man (1958)                                 18'
    fl; timp+1, hp, pf, cel, str                             CFP

GLASS, PHILIP   (1937-      )

Music in Similar Motion (1969)                          12'
    3*3*4=2; 4221; org, str                            DVG

Company (1983)                                          8'
    str                                                DVG

Civil Wars:  Rome Section (1984)                        90'
    soli s, a, t, bar, b; satb cho; 2*23*2;            DVG
    4331; 3perc, hp, str

Dance from "Akhnaten" (1984)                            6'
    223*2; 2231; 3perc, str (no vlns)                  DVG

Hymn to the Sun from "Akhnaten" (1984)                  9'
    solo countertenor; satb cho (offstage);           DVG
    2222; 2231; str (no vlns)

Music from "Civil Wars" (1984)                          28'
    satb cho(opt); 2*23*2; 4331; timp+4, str          DVG

Concerto for Violin (1987)                              30'
    solo vln; 1*23*2; 4331; timp+5, hp, str           DVG

The Light (1987)                                        24'
    3*23*2; 4331; timp+4, 2hp, pf, str                DVG

The Canyon (1988)                                       18'
    2*23*2; 4331; timp+8, str                         DVG

Itaipu (1988)                                           38'
    satb cho; 3*333*; 6431; 4perc, hp,                DVG
    pf, str


GODFREY, DANIEL   (1949-      )

Rhapsody for Large Orchestra (1973)                     10'
    3*4*4=3*; 3323; 5perc, hp, str                    ACA

Concentus (1985)                                        14'
    1=1*11; 1110; timp/perc, str                      MG

Mestengo (1988)                                         11'
    3*3*3*3*; 4331; timp+4, hp, str                   MG

GOEB, ROGER   (1914-     )

Concertino I for Orchestra (1946)                18'
   223*2; 4331; timp, str                        ACA

Fantasy for Oboe and Strings (1947)             6'
   solo ob; str                                  AMP

Prairie Songs (1947)                            11'
   2222; 2210; timp+3, str                       PS

Concertant I (1948)                             14'
   soli fl, ob, cl; str                          ACA

Romanza (1948)                                  12'
   str                                           ACA

Symphony No. 3 (1950)                           24'
   3*3*3*2; 4331; timp+2, cel, str               ACA

Concertant II (1951)                            12'
   solo bsn (or vc); str                         ACA

Concertant IV (1951)                            16'
   solo cl; timp+2, pf, str                      ACA

American Dance No. 1 (1952)                     3'
   str                                           ACA

American Dance No. 2 (1952)                     3'
   str                                           ACA

American Dance No. 3 (1952)                     3'
   str                                           ACA

American Dance No. 4 (1952)                     3'
   2121; 2220; timp, str                         ACA

American Dance No. 5 (1952)                     3'
   2122; 2110; timp, str                         ACA

Concerto for Violin and Orchestra (1953)        19'
   solo vln; 2222; 3210; timp+1, pf, str         ACA

Concerto for Piano and Orchestra (1954)         18'
   solo pf; 2121; 2200; timp+1, str              ACA

Fantasy for Piano and Strings (1955)            10'
   solo pf; str                                  ACA

Concertino II for Orchestra (1956)                          15'
   2222; 4231; timp+1, pf, str                      ACA

Symphony No. 4 (1956)                                       25'
   3*3*3*2; 4331; timp+3, str                       ACA

Sinfonia I (1957)                                          12'
   2222; 4221; timp+1, str                          ACA

Concertino III for Orchestra (1959)                        17'
   2222; 4231; timp+1, pf, str                      ACA

Iowa Concerto (1959)                                       16'
   1111; 1110; timp+1, str                          ACA

Sinfonia II (1962)                                        15'
   2222; 4221; timp+1, str                          ACA

Symphony No. 5 (1981)                                      24'
   3*3*3*2; 4331; 4perc, str                        ACA

Caprice for Orchestra (1982)                                8'
   3*3*3*2; 4331; 2perc, str                        ACA

Divertissement for Strings (1982)                           8'
   str                                              ACA

Memorial (1982)                                             8'
   3*3*3*2; 4331; timp+3, str                       ACA

Fantasia for Orchestra (1983)                              11'
   3*3*3*2; 4331; 3perc, str                        ACA

Essay for Orchestra (1984)                                  8'
   3*3*3*2; 4331; 3perc, str                        ACA

Gambol (1984)                                               5'
   3*3*22; 4331; timp+3, str                        ACA

Symphony No. 6 (1987)                                      23'
   3*3*3*2; 4331; 3perc, str                        ACA


### GOLDSTEIN, MALCOLM  (1936-        )

"a breaking of vessels, becoming song" (1981) 15'
   solo fl; ww; br; perc, str                       MS
   N.B.  Number of performers is unspecified.

Cascades of the Brook:
   Bachwasserfall (1985)                              15'
   solo vln; 1111; a sax; 0000; hpsd, str          MS

Pond:  earth's eye, the mirror (NA)                20'
   ww; br; perc, str (all unspecified)             MS


      GOOCH, WARREN

Ontogeny (1975)                                    17'
   timp+3, hp, pf, cel, str                        MS

Restless Landscape (1984)                           9'
   2222; 2220; timp, str                           MS

Wisdom - cantata (1989)                            35'
   soli mez, bar; satb cho, pf, str                MS

One Star, Ours (1990)                               8'
   satb cho; 2222; 4220; timp+2, str               MS


      GOODE, DANIEL   (1936-      )

Phrases of the Hermit Thrush (1980)                 7'
   solo cl; 2fl; str                               SP


      GOODENOUGH, FORREST   (1918-      )

Two Essays for Orchestra (1945)                     7'
   1121; 2221; timp+1, str                         ACA

Choral Fantasy (1953)                               9'
   2222; 4331; timp+1, str                         ACA

Elegy (1960)                                        6'
   2222; 2221; timp+1, str                         ACA


      GOODWIN, GORDON R.   (1941-      )

Codes for Orchestra (1969)                         16'
   2222; 4331; 3perc, str                          CMP

Kerr County Kick (1979)                            10'
   2202; 2000; str                                 CMP

Palmetto Symphony (1989)                              24'
  3*222; 4331; timp+3, hp, pf, str               CMP


## GOOSSEN, FREDERIC (1927-    )

Corybant (1954)                                        4'
  1112; 1110; timp+2, pf, str                     ACA

Litanies (1963)                                       21'
  2222; 4230; timp+2, str                         ACA

Concerto for Viola and Orchestra (1965)              20'
  solo vla; 2222; 4220; timp+1, str               ACA

Entertainments (1965)                                  7'
  2222; 4220; timp+1, str                         ACA

Stanzas and Refrains (1970)                           25'
  0000; 4331; timp, str                           ACA

Hae: In memoriam Thomas Mann (1971)                  10'
  3*223*; 4331; timp+1, str                        ACA

Dance Measures (1972)                                 12'
  2222; 2200; timp, str                           ACA

Orpheus Singing (1972)                                10'
  0100; 1000; timp, str                           ACA

Symphony No. 2 (1977)                                 25'
  2222; 4231; timp+4, str                         ACA

Music for Orchestra (1979)                            13'
  2223*; 4331; timp+3, str                         ACA

Grimmtales (1980)                                     40'
  2223*; 4331; timp+3, str                         ACA

Prospero's Spell (1982)                               12'
  2223*; 4331; timp+2, str                         ACA


## GOTTLIEB, JACK (1930-    )

Pieces of Seven: Overture (1962)                       8'
  3*23*3*; 4231; timp+1, str                        GS

Articles of Faith (1965)                              15'
  23*3*2; 4321; timp+2, pf, str, tape               TP

GOTTSCHALK, ARTHUR  (1952-    )

Communiqué (1975)                                              12'
  3*33*3*; a sax; 4331; t tba; timp+3,              MS
  hp, str

Beati Omnes (1978)                                            18'
  ttbb cho; 3*33*3*; 4331; timp+3, hp, str          MS

Blue Fantasy (1986)                                          12'
  solo vln; 2222; 2000; timp+1, hp,                 MS
  cel, str

Infinity (1991)                                              24'
  4*4*4*4*; 4331; timp+2, hp, cel, str              MS


GOULD, MORTON  (1913-    )

Concerto for Piano and Orchestra (1934)                      20'
  solo pf; 1*111; 2210; timp+2, str                 GS

Foster Gallery Suite (1939)                                  18'
  3*3*3*3*; 4331; timp+2, hp, bj, str               GS

Lincoln Legend (1942)                                        18'
  2*2*3*2; 4331; timp+2, hp, str                    GS

Symphony No. 1 (1943)                                        32'
  3*3*3*3*; 4331; timp+3, hp, str                   GS

Symphony No. 2 on Marching Tunes (1944)                      31'
  3*3*3*3*; 4331; timp+3, hp, str                   GS

Concerto for Orchestra (1945)                                18'
  3*3*4=3*; a,t sax; 4331; timp+3,                  GS
  hp, pf, str

Harvest (1945)                                               12'
  vib, hp, str                                      GS

Minstrel Show (1946)                                          8'
  2*223; 4331; timp+1, hp, str                      GS

Holiday Music (1947)                                         16'
  2*2*22; 4331; timp+3, hp, pf/cel, str             GS

Symphony No. 3 (1947)                                        36'
  3*3*3=3*; 4331; timp+3, hp, cel, str              GS

Philharmonic Waltzes (1948)                        9'
  2*23*3*; 4331; timp+3, hp, pf, str               GS

Fall River Legend - suite (1949)                  24'
  2*222; 4230; timp+2, pf, str                     GS

Serenade of Carols (1949)                         15'
  3*23*2; 2200; hp, str (4-2-2-0)                  GS

Big City Blues (1950)                              5'
  2*1*21; 4331; timp+1, hp, pf, str                GS

Family Outing (1951)                              15'
  2*2*22; 4230; timp+2, pf, str                    GS

Tap Dance Concerto (1952)                         16'
  solo tap dancer; 2*222; 4200; timp, str          GS

Dance Variations (1953)                           23'
  soli 2pf; 2*2*22; 4331; timp+3, str              GS

Showpiece (1954)                                  19'
  3*3*4=3*; 6331; timp+4, hp, pf/cel, str          GS

Declaration Suite (1956)                          19'
  3*2*22*; 4331; timp+2, hp, str                   GS

Hoofer Suite
  (For Tap Dancer and Orchestra) (1956)           11'
  1*121; 2221; timp+1, str                         GS

Declaration
  (Declaration of Independence) (1957)            30'
  2narr; male speaking cho; 3*2*22*; 4331;         GS
  timp+3, hp, pf, str

Jekyll and Hyde Variations (1957)                 22'
  3*3*4=3*; 6331; 3perc, hp, pf/cel, str           GS

Dialogues (1958)                                  22'
  solo pf; str                                     GS

Rhythm Gallery (1959)                             24'
  narr; 2*2*22; 3221; timp+1, hp, pf, str          GS

Festive Music (1965)                              11'
  3*23*2; 4331; timp+3, hp, str,                   GS
  offstage tpt

Columbia:   Broadsides for Orchestra (1967)      13'
    3*3*4=3*; 4331; timp+3, hp, str               GS

Venice for Double Orchestra (1967)               30'
    orch 1:   2*2*2*2*; 3221; timp+1, hp, str     GS
    orch 2:   2*121; 3230; timp+1, hp, str

Vivaldi Gallery (1968)                           27'
    solo str qt; 2*222; 2220; hp, str             GS

Soundings (1969)                                 18'
    3*3*3=3*; 4331; timp+3, hp, cel, str          GS

Troubador Music (1969)                           24'
    soli 4gtr; 2*2*22; 2222; 2perc, str           GS

American Ballads (1976)                          33'
    3*2*3=2*; 4331; timp+3, hp, str               GS

Symphony of Spirituals (1976)                    33'
    3*3*3=3*; 4331; timp+1, hp, pf, str           GS

Elegy from "Holocaust" (1978)                     4'
    str                                           GS

"Holocaust" - suite (1978)                       21'
    2*2*2+2*; 4331; timp+2, hp, pf, str           GS

Cheers! (Celebration March) (1979)                5'
    3*3*3*3*; 4431; timp+1, hp, str               GS

Burchfield Gallery (1981)                        27'
    3*3*3+3*; 4331; timp+3, hp, pf, str           GS

Celebration Strut (1981)                          3'
    3*23*2; 4331; timp+1, hp, str                 GS

Housewarming (1982)                               9'
    3*3*3=3*; 4331; timp+4, hp, cel, str          GS

Audobon (unfinished ballet by G. Balanchine)
    (1983)                                        83'

    1.   Apple Waltzes                            18'
         3*2*3*3*; 4331; timp+1, hp,
         pf/cel, str                              GS

    2.   Bird Movements                           12'
         3=2*3=3*; 0001; perc, b gtr/db           GS

3.  Chorales and Rags (Finale )                     6'
    3*2*33*; 4331; perc, hp, pf/cel, str   GS

4.  Concerto Grosso (4 mvts)                        19'
    soli 4vln; 3*2*3*2*; 4331; timp+1,      GS
    hp, str

5.  Fire Music                                      4'
    3*3*4=3*; 4331; perc, wind machine,     GS
    elec kybd, str, tape

6.  Indian Attack                                   3'
    3*2*3+3*; 4331; timp+1, str             GS

7.  Night Music                                     5'
    3*2*3*3; 0000, perc, hp, gtr, str       GS

8.  Scherzo                                         3'
    3*2*3=2*; 4331; timp, hp, pf, str       GS

9.  Serenade                                        8'
    223*2; 0000; hp, str                    GS

10. Tribal Dance                                    5'
    3*3*4=3*; 4331; timp+1, hp, pf, str     GS

Flourishes and Galop (1983)                         4'
    3*3*3*3*; 4331; timp+1, hp, str         GS

American Sing
    (settings of folk songs) (1984)                 16'
    solo s, mez, t, bar; 3*333*; 4331;      GS
    timp+2, hp, str

Concerto for Flute and Orchestra (1984)             34'
    solo fl; 2*333*; 4331; timp+3, hp,      GS
    cel, str

Quotations (1984)                                   23'
    ssaattbb cho; 2222; 4331; timp+3,       GS
    hp, pf, str

Classical Variations on Colonial
    Themes (1986)                                   14'
    2*222; 4220; timp+3, hp, str            GS

Notes of Remembrance (1989)                         8'
    2*223; 4331; timp+1, hp, str            GS

Cinerama Holiday - suite (NA)                                    15'
  2121; 2221; timp+2, hp, pf/cel, str                  GS

Guajira for Clarinet and Orchestra (NA)                          3'
  solo cl; 22*12; 2000; perc, hp, str                  GS

A Homespun Overture (NA)                                         6'
  3*23*2; 4331; timp+2, hp, bj, str                    GS

Sarajevo Suite (NA)                                              13'
  2*121; 2221; timp+1, hp, pf/cel, str                 GS


      GRANT, JAMES (1954-    )

Concerto Fantasy for Percussion and
  Orchestra (1991)                                      26'
  solo perc; 2222; 4231; perc, str                     MS

Lament for String Orchestra (1991)                              8'
  str                                                  MS


      GRANT, PARKS  (1910-    )

Suite No. 1, op. 21 (1946)                                      11'
  str                                                  ACA

Rhythmic Overture, op. 23 (1947)                                7'
  3*3*3*3*; 4231; timp+1, str                          ACA

Dramatic Overture, op. 26 (1948)                                10'
  3*3*3*2; 4331; timp+1, pf/cel, str                   ACA

Homage Ode, op. 30 (1948)                                       8'
  2222; 4231; timp+1, str                              ACA

Scherzo for Flute and Orchestra (1949)                          7'
  solo fl; 0121; 2100; perc, pf/cel, str               ACA

A Mood Overture, op. 36 (1950)                                  10'
  2222; 4231; timp+1, str                              ACA

Instrumental Motet, op. 42 (1952)                               7'
  str                                                  ACA

Suite No. 2, op. 43 (1952)                                      10'
  str                                                  ACA

A Quiet Piece, op. 47b (1953)                        6'
  str                                      ACA

Lyrical Overture, op. 50 (1955)                     10'
  3*3*3*2; 3231; timp, str                 ACA

A Musical Tribute, op. 50, No. 2 (1955)             14'
  3*23*2; 4221; timp+2, str               ACA

Suite No. 3, op. 53 (1956)                          24'
  str                                      ACA

Symphony No. 3, op. 54 (1957)                       21'
  3*3*3*3*; 4331; timp+1, hp, pf/cel, str  ACA

Character Sketches, op. 58 (1963)                   19'
  2222; 4231; timp+1, str                  ACA


     GRANTHAM, DONALD  (1947-    )

Kyng Celestial (1981)                               10'
  solo s; 0201; 0000; 3perc, hp,           MS
  3handbells, str

El Album de los Duendecitos (1982)                  15'
  1*2*2=2; 2100; perc, pf/cel, str         TP

Fiddler's Fancy (1986)                              30'
  solo bar; satb cho; 3*23*3*; 4231;       MS
  timp+2, hp, pf/cel, str

Invocation and Dance (1986)                          8'
  3*23*3*; 4231; timp+2, hp, pf/cel, str   MS


     GREEN, GEORGE  (1930-    )

Prologue and Fugue (1956)                           12'
  2222; 4231; timp+1, hp, pf, str          SEE

Passacaglia (1957)                                   6'
  2222; 2200; perc, str                    SEE


     GREENBERG, LAURA  (1942-    )

Concert Music (1976)                                12'
  1010; 1100; perc, pf, str                ACA

GROFÉ, FERDE   (1892-1972)

Grand Canyon Suite (1931)                                31'
  3*3*3*3*; 4331; timp+3, hp, pf/cel, str        LML

Atlantic Crossing (1950)                                 28'
  narr(opt); satb cho; 3*3*3*2; 4331;            TP
  timp+5, hp, pf, cel, str

Death Valley Suite (1957)                                16'
  3*3*3*3*; 4331; timp+4, hp, cel, str           TP

Niagara Falls Suite (1960)                               25'
  3*3*3*3*; 4331; timp+4, hp, pf, cel, str       TP

World's Fair Suite (1963)                                36'
  3*3*3*3*; 4331; timp+4, hp, pf, str           TP

Hollywood Suite (1965)                                   22'
  3*3*3*3*; 4331; timp+3, hp, str               TP


GROSS, ROBERT   (1914-1983)

Aria, Prelude and Fugue (1952)                           9'
  2122; 2221; timp, str                          ACA

Resonants for Divided Orchestra (1977)                   10'
  3*3*4=2; 4221; timp+3, hp, str                 ACA


GRUENBERG, LOUIS   (1884-1964)

The Enchanted Isle, op. 11 (1927; rev 1933)   16'
  3*3*3*2; 4331; timp+2, hp, cel, str            FLE

Jazz Suite, op. 28 (1927)                                15'
  3*3*3*3*; 4331; timp+3, hp, cel, str           MG

Piano Concerto No. 2, op. 41
  (1938; rev 1963)                               33'
  solo pf; 3*3*3*3*; 4331; timp+1,               FLE
  hp, cel, str

Symphony No. 2, op. 43
  (1941; rev 1953, 1961)                         30'
  3*3*3*3*; 4331; timp+2, hp, pf/cel, str        FLE

Symphony No. 3, op. 44 (1941; rev 1964)   30'
  3*3*3*3*; 4331; timp+2, hp, pf/cel, str        FLE

White Lilacs (orch'd by G. Schuller) (1944)        31'
   3*3*3*3*; 4331; timp+3, hp, str                    MG

Americana - Suite for Orchestra,
   op. 48 (1945)                                       20'
   3*3*3*3*; 4331; timp+2, hp, pf, cel, str       FLE


GRYC, STEPHEN   (1949-      )

Three Fantasies for Orchestra (1983)               15'
   3*3*3*3*; 4331; 4perc, hp, pf/cel, str         MS

Neon Night (1984)                                   8'
   3*3*3+3*; 4331; 4perc, pf, str                 MS

The Moon's Mirror:  Three Nocturnes (1985)         16'
   solo fl/a fl; perc, str                        MS

A Dance Concerto (1989)                            15'
   solo cl; 2*222; 2210; 2perc, pf/cel, str       MS


GUTCHE, GENE   (1907-      )

Holofernes Overture, op. 27 (1958)                  9'
   3(picc, b fl)3*3*3*; a sax; 4431;              HG
   timp+3, str

Concertino for Orchestra, op. 28 (1958)            19'
   11*11*; 1111; 2perc, str                       HG

Rondo capriccioso, op, 29 (1958)                    7'
   1110; 1110; 3perc, 2hp, str                    ACA

Symphony No. 4, op. 30 (1958)                      13'
   2222; 4341; timp+1, hp, cel, str               HG

Timpani Concertante, op. 31 (1959)                  7'
   solo timp; 3*3*3=3*; 4331; perc, str           HG

Symphony No. 5, op. 34 (1961)                      22'
   str                                            HG

Bongo Divertimento, op. 35 (1961)                   9'
   solo perc; 1111; 1100; str                     HG

Raquel, op. 38 (1964)                               8'
   3*3*3*3; 4431; timp+2, str                     HG

Rites in Tenochtitlan, op. 39 (1965)                18'
   1*1*11*; 2100; timp+2, str                       HG

Hsiang Fei, op. 40 (1965)                           15'
   0000; 4431; timp+3, hp, str                      HG

Gemini, op. 41 (1965)                               15'
   solo pf(4-hands); 3*3*3*3*; 4331;                HG
   timp+3, str

Aesop Fabler Suite, op. 43 (1965)                   18'
   3*3*3=3*; 4431; timp+2, str                      HG

Symphony No. 6, op. 45 (1967)                       28'
   3*3*3=3*; 4431; timp+3, hp, cel, str             HG

Concerto for Violin and Orchestra,
   op. 36 (1968)                                    20'
   solo vln; 2*2*22*; 2220; timp+1, hp, str         HG

Epimetheus USA, op. 46 (1968)                       10'
   3*3*3*3*; a sax; 4431; timp+3, str               HG

Icarus, op. 48 (1975)                               30'
   3*3*3*3*; 4331; timp+6, str                      REG

Bi-Centurion, op. 49 (1975)                         12'
   3*3*3*3*; 4331; timp+4, str                      REG

Perseus and Andromeda XX, op. 50 (1977)             22'
   3*3*3*3*; a sax; 4431; timp+3, str               REG

Helios Kinetic, op. 52 (1978)                       18'
   3*3*3*3*; a sax; 4431; timp+4, str               HG


          GYRING, ELIZABETH  (1906-1972)

Adagio for Orchestra (1955)                          7'
   1011; 0100; str                                  ACA

HAGEN, DARON ARIC  (1961-    )

Prayer for Peace (1981)                                    19'
    str                                                    ECS

A Handful of Days (1982)                                   16'
    2*2*2*2*; 4331; timp+1, 2hp, pf/cel, str               ECS

Instants (1982)                                            13'
    1*211; 2100; timp, pf, str                             ECS

A Stillness at Appomattox (1982; rev 1989)                10'
    2*2*2*2; 2220; perc, hp, str                           ECS

Concerto for Violin and Orchestra (1983)                  17'
    solo vln; 2=2*2*2; 22(cnt)20; timp, str                ECS

Stanzas for Cello and Orchestra (1983)                    12'
    solo vc; 1*101; 1000; pf, str                          ECS

A Walt Whitman Requiem (1984)                              22'
    solo s; satb cho; str                                  ECS

Companion Piece (1985)                                     13'
    1*211; 2110; timp+1, str                               ECS

Symphony No. 1 (1985; rev 1988)                           22'
    3*3*3*3*; 44(cnt, flu hn)31; timp+1, hp,               ECS
    pf/cel, str

Fresh Ayre (1987)                                          6'
    3(2picc)3*3*3*; 4331; timp+3, hp, str                  ECS
    N.B.  First movement of Symphony No. 2.

Grand Line:
    A Tribute to Leonard Bernstein (1987)                 11'
    2*222; 2220; timp+1, pf/cel, str                       ECS

Introduction and Cortege (1987)                           8'
    2*2*2*2; 2221; timp+1, hp, str                         ECS

Lyric Variations (1987)                                   13'
    3(2picc)3*3*3*; 4331; timp+3, hp, str                  ECS
    N.B.  Second movement of Symphony No. 2.

Symphony No. 2 (1987-1989)                                    31'
  3(2picc)3*3*3*; 4331; timp+3, hp, str                      ECS

Adagietto for Strings (1988)                                  5'
  str                                                        ECS

Common Ground (1989)                                         12'
  3=3*3*3*; 43(cnt)31; 3perc, hp,                           ECS
  pf/cel, str
  N.B.  Third movement of Symphony No. 2.

Heliotope (1989)                                             9'
  2*2*2(a sax, b cl)2; 2220; 2perc,                         ECS
  hp, pf/cel, str


          HAILSTORK, ADOLPHUS (1941-    )

Celebration (1974)                                           3'
  3*3*3*2; 4331; timp+5, str                                 MMB

Epitaph (In memoriam Martin Luther King, Jr.)
  (1979)                                                     6'
  3*223*; 4331; timp+2, hp, str                              MS

Sport of Strings (1982)                                      6'
  str                                                        MS

An American Port of Call (1984)                             8'
  3*223*; 4331; timp+3, hp, str                              MS

Done Made My Vow (1985)                                     40'
  satb cho; 3*222; 4331; timp+5, str                         MS

Essay for Strings (1986)                                    6'
  str                                                        MS

Songs of Isaiah (1987)                                     13'
  satb cho; 2222; 2220; timp+1, str                          MMB

Symphony No. 1 (1988)                                      20'
  2222; 2210; str                                            MS

Four Spirituals (1989)                                     15'
  soli 2s(or s, t); 1111; 1111; timp+1, str   MS

I Will Lift Up Mine Eyes (1989)                            18'
  solo t; satb cho; 1111; 1111;                            MS
  timp+1, hp, str

My Lord what a Mourning (1989)                    8'
   2222; 2211; timp, str                          MMB

Sonata da chiesa (1991)                          20'
   str                                            MS


           HAIMO, ETHAN   (1950-    )

Symphony for Strings (1988)                       14'
   str                                            MS


           HAINES, EDMUND   (1914-1974)

Informal Overture (1948)                          7'
   2*223*; 0000; timp+1, pf, str                  CF

Rondino and Variations (1956)                     15'
   2*2*22; 4230; timp+1, pf, str                  CF

Three Dances for Orchestra (1962)                 11'
   2*2*22; 4330; timp+2, hp, str                  CF


           HANDEL, DARRELL   (1933-    )

Low Country Hauntings (1976)                      20'
   soli s, a, t, b; 2223*; 5231; timp+3,          MS
   hp, pf, str

Acquainted with the Night (1982)                  22'
   solo mez; 3perc, hp, pf, str                   MS

Kyushu Impressions (1991)                         18'
   2222; 4231; 3perc, hp, pf, str                 MS


           HANNAY, ROGER   (1930-    )

Dramatic Overture (Homage to Schoenberg)
   (1951; rev 1981)                               8'
   3*223*; 3231; timp+1, str                      MS

Cantata (1952)                                    12'
   solo t; satb cho; 2222; 2220; timp, str        MS

Symphony No. 1 (1953; rev 1973)                   20'
   1111; 1110; timp, str                          MS

Music for Strings (1955)                                 10'
   str                                                     MS

Symphony No. 2 (1956)                                    25'
   3*3*23*; 4331; timp+2, hp, pf, str                    MS

Concertino for Organ and Strings (1957)                   6'
   solo org; str                                         MS

Lament (1957)                                             5'
   solo ob; str                                          RMP

Prelude and Dance (1959)                                  6'
   1111; 1110; perc, str                                 MS

Requiem:  When Lilacs Last in the
   Dooryard Bloom'd (1961)                               40'
   solo s; satb cho; 3*2*23*; 4331; timp+2,              MS
   hp, cel, str

Abstraction for Chamber Orchestra (1962)                  7'
   1*12*1; 0110; timp+10, hp, pf, cel, gtr,              MS
   str (1-0-1-1)

Symphony No. 3
   "The Great American Novel" (1967-1977)                35'
   satb cho; 4*3*3*2; 4431; timp+4, str                  MS

Fragmentation (1968)                                      NA
   2222; 2221; perc, hp, pf, cel, str                    MS

Sonorous Image (1968)                                     6'
   3*223*; 4431; 4perc, hp, pf, str                      MS

Sayings for Our Time (1969)                              14'
   satb cho; 223*2; 4331; 4perc, pf, str                 MS

Listen (1971)                                             9'
   23*3*2; 4431; 6perc, str                              MS

Celebration (1975; rev 1980)                              7'
   2222; 4331; perc, hp, pf, str, tape                   MS

Suite "Billings" (1975)                                  10'
   2222; 2221; timp+1, str                               MS

Symphony No. 4 "American Classic" (1977)                 37'
   soli s, a, t, b; 2222; 2221; timp+4, str              MS

The Age of Innocence (1983)                      14'
   23*22; 2231; timp+1, pf, str                  MS

Symphony No. 5 (1988)                            35'
   3*2*22; 4331; timp+2, hp, str                 MS
   N.B.  The individual movements "Arctic
   Stellar Night", "Echos and Patterns",
   "Illusions in Time Velocity" and "Epilogue"
   may be performed separately.

A Farewell to Leonard Bernstein (1990)            5'
   11*11; 1110; str                              MS

Symphony No. 6 (1991)                            20'
   str                                           MS

Summer Festival Overture (NA)                     5'
   3*222; 3331; timp+2, hp, str                 ACA


      HANSEN, TED  (1935-    )

Three Movements for Orchestra (1968)             19'
   3*222; 4331; timp+1, str                     SEE

Symphony No. 1 (1975)                            35'
   2222; 4331; timp, pf, str                    SEE

Contrasts for English Horn and
   Orchestra (1984)                             23'
   solo eh; str                                 SEE

Contrasts for Alto Saxophone and
   Orchestra (1985)                             15'
   solo a sax; 2222; 0000; str                  SEE


      HANSON, HOWARD  (1896-1981)

Symphony No. 1 "Nordic", op. 21 (1922)           28'
   3*223*; 4331; timp+2, hp, str                CF

Lux aeterna, op. 24 (1923)                       15'
   3*223*; 4331; timp+2, 2hp, str               CF

Lament for Beowulf, op. 25 (1925)                19'
   satb cho; 3*223*; 4331; timp+1, hp, str      CF

Pan and the Priest, op. 26 (1925-1926)           11'
   3*3*23*; 4331; timp+1, pf, str               CF

Symphony No. 2 "Romantic", op. 30 (1930)          27'
   3*3*22; 4331; timp+2, hp, str                      CF

Symphony No. 3, op. 33 (1937-1938)                35'
   3*3*3*3*; 4331; timp, str                          CF

Concerto for Organ, Harp and
   Strings, op. 22, No. 3 (1941)                  15'
   soli org, hp; str                                  CF

Symphony No. 4 "Requiem", op. 34 (1943)           22'
   3*223*; 4331; timp+2, hp, str                      CF

Serenade, op. 35 (1945)                            6'
   soli fl, hp; str                                   CF

Concerto for Piano and Orchestra,
   op. 36 (1948)                                  20'
   solo pf; 3*222; 4331; timp+3, str                  CF

Pastorale, op. 38 (1949)                           6'
   ob, hp, str                                        CF

Cherubic Hymn, op. 37 (1950)                      12'
   satb cho; 3*222; 4331; timp+1, pf, str             CF

Fantasy-Variations on a Theme of Youth,
   op. 40 (1951)                                  12'
   solo pf; str                                       CF

Symphony No. 5 "Sinfonia Sacra",
   op. 43 (1954)                                  16'
   3*3*22; 4331; timp+3, hp, str                      CF

Elegy in Memory of Serge Koussevitsky (1956)      12'
   2*2*22; 4331; timp, hp, str                        CF

Mosaics (1957)                                    10'
   3*3*3*3*; 4331; timp+2, hp, pf, str                CF

Song of Democracy, op. 44 (1957)                  12'
   satb cho; 3*3*22; 4331; timp+2,                    CF
   hp, cel, str

Bold Island Suite (1958)                          28'
   3*3*22; 4331; timp+3, hp, pf, str                  CF

Suite, op. 46 (1961)                              13'
   3*222; 4331; timp, hp, str                         CF

For the First Time (1963)                              16'
   2*222; 2000; perc, hp, pf, str                    CF

Song of Human Rights, op.49 (1963)                     12'
   satb cho; 3*222; 4331; timp+1, str              CF

Summer Seascape II (1965)                               9'
   solo vla; str                                    CF

Dies Natalis I (1967)                                  12'
   3*3*3*3*; 4331; timp+2, str                      CF

Symphony No. 6 (1967)                                  20'
   3*3*3*3*; 4331; timp+3, str                      CF

Two Psalms (CXXI, CL) (1968)                            9'
   solo bar; satb cho; 3*222; 4331; timp, str  CF

Streams in the Desert (1969)                           12'
   satb cho; 3*223*; 4331; timp+3,                  CF
  hp, pf, str

The Mystic Trumpeter (1970)                            16'
   3*3*23*; 4331; timp+2, hp, pf, str               CF

Lumen in Christo (1974)                                13'
   satb cho; 2222; 2220; timp+1, pf/cel, str  CF

New Land, New Covenant - cantata (1976)                70'
   soli s, bar; narr; satb cho; children's          CF
  cho(opt); 3*222; 4331; timp+2, hp, cel, str

Symphony No. 7 "A Sea Symphony" (1977)                 17'
   3*3*3*3*; 4331; timp+1, hp, str                  CF


    HARBISON, JOHN   (1938-      )

Sinfonia for Violin and Orchestra (1963)               10'
   solo vln; 1111; 1110; str                        AMP

The Merchant of Venice (1971)                          12'
   str                                              AMP

Elegiac Songs (1974)                                   20'
   solo mez; 2*22(s sax)2; 2000; perc, str     AMP

Diotima (1976)                                         18'
   3*23*3*; 4331; timp+1, hp, cel, str              AMP

Concerto for Piano and Orchestra (1978)          20'
    solo pf; 2222; 2221; perc, hp, str          AMP

Concerto for Violin and Orchestra (1980)         28'
    solo vln; 2222; 2221; timp+1, hp, pf, str   AMP

Snow Country (1981)                              12'
    solo ob; str                                AMP

Symphony No. 1 (1981)                            23'
    3=3*3*3*; 4231; timp+6, hp, str             AMP

Ulysses' Bow (1983)                              33'
    3*3*4=2*; 4231; timp+4, hp, str             AMP

Ulysses' Raft (1983)                             47'
    3*3*4=2*; 4231; timp+4, hp, str             AMP

Concerto for Oboe, Clarinet and
    Strings (1985)                               13'
    soli ob, cl; str                            AMP

Confinement (1985)                               15'
    11*1*0; a sax; 0110; perc, pf, str          AMP

Remembering Gatsby
    (Foxtrot for Orchestra) (1985)               8'
    3*3*3(s sax)3*; 4331; timp+1,                AMP
    dmst, pf, str

The Flight Into Egypt (1986)                     14'
    soli s, bar; satb cho; 03*01; 0030;         AMP
    org, str

Symphony No. 2 (1987)                            20'
    3*3*4=3*; 4431; timp+3, hp, pf, str         AMP

Concerto for Double Bass and
    Orchestra (1988)                             20'
    solo db; 2222; 4331; timp, str              AMP

Concerto for Viola and Orchestra (1989)          15'
    solo vla; 2*2*2*2; 2200; timp+1,            AMP
    hp, cel, str

HARRIS, DONALD   (1931-      )

Fantasy (1957)                                              8'
   solo vln; 2222; 2220; timp+1,                      JOB
   hp, cel, str

Symphony in Two Movements (1958-1961)                     16'
   3*3*4=3*; 4331; timp+6, hp, cel, str               ELK

On Variations (1976)                                      15'
   12*01; a,t sax; 1110; mar, 2vib, xyl, str   JOB


HARRIS, MATTHEW   (1956-      )

Illuminations (1978)                                      11'
   23*3*3*; 4231; timp+1, 2hp, cel, str               ACA

Music for Orchestra (1982)                                10'
   23*3*2; 4331; timp+5, 2hp, pf, cel, str            ACA

Invitation to the Waltz (1986)                             7'
   str                                               ACA

Ancient Greek Melodies (1987)                             18'
   2222; 2220; timp+3, str                           ACA


HARRIS, ROY   (1898-1979)

Farewell to Pioneers (1935)                               11'
   4*3*3*3; 4331; timp, str                           GS

When Johnny Comes Marching Home (1935)                     8'
   4*3*3*3*; 4331; euph; timp+2, str                  GS

Prelude and Fugue (1936)                                  14'
   str                                               GS

Three Symphonic Essays (1937)                             15'
   3*3*3*2; 4331; timp+2, hp, pf, str                 GS

Symphony No. 3 (1938)                                     18'
   3*3*3*2; 4332; 2timp+4, str                        GS

Challenge (1940)                                          NA
   satb cho; 3*3*4*3*; 4431; timp+3, str             GS

Folksong Symphony (Symphony No. 4) (1940)        43'
   satb cho; 3*3*4*3*; 4331; timp+3, pf, str     GS

Folksong Symphony:  Two Interludes (1940)        38'
   3*3*4*3*; 4331; timp+3, pf, str                GS

Memories of a Child's Sunday (1945)              11'
   3*3*3*3; 2331; timp+3, hp, str                 CF

Blow the Man Down (1946)                         15'
   soli ca, bar; satb cho; 223*1; 2331;           CF
   timp, hp, pf, str

Celebration:  Variations on a Timpani Theme
   from Howard Hanson's "Symphony No. 3"
   (1946)                                         11'
   4*3*3*4*; t,bar sax; 2331; timp+2,              CF
   pf, str

Concerto for Two Pianos and Orchestra (1946)     25'
   soli 2pf; 3*3*3(t sax)3; 4331; timp+1,         CF
   hp, str

Melody (1946)                                    10'
   23*3*3; 4331; timp+4, hp, str                  CF

Radio Piece (1946)                                8'
   solo pf; 2*2*2*2; 1110; timp+2, str            CF

The Quest (1947)                                 15'
   3*3*3*3; 4331; timp+1, hp, str                 CF

Theme and Variations for Accordion and
   Orchestra (1947)                               18'
   solo acc; 113*1; t sax; 1121; timp+2,          CF
   hp, str

Concerto for Violin and Orchestra (1949)         25'
   solo vln; 3*3*3*3; 4331; timp+1,               CF
   hp, pf, str

Kentucky Spring (1949)                           10'
   3*3*3*3; 4331; timp+3, hp, pf, str             CF

Cumberland Concerto (1951)                       18'
   3*3*4*3; 5431; timp+1, pf, str                 FC

Fantasy for Piano and Orchestra
   (1951; rev 1955)                               15'
   solo pf; 2*2*2*1; 2331; timp+2, hp, str        AMP

Symphony No. 7 (1952)                                      19'
   3*3*3*3; 3331; timp+2, hp, str                      AMP

Symphonic Epigram (1954)                                   12'
   3*3*3*3; 4331; timp+1, hp, pf, str               AMP

Give Me the Splendid Silent Sun (1956)                     15'
   solo bar; 3*3*3+3*; 4331; timp+1, pf, str      AMP

Ode to Consonance (1956)                                   10'
   2*2*32; 2321; euph; timp+2, hp, str             AMP

Elegy (1958)                                                6'
   3*3*23; 4331; timp+1, hp, str                   AMP

Symphony No. 8 (St. Francis Symphony) (1962)               23'
   3*3*3*3*; 4331; timp+1, hp, str                 AMP

Symphony No. 9 (1962)                                      27'
   4*3*4*4*; 6441; euph; timp+1, hp, pf, str     AMP

Epilogue to "Profiles in Courage:
   JFK" (1964)                                      10'
   3*3*3*3; 4331; timp+3, str                      AMP

Horn of Plenty (1964)                                      10'
   solo tpt; 3*3*3*3; 4331; euph;                  AMP
   timp+1, str

Salute to Youth (1964)                                     12'
   3*24*2; 4331; timp+1, str                       AMP

Symphony No. 11 (1967)                                     19'
   4*4*4*4*; 6442; euph; timp+1, hp,               AMP
   pf, cel, str

Pere Marquette Symphony
   (Symphony No. 12) (1968)                         45'
   solo t; 3*3*3*4*; 5331; euph; timp+4, str   AMP


HARRIS, RUSSELL  (1914-    )

Swanee River Variations, op. 29 (1946)                     24'
   3222; s sax; 4231; timp+3, cel,                 ACA
   glock, str

Minnesota Centennial Prelude, op. 33 (1958)                 7'
   3222; 4231; timp+3, pf, glock, str              ACA

Three Movements for Orchestra, op. 40 (1969)    10'
    1*202; 2000; hpsd, str                          ACA

Variations-Pastorale-Dance, op. 41 (1970)       11'
    2202; 2000; hpsd, str                           ACA


            HARRISON, LOU  (1917-    )

Symphony No. 3 (1937-1982)                      30'
    3*3*3*3*; 4331; 3perc, hp, tack pf,          CFP
    cel, str

Mass to St. Anthony (1939-1954)                 25'
    satb cho; tpt; hp, str                          PS

Elegiac Symphony (1941-1975)                    31'
    3*3*33*; 4331; timp+3, 2hp, pf, tack pf,     PS
    cel, org, str

Easter Cantata (1943-1956)                      12'
    satb cho; tpt; hp, str                          MS

Suite No. 1 (1947)                              20'
    str                                             CFP

Suite No. 2 (1948)                              17'
    str                                             PS

Symphony on G (1948-1961)                       35'
    2330; 2220; timp+5, 2hp, pf, str                PS

The Marriage at the Eiffel Tower (1949)         22'
    2222; 0220; perc, pf, str                       CFP

Seven Pastorales (1952)                         7'
    2101; 0000; hp, str                             PS

Four Strict Songs (1955)                        14'
    soli 8bar; 2tbn; perc, pf, str                  AMP

Suite for Symphonic Strings (1960)              20'
    str                                             CFP

Pacifika Rondo (1963)                           25'
    fl, picc, niguk piris(or s sax/a sax/cl),    PS
    3tbn, jahla(or cel), vib,
    sheng(or psaltery), kayageum(or hp/psaltery),
    hpsd, org, 5perc(pale, b dr, chango, daiko,
    elephant bells, jahlataranga, gongs), str

Symphony No. 4 (1985)                              45'
  solo t; 3*3*3*3*; 4331; perc, hp,              PS
  tack pf, cel, str

Piano Concerto (1985)                             25'
  solo pf; 3tbn, 4perc, 2hp, str                 CFP


          HART, WELDON   (1911-1957)

Symphony No. 1 (1946)                             22'
  3*222; 4331; timp+2, str                        CF


          HARTKE, STEPHEN   (1952-    )

Symphony No. 1 (1974-1976)                        21'
  3=3*24; 2a sax; 44(picc)31; 3perc, str         FLE

The Bull Transcended (1981)                        6'
  str                                             PS

Two Songs for an Uncertain Age (1982)             16'
  solo s; 3*3*3*3*; 4331; timp+2, hp,            MMB
  pf, cel, str

Alvorada (1983)                                   18'
  str                                            MMB

Maltese Cat Blues (1986)                          16'
  3*3*3+3; 4331; 4perc, str                      MMB

Precession (1986)                                  4'
  11*11; 1100; 2perc, pf, str (1-1-1-1)          MMB

Pacific Rim (1988)                                10'
  2*3*2+2; 4220; perc, str                       MMB

Symphony No. 2 (1991)                             23'
  2222; 2200; perc, hp, cel, str                 MMB


          HARTLEY, WALTER   (1927-    )

Ballet Music for Orchestra (1949)                 14'
  2*2*22; 4231; timp+1, hp, str                  FEM

Sinfonietta (1950)                                12'
  3*222; 4231; timp+1, hp, pf, str               FEM

Three Patterns for Small Orchestra (1951)    5'
  2222; 2210; timp+1, hp, str    FEM

Triptych (1951)    15'
  2*2*22; 2210; timp+3, str    FEM

Concerto for Piano and Orchestra (1952)    19'
  solo pf; 3*2*22; 4331; timp+2, str    FEM

Elegy for Strings (1952)    4'
  str    FEM

Chamber Symphony (1954)    13'
  1*111; 2110; hp, str    GAL

Concert Overture (1954)    8'
  2*222; 4231; timp+1, str    FEM

Scenes from Lorca's "Blood Wedding" (1956)    15'
  2222; 4231; timp+1, hp, str    ACC

Sonatina for Trumpet and
  Small Orchestra (1956)    6'
  solo tpt; 2222; 2210; timp, str    ACC

Elizabethan Dances (1962)    4'
  2222; 2220; timp+3, str    FEM

Sinfonia No. 2 (1962)    12'
  2*222; 4331; timp+2, str    FEM

Festive Music for Orchestra (1963)    4'
  2222; 4231; timp+3, str    FEM

Partita for Chamber Orchestra (1964)    16'
  1111; 2100; str (1-1-1-0)    GAL

Psalm for Strings (1964)    5'
  str    TP

Variations for Orchestra (1973)    10'
  3*222; 4331; timp+4, str    FEM

Rhapsody for Tenor Saxophone and
  String Orchestra (1979)    8'
  solo t sax; str    DRN

Euphonium Concerto (1980)    11'
  solo euph; 2222; 2211; timp+1, str    ACC

Concertante for Timpani (1981-1982)                8'
    solo timp; 2*222; 4231; perc, str             GAL

Symphony No. 3 (1983)                              14'
    3*3*3*3; 4331; timp+1, hp, str                 GAL

Sinfonia No. 7 (1986)                              8'
    2*12*1; 2211; timp+2, str                      KAL

Concerto No. 2 for Alto Saxophone and Small
    Orchestra (1989)                               11'
    solo a sax; 2121; 2210; timp+1, str            DRN

Fantasia for Tuba and Chamber
    Orchestra (1989)                               9'
    solo tba; 2*121; 2210; str                     WJ


        HASS, JEFFREY  (1953-    )

Chimera (1989)                                     13'
    3*3*3*3*; 4331; timp+4, hp, pf/cel, str        MMB

City Life (1990)                                   10'
    1*1*10; 1110; perc, pf, amp str (2-1-1-1)      MMB


        HAUBIEL, CHARLES  (1892-1978)

1865 A.D. (1945)                                   5'
    3*3*22; 4331; timp+1, hp, str                  TCP

Father Abraham - cantata (1945)                    6'
    soli 2a, t, b; satb cho; 213*1; 2331;          TCP
    timp+1, hp, str

Pioneers:  A Symphonic Saga of Ohio (1946)         18'
    3*3*22; 4331; timp+4, hp, str                  ELK

American Rhapsody (1948)                           10'
    3*3*22; 4331; timp+4, hp, str                  TCP

Portals (1963)                                     33'
    2*121; 2110; timp, hp, str                     TCP

Heroic Elegy (1965)                                12'
    3*3*3*2; 4331; timp+2, hp, str                 FLE

Gothic Variations (1968)                                    17'
  solo vln; 2*222; 2220; timp+1, hp, str          TCP


HAUFRECHT, HERBERT   (1909-    )

The Little Red Hen (1945)                                   12'
  narr; 1110; 2110; cel, str                       ACA

A Walk in the Forest (1951)                                 6'
  narr; 1111; 1100; perc, str                      ACA

When Dad was a Fireman (1953)                               14'
  23*3*3*; 4331; timp+1, str                        ACA

Suite for Orchestra (1959)                                  14'
  3*23*2; 4331; timp+1, str                         ACA

Divertimento (1982)                                         13'
  solo gtr; 2221; 2210; perc, str                  ACA

Suite on Catskill Mountain Tunes (1986)                     12'
  1222; 2000; str                                  ACA


HAXTON, KENNETH   (1919-    )

Moses (1965)                                                80'
  soli s, a, t, b; narr; satb cho; 2222;          ACA
  4331; timp+1, hp, pf, str

Chorale Prelude and Fugue (1970)                            11'
  223*2; 4331; timp, str                           ACA

Elegy (1971)                                                10'
  2222; 4231; timp+1, str                          ACA

A Psalm Cycle (1972)                                        45'
  soli s, t; satb cho; 2222; 4331; timp+1,         ACA
  hp, pf, str

Concerto No. 1 for Piano and
  Orchestra (1973)                                 45'
  solo pf; 23*3*2; 4331; timp+1, str               ACA

A Rose for Emily (1973)                                     7'
  223*2; 4231; timp+1, str                         ACA

Largo (1979)                                                9'
  str                                              ACA

Fugue (1981)                                                    4'
   2222; 4331; timp+1, str                       ACA

Music for English Horn and Strings (1982)      7'
   solo eh; str                                  ACA

Involvement (1984)                                             8'
   223*3*; 4331; timp+1, str                     ACA

Welty Women - Suite for Orchestra (1985)       43'
   23*3*2; 4331; timp+1, pf, str                 ACA


     HAYS, DORIS   (1941-    )

Southern Voices for Orchestra (1981)           18'
   solo s; 4*3*3*3*; 4331; timp+2, pf, str       CFP


     HAZZARD, PETER   (1949-    )

Harwichport Interlude (1971)                                   4'
   214=0; 1110; timp+1, str                      SEE


     HEATH, JIMMY   (1926-    )

Afro-American Suite of Evolution (1975)        60'
   soli s, t, bar, b; 0000; 2a,2t,bar sax;      MJQ
   0441; 2perc, dmst, pf, gtr, str


     HEIDEN, BERNHARD   (1910-    )

Concerto for Small Orchestra (1949)            18'
   1121; 2100; str                               AMP

Euphorion (1949)                                               12'
   3*222; 4331; timp+1, str                      AMP

Symphony No. 2 (1954)                                          24'
   3*222; 4331; timp+1, str                      AMP

Memorial (1955)                                                14'
   2222; 4231; timp+1, str                       AMP

Triple Concerto (1957)                                         27'
   soli pf, vln, vc; 2222; 4330; timp, str       AMP

Variations for Orchestra (1960)     16'
   3\*3\*3\*3\*; 4331; timp+3, hp, str     AMP

Envoy (1963)     8'
   3\*3\*3\*3\*; 4331; timp+1, str     AMP

Concertino for String Orchestra (1967)     18'
   str     AMP

Concerto for Cello and Orchestra (1967)     16'
   solo vc; 3\*222; 4330; timp+1, str     AMP

Concerto for Horn and Orchestra (1969)     15'
   solo hn; 2222; 0210; timp+1, str     AMP

Partita (1970)     18'
   2\*2\*3=2\*; 4431; timp+1, hp, str     AMP

Concerto for Tuba and Orchestra (1976)     17'
   solo tba; 3\*222; 4330; 2perc, str     PS

Triptych (1982)     10'
   solo bar; 3\*3\*3\*3\*; 4331; timp+3, hp, str   AMP

Recorder Concerto (1987)     19'
   solo rec; 0201; 2000; str     MMB

Salute for Orchestra (1989)     8'
   3\*2\*22; 4231; timp+2, str     MMB


     HEILNER, IRWIN   (1908-1991)

Suite for Harp and Chamber Orchestra (1946)     18'
   solo hp; 113(s,a,t sax)0; 2200;     ACA
   timp+2, str

Concerto in Memory of Dvorak (1952)     18'
   solo vln; 2222; 4330; timp+2, str     ACA


     HELLERMANN, WILLIAM   (1939-    )

Time and Again (1969)     13'
   2222; 4220; timp+1, hp, pf, str     MER

Anyway (1977)     15'
   2222; 4220; 2perc, hp, pf, str     ACA

HELM, EVERETT   (1913-      )

Brasiliana - Suite for Orchestra (1946)          12'
   3*23*3*; 4331; timp+2, hp(opt), str           FLE

Concerto No. 1 for Piano and
   Orchestra (1951)                              24'
   solo pf; 3*222; 4321; timp+2, str             SCH

Italian Suite (1952)                             12'
   2*111; 2220; str                              BB

Three Gospel Hymns (1953)                        16'
   3*222; 4320; timp+1, str                      AMP

Concerto No. 2 for Piano and
   Orchestra (1956)                              15'
   solo pf; 2221; 2210; 2perc, str               BB

Serenade (1957)                                  14'
   soli eh, cl, bsn; str                         BB

Concerto for Five Solo Instruments
   and Strings (1958)                            15'
   soli fl, ob, bsn, tpt, vln; str               SCH


HELPS, ROBERT   (1928-      )

Symphony No. 1 (1957)                            22'
   3*3*3*3*; 4331; timp+1, pf, str               AMP

Cortege (1963)                                   10'
   2222; 4231; timp+1, str                       ACA

Concerto for Piano and Orchestra (1969)          20'
   solo pf; 23*3*2; 3431; timp+1, hp, str        CFP

Concerto No. 2 for Piano and
   Orchestra (1976)                              14'
   solo pf; 3*3*3*3*; 4231; timp+1, hp, str      AMP

Gossamer Noons (1977)                            18'
   solo s; 2222; 4330; timp+1, pf, str           CFP


HEMMER, EUGENE   (1929-1977)

Sunshine Games (1954)                            17'
   2221; 2110; timp+3, hp, cel, str              TP

The Midnight Ride of Paul Revere (1955)          10'
  3*3*3*3*; 4331; timp+1, hp, str               TP

The Voice of the Grand Piano
  Concertino for Piano and Orchestra (1956)     25'
  solo pf; 3*3*3*2; 4331; timp+3, hp,           TP
  cel, str

A Festival of Spirituals (1957)                 12'
  solo bar; ttbb cho; 1121; 2210; timp, str     TP

Idyll for Oboe and Orchestra (1958)              7'
  solo ob; 1111; 2010; timp, cel, str           TP


        HENNAGIN, MICHAEL  (1936-      )

Passacaglia for Orchestra (1960)                11'
  2*101; 2330; 3perc, hp, pf/cel, str           MS

A Summer Overture (1963)                         7'
  2*222; 4220; 3perc, hp, pf, str               MS

Symphonic Essay (1963)                          22'
  3*2*3*2; 4331; 4perc, hp, pf/cel, str         MS

Explorations for Orchestra (1970)               10'
  2222; 2221; 2perc, str, tape(opt)             MS

Variations on an Oh so Familiar Tune (1970)     17'
  ssaattbb cho; 1111; 1210; 2perc, pf,          MS
  str (no vc, db)

A Meditation (1982)                             12'
  satb cho; 1111; 1110; perc, hp, pf,           MS
  str (2-1-1-1)

A Song of Songs (1988-1989)                     40'
  soli s, bar; satb cho; 3333; 4331;            MS
  timp+3, hp, pf, str


        HERMAN, MARTIN

Cantos (1980)                                   13'
  1*11*0; 111(b tbn)0; perc, hp, gtr, str       MS

Canticle for the Sacred Heart (1981)            20'
  satb cho; 1=11*1; 111(b tbn)0; perc, hp,      MS
  8 handbell players, str

Interludes from "The Scarlet Letter" (1985)    12'
   3*3*3*3*; 4221; timp+3, hp, pf/cel, str     MS

Scripts for a Pageant (1986)                    16'
   solo s; DX-7 synth, hurdy-gurdy,             MS
   str, tape

Hawthorne Symphony (1987-1989)                  22'
   3*3*3*3*; 4221; timp+3, hp, pf/cel, str     MS

...from The River Why (1989)                    30'
   narr; 2*2*2*2; 2220; perc, pf, str          MS


         HERRMANN, BERNARD   (1911-1975)

A Portrait of Hitch - suite (1969)               8'
   3*23*2; 4000; timp, 2hp, str                TP


         HERVIG, RICHARD   (1917-    )

Trio Concertino (1956)                          13'
   soli cl, pf, vln; 3*222; 4231; timp, str    MS

Music for a Concert (1959)                       8'
   3*3*22; 4331; timp+1, hp, pf, str           ACA

Symphony (1960)                                 18'
   3*222; 4331; timp+1, pf, str                MS

In those Days (1987)                            15'
   2*222; 4431; timp+5, hp, pf, str            MS


         HEUSSENSTAMM, GEORGE   (1926-    )

Chamber Symphony, op. 16 (1963)                 12'
   1111; 1110; perc, str (2-1-1-1)             SEE

Litany of L.H., op. 24 (1967)                   35'
   satb cho; 1111; 1110; perc, str (1-0-1-1)   SEE

Das Dreieck, op. 27 (1968)                      17'
   1111; 1000; 2perc, str (1-1-1-0)            SEE

Scherzo, op. 31 (1969)                          10'
   1111; 1111; 2perc, str                      SEE

Seventeen Impressions, op. 35 (1970)           19'
    1110; 1000; timp+5, pf, str (1-1-1-1)       SEE


    HEWITT, HARRY DONALD  (1921-    )

N.B.  Mr. Hewitt's works are contained in two
sections.  The symphonies are listed by number.
The remainder of his works are listed by year
of commencement.

Symphony No. 4, op. 59 (1941-1952)              25'
    2*233*; 4330; timp+2, pf, cel(opt), str     FLE

Symphony No. 5, op. 74 (1945-1946)             32'
    2*2*22*; 2220; timp+1, pf/cel, str          FLE

Symphony No. 6, op. 82 (1952; rev 1976)        19'
    3*223*; 4221; timp+3, str                   FLE

Symphony No. 7, op. 91 (1946-1950)             26'
    2(2picc)2*22; 4220; timp, str               FLE

Symphony No. 8, op. 103 (1948-1952)            28'
    2*222; 4220; timp+2, str                    FLE

Symphony No. 9, op. 112 (1945-1950)            55'
    4*4*4*3*; 4431; timp+1, pf, str             FLE

Symphony No. 10, op. 121 (1946-1949)           45'
    3333; 4331; timp+3, pf, cel, str            FLE

Symphony No. 11, op. 133 (1946-1950)           25'
    3322; 4230; timp+3, hp, pf, cel, str        FLE

Sympnony No. 13, op. 150 (1946-1950)           35'
    2222; 2220; timp+2, str                     FLE

Symphony No. 14, op. 162 (1946-1950)           35'
    3*3*33*; 4321; timp+3, str                  FLE

Symphony No. 15, op. 171, (1949-1951)          26'
    3*3*3*3*; 4431; timp+1, str                 FLE

Symphony No. 16, op. 180 (1955-1977)           36'
    2*122; 2221; timp+2, hp, cel, str           FLE

Symphony No. 18, op. 200
    (1952-1956; rev 1978)                       22'
    2*3*2+3*; 4221; timp+1, hp, cel, str        FLE

Symphony No. 19, op. 212 (1953-1955)                          22'
  2(2picc)3*3*2; 2220; timp+3, str                            FLE

Symphony No. 22, op. 446 (1975)                              23'
  3*3*33*; 4321; timp+3, str                                  FLE

Symphony No. 23, op 450 (1978-1981)                          19'
  2223; 4221; timp+3, cel(opt), str                           FLE

Symphony No. 24, op. 462 (1955-1982)                         32'
  3(3picc)23+2; 4221; timp+3, str                             FLE

Symphony No. 25, op. 464 (1977-1983)                         17'
  334+3*; 4331; 3perc, str                                    FLE

Symphony No. 26, op. 466 (1978-1982)                         27'
  satb cho; 3*3*33*; 4331; timp+3, cel, str                   FLE

Symphony No. 27, op. 458 (1982)                              28'
  22*3*3*; 4231; timp+3, cel, str                             FLE

Symphony No. 31, op. 476 (1982-1986)                         26'
  2(2picc)3*3+3*; 4221; timp+4, hp,                           FLE
  cel, str

Symphony No. 32, op. 478 (1984)                              21'
  2*2*22; 3321; timp+2, cel,str                               FLE

Prelude to "A New Testament",
  op. 53, No. 5 (1945)                                        8'
  2101; 1100; pf, str                                         FLE

When Spring is Near, op. 281, No. 34
  (1946; rev 1987)                                            5'
  str                                                         FLE

Taming of the Shrew - Overture,
  op. 53, No. 6 (1948)                                        8'
  1111; 1100; timp, str                                       FLE

A Good-Natured Overture,
  op. 57, No. 1 (1948)                                        6'
  2222; 4220; timp, str                                       FLE

Ode, op. 26, No. 1 (1949)                                    8'
  str                                                         FLE

Earth Songs, op. 283 (1949-1959)                             40'
  str                                                         FLE

Night of Hecate, op. 26, No. 6 (1950)           4'
   str                                             FLE

Concerto Grosso No. 1, op. 184, No. 1 (1950)    6'
   solo str qnt; str                               FLE

Concerto Grosso No. 2, op. 184, No. 2 (1950)    11'
   double str orch                                 FLE

Concerto Grosso No. 3, op. 184, No. 3 (1950)    5'
   double str orch                                 FLE

Concerto Grosso No. 4, op. 184, No. 4 (1950)    6'
   double str orch                                 FLE

Under the Birches, op. 242 (1950-1960)          16'
   str                                             FLE

The Flowers Have No Mothers,
   op. 281, No. 37 (1950)                          3'
   str                                             FLE

Sinfonia No. 2, op. 40, No. 2 (1951)            12'
   2221; 2200; timp+1, hp, str                     FLE

Seven, op. 196, No. 1 (1951-1954)               10'
   2(2picc)2*3+2; 2220; timp+1, hpsd, str          FLE

Divertimento No. 1, op. 231, No. 1 (1951)       12'
   2hn; str                                        FLE

To a Green Soul, op. 279, No. 1 (1951)          15'
   2*2*22; 2220; timp, hp, str                     FLE

The Wheel, op. 294, No. 1 (1951-1968)           5'
   3*3*3*3*; 4221; timp+4, str                     FLE

The Sad Snowman - suite,
   op. 170b (1952-1980)                            14'
   str                                             FLE

Moonscapes, op. 216 (1952-1977)                 18'
   4(2picc)14*2; 4240; timp+4, str                 FLE

The Quiet Journey, op. 281, No. 28 (1953)       5'
   timp, str                                       FLE

Dark Journey, op. 25, No. 7 (1954)              3'
   str                                             FLE

A Summer in Blue and Green, op. 201a (1954)     9'
    2122; 2100; 2perc, 2hp, str                 FLE

Scars on the Clock's Face,
    op. 281, No. 27 (1954)                       3'
    1*111; 0100; perc, str                      FLE

At the Gate of the Kingdom of Fools,
    op. 350, No. 1 (1954-1964)                  12'
    11*00; 1000; pf, str                        FLE

The Golden Door, op. 279, No. 2 (1956)          7'
    8(2picc)2(2eh)30; 6330; perc, str           FLE

Aunt Frieda's Stove,
    op. 329, No. 2 (1956-1986)                   9'
    1122; 2010; hp(opt), glock, str             FLE

Anglesley Abbey, op. 380 (1957-1959)            18'
    2121; 2000; timp+1, hp, str                 FLE

Night Without Neon, op. 281, No. 5 (1958)        6'
    1=011; 1110; timp+2, str                    FLE

Haunted House,
    op. 329, No. 1 (1958; rev 1978)              7'
    2*111; 2010; timp+1, hp, cel, str           FLE

In Other Gardens, op. 203 (1960-1980)           24'
    2112; 2110; timp, str                       FLE

The Magic Fountain - suite from ballet
    op. 422 (1966; rev 1986)                    28'
    2222; 4320; timp+1, hp, str                 FLE

Yugen, op. 426, No. 1 (1967)                    var
    4(2picc)2*22; 4221; timp+3, pf, str         FLE

Wizard's Eggs, op. 425, No. 1 (1968)             8'
    3*232; 4321; timp+2, 2pf, str               FLE

Return of the White-Throat,
    op. 333, No. 2 (1969-1979)                  10'
    33*32; 4220; timp+2, str                    FLE

The Stars Will Heal Us,
    op. 420, No. 1 (1969)                       10'
    solo vln (opt); 6(6picc, 2opt)222; 3220;    FLE
    2perc, 2pf, str

Concerto for Piano and Orchestra   No. 2,
  op. 435 (1970)                                                      40'
  solo pf; 3*3*22; 2220; timp+1, str                                 FLE

Return of the Night-Hawk,
  op. 333, No. 2 (1974)                                               7'
  221(a cl)2; 4111; perc, hp(opt), pf, str                           FLE

Entering, op. 165, No. 1 (1975-1986)                                 4'
  0222; 4210; timp, glock, str                                       FLE

The Loveliness of Longwood,
  op. 369 (1975-1987)                                                 40'
  2222; 2220; timp, hp, cel, str                                     FLE

Haven, op. 426, No. 3 (1975)                                         9'
  6666 (all opt); 6777; timp+1, pf, str                             FLE
  N.B. Strings are divisi in 30 parts.

Satori, op. 425, No. 2 (1976)                                        3'
  22*2+2; 4011; perc, pf, str                                        FLE

Morning of the Moss Roses, op. 449 (1976)                           27'
  str                                                                FLE

Concertino for String Bass and
  Small Orchestra, op. 455 (1977)                                   18'
  solo db; 1111; 2000; timp+1, str                                  FLE

Now That I Am God, op. 156, No. 2 (1978)                            5'
  21*40; 0002; 5perc, hp, str                                        FLE

Fantasia on Old Welsh Airs,
  op. 327, No. 1 (1979)                                              9'
  str                                                                FLE

Fantasia on Old British Airs,
  op. 327, No. 2 (1979)                                              11'
  str                                                                FLE

The Triumph of Flora, op. 431 (1979)                                22'
  3(3picc)3(2eh)33; 4330; timp+3, hp, str                           FLE

Fantasia for Oboe, Two Horns and Strings,
  op. 213, No. 4 (1980-1985)                                         6'
  0100; 2000; str                                                    FLE

Beautiful Morris, op. 417b (1980)                                   30'
  2222; 2221; timp+1, str                                            FLE

In the Sun, op. 434 (1980-1982)                              14'
  3*2*3*2*; 4331; timp+3, hp, cel, str                       FLE

Concerto for Guitar and Orchestra,
  op. 463 (1981)                                             25'
  solo gtr; 2*222; 2222; perc, str                          FLE

A Tribute to Three Masters,
  op. 284, Nos. 1-3 (1982-1985)                              5'
  2*1*31; 0000; 3perc, hp, cel, str                         FLE

Folk Fantasia No. 3, op. 327, No. 3 (1985)                   4'
  str                                                        FLE

The Good Samaritan, op. 275, No. 2 (1986)                    5'
  ssaattbb cho; 1011; 2321; 3perc, str                      FLE

Beyond the Blue Mountains,
  op. 425, No. 2 (1986)                                      9'
  02*21; 2111; 3perc, str                                   FLE


            HIBBARD, WILLIAM   (1939-1989)

Processionals (1980)                                         12'
  3*23*2; 4231; str                                         AMP

Concerto for Viola and Orchestra (1981)                      23'
  solo vla; 2+2*2*1; 0430; 3perc,                           AMP
  hp, pf, str

Sinfonia on Expanding Matrices (1983)                        8'
  str                                                        ACA


            HILL, JACKSON   (1941-    )

Variations for Orchestra (1964)                              13'
  2222; 4331; timp+2, str                                   FLE

Mosaics (1965)                                               15'
  2222; 4331; timp+2, pf, str                               FLE

Ceremonies of Spheres (1973)                                 20'
  3*3*3*3*; 4321; timp+2, str                               FLE

Paganini Set (1973)                                          8'
  1201; 2000; str                                           FLE

Sangraal (1977)                                              9'
    2222; 4231; timp+1, hp, str                            FLE

Chambers (1988)                                             12'
    1121; 1000; pf, str                                     MS

Toccata Nipponica (1989)                                   12'
    2222; 2210; perc, pf, str                               MS

Secrets (Himitsu) (1990)                                    7'
    1121; 1000; pf, str                                     MS

Symphony No. 1
    (Sinfonia Nipponica) (1988-1990)                       33'
    2222; 2210; pf, str                                     MS

Symphony No. 2
    (Sinfonia Canonica) (1986-1990)                        40'
    2222; 4321; perc, str                                   MS


        HILLER, LEJAREN  (1924-      )

Divertimento for Chamber Ensemble,
    op. 25 (1958)                                          37'
    1*1*11; 1110; timp+4, cel, gtr, str                    TP

A Preview of Coming Attractions (1975)                     14'
    3*3*3*3*; 4431; timp+3, hp, str                        TP

A Triptych for Hieronymous (NA)                            41'
    1101; a,t sax; 0222; 3perc, hp, hpsd,                  TP
    mand, gtr, cel, str, tape, actors,
    dancers, films, lantern slides


        HILLIARD, JOHN  (1947-      )

The Grand Traverse (1975)                                  20'
    solo tpt/flu hn; 223*2; 2331; hp, str                 ACA

Symphony in Two Movements (1983)                           22'
    3*3*3*3*; s sax; 4331; timp+5, 2hp,                   ACA
    cel, str

Symphony of Nocturnes (1991)                               18'
    3*3*3*2; 4331; 5perc, hp, pf/cel, str                ACA

HOAG, CHARLES  (1931-      )

November 22, 1963 (1964)                                    9'
    solo ob; str                                           MS

Fantasy on a Bach Chorale (1966)                           12'
    223*2; 4331; timp+2, str                               FLE

Encounter for Orchestra (1967)                             11'
    2222; 4231; timp+1, str                                FLE

Symphonic Movement (1970)                                  10'
    3*3*3*2; 4331; timp+2, hp, pf, str                     MS

Concerto for Double Bass and
    Orchestra (1978)                                       18'
    solo db; 223*2; 4331; timp+1, gtr, str                 MS

Pianoplay II (1987)                                        14'
    solo pf; 223*2; 4331; timp+2, str                      MS

Cloud Tango (1990)                                         12'
    3*3*3*2; 4331; timp+2, str                             MS

When the Yellow (Dream) Leaves Fell (1990)                 12'
    2222; 2200; perc, str                                  MS

Ephemeral Gestures (1991)                                  12'
    solo bsn; 2*2*2*1; 1100; perc, str                     MS

An After-Intermission Overture (NA)                        10'
    2222; 4331; timp+1, pf, str                            GS

A Vinland Narrative (NA)                                   12'
    3*23*2; 4231; timp+2, hp, str                          MS


HODKINSON, SYDNEY  (1934-      )

Laments (1957)                                             8'
    1111; 0000; str                                        ACA

Dynamics (Five Miniatures) (1960)                          5'
    2222; 4231; 3perc, pf, str                             ACA

Caricatures (1966)                                         8'
    2222; 4331; timp+2, hp, str                            RIC

Fresco (Symphony No. 1) (1968)                             20'
   3*3*3*3*; a sax; 4331; timp+3, hp,                    JOB
   pf/cel, elec gtr, str

Drawings:   Set No. 7 (1970)                               4'
   str                                                    TP

Drawings:   Set No. 8 (1970)                               4'
   str                                                    TP

Stabile (1970)                                             9'
   3*222; 4331; timp+2, pf, str                           JOB

Valence (1970)                                             7'
   1212; 2000; 2perc, str                                 JOB

Epigrams (1971)                                            10'
   333+3; t sax; 4431; timp+3, hp, pf, str                MER

November Voices (1975)                                     11'
   soli s, t; narr; 2010; 2321; 3perc, hp,                TP
   str (1-0-2-1)

Celestial Calendar (1976)                                  12'
   str                                                    ACA

Edge of the Olde One (1976)                                28'
   solo elec eh; 2perc, str                               MER

Missa Brevis (1978)                                        20'
   satb cho; 2222; 2200; perc,                            MER
   handbells, str

Chansons de Jadis (1978-1979)                              28'
   solo s (or t); 2222; 2200; 2perc, str                  MER

Sinfonia concertante (Symphony No. 5) (1980)  18'
   1212; 2000; pf, str                                    MER

Tango, Boogie and Grand Tarantella (1980)                 10'
   solo db; 2*222; 4221; timp+2, hp, str                  MER

Bumberboom (Scherzo diabolique) (1982)                    15'
   3=3*3=3*; 4331; timp+3, hp, str                        AMP

Burning Bell (1985)                                        7'
   2narr; 2121; 2211; timp+3, str                         ACA

Cantata Appalachia (1987)                            45'
    soli s, bar; satb cho; 2*2*2*2*; 2111;           AMP
    2perc, hp, cel, str

Symphony No. 6 (1988)                                30'
    solo vln; 2222; 4331; timp+1, hp,                MER
    pf, cel, str

Epitaphium (1990)                                    13'
    3*332*; 4331; timp+3, hp/cel, str                MER

Overture - A Little Travelin' Music
    (The Can Opener) (1991)                          9'
    2*222; 4331; timp+4, hp, str                     MER


              HOFFMANN, RICHARD   (1925-     )

Violin Concerto (1948)                               15'
    solo vln; 3*3*3*3*; 4331; timp+3, str            MS

Orchestra Piece No. 1 (1952)                         7'
    1111; 2110; perc, str                            CFP

Piano Concerto (1953-1954)                           17'
    solo pf; 3*3*3*3*; 4331; timp+4, str             MS

Cello Concerto (1956-1959)                           16'
    solo vc; 3*3*3*3*; 3431; 6perc,                  BOE
    hp, pf, str

Orchestra Piece No. 2 (1961)                         20'
    22*2*2*; 2221; timp+4, hp, 2pf, str              UE

Memento Mori (1966-1969)                             25'
    ttbb cho; 002(b cl, cb cl)4*; 0031;              BOE
    perc, hp, 2pf, str (0-0-12-12)

Music for Strings (1970-1971)                        22'
    solo vln; str                                    BOE

Stouffler (1975-1976)                                15'
    3*3*3*3*; 4331; timp+3, hp, pf, str,             MS
    16 track tape
    N.B.  Performed without conductor.

Lacrymosa '91 (1990)                                 10'
    ssaattbb cho; 3*3*3*3*; 4331; timp+3,            MS
    hp, pf, str

HOGG, MERLE   (1922-      )

Concerto for Trombone and Orchestra
   (1954; rev 1967)                                                   18'
   solo tbn; 1121; 2000; str                                         MGP


HOIBY, LEE   (1926-      )

Pastoral Dances, op. 4 (1950)                                         NA
   solo fl; 1*121; 2100; timp, hp, str                               RVM

Noctambulation, op. 2 (1952)                                          7'
   3*222; 4331; timp, hp, str                                        RVM

Second Suite for Orchestra, op. 8 (1953)                             17'
   3*3*3*2; 4331; timp+2, hp, cel, str                               RVM

Study in Design, op. 9 (1953)                                         5'
   str                                                                BH

Overture to a Farce, op. 15 (1958)                                    7'
   3*222; 4331; timp+1, hp, str                                      RVM

A Hymn of the Nativity, op. 19 (1960)                                30'
   soli s, bar; satb cho; 2*2*2*2; 2221;                             RVM
   timp+2, hp, str

The Tides of Sleep, op. 22 (1961)                                    10'
   solo bar; 223*2; 4331; timp+2, hp,                                 BH
   cel, str

After Eden, op. 25 (1967)                                            17'
   2*2*2*2; 4331; timp+2, hp, pf/cel, str                            RVM

Landscape, op. 26 (1968)                                             20'
   2*2*2*2; 4331; timp+2, hp, pf, str                                RVM

Where The Music Comes From (1972)                                    4'
   solo s; 2020; 0000; hp, str                                        GS

Galileo Galilei, op. 29 (1975)                                       55'
   soli 7vv; satb cho; 3*3*3*2; 4331;                                RVM
   timp+2, hp, cel, str

Hymn to the New Age (1976)                                           4'
   satb cho; 2*222; 4321; timp+2, hp,                                RVM
   org, str

Music for a Celebration, op. 30 (1976)            10'
  2*222; 4331; timp+2, hp, cel, str            TP

A Christmas Carol (1977)                           5'
  satb cho; 2222; 4221; timp+1, hp, str      RVM

Concerto No. 2 in D, op. 33 (1979)               30'
  solo pf; 2*2*2*2; 2210; perc, str           RVM

The Serpent (1979)                                 4'
  solo s; 2*111; 0001; perc, hp, str          PS

Serenade, op. 44 (1986)                           11'
  solo vln; 2*121; 2100; hp, str             RVM

I Have a Dream, op. 46 (1987)                     10'
  solo bar; 1121; 2220; timp+1, hp, str      RVM

Rock Valley Narrative, op. 50 (1989)             11'
  2*2*2*2; 4321; timp+1, str                  RVM

The Nations Echo Round, op. 55 (1991)            15'
  sa cho; 2*2*2*2; 4321; timp+1,             RVM
  hp, pf, str


### HOLLINGSWORTH, STANLEY (1924-    )

Stabat Mater (1957)                                9'
  satb cho, 2222; 2210; timp, hp, pf, str    GS

Divertimento (1972)                               12'
  2*222; 4221; timp+3, hp, pf, str          BEL

Concerto for Piano and Orchestra (1979)          15'
  solo pf; 2*22*2; 2100; timp+2, str        BEL

Concerto for Violin and Orchestra (1980)         15'
  solo vln; 2*22*2; 2100; str                GS

Three Ladies by the Sea (1982)                   10'
  narr; 2111; 0200; timp+1, hp,             BEL
  pf, cel, str


### HOLT, DARRELL (1941-    )

Symphony Concertante (1966)                       15'
  1111; 1100; str                             MS

Songs of Love (1984)                                        6'
    solo tbn; 2222; 4231; timp+1, str                      MS


        HOPKINS, JAMES  (1939-      )

Dance Suite (1960)                                         16'
    1*1*1*1; 2110; perc, hp, pf, str                       MS

Theatrikomelos (1962)                                      16'
    2*1*11; 2110; 2perc, hp, pf, str                       MS

Elegy and Dithyramb (1963)                                21'
    3*3*22; 4331; 3perc, hp, pf, str                       MS

Concerto for Two Pianos and Orchestra (1964)  13'
    soli 2pf; 3*2*22; 4331; 2perc, hp, str                 MS

Symphony No. 1 (1964)                                     15'
    4*33=3*; 4331; 3perc, 2hp, pf/cel, str                 MS

Three Pieces for Orchestra (1965)                         12'
    4*4(eh, hklph)33*; 4441; timp+3,                       MS
    hp, pf, str

Variations for Orchestra (1966)                           10'
    3*2*2*2; 4331; 2perc, hp, pf/cel, str                  MS

Phantasms (1968)                                          18'
    solo s; 5(4picc,a fl)3*3*3*; 4441;                     MS
    timp+4, 2hp, pf, cel, hpsd, b gtr, str

Revelations and Transformations (1969)                    12'
    2=11*1; 1230; 2perc, hp, pf, cel, str                  MS

Visions of Hell (Symphony No. 4) (1975)                   21'
    3*3*3*3*; 4331; timp+4, pf/cel, str                    MS

Concert Variations for Violin, Piano
    and Orchestra (1977)                                   21'
    soli vln, pf; 2*222; 4331; 3perc, hp, str  MS

Concerto for Contrabass and Orchestra (1977)  16'
    solo db; 2*2*22; 4231; 3perc, hp, str                  MS

Symphony No. 5 (1978)                                     19'
    4=3*4*4*; 4441; timp+3, hp, pf/cel,                    MS
    org, str

Voces Organi (1979)                                    15'
    solo org(4 hands); 2perc, str                       MS

Fantasy on `Cortege et Litanie' (1990)                 13'
    2*2*2*2*; 2211; 2perc, hp, pf/cel, str              MS


        HORBAN, WALTER  (1941-    )

Australis (1989)                                        8'
    solo fl; str                                       MMB


        HORVIT, MICHAEL  (1932-    )

Symphony No. 1 (1959)                                   25'
    2222; 4231; timp+1, str                            SHA

Toccatina (1968)                                        3'
    2222; 2330; timp+2, str                            SHA

The Gardens of Hieronymus B. (1976)                    12'
    3*3*3*3*; 4331; timp+1, hp, str                    SHA


        HOVHANESS, ALAN  (1911-    )

Storm on Mt. Wildcat (1931)                             6'
    2222; 4331; timp+1, str                            MS

Monadnok, op. 2, No. 1 (1935)                          5'
    2222; 4331; timp, str                              CFP

Missa Brevis, op. 4 (1935)                             12'
    solo b; satb cho; org, str                         CFP

Concerto for Cello and Orchestra,
    op. 17 (1936)                                      25'
    solo vc; 2222; 4330; timp, hp, str                 CFP

Psalm and Fugue, op. 40a (1940)                        6'
    str                                                CFP

Alleluia and Fugue, op. 40b (1940)                     10'
    str                                                MS

Armenian Rhapsody No. 2, op. 5 (1944)          5'
  str                                          MS

Celestial Fantasy, op. 44 (1944)              7'
  str                                          MS

Armenian Rhapsody No. 1, op. 45 (1944)        5'
  perc, str                                    PS

Lousadzak "The Coming of Light",
  op. 48 (1944)                               18'
  solo pf; str                                 PS

Khrimian Hairig, op. 49 (1944)                9'
  solo tpt; str                                CFP

Elibris "God of Dawn", op. 50 (1944)          10'
  solo fl; str                                 PS

Tzaikerk "Evening Song", op. 53 (1945)        10'
  soli fl, timp, vln; str                      PS

Anahid, op. 57 (1945)                         14'
  11*00; 0100; timp+1, str                     CFP

Prayer of St. Gregory, op. 62b (1946)         4'
  solo tpt; str                                BRO

Kohar, op. 66, No. 1 (1946)                   8'
  11*00; 1000; timp, str                       CFP

Agori, op. 66, No. 2 (1946)                   10'
  soli fl, eh, bsn, tpt; timp, str             FUJ

Symphony No. 8 "Arjuna", op. 179 (1947)       25'
  11*11; 1000; timp, pf, str                   CFP

Angelic Song, op. 19 (1948)                   12'
  solo s (or t); hn; str                       CFP

Avak the Healer, op. 64 (1948)                20'
  solo s; tpt; str                             PS

Haroutiun, op. 71 (1948)                      10'
  solo tpt; str                                CFP

Sosi "The Forest of Prophetic Sound",
  op. 75 (1948)                               10'
  solo vln; hn; timp, tam-tam, pf, str         PS

30th Ode of Solomon, op. 76 (1948)                30'
   solo bar; satb cho; tpt, tbn; str             CFP

Zartik Parkim, op. 77 (1949)                      15'
   1020; 2200; timp+1, pf, str                   PS

Artik, op. 78 (1949)                              15'
   solo hn; str                                  CFP

Janabar, op. 81 (1949)                            35'
   soli tpt, pf; str                             PS

Concerto No. 3 "Diran", op. 94 (1949)             6'
   solo tbn; str                                 RKI

Symphony No. 9 "St. Vartan", op. 180 (1950)       40'
   0000; a sax; 1410; timp+2, pf, str            PS

Concerto No. 1 "Arevakal", op. 88 (1951)          15'
   2222; 2200; timp+1, hp, str                   AMP

Concerto No. 2, op. 89a (1951)                    20'
   solo vln; str                                 CFP

Shepherd of Israel, op. 192 (1951)                12'
   solo t; 1000; 0100; str                       IMI

Talin, op. 93 (1952)                              14'
   solo vla; str                                 AMP

As on the Night, op. 100, No. 2 (1952)            5'
   solo s; 0200; 2000; hp, cel, str              AMP

Partita, op. 98, No. 1 (1953)                     12'
   solo pf; str                                  CFP

Concerto No. 4, op. 98, No. 2 (1953)              14'
   32*22; 4231; timp, hp, str                    CFP

Easter Cantata, op. 100, No. 4 (1953)             16'
   solo s; satb cho; 0200; 2300; perc,           AMP
   hp, cel, str

Concerto No. 6, op. 114 (1953)                    35'
   solo hca; str                                 PS

Canticle, op. 115 (1953)                          10'
   solo s; ob; xyl, hp, cel, str                 CFP

Concerto No. 7, op. 116 (1953)                      20'
    2222; 4231; timp+1, hp, cel, str                AMP

Symphony No. 5, op. 170 (1953; rev 1963)            10'
    2222; 4331; timp+1, hp, cel, str                CFP

Vision from High Rock, op. 123 (1954)               11'
    2222; 2200; timp+1, hp, cel, str                CFP

The Stars, op. 126 (1954)                            6'
    solo s; satb cho; eh; hp, cel, str              CFP

Symphony No. 13, op. 190 (1954)                     20'
    11*11; 1000; timp+3, hp, str                    CFP

The Beatitudes, op. 100, No. 3 (1955)                8'
    satb cho; 0200; 2000; hp, cel, str              AMP

Symphony No. 2 "Mysterious Mountain",
    op. 132 (1955)                                  17'
    3*3*3*3*; 5331; timp, hp, cel, str              AMP

Anabasis, op. 141 (1955)                            45'
    soli s, bar; narr; satb cho; 12*10; 2100;       CFP
    timp+1, hp, str

Ad Lyram, op. 143 (1955)                            12'
    soli s, a, t, b; ssaattbb cho; 33*3*3*;         CFP
    5331; timp+1, hp, str

Symphony No. 3, op. 148 (1956)                      22'
    3*3*3*3*; 5331; timp+1, hp, str                 CFP

Concerto No. 8, op. 117 (1957)                      20'
    2222; 2210; timp+1, hp, str                     CFP

Meditations on Orpheus, op. 155 (1957)              14'
    3*3*3*3*; 4331; timp+1, hp, cel, str            CFP

Magnificat, op. 157 (1958)                          28'
    soli s, a, t, b; satb cho; 0200; 2210;          CFP
    perc, hp, str

In Memory of an Artist,
    op. 163 (1958; rev 1968)                         7'
    str                                             CFP

Blue Flame, op. 172 (1959)                          26'
    soli s, t, b; satb cho; 2222; 4231;             CFP
    timp+1, hp, str

Symphony No. 6 "Celestial Gate",
  op. 173 (1959)                                    18'
  1111; 1100; timp+1, hp, str                      CFP

Concerto for Accordion and Orchestra,
  op. 174 (1959)                                    10'
  solo acc; 2222; 2000; timp, hp, str               CFP

Symphony No. 10 "Vahaken", op. 184 (1959)          18'
  11*11; 1110; timp+2, hp, str                      CFP

Fuji, op. 182 (1960; rev 1964)                     12'
  ssa cho; fl; hn; str                              CFP

Symphony No. 11 "All Men Are Brothers",
  op. 186 (1960; rev 1969)                          29'
  3*3*3*3*; 4331; timp+2, hp, str                   CFP

Symphony No. 12, op. 188 (1960)                    25'
  satb cho; 1000; 0200; timp+2, hp,                 CFP
  str, tape(opt)

Mountain of Prophecy, op. 195 (1961)               10'
  3*3*22; 4331; timp+1, 2hp, str                    CFP

Wind Drum, op. 183 (1962)                          26'
  unis male cho; dancers; fl; timp+2,               CFP
  hp, str

Symphony No. 15 "Silver Pilgrimmage",
  op. 199 (1962)                                    20'
  2222; 4331; 3perc, hp, str                        CFP

Symphony No. 16, op. 202 (1962)                    16'
  timp+2, 6 Korean instr (kayakeum, janggo,         CFP
  zwago, 3pyunjong), hp, str

Symphony No. 18 "Circe", op. 204a (1963)           15'
  2222; 2231; timp+2, hp, cel, str                  CFP

In the Beginning was the Word,
  op. 206 (1963)                                    27'
  soli a, b; satb cho; 12*10; 0110;                 CFP
  3perc, hp, str

Variations and Fugue, op. 18 (1964)                13'
  3*3*22; 4331; timp+1, hp, glock, str              CFP

Meditation on Zeami, op. 207 (1964)                18'
  3*3*3*3; 4331; timp+3, hp, str                    CFP

Floating World "Ukiyo", op. 209 (1964)            12'
   3*3*22; 4331; timp+3, hp, cel, str             CFP

Island Sunrise, op. 107 (1965)                     5'
   3*3*3*3*; 4331; timp+6, 2hp, cel, str          CFP

Fantasy on Japanese Woodprints,
   op. 211 (1965)                                 15'
   solo xyl; 3*222; 4331; timp+3,                 CFP
   hp, cel, str

The Holy City, op. 218 (1965)                      8'
   solo tpt; chime in A, hp, str                  CFP

Ode to the Temple of Sound, op. 216 (1966)        14'
   3*3*22; 4331; timp+1, hp, cel, str             CFP

Symphony No. 19 "Vishnu", op. 217 (1966)          30'
   3*3*3*3*; 4331; timp+6, 2hp, cel, str          CFP

Fra Angelico, op. 220 (1967)                      16'
   3*3*3*3*; 4331; timp+4, 2hp, cel, str          CFP

Adoration, op. 221 (1968)                         21'
   solo fem v (or fem cho with soli s, a          CFP
   or male cho with soli t, b); 1110;
   0110; chimes, cel, str

Praise the Lord with Psaltery,
   op. 222 (1968)                                 21'
   satb cho; 3*23*3*; 4331; perc,                 CFP
   hp, cel, str

Vibration Painting, op. 226 (1968)                12'
   str                                            CFP

Lady of Light, op. 227 (1969)                     38'
   soli s, bar; satb cho; 11*22; 2200;            CFP
   timp+3, hp, str

Shambala, op. 228 (1969)                          33'
   soli vln, sitar; 3*222; 4331; timp+4,          CFP
   hp, str

A Rose for Miss Emily, op. 229, No. 2 (1969)      30'
   1*111; 1111; timp+1, pf, str                   CFP

And God Created Great Whales, op. 229 (1970)      12'
   3*222; 4331; timp+4, 2hp, str, tape            CFP

Symphony No. 21 "Etchmiadzin",
  op. 234 (1970)              15'
  2tpt; timp+2, str        CFP

Symphony No. 22 "City of Light",
  op. 236 (1971)             21'
  3*23*3*; 4331; timp+3, hp, str  CFP

Khorhoort Nahadagats, op. 251 (1972)  50'
  solo oud(or gtr or lute); str  PS

Concerto for Harp and Strings,
  op. 267 (1973)             11'
  solo hp; str          ACA

Symphony No. 24 "Majnun", op. 273 (1973)  38'
  solo t; solo vln; satb cho; tpt; str  AMP

Symphony No. 25 "Odysseus", op. 275 (1973)  36'
  1*110; 1111; timp+1, str  PS

The Way of Jesus, op. 278 (1974)  85'
  soli s, t, b; satb cho; 3*222; 4331;  PS
  timp+4, hp, str

Symphony No. 26 "Consolation",
  op. 280 (1975)             35'
  3*222; 3431; timp+4, hp, str  PS

Ode to Freedom, op. 284 (1976)  12'
  solo vln; 3*222; 4331; timp+4, hp, str  FUJ

Symphony No. 27, op. 285 (1976)  35'
  1100; 1100; timp+2, str  FUJ

Symphony No. 28, op. 286 (1976)  26'
  11*00; 0100; timp, str  FUJ

Symphony No. 29, op. 289 (1976)  25'
  solo euph; 3*222; 4331; timp+4, hp, str  FUJ

Symphony No. 30, op. 293 (1976)  20'
  1100; 0100; str  FUJ

Symphony No. 31, op. 294 (1976)  30'
  str  FUJ

Symphony No. 32 "The Broken Wings",
  op. 296 (1977)             33'
  1110; 1100; perc, str  FUJ

Symphony No. 33, op. 307 (1977)                    35'
    101*0; 0110; perc, str                          FUJ

Symphony No. 34, op. 310 (1977)                    20'
    solo b tbn; str                                 FUJ

Adoration, op. 221 (1978)                           21'
    solo s (or t); 1110; 0110; chimes,              CFP
    cel, str

Symphony No. 35 for Two Orchestras,
    op. 311 (1978)                                  35'
    orch 1:  Korean instr:  sogeum, daegeum,        FUJ
    piri, haegeum, keomongo, ahjaeng, janggu,
    jwago, 2pyeon kyeong
    orch 2:  33*3*3*; 4332; timp+4, hp, str

Symphony No. 36, op. 312 (1978)                    30'
    solo fl; 3*3*3*3*; 4331; timp+3, hp, str        FUJ

Symphony No. 37, op. 313 (1978)                    30'
    2222; 4331; timp+1, hp, str                     FUJ

Symphony No. 38, op. 314 (1978)                    52'
    solo s; fl; tpt; str                            FUJ

Symphony No. 39, op. 321 (1978)                    30'
    solo gtr; 3*3*22; 4331; timp+2, hp, str         FUJ

Symphony No. 40, op. 324 (1979)                    15'
    0000; 1211; timp, str                           FUJ

Symphony No. 41, op. 330 (1979)                    15'
    0000; 1210; str                                 FUJ

Symphony No. 42, op. 332 (1979)                    20'
    1000; 0110; str                                 FUJ

Symphony No. 43, op. 334 (1979)                    18'
    0100; 0100; timp, str                           FUJ

Concerto for Guitar, op. 325 (1980)                30'
    solo gtr; 3*3*22; 4331; timp+3, str             FUJ

Copernicus, op. 338 (1980)                          7'
    2222; 4330; timp+3, hp, str                     FUJ

Symphony No. 44, op. 339 (1980)                    18'
    1100; 0100; timp+1, str                         FUJ

Greek Rhapsody No. 2, op. 341 (1980)              12'
   3*222; 4331; timp, str                        CFP

Revelation of St. Paul, op. 343 (1980)            70'
   soli s, t, bar; satb cho; 3*222; 4331;         FUJ
   timp+2, hp, str

Concerto for Soprano Saxophone,
   op. 344 (1980)                                 15'
   solo s sax; str                                FUJ

Symphony No. 48 "Vision of Andromeda",
   op. 335 (1982)                                 30'
   3*222; 4331; timp+4, hp, str                   FUJ

Symphony No. 50 "Mount St. Helens",
   op. 360 (1982)                                 25'
   3*3*22; 4331; timp+4, hp, str                  CFP

Symphony No. 51, op. 364 (1982)                   17'
   tpt; str                                       MS

Symphony No. 52 "Journey to Vega",
   op. 372 (1983)                                 30'
   1111; 2211; timp, str (solo or section)        MS

Symphony No. 54, op. 378 (1983)                   17'
   2222; 4331; timp, str                          MS

Symphony No. 55, op. 379 (1983)                   20'
   3*222; 4331; timp+1, hp, pf, str               MS

Symphony No. 56, op. 380 (1983)                   17'
   3*222; 4331; timp, pf, str                     MS

Symphony No. 57 "Cold Mountain",
   op. 381 (1983)                                 37'
   solo s or t; cl; str (solo or section)         FUJ

Symphony No. 58 "Symphony Sacra",
   op. 389 (1985)                                 20'
   soli s, bar; 1000; 1100; timp+1, hp, str       MS

Guitar Concerto No. 2, op. 394 (1985)             14'
   solo gtr; str                                  MS

Symphony No. 59, op. 395 (1985)                   40'
   3322; 4331; timp+4, hp, str                    FUJ

Symphony No. 60, op. 396 (1985)
 "To the Appalachian Mountains"                30'
 3*3*22; 4331; timp+4, hp, str                 FUJ

Symphony No. 61, op. 397 (1986)                15'
 3*222; 4331; timp+4, hp, str                  MS

HOWE, HUBERT, JR.  (1942-    )

Scherzo (1975)                                 12'
 223*2; 4221; str                              ACA

Elegy for Strings (1987)                       5'
 str (6-2-3-1, all separate parts)             ACA

Concerto for Piano and Strings (1989)          9'
 solo pf; str (each section divisi)            ACA

Symphony (1989)                                40'
 2222; 4221; str                               ACA

Essay (1990)                                   19'
 23*3*2; 4221; pf, str                         ACA

HUGGLER, JOHN  (1928-    )

Elegy, op. 2 (1952)                            6'
 2222; 2330; timp+1, str                       CFP

Concerto for Horn and Orchestra,
 op. 17 (1957)                                 11'
 solo hn; 2220; 0000; timp+1, str              CFP

Toccata (1958)                                 3'
 2222; 2331; perc, hp, str                     MS

Ecce Homo, op. 30 (1959)                       15'
 4=4*4*3*; 4331; timp+1, hp, str               CFP

Concerto for Violin and Orchestra,
 op. 31 (1960)                                 14'
 solo vln; 2021; 0331; timp+1, hp, str         CFP

Divertimento for Viola and Orchestra,
 op. 32 (1960)                                 11'
 solo vla; 3021; 0230; timp+1, hp,             CFP
 str (no vla)

"D" into Blossom, op. 36 (1960)                        6'
   3221; 4230; timp+1, hp, str                    CFP

Cantata, op. 50 (1962)                                 5'
   satb cho; 3033; 2330; perc, str                CFP

Sculptures, op. 39 (1964)                             14'
   solo s; 4030; 4660; timp+4, pf, str            CFP

Music in Two Parts, op. 64 (1965)                     14'
   4030; 4430; timp+1, hp, str                    CFP

Desert Forms, op. 65 (1965)                            7'
   3(a rec)022; 4331; timp+1, hp, str             CFP

Elaborations, op. 69 (1966)                           10'
   solo a sax; 2222; 4331; timp+1, hp, str        ACA

Variations for Orchestra, op. 73 (1970)               14'
   2*222; 4330; timp+1, hp, str                   CFP

Seven Songs, op. 74 (1972)                            18'
   solo s; 2222; 4330; timp+1, hp, str            CFP

Symphony in Three Movements (1980)                    20'
   222*2; 4331; timp+2, hp, str                   CFP

Continuum (1986)                                      10'
   2222; 2330; 3perc, hp, str                      MS


## HUNT, FREDERICK (1906-1967)

Symphony in G Minor (1964)                            24'
   2*222; 4230; timp, str                         FLE

Doric Concerto (1965)                                 NA
   soli s sax, a sax; 1111; 2000; hp, str         FLE

Canzona for Chamber Orchestra (1967)                  NA
   12*22; 2100; str                               FLE


## HUNT, MICHAEL (1945-    )

Theme in Two Moods (1971)                              4'
   2222; 4231; 2perc, pf, str                     MMB

Asymptopia I (1972)                                    7'
   3*221; 2231; 3perc, pf, str                    MMB

Asymptopia II (1972)                                          8'
    3*221; 2231; 3perc, pf, str                              MMB

Con Cordes (1987)                                            7'
    str                                                      MMB

Hidden Walls of Time (1987)                                  28'
    3perc, str                                               MMB

Lento (1988)                                                 9'
    str                                                      MMB

Emerald Reflections (1989)                                   12'
    2*2*22; 4231; 2perc, str                                 MMB


        HUSA, KAREL   (1921-      )

Three Fresques (1947)                                         13'
    solo vla; 0100; 1000; pf, str                            MS

Divertimento (1948)                                          15'
    str                                                      SCH

Concertino for Piano and Orchestra (1949)                    16'
    solo pf; 2222; 2200; timp+1, str                         SCH

Musique d'amateurs (1952)                                    15'
    0100; 0100; perc, str                                    SCH

Portrait (1953)                                              11'
    str                                                      SCH

Symphony No. 1 (1953)                                        26'
    3*3*3*2*; 4331; timp+3, 2hp, pf, str                     SCH

Festive Ode (1955)                                           4'
    satb cho; 3*3*3*3*; 4331; timp+2, str                    HG

Four Little Pieces (1955)                                    14'
    str                                                      SCH

Fantasies (1956)                                             19'
    1*110; 0300; perc, pf, str                               SCH

Poem for Viola and Chamber Orchestra (1959)                  13'
    solo vla; 0100; 1000; pf, str                            SCH

Elegie et Rondeau (1961)                                     10'
    solo a sax; 2222; 2200; 6perc, pf, str                   LED

Mosaiques (1961)                                                15'
    2*2*2*1; 2220; timp+4, hp, cel, str                        SCH

Fresco (1963)                                                  11'
    3*3*3*3*; 4331; timp+2, hp, pf, str                        AMP

Serenade (1963)                                                16'
    1111; 1000; xyl, hp(or pf), str                            LED

Concerto for Brass Quintet and
    String Orchestra (1965)                                    24'
    solo br qnt; str                                           AMP

Music for Prague, 1968 (1969)                                  19'
    3*3*3*3*; 4431; timp+4, hp, pf, str                        AMP

Two Sonnets by Michaelangelo (1971)                            16'
    3*3*22; a sax; 4331; timp+2, hp, str                       AMP

Apotheosis of this Earth (1972)                                25'
    satb cho; 4*4*4*3*; 4441; timp+2, str                      AMP

The Steadfast Tin Soldier (1974)                               26'
    narr; 2*222*; a sax; 221(b tbn)0;                          AMP
    timp+3, hp, str

Monodrama: Portrait of an Artist (1976)                        23'
    3*3*3*3*; 4331; timp+4, hp, str                            AMP

An American Te Deum (1976-1977)                                45'
    solo bar; satb cho; 3*3*3*3*; 4431;                        AMP
    timp+4, str

Pastorale (1979)                                               7'
    str                                                        AMP

The Trojan Women - ballet suite (1980)                         22'
    2*2*2*2*; 221(b tbn)0; timp+3,                             AMP
    hp, pf, str

Symphony No. 2 "Reflections" (1983)                            20'
    2*2*2*2*; 2200; timp+2, hp, str                            AMP

Symphonic Suite (1984)                                         19'
    3*33*3*; 4331; timp+4, hp, pf, str                         AMP

Concerto for Orchestra (1986)                                  39'
    3=3*3*3*; 5431; timp+5, hp, pf, str                        AMP

Concerto for Organ and Orchestra (1987)          21'
   solo org; 3tpt; 2perc, str                    GS

Concerto for Trumpet and Orchestra (1987)        20'
   solo tpt; 2*22*2*; 2200; timp+3, hp, str      GS

Concerto for Violoncello and
   Orchestra (1988)                              28'
   solo vc; 3*3*3*3*; 4331; timp+3, hp, str      MS


          HUTCHESON, JERE  (1938-    )

Transitions for Orchestra (1972)                 10'
   2222; 2221; 2perc, str                        SEE

Metaphors (1985)                                 14'
   3*3*3*2; 4331; timp+2, cel, str               ACA

Concerto for Violin and
   Small Orchestra (1987)                        18'
   solo vln; 1111; 1110; timp, cel, str          ACA


          HUTCHISON, WARNER  (1930-    )

Prairie Sketch (1956)                            5'
   2122; 1210; str                               SEE

Psalm CXLII (1957)                               6'
   solo s; 323*2; 4331; timp+2, str              CCM

The Prairie Grass Dividing (1958)                6'
   solo s; 223*3*; 4331; str (divisi)            CCM

Prologue for Symphony Orchestra (1959)           5'
   223*2; 4331; str (divisi)                     CCM

Lyric Piece (1962)                               3'
   str                                           CCM

Let Us Be Grateful (1964; rev 1976)              4'
   satb cho; 223*2; 4221; timp+2, str            CCM

The Sacrilege of Alan Kent (1971)                22'
   solo bar; 33*3*3*; 4331; timp+6,              SEE
   str (div a 3+4), tape

Three Love Songs (1973; orch'd 1988)                11'
    solo s (or t); 223*2; 2000; 2perc,            CCM
    hp, str

Death-Words from the Cherokee (1976)                18'
    solo s; 223*0; 0000; 2perc, gtr,              CCM
    str, tape

Varied Carols
    I Hear America Singing (1986)                 11'
    1121; 2210; timp+3, str                       CCM
    OR:   2122; 2210; timp+2, hp, synth, str

The Desert Shall Bloom as the Rose (1988)           6'
    323*2; 4331; timp+2, hp, cel, str             KJO

Tombeau for Leonard Bernstein (1991)                6'
    cl; 2perc, str                                CCM

IANNACCONE, ANTHONY   (1943-     )

Suite (1962)                                            19'
  3*3*3*3*; 4331; timp+2, hp, str                      MS

Magnificat (1963)                                      26'
  solo 4vv; satb cho; 3*3*3*3*; 4331;                  SEE
  timp+4, 2hp, pf, cel, str

Symphony No. 1 (1965)                                  47'
  3*3*3*3*; 8431; timp+4, hp, str                      MS

Symphony No. 2 (1966)                                  23'
  3*3*3*3*; 4331; timp+2, hp, str                      MS

Lysistrata (1968)                                       9'
  3*3*3*3*; 4331; timp+2, hp, pf, cel, str             SEE

Concertino for Violin and Orchestra (1969)            18'
  solo vln; 2222; 2220; timp+3, hp,                    MS
  pf/cel, str

The Prince of Peace (1970)                             37'
  solo 4vv; satb cho; 324=2; 4331; timp+2,             CF
  hp, pf/cel, str

Divertimento (1983)                                    11'
  3*23*2; 4331; timp+3, hp, pf/cel, str                TP

Night Rivers (1990)                                    15'
  323*2; 4331; timp+3, hp, pf, cel, str                TP


IMBRIE, ANDREW   (1921-     )

Ballad in D (1947)                                      7'
  3*3*3*2; 4331; timp+1, pf, str                       SHA

On the Beach at Night (1949)                            5'
  satb cho; 002*0; 0000; str                           SHA

Three Songs (1949)                                     10'
  1.  Mabel Osborne                                    SHA
  2.  Spectral Lovers
  3.  The Telephone
  solo s; 2222; 2200; timp, hp, str

Concerto for Violin and Orchestra (1954)          37'
    solo vln; 3*3*3*3*; 4331; timp+1,              SHA
    hp, cel, str

Little Concerto for Piano (1956)                  11'
    solo pf(4 hands); 3*222; 2221; timp,          SHA
    xyl, str

Legend (1959)                                     12'
    3*3*3*3*; 4331; timp+1, hp, cel, str          SHA

Symphony No. 1 (1965)                             33'
    3*3*3*3*; 4331; timp+1, hp, cel, str          SHA

Chamber Symphony (1968)                           18'
    111+1; 1110; hp, pf, str                      SHA

Symphony No. 2 (1970)                             21'
    3*3*3*3*; 4331; 2perc, 2hp, cel, str          SHA

Symphony No. 3 (1970)                             20'
    3*3*3*3*; 4331; timp+1, 2hp, cel, str         SHA

Concerto for Cello and Orchestra (1972)           30'
    solo vc; 4*3*4=3*; 4331; timp+1, hp,          SHA
    cel, str

Concerto No. 1 for Piano and
    Orchestra (1973)                              16'
    solo pf; 1121; 2100; timp+4, pf, str          SHA

Concerto No. 2 for Piano and
    Orchestra (1974)                              26'
    solo pf; 23*3*3*; 4331; timp+3, hp,           SHA
    cel, str

Concerto for Flute and Orchestra (1977)           30'
    solo fl; 3*3*3*3*; 4331; perc, hp,            SHA
    cel, str

Prometheus Bound (1980)                           35'
    soli s, t, bar; satb cho; 3*3*3*3*; 4331;     MS
    timp+2, pf, str

Requiem: In Memoriam
    John H. Imbrie (1962-1981) (1984)             27'
    solo s; satb cho; 3=3*3*3*; 4331; timp+1,     SHA
    hp, cel, mand, str

INCE, KAMRAN    (1960-     )

Concerto for Piano and Orchestra (1984)          19'
    solo pf; 3*222; 4231; timp+3, str            EAM

Infrared Only (1985)                             10'
    3*233; 4331; timp+3, hp, str                 EAM

Before Infrared (1986)                           10'
    3*233; 4331; timp+3, hp, str                 EAM

Ebullient Shadows (1987)                         14'
    4*344; 4331; timp+3, hp, pf, str             EAM

Deep Flight (1988)                               11'
    1111; 2231; timp+1, pf, str                  EAM

Symphony No. 1 "Castles in the Air" (1989)       28'
    3*3*3*3*; 4331; timp+3, pf, str              EAM


IVEY, JEAN EICHELBERGER    (1923-     )

Little Symphony (1948)                           15'
    3*3*22; 4331; timp+1, str                    CF

Passacaglia for Chamber Orchestra (1954)         5'
    1111; 1110; timp+1, str                      CF

Festive Symphony (1955)                          12'
    2222; 4331; timp+3, str                      AMC

Overture for Small Orchestra (1955)              5'
    2222; 2000; str                              CF

Ode for Orchestra (1965)                         7'
    2222; 4231; perc, str                        CF

Tribute: Martin Luther King (1969)               28'
    solo bar; 3*3*3*3*; 4331; perc, str          CF

Circling (1972)                                  10'
    3*3*3*3*; 4331; 2perc, hp, pf, str           CF

Forms in Motion (1972)                           25'
    3*3*3*3*; 4331; timp+3, hp, pf/cel, str      CF

Testament of Eve (1976)                          25'
    solo mez; 2222; 4231; timp+1, hp,            CF
    cel, str, tape

Sea Change (1979)                                          20'
   3*3*3*3*; 4331; timp+4, hp, str,                    CF
   4-channel tape

Voyager: for Solo Cello and Orchestra (1987)    25'
   solo vc; 3*3*3*3*; 4000; timp+2, cel, str    CF

Short Symphony (1988)                                      15'
   3*3*3*3*; 4331; timp+3, hp, str              CF

JACOBI, FREDERICK  (1891-1952)

Concerto for Piano and Strings (1946)          17'
   solo pf; str                                    TP

Two Pieces in Sabbath Mood (1946)              10'
   12*2*1; 2210; timp+2, str                       FLE

Symphony No. 2 in C  (1947)                     21'
   3*3*3*3*; 4331; timp+3, hp, cel, str             FLE

Music Hall Overture (1948)                      6'
   2*222; 4331; timp+4, hp, pf, str                LEE


JACOBS, KENNETH  (1948-    )

"Caravans" (Symphony No. 1) (1979)             19'
   str, tape                                       NSE

"Gestures in the Face of Time"
   (Symphony No. 2) (1985)                         41'
   solo s; 1111; 2121; timp+1, str                 NSE

"Gypsy Nights" (Symphony No. 3) (1987)         20'
   2222; 4231; timp+1, str                         NSE

Concerto for Orchestra (1991)                  25'
   2222; 4231; timp+1, str                         NSE


JAFFE, STEPHEN  (1954-    )

Three Yiddish Songs (1975; rev 1977)           23'
   solo mez; 2021; 211(bs)0; perc, hp,             TP
   pf/cel, str (2-1-1-1)

Three Images (1979)                            16'
   solo vv; narr; satb cho; 4tbn; perc, str        TP

Four Images (1983)                             21'
   3=3*3*3*; 43*21; 4perc, 2hp, pf/cel, str        TP

The Rhythm of the Running Plough
   (1985; rev 1988)                                14'
   1=111; 1000; 2perc, hp, str                     TP

Autumnal (1986)                                          24'
    2*2*2*2; 4221; timp+2, str                           TP


            JAGER, ROBERT   (1939-    )

Concerto Grosso
    (for Dance Band and Orchestra) (1964)                17'
    dance band: 2a, 2t, bar sax; 4tpt, 4tbn;             ELK
    pf, db, dmst
    orch: 3*222; 4331; timp+1, str

Three Pieces for Orchestra (1965)                         5'
    2222; 2220; timp+1, str                              ELK

The War Prayer (1973)                                    14'
    narr; 3*23*2; 4331; timp+3, hp, str                  MS

A Child's Garden of Verses (1976)                        12'
    2122; 2220; 2perc, str                               MS

Concerto for Tuba and Orchestra (1979)                   13'
    solo tba; 3*23*2; 4330; timp+3, hp, str              ELK

Symphony No. 3 (1990)                                    18'
    3*3*3*3*; 4331; timp+3, pf, str                      MS


            JAMES, CHRISTOPHER   (1951-    )

Lohengrin Follies (1985)                                 18'
    3*3*3*3*; 4331; timp+3, hp, str                      NOA


            JAMES, PHILIP   (1890-1975)

Symphony No. 2 (1946)                                    27'
    6*223*; 4331; timp+1, hp, str                        TP

Miniver Cheever and Richard Corey (1947)                 11'
    3*3*22; 2200; timp+1, str                            TP

Chaumont (1948)                                          10'
    3*3*22; 2200; timp, hp, str                          TP

Passacaglia (1951; orch'd 1956)                           7'
    3*223*(opt cbsn); 4331; timp+1, hp, str              FLE

Overture to a Greek Play (1952)                          12'
    3*223*; 4331; timp+1, hp, pf, str                    FLE

JANSON, THOMAS   (1947-    )

Revelations for Orchestra (1970)                  8'
  4*24=2; 4331; timp+3, hp, pf/hpsd, str          MS

Departures (1975)                                20'
  3=3*3*3*; 4231; 3perc, pf/cel, str             MS

Concerto for Organ and Chamber
  Orchestra (1976)                               30'
  solo org; 1111; 0000; perc, str                MS

Symphonia (Musica Ficta) (1979)                  30'
  2*2*2*2; 2110; timp+1, hp, str                 MS

Variations for Orchestra (1982)                  19'
  12*12; 2100; 2perc, hp, mus saw(opt), str      MS

Nocturne (1989)                                  15'
  1121; 1111; 2perc, hp, str                     MS

Skyscape (1991)                                   5'
  223*2; 2231; 2perc, str                        MS


JAZWINSKI, BARBARA   (1950-    )

Music for Symphony Orchestra (1970)               6'
  4*4*4*4*; 6331; 4perc, str                     ACA

Overture in the Classical Style (1970)            7'
  2111; 4200; timp, str                          ACA

Essay for Soprano and Orchestra (1972)            9'
  solo s; 2220; 4300; 2perc, pf, str             ACA

Music for Symphony Orchestra (1973)              16'
  3*3*3*3*; 4221; 2perc, pf, str                 ACA

Music for Chamber Orchestra (1974)               10'
  1111; 1100; 2perc, pf, str                     ACA

Cantique de Saint-Jean (1976)                     8'
  satb cho; 3*222; 1100; 2perc, hp, pf, str      ACA

Concerto for Cello and Orchestra (1980)          18'
  solo vc; 1111; 1110; 2perc, pf, str            ACA

Stryga (1984)                                    32'
  3*3*3*3*; 6321; 3perc, pf, str                 ACA

### JENNI, DONALD MARTIN   (1937-      )

Concertino for Piano and Orchestra
  (1953; rev 1958)                                17'
  solo pf; 2222; 2110; timp+1, str               ACA

Frescamento (1953)                                7'
  2222; 4321; timp+1, hp, str                    ACA

Elegy and Dance (1961)                            5'
  1121; 1110; timp+2, str                        ACA

Divertimento (1961)                              17'
  2222; 2221; timp, str                          ACA

From the Top - Variantics on a Tune
  for Young Orchestra (1961)                      6'
  2222; 4231; timp+1, str                         MS

In Memoriam Fratris Catulli (1962)                8'
  str                                            ACA

Inventio Super Nomen (1965)                      10'
  1111; 1110; timp+2, pf, gtr, str               ACA

Le Kaleidoscope de Gide (1966)                    8'
  1221; 0000; timp+2, pf, cel, hpsd, str         ACA

R-music - Asphodel (1969)                         8'
  2+020; 0020; 5perc, hp, pf, cel, toy pf,       ACA
  str (0-0-5-4)

Eulalia's Rounds (1971)                           9'
  5(picc, 2a fl, b fl)23*3*; 5440; timp+10,      ACA
  hp, pf, toy pf, cel, hpsd, str

Chopiniana (1973)                                 8'
  solo pf; 3*2*22; 2100; perc, hp, str           AMP

Get Hence, Foule Griefe (1975)                    7'
  solo t; 2+2*22; 1000; perc, str (divisi)        MS

Canticum beatae virginis (1979)                   8'
  solo mez; solo tpt; org, str                   ACA

This is the Year (1986)                           5'
  3satb cho; band:  2*111; a,t,bar sax;           MS
  23(3cnt)32; euph; perc
  orch:  2*122; 2200; perc, hp, cel,
  glock, str

Romanza (1987)                                                         7'
    solo vc; 3*222; 4330; perc, pf, str                          MS


### JOHNSON, A. PAUL   (1955-   )

Be Well Mov'd (1972)                                                  var
    narr; solo vln; large orch (number and                      ACA
    size vary)

Noche oscura del Alma (1976)                                          22'
    satb cho; 3*23*3*; 4331; hp, org, str                       ACA

Cento (1984)                                                         40'
    3*3*4(a sax)3*; 6331; 4perc, pf, str                        ACA


### JOHNSON, HUNTER   (1906-   )

Music for String Orchestra (1949-1954)                               8'
    str                                                         GAL

Letter to the World - suite (1958)                                   23'
    2222; 2220; timp+1, pf, str                                 ECS

North State Suite (1963)                                             14'
    3*232; 4331; timp+2, hp, cel, str                           GAL

Past the Evening Sun (1964)                                          9'
    2222; 4220; timp+1, hp, cel, str                            GAL


### JOHNSON, TOM   (1939-   )

Fission (1966)                                                       6'
    2111; 1031; 2perc, str                                      AMP

The Secret of the River (1966)                                      7'
    2*222; 4230; 2perc, str                                     AMP

Five Americans (1969)                                               12'
    223*2; 4330; timp+1, str                                    AMP


### JOHNSTON, BENJAMIN   (1926-   )

Passacaglia and Epilogue (1960)                                      NA
    2*222*; 3331; perc, hp, pf/cel, str                         SMI

Journeys (1988)                                         NA
   ssatb cho; 3*3*3*3*; 5531; timp+2,        SMI
   hp, str

Symphony in A (1988)                                    NA
   1*111; 1110; timp, str                     SMI


      JONES, SAMUEL  (1935-     )

In Retrospect (1959)                                    8'
   3*3*22; 2210; timp, glock, str              CF

Chaconne and Burlesque (1960)                          12'
   3*3*3*3*; 4331; timp+2, hp, pf, str          CF
   N.B.  Movements 2 & 3 of Symphony No. 1.

Symphony No. 1 (1960)                                  27'
   3*3*3*3*; 4331; timp+3, hp, pf, cel, str     CF

Elegy for String Orchestra (1963)                      6'
   str                                         CF

Overture for a City (1964)                             9'
   3*3*3*3*; 4331; timp+2, hp, str             CF

Let Us Now Praise Famous Men (1972)                    16'
   4*3*3*3*; 4331; timp+4, hp, str             CF

Fanfare and Celebration (1980)                         5'
   4*4*4*4*; 5442; timp+1, hp, str             CF

A Symphonic Requiem (Variations on a Theme
   of Howard Hanson) (1983)                    22'
   3*3*3*3*; 4331; timp+3, hp, str             CF

Listen Now, My Children (1985)                         11'
   3*3*22; 4331; timp+3, hp, str               CF

The Trumpet of the Swan (1985)                         19'
   satb cho; 3*2*2*2*; 4331; timp+3, hp, str   MMB

Canticles of Time (Symphony No. 2) (1990)              28'
   satb cho(divisi at times); 2*3*3*2*;        MMB
   4431; timp+5, hp, str

Palo Duro Canyon (Symphony No. 3) (1991)               23'
   3*3*3*3*; 4331; timp+4, hp, str             CF

KALBFLEISCH, RODGER  (1955-    )

Eruptions (Symphony No. 1) (1980)                    20'
    soli 3perc, db; 3*23*3*; 4331; str              MMB

Junctures (Symphony No. 2) (1982)                    10'
    2222; 3220; pf, str, tape recorders,            MMB
    microphone

KALLMAN, DANIEL  (1956-    )

Spring Flings (1989)                                 11'
    1221; 2000; perc(opt), str                      MMB

Trinity Canticles (1989)                             19'
    3*3*3*2; 4331; timp+3, hp, str                  MMB

KARCHIN, LOUIS (1951-    )

Songs of John Keats (1984)                           10'
    solo s; 2223*; 1100; 2perc, hp, str             CFP

Five Orchestral Songs (1985)                         17'
    solo s; 3*23*3*; 4221; 4perc, str               ACA

KARLINS, MARTIN W.  (1932-    )

Concert Music No. 1 (1959)                           14'
    3*3*3*3*; 4331; timp+2, str                     ACA

Concert Music No. 2 (1960)                           14'
    satb cho; 2222; 4231; timp, hp, str             ACA

Concert Music No. 4 (1964)                            4'
    3*23*2; 3211; 2perc, pf, str                    ACA

Concert Music No. 5 (1973)                           12'
    3*3*3*3*; a,t,bar sax; 4422;                    SEE
    timp+5, pf, str

Symphony No. 1 (1980)                                19'
    22*2*2*; 2200; timp+1, str                      ACA

Catena No. 1 (1981)                                      13'
    solo cl; 0100; 0110; pf, str                        ACA

Concerto for Alto Saxophone and
    Orchestra (1982)                                     21'
    solo a sax; 2222; 2220; timp+2, str                 ACA

Catena III (1983)                                        20'
    solo hn; 222(a sax, t sax)2; 3331;                  ACA
    timp+2, str


        KARPMAN, LAURA   (1959-    )

Theme and Variations (1983)                              14'
    solo pf; 2*2*2*1; 1000; perc, str                   MMB

Duets, Trios, Quintets (1985)                            12'
    soli fl, ob, cl, bsn; str                           MMB

Six of one Half, a Dozen of the Other (1986)   9'
    23*3*2; 0221; perc, pf, str                         ACA


        KAUFMAN, FREDERICK   (1936-    )

Symphony No. 3 (1974)                                    14'
    soli perc; str                                      ACA

When the Twain Meet (1981)                               17'
    2222; 2200; timp, str                               ACA

Kaddish Concerto (1984)                                  15'
    solo vc; str                                        ACA

American Symphony No. 5 (1986)                           22'
    224=2; 4331; euph; timp+1, hp, str                  ACA

Concerto for Clarinet and Strings (1987)       15'
    solo cl; str                                        ACA

Dance of Death (1989)                                     7'
    2*2*2*2*; 2200; timp, str (6-6-4-4-2)               ACA


        KAY, HERSHY   (1919-1981)

Funérailles (1946)                                        9'
    3*3*3*3; 4331; timp+2, hp, str                      BH

Cakewalk - ballet suite
    (after L.M. Gottschalk) (1951)                24'
    2*22*2; 4231; timp+3, hp, pf/cel, str         BH

Western Symphony (1954)                          25'
    2*23=0; 4331; timp+2, hp, pf/cel, str         BH

Stars and Stripes - ballet suite
    (after J.P. Sousa) (1958)                     NA
    3*23=2; 4421; euph; 4perc, hp, str            BH

The Clowns (1968)                                26'
    2222; 4331; timp+1, hp, cel, str              BH

Suite (pieces by Orlando Gibbons) (NA)           12'
    3*3*3*3; a sax; 4331; timp, str               BH


            KAY, ULYSSES  (1917-      )

Danse Calinda - ballet suite (1941)              14'
    2*1*21; 2220; timp+1, pf, str                 PEM

Of New Horizons - overture (1944)                8'
    3*3*3*3*; 4331; timp+2, hp, pf/cel, str       CFP

Suite (1945)                                     17'
    3*3*3*3*; 4331; perc, pf, str                 AMP

Brief Elegy (1946)                               5'
    solo ob; str                                  MCA

A Short Overture (1946)                          7'
    2222; 2220; timp+2, str                       MCA

Ancient Saga (1947)                              8'
    solo pf; str                                  CF

Danse Calinda - ballet suite (1947)              14'
    3*221; 2220; timp+2, pf, str                  CF

Song of Jeremiah - cantata (1947)                13'
    solo b-bar; satb cho; 3*3*22; 2221;           CF
    timp+2, hp, pf, str

Concerto for Orchestra (1948)                    18'
    3*222; 4331; timp+3, str                      CF

Portrait Suite (1948)                            18'
    3*222; 4331; timp, str                        CF

The Quiet One - film suite (1948)                16'
  1*111; 1110; timp+2, pf, str                     PEM

Pieta (1950)                                      7'
  solo eh; str                                      CF

Sinfonia in E (1950)                             20'
  3*222; 4331; timp, str                            CF

Serenade (1954)                                  18'
  2222; 4331; timp, str                             AMP

Six Dances (1954)                                20'
  str                                               BRO

Phoebus Arise - cantata (1959)                   30'
  soli s, bar; satb cho; 1121; 2210;                TP
  timp+3, pf/cel, str

Of New Horizons (1961)                            8'
  3*222; 4331; timp+1, hp, pf/cel, str              CFP

Trigon (1961)                                    12'
  3*3*4=3*; 4441; timp+3, hp                        CFP

Choral Triptych - cantata (1962)                 15'
  satb cho; str                                     AMP

Fantasy Variations (1963)                        15'
  2222; 4331; timp+1, str                           MCA

Inscriptions from Whitman (1963)                 25'
  satb cho; 2222; 4331; timp+2, hp, str             CF

Umbrian Scene (1963)                             13'
  2222; 4331; timp+1, hp, str                       LEE

Reverie and Rondo (1964)                          7'
  3*222; 4331; timp+2, str                          PEM

Presidential Suite (1965)                        12'
  3*222; 4331; timp+1, str                          CF

Markings: A Symphonic Essay (1966)               18'
  3*3*3*3*; 4331; timp+1, str                       MCA

Aulos (1967)                                      8'
  solo fl; 2hn; perc, str                           CF

Scherzi musicali (1968)                              17'
    1111; 1000; str                                  MCA

Theater Set (1968)                                   15'
    3*3*3*2; 4331; timp+1, hp, str                   MCA

Once there was a man (1969)                          17'
    satb cho; narr; 3*23*2; 4331;                    CF
    timp+2, hp, str

Quintet Concerto (1974)                              17'
    solo br qnt; 3*23*2; 3110; timp+2, str           CF

Southern Harmony (1975)                              20'
    3*3*3*3*; 4331; timp+2, str                      CF

Chariots; Orchestra Rhapsody (1979)                  15'
    3*3*3*3; 4331; timp+3, hp, str                   PEM


        KEATS, DONALD   (1929-      )

Concert Piece (1952)                                 12'
    2222; 4231; timp+2, str                          MS

Symphony No. 1 (1957)                                25'
    23*3+3*; 4231; timp+2, hp, str                   GAL

An Elegiac Symphony
    (Symphony No. 2) (1962; rev 1973)                20'
    3*3*3*3*; 4331; timp+1, cel, str                 BH

Branchings (1976)                                    7'
    3*3*3*2; 4331; timp+1, hp, str                   MS

Concerto for Piano and Orchestra (1990)              37'
    solo pf; 3*3*3*3*; 4331; 3perc, hp, str          MS


        KECHLEY, DAVID   (1947-      )

Second Composition for Large
    Orchestra (1967)                                 10'
    4(2picc)3*3*3; 4331; timp+3, hp, pf, str         PVP

Four Horsemen of the Apocalypse (1969)               25'
    3*3*3*3*; 4331; timp+3, hp, pf/cel, str          MS

Faint Harps and Silver Voices (1974)                 26'
    solo s, b; satb cho; 2perc, hp, pf, str          PVP

Five Ancient Lyrics (1976)                          18'
    solo s; hp, str                                 PVP

The Funky Chicken (1976)                            4'
    str                                             PVP

Lightning Images (1978)                             16'
    3*3*3*3*; 4331; timp+3, 2hp, pf/cel, str        PVP

Silver Tears (1978)                                 5'
    solo picc; str                                  PVP

Concerto for Violin and Strings (1979)              29'
    solo vln; str                                   PVP

Alexander and the Wind-Up Mouse (1981)              17'
    narr; 3*3*3*3*; 4331; hp, pf/cel, str           PVP

Clocks and More Clocks (1981)                       13'
    narr; 3*3*3*3*; 4331; timp+4, hp, pf, str       PVP

Pathways:  Symphony in Four Movements (1981)        31'
    3*3*3*3*; 4331; timp+3, hp,                     PVP
    pf/cel/elec pf, str

Concerto for Alto Saxophone (1984)                  17'
    solo a sax; 2*2*2*2; 2220; 2perc,               PVP
    hp, pf, str


            KELLER, HOMER  (1915-    )

Overture (1947)                                     4'
    3222; 4331; timp+1, str                         CF

Symphony No. 2 (1948)                               16'
    2*34=3*; 4331; timp+4, hp, pf, str              ACA

Concerto for Piano and Orchestra (1949)             15'
    solo pf; 2222; 2110; timp+1, str                CF

Symphony No. 3 (1955)                               22'
    23*3*3*; 4331; timp+4, hp, pf, str              ACA

Sonorities (1970)                                   12'
    3*3*22; 4331; timp+1, hp, pf, str               ACA

Magnificat (NA)                                     5'
    satb cho; 2222; 4341; timp, db                  ACA

KELLY, ROBERT    (1916-      )

Rounds for String Orchestra, op. 13 (1947)    6'
    str                                       ACA

A Miniature Symphony
    (Symphony No. 1), op. 14 (1948)           10'
    1111; 2110; timp, str                     GAL

Symphony No. 2, op. 33 (1958)                 28'
    3*3*3*2*; 4331; timp+1, hp, str           ACA

Concerto for Violin, Cello and Orchestra,
    op. 38 (1960)                             24'
    soli vln, vc; 2222; 2220; timp+1,         ACA
    cel, str

The Legend of the Maize (1962)                15'
    3*222; 4322; timp+1, hp, pf/cel, str      ACA

Symphony No. 3 in D Minor (1964)              32'
    3*3*3*3*; 4331; timp+3, str               ACA

Emancipation Symphony, op. 39 (1965)          15'
    2222; 4331; timp+2, str                   ACA

Colloquy, op. 43 (1971)                       13'
    1111; 2110; 2perc, str                    ACA

Concerto for Violin and Orchestra,
    op. 46 (1973)                             23'
    solo vln; 2222; 4330; timp+1, str         GAL

Concerto for Violoncello and Orchestra,
    op. 51 (1974)                             18'
    solo vc; 2222; 2220; timp+2, hp, str      ACA

Concerto for Viola and Orchestra,
    op. 53 (1976)                             22'
    solo vla; 2222; 2220; timp+3, str         ACA

Concertino, op. 54 (1977)                     12'
    2222; 2200; perc, str                     ACA

Garden of Peace, op. 56 (1979)               9'
    str                                       ACA

Concerto for Violin and Viola, op. 57 (1980) 22'
    soli vln, vla; 2222; 2000; str            ACA

Shenandoah Variations, op. 59 (1981)          8'
   str                                           ACA

Fantasia, op. 62 (1984)                       16'
   solo hp; str                                  ACA


      KENNEDY, JOHN BRODBIN  (1934-    )

Lyric Ode (1960)                              9'
   str                                           BH

Symphonic Fantasy (1964)                      14'
   3*3*3*3*; 4331; timp+3, hp, pf, cel, str     BH

Symphony in Two Movements (1966)              22'
   3*3*3*3*; 4331; timp+1, hp, pf, cel, str     BH

Two Sonnets from Shakespeare (NA)             10'
   1111; 0000; str                               BH


      KERNIS, AARON JAY  (1960-    )

Dream of the Morning Sky (1983)               23'
   solo s; 3*3*3*2*; 4331; timp+1, hp,           AMP
   pf/cel, str

Morning Songs (1983)                          15'
   solo bar; 1=02*1; 1000; perc, hp,             AMP
   str (1-1-1-0 or multiples)

Mirror of Heat and Light
   (Cycle V, Part 2) (1985)                      16'
   3*3*3=2; 4331; timp+1, hp, pf, str            AMP

Barbara Allen (1988)                          5'
   solo s; 1111; 1000; 2perc, hp, str            AMP

Invisible Mosaic III (1988)                   13'
   3*3*3=3*; 4331; timp+4, hp, pf/cel, str      AMP

Symphony in Waves (1989)                      35'
   1*2*1=2*; 31*00; perc, pf/cel, str           AMP

Simple Songs (1991)                           20'
   solo s (or t); 1*100; 1000; perc, hp,         AMP
   str (2-1-1-1 or multiples)

KESSNER, DANIEL (1946-    )

Strata (1971)                                          14'
    3*3*3*3*; 4331; 4perc, hp, pf, cel, str           MS

Mobile (1973)                                         11'
    3*3*3*3*; 4331; 4perc, hp, pf, cel, str           MS

The Telltale Heart - Monodrama for Tenor and
    Orchestra (1975-1978)                            40'
    solo t; 111*0; 201(b tbn)0; 2perc,               MS
    hp, pf, str (soli or small sections)

Romance; Orchestral Prelude No. 1 (1979)             10'
    3*3*3*3*; 4331; 2perc, str                       MS

Raging; Orchestral Prelude No. 2 (1981)               9'
    3*3*3*3*; 4331; 2perc, str                       MS

    N.B. The two preludes, "Romance" and
    "Raging", may be performed together
    as a two-movement work.

Piano Concerto (1986)                                33'
    solo pf; 2222; 2221; 2perc,hp, str               MS

Breath - for cello and orchestra (1991)              21'
    solo vc; 2222; 2221; 2perc, str                  MS


        KEYES, NELSON   (1928-1987)

Concerto Grosso (1963)                               15'
    soli 2vln, vla, vc, db; str                      MMB


        KIEVMAN, CARSON   (1949-    )

String (A Condition Attached to the Plan)
    Rumble (A Fight Between Two Teenaged Gangs):
    a semi-aleatoric piece for strings (1972)  var
    str                                              AMP

Hollowangels (1975)                                  38'
    3*24*3*; 3221; timp+1, hp(amp), pf/cel,         ICP
    elec gtr, str

Overture, Prologue and Prelude
  (from "California Mystery Park") (1980)   40'
  1=11*1*; 1211; 4perc, hp, pf/hpsd,     ICP
  gtr/elec gtr, str

Prologue
  (from "California Mystery Park") (1980)   15'
  1+11*1; 1211; 4perc, hp, pf,        ICP
  elec gtr, str

Prisoners of Conscience
  (Piano Concert No. 1) (1981)        25'
  solo pf; 2*23=1*; 2211; timp,      ICP
  choir bells, str

Concerto for Percussion, Piano and
  Small Orchestra (1983)           25'
  soli perc, pf; 012*0; 101(b tbn)0; perc,  ICP
  pf, str, tape

Suite, Intelligent Systems (1983)     25'
  112*0; 2111; 2perc, kybd, str, tape(opt)  ICP

Aspen Symphony (Symphony No. 1) (1987)   33'
  22*3*2*; 3221; 2perc, hp, str      ICP

Suite No. 2 (California Mystery Park) (1987) 15'
  1=11*1*; 1211; 4perc, hp, pf/hpsd,   ICP
  gtr/elec gtr, str

Overture from "Hamlet" (1988)       20'
  1120; 2211; 2perc, pf, str, tape    ICP

Fanfare for Everyman (1990)        5'
  333*3*; 5300; timp+3, str        ICP

Excerpts from Orchestra Suite No. 4 (1991)  8'
  2*23*2; 1021; timp+2, synth, str    ICP

Happybirthdaytou (1991)          3'
  3333; 4321; timp+3, str         ICP

Symphony No. 2 (1991)           40'
  satb cho; 3(picc, b fl)3*3*3*; 4331;  ICP
  timp+3, 2hp, str

Funeral March (from "Hamlet") (NA)    8'
  2232; 4321; timp+2, synth, str    ICP

KING, JOHN   (1953-    )

Orchestravariations (1982)                         20'
  2223*; 4030; str                                 ACA

Sinfonietta (1985)                                 16'
  2222; 2200; timp+2, 2hp, str                     ACA


KIRCHNER, LEON   (1919-    )

Sinfonia (1951)                                    20'
  3*3*3*3*; 4331; timp+1, hp, pf, cel, str         AMP

Concerto No. 1 for Piano and
  Orchestra (1953)                                 25'
  solo pf; 3*3*3*3*; 4331; timp+1, cel, str        AMP

Toccata (1955)                                     14'
  0111; 1110; perc, cel, str                       AMP

Concerto No. 2 for Piano and
  Orchestra (1963)                                 30'
  solo pf; 3*3*3*3*; 4331; timp+5, cel, str        AMP

Music for Orchestra (1969)                         14'
  3*3*3*3*; 4331; timp+5, pf/cel, str              AMP

Music for Flute and Orchestra (1978)               13'
  solo fl; 3*3*3*3*; 4331; timp+5, hp,             AMP
  pf/cel, Fender b gtr, str


KIRK, THERON   (1919-    )

Divertimento (1952)                                5'
  1110; 2000; timp, str                            MS

Symphony No. 1 (1952)                              21'
  2*222; 3231; timp+3, str                         MS

Ballet Music - suite (1953)                        6'
  2*222; 4331; timp+3, str                         FLE

Adagietto (1954)                                   6'
  11*11; 2000; timp, cel, str                      PAP

Carol Service with Nine Lessons (1954)             30'
  solo s; 2020; 0220; str                          BEL

Intrada (1954)                                              5'
    2*222; 4230; timp+2, str                               CF

Vignettes (1954)                                           7'
    2*220; 4220; timp+2, str                               BEL

Fantasy and Frolic (1955)                                 10'
    solo pf; 2*222; 2331; timp+2, str                      FLE

Saga of the Plains (Symphony No. 2) (1959)                19'
    3*2*3*2; 4331; timp+2, hp, str                         CF

Concerto Grosso for Piano and Strings (1960)              12'
    solo pf; str                                           MS

Concerto for Orchestra (1960)                             12'
    2222; 4331; timp+1, pf, str                            TP

An Orchestra Primer
    (for young audiences) (1961)                          13'
    narr; 2222; 4231; 2perc, str                           OXF

King David's Deliverance (1962)                           12'
    satb cho; 3*222; 4331; timp+4, str                     BEL

Night of Wonder (1962)                                    30'
    satb cho; str                                          SHA

Dance of the Border (1963)                                 6'
    2*222; 4331; timp+3, str                               MS

Prayers from the Ark:  Five Songs (1963)                  11'
    solo mez (or bar); 2120; 2000; hp, str                 HMI

Prayers from the Ark (1963)                               37'
    soli s, t, bar; 3*222; 4331; timp+3,                   HMI
    hp, str

Hemis Dance (1967)                                         6'
    perc, str                                              CF

Latham  Suite (1987)                                       9'
    str                                                    OXF


        KITZKE, JEROME P.  (1955-      )

The Rime of the Ancient Mariner (1976-1979)               90'
    soli t, bar; satb cho; 3*3*3=3*; 6432;                 AMC
    timp+1, 2hp str (26-26-15-10-9)

And Miles to go Before I Sleep (1980)                13'
  solo s; ssaa cho; 2020; 1000; euph;               ACA
  2perc, hp, pf, handbells, str

The Snow Crazy Copybook (1980)                      14'
  2222; 2200; 2perc, elec pf; cel, str              ACA


        KNEHANS, DOUGLAS  (1957-     )

Five Orchestral Songs to Poems of
  Sylvia Plath (1983)                               16'
  solo s; 3*3*4*3*; 4231; timp+2,                   AUS
  hp, pf, str

Passacaglia (1983)                                   9'
  3*3*3*3*; 4231; timp+2, pf/cel, str               AUS

Concerto for Guitar, Orchestra and
  Concertante (1990)                                27'
  soli gtr, hpsd; 1*11*0; a sax; picc tpt,          AUS
  b tbn, tba; 2perc, str

Hell's Response (Concerto for Clarinet and
  Orchestra (1991)                                  22'
  solo cl; 223*2; 2221; timp+4, hp, pf, str         AUS


        KNIGHT, ERIC  (1932-     )

Americana Overture (1977)                            6'
  3*3*3*3*; 4431; timp+3, dmst, hp, pf, str         GS

Kidnapped:  Overture (A Symphony in Four
  American Idioms) (1977)                           24'
  3*3*3*3*; 4431; timp+3, dmst, hp, pf, str         GS

Three Musical Elements for Orchestra:
  Earth, Water, Space (1979)                        12'
  3*23*2; 4331; timp+3, hp, pf, str                 GS

Canadian Tribute (1980)                             10'
  2*222; 4431; timp+7, dmst, hp, pf, str            GS

The Great American Bicycle Race (1983)               6'
  3*3*3*3*; 4431; timp+4, hp, pf, str               GS

KNOX, CHARLES (1929-    )

Concert Music for Bassoon and
   Orchestra (1959)                                9'
   solo bsn; 2221; 4231; timp, str                 MS

Overture in F (1960)                               6'
   3*3*3*3*; 4331; timp+2, str                      MS

Ballad Suite (1961)                                8'
   2222; 4231; timp+1, str                         MS

Concert Piece for Piano and Orchestra (1963)    8'
   solo pf; 3*3*3*3*; 4331; timp+1, str             MS

Paseos (1978)                                      5'
   2220; 0200; str                                 MS

Brazen (1982)                                      7'
   3*23*2; 4331; timp+1, str                       MS


          KOBLITZ, DAVID  (1948-    )

Trism (1971)                                       7'
   223*2; 3331; 4perc, hp, pf, str                 MG

Gris-Gris (1973)                                   8'
   3+03+0; 2300; 4perc, pf/cel,                    MG
   elec gtr, str


          KOCH, FREDERICK  (1924-    )

River Journey (1955)                              15'
   3*3*23*; 4320; timp+5, hp, pf, cel, str         CF

Concertino for Alto Saxophone and
   Orchestra (1963)                               14'
   solo a sax; 3*222; 3220; timp+1,                SEE
   hp, pf, str

Variations for Orchestra with Piano (1963)      7'
   3*3*23*; 2221; timp+3, hp, pf, cel, str         MS

Short Symphony No. 1 (1965)                       20'
   23*22; 2221; timp+1, hp, pf, cel, str           SEE

Symphonic Suite:   Phase No. 1 (1969)            20'
  solo mez (or bar); 3*222; 2210; timp+1,       MS
  hp, pf/cel, str

Memorial (1970)                                  5'
  23*22; 2210; perc, cel, str                    SEE

Dance Overture (1971)                            5'
  3*23*2; 2210; timp+2, hp, str                  SEE

Veltin Fantasy (1971)                            10'
  solo ob; str                                   SEE

Overture for America (1974)                      8'
  2222; 2220; timp+1, hp, str, tape              SEE

Concerto sonica (1976)                           15'
  soli 2pf; 2222; 4220; timp+1, hp, str          SEE

Concerto for Acoustic/Electric Piano
  and Orchestra (1987)                           20'
  solo pf/elec pf; 23*22; 2210; timp+1,          MS
  hp, str


     KOGAN, ROBERT  (1940-    )

Gemini (1977)                                    22'
  soli vib, mar; 203*1; 2220; timp, str          MS


     KOHN, KARL  (1926-    )

Sinfonia concertante (1951)                      20'
  solo pf; 2222; 2231; timp, str                 CF

Castles and Kings
  Suite for Children (1958)                      11'
  3*222; 3221; timp+2, str                       CF

Three Scenes for Orchestra (1960)                12'
  3*3*3*3*; 4231; timp+1, hp, cel, str           CF

Concerto mutabile (1962)                         13'
  solo pf; 1111; 1230; str                       CF

Interludes (1964)                                12'
  3*222; 3231; timp+2, str                       CF

Episodes (1966)                                    11'
    solo pf; 2222; 4221; timp+1, hp, str          CF

Interlude I (1969)                                  5'
    str                                            CF

Interlude II (1969)                                 7'
    solo pf; str                                   CF

Centone per Orchestra (1973)                       30'
    3*3*3*3*; 4221; timp+3, hp, pf, str            CF

Concerto for Horn and Small Orchestra (1974)       25'
    solo hn; 1112; 0000; vib, pf, str              CF

Waldmusik - Concerto for Clarinet and
    Orchestra (1979)                               23'
    solo cl; 1*2*02; 2000; pf, str                 CF

Time Irretrievable (1983)                          25'
    3*222; 4231; timp+2, str                       CF

Lions on a Banner - Seven Sufi Texts (1988)        24'
    3*222; 4231; timp+1, hp, pf, str               PTP

Return (Rueckgabe) (1990)                          10'
    0000; 2221; 3perc, str                         PTP


            KOHS, ELLIS  (1916-      )

Concerto in One Movement (1941)                    15'
    2222; 4331; perc, str                          ACA

Concerto for Piano and Orchestra (1945)            16'
    solo pf; 3*222; 4331; timp+1, str              ACA

Legend (1946)                                       5'
    solo ob; str                                   AMP

Passacaglia (1946)                                  6'
    solo org; str                                  ACA

Concerto for Violoncello and Orchestra
    (in one movement) (1947)                       12'
    solo vc; 2222; 2000; str                       ACA

Psalm XXV (1947)                                   10'
    satb cho; 2222; 2220; str                      ACA

Chamber Concerto for Viola and
   Strings (1949)                                      20'
    solo vla; str (2-2-2-2-1) or str orch          ACA

Symphony No. 1 (1950)                                  16'
   1111; 1110; timp, str                            ACA

Lord of the Ascendant (1955)                          120'
   soli 7vv; satb cho; 3*3*3*3*; 4331;              ACA
   timp+1, hp, pf, org, str, 8 dancers

Symphony No. 2 (1956)                                  25'
   satb cho; 2222; 2221; timp+1, hp, str            ACA

Four Orchestral Songs (1959)                           12'
   soli s, b-bar; 2222; 2231; perc, hp, str         ACA

Concerto for Violin and Orchestra (1981)               24'
   solo vln; 3*3*3*3*; a sax; 4331;                 ACA
   timp+2, hp, str


      KOLB, BARBARA  (1939-      )

Soundings (1972)                                       16'
   3*3*3*3*; 3000; 2perc, 2hp,                      BH
   str(no db), tape
N.B.  Requires two conductors for performance.

Grisaille (1979)                                       11'
   4*3*4=3*; 4331; 5perc, str                       BH

Sequela (1983)                                         12'
   str                                              CF

Cross Winds (1985)                                     13'
   223*2; a sax; 3220; perc, str                    BH

Yet that things go round (1987)                        14'
   2*22*2; 2210; timp+2, pf, str                    BH

The Enchanted Loom (1989)                              18'
   3*3*3*3*; 4331; timp+3, hp, str                  BH

Voyants (1990)                                         NA
   solo pf; 1111; 1110; str (2-1-1-1)               BH

KORF, ANTHONY   (1951-      )

Nascent Glimmers (1978)                                       NA
    4=23*2; 4231; timp+1, pf, str                            AMC

Symphony in the Twilight (1985)                              27'
    4*2*3*1; 4221; timp+4, hp, pf/cel, str                  ACA

Symphony No. 2 (Blue Note) (1987)                            27'
    2222; 2220; timp+1, pf/synth; str                       ACA

Requiem (1989)                                               20'
    narr; satb cho; 4=2*22; 4221; timp+2,                   ACA
    hp, pf, synth, str


KORTE, KARL   (1928-      )

Symphony No. 2 (1961)                                        20'
    3*3*3*3*; 4331; timp+5, hp, str                          MS

Mass for Youth (Missa St. Dominick) (1963)                  20'
    satb cho; 2*222; 2221; timp+1, hp, str                  GAL

Southwest (A Dance Overture) (1963)                         10'
    3*222; 4331; 4perc, hp, pf, str                          MS

Symphony No. 3 (1968)                                        20'
    3*3*4=3*; 4331; timp+4, hp, pf, str                     SEE


KOUTZEN, BORIS   (1901-1966)

Concert Piece for Cello and Strings (1946)                  12'
    solo vc; str                                             TP

Concerto for Violin and Orchestra (1946)                    25'
    solo vln; 3*222; 4230; timp+1, hp, str                  FLE

Sinfonietta (1947)                                          16'
    1111; 1100; pf, str                                      TP

Viola Concerto (1949)                                       14'
    solo vla; 1010; 0000; str                               AME

Divertimento (1956)                                         15'
    2222; 2210; timp+1, hp, str                             FLE

Concertino for Piano (1959)                                 15'
    solo pf; str                                            BTN

Elegiac Rhapsody (1961)              11'
   1121; 2110; timp, str          BTN

Fanfare, Prayer and March (1961)    13'
   11*21; 1110; timp+2, pf, str    BTN


       KOYKKAR, JOSEPH  (1951-   )

Chamber Symphony (1975)           15'
   0111; 1000; str              SEE

Kinesis (1976)                    5'
   3*2*4=2; 4331; 4perc, str      SEE

Evocations (1981)               6'
   3*23*2; 4331; timp+4, pf, str   BEL

Composite (1983)                15'
   3*232; 4331; timp+1, pf, str    MMB


       KRAFT, LEO  (1922-   )

Overture in G (1947)            8'
   2122; 2220; timp+1, str       TP

Concerto No. 1 (1951)           16'
   soli fl, cl, tpt; str        CF

A Proverb of Solomon (1953)      6'
   satb cho; 2222; 2200; str     TP

Larghetto in Memory of Karol Rathaus (1955)  5'
   timp, str                  TP

Variations for Orchestra (1958)    17'
   3*3*3*2; 4330; timp, str      CF

Three Pieces for Orchestra (1963)   18'
   3*3*3*2; 4331; timp+2, str    CF

Concerto No. 4 (1979)           18'
   solo pf; 1111; a sax; 1110; perc,   PM
   str (2-1-1-1)
   N.B.  May also be performed with a larger
   complement of strings.

Chamber Symphony (1980)                                    17'
   1111; 1110; str (2-1-1-1)                              PM
   N.B.  May also be performed with a larger
   complement of strings.

Symphony in One Movement (1985)                            14'
   3*3*4=3*; 4330; timp+2, str                        CF

Clarinet Concerto (1986)                                   15'
   solo cl; 2=21+1; a sax; 2110; perc, str            CF


      KRAFT, WILLIAM  (1923-    )

Three Miniatures for Percussion and
   Orchestra (1958)                                    4'
   soli timp+3; 3*23*3*; 4331; str                    NMW
   OR:  solo perc; 2222; 2220; str

A Simple Introduction to the
   Orchestra (1958)                                    4'
   3*3*3*3*; 4221; timp+1, hp, pf, str                NMW

Concerto Grosso (1961)                                     13'
   soli fl, bsn, vln, vc; 3*4*4*3*; 4331;             NMW
   timp+1, hp, pf, str

American Carnival Overture (1962)                          5'
   3*3*3*2; 4231; timp+1, hp, pf/cel, str             NMW

Silent Boughs (1963)                                       19'
   solo s; str (3-3-2-2-1 minimum)                    NMW

Concerto for Four Percussion Soloists
   and Orchestra (1964)                                18'
   soli 4perc; 2222*; 4221; hp, pf/cel, str           NMW

Contextures:  Riots - Decade '60 (1967)                    16'
   solo jazz qt; 44*4(a sax)4*; 4441;                 NMW
   timp+1, hp, pf, str

Concerto for Piano and Orchestra (1972-1973)  25'
   solo pf; 3*3*3*3; 4332; timp+1, hp, str            NMW

Tintinnabulations:  Collage No. 3 (1974)                   10'
   3*222; 4331; timp+3, hp, cel, str                  NMW

Dream Tunnel (1976)                                        15'
   narr; 2*2*2*2; 3220; 2perc, pf/cel, str            NMW

Concerto for Tuba with Three Chamber Groups
  and Orchestra (1979)                                 18'
  solo tba; 3*3*3*3*; 4330; timp+3,                    NMW
  hp, pf/cel, str

Settlers Suite (1981)                                  15'
  1111; 2220; timp+1, pf, str                          NMW

Double Play for Violin, Piano and
  Chamber Orchestra (1982)                             17'
  soli pf, vln; 12*1*2; 2100; perc, str                NMW

Fire and Ice - suite from film (1982)                  22'
  2*3*22; 4331; timp+1, hp, pf/cel, str                NMW

Concerto for Timpani and Orchestra (1983)              23'
  solo timp; 2*2*22; 4331; 3perc, hp,                  NMW
  pf/cel, str

Interplay (1984)                                       17'
  3(2picc)3*3*3*; 4331; timp+3, hp,                    NMW
  pf/cel, str
  N.B.  Requires six offstage crotale players.

Of Ceremonies, Pageants and
  Celebrations (1986; rev 1987)                        12'
  3*3*3=2; 4331; timp+3, hp, pf/cel, str               NMW
  N.B.  Optional six offstage crotale and
  chime players.

Contextures II:  The Final Beast (1986)                31'
  soli s, t; boys cho; 4(2picc,a fl)4*4=3*;            NMW
  4441; timp+6, hp, pf/cel, str
  N.B.  Requires an old music group, with the
  suggested instrumentation:  hurdy-gurdy,
  small hand bells, vielle, crumhorn, viola da
  gamba, medieval harp, rebec, lute, low drum,
  bass and treble recorders, tambourine, flute.

A Kennedy Portrait (1988)                              18'
  narr; 3*3*3*3; 4331; timp+3, hp,                     NMW
  pf/cel, str

Veils and Variations (1988)                            27'
  solo hn; 3=3*3*3; 4331; timp+3, hp,                  NMW
  pf/cel, str

Vintage Renaissance (1989)                             12'
  3*3*33*; 4331; timp+3, hp, pf/cel, str               NMW

Fanfare Vintage 90-91 (1990)                    5'
   3*3*23; 4231; timp+3, hp, str               NMW


   KRAMER, JONATHAN   (1942-    )

Moments In and Out of Time (1981-1983)         29'
   3*3*4=3*; 4331; timp+3, hp, pf, str          GS

No Beginning, No End (1983)                     10'
   satb cho; 2*2*22; 2211; timp+1, str         MMB

Musica pro Musica (1987)                        16'
   2=2*2*2*; 2210; timp+2, str                 MMB

About Face (1989)                               16'
   3(2picc)3*3=3*; 4331; timp+3, hp, str       MMB


   KREMENLIEV, BORIS   (1911-    )

Study for Orchestra (1947)                      5'
   1+2*3*2*; 2210; timp+1, hp, str             FLE

Bulgarian Rhapsody (1952)                       14'
   3(2picc)3*22; 4331; timp+3, hp, str         FLE


   KRENEK, ERNST   (1900-    )

Symphonic Piece, op. 86 (1939)                  16'
   str                                          UE

Little Concerto, op. 88 (1939-1940)            10'
   soli pf, org (or pf); 1010; 0000; str        UE

Cantata for Wartime, op. 95 (1943)             12'
   ssaa cho; 2222; 4220; timp+1, str            UE

Symphonic Elegy in Memoriam Anton Webern,
   op. 105 (1946)                               12'
   str                                          TP

Piano Concerto No. 3, op. 107 (1946)           19'
   solo pf; 223*2; 4221; timp+1, hp, str       EAM

Symphony No. 4, op. 113 (1947)                  30'
   3*3*3*3*; 4331; timp+1, pf, str             MS

Five Short Pieces, op. 116 (1948)                10'
  str                                              BAR

Symphony No. 5, op. 119 (1949)                   22'
  223*2; 4221; timp+1, str                        EAM

Double Concerto, op. 124 (1950)                  20'
  soli vln, pf; 1111; 2100; str                   EBM

Piano Concerto No. 4, op. 123 (1950)             20'
  solo pf; 222*2; 4220; 2perc, str                BAR

Concerto for Harp and Orchestra,
  op. 126 (1951)                                  19'
  solo hp; 1111; 2100; str                        UE

Concerto for Two Pianos and Orchestra,
  op. 127 (1951)                                  16'
  soli 2pf; 2*222; 4221; timp+1, str              BAR

Medea, op. 129 (1952)                            16'
  solo mez; 2*222; 4221; 2perc, str               BAR

Brazilian Sinfonietta, op. 131 (1952)            14'
  str                                             EAM

Cello Concerto No. 1, op. 133 (1953)             22'
  solo vc; 2*222; 4220; timp+1, hp, str           EAM

Scenes from the West, op. 134 (1953)             15'
  313*1*; a,t sax(opt); 2320; timp+4,             TP
  pf(opt), str

Symphony "Pallas Athene", op. 137 (1954)         24'
  2222; 4220; timp+3, hp, pf, cel, str            EAM

Violin Concerto No. 2, op. 140 (1954)            26'
  solo vln; 2222; 4220; timp+2,                   EAM
  hp, cel, str

Eleven Transparencies, op. 142 (1954)            18'
  2222; 4221; timp+3, hp, str                     EAM

Suite for Flute and Strings, op. 147a (1954)     6'
  solo fl; str                                    BRO

Capriccio for Cello and Orchestra,
  op. 145 (1955)                                  11'
  solo vc; 1111; 1110; timp+3, hp, cel, str       EAM

Seven Easy Pieces, op. 146 (1955)                            8'
   str                                                        SCH

Suite for Clarinet and Strings,
   op. 148a (1955)                                         8'
   solo cl; str                                            BRO

Ich singe wieder, wenn es tagt,
   op. 151 (1956)                                          5'
   satb cho; str                                           SCH

Divertimento, op. 158 (1956)                                 7'
   223*2; 2220; timp+1, str                                BRO

Circle, Chain and Mirror, op. 160 (1957)                    16'
   2*222; 2221; timp+1, hp, str                            BAR

A Question of Time, op. 170 (1959)                          18'
   1*1*1*1*; 1111; 4perc, hp, pf, cel, gtr,                EAM
   str (solo or section)

From Three Make Seven "Aus Drei Mach Sieben",
   op. 177 (1961)                                         12'
   2*222*; 4221; 2perc, hp, pf, str                        BAR

Ausgerechnet und verspielt, op. 179 (1961)                   6'
   1110; 0110; 2perc, hp, 2pf, cel, hpsd,                  BAR
   gtr, harmonium, str (1·1·1·0)

Nach wie vor der Reihe nach, op. 182 (1962)                  8'
   2narr; 2*222; 4221; 10perc, hp, cel,                    BAR
   gtr, str

To believe and to know, op. 194 (1965)                      28'
   4narr; satb cho; 223*3*; 4221; timp+4,                  MS
   hp, pf, cel, harmonium, gtr, str

Horizon Circled, op. 196 (1967)                             20'
   2*23*2; 4221; timp+4, hp, pf, str                       BAR

Perspectives, op. 199 (1967)                                20'
   2*2*32; 4321; timp+3, hp, pf, cel,                      EAM
   elec gtr; str
   offstage:  prep pf, vib, 2glock, thundersheet

Exercises of a Late Hour, op. 200 (1967)                    18'
   1*021; 1110; timp+3, hp, pf, gtr,                       EAM
   str, tape

Instant Remembered, op. 201 (1968)          15'
   solo s; narr; 2*02*0; 2220; timp+7,     EAM
   hp, pf, cel, gtr, str (1-1-1-0), tape

Six Profiles, op. 203 (1968)            12'
   2*23*2*; 4221; timp+6, hp, pf, cel, str   EAM

Fivefold Enfoldment, op. 205 (1969)        13'
   3*24*3*; 4321; 9perc, hp, 2pf, cel,    EAM
   elec gtr, str

Mass "Give Us Peace", op. 208 (1970)       20'
   soli s, a, t, b; satb cho; 0011; 1100;   BAR
   perc, org, str

Kitharaulos, op. 213 (1971)             20'
   soli ob/eh/ob d'am, hp; perc, pf, str   EAM

Static and Ecstatic, op. 214 (1972)        10'
   11110; 0110; perc, pf, str           EAM

Von vorn herein, op. 219 (1974)          10'
   1120; 1010; pf, cel, str             UE

Auf-und Ablehnung, op. 220 (1974)         18'
   2*23*3*; 4431; 5perc, hp, pf, cel, str  BAR

Anniversary Cantata, op. 221 (1975)        25'
   soli mez, bar; narr; satb cho; 1*1*1*0;  UE
   0110; perc, hp, pf, str

The Dissembler - monologue, op. 229 (1978)   20'
   solo bar; 1*1*11; 1110; 4perc, hp,    BAR
   pf, cel, str

Concerto for Organ and String Orchestra,
   op. 230 (1979)                      10'
   solo org; str                    UE

In the Valley of Time, op. 232 (1979)     14'
   1111; 1110; 3perc, pf, gtr, str       BAR

The Arc of Life, op. 234 (1981)          17'
   1*1*11; 1110; timp+5, pf, str       BAR

Organ Concerto, op. 235 (1982)          25'
   solo org; 2*2*2*2; 4221; timp+1, hp, str  BAR

Cello Concerto No. 2, op. 236 (1982)       20'
   solo vc; 2*202; 4220; 3perc, hp, str   BAR

Opus sine nomine, op. 238 (1986-1988)          NA
    soli s, mez, 2t, bar; narr; satb cho;       MS
    223*3*; 4441; 4perc, hp, pf, cel, 3gtr, str


        KRIEGER, ARTHUR   (1945-      )

Remnants (1983)                                15'
    3*3*3*3*; 6231; timp+5, pf, str            ACA

Riverside Variations (1989)                    10'
    3*3*3*3*; 4231; timp+3, hp, pf, str        ACA


        KRIESBERG, MATHIAS   (1953-      )

Short Symphony (1978)                          11'
    3=3*3=3*; 4331; timp+3, hp, str            AMP

Parte sin Novedad (1985)                       20'
    solo mez; 2222; 2211; 2perc,               ANM
    str (2-2-2-1)


        KROEGER, KARL   (1932-      )

Chorale for Orchestra (1958)                    6'
    2222; 4231; timp+1, str                    MS

Sinfonietta No. 1 (1958)                       13'
    223*2; 4331; timp+1, hp, str               MS

Concerto da Camera for Oboe and
    Strings (1961)                             11'
    solo ob; str                               MS

Dramatic Overture (1964)                       10'
    2222; 4231; timp+1, str                    MS

Sinfonietta for String Orchestra (1965)        15'
    str                                        FLE

Suite No. 1 (1965)                             30'
    3*3*3*3*; 4331; timp+1, hp, pf/cel, str    FLE

"Dark of the Moon" Concert Suite (1966)        25'
    2222; 4331; timp+1, hp, str                FLE

Five Bagatelles (1967)                         12'
    solo pf; 2121; 0000; str                   MS

Suite for Chamber Orchestra (1967)              15'
   2121; 2100; str                              FLE

Pax vobis - cantata (1976)                45'
   soli s, bar; satb cho; 2121; 2220;     ACA
   timp, str

Concert Overture (1980)                   11'
   2222; 4231; timp+1, str                 FLE

Moravian Praise (1980)                   12'
   satb cho; 2222; 2200; timp, str       MS


      KUBIK, GAIL  (1914-1984)

Choral Suite No. 1
   (from "A Mirror in the Sky") (1946)    16'
   narr; satb cho; 2222; 2221; perc, pf, str  TP

Choral Suite No. 2
   (from "A Mirror in the Sky") (1946)    16'
   narr; satb cho; 2222; 2221; perc, pf, str  TP

Folk Song Suite (1946)                  10'
   1121; 2210; 3perc, pf, str             PS

A Mirror in the Sky (1946)             TP

   1.  Audubon's Creed              10'
   2.  Choral Suite No. 1          16'
   3.  Choral Suite No. 2          16'
   4.  My Lord's a Forefended Place   7'
   5.  Overture                    10'
   solo vv; satb cho; 2*222; 2221; perc,
   pf, str

Music for Dancing (1946)               9'
   1=121; 2210; timp+1, str             PS

Bachata (1947)                       5'
   2222; 3331; timp+4, pf, str           PS

Symphony No. 1 (1947-1949)           38'
   3*3*3*3*; 4331; timp+6, pf, cel, str  PS

Symphonic concertante (1952; rev 1953)   25'
   soli vla, tpt, pf; 3*23*3*; 2110;     TP
   perc, str

Thunderbolt Overture (1953)                      7'
  3*3*3*3*; 4331; timp+1, pf/cel, str       TP

Symphony No. 2 (1955)                           34'
  2222; 4331; timp+2, pf, cel, str          ECS

Symphony No. 3 (1956)                           15'
  3*3*3*3*; 4331; timp+3, pf/cel, str       AMP

Scenario for Orchestra (1957)                   25'
  4*3*4=3*; 4331; perc, 2pf, str            TP

Divertimento No. 1 (1959)                       16'
  2221; 1110; perc, pf, cel, str            TP

A Christmas Set (1968)                          30'
  satb cho; 1*121; 1210; 2perc, hp,         ECS
  pf, str (0-2-1-1)

Pastorale and Spring Valley Overture (1973)      6'
  2*2*2=2; 3220; timp+1, pf, str            ECS

Magic, Magic, Magic! (1976)                     18'
  soli a, t; narr; satb cho; 224=2; 4330;   GS
  3perc, pf, str


     KUPFERMAN, MEYER  (1926-    )

Concerto for Piano and Orchestra (1948)         13'
  solo pf; 2*2*2*2*; 4331; timp+4, str      SS

Libretto for Orchestra (1948)                   18'
  2*2*2*2*; 4331; timp+1, hp, cel, str      EMI

Little Symphony (1952)                          22'
  1*202; 2000; str                          GS

Ostinato Burlesco (1954)                         8'
  2*2*2*2*; 4331; timp+3, hp, pf, str       EMI

Symphony No. 4 (1955)                           26'
  2*2*2*2; 4330; timp+1, hp, str            GS

Symphony No. 3 (1956)                           23'
  2*2*2*2*; 4330; timp+2, hp, str           EMI

Variations for Orchestra (1959)                 13'
  2*222; 4231; timp+4, hp, cel, str         EMI

Festivals (1962)                                              13'
    2*2*22; 4230; timp+5, hp, str                            EMI

Six Epilogues (1967)                                          9'
    2222; 4331; timp+2, hp, str                              SS

Sculptures (1971)                                            15'
    2*2*2*2*; 4331; timp+1, hp, str                          SS

Yin-Yang Symphony (1972)                                     43'
    3*3*3*3*; 6431; timp+3, hp, pf, str                      EMI

Concerto for Violoncello, Tape and
    Orchestra (1974)                                         30'
    solo vc; 2222; 4231; timp+2, hp,                         AMC
    str, tape

Symphony for Twelve (1974)                                   30'
    1111; 0110; perc, elec hpsd,                             SS
    str (1-1-1-1)

Symphony No. 7 (1974)                                        24'
    2*2*2*2*; 4331; timp+2, hp, str                          SS

Sinfonia Brevis (1975)                                       14'
    2*2*2*2*; 4331; timp+2, hp, str                          SS

Sound Objects No. 10 (1979)                                  10'
    1111; 1110; perc, str (1-1-1-1)                          SS

Rhapsody for Guitar and Orchestra (1980)                     14'
    solo gtr; 1111; 1110; timp+1, str                        SS

Sound Phantoms No. 8 (1980)                                  14'
    3*3*3(s sax)2; 4331; timp+2, hp, str                     SS

Symphony No. 9 (1980)                                        20'
    2222; 4210; timp+2, hp, str                              SS

Symphony No. 10:  FDR (1981)                                 45'
    2222; 4331; hp, pf, str                                  EMI

Concerto for Tuba and Orchestra (1982)                       23'
    solo tba; 2*2*2*2*; 4331; timp+2,                        SS
    hp, cel, str

Symphony No. 11 (1983)                                       18'
    3*3*3*3*; 4331; timp+2, hp, pf, str                      SS

Concerto for Clarinet and Orchestra (1984)     24'
    solo cl; 2*2*2*2*; 4210; timp+1,             SS
    hp, pf, str

Overture for Double Orchestra (1987)           20'
    2*2*22; 221(b tbn)0; timp+2,                 SS
    2elec hpsd, str
    N.B.   Requires two conductors for performance.

Wings of the Highest Tower (1987)              15'
    2*2*3*2*; 421(b tbn)0; timp+2, hp,           SS
    pf, str

Jazz Symphony (1988)                           25'
    solo mez; solo a sax; 2+2*2*2*; 4331;        SS
    timp+3, hp, pf, str

Savage Landscape (1989)                        12'
    3*3*3*3*; 6431; timp+4, hp, str              SS

"Markings" for Orchestra (1990)                12'
    3*3*3*3*; 4331; timp+2, hp, str              SS

Symphonic Odyssey (1990)                       21'
    3*3*3*3*; 6431; timp+3, hp, pf, str          SS

Double Concerto for Two Clarinets and
    Orchestra (1991)                           25'
    soli 2cl; 2*2*2*2*; 4331; timp+2, hp, str   SS

Concerto for Trumpet and
    Chamber Orchestra (NA)                     15'
    solo tpt; 1*02*0; 0000; timp+4, pf, str     SS


            KUREK, MICHAEL   (1955-    )

Chimera (1985)                                 15'
    3*3*3*3*; 4331; timp+3, hp, pf, cel, str    MS

Concerto for Harp and Orchestra (1991)         20'
    solo hp; 2222; 4000; timp+2, pf/cel, str    MS


            KURKA, ROBERT  (1921-1957)

Serenade, op. 25 (1954)                        20'
    2*222; 2200; timp, str                       GS

Julius Caesar - overture, op. 28 (1955)          9'
   3*222; 4221; timp, str                        GS

Concertino for Two Pianos, op. 31 (1956)        15'
   soli 2pf; tpt obbl; str                       GS

Concerto for Marimba and Orchestra,
   op. 34 (1957)                                 20'
   solo mar; 2*222; 2210; timp+1, str            GS

Ballad, op. 36 (1957)                            8'
   solo hn; str                                  GS

Symphony No. 2, op. 24 (1957)                   22'
   3*3*3*3*; 4331; timp+3, str                   GS

Concerto for Violin and Orchestra,
   op. 8 (NA)                                    15'
   solo vln; 2222; 2000; str                     GS

Music for Orchestra, op. 11 (NA)                17'
   3*33*3*; 4331; timp+1, hp, cel, str           GS

LADERMAN, EZRA (1924-    )

| | | |
|---|---|---|
| Concerto for Piano and Orchestra (1957)<br>solo pf; 2222; 4330; timp+2, str | 26'<br>GS | |
| Stanzas (1961)<br>2121; 1110; timp+2, org, str | 21'<br>OXF | |
| Symphony No. 1 (1963)<br>3*3*4=3*; 4341; timp+5, str | 27'<br>GS | |
| Magic Prison (1967)<br>2narr; 223*2; 4330; timp+2, hp, org, str | 25'<br>OXF | |
| Symphony No. 2 "Luther" (1967)<br>3333*; 4331; timp+3, hp, cel, org, str | 25'<br>GS | |
| Celestial Bodies (Flute Concerto) (1968)<br>solo fl; str | 20'<br>OXF | |
| Concerto for Orchestra (Satire) (1968)<br>3*3*3*3*; 4331; timp+2, hp, cel, str | 24'<br>OXF | |
| Symphony No. 3 "Jerusalem" (1973)<br>3*3*3*3*; 4331; timp+3, hp, str | 40'<br>GS | |
| "Visions - Columbus" (1976)<br>solo b-bar; 3*3*3*3*; 4330; timp+1,<br>hp, str | 25'<br>GS | |
| Concerto for Viola and<br>Chamber Orchestra (1977)<br>solo vla; 1*212; 2000; pf, str | 30'<br>GS | |
| Concerto for Violin and Orchestra (1978)<br>solo vln; 3*23*3*; 4230; timp+2, str | 27'<br>GS | |
| Concerto for String Quartet and<br>Orchestra (1980)<br>solo str qt; 3*223*; 4230; timp, str | 25'<br>GS | |
| Summer Solstice (1980)<br>2222; 2221; timp+4, cel, str | 17'<br>GS | |
| Symphony No. 4 (1981)<br>3*3*3*3*; 6441; timp+3, str | 30'<br>GS | |

Concerto for Flute, Bassoon and
  Orchestra (1982)                        29'
  soli fl, bsn; 3*3*3*2; 4230; timp+2,     GS
  hp, str

Symphony No. 5 "Isaiah" (1982)        36'
  4=4*4*4*; 4431; timp+3, str       GS

Sonore (1983)                   21'
  3+3*4=3*; 44(picc tpt)31; timp+4, str  GS

Concerto for Violoncello and
  Orchestra (1985)                   29'
  solo vc; 3*222; 4231; timp+3, str   GS

Pentimento (1985)              29'
  3*3*3=3; 4331; timp+3, pf/cel, str  GS

Symphony No. 6 (1985)          28'
  3=3*4=3*; 44(picc tpt)31; timp+4, str  GS

Concerto for Flute and Orchestra (1986)  29'
  solo fl; 3*3*3*3*; 4230; timp+3, str  GS

Concerto for Violin, Violoncello and
  Orchestra (1986)                   42'
  soli vln, vc; 2222; 4230; timp+3, hp, str GS

Sanctuary
  An Original Theme and Variations (1986)  19'
  3*3*3*3*; 4331; timp+3, hp, str   GS

Symphony No. 7 (1986)          40'
  3*3*3*3*; 4331; timp+3, str     GS

Sinfonia Concertante (1988)       28'
  soli picc, eh, b cl, tpt, b tbn; 2222;  GS
  4220; timp+4, str

Concerto for Chamber Orchestra (1989)  20'
  2222; 2210; 2perc, str          GS

Concerto for Double Orchestra
  "A Play Within A Play" (1989)     35'
  3*3*3*3*; 4331; timp+1, str     GS

Concerto No. 2 for Piano and
  Orchestra (1989)                   27'
  solo pf; 2222; 4220; timp+3, str   GS

Citadel (1990)                                      20'
   3*3*22; 4330; timp+3, str                   GS

And David Wept (NA)                                 50'
   solo mez, t, b-bar; 1121; 2100; 2perc,       OXF
   pf/hpsd, str

Double Helix (NA)                                   12'
   soli fl, ob; str                             OXF

A Single Voice (NA)                                 10'
   solo ob; str                                 OXF


     LA MONTAINE, JOHN  (1920-    )

Songs of the Rose of Sharon, op. 6 (1948)          14'
   solo s; 2223*; 4231; timp, hp, str           BRO

Canons, op. 10a (1956)                             10'
   2*23*2*; 4220; timp+1, hp, cel, str          CF

Sonnets for Orchestra, op. 12a (1957)              12'
   solo high or med v; 2222; 4331;              FRE
   timp+1, str

Recitative, Aria and Finale, op. 16a (1957)        NA
   str                                          FRE

Jubilant Overture, op. 20 (1957)                   7'
   3*223*; 4331; timp+2, str                    FRE

Colloquy, op. 21 (1957)                            14'
   str                                          FRE

Passacaglia and Fugue, op. 21a (1957)              NA
   str                                          FRE

Concerto for Piano and Orchestra,
   op. 9 (1958)                                 30'
   solo pf; 3*3*3*3*; 4330; timp+4, str         GAL

Fragments from the Song of Songs,
   op. 29 (1959)                                30'
   solo s; 2222; 4331; timp+1, hp, pf, str      FRE

Come into My Garden, op. 29a (1959)                5'
   3*2*11; 0000; hp, pf, str                    FRE

Overture: From Sea to Shining Sea,
   op. 30 (1960)                             8'
   3*223*; 4340; timp+3, str          FRE

Novellis, Novellis, op. 31 (1960)      45'
   soli 8vv; satb cho; 23*13*; 0330; timp+1,  FRE
   hp, hpsd, org(opt), str

A Summer's Day, op. 32 (1961)         6'
   1110; 1100; hp, str              GS

Birds of Paradise, op. 34 (1964)      13'
   solo pf; 3*3*22; 4331; timp, hp, str    CF

Mass of Nature, op. 37 (1966)         NA
   satb cho; 3*2*3+2*; 4331; timp+2, hp, str  FRE

Wilderness Journal (Symphony for Bass-Baritone,
   Organ and Orchestra), op. 41 (1972)   45'
   solo b-bar; 2*1*2+1; 1220; 3perc, hp, pf,  FRE
   org, str, tape

Be Glad Then America - A Decent Entertainment
   from the Thirteen Colonies, op. 43 (1973) 80'
   soli 4vv; satb cho; 3*223*; 4331;      FRE
   timp+2, str

Overture: An Early American Sampler,
   op. 34a (1974)                        8'
   3*223*; 4331; timp+2, str          FRE

Concerto for Flute and Orchestra,
   op. 48 (1978)                        25'
   solo fl; 2*2*2+2*; 0320; timp+2, hp, str  FRE

Two Scenes from the Song of Solomon,
   op. 49 (1979)                        10'
   solo fl; 3*2*11; 0000; hp, pf, str     FRE

The Whittier Service, op. 45 (1981)    30'
   satb cho; 0000; 4331; timp(opt),       FRE
   org(opt), gtr, str

Concerto for String Orchestra, op. 51 (1981) NA
   str                                  FRE

Symphonic Variations, op. 50 (1982)    19'
   solo pf; 223*2; 2320; 2perc, str       FRE

Concerto II for Piano and Orchestra,
    op. 55 (1983)                                          32'
    solo pf; 2*2*3=2*; 2220; timp+2, str                  FRE

The Marshes of Glynn, op. 53 (1984)                       18'
    solo b; satb cho; 1*1*2+1; 1100;                      FRE
    2perc, hp, str

Concerto III for Piano and Orchestra,
    op. 56 (1986)                                          20'
    solo pf; 2*2*3=2*; 2221; timp+2, str                  FRE

Concerto IV for Piano and Orchestra,
    op. 59 (1989)                                          28'
    solo pf; 3*3*4=3*; 4330; timp+2, str                  FRE


                  LANG, DAVID  (1957-      )

Eating Living Monkeys (1985-1987)                           8'
    3*3*3*3; 4331; 4perc, hp, pf, str                      MG

Bonehead (1990)                                           18'
    3*3*3*3*; 2bar sax; 0000; 4perc, hp,                  NOV
    pf, b gtr, str

International Business Machine (1990)                       5'
    3*333; 4331; 4perc, hp, cel, str                      NOV


                  LANGE, ARTHUR  (1889-1956)

American Pastorale No. 1 (1947)                           12'
    3*3*3*2; 4331; timp+1, hp, cel, str                   FLE

American Pastorale No. 2 (1947)                           14'
    3*3*3*2; 4331; timp+2, hp, cel, str                   FLE

Symphony No. 1 (1948)                                     23'
    3*2*22; 4331; timp+1, hp, cel, str                    FLE

American Pastorale No. 3 (1951)                           13'
    22*22; 4331; timp+1, hp, cel, str                     FLE

Arabesque (1953)                                          13'
    solo hp; 1121; 2200; timp+1, str                      FLE

Atoms for Peace - overture (1955)                         10'
    2*2*3*2; 4331; timp+1, str                            FLE

Divertimento for String Orchestra (1956)          8'
  str                                             FLE


        LANKESTER, MICHAEL

Seven Nursery Rhymes (1983)                       20'
  2*22*2; 2110; timp+2, hp, str                   MMB
  N.B.  Requires audience participation.

Two Christmas Carols (1983)                        6'
  1+22*2; 4230; 2perc, hp, str                    MMB
  N.B.  Requires audience participation.

Make Your Own Orchestra (1984)                     16'
  soli bamboo fl, drinking straw,                 MMB
  hosepipe in F, bottles, broomstick bass;
  2(bamboo fl)2(drinking straw)22;
  3(hosepipe in F)201; 3perc(2 bottles),
  hp, str (principal bass plays broomstick)
  N.B.  The solo "instruments" are available
  on rental from the publisher.

The Time Machine (1989)                            7'
  narr; 1*111; 2110; perc, str                    MMB


        LAROCCA, FRANK  (1951-    )

The Pure Fury (1989)                              20'
  solo t; 3*3*3*2; 3000; timp+2, hp, str          MS


        LARSEN, LIBBY  (1950-    )

Tom Twist (1975)                                   8'
  narr; 2*12=2; a sax; 1100; 2perc, hp, pf,       ECS
  str, mime

Weaver's Song and Jig (1978)                       9'
  1*111; 1000; perc, str                          ECS

Pinions (1982)                                    15'
  solo vln; 1111; 1000; pf, str                   ECS

Overture:  Parachute Dancing (1984)                7'
  2*222; 4231; timp+3, pf, str                    ECS

Coriolis (1985)                                              12'
   3*23*3*; 4231; timp+3, pf/cel, str          ECS

In A Winter Garden (1985)                                    40'
   soli mez, t; satb cho; 1*100; 0000;         ECS
   3perc, hp, str

Symphony No. 1 "Water Music" (1985)                          19'
   3*23*0; 4331; timp+3, hp, pf/cel, str       ECS

Coming Forth Into Day
   (Symphony No. 2) (1986)                     45'
   2*222*; 4331; 2perc, hp, str                ECS

Deep Summer Music (1986)                                      8'
   2*212; 4130; timp+2, str                    ECS

What the Monster Saw (1987)                                  14'
   1*11*1*; 1100; perc, pf, DX-7 synth, str    ECS

Collage: Boogie (1988)                                        5'
   3*23=2; 4331; timp+3, kybd, str             ECS

Concerto for Trumpet and Orchestra (1988)                   25'
   solo tpt; 2*222; 4231; 3perc, cel, str      ECS

Concerto: Cold, Silent Snow (1989)                          27'
   soli fl, hp; 2*222; 2000; 2perc, str        ECS

Symphony No. 3 "Lyric" (1990)                               40'
   3(2picc)3*3(s,a,b cl)3*; 4331; timp+3,      ECS
   hp, pf, cel, synth, str


      LASSER, PHILIP   (1963-    )

Southern Landscapes (1987)                                   7'
   3*23*3*; 4230; perc, vib/xyl, hp, str       NOA


      LAUFER, BEATRICE   (1923-    )

Symphony No. 1 (1945)                                        21'
   3*23*2; 4220; timp+1, hp, cel, str          BEL

Festival and Frolic -
   Two Orchestral Dances (1954)                12'
   2*222; 4220; timp+1, hp, cel, str           MS

Small Concerto for Chamber Orchestra (1960)        15'
    1111; 1000; pf, str                            MS

Symphony No. 2 (1960)                              20'
    3*23*2; 4331; timp+1, hp, str                  MS

Concerto for Flute, Oboe, Trumpet and
    Strings (1962)                                 10'
    soli fl, ob, tpt; str                          MS

Cry! - An Orchestral Prelude (1965)               6'
    2*122; 2321; timp+2, str                       MCA

In the Throes (1965)                              9'
    2*122; 2321; timp+2, str                       MCA

Resolution (1965)                                 6'
    2*122; 2321; timp+2, str                       MCA

    N.B.  "Cry!", "In the Throes", and "Resolution"
    are constituent parts of the "Orchestral
    Trilogy."

Everest:  A Fugue for Orchestra (1966)            8'
    3*23*2; 4331; timp+1, hp, str                  MS

Overture for Orchestra (Crucible) (1972)          9'
    3*3*3*2; 4331; timp+3, cel, str                MS

And Thomas Jefferson... (1974)                    60'
    solo bar; ssaattbb cho; 3*3*3*2; 4331;         MS
    timp+3, hp, str

Prelude and Fugue (1975)                          9'
    3*23*2; 4331; timp+3, hp, str                  MS

Prologue and Epilogue (1980)                      8'
    3*3*3*2; 4331; timp+2, hp, str                 MS


        LAVENDA, RICHARD  (1955-      )

Star Shadow (1983)                                18'
    3*3*3*3*; 4230; timp+3, hp, str                MMB

Affinities (1988)                                 8'
    3=3*3*3*; 4331; timp+3, hp, str                MS

Free Fall (1989)                                  15'
    2=1*2*1; 2110; 2perc, hp, str                  MS

LAYTON, BILLY JIM   (1924-      )

An American Portrait, op. 2 (1953)                    12'
  3*3*3*2; 4331; timp+2, str                        GS

Dance Fantasy, op. 7 (1964)                           26'
  3*3*3*3*; 4331; timp+4, hp, pf, cel, str    GS


LAZAROF, HENRI   (1932-      )

Piccola serenata (1959)                                7'
  2222; 2200; timp, str                             IMI

Viola Concerto (1960)                                 23'
  solo vla; 32*2*2*; 4331; timp+2,                  IMI
  hp, pf, str

Concerto for Piano and
  Twenty Instruments (1961)                         18'
  solo pf; 002*2; 2100; str (0-6-4-2)               IMI

Odes for Orchestra (1963)                             10'
  212*2*; 1111; timp+1, hp, pf, cel, str      AMP

Rhapsody for Violin and Orchestra (1966)             10'
  solo vln; 3*222; 2220; timp+1,                    AMP
  hp, pf, str

Structures sonores (1966)                             28'
  3*3*3*3*; 4431; timp+3, hp, pf, cel, str    AMP

Mutazione (1967)                                      13'
  3*3*3*3*; 4331; timp+1, 2hp, pf, cel, str   AMP

Concerto for Cello and Orchestra (1968)              18'
  solo vc; 3+3*3*3*; 4431; timp+1,                  AMP
  hp, pf/cel, str

Omaggio (1968)                                        16'
  2+2*2*0; 1110; timp+4, hp, pf,                    AMP
  cel, str (0-1-1-1)

Textures (1970)                                       23'
  solo pf; 2+2*2*0; 2221; timp+4, hp, cel,    AMP
  harmonium, str

Konkordia (1971)                                      13'
  str                                               AMP

Concerto for Flute and Orchestra (1973)            22'
    solo fl; 203*0; 4220; 3perc, hp, pf,            GS
    pf/cel, harmonium, str

Spectrum for Trumpet and Orchestra (1973)          15'
    solo tpt; 4*4*4*4*; 4231; 4perc, hp, pf,        MER
    str (no vln, vla), tape

Ritralto (1974)                                    10'
    2222; 3210; timp+1, hp, pf/cel, str            AMP

Volo for Viola and String Orchestra (1975)         26'
    solo vla; str                                  MER

Chamber Symphony (1976)                            18'
    1202; 2000; str                                MER

Concerto for Orchestra (1977)                      21'
    4*4*4*4*; 6441; timp+3, 2hp, pf, cel, str      MER

Symphony (1978)                                    23'
    3*3*3*3*; 5331; timp+3, hp, pf, str            TP

Sinfonietta (1981)                                 18'
    2222; 2200; perc, str                          MER

Poema (1986)                                       11'
    33*3*3; 4331; timp+3, hp, pf/cel, str          MER

Second Concerto for Orchestra: Icarus (1986)       22'
    4*4*4*4*; 6431; 2timp+2, hp, pf/cel, str       MER

Concerto for Violin and Orchestra (1987)           25'
    solo vln; 22*2*2; 2200; 2perc, hp,             MER
    pf/cel, str (8-6-4-4-2)

Tableaux (after Kandinsky) (1989)                  27'
    solo pf; 4=4*4*4*; 6431; timp+4, hp,           MER
    str (16-14-12-12-10)

Clarinet Concerto (1990)                           22'
    solo cl; 2perc, hp, str (8-6-4-4-2)            MER


           LE BARON, ANNE  (1953-    )

Three Movements for Orchestra (1973)               16'
    5perc, str                                     ACA

Strange Attractors (1987)                                    13'
    2*2*2+2*; 4331; timp+3, hp, pf/cel, str            MMB


                LEE, DAI-KEONG   (1915-       )

Symphony No. 1 (1945)                                        20'
    3*222; 4331; timp+1, str                           BEL

Concerto for Violin and Orchestra (1947)                    24'
    solo vln; 2222; 4231; timp+1, str                  BEL

Waltzing Matilda - suite from ballet (1951)                 15'
    3*222; 4331; timp+2, str                           CF

Symphony No. 2 (1952)                                       22'
    3*222; 4331; timp+1, str                           BEL

Teahouse of the August Moon - suite (1954)                  14'
    3*3*22; 4331; timp+3, hp, str                      BEL

Polynesian Suite (1958)                                     15'
    4*3*23*; 4331; timp+1, str                         BEL

Canticle of the Pacific (1968)                              15'
    satb cho; 3*222; 4331; timp+2, str                 BEL

Overture for Chamber Orchestra (NA)                          7'
    1121; 2210; timp, str                              BH

Peter and his Magic Flute (NA)                              10'
    narr; 1121; 2221; perc, hp, cel, str               BH


                LEE, THOMAS OBOE   (1945-       )

Phantasia for Elvira Shatayev (1981)                        20'
    solo s; 1*212; 21(fl hn)21; 2perc,                 MG
    hp, pf, str

Morango - Almost a Tango (1984)                              8'
    str (6-5-4-4-2)                                    DFM

Harp Concerto (1985)                                        19'
    solo hp; 1*120; 2200; 2perc, str                   MG

Concertino (1986)                                           15'
    solo tpt; timp, str (6-5-4-4-2 minimum)            DFM

Jana... An American Overture (1991)                    12'
   3(3picc)223; 4231; 2perc, pf, str                 DFM


     LEES, BENJAMIN  (1924-    )

Profile (1952)                                          7'
   3*23*3*; 4331; timp+4, str                         EWM

Declamations (1953)                                     9'
   solo pf; str                                       EWM

Piano Concerto No. 1 (1953)                            24'
   solo pf; 3*3*3*3*; 4331; timp+2, str               BH

Symphony No. 1 (1953)                                  19'
   3*3*3*3*; 4331; timp+1, pf, str                    BH

Divertimento Burlesca (1957)                           22'
   2*2*22; 2210; timp+1, hp, str                      BH

Interlude (1957)                                       12'
   str                                                BH

Symphony No. 2 (1958)                                  22'
   2*2*22; 4331; timp+1, hp, str                      BH

Violin Concerto (1958)                                 24'
   solo vln; 3*3*3*3*; 4331; timp+2, str              BH

Concertante breve (1959)                               16'
   0100; 2000; pf, str                                BH

Concerto for Orchestra (1959)                          24'
   3*3*3*3*; 4331; timp+3, pf, cel, str               BH

Prologue, Capriccio and Epilogue (1961)               10'
   3*3*3*2; 4231; timp+3, str                         BH

Vision of Poets (1961)                                 40'
   soli s, t; satb cho; 3*3*3*3*; 4331;               BH
   timp+3, hp, cel, str

Oboe Concerto (1963)                                   17'
   solo ob; 2*022; 2000; timp+2, str                  BH

Concerto for String Quartet and
   Orchestra (1964)                                   23'
   solo str qt; 2*2*22; 4331; timp+3, str             BH

Spectrum (1964)                                          10'
   2*222; 2210; 2perc, pf, str                          BH

Concerto for Chamber Orchestra (1966)                   18'
   2*2*2*2*; 2200; timp+2, str                          BH

Piano Concerto No. 2 (1966)                             25'
   solo pf; 3*33*3*; 4331; timp+4, str                  BH

Silhouettes (1967)                                      15'
   1*1*11; 1110; timp+2, hp, pf, str                    BH

Symphony No. 3 (1968)                                   26'
   3*3*3*3*; t sax; 5431; timp+5, cel, str              BH

The Trumpet of the Swan (1972)                          17'
   narr; 2*2*22; 4331; timp+4, str                      BH

Etudes (1974)                                           20'
   2*22*2*; 4331; timp+3, cel, str                      BH

Passacaglia for Orchestra (1975)                        13'
   3*223*; 4331; timp+3, pf, str                        BH

Concerto for Woodwind Quintet and
   Orchestra (1976)                                     22'
   solo ww qnt; 0000; 2230; timp+4, cel, str  BH

Variations for Piano and Orchestra (1976)               23'
   solo pf; 3*223*; 4331; timp+3, str                   BH

Scarlatti Portfolio - ballet (1978)                     25'
   2222; 2210; timp+1, str                              BH

Mobiles (1980)                                          20'
   2*22*2*; 2200; timp+4, hp, cel, str                  BH

Double Concerto (1982)                                  20'
   solo vc, pf; 2*222*; 4331; timp+1, str               BH

Concerto for Brass Choir and Orchestra (1983) 26'
   3*000; 4331; timp+1, cel, str                        BH

Portrait of Rodin (1984)                                17'
   3*33*3*; 4331; timp+3, hp, cel, str                  BH

Symphony No. 4 "Memorial Candles" (1985)                60'
   solo mez; solo vln; 3*333*; 4431; timp+4,  BH
   hp, cel, str

Symphony No. 5 (Kalmar Nyckel) (1986)                26'
   3*33*3*; 4331; timp+3, hp, str                    BH


LEICHTLING, ALAN  (1947-    )

Symphony No. 1, op. 35 (1965)                         60'
   4=4*4=4*; 4441; timp+5, 2hp, pf, cel, str         AMC

Concerto for Chamber Orchestra (1966)                20'
   102*0; 1110; 4perc, str                           SEE

Symphony No. 2 (1966)                                 22'
   3*3*3*3*; 4331; timp+6, hp, str                   SEE

Concerto for Viola and Orchestra
   (1968; rev 1982)                                  33'
   solo vla; 223*2; 4221; timp+3, hp, str            SEE

Fantasy Piece No. 5 (1979)                            10'
   3*3*3*3*; 4331; timp+3, hp, cel, str              SEE

Capriccio (1980)                                      14'
   1212; 2000; timp+1, cel/hpsd, str                 SEE

Concerto for Violin, Cello, Piano and
   Orchestra (1980)                                  39'
   solo vln, vc, pf; 3*3*4=3*; 4331; perc,           SEE
   hp, str

Symphony No. 3 (1980)                                 20'
   3*3*3*3*; 4331; timp+1, hp, str                   SEE

Eleven Songs "Shropshire" (1984)                      45'
   solo bar; 113*2; 2220; perc, hp, pf, str          SEE


LENNON, JOHN ANTHONY  (1950-    )

Metapictures (1981)                                   13'
   2*12*1; 2110; 3perc, hp, pf, cel, str             ECS

Symphonic Rhapsody (1984)                             20'
   solo a sax; 4*23*3*; 4321; 3perc,                 ECS
   hp, pf, str

Spectra (1987)                                        24'
   3*3*8*3*; 4321; 3perc, hp, pf, cel, str           ECS

Suite of Fables (1989)                                    15'
    narr; 4*23*2; 4321; 3perc, hp,                        ECS
    pf, cel, str

Zingari - Concerto for Guitar (1991)                      18'
    solo gtr; 3*3*22; 4310; 3perc,                        ECS
    hp, cel, str


### LENTZ, DANIEL

10 Minus 30 Minutes (1970)                                20'
    str                                                   LTZ

The Crack in the Bell (1985)                              16'
    solo v; 1000; 1111; 2perc, pf,                        LTZ
    3kybd, str (1-1-1-1), electronics

An American in L.A. (1987)                                19'
    4*4*4*4*; 4441; timp+4, 2hp,                          LTZ
    pf, kybd, str

Apache Wine:  White, Blush, Red (1988)                    15'
    1211; 3100; perc, kybd, str                           LTZ


### LEON, TANIA  (1943-    )

Concerto criollo (1977)                                   20'
    solo pf; 2222; 4430; timp+3, str                      PS

The Golden Windows (1982)                                 30'
    1=1*00; 0100; 2perc, pf, hpsd, str                    PS

Bata (1985)                                               12'
    2*2*2*2; 2221; 2perc, hp, pf, cel, str                PS

Kabiosile (1988)                                          8'
    solo pf; 2*2*2*2*; 4230; timp+2, str                  PS


### LERDAHL, ALFRED  (1943-    )

Aftermath (1973)                                          30'
    soli s, mez, bar; 2121; 0000; 2perc,                  BOE
    hp, str (1-1-2-0)

Chords (1974; rev 1983)                                   15'
    3*3*3*3*; 3330; 5perc, str (0-3-3-3)                  BOE

Beyond the Realm of the Bird (1981-1984)        13'
    solo s; 2222; 1110; 2perc, hp, pf, str      BOE

Cross-Currents (1987)                           10'
    3*333; 4231; 4perc, hp, pf, str             BOE

Waves (1988)                                    15'
    2*222; 2000; str (5-4-3-3-1)                BOE


        LESEMANN, FREDERICK

Scherzo for Orchestra (1960)                     6'
    2*22*2; 4231; timp+1, hp, pf, str           MS

The Garden of the Prosperine -
    cantata (1966-1969)                         35'
    solo mez, bar; satb cho; 1*1*1*1*; 1111;    MS
    3perc, hp, str (2-1-1-1)

Symphony in Three Movements (1971)              22'
    4*3*3*4*; 4332; timp+1, hp, pf, str         TP

Orchestra Music (1976)                          NA
    3*3*3*3*; 4331; perc, pf, str               MS

Legends:  An Orchestral Suite after the U.S.
    Bicentennial (1977)                         22'
    3*3*3*3*; 4331; 2perc, pf, str              MS

Seven Pieces for String Orchestra and
    Electronic Tape (1980)                      15'
    str (6-6-4-4-2 minimum), stereo tape        MS


        LE SIEGE, ANNETTE

Montage (1975)                                  15'
    3*3*3*2; 4330; 4perc, str                   SEE

Star Gazers (1982)                              15'
    3*222; 4221; timp+3, str                    SEE

Sapphire Seesaw (1987)                          15'
    3*3*3*3*; 4331; timp+3, str                 SEE

LESSARD, JOHN  (1920-      )

Box Hill Overture (1946)                        9'
    3*222; 4221; timp, str                      ACA

Cantilena (1947)                                6'
    solo ob; str                                ACA

Little Concert (1947)                          12'
    3*23*2; 4220; timp, str                     ACA

Serenade No. 1 for Strings (1953)               3'
    str                                         ACA

Serenade No. 2 for Strings (1957)               3'
    str                                         ACA

Suite (1959)                                   12'
    223*2; 4320; timp+1, str                    ACA

Sinfonietta concertante (1961)                 15'
    2020; 2210; str                             ACA

Concerto for Harp and Orchestra (1963)         14'
    solo hp; 2121; 2310; str                    ACA

Pastimes and an Alleluia (1975)                15'
    2111; 2220; 2perc, hp, pf/cel, str,         ACA
    taped voice


LEVI, PAUL ALAN  (1941-      )

Symphonic Movement (1972)                      12'
    2222; 2321; timp+3, hp, str                 MER

Stringalevio (1973)                             4'
    solo timp; str                              ACA

The Natural History of the
    Water Closet (1976)                        25'
    satb cho; 1011; 1110; timp+1, hp, str       ACA

Transformations of the Heart (1987)            12'
    2222; 2220; 2perc, hp, str                  ACA

Songs for the Synagogue (1989)                 25'
    solo vln; cantor; children's cho;           ACA
    satb cho; str

LEVIN, TODD   (1961-      )

Turn extended dance mix (1987)                          17'
  3(2picc)3*3=2; 4331; 4perc, pf, str                    NOA


LEVY, FRANK   (1930-      )

Symphony No. 1 (1969)                                   18'
  2121; 2221; timp+1, gtr, str                          SEE


LEVY, MARTIN DAVID   (1932-      )

Caramoor Festival Overture (1959)                       12'
  2222; 4231; timp+4, hp, str                           BH

For the Time Being -
  Christmas Oratorio (1959)                            105'
  soli 2s, mez, t, bar, b; satb cho;                    BH
  3*3*3*3*; 4431; timp+2, hp, pf,
  cel, org, str

Symphony No. 1 (1960)                                   24'
  3*3*3*3*; 4331; timp+4, hp, pf/cel, str               BH

Kyros - Dance Poem (1961)                               20'
  2222; 3220; timp+4, hp, pf(offstage), str            BH

One Person - cantata (1962)                             20'
  solo ca; 2222; 4231; timp+4, hp,                      BH
  pf, cel, str

Concerto No. 1 for Piano and
  Orchestra (1970)                                     22'
  solo pf; 2*222; 4230; timp+4, hp,                     BH
  elec gtr, str

Trialogus I (1972)                                      18'
  0000; 3000; hp, pf, org, str                          BH

Trialogus II (1972)                                     15'
  1211; 1110; hp, org, str                              BH

In Memoriam:  W. H. Auden (1974)                        22'
  solo t; 1111; 1000; elec pf, org, str                BH

Canto de los Marranos (1977)                            25'
  solo s; 2222; 2110; timp+4, hp, pf, str              BH

Masada - oratorio (1987)                                      100'
   solo t; narr; satb cho; 3*222; 4331;            SSM
   timp+4, hp, pf, cel, str

Arrows of Time (1988)                                         14'
   soli 4perc; 3*222; 4331; timp, hp,              SSM
   glock(or cel), str
   N.B.  Three offstage trumpets (doubling on
   percussion instruments) are also required.

Pascua Florida (1988)                                         13'
   3*222; 4231; timp+2, hp, str                    SSM


        LEWIN, DAVID  (1933-    )

Essay on a Subject by Webern (1958)                           10'
   1111; 2100; str (4-4-3-3-0)                      MS

Fantasy - Adagio (1963-1966)                                  15'
   solo vln; 2222; 4231; timp, str                 MS


        LEWIN, FRANK  (1925-    )

Evocation (1960)                                              18'
   2222; 4200; timp+1, str                         ACA

Concerto on Silesian Tunes (1965)                            20'
   solo vla; 2222; 2000; timp+1,                   ACA
   hp, cel, str


        LEWIS, JAMES  (1938-    )

(...the errant note to seize) (1987)                          9'
   22*3*2; 4231; timp+1, pf/cel, str               MG
   OR:  22*3*2; 2211; perc, hp, pf/cel, str


        LEWIS, JOHN  (1920-    )

England's Carol (1960)                                        7'
   soli pf, db, vib, dmst; 1111; 0000;             MJQ
   hp, str

Original Sin (1961)                                           24'
   222*1; 2110; timp+2, dmst, str                  MJQ

Concert Piece (NA)                                   20'
    soli pf, db, vib, dmst; 3*222; 4321;            MJQ
    perc, hp, str

Fanfare - Salute to Basie (NA)                        5'
    333*3*; 4431; timp+1, vib, hp, bells, str       MJQ

Jazz Ostinato (NA)                                    6'
    soli pf, db, vib, dmst; 3*3*3*3*; 4431;         MJQ
    timp+1, hp, cel, str

Na Dubrovacki (NA)                                   20'
    soli pf, gtr, vib, dmst; str                    MJQ

The Queen's Fancy (NA)                                5'
    soli pf, db, vib, dmst; 1111; 2321;             MJQ
    timp, hp, str

The Spiritual (NA)                                    7'
    soli pf, db, vib, dmst; 3*3*3*3*; 4431;         MJQ
    timp+1, hp, cel, str


        LEWIS, PETER TOD   (1932-1982)

Evolution (1961)                                     10'
    1111; 2111; timp+2, str                         MER

Images:  In Memoriam James Agee (1962)              15'
    narr; 1111; 1000; pf, str (2-1-1-1)             ACA
    OR:  narr; 3*3*3*3*; 4331; perc, hp, pf, str

Espejo (1966)                                         8'
    1111; 2110; str                                 ACA

Fragments/Hedgehogs (1978)                            8'
    3*3*4=2; 2231; timp+1, pf, str, tape            ACA


        LEWIS, ROBERT HALL   (1926-    )

Prelude and Finale (1959)                            14'
    1111; 1100; perc, str                           TP

Designs (1963)                                       14'
    3*3*3*2; 4331; timp+1, hp, str                  TP

Three Pieces for Orchestra (1965)                     7'
    3*3*3*3*; 4331; timp+1, cel, str                TP

Concerto for Chamber Orchestra
    (1967; rev 1972)                                     15'
    2221; 1110; perc, hp, str                            TP

Symphony No. 2 (1971)                                    21'
    3*3*3*3*; 4331; timp+1, hp, str                      TP

Nuances II (1975)                                        24'
    3*3*3*3*; 4331; timp+4, hp, pf/cel, str              TP

Moto (1980)                                              15'
    3*3*3*3*; 4331; timp+4, hp, pf/cel,                  TP
    acc, str

Atto (1981)                                              12'
    str                                                  TP

Three Movements of Hieronymus Bosch (1983)               23'
    3*3*3*3*; 4331; timp+4, hp, pf, cel,                 TP
    mand, cimbalom, str

Destini (1985)                                           13'
    3*3*3*3*; 4000; hp, str                              TP

Concerto (1987)                                          26'
    2tpt; hp, kybd, str                                  TP

Invenzione (1988)                                        18'
    3*3*3*3*; 4331; timp+4, hp, pf, cel, str             TP

Symphony No. 4 (1990)                                    19'
    3*3*3*3*; 4331; timp+4, hp, pf, cel, str             TP


            LIEBERMAN, DAVID  (1962-    )

June 28, 1982 - Hotel Jerome (1986)                      8'
    3*3*22; 4221; 2perc, hp, str                         ACA


            LIEBERMAN, GLEN  (1947-    )

Beards of a Father (1978)                                12'
    213*1; 1100; perc, pf, str                           ACA

Lighted Stones (1983)                                    23'
    solo pf; str                                         ACA

LIEBERSON, PETER   (1946-     )

Three Songs (1982)                                           10'
    solo s; 1111; 1110; hp, pf, str (2-1-1-0)   AMP

Piano Concerto (1980-1983)                                   45'
    solo pf; 3*3*3*3*; 4331; timp+6,            AMP
    hp, cel, str

Drala for Orchestra (1986)                                   17'
    3=23+3*; 4331; timp+6, hp, pf, str          AMP

Gesar Legend (1988)                                          18'
    4*2*3*4*; 4331; timp+4, hp, pf/cel, str     AMP


LIEUWEN, PETER   (1953-     )

Angelfire (1989)                                             16'
    2*2*22; 4231; timp+3, hp, pf/cel, str       MMB


LIFCHITZ, MAX   (1948-     )

Tiempos (1969)                                               10'
    1011; 0110; 2perc, hp, pf/elec org;         NSE
    str (1-1-1-1)

Globos (1971)                                                9'
    soli hn, tpt, tbn; 1111; 0000; 2perc,       NSE
    hp, pf/cel, str (1-1-1-1)

Roberta (1972)                                               14'
    1110; 1000; pf, str (4-2-2-1)               NSE

Sueños (1974)                                                15'
    1111; 2000; perc, pf, str (1-1-1-1)         NSE

Intervencion (1976)                                          22'
    solo vln; 1111; 2000; timp+1, pf, str       NSE

Expressions (1982)                                           12'
    str                                         NSE

Yellow Ribbons No. 8 (1982)                                  6'
    3*222; 4231; 2perc, str                     NSE

Yellow Ribbons No. 9 (1982)                                  12'
    2222; 4331; 2perc, str                      NSE

Yellow Ribbons No. 12 (1982)                      6'
   2223*; 3000; str (0-1-1-1)                    NSE

Yellow Ribbons No. 17 (1983)                     10'
   2222; 2200; perc, hp/pf, str                  NSE

Yellow Ribbons No. 18 (1983)                      9'
   soli vln, db; 3*222; 4231; 2perc, str         NSE

Night Voices No. 5 (1984)                        14'
   solo fl; 0111; 0000; pf, str (1-1-1-1)        NSE

Night Voices No. 6 (1985)                        14'
   solo bsn; 1110; 1000; perc, str (1-1-1-1) NSE

Night Voices No. 10 (1989)                       12'
   solo vln; 2220; 0000; 2perc,                  NSE
   str (0-1-1-1)

Piano Concerto (1989)                            18'
   solo pf; 3*3*3*2*; 4331; 3perc, str           NSE


          LINDENFELD, HARRIS  (1945-    )

And the Eagles (1980)                            13'
   satb cho; 3*3*3*4*; 4340; timp+1, str         ACA


          LIPTAK, DAVID  (1949-    )

Beginnings (1982)                                10'
   1212; 2110; perc, pf, str                     ACA

Ellipses (1984)                                  13'
   str                                           ACA

Loner (1988)                                      7'
   3*223*; 4231; timp+1, str                     NOR

Resoundings (1990)                                7'
   3*3*4=3*; 4331; timp+4, hp, str               NOR


          LISTER, RODNEY  (1951-    )

Inglorious Fourth (1987)                         15'
   solo mez; 2*1*22; 1100; perc, hp, str         MG

LOCKWOOD, NORMAND   (1906-      )

Weekend Prelude (1945)                                      8'
    3*3*3*3*; 4331; timp+2, hp, str                        ACA

The Closing Doxology (1952)                                9'
    satb cho; 3*3*5*3*; a,t,bar sax; 4442;                 BRO
    timp+6, str

Prairie (1952)                                            25'
    satb cho; 3*3*3*2; 4321; timp+2, str                   BRO

Magnificat (1953)                                         20'
    solo s; satbb cho; 2221; 2211; timp, str              ACA

Children of God - oratorio (1956)                        100'
    soli 5vv; satb cho; 3*3*3*3*; 4331;                    MS
    timp+2, str

Give me the Splendid Silent Sun (1957)                    10'
    satb cho; 2222; 2201; timp+1, str                      ACA

Light out of Darkness (1957)                              45'
    solo bar; satb cho; 3*3*3*3*; 4331;                    MS
    timp+2, str

Concerto for Oboe (1967)                                  20'
    solo ob; 2hn; timp+2, str                              ACA

Concerto for Organ and
    Chamber Orchestra (1973)                              25'
    solo org; 2*200; 2200; timp+1, str                     MS

Concerto for Piano and Orchestra (1973)                   25'
    solo pf; 1111; 1110; timp, str                         ACA

Symphony for String Orchestra (1975)                      14'
    str                                                    ACA

Mass for Children and Orchestra (1976-1977)               25'
    children's cho; 2222; 2210; perc, str                  ACA

Symphony for Large Orchestra (1979)                       20'
    3*3*3*3*; 4331; timp+3, hp, cel, str                   MS

Panegyric (1979-1980)                                     10'
    solo hn; str                                           MS

Concerto for Two Harps and Orchestra (1981)               30'
    soli 2hp; 2111; 2110; 2perc, cel, str                  ACA

Prayers and Fanfares (1982)                          20'
    0000; 4331; timp, str                            MS

Thought Of Him I Love (1982)                         25'
    satb cho; 2222; 2210; timp, str                  MS


            LOMBARDO, ROBERT  (1932-    )

Aphorisms (1968)                                     8'
    2222; 2221; 3perc, hp, str                       ACA

Threnody (1972)                                      9'
    str                                              ACA

Mesto (1978)                                         9'
    solo bsn; str                                    ACA

Sicilian Lyric (1980)                                10'
    soli timp+3; 2222; 2221; hp, pf, str             ACA


            LONDON, EDWIN  (1929-    )

Overture to "The Imaginary Invalid"
    (1959; rev 1969)                                 5'
    101*1; 0100; str                                 EAM

The Iron Hand (1975)                                 16'
    soli mez, b-bar; narr; satb cho;                 MS
    3*3*3*3*; 4331; 2perc, hp, pf, str

Hast Thou Not? (1977)                                9'
    satb cho; br qnt; str                            MS

Paraleipsis (1980)                                   16'
    3*3*3*3*; 4331; hp, pf, 2perc, str               MS

Moon Sound Zone (1981)                               var
    satb cho; triangle, str                          CFP
    N.B.  Duration should not be less than 10'.

Be Bop Dreams (1983)                                 8'
    solo hn; perc, hp, kybd, str                     CFP

According to the Number (1984)                       7'
    ssaattbb cho; 1+010; 0000; vib,                  MS
    hp, bells, str

In Heinrich's Shoes (1985)                                    30'
   1=1*2(b cl, s sax)0; 1220; 3perc, str        CFP

Peter Quince at the Clavier (1987)                           30'
   solo t; 3*23*2; 4331; 3perc, hp, pf/cel,     CFP
   str (10-8-6-5-3)

In Memoriam (1989)                                           11'
   1111; 1110; perc, hp, 2elec kybd,            MS
   str (2-1-1-1)

Two A' Marvells for Words (1990)                             25'
   solo b-bar; 2*13*1; 2110; 2perc,             CFP
   hp, kybd, str


     LOOS, ARMIN   (1904-1971)

Symphony:   In Memoriam F. Busoni (1945)                     35'
   3*222; 4331; timp+2, hp, str                 MOB

Psalm CXX (1963)                                             6'
   satb cho; tbn; timp+1, str                   MOB

Percepts (1968)                                              14'
   1111; 0221; cel, str                         MOB

Aquaries (1970)                                              14'
   str                                          MOB


     LOPATNIKOFF, NIKOLAI   (1903-1976)

Two Russian Nocturnes, op. 25 (1939)                         8'
   22*3*2; 4000; perc, hp, str                  AMP

Concerto for Violin and Orchestra,
   op. 26 (1941)                                22'
   solo vln; 2222; 3200; perc, str              AMP

Sinfonietta, op. 27 (1942)                                   16'
   1111; 1100; perc, pf, str                    AMP

Concerto for Two Pianos and Orchestra,
   op. 33 (1951)                                20'
   soli 2pf; 2222; 2220; timp+1, str            MCA

Divertimento, op. 34 (1951)                                  19'
   2222; 2220; timp+1, pf, str                  MCA

Symphony No. 3, op. 35 (1954)                          35'
    2222; 4321; timp+2, hp, pf, str                    MCA

Variazioni Concertante, op. 38 (1958)                 20'
    2222; 4331; timp+1, hp, pf, str                    MCA

Music for Orchestra, op. 39 (1958)                    13'
    2222; 4231; timp+1, hp, str                        MCA

Festival Overture, op. 40 (1960)                      11'
    3*3*3*3*; 4331; timp+2, hp, pf, str                MCA

Concerto for Orchestra, op. 43 (1964)                 19'
    3*3*3*2*; 4331; timp+1, str                        CFP


            LO PRESTI, RONALD   (1933-1985)

Elegy (1955)                                          12'
    satb cho; 2*222; 4331; timp, str                   SWP

The Masks (1956)                                       5'
    2222; 4330; timp, str                              CF

Tribute (1961)                                         6'
    satb cho; 3*222; 4331; euph; timp+1, str          SWP

Nocturne for Viola and
    String Orchestra (1965)                            7'
    solo vla; str                                      SWP

    N.B.  Inquiries regarding the works listed
    above or others by Mr. LoPresti may be
    directed to Southwest Publishers.


            LOVENDUSKY, JAMES  (1957-    )

Metathesis (1981)                                     15'
    3*3*3*2; 4220; 2perc, str                          ACA


            LUBET, ALEX  (1954-    )

La Armonia del Mundo (1985)                           12'
    2222; 4331; 2perc, pf, str                         MS

Concerto for Organ and Strings (1988)                12'
    solo org; str                                      MS

LUBIN, ERNEST  (1916-     )

Pavane for Flute and Strings (1945)                    8'
  solo fl; str                                         FLE

A Tragic Overture (1948)                               6'
  3*23+3*; 4331; timp, str                             FLE

Variations & Epilogue, op. 31 (1973)                   19'
  solo vc; 3*222; 2200; timp+1, hp, str                EBM
  N.B.  This work was originally written
  in 1946.  It was extensively revised and
  orchestrated in 1973.


LUEDEKE, RAYMOND

Chamber Symphony No. 1 (1971)                          17'
  213*2; 1101; perc, str                               ACA

Four Cantos (1974)                                     16'
  2222; 4231; 4perc, str                               ACA

Concerto for Saxophone Quartet and
  Orchestra (1977)                                     23'
  solo sax qt; 2*222; 4231; timp, str                  ACA

The Moon in the Labyrinth (1984)                       25'
  str                                                  ACA

Tales of the Netsilik (1988)                           35'
  narr; 2222; 4231; timp+2, hp, pf/cel, str  ACA


LUENING, OTTO  (1900-     )

Three Songs (1917-1922)                                5'
  solo s; 2*221; 2000; perc, hp, cel, str              ACA

Concertino for Flute (1923)                            12'
  solo fl; hp, cel, str                                CFP

Music for Orchestra (1923)                             12'
  2222; 4230; timp+1, str                              HG

Symphonic Fantasia No. 1 (1924)                        18'
  3*3*23*; 4331; timp+1, hp, pf,                       ACA
  cel, org, str

Serenade for Three Horns and Strings (1927)    8'
  3hn; str                                       HG

Short Symphony (1929-1980)                       8'
  2222; 4330; perc, str                          ACA

Two Symphonic Interludes (1935)                  9'
  33*3*3*; 4331; timp+2, hp, pf, str             CFP

Elegy for the Lonesome Ones (1937; rev 1974)    6'
  cl; str                                        ACA

Prelude to a Hymn Tune by
  William Billings (1937)                        10'
  1111; 1000; pf; str                            CFP

Suite for String Orchestra (1937)                20'
  str                                            BH

Serenade for Flute and Strings (1940)            8'
  solo fl; str                                   HG

Pilgrim's Hymn (1946)                            4'
  satb cho; 1111; 2110; perc, pf, str            TP

Prelude:  World Without People (1946)            14'
  1111; 2210; pf, str                            HG

Symphonic Fantasia V (1948-1985)                 6'
  4*3*3*3*; 4331; 2perc, hp, pf, str             ACA

Symphonic Fantasia II (1949)                     17'
  3*3*3*3*; 4331; timp+1, hp, pf, str            ACA

Kentucky Concerto (1951)                         20'
  2222; 4230; timp+1, pf, str                    HG

Legend for Oboe and Strings (1951)               12'
  solo ob; str                                   HG

Poem in Cycles and Bells (1954)                  14'
  2222; 4230; 2perc, hp, str, tape               CFP
  N.B.  Composed in collaboration with
  V. Ussachevsky.

Rhapsodic Variations (1954)                      17'
  2*222; 4230; perc, str                         CFP
  N.B.  Composed in collaboration with
  V. Ussachevsky.

Wisconsin Suite (1954)                                            8'
  2*222; 2220; timp+1, pf, str                         HG

Lyric Scene (1958)                                               7'
  solo fl; str                                          CFP

Fantasia (1959)                                                  10'
  solo str qt; 2222; 2200; timp+1, pf, str              CFP

Concerted Piece (1960)                                           9'
  2*222; 4220; perc, str, tape                          CFP
  N.B.  Composed in collaboration with
  V. Ussachevsky.

Synthesis (1962)                                                 9'
  2*222; 2230; 2perc, pf, str, tape                     CFP
  N.B.  Composed in collaboration with
  V. Ussachevsky.

Fantasia for String Orchestra (1966)                             8'
  str (vln I-div a 2; vln II-div a 6;                   HG
  vla-div a 5; vc-div a 4)

Symphonic Fantasia III (1969-1982)                               3'
  2*2*2*2*; 1111; perc, pf, str                         ACA

Symphonic Fantasia IV (1969-1981)                                9'
  2221; 1111; 2perc, pf, str                            ACA

Sonority Forms No. 1 (1973)                                      14'
  4*23*2; 4331; 4perc, hp, pf, str                      ACA

Symphonic Interlude No. 3 (1975)                                 10'
  3*3*23*; 4330; timp+1, str                            SG

A Wisconsin Symphony (1975)                                      30'
  2*3*3*3*; t sax; 4331; timp+3, hp,                    ACA
  pf, str, tape

Potawatomi Legends (1980)                                        18'
  1*111; 1110; 3perc, 2pf, str (no vln 2)               ACA

Sonority Forms II (1983)                                         17'
  3*3*3*2; 4331; 3perc, pf, str                         ACA

Symphonic Fantasia VI (1985)                                     13'
  4*3*3*3*; 4331; 2perc, pf, str                        ACA

Symphonic Interlude No. 4 (1985)                                 8'
  2*2*2*2*; 1111; perc, hp, cel, str                    ACA

Symphonic Fantasia VII (1986)                     6'
    2222; 2200; timp+1, pf, str                   ACA

Symphonic Fantasia VIII (1986)                    5'
    2222; 2200; timp+1, pf, str                   ACA

Symphonic Interlude No. 5 (1986)                  6'
    3*222; 4331; timp+1, hp, str                  CFP

Symphonic Fantasia IX (1989)                     12'
    2*2*2*2*; 1111; timp+1, str                   ACA

Symphonic Fantasia X (1990)                       6'
    2*222; 2220; perc, pf, str                    ACA


             LUKE, RAY  (1928-      )

Suite for Orchestra (1958)                       10'
    3*222; 4331; timp+2, hp, str                  OXF

Symphony No. 2 (1961)                            16'
    3*3*3*3*; 4331; timp+3, hp, pf, str           OXF

Symphony No. 3 (1963)                            19'
    3*23*2; 4331; timp+3, hp, pf, str             OXF

Concerto for Bassoon and Orchestra (1965)        17'
    solo bsn; 223*1; 4331; timp+2, hp, str        OXF

Symphonic Dialogues (1965)                       14'
    soli ob, vln; 21*21; 0000; timp+2,            OXF
    hp, str

Second Suite for Orchestra (1967)                13'
    3*3*3*2; 4331; timp+2, hp, pf, str            MS

Concerto for Piano and Orchestra (1968)          20'
    solo pf; 3*3*3*3*; 4331; timp+3, str          OXF

Symphonic Songs (1968)                           12'
    solo mez; 3*23*2; 4000; timp+1,               MS
    hp, pf, str

Incantation (1969)                               NA
    soli vc, hp; str                              MS

Symphony No. 4 (1970)                            24'
    2222; 4331; timp+2, hp, pf, str               OXF

Compressions (1972)                                              16'
   2*222; 4331; timp+3, hp, pf, str, tape              MS

Concert Overture: Summer Music (1975)                            8'
   3*3*3*2; 4331; timp+2, hp, pf, str                  MS

Plaintes and Dirges (1982)                                       6'
   satb cho; 3*23*3*; 4331; timp+7,                    MS
   hp, pf, str

Quartz Mountain (1988)                                           12'
   3*233; 4331; timp+2, str                            MS

Symphonic Dialogues II (1988)                                    21'
   solo s; soli vln, ob, hpsd; str                     MS

Sinfonia Concertante for
   Two Orchestras (1990)                               20'
   4*4*44; 8661; timp+8, 2hp, pf, str                  MS

Third Suite for Orchestra (1990)                                 20'
   3*3*3*3*; 4331; timp+3, hp, pf, str                 MS

Cantata Concertante (1991)                                       20'
   soli ww qnt, br qnt, str qt; 3satb cho;             MS
   2222; 4331; timp+3, hp, str


### LUNDBORG, ERIK  (1948-    )

Concerto for Piano and Orchestra (1980)                          16'
   solo pf; 2222; 4231; timp+3, hp, str              ACA

Scherzo (1989)                                                   12'
   3*3*3*3*; 4231; timp+2, hp, pf/cel, str          ACA


### LYBBERT, DONALD  (1923-1981)

Concert Overture (NA)                                            10'
   3*23*2; 4331; timp+1, pf, str                     ACA

MACBRIDE, DAVID

| | |
|---|---|
| Produce (1971) | 10' |
| 23*23*; 2221; timp+4, hp, str | ACA |

| | |
|---|---|
| Once Removed (1972) | 6' |
| str | ACA |

| | |
|---|---|
| See what happens (1976) | 17' |
| 2222; 3330; 3perc, hp, cel, str | ACA |

| | |
|---|---|
| Four Sonnets (1979) | 20' |
| 2121; a sax; 1210; 2perc, cel, str | ACA |

| | |
|---|---|
| Four Sonnets of Feng Zhi (1981) | 18' |
| soli 2vv; satb cho; 3*3*3*3*; 4331; | ACA |
| timp+3, hp, pf/cel, str | |

| | |
|---|---|
| Elegies (1982) | 12' |
| solo hp; str | ACA |

| | |
|---|---|
| Parallex (1983) | 20' |
| 3*3*3*2; 4331; 4perc, hp, pf, cel, str | ACA |

| | |
|---|---|
| Measuring the Future (1985) | 14' |
| 3*3*3*3*; 4331; timp+3, str | ACA |
| N.B.  Requires two conductors for performance. | |

| | |
|---|---|
| Dance Interlude (1987) | 6' |
| 2222; 4430; 4perc, str | ACA |

| | |
|---|---|
| 1010 (1987) | 14' |
| 2222; 1210; 2perc, str | ACA |

MACINNES, DONALD  (1923-    )

| | |
|---|---|
| Dialogues for Orchestra (1960) | 8' |
| 2222; 2231; timp+1, pf, str | TP |

| | |
|---|---|
| "Intersections" (1963; rev 1968) | 7' |
| 2222; 2231; timp+1, hp, str, tape | EBM |

| | |
|---|---|
| In Memoriam JFK (1964) | 5' |
| 1010; 2020; timp+1, str | TP |

Four Miniatures (1965)                              7'
   str                                               EBM


    MACKEY, STEVEN   (1956-     )

The Big Bang and Beyond (1984)                      20'
   2*2*2*2*; 2221; timp+3, hp, pf, str             MG

Square Holes, Round Pegs (1987)                     11'
   2222; 2200; timp+1, hp, pf,                     MG
   str (8-8-6-6-4)


    MAGGIO, ROBERT   (1964-     )

The Hand Prints of Sorcerers (1987)                 10'
   2*222; 4331; timp/perc, pf, str                 NOA
   N.B.  Formerly titled "An Exorcism."


    MAHLER, DAVID   (1944-     )

Three Pieces after Charles Ives (1990)             10'
   2*120; 0110; perc, pf, str                      FPM


    MAILMAN, MARTIN   (1932-     )

Autumn Landscape (1954)                             8'
   2222; 2210; timp, hp, str                       BEL

Prelude and Fugue No. 1 (1959)                      9'
   3*222; 4431; timp+5, hp, str                    BEL

Gateway City Overture (1960)                        7'
   2222; 4331; timp+5, hp, str                     BEL

Alleluia (1961)                                     4'
   unis satb cho; 3*24=1; 2a,t,bar sax;            KAL
   4531; timp+1, str

Suite in Three Movements (1961)                    12'
   4*23*2; 4331; timp+6, hp, str                   BEL

Prelude and Fugue No. 2 (1963)                     10'
   2211; 2221; timp+1, str                         BEL

Sinfonietta (1964)                                 14'
   3*222; 4331; timp+1, hp, str                    BEL

Partita for String Orchestra (1966)                    9'
   str                                                    BEL

Generations (1969)                                     10'
   3str orch                                              BEL

Symphony No. 1 (1969)                                  17'
   3*23*2; a sax; 4331; timp+6, str                       BEL

Requiem, Requiem (1970)                                40'
   soli s, a, t; narr; satb cho; 3*3*3*3*;                BEL
   4331; timp+5, hp, pf, str

Symphony No. 2 (1979)                                  24'
   3*3*3*2; 4231; timp+4, hp, pf, str                     BH

Concerto for Violin and Orchestra (1982)               17'
   solo vln; 2222; 4211; timp+3, hp, str                  BH

Symphony No. 3 (1983)                                  25'
   3*3*3*3*; 4231; timp+5, hp, pf, str                    BH

Elegy for String Orchestra (1985)                      8'
   str                                                    MS

Mirror Music (1987)                                    16'
   2*2*22; 4231; timp+2, hp, pf, str                      MS

Love Letters from Margaret (1991)                      22'
   solo s; 2222; 1111; timp+1, hp, pf, str                CF


       MAMLOK, URSULA  (1928-    )

Concerto for String Orchestra (1950)                   29'
   str                                                    ACA

Grasshoppers - Six Humoresques (1956)                  7'
   3*222; 4321; timp+2, str                               ACA

Four German Songs (1957)                               7'
   solo mez; pf, str                                      ACA

Oboe Concerto (1976)                                   12'
   solo ob; 3*03*3*; 4331; 2perc, 2hp,                    ACA
   cel, mand, str
   OR:  2022; 2211; 2perc, str

Concerto for Soprano Saxophone and
  Chamber Orchestra (1991)                    12'
  solo s sax; 2222; 3211; timp+2,             ACA
  hp, pf, str


MANDELBAUM, JOEL  (1932-    )

Convocation Overture (1951)                    6'
  2222; 2210; timp+1, str                     MS

Concerto for Piano and Orchestra (1953)       28'
  solo pf; 2222; 2220; timp+1, str            MS

Sursum corda (1960)                           17'
  22*22; 3220; timp+2, hp, str                MS

Sinfonia concertante (1962)                   28'
  soli ob, hn, vln, vc; 2022; 2200;           MS
  timp+2, str

Memorial (1965)                                7'
  str                                         MS

Concerto for Trumpet and Orchestra (1970)     20'
  solo tpt; 3*2*3*2; 4130; timp+2, hp, str    MS

Song Cycle: She (1975)                        17'
  soli s, bar; 2222; 4230; timp+1, str        MS

Sea Surface Full of Clouds (1979)             16'
  soli s, a, t, b; satb cho; 2222; 4231;      MS
  timp+2, hp, str

Creations for Cello and Orchestra (1985)       9'
  solo vc; 2222; 2100; perc, str              MS

A Mourner's Kaddish (1987)                    15'
  solo s; satb cho; 6222; 4231; timp+1,       MS
  hp, str


MARSHALL, INGRAM

Spiritus (1983)                               18'
  4fl(amp); perc, hpsd, str                   IBU

Sinfonia "Dolce far Niente" (1988)            21'
  2*3*3*3*; 4331; timp+4, 2hp, pf, str        IBU

A Peaceable Kingdom (1990)                       16'
    2*2*2+2; 0000; elec kybd, str, tape          IBU


        MARTINO, DONALD   (1931-      )

Portraits (1955)                                 38'
    soli mez, bar; satb cho; 223*3*; 4231;       DAN
    perc, hp, pf, cel, str

Contemplations (1956)                            16'
    223*3*; 4231; 3perc, hp, cel, str            DAN

Concerto for Piano and Orchestra (1965)          29'
    solo pf; 3*23*3*; 4231; euph; timp+1,        ION
    hp, pf/cel, str

Mosaic for Grand Orchestra (1967)                15'
    4*4*4=4*; 4441; 6perc, 2hp, cel,             DAN
    elec org, elec gtr, str

Concerto for Violoncello and
    Orchestra (1972)                             23'
    solo vc; 3*3*3*3*; 4431; timp+5, hp,         DAN
    pf/cel, str

Paradiso Choruses (1974)                         24'
    soli 3s, 4mez, 3t, 2bar; children's cho;     DAN
    satb cho; 3*3*3*4*; 4441; timp+4, hp,
    elec pf, org, str, tape

Ritorno (1976)                                   15'
    23*3*2; 4331; timp+4, hp, pf, cel, str       DAN

Triple Concerto (1977)                           25'
    soli cl, b cl, cb cl; 1102; 1120; 2perc,     DAN
    pf, str (2-1-1-1)

The White Island (1985)                          24'
    satb cho; 1121; 2120; 2pf, str               DAN

Concerto for Alto Saxophone and
    Orchestra (1987)                             24'
    solo a sax; 1212; 3110; 2perc, pf, str       DAN


        MATALON, MARTIN   (1962-      )

Variations for Orchestra (1987)                  10'
    3=3*3=3*; 4331; 5perc, 3hp, pf, str          NOA

MATHEW, DAVID

Six for Twenty-Seven (1972)                         6'
   2222; 2121; 3perc, str                         SEE


MATTHEWS, WILLIAM   (1950-    )

Larchwood (1976)                                    17'
   3*23*2; 4231; 3perc, hp, pf, cel, str         ACA


MAVES, DAVID   (1937-    )

Overture to an Opera (1963)                         8'
   3*23*3*; 4331; timp+3, cel, str               MMB

Concerto for Percussion and Orchestra (1972)   15'
   solo perc; 3*23*2; 4221; hp, str              TP

Symphony No. 2 (1973)                               17'
   3*3*3*3*; 4331; timp+3, hp, str               MMB

Symphony No. 3 (1977)                               13'
   3*2*3*2; 4331; timp+1, hp, pf, str             CF

Concerto for Organ and Orchestra (1980)        7'
   solo org; 0201; 0100; hpsd, str               MMB

Concerto for Two Pianos and Orchestra (1983)   15'
   soli 2pf; 3*3*3*2; 4331; timp+4, str          MMB


MAY, ROBERT   (1962-    )

Orpheus (1986)                                      14'
   3*3*23*; 4331; 2perc, pf, str                 NOA


MAYER, WILLIAM   (1925-    )

The Greatest Sound Around (1955)               14'
   solo mez (or bar); narr; 2222; 2220;          GS
   timp+1, str

Andante for Strings (1956)                          6'
   str                                           MCA

Concert Piece (1956)                                9'
   solo tpt; perc, str                           BH

Hello World (1956)     26'
   narr; dancer(opt); 2222; 3220; perc,     BH
   pf, str

Two Pastels (1961)     12'
   3*3*3*3*; 4331; timp+2, pf/cel, str     MCA

Overture for an American (1962)     10'
   3*3*3*3*; 4331; timp+2, hp, pf, str     BH

Scenes from "The Snow Queen" - suite (1966)     14'
   2*222; 4331; timp+2, hp, pf, str     TP

Letters Home (American and Vietnamese
   Soldiers) (1968)     8'
   solo vv; narr; satb cho; 2*2*2*2; 2220;     TP
   timp+1, hp, pf/cel, str

Eve of St. Agnes (1969)     14'
   soli s, mez, bar; satb cho; 2222; 2220;     TP
   timp+3, hp, pf, str

Back Talk (1970)     4'
   1111; 1110; timp+1, pf, str     TP

Octagon (1971)     29'
   solo pf; 2*2*2=2*; 2221; timp+2, hp,     MCA
   org, str

Spring Came On Forever (1975)     30'
   soli mez, t, bar; satb cho; 2222; 2200;     MS
   timp+2, hp, pf, str

Inner and Outer Strings (1982)     8'
   solo str qt; str     MOB

Of Rivers and Trains (1988)     15'
   3*3*22; 4331; timp+2, hp, pf/cel, str     TP

## MCBETH, WILLIAM FRANCIS (1933- )

Symphony No. 1 (1955)     47'
   3*222; 4331; timp+3, str     MS

Pastorale (1956)     NA
   3*222; 4331; timp+3, str     MS

Suite on a Biblical Event (1956)     10'
   3*222; 4331; timp+3, str     MS

Symphony No. 2 (1957)                                    15'
   3*222; 4331; timp+1, pf, str                        MS

Overture (1959)                                          10'
   3*222; 4331; timp+2, str                            MS

Quanah (1960)                                            7'
   2*222; 2210; timp+2, hp, str                        SMC

Pastorale and Allegro (1961)                            12'
   2*222; 2210; timp+2, str                            MS

Allegro agitato (1962)                                  12'
   2*222; 2210; timp+2, str                            SMC

Symphony No. 3 (1963)                                   25'
   2*222; 4331; timp+4, str                            SMC

Symphony No. 4 (1970)                                   15'
   3*232; 4331; timp+5, str                            SMC

Grace, Praeludium and Response (1975)                   8'
   3*232; 4331; timp+4, str                            SMC

The Badlands (1976)                                     7'
   3*232; 4331; timp+5, str                            SMC

Kaddish (1977)                                          7'
   3*232; 4331; timp+4, str                            SMC


      MCBRIDE, ROBERT  (1911-     )

Concerto for Doubles (1947)                             14'
   soli cl/b cl, a sax; 1100; 2a,t,bar sax;      ACA
   1341; hp, pf, gtr, str

Variety Day (1948)                                      13'
   solo vln; 2222; 2220; timp+1, hp, pf, str     ACA

March of the Be-Bops (1949)                             3'
   3*222; 4331; timp, hp, pf, str                ACA

Ill Tempered (1951)                                     3'
   solo pf; 3*3*3*1; a sax; 1110; perc,          ACA
   gtr, str

Brown Ukelele (1952)                                    3'
   solo boingaphone; str                         ACA

Nothing Else Matters (1952)                       2'
   2121; a sax; 2110; perc, hp, pf, gtr, str   ACA

Stringitis (1952)                                 3'
   1121; 4330; perc, hp, pf, str              ACA

Variations on an Unknown Theme (1952)             3'
   str                                        ACA

We are alone (1952)                               2'
   2121; a sax; 2110; perc, hp, pf, gtr, str   ACA

Pumpkin Eater's Little Fugue (1955)               4'
   str                                        AMP

Fantasy on a Mexican Christmas Carol (1956)       6'
   3*3*3*3*; 4331; timp+3, hp, pf, str         ACA

Pioneer Spiritual (1956)                          5'
   2222; 4231; timp+1, hp(or pf), str          ACA

Panorama of Mexico (1960)                         8'
   3*3*3*3*; 4331; timp+2, hp, str             ACA

Overture on Whimsical Tunes (1962)                5'
   2222; 4331; timp+1, pf/cel, str             ACA

Symphonic Melody (1968)                           8'
   2222; 4331; timp+3, str                    ACA

Folksong Fantasy (1973)                           6'
   3*3*3*3*; 4331; timp+3, hp, str             ACA

Light Fantastic (1976)                            4'
   3*3*22; 4331; timp+3, hp, str               ACA


      MCCULLOH, BYRON  (1927-    )

Concerto for Trombone and Orchestra (1949)        8'
   solo tbn; 2222; 2201; timp+1, pf, str       SEE

Concerto for Orchestra (1951)                     18'
   3*222; 4331; timp+2, pf, str                MS

Two Pieces for Orchestra (1953)                   11'
   3*3*3*3*; 4331; timp+3, hp, str             MS

Symphony Concertante for Timpanist and
  Orchestra (1973)                                    25'
  solo 5timp/4 roto-toms/8tom-toms;                   CF
  3*3*3*3*; 4331; 3perc, pf/cel, str

Concerto for Large Trombone and Small
  Orchestra (1974)                                    15'
  solo tbn (or b tbn); solo hpsd(amp);                CF
  1*111; 1100; perc, hp, str

Symphony No. 1 (1975)                                 22'
  3*3*3*3*; 4331; timp+3, hp, cel, str                CF

Six Songs (1976)                                      19'
  solo bar; 1111; 1000; perc, pf, str                 CF

Concerto for Cello and Orchestra (1981)               25'
  soli vc; 3*3*3*3*; 4231; timp+4, hp, str            ACC

Concerto No. 1 for Trumpet and
  Orchestra (1983)                                    22'
  solo tpt; 2222; 2110; timp+4, pf, str               ACC

Vox Humana - cantata (1985)                           25'
  solo s; satb cho; 2222; 2211; timp+2, hp,           ACC
  pf(or synth), str


          MCDERMOTT, VINCENT   (1933-    )

Siftings upon Siftings (1976)                         11'
  3*3*3*3*; 4331; timp+2, hp, pf, str                 TJP


          MCDONALD, HARL   (1899-1955)

Song of a Free Nation (1945)                          3'
  solo s; 3*3*3*3*; 3331; timp+1, str                 ELK

God Give Us Men (1950)                                9'
  satb cho; 3*232; 4321; timp+1, str                  ELK

Overture for Children (1950)                          15'
  4*333*; 4331; timp+4, hp, str                       ELK


          MCKAY, NEIL   (1924-    )

Fantasy on a Quiet Theme (1956)                       9'
  1*111; 2110; perc, hp, str                          GS

Symphony No. 1 (1956)                          20'
    3*13*3*; a sax; 4331; timp+2, str          KAL

Dance Overture (1966)                          10'
    3*222; 4331; timp+4, str                   GS

Structure (1968)                               8'
    3*222; 4331; timp+4, str                   MS

Kaleidoscope (1971)                            8'
    1111; 1100; perc, pf, str                  GS

Ritual (1973)                                  8'
    1111; 1110; 2perc, pf, str                 MS

Parables of Kyai Gandrung (1976)               22'
    3*222; 4331; timp+4, gamelan, str          MS

Fantasy on Sea Themes (1981)                   12'
    3*222; 4331; timp+3, str                   MS

Jubilee -
    Variations on an American Theme (1983)     12'
    3*222; 4331; timp+3, str                   MS

Evocations (1984)                              8'
    3*222; 4331; timp+5, str                   MS

Voice of the Phoenix (1984)                    20'
    solo koto; 3*222; 2110; timp+2, str        MS

Lamentations of Joseph (1987)                  17'
    satb cho; str                              MS

Concerto for Orchestra (1991)                  22'
    3*3*3*3*; 4331; timp+4, hp, pf, str        MS


        MCKINLEY, WILLIAM THOMAS   (1938-    )

Orchestral Study (1963)                        10'
    112*2*; 2121; timp+5, str                  MMC

Triple Concerto (1970)                         20'
    solo jazz trio:  pf, db, dmst; 2*222*;     MMC
    2221; 5perc, str

Concerto No. 1 for Piano and
  Orchestra (1974)                                    17'
  solo pf; 4=3*4(4b cl, cb cl)4(2cbsn);              MMC
  4332; timp+6, str

Concerto for Orchestra (1974)                         10'
  4*3*3*3*; 4332; timp+3, str                        MMC

Concertino for Orchestra (1976)                        8'
  4*5*4*3*; 4221; timp+2, str                        MMC

Concerto for Violoncello and
  Orchestra (1976)                                    55'
  solo vc; 3*3*3*3*; 4221; timp+4, str               MMC

October Night (1976)                                   8'
  22*2*2*; 4221; 3perc, str                          MMC

Rhapsody for Clarinet and Orchestra (1976)            10'
  solo cl; 4*3*3*4*; 4242; timp+2, str               MMC

Symphony No. 1 (1976)                                  14'
  3*4*4*4*; 4221; timp+3, str                         MG

Concerto No. 1 for Clarinet and
  Orchestra (1977)                                    23'
  solo cl; 3*3*3*3*; 4221; timp+2, str                MG

Concerto No. 1 for Viola and
  Orchestra (1978)                                    18'
  solo vla; 3*3*3*3*; 2221; timp+2, str              MMC

Symphony No. 2
  "Of Time and Future Monuments" (1978)              38'
  6*3*5*4*; 4442; timp+2, str                        MMC

Blues Lament (1981)                                    2'
  solo cl; 2222; 4221; perc, str                     MMC

The Mountain (1982)                                   12'
  3*3*3*3*; 2100; perc, str                          MMC

"Lucy" Variations (1983)                              22'
  soli cl, vln; 2222; 2100; timp+1, str              MMC

Symphony for Thirteen Players (1983)                  16'
  1*1*11; 1110; perc, str (2-1-1-1)                  MMC

Summer Dances (1984)                                  11'
  solo vln; 1111; 1110; perc, str                    MMC

Symphony No. 3 (1984)                            21'
   2222: 2200; perc, str                    MMC

Concerto No. 2 for Viola and
   Orchestra (1985)                           38'
   solo vla; 3*3*3*3*; 2200; perc, str       MMC

Sinfonia Concertante (1985)                      18'
   soli perc, pf, vln, vc; 3*3*3*3*; 4222;   MMC
   perc, str

SinfoNova (1985)                                 16'
   str                                       MMC

Symphony No. 4 (1985)                            24'
   2*222*; 2200; timp+2, str                 MMC

American Blues (1986)                            24'
   soli cl, vib; 2222; 4221; timp+1, str     MMC

Boston Overture (1986)                           9'
   3*3*3*3*; 5431; timp+2, org(opt), str     MMC

Concerto for Flute (1986)                        26'
   solo fl; str                              MMC

Adagio for Strings (1987)                        21'
   str                                       MMC

Piano Concerto No. 2 "The Oleary" (1987)         16'
   solo pf; 3*223*; 4221; timp+2, str        MMC

Concerto for Horn and Orchestra (1988)           19'
   solo hn; 3*3*4*4*; 4331; timp+2, str      MMC

Miniature Portraits (1988)                       15'
   soli tpt, bsn; str                        MMC

Symphony No. 5 (1988)                            19'
   3*3*3*4*; 4331; timp+2, str               MMC

Tenor Rhapsody (1988)                            13'
   solo t sax; 23*3*3*; 4221; timp+2, str    MMC

Can You Sing Me A Song (1989)                    30'
   soli t sax, pf, db, dmst; small fem cho;  MMC
   2*3*3*3*; 4321; timp+2, str

Chamber Symphony No. 2 (1989)                    16'
   1*1*11; 1110; timp+2, str                 MMC

Concerto No. 2 for Clarinet and
   Orchestra (1990)                     22'
   solo cl; 2*222; 2221; timp+2, str    MMC

Jubilee Concerto (1990)             20'
   solo br qnt; 4*4*4*4*; 4221; timp+2, str   MMC

New York Overture (1990)           12'
   2*222; 2200; timp+2, str        MMC

Symphony No. 6 (1990)             33'
   3*3*3*4*; 4331; timp+4, str      MMC


      MCLEAN, EDWIN  (1951-    )

Big Variations (1977)             8'
   2020; 1110; xyl, str          ACA

Big City Ballads (1988)           14'
   soli a sax, t sax, bar sax; 223*2; 4321;   ACA
   timp+3, str


      MCLEAN, PRISCILLA  (1942-    )

Variations and Mosaics on a Theme
   of Igor Stravinsky (1967-1969; rev 1975)   20'
   3*3*23*; 4220; timp+3, hp, cel, str    MLC

A Magic Dwells (1986)            15'
   3*222; 2210; timp+1, pf, str, tape    MLC

Voices of the Wild (1988)          14'
   solo v; 2*223*; 2421; timp+3, str,     MLC
   elec instr

Everything Awakening Alert and Joyful (1991)  18'
   narr; 2*222; 2210; timp+1, str      MLC


      MCLENNAN, JOHN STEWART  (1915-    )

Celebration (1964)              15'
   3*223*; 4331; perc, str         MG

Triptych (1974)                14'
   23*23*; 4331; timp, str         MG

### MCPHEE, COLIN   (1900-1964)

Transitions (1951)                                                14'
   3*3*22; 4331; timp+1, pf, str                    AMP

Symphony No. 2 "Pastorale" (1957)                                 22'
   2222; 4231; timp+2, hp, pf, str                  AMP


### MCTEE, CINDY   (1953-    )

On Wings of Infinite Night (1985)                                 9'
   333*3*; 4331; timp+3, hp, pf, str                MMB

Circuits (1990)                                                   6'
   3*3*3*3*; 4331; timp+2, pf, str                  MMB
   OR:   2222; 2210; timp+2, pf, str


### MCVOY, JAMES   (1946-    )

Reflections for Orchestra (1971)                                  15'
   22*2*2; 4221; timp+2, str                        FLE

Orion - ballet (1976)                                             40'
   2*222; 4331; timp+2, hp, pf, str                 FLE

A Summer Overture (1982)                                          10'
   2222; 2200; timp, str                            FLE

Elegy for Strings (1986)                                          8'
   str                                              MS

Spring Fancies (1988)                                             15'
   2222; 4211; timp+1, str                          MS


### MECHEM, KIRKE   (1925-    )

Symphony No. 1, op. 16 (1959)                                     24'
   3*23*2; 4331; timp+4, hp, str                    BH

Haydn's Return:  Fugue and Variations on the
   "Farewell Symphony", op. 18 (1960)               13'
   3*222; 4331; timp+1, hp, str                     TP

The King's Contest, op. 42 (1962; rev 1972)                       26'
   soli mez, t, bar, b; 3*3*3*3*; 4331;             GS
   timp+4, hp, str

Symphony No. 2, op. 29 (1966; rev 1968)          32'
3*3*3*3*; 4331; timp+4, hp, str                  BH

The Jayhawk, op. 43 (1974)                         8'
3*23*2; 4331; timp+2, pf, str                    GS

Speech to a Crowd, op. 44 (1974)                 15'
solo bar; 3*23*2; 4331; timp+4, hp,             NMP
cel, str

Songs of the Slave, op. 51b (1991)               27'
solo b-bar; satb cho; 3*3*3*3*; 4331;            GS
timp+4, hp, str

Singing is so Good a Thing (NA)                  26'
satb cho; 1*101; 1100; 2perc, hpsd,             CFP
gtr, str


         MEKEEL, JOYCE  (1931-    )

Toward the Source... (1975)                      17'
satb cho; 33*22; 4211; 2perc, str                MS

Vigil (1977; rev 1986)                           10'
6*24*2; 4211; timp+2, hp, pf, str                MG

Obscurities of Order (1988)                      15'
2222; 2222; 3perc, str                           MS

Quilt (1988)                                     18'
4*4*4*2; 2222; perc, str                         MS


         MELBY, JOHN  (1941-    )

Concerto for Computer Synthesized Tape and
Orchestra (1987)                                 19'
solo tape; 3*3*3*2; 4331; timp+3,               MER
2hp, str


         MELZER, PAUL  (1957-    )

The Altered Constellation (1989)                 10'
33*3*3*; 4331; timp+3, hp, str                   FB

MENNIN, PETER   (1923-1983)

Symphony No. 2 (1944)                              15'
   3*3*22; 4331; timp+2, str                       GS

Folk Overture (1945)                               8'
   2*222; 4331; timp+3, str                        HAR

Sinfonia (1946)                                    15'
   4*3*3*3*; 4431; timp+3, str                     CF

Symphony No. 3 (1946)                              20'
   3*222; 4331; timp+3, str                        HAR

Fantasia for Strings (1947)                        9'
   str                                             HAR

Symphony No. 4 "The Cycle" (1948)                  23'
   satb cho; 3*222; 4331; timp+2, str              CF

Symphony No. 5 (1950)                              22'
   3*222; 4331; timp+3, str                        CF

Concerto "Moby Dick" (1952)                        12'
   3*3*3*2; 4331; timp+4, str                      CF

Symphony No. 6 (1953)                              26'
   3*3*22; 4231; timp+2, str                       CF

Concerto for Violoncello and
   Orchestra (1956)                                25'
   solo vc; 3*222; 4231; timp+1, str               GS

Concerto for Piano and Orchestra (1958)            27'
   solo pf; 3*222; 4231; timp+1, str               GS

Canto for Orchestra (1963)                         9'
   3*3*22; 4331; timp+2, str                       CF

Symphony No. 7 "Variation Symphony" (1963)         25'
   3*3*3*3*; 4331; timp+3, str                     CF

Cantata de virtue:
   Pied Piper of Hamlin (1969)                     42'
   soli t, bar; narr; ssaattbb cho;                GS
   children's cho; 4*3*3*3; 4331; timp+1, str

Symphony No. 8 (1973)                              26'
   3*3*3*3*; 4431; timp+4, str                     GS

Symphony No. 9 "Sinfonia Capricciosa" (1981)    20'
    3*2*3*3*; 4331; timp+4, str                   GS

Concerto for Flute and Orchestra (1983)         19'
    solo fl; 3*3*3*3*; 4331; timp+1, str         GS

The Christmas Story (NA)                         24'
    soli s, t; satb cho; 0000; 0220;             CF
    timp, str


            MENNINI, LOUIS  (1920-    )

Andante and Allegro energico (1948)             16'
    3*222; 4231; timp+2, str                     BH

Arioso (1948)                                    7'
    str                                          BRO

Overtura breve (1949)                           7'
    3*222; 4331; timp+2, str                     BH

Cantilena (1950)                                9'
    3*222; 4331; timp+2, str                     BH

Symphony No. 2 "Da Festa" (1963)                22'
    3*222; 4331; timp+1, str                     FLE


          MENOTTI, GIAN CARLO   (1911-    )

Baba's Aria from "The Medium" (1945)            5'
    solo ca; 1111; 1100; pf(4-hands), str        GS

The Black Swan from "The Medium" (1945)         5'
    solo ca; 1111; 1100; perc,                   GS
    pf(4-hands), str

Monica's Waltz from "The Medium" (1945)         5'
    solo s; 1111; 1100; perc,                    GS
    pf(4-hands), str

Piano Concerto in F (1945)                       28'
    solo pf; 3*222; 4331; timp+2, str            RIC

Sebastian - suite from the ballet (1945)         20'
    1121; 2220; timp+2, hp, pf, str              FC

Errand into the Maze - ballet (1947)             20'
    1111; 1000; timp+1, pf, str                  GS

Lucy's Aria from "The Telephone" (1947)        4'
    solo s; 1111; 1100; perc, pf, str          GS

Lullaby from "The Consul" (1949)               5'
    solo s; 1111; 2110; hp, pf, str            GS

Magda's Aria from "The Consul" (1949)          5'
    solo s; 1111; 2210; perc, hp, pf, str      GS

Apocalypse (1951)                              24'
    3*3*3*3*; 6431; timp+1, 2hp, pf, cel, str  GS

Introduction, March and Shepherd's Dance
    from "Amahl and the Night
    Visitors" (1951)                           7'
    1211; 1100; perc, hp, pf, str              GS

Concerto for Violin and Orchestra (1952)       24'
    solo vln; 3*222; 2200; timp+1, hp, str     GS

The Death of Bishop Brindisi (1963)            30'
    satb cho; 3*23*2; 4331; timp+1, hp,        GS
    2pf, str

Lewisohn Stadium Fanfare (1965)                5'
    0000; 4331; timp+1, str                    GS

Triplo Concerto a Tre (1968)                   20'
    soli ob, cl, bsn, perc, hp, pf, vln,       GS
    vla, vc; 2222; 2231; timp+1, hp, pf, str

Fantasia for Cello and Orchestra (1975)        30'
    solo vc; 3*3*3*2; 4231; timp+1, hp, str    GS

Landscapes and Remembrances (1976)             45'
    soli s, a, t, b; satb cho; 3*3*3*2; 4331;  GS
    timp+1, hp, pf, str

Symphony No. 1 "The Halcyon" (1976)            30'
    3*3*3*2; 4231; timp+1, hp, pf, str         GS

Miracles (1979)                                17'
    boys cho (or ssaa cho); 2222; 2210; perc,  GS
    hp, str

Missa O Pulchritudo in Honorem Sacratissimi
    Cordis Jesus (1979)                        45'
    soli s, mez, t, bar; satb cho; 3*23*2;     GS
    4331; timp+2, hp, str

A Song of Hope (1980)                                          10'
    solo bar; satb cho; 3*3*3*2; 4331;                        GS
    timp+2, hp, pf, str

Muero, Porque no Muero - cantata (1982)                       15'
    solo s; satb cho; 3*3*3*2; 0000; 5perc,                   GS
    hp, str

Concerto for Double Bass and
    Orchestra (1983)                                          23'
    solo db; 3*23*2; 4231; timp+1, hp, str                   GS

"Goya" Suite (1987)                                           25'
    3*3*3*2; 4331; timp+1, hp, str                           GS

For the Death of Orpheus (1990)                               11'
    solo t; satb cho; 3*3*3=3*; 4331;                        GS
    4perc, hp, str

Llama de Amor Viva (1991)                                     10'
    solo bar; satb cho; 3*3*3*2; 4331;                       GS
    timp+2, hp, pf, str


        MERRYMAN, MARJORIE   (1952-    )

The River Song (1981)                                         10'
    2222; 2220; 2perc, str                                   ANM

In the Dreamtime (1990)                                       12'
    2222; 4231; timp+1, str                                  MG


        MEYER, JAMES

Three American Visions (1987)                                 23'
    3*3*3*3*; 4331; timp+3, hp, str                          MMB

Festival Overture (1990)                                      13'
    3*23*2; 3331; timp+3, str                                MMB


        MEYEROWITZ, JAN   (1913-    )

The Glory Around His Head (1955)                              20'
    solo bar; satb cho; 2*2*22; 4331; timp+1,                BRO
    hp, org, str

Esther Midrash - Symphony (1957)                             26'
    3*3*33; 4331; timp+1, hp, str                            BRO

Silesian Symphony (1957)                        17'
    str                                         BRO

Flemish Overture (1959)                         11'
    3*3*3*3*; 4331; perc, hp, str               AMP
    OR:  2222; 4221; perc, hp, str

Oboe Concerto (1962)                            21'
    solo ob; 2022; 4220; perc, hp, str          SIK

Flute Concerto (1963)                           20'
    solo fl; 1222; 4000; timp+1, str            SZG

Six Pieces for Orchestra (1967)                 18'
    2222; 4330; perc, hp, str                   SZG

Sinfonia brevissima (1968)                      11'
    3*3*3*3*; 4331; timp+2, hp, str             SZG

Seven Pieces for Orchestra (1974)               26'
    3*23*2; 4331; timp+2, hp, str               SZG

Cinque Pezzi da Machaut (1978)                  18'
    3*222; 4230; timp+2, hp(opt),               SZG
    org(opt), str

Fünf Geistliche Lieder (1983)                   13'
    solo bar; 2222; 4231; timp+1, hp, str       SIK

Tre Pezzi Romantici (1985)                      17'
    2222; 2100; timp, str                       SZG


            MILBURN, ELLSWORTH  (1938-    )

Voussoirs (1970)                                15'
    3=3*3=3*; 4331; timp+4, pf/cel, str         MMB

Prologue:  Venosa (1973)                        5'
    ssatb cho; 2222; 2220; timp+1, hp, str      MMB

The Armies of the Night (1975)                  3'
    3*3*3*3*; 4431; timp+2, hp, pf, str         MMB

Chiaroscuro (1984)                              14'
    1*221; 2100; timp+2, hp, pf/cel, str        MMB

Salus...Esto (1984)                             12'
    3*221; 4431; timp+3, hp, pf, str            MMB

MILLER, DENNIS (1951-    )

Piece in Three Parts for Chamber
  Orchestra (1981)             14'
  2222; 1111; str          MS


MILLER, EDWARD (1930-    )

Orchestral Changes (1966)        6'
  3*3*3*3*; 4331; 3perc, hp, cel, str  ACA

Reflections at the Bronx Zoo (1966)   9'
  2*223*; 4322; 3perc, hp, str   ACA

Anti-Heroic Amalgam (1969)      6'
  3*3*3*3*; 4322; 3perc, hp, str  ACA

Orchestral Fantasies (1968)     16'
  3*4*3*3*; 4322; perc, hp, str  ACA

Anacrusis (1975)            10'
  4*4*4=3*; 6431; 3perc, hp, str  ACA

Images from the Eye of a Dolphin (1989)  10'
  2(2 picc)22*2; 1110; perc, hp, synth, str ACA

Music for Orchestra (NA)       12'
  2*23*2; 3231; timp+1, pf, str  GS


MILLS, CHARLES (1914-1982)

Symphony No. 1 in E minor (1939)   24'
  3*3*4*4*; 4332; timp+4, pf, str  ACA

Symphony No. 2 in C Major (1940)   30'
  3*3*4*4*; 4332; timp+3, pf, str  ACA

Symphony No. 3 in D minor (1946)   24'
  3*3*3*3*; 4431; timp+1, hp, str  ACA

Concerto for Piano and Orchestra (1948)  25'
  solo pf; 3*3*22; 4331; perc, str  ACA

Theme and Variations (1951)     13'
  3*3*3*4*; 4431; timp, 2hp, str  ACA

Toccata in C (1951)         6'
  3*3*3*3*; 4331; timp, xyl, hp, str  ACA

Prelude and Fugue (1952)                              8'
    4*3*4=3*; 4431; timp, hp, str                     ACA

Prologue and Dithyramb (1954)                         8'
    str                                               ACA

Concertino for Oboe and Strings (1957)               12'
    solo ob; str                                      ACA

Symphony No. 4 "Crazy Horse" (1958)                  18'
    3*3*3*3*; 4430; timp, str                         ACA

Serenade (1960)                                       8'
    1111; 1000; str                                   ACA

In a Mule Drawn Wagon (1969)                          5'
    str                                               ACA

Symphonic Ode (1976)                                  6'
    str                                               ACA

Symphony No. 5 (1980)                                16'
    str                                               ACA


            MITCHELL, DARLEEN  (1946-     )

And still... (1984)                                  22'
    solo hn; 2222; 2220; 4perc, str                   ACA


            MITCHELL, LYNDOL  (1923-1963)

Overture for Orchestra (1950)                         NA
    2*222; 4331; timp+1, str                          FLE

Melody for Strings (1951)                             8'
    str                                               FLE

Toccata for Violin and Orchestra (1952)               8'
    solo vln; 2*222; 4331; timp+1, str                FLE

Kentucky Mountain (1956)                             12'
    2*222; 4230; timp+1, str                          FLE

Concerto Grosso for Three Trombones and
    Orchestra (1961)                                 15'
    soli 3tbn; 1111; 2100; str                        FLE

MOBBERLY, JAMES  (1954-    )

Aquaria (1978)                                          9'
    4*222; 4431; 4perc, hp, pf, str                    MMB

Synthesis (1981)                                       13'
    3=2*3*2*; 4431; timp+3, hp, cel, str               MMB


MOEVS, ROBERT  (1920-    )

Endymion (1948)                                        35'
    3*3*23*; 2210; timp+3, str                         MS

Introduction and Fugue (1949)                          18'
    3*3*23*; 2220; timp+1, str                         MS

Overture (1950)                                        13'
    3*3*3*3*; 4331; timp+3, 2hp, str                   MS

Fourteen Variations (1952)                             16'
    3*3*23*; 4331; timp+3, str                         LOC

Three Symphonic Pieces (1955)                          26'
    3*3*3*3*; 4331; timp+2, hp, str                    TP

Attis (Catullis) (1958-1963)                           46'
    soli s, t; ssat cho; 3*3*3=3*;                     TP
    43(b tpt)31; timp+5, hp, pf, cel, str

Concerto Grosso (1960-1968)                            20'
    solo pf; 3*3*3=3*; 4331; timp+7, str               RIC

Et occidentum illustra (Dante) (1964)                  19'
    satb cho; 3*3*3=3*; 4330; timp+6,                  TP
    hp, pf, str

Main-travelled Roads
    (Symphonic Piece No. 4) (1973)                     12'
    3*3*3*3*; 4331; timp+3, str                        TP

Prometheus:
    Music for Small Orchestra I (1980)                 10'
    2*22+2; 2200; timp+1, hp, str                      TP

Pandora:
    Music for Small Orchestra II (1983)                13'
    2*223*; 2100; timp, xyl, hp, pf, str               TP

Symphonic Piece No. 5 (1984)                              10'
   3*3*3*3*; 4331; timp+2, str                       TP

Symphonic Piece No. 6 (1986)                              11'
   3*3*3*3*; 4331; timp+3, str                       MS


### MOLLICONE, HENRY  (1946-    )

Fantasy for Piano and Orchestra (1967)                    10'
   solo pf; 2222; 0000; perc, cel, str             ACA

Suite from "Young Goodman Brown" (1971)                   17'
   3*3*3*4*; 4331; timp+5, hp, pf, cel, str        ACA


### MOLS, ROBERT  (1921-    )

Andante and Allegro (1962)                                8'
   2*222; 4230; timp+1, str                        MOL

Symphony No. 1 (1962)                                     19'
   2222; 2210; timp+1, str                          MOL

Cantilena (1966)                                          6'
   solo ob; hp, str                                MOL

Symphony No. 2 (1967)                                     16'
   3*3*3*2; 4331; timp+2, hp, pf, str              MOL

Serenade for Alto Saxophone and
   Strings (1975)                                   10'
   solo a sax; str                                  MOL


### MONELLO, SPARTACO  (1909-    )

Symphony No. 1, op. 9 (1946)                              40'
   3*222; 4331; timp+1, str                         FLE

Symphony No. 2, op. 11 (1947)                             28'
   str                                              FLE

Concerto Grosso, op. 15 (1950)                            19'
   solo pf; str                                     FLE

Country Dance, op. 18 (1951)                              9'
   3*222; 3220; timp+1, str                         FLE

Concerto for Orchestra, op. 26 (1955)          20'
   2222; 2200; timp+1, str                     FLE

Divertimento for Orchestra, op. 33 (1964)       5'
   3*14+1; a,t sax; 2331; timp+1, str          FLE


        MONTAGUE, STEPHEN   (1943-    )

Voussoirs (1972)                               28'
   4*4*4=4*; 5431; 7perc, str, tapes           UMP

Sound Round (1973)                             20'
   4*3*3*3*; 4331; str, digital delay          EM

Varshavian Spring (1973; rev 1980)             20'
   satb cho; 2020; 2020; 2perc, str            EM

At the White Edge of Phrygia (1983)            19'
   1111; 1110; 3perc, pf, str (solo or sect)   UMP

From the White Edge of Phrygia (1984)          19'
   2222; 4231; 4perc, pf, str                  UMP

Prologue (1984)                                10'
   2222; 4231; 4perc, pf, cel, str             UMP

Piano Concerto (1988)                          30'
   solo pf; 1*1*11; 1110; 3perc,               UMP
   str (6-6-5-4-2)


        MOORE, CARMAN   (1936-    )

Sinfonia (1964)                                10'
   2*222; 4221; timp+1, str                    SJM

Catwalk - ballet (1966)                        15'
   2*3*22; 0331; 2perc, str                    SJM

Gospel Fuse (1974)                             23'
   soli 2s, 2a; 3*3*33*; s sax; 4331;          PS
   timp+4, hp, pf, elec org, b gtr, str

Wildfires and Field Songs (1974)               21'
   4*5*4*4*; a sax; 4441; timp+3, hp, str      PS

The American Nebula - cantata (1976)           35'
   satb cho; 2*14=1; a,t,bar sax; 4210;        PS
   3euph; timp+6, hp, pf, synth, elec gtr, str

Tone Roads to HK:  Four Movements for a
    Fashionable Five-Toed Dragon (1976)              55'

    1. Overture - Tone Roads #1A                      3'
    2. Pastorale - Tone Roads #1B                     11'
    3. Urban Walk - Tone Roads #2                     15'
    4. Colors - Tone Roads #3                         10'
    5. Folk Energy - Tone Roads #4                    13'

    jazz ensemble:  fl/s sax/t sax, elec gtr,  PS
    dmst, db(or b gtr), kybds (pf, elec pf,
    hpsd, synth)
    orch:  solo vln; 2=2*11; 0000; 2perc, hp, str
    N.B.  The individual movements are published
    separately and are available for performance.

Hit (1978)                                           23'
    3*3*3*2; 4331; timp+5, str                        PS

Concerto for Blues Piano and
    Orchestra (1982)                                 20'
    solo pf; 3*3*3*0; a sax; 2321; timp+1,           SJM
    dmst, hp, str

Concerto for Jazz Violin and
    Orchestra (1987)                                 15'
    solo vln; 3*120; 3220; timp+3, str               PS


        MOORE, DOUGLAS  (1893-1969)

Symphony No. 2 in A (1945)                           22'
    3*23*2; 4231; timp+1, hp, str                    GS

Farm Journal - suite (1947)                          13'
    2222; 2100; timp+1, str                          CF

Cotillion Suite (1952)                               15'
    str                                              CF


        MORRIS, ROBERT  (1943-    )

Syzygy (1966)                                        12'
    3*33*3; 4331; 3perc, pf, str                     MSM

Continua (1969)                                      20'
    3*33*3*; 4331; 5perc, pf, str                    MSM

Streams and Willows (1972)                                16'
    solo fl; 3*333; 0000; 3perc, pf, str                  MSM

Tapestries (1976)                                         21'
    2*2*2*2*; 2211; 3perc, pf,                            MSM
    str (4-4-3-2-1)

Interiors (1977)                                          15'
    2222; 2111; perc, pf(4-hands), str                    MSM

Clash (1987)                                              6'
    2222; 2221; 2perc, pf, str                            MSM


            MORYL, RICHARD (1929-     )

Multiples (1968)                                          12'
    2perc, hp, pf, str (3-3-2-2-1)                        JC

Total (1969)                                              13'
    3*222; 3321; timp+2, str (6-6-6-6-3)                  JC

Illuminations (1970)                                      21'
    solo s; 4satb cho; 1111; 2220; timp+3,                JC
    pf, str (1-1-1-1)
    N.B.  Choruses play small bells, tuning forks,
    wind chimes and chromatic pitch pipes.

Balloons (1971)                                           14'
    soli 2perc; 1111; 2221; pf; transistor                MS
    radios
    N.B.  Intended for young people's concerts,
    with audience participation.

Volumes (1971)                                            14'
    solo pf; largest orch available                       JC

Chroma (1972)                                             13'
    1111; 1110; timp+3, hp, pf, str (1-1-1-0)             MS

Loops (1973)                                              var
    large homogenous group of instruments                ACA
    in various antiphonal placements; tape

Meta (1973)                                               var
    any instruments and lights                           ACA

Particles (1974)                                          var
    high version:   4picc; 2perc, pf, str                ACA
    low version:   2 cb cl, 2 cbsn; 3tbn, tba;
    pf, 8-20 db

Strobe (1974)                                             20'
    large orchestra, any instrumentation                 ACA

The Untuning of the Skies (1981)                         15'
    3*3*3*3*; 4331; timp+3, hp, pf, str                  MS

The Pond (1984)                                          15'
    solo fl; 2perc, pf, str                              ACA


## MOSS, LAWRENCE  (1927-    )

Scenes for Small Orchestra (1961)                        8'
    2222; 4200; perc, str                                SEE

Ariel (1969)                                            10'
    solo s; 3*222; 4231; 2perc, hp,                      CF
    pf/cel, str

Paths (1970)                                             10'
    3*3*3*3*; 6331; 5perc, str                           CF

Symphonies for Brass Quintet and
    Chamber Orchestra (1977)                             18'
    solo br qnt; 2111; 1110; 3perc, pf, str              SEE


## MOURANT, WALTER  (1910-    )

Idyl (1948)                                               7'
    solo fl; str                                         ACA

Burlesque (1953)                                          3'
    solo cl; perc, cel, str                              ACA

Dark Forest (1953)                                        5'
    perc, hp, str                                        ACA

Blue Haze (1954)                                          4'
    solo cl; str                                         ACA

Elm Street, Fairbury, Illinois (1954)                    8'
    solo eh; str                                         ACA

The Pied Piper (1954)                                        4'
  solo cl; cel, str                                ACA

Air and Scherzo (1955)                                       7'
  solo ob; hp, str                                 AMP

Sleepy Hollow Suite (1955)                                   12'
  hp, str                                          AMP

Three New Hampshire Idylls (1956)                            9'
  solo cel; str                                    ACA

Valley of the Moon (1956)                                    3'
  str                                              AMP

Concertino for Clarinet and Orchestra (1957)                14'
  solo cl; 2222; 2200; 2perc, hp, str             ACA

Four Garden Scenes (1958)                                    12'
  2122; 2000; perc, hp, str                       ACA

Aria for Orchestra (1960)                                    15'
  3*3*3*3*; 4331; timp+1, hp, str                 ACA

Pizzicato Polka (1960)                                       3'
  str                                              ACA

Whistler's Father (1960)                                     3'
  2222; 2330; timp+1, hp, cel, str                ACA

Remembrance of Things Past (1961)                            9'
  solo ob; hp, str                                 ACA

Blue Horizons (1963)                                         2'
  solo hp; str                                     ACA

Prelude and Rondo (1963)                                     9'
  cl; hp, str                                      ACA

The Marble Faun (1968)                                       6'
  solo ob; str                                     ACA

Fantasia for Trumpet and Orchestra (1969)                   10'
  solo tpt; 2222; 4331; timp+2, hp, str           ACA

Song of the Caribbean (1972)                                 9'
  2222; 4331; timp+2, hp, cel, str                ACA

Mountain Air (1973)                                          3'
  solo fl; perc, str                              ACA

Serenade (1975)                                         4'
  2222; 2220; perc, str                       ACA

Song for Strings (1976)                                 5'
  str                                          ACA

Flea Dance (1979)                                       14'
  2222; 4330; 2perc, hp, str                  ACA

Fantasy for Strings (1981)                              4'
  str                                          ACA

Spring Idyll (1983)                                     4'
  solo fl; str                                 ACA

Three Acts from "Punch and Judy" (1988)                 8'
  2222; 4331; timp+1, pf, str                 ACA

Ecstasy (NA)                                            4'
  solo cl; hp, cel, str                        AMP


    MOYLAN, WILLIAM  (1956-    )

Concerto for Bass Trombone and
  Orchestra (1979)                             15'
  solo b tbn; 2222; 4111; 4perc, str           SEE

Two Movements for String Orchestra (1980)               11'
  str                                          SEE


    MUCZYNSKI, ROBERT  (1929-    )

Concerto for Piano and Orchestra,
  op. 7 (1954)                                  17'
  solo pf; 3*222; 4321; timp+1, hp, str        SHA

Dovetail Overture, op. 12 (1960)                        5'
  3*222; 4331; timp+1, str                    GS

Dance Movements, op. 17 (1963)                          14'
  1111; 1110; timp+1, hp, cel, str            GS

Symphonic Dialogues, op. 20 (1965)                      8'
  3*222; 4331; timp+1, hp, str                GS

Charade, op. 28 (1971)                                  7'
  3*222; 4331; timp+3, str                    GS

Serenade for Summer, op. 38 (1976)　　8'
　0101; 1000; timp, hp, cel, str　　　TP

Symphonic Memoir, op. 39 (1978)　　17'
　3*3*4(2b cl)3*; 4331; timp+1, hp, pf, str　TP

Concerto for Alto Saxophone and
　Orchestra, op. 41 (1981)　　　　18'
　solo a sax; 1111; 1100; timp+2, pf, str　TP


　　　MURRAY, J.D. BAIN

Epitaph for Strings (1972)　　　　8'
　str (5-5-4-3-2, desks)　　　　　MS

Evocations -
　Song Cycle on Primitive Prayers (1982)　20'
　solo s; 11*1*1; 1220; 2perc, str　　MS

City of Cities - song cycle (1985)　　16'
　solo s; 111*1; a sax; 1000; perc, pf, str　MS


　　　MUSGRAVE, THEA　(1928-　　)

Cantata for a Summer's Day (1954)　　33'
　soli s, a, t, b; narr; 1010; 0000; str　NOV

Obliques (1958)　　　　　　　10'
　2222; 4331; timp+2, hp, cel, str　　CHE

Scottish Dance Suite (1959)　　　8'
　2222; 4231; timp+2, hp, str　　　CHE

Triptych (1959)　　　　　　　10'
　solo t; 2211; 3200; 3perc, hp,　　CHE
　pf/cel, str

The Phoenix and the Turtle (1962)　　18'
　satb cho; 23*3*2; 4331; timp+3, hp, str　CHE

Theme and Interludes (1962)　　　11'
　213*1; 2210; timp+2, hp, str　　　NOV

The Five Ages of Man (1963)　　　27'
　2222; 4331; timp+3, pf, str　　　CHE

Nocturnes and Arias (1966)　　　21'
　223*3*; 4331; timp+2, hp, str　　CHE

Concerto for Orchestra (1967)                          20'
    3*3*3*3*; 4331; timp+3, hp, str                    CHE

Concerto for Clarinet and Orchestra (1968)            22'
    solo cl; 3*3*13*; 4331; timp+3,                    CHE
    hp, acc, str

Night Music (1968)                                     18'
    1201; 2000; str                                    CHE

Memento Vitae
    (Concerto in Homage to Beethoven) (1970)           18'
    2222; 4331; timp, str                              CHE

Concerto for Horn and Orchestra (1971)                22'
    solo hn; 2222; 4210; 3perc, str                   CHE

Viola Concerto (1973)                                  23'
    solo vla; 1221; 3210; perc, hp, str               NOV

Orfeo ll (1975)                                        14'
    solo fl; str                                       NOV

Monologues of Mary,
    Queen of Scots (1977-1982)                         22'
    solo s; 23*22; 3210; timp+2, hp, org, str         NOV

From One to Another (1980)                             10'
    solo vla; str                                      NOV

Peripeteia (1981)                                      15'
    2222; 4231; timp+2, hp, str                        NOV

Moving into Aquarius (1984)                            16'
    2222; 4331; timp+3, pf, str                        NOV

Echoes through Time (1988)                             32'
    sa cho; speaking cho; 3 dancers(opt);             NOV
    1121; 1000; timp+1, hp, pf/synth,
    str (2-1-1-1)

The Seasons (1988)                                     22'
    2222; 2200; timp+1, pf, str                        NOV

Rainbow (1990)                                         12'
    2222; 4331; timp+3, hp, synth, str                NOV

Song of the Enchanter (1990)                            4'
    2222; 2230; timp+2, hp, pf, str                    NOV

NABOKOV, NICOLAS (1903-1978)

The Return of Pushkin - elegy (1948)             25'
    solo s(or t); 2222; 4300; timp+1, str         FC

Concerto corale (1950)                            17'
    soli fl, pf; str                              FC

La vita nuova (1951)                              30'
    solo s (or t); 2222; 4221; timp+1,            FC
    hp, pf, str

Les hommages (1953)                               22'
    solo vc; 2222; 4110; timp+1, hp,              FC
    pf, cel, str

Symboli Chrestiani (1956)                         17'
    solo bar; 2002; 2200; timp+1, hp,             FC
    pf, cel, str

The Last Flower - symphonic suite (1957)          25'
    narr (opt); 2222; 4220; timp+1, pf, str       FC

Studies in Solitude (1961)                        15'
    223*2; sax; 4110; timp+1, hp,                 FC
    pf, cel, str

Quatre Poèmes (B. Pasternak) (1961)               15'
    solo bar; 2222; 2220; timp+1, hp,             RIC
    pf, cel, str

Six Lyric Songs (Akhmatova:  Requiem) (1966)      14'
    solo s; 0121; 2220; timp+1, pf, cel, str      BB

Symphonic Variations (1967)                       38'
    3*3*3*3*; 4331; timp+1, hp, pf, cel, str      MPB

Prelude, Variations and Finale on a
    Theme by Tchaikovsky (1968)                   30'
    solo vc; 2*122; 4220; timp+1, hp,             MPB
    pf, cel, str

Symphony No. 3 "A Prayer" (1968)                  18'
    3*3*3*3*; 4331; timp+1, hp, pf, cel, str      MPB

The Hunter's Picnic - symphonic suite
   from the ballet Don Quichotte (1973)        23'
   3*3*3*3*; 4331; timp+1, hp, pf, str         SEE

Don Quichotte - ballet (NA)                    30'
   3*3*3*3*; 4331; timp+1, hp, pf, cel, str    MPB


           NANCARROW, CONLON   (1912-     )

Piece No. 2 for Small Orchestra (1986)         NA
   0111; 1110; 2pf, str                        SMI


           NANES, RICHARD

Concerto Grosso (1983)                         14'
   soli hn, tpt, tbn; 2222; 1110; timp, str    DLF

Rhapsody pathétique (1985)                     24'
   solo vln; 3*3*3*3*; 4332; timp, str         DLF

Symphony No. 1 in B-flat (1985)                24'
   43*33; 4532; timp+4, hp, str                DLF

Symphony No. 2 in B (1986)                     29'
   4*33*3; 4532; timp+3, 2hp, org, str         DLF


           NEIKRUG, MARC   (1946-     )

Concerto for Piano and Orchestra (1966)        24'
   solo pf; 2222; 2000; 2perc, hp, str         EAM

Concerto for Clarinet and Orchestra (1967)     16'
   solo cl; 3*3*03*; a,t sax; 4331; perc,      EAM
   2hp, cel, str

Fantasy for Orchestra (1972)                   13'
   3*3*33*; 5231; 4perc, 2hp, cel, str         EAM

Eternity's Sunrise (1980)                      14'
   4*4*5=4; 4331; timp+4, hp, pf, cel, str     HC

Mobile (1981)                                  17'
   213*0; 0000; 2perc, pf, str (2-1-1-1)       HC

Concerto for Violin and Orchestra (1982)       21'
   solo vln; 3*33+3*; 4331; timp+4,            HC
   hp, pf/cel, str

Chetro Ketl (1986)                                    15'
    12*22; 2200; timp/perc, str                       HC

Concerto for String Quartet and
    Orchestra (1987)                                  15'
    solo str qt; 1212; 2100; timp/perc, str           HC

Nachtlieder (1988)                                    18'
    solo s; 3=2*2*3*; 4221; timp+3,                   HC
    hp, pf/cel, str

Concerto for Flute and Orchestra (1989)               20'
    solo fl; 3*33*3*; 4321; timp+3,                   HC
    hp, pf/cel, str


                NELHYBEL, VACLAV  (1919-     )

Étude symphonique (1949)                              12'
    3*3*3*3*; 4331; timp+2, pf, str                   MS

Viola Concerto (1962)                                 18'
    solo vla; 2222; 3110; 2perc, str                  BTA

Dies Ultima (1967)                                    16'
    soli s, t, bar; satb cho; speaking cho;           ECK
    jazz band; 3*3*3*3*; 4331; timp+2, pf, str

Houston Concerto (1967)                               25'
    solo str qt; 4*3*4=3*; 4441; timp+5, str          ECK

Music for Orchestra (1967)                            9'
    3*23*2; 0000; str                                 FC

Movement for Orchestra (1968)                         9'
    3*23*2; 0000; str                                 BEL

Sine nomine (1968)                                    10'
    soli s, a, t, b; satb cho;                        FC
    4*26(b cl,2cb cl)2; 3551; 2timp+7,
    org, str, tape

Two Movements for Chamber Orchestra (1970)            9'
    solo pf; 1111; 1100; str                          MS

A Mighty Fortress (1972)                              8'
    3*221; 0000; str                                  ECK

Polyphonies (1972)                                    18'
    4*4*4*4; 4441; timp+5, pf, str                    ECK

Aegean Modes (1973)                                        4'
   213*1; 1211; str                                        ECK

Slavonic Triptych (1976)                                   3'
   3*121; 2331; timp+3, str                                ECK

Concerto Spiritoso No. 4:
   Variants on B-A-C-H (1977)                              20'
   solo med v; solo str qt; 2230; 2220;                    EAM
   timp+3, str, tape

Fables for All Time (1980)                                 65'
   soli s, a, t, b; 3*3*3*3*; 4331;                        MS
   timp+2, pf, str

Campus Concertante (1981)                                  10'
   2222; 2210; str                                         BTA

Let There Be Music (1982)                                  45'
   soli s, a, t, b; 3*3*3*3*; 4331;                        MS
   timp+2, pf, str


                NELSON, BRADLEY   (1950-      )

Recantation (1975)                                         17'
   solo v; 1121; 2211; 4perc, str                          SEE

The Feast of Lights (1986)                                 50'
   solo s; satb cho; 3*222; 2331; 4perc, str  MS

Jesus, The Very Thought of Thee (1990)                     4'
   str                                                     MS


                NELSON, LARRY   (1944-      )

Variations for Orchestra (1974)                            18'
   3*2*4=2; 4320; timp+3, str                              FLE


                NELSON, RON   (1929-      )

Savannah River Holiday (1953)                              9'
   3*222; 4331; timp+4, hp, pf, str                        CF

Sarabande - for Katherine in April (1954)                 6'
   22*22; 2200; 3perc, hp, str                             BH

The Christmas Story (1958)                          31'
   solo bar; narr; satb cho; 2222; 2331;      BH
   timp+1, hp, cel, org, str

Fanfare for a Festival (1960)                       3'
   satb cho; 3*222; 4331; timp+1, str          BH

Jubilee (1960)                                      6'
   3*222; 4331; timp+6, hp, str                BH

This is the Orchestra (1960)                        22'
   narr; 2222; 4331; timp+1, hp, str           BH

Toccata for Orchestra (1962)                        10'
   2*202; 4331; timp+2, hp, pf, cel, str       BH

What is Man? - oratorio (1967)                      57'
   soli s, bar; narr; satb cho; 2222;          BH
   4331; timp+2, hp, pf, org, str, tape

Rocky Point Holiday (1969)                          8'
   2222; 4331; timp+1, hp, str                 BRO

Trilogy - JFK - MLK - RFK (1969)                    26'
   solo s; 2222; 2211; timp+2, hp,             BH
   pf, str, tape

Vox Aeterna Amoris (1971; rev 1975-1981)            35'
   solo mez; 3*3*3*3*; 4331; timp+4,            NOA
   hp, cel, str

Five Pieces for Orchestra - after paintings
   by Andrew Wyeth (1976)                       22'
   3*3*3*3*; 4331; timp+2, hp, pf, str          BH

Meditation and Dance (1977)                         13'
   narr; 3*222; 4331; timp+1, hp, pf, str       BH

Fanfare for a Celebration (1983)                    4'
   3*222; 4331; timp+2, str                     BH

Danza Capriccio (1988)                              12'
   solo a sax; 3*3*3*3*; 4331; str (no vlns)    LDW

Elegy for Strings (1988)                            6'
   str                                          MS

Fanfare for the Hour of Sunrise (1989)              3'
   3*222; 4331; str (no vlns)                   LDW

NEWELL, ROBERT  (1940-    )

Edifice in memoriam (1962)                            5'
    2122; 2220; 3perc, pf, str (no vla)              ACA

Concerto for Piano and Orchestra (1965)             15'
    solo pf; 1111; 2100; 2perc, gtr, str            ACA

Modular Melliphony (1977)                            20'
    5=2*2*2; 4331; 4perc, str                       ACA
    N.B.  Requires two conductors for performance.

Viola-Mobile (1978)                                  15'
    solo vla; 1111; 2211; perc, str                 ACA

Four-Fold World View (1980)                          13'
    222(t sax)2; 4431; 3perc, hp, str               ACA

Visions and Dreams (1986)                            19'
    solo bar; satb cho; 2222; 4331;                 ACA
    3perc, str

Solo Suite II (1990)                                 21'
    soli fl, timp, vln; 2222; 3230;                 ACA
    timp+2, str
    N.B.  Soloists are drawn from the orchestra.


NEWLIN, DIKA  (1923-    )

Triple Play (1948)                                   15'
    1111; 2100; str                                 ACA


NEWMAN, THEODORE S.  (1933-1975)

Divertimento for Chamber Orchestra,
    op. 10 (1959)                                    10'
    3*222; 2220; timp+1, hp, str                    FLE

Hymn for String Orchestra, op. 11 (1959)             5'
    str                                             KAL
    N.B.  Also known as "Psalm for String
    Orchestra."

Fanfare for Orchestra, op. 17 (1959)                 4'
    3*3*3*3*; 4331; timp+1, str                     FLE

Toccata for Orchestra (1959)                         12'
    3*3*3*3*; 4331; timp+1, pf, str                 KAL

Symphonic Prelude (1960)      NA
   3*3*3*3*; 4331; timp+2, hp, pf, str    KAL

Symphony No. 1 in F-sharp (1960)    48'
   3*33*3*; 4331; timp+1, hp, pf, str    KAL

Discourse for Orchestra (1961)     14'
   3*222; 2220; timp+1, str      KAL

Song for Strings and Harp (1962)    5'
   hp, str             FLE

Concerto for Organ and Orchestra (1963)   NA
   solo org; 1*1*1*1; 1220; timp+1, str   FLE

Nocturne for Clarinet and Strings (1963)   NA
   solo cl; str           FLE

Overture-Fantasy (1963)        15'
   2*22*2; 2220; timp+1, pf/cel, str    FLE

Cain - ballet (1967)          19'
   2*121; 2110; timp+1, pf, cel, str    KAL

"B" for Orchestra (1970)        6'
   3*3*3*3*; 4331; timp+1, hp, pf, str    KAL

Double Piece for Orchestra (1972)    4'
   3*3*3*3*; 4331; timp+1, hp, pf, str    KAL

Presto (1972)               4'
   3*3*3*3*; 4331; timp+2, hp, pf, str    KAL


NIELSON, LEWIS J.   (1950-    )

Concerto for Viola and Orchestra (1980)   20'
   solo vla; 2221; 4240; 5perc, hp, str   ACA

Concerto for Percussion and Orchestra (1984)   30'
   solo perc; 2122; 2221; 4perc, str    ACA

Fantasia (1986)              19'
   solo perc; 1111; 1110; str      ACA

Timpani Concerto (1987)        25'
   solo timp; 2222; 2221; 2perc, str    ACA

Concerto for Violin and Orchestra (1989)   25'
   solo vln; 2222; 2221; 3perc, str    ACA

NIN-CULMELL, JOAQUIN  (1908-      )

Concerto for Piano and Orchestra (1946)          20'
    solo pf; 2222; 4230; timp, str               EME

Tres Piezas Antiquas Españolas (1959-1961)       13'
    23*22; 4331; timp+1, str                     EME

Differencias (1962)                               9'
    3*3*22; 4231; timp+2, cel, str               EME

Concerto for Cello and Orchestra (1963)          20'
    solo vc; 0200; 2000; str                     EME

Cantate de José Prados (1965)                    16'
    solo v; hpsd/pf, str                         GS

Six Chansons Populaires Sephardiques (1982)      11'
    solo v; 2222; 4220; timp+1, str              GS


NIXON, ROGER  (1921-      )

Air for Strings (1953)                            6'
    str                                          TP

Concerto for Viola and Orchestra (1969)          30'
    solo vla; 3*3*22; 4230; timp+1,              CF
    hp, cel, str

Mooney's Grove Suite (NA)                        20'
    2222; 4330; timp+1, hp, cel, str             MS


NORTH, ALEX  (1910-      )

Revue (1946)                                     16'
    solo cl; 3*3*3*2; 4331; timp+6, hp,          TP
    pf, cel, str

A Streetcar Named Desire - suite (1951)          30'
    1*121; 1110; perc, pf, str                   GS


NOWAK, ALISON  (1948-      )

Blend (1980)                                     17'
    3*221; 2211; 2perc, str                      ACA

O'BRIEN, EUGENE   (1945-    )

Symphony (1969)                                              15'
   3*3*3*3*; 4331; timp+2, str                              MS

Concerto for Violoncello and
   Orchestra (1971)                                         20'
   solo vc; 2222; 2200; 2perc, str                         MS

Dédales (1973)                                              15'
   solo s; 1120; a sax; 2100; 2perc, hp,                   MMB
   pf/cel, elec org, mand, str

Rites of Passage (1978)                                     15'
   3*3*3*3*; 4331; timp+4, hp, pf,                          MS
   elec org, str

Dreams and Secrets of Origin (1983)                         12'
   solo s; 2222; 2210; timp+2, str                          MS

Mysteries of the Horizon (1987)                             16'
   1+01*0; 1110; pf, str (4-3-3-3-2)                        MMB

Concerto for Alto Saxophone and
   Orchestra (1991)                                         19'
   solo a sax; 3*3*3*3*; 4331; 5perc,                       MMB
   pf, str


OGDON, WILL   (1921-    )

Five Comments and Capriccio (1979)                          12'
   3*23*3*; 4221; 3perc, hp, cel, str                      ANM

Five Preludes (1985)                                        10'
   solo vln; 1110; 1110; 2perc, str                        ANM


OLAN, DAVID   (1948-    )

Symphony (1984)                                             22'
   2222; 4231; timp+1, hp, pf, str                         ACA

### OLIVEROS, PAULINE   (1932-     )

To Valerie Solanas and Marilyn Monroe:
    In Recognition of their Desperation (1970) 30'
    from 6 players to large orchestra          SMI

Tashi gomang (1981)                            20'
    56 players                                 SMI

The Well and the Gentile (1983)                var
    indeterminate instrumentation              DLP

The New Sound Meditation (1989)                var
    indeterminate instrumentation              DLP


### ORLAND, HENRY   (1918-     )

Concerto for Bassoon and String Orchestra,
    op. 17 (1948)                              9'
    solo bsn; str                              MCA

Symphony No. 3, op. 19 (1948)                  16'
    3*3*3*3*; 2200; timp, str                  MCA

Symphony No. 4 (1961)                          25'
    male reciter; high fem v; str              SEE

Double Concerto, op. 26 (1962)                 16'
    soli fl, eh; str                           MCA

Christmas Candlelight, op. 29 (1964)           15'
    satb cho; 2222; 2221; 2perc, str           SEE

Christmas Legend, op. 30 (1965)                6'
    satb cho; 2222; 2230; perc, str            SEE

Initial, op. 33 (1966)                         4'
    2222; 4231; timp, str                      SEE

Epigram, op. 37 (1975)                         3'
    3*3*3*2; 2231; perc, str                   SEE


### ORREGO-SALAS, JUAN   (1919-     )

Symphony No. 3, op. 50 (1961)                  24'
    3*3*3*3*; 4231; timp+3, hp, str            MMB

```
Concerto a tre, op. 52 (1962)                        37'
    soli vln, vc, pf; 3*222; 4220;                   MMB
    timp+3, str

América, No en vano Invocamus Tu Nombre,
    op. 57 (1966)                                    15'
    soli s, bar; ttbb cho; 3*23*3*; 4231;            MMB
    timp+2, hp, pf, str

Symphony No. 4, op. 59
    "Of the Distant Answer" (1966)                   22'
    3*3*3*3*; 4331; timp, hp, str                    MMB
    offstage:  2hn, tpt

Missa "In tempore Discordiae", op. 64 (1969)         72'
    solo t; satb cho; 4*04*0; 0040; 5perc,           MMB
    pf, str

Variaciones Serenas, op. 69 (1971)                   14'
    str                                              MMB

The Days of God, op. 73 (1977)                       78'
    soli s, a, t, b; satb cho; 3*23*3*;              MMB
    4331; timp+5, hp, pf, str

Concerto for Oboe and String Orchestra,
    op. 77 (1980)                                    17'
    solo ob; str                                     MMB

Bolivar, op. 81 (1982)                               20'
    satb cho; 3*3*3*3*; 4331; timp+4, hp, str        MMB

Violin Concerto, op. 86 (1984)                       20'
    solo vln; 3*3*3*2; 4231; timp+3,                 MMB
    hp, cel, str

Ash Wednesday, op. 88 (1984)                         12'
    solo mez; str                                    MMB

Piano Concerto No. 2, op. 93 (1985)                  30'
    solo pf; 3*3*3*2; 4331; timp+2, hp, str          MMB

Riley's Merriment - Scherzo for Orchestra,
    op. 94 (1986)                                     9'
    3*23*2; a sax; 4331; 3perc, pf, str              MMB

Fanfare for Large Orchestra, op. 97 (1988)            2'
    3*3*3*2; 4331; 2perc, str                        MMB
```

ORTIZ, WILLIAM (1947-    )

Kantuta, Ritual para Orquesta (1976)                15'
    3*222; 4221; timp+4, str                        ACA

Elegia a los Inocentes Caidos (1978)               10'
    2222; 2201; timp+3, str                         ACA

Antillas (1981)                                     15'
    1111; 1000; perc, pf, str                       ACA

Resonancia Esfercia (1982)                          18'
    orch  1:  1121; 2120; perc, str                 ACA
    orch  2:  1101; a sax; 2111; perc, str


OTT, DAVID (1947-    )

Genesis II (1980)                                    7'
    3*23*2; 4331; timp+3, pf, str                   MMB

Commemoration and Celebration Overture (1982) 10'
    223*2; 4331; timp+3, str                        MMB

Cornerstone of Loveliness (1982)                    55'
    soli s, mez, t; satb cho; 2222; 4231;           MMB
    timp+3, hp, str

Piano Concerto No. 1 (1983)                         37'
    solo pf; 2*2*3*2; 4331; timp+2, str             MMB

From Darkness Shines (1984)                         15'
    3*23*2; 4331; timp+3, hp, pf, str               MMB

Percussion Concerto (1984)                          23'
    solo perc; 3=2*3*2*; 4331; timp+3,              MMB
    hp, pf, str

Short Symphony (Symphony No. 1) (1984)              18'
    2222; 2221; timp+1, hp, str                     MMB

Cello Concerto (1985)                               30'
    solo vc; 2*222; 2230; timp+1, hp, pf, str   MMB

The Water Garden (1985)                              9'
    3*3*33*; 4331; timp+3, hp, pf/cel, str          MMB
    OR:  1111; 1110; timp+1, hp, str

Celebration at Vanderburgh (1987)                   13'
    3*3*3*2; 4331; timp+3, hp, str                  MMB

Concerto for Two Violoncellos and
   Orchestra (1987)                                        19'
   soli 2vc; 3*223*; 4331; timp+2, hp, str       MMB
   OR:  soli 2vc; 1111; 2110; timp+2, hp, str

Saxophone Concerto (1987)                                  19'
   solo a sax; 2=2*22; 2110; timp+2,              MMB
   hp, pf, str

Vertical Shrines (1988)                                    32'
   3*23*3*; 4431; timp+3, hp, pf, str             MMB

Visions (1988)                                             24'
   1121; 2110; timp+1, hp, pf, str                MMB

Concerto for Alto Flute and Strings (1989)     20'
   solo a fl; str                                 MMB

The Twelve Days of Christmas (1989)            12'
   satb cho; 3*222; 4331; timp+3, hp, str         MMB

Viola Concerto (1989)                                      22'
   solo vla; 3*223*; 4331; timp+2, hp, str        MMB

Concerto for Three Brass and
   Orchestra (1990)                               21'
   soli hn, tpt, tbn; 3*222; 3221;                MMB
   timp+2, hp, str

Music of the Canvas (1990)                                 20'
   3*23*3*; 4331; timp+3, hp, str                 MMB

String Symphony (1990)                                     15'
   str                                            MMB

Symphony No. 2 (1990)                                      35'
   3*23*3*; 4331; timp+3, hp, str                 MMB

Wild Orchid Overture (1990)                                4'
   2222; 2220; timp+2, str                        MMB

Behold Spring (1991)                                       9'
   3*23*3*; 4331; timp+3, hp, str                 MMB

Concerto for Tenor Saxophone and
   Orchestra (1991)                               23'
   solo t sax; 3*23*3*; 4331; timp+3,             MMB
   hp, str

OTT, JOSEPH   (1929-1990)

Music for Chamber Orchestra (1967)              26'
    1212; 2000; str                            AMP

Matrix IX (1989)                                12'
    2222; 2232; timp+1, pf, str                CBP

Premise for Orchestra (NA)                      15'
    3*3*3*2; 2210; timp+1, str                 ELK

    N.B.  This is a partial listing.
    Inquiries regarding these and other
    works by Mr. Ott may be directed to
    Jenika Ott at Claude Benny Press.


OVERTON, HALL   (1920-1972)

Symphonic Movement (1950)                        8'
    3*23*2; 2220; timp+2, pf, str              ACA

Nonage (1951)                                   15'
    1111; 1100; pf, str (2-1-1-1)              ACA

Symphony for Strings (1955)                     21'
    str                                        CFP

Symphony No. 2 (1962)                           13'
    3*222; 4331; timp+1, hp, str               CFP

Interplay (1964)                                 9'
    2222; 2220; timp+2, pf, str                ACA

Sonorities (1964)                                7'
    2222; 2421; timp+2, vib, str               MJQ

Rhythms (1965)                                  12'
    solo vln; 1111; 1100; 2perc, pf, str       ACA

Pulsations (1972)                               17'
    1011; 1110; perc, hp, pf, str (1-0-1-1)    ACA

PACCIONE, PAUL

Our beauties are not ours (1978; rev 1990)   10'
   2222; 2200; str   ACA


PACKALES, JOSEPH  (1948-  )

Cassandra's Monologue from
  "Agamemnon" (1968)   15'
  solo s; 2222; 4331; timp+2, str   MS

Five Anagogic Dances (1983)   23'
  4*4*4*4*; 4331; timp+4, str   MS

Concerto for Piano and Orchestra (1985)   18'
  solo pf; 3*23*2; 4331; 5perc, str   MS

Variations on a Romantic Theme (1986)   24'
  2222; 4331; perc, str   MS

Ciudad del Sol (1989)   15'
  4*4*4*4*; 6441; timp+5, hp, pf, cel, str   MS


PALANGE, LOUIS  (1917-1979)

Concerto for Piano and Orchestra
  "Romantic" (1949)   30'
  solo pf; 2222; 4331; timp, str   FLE

Don Juan's Coda - Symphonic Poem (1972)   10'
  3*3*22; 4331; timp+1, hp, str   FLE


PALMER, ROBERT  (1915-  )

Variations, Chorale and Fugue
  (1947; rev 1954)   35'
  2222; 4231; timp+2, str   PS

Abraham Lincoln Walks at Midnight (1948)   12'
  satb cho; 32*22; 4331; timp, str   PS

Chamber Concerto (1949)   13'
  soli ob, vln; str   PS

Memorial Music (1960)                        13'
    1111; 2110; str                          PS

Symphony No. 2 (1966)                        25'
    2222; 4330; timp+2, str                  MS

A Centennial Overture (1968)                 7'
    3*3*3*3*; 4331; timp+1, pf, str          MS

Concerto for Piano and
    String Orchestra (1969)                  19'
    solo pf; timp, str                       MS

Concerto for Two Pianos and
    Percussion (1991)                        NA
    soli 2pf, 4perc; double string orchestra MS


PANERIO, ROBERT M., SR.

Ensenada (1969)                              NA
    223*2; 4330; timp+2, str                 CF

Rustic Dance (1970)                          NA
    223*2; 4330; timp+2, str                 MS

Te Deum (1990)                               NA
    solo bar; ssaattbb cho; 223*2; 4330;     MS
    timp+2, hp, str


PARCHMAN, GEN  (1929-    )

Violin Overture (1959; rev 1974)             14'
    3*3*3*3*; 4321; timp+3, str              SEE

Elegy for Orchestra (1960)                   5'
    2222; 4331; 3perc, str                   SEE

Symphony No. 1 for String Orchestra (1960)   20'
    str                                      SEE

Twelve Variations on an
    Original Theme (1960)                    20'
    soli 2pf; 2222; 2321; timp+3, str        SEE

Concerto for Percussion Ensemble and
    Orchestra (1961)                         13'
    solo perc ens; 3*3*3*3*; 4331; timp,     SEE
    hp, str

Concerto for Percussion and
   Orchestra No. 2 (1961)           11'
     soli 7perc; 3*3*3*2; 4331; str    SEE

Concerto for Piano and Orchestra (1961)   13'
     solo pf(4 hands); 3*3*3*3*; 4321;    SEE
     timp+3, str

Adagio for Strings (1962)          5'
     str    SEE

Little Fugue (1962)          3'
     3*233; 4341; 2perc, str    SEE

Sonata for Little Symphony (1962)    16'
     1111; 1110; perc, str    SEE

Winsel Overture (1962)         7'
     3*3*3*3*; 4331; timp+3, str    SEE

Concerto for Timpani (1963)       15'
     solo timp; 3*3*3*3*; 4431; str    SEE

Concerto No. 2 for Two Pianos and
   Orchestra (1963)          14'
     soli 2pf; 3*3*3*3*; 4321; timp+3, str    SEE

Concerto for Marimba (1964)       14'
     solo mar; 23*3*3*; 4432; timp+3, str    SEE

Essay for Orchestra (1964)        5'
     3*3*3*3*; 4421; timp+4, str    SEE

Dramatic Overture (1965)         5'
     3*3*3*3*; 4422; timp+4, str    SEE

History of Music (1965)         NA
     narr; 3*3*3*2; 4431; 2perc, hp, pf, str    SEE

Study for Orchestra (1967)        8'
     3*3*3*3*; 4332; timp+4, hp, str    SEE

Symphony for Chorus and Orchestra (1967)   NA
     satb cho; 3*23*3*; 4431; perc, hp, str    SEE

Concerto for Soprano Voice and
   Orchestra (1972)          15'
     solo s; 3*3*3*3*; 4431; timp+4, hp, str    SEE

Symphony No. 5, op. 93 (1979)                     12'
   2222; 2200; timp+1, str (5-4-3-3-2)            SEE

Concerto for Five Percussion and
   Orchestra (NA)                                 11'
   soli 5perc; 3*3*3*3*; 4331; timp, str          SEE

Petit Symphony (NA)                               10'
   str                                            SEE

Symphony No. 3 (NA)                               26'
   3*3*3*3*; 4332; timp+4, str                    SEE


              PARK, JAMES  (1942-     )

Rondo con Fantasia Concertante (1982)             16'
   1101; 0000; str                                ACA

Gawain's Passage (1985)                           14'
   3*3*02; 2200; timp+1, str                      ACA

Out Island:
   Fantasy for String Orchestra (1987)            10'
   str                                            ACA

Second Fantasy for String Orchestra (1989)        15'
   str                                            ACA


           PARKER, ALICE STUART  (1925-     )

Seven Carols for Christmas (1975)                 17'
   solo s; satb cho; 2222; 2210; timp, str        CF

Gaudete:  Six Latin Christmas Hymns (1976)        22'
   satb cho; 3333; 4321; timp+1, hp, str          ECS

Journeys:  Pilgrims and Strangers (1976)          50'
   soli s, bar; satb cho;                         HMI
   jazz group:  cl, tpt, tbn, tba, dmst;
   3*3*3*3*; 4231; timp+1, hp, str

Commentaries (1978)                               40'
   ssaa cho; 2222; 2221; timp, hp, str            HMI

Revolutionary Overture (1984)                      5'
   2*222; 2231; timp+3, str                       MS

Songs from the Dragon Quilt (1984)                        50'
    solo s; narr; satb cho; 2222; 2221;                   MS
    timp+1, hp, str

Earth, Sky and Spirit (1986)                              18'
    children's cho; 3*3*3*3*; 4331;                       ECS
    timp+3, hp, str

Our Native Land (1986)                                    8'
    satb cho; 2222; 2221; timp+1, str                     MS

The World's One Song (1990)                               40'
    solo s; satb cho; 2222; 4321; timp+1, str             MS

That Sturdy Vine (1991)                                   40'
    solo s; satb cho; children's cho; 2222;               MS
    2220; timp, str


        PARMENTIER, F. GORDON   (1923-      )

Double Entendre (1961)                                    10'
    2222; 4320; perc, hp, str                             ACA

From the Diary of a Northern Window (1963)                18'
    satb cho; 2222; 4230; timp+1,                         ACA
    hp(or pf), str

Eclipse (1971)                                            12'
    solo b-bar; satb cho; 23*3*3*; 4330;                  ACA
    perc, org(opt), str

Symphony III (1976)                                       33'
    2223*; 4330; timp+1, hp, cel, str                     ACA

Concerto for Piano - Mirrors (1980)                       20'
    solo pf; 2222; 0220; timp, str                        ACA


        PARRIS, ROBERT   (1924-      )

Fantasy on Two Themes (1952)                              NA
    1111; 2200; timp+1, str                               ACA

Symphony No. 1 (1952)                                     25'
    1110; 2200; timp+1, str                               ACA

Alas for the New Day (1954)                               15'
    solo t; satb cho; 2222; 2110; timp, str               ACA

Concerto for Piano and Orchestra (1954)            20'
    solo pf; 1111; 2100; str                         ACA

Concerto for Viola and Orchestra (1956)            20'
    solo vla; 1111; 2111; perc, str                  ACA

Concerto for Violin and Orchestra (1958)           20'
    solo vln; 2222; 4231; timp+1, hp, str            ACA

Concerto for Five Kettledrums and
    Orchestra (1961)                                 15'
    solo timp; 3*222; 4230; str                      CFP

Concerto for Flute and Orchestra (1964)            12'
    solo fl; 024=0; 4231; timp+3, pf, str            ACA

Concerto for Trombone (1964)                       17'
    solo tbn; 1110; 0000; perc, pf, str              ACA

The Phoenix (1969)                                 24'
    solo timp; 3*3*4=3*; 4331; perc, hp,             CFP
    pf/cel, str

Angels (1974)                                      25'
    3*23*2; 4331; timp+5, hp, pf, cel, str           ACA
    N.B.  Formerly titled "The Messengers."

The Unquiet Heart (1981)                           10'
    solo vln; 3*222; 4231; 5perc, hp,                ACA
    pf/cel, str

Chamber Music for Orchestra (1984)                 24'
    3*24=3*; 4331; 4perc, hp, cel, str               ACA

Symphonic Variations (1987)                        25'
    3*23*3*; 4431; timp+4, hp, pf, cel, str          ACA


      PARSI, HECTOR CAMPOS  (1922-    )

Divertimento del Sur (1953)                        22'
    soli fl, cl; str                                 PS

Rapsodia elegiaca (1960)                           8'
    str                                              PS

PARWEZ, AKMAL   (1948-     )

Punjab - Land of Five Rivers (NA)                            35'
  1+111; t sax; 0000; timp+1, hp, str                       SEE


PASATIERI, THOMAS   (1945-     )

Three Poems of James Agee (1973)                             8'
  solo mez (or bar); 1111; 1110;                            BEL
  timp+1, hp, str

Rites de Passage (1974)                                     11'
  solo mez (or bar); 2*222; 2110;                            TP
  timp+1, hp, str

Permit Me Voyage - cantata (1976)                           16'
  solo s; satb cho; 2*2*2*2*; 4221;                         BEL
  timp+2, str

Three Sonnets from the Portuguese (1981)                    12'
  solo mez (or bar); str                                     GS

Three Sisters - "Portrait" (1987)                           14'
  2*2*2*2*; 4231; timp+1, hp, str                            GS

Sieben Lehmannlieder (1989)                                 26'
  solo v; 2222; 4221; timp+1, hp, str                        TP


PATTERSON, DAVID

The Five Degrees (1985)                                     18'
  solo a (or t); pf, glock, str                              MS


PAULUS, STEPHEN   (1949-     )

Canticles:  Songs and Rituals for Easter and
  the May (1977)                                             35'
  soli s, mez; narr; satb cho; 1111;                        EAM
  2210; timp+1, org, str

North Shore (1977)                                          35'
  soli mez, bar; satb cho; 2021; 2210;                      EAM
  timp+2, hp, pf/cel, str (1-0-1-1)

Letters for the Times (1980)                                15'
  soli s, t, bar; satb cho; 1111; 0000;                     EAM
  3perc, pf, str (2-1-1-0)

Spectra (1980)                                                    15'
  1121; 2110; timp+2, str                                         EAM

So Hallow'd is the Time -
  A Christmas Cantata (1981)                                      40'
  soli s, t, bar; boy s; satb cho; 1111;                         EAM
  1310; timp+1, hp, org, str

Divertimento for Harp and
  Chamber Orchestra (1982)                                       12'
  solo hp; 1111; 0000; timp+1,                                   EAM
  str (6-6-4-4-2)

Translucent Landscapes (1982)                                    18'
  2121; 2110; timp+1, hp, pf, str                                EAM

Concerto for Orchestra (1983)                                    25'
  3*3*33*; 4431; timp+1, hp, pf/cel, str                         EAM

Seven Short Pieces for Orchestra (1983)                          13'
  3*33*3*; 4331; timp+3, hp, pf/cel, str                         EAM

Ordway Overture (1985)                                           5'
  3*333; 4331; timp+2, str                                       EAM

Reflections:  Four Movements on a Theme of
  Wallace Stevens (1985)                                         22'
  1212; 2100; timp+1, pf, str                                    EAM

"The Postman Always Rings Twice" (1986)                          22'
  3*333; a sax; 4331; timp+3, hp, pf, str                        EAM

Symphony in Three Movements
  (Soliloquy) (1986)                                             30'
  3*333; 4331; timp+3, hp, pf/cel, str                           EAM

Ground Breaker
  An Overture for Construction Instruments
  and Orchestra (1987)                                           7'
  2*222; 4331; timp+1,                                           EAM
  construction ens, str

Violin Concerto (1987)                                           25'
  solo vln; 3*333; 4321; timp+3,                                 EAM
  hp, pf, str

Voices (1988)                                                    40'
  solo s (or t); satb cho; 3*333; 4331;                          EAM
  timp+3, hp, pf, str

Christmas Tidings (1989)                          15'
   satb cho; str                           EAM

Concertante (1989)                               11'
   3*333; 4331; timp+3, pf, str           EAM

Night Speech (1989)                              20'
   solo bar; 3*333; 4331; timp+3,          EAM
   hp, pf, str

Street Music (1989)                               4'
   2222; 4331; timp+2, str                EAM

Symphony for Strings (1989)                      22'
   str                                    EAM

Suite from "Harmoonia" (1990)                     5'
   narr; 2222; 4331; timp+3, hp, pf, str  EAM

Sinfonietta (1991)                               12'
   3333; 4331; timp+3, hp, str            EAM

Trumpet Concerto (1991)                          25'
   solo tpt; 3333; 4331; timp+3,          EAM
   hp, pf/cel, str

Voices from the Gallery (1991)                   30'
   narr; 1111; 1100; timp/perc, str       EAM


      PEASLEE, RICHARD   (1930-    )

Nightsongs (1974)                                10'
   soli flu hn, hp; str                   MG

October Piece (1974)                             15'
   solo rock group; 2222; 4331; timp+4,   ECS
   hp, str

Suite for Guitar and Strings (1980)              20'
   solo gtr; str                          MS

Afterlight (1985)                                18'
   2222; 4331; timp+3, hp, pf, str        LML

Tarantella (1988)                                 3'
   2222; 2221; timp+2, hp, str            MS

PEHRSON, JOSEPH   (1950-      )

Regions (1973)                                              7'
    3*3*3*3*; 4331; timp+3, hp, pf, str                    SEE

Manhattan Plaza Painting (1988)                            5'
    2222; 4331; timp+1, hp, str                            SEE


PELLEGRINI, ERNESTO   (1932-      )

Seven Statements in 3/4 Time (1963)                        10'
    3*3*3*3*; 4331; 4perc, str                             MS

Memorie for Alto/C Flute and
    Orchestra (1985)                                       18'
    solo fl/a fl; 2222; 4331; 4perc,                       MS
    hp, cel, str

Violin Concerto (1986)                                     45'
    solo vln; 3*3*3*3*; 4231; 4perc,                       MS
    hp, cel, str

Piano Concerto (1988)                                      35'
    solo pf; 2222; 4231; 3perc, hp, str                    MS


PENN, WILLIAM   (1943-      )

Spectrums, Confusions and Sometime -
    Moments Beyond the Order of Destiny (1969) 9'
    4*2*3*3*; 4321; 3perc, hp, pf, str                     TP

Symphony (1971)                                            20'
    4*23*3*; 4431; 4perc, hp, pf, str                      MS


PERERA, RONALD   (1941-      )

Mass (1967)                                                25'
    soli s, t, b; 1*111; 1120; 2perc, hp, str  MS

Chanteys (1976; rev 1979)                                  11'
    3*3*3*3*; 4331; timp+3, hp, cel, acc, str  ECS

The White Whale (1981)                                     30'
    solo bar; 1*12*2*; 1110; 2perc, hp,                    ECS
    pf/cel, str

The Saints:
  Three Pieces for Orchestra (1990)                    9'
  2*22(s sax)2; a,t sax; 2221; timp+1, pf,           ECS
  bj, str, tape, audience participation


          PERLE, GEORGE  (1915-    )

Three Movements for Orchestra (1960)                 16'
  4*3*3*2; 4331; timp+1, hp, pf, cel, str            TP

Six Bagatelles (1965)                                 6'
  3*3*3*3*; 4331; timp+1, hp, cel, str               TP

Concerto for Cello and Orchestra (1966)              17'
  solo vc; 2222; 4331; timp+2, hp, cel, str  TP

Songs of Praise and Lamentation (1974)               39'
  soli s, a, t, b; ssaattbb cho; 4*3*3*3*;           BOE
  4441; timp, hp, cel, str

A Short Symphony (1980)                               15'
  3*3*23*; 2431; timp+1, hp, cel, str                BOE

Dance Fantasy (1986)                                 10'
  3*3*33*; 4331; timp+2, hp, pf, cel, str            GAL

Sinfonietta I (1987)                                 14'
  1212; 2100; timp, xyl, str                         GAL

Concerto for Piano and Orchestra (1990)              25'
  solo pf; 4*4*4*4*; 4431; timp+2,                   GAL
  hp, cel, str

Sinfonietta II (1990)                                15'
  2(2picc)2*2+2*; 2210; timp+2, hp, str              GAL


          PERLONGO, DANIEL  (1942-    )

Myriad (1968)                                         9'
  4*3*3*3*; 4431; timp+5, 2hp, cel, str              ACA

Ephemeron (1972)                                     15'
  4*3*3*3*; 4431; timp+5, hp, str                    ACA

Variations for Orchestra (1973)                      10'
  2222; 2110; hp, pf, str                            ACA

Voyage for Orchestra (1975)                          14'
  2222; 2110; hp, pf, str                          ACA

Concertino for Small Orchestra (1980)                12'
  1111; 1110; hp, pf, str                          ACA

Lake Breezes (1990)                                  17'
  1111; 1110; pf, str                              ACA


     PERRY, JULIA   (1924-1979)

A Short Piece for Large Orchestra (1952)             8'
  3*3*3*3*; 4321; timp+3, hp, pf/cel, str          PS

Concerto No. 2 for Piano and
  Orchestra (1955)                                  24'
  solo pf; 3*23*2; a sax; 4320; timp+2, str        PS

Frammenti dalle lettere de
  Santa Caterina (1957)                             10'
  solo s; satb cho; 12*2*2*; 1110;                 PS
  timp+2, hp, str

Hommage to Vivaldi (1959; rev 1964)                  8'
  3*222; 4220; euph; timp+3, hp, str              PS

Concerto for Violin and Orchestra (1964)             23'
  solo vln; 2*222; t sax; 3220; timp+3,           PS
  hp, pf, str

Symphony No. 4 (1964-1968)                           30'
  3*23*2; t sax; 4230; euph; 4perc,               PS
  hp, pf, cel, str

Piano Concerto in
  Two Uninterrupted Speeds (1969)                  25'
  solo pf; 223+2; 4320; timp+2, str               PS


    PERSICHETTI, VINCENT   (1915-1987)

Concerto for Piano and Orchestra,
  op. 16 (1941)                                     10'
  solo pf; 2222; 2200; timp, str                  ELK

Dance Overture, op. 20 (1942)                        8'
  3*3*3*3*; 4431; timp+1, pf, str                 ELK

Fables for Narrator and Orchestra,
   op. 23 (1943)                                            22'
   narr; 3*3*3*3*; 4331; timp+1, pf, str                   CF

Symphony No. 3, op. 30 (1946)                                  28'
   3*3*3*3*; 4331; timp+1, pf, str                        ELK

Serenade No. 5, op. 43 (1950)                                 11'
   2222; 4231; timp, str                                  ELK

Fairy Tale, op. 48 (1950)                                     11'
   2222; 4231; timp+2, str                                CF

Symphony No. 4, op. 51 (1951)                                 23'
   3*3*3*2; 4231; timp+1, str                             ELK

Symphony for Strings, op. 61
   (Symphony No. 5) (1953)                                22'
   str                                                    ELK

Symphony No. 7 "Liturgical", op. 80 (1958)                    28'
   4*3*4=3*; 4331; timp+3, str                            ELK

Concerto for Piano and Orchestra,
   op. 90 (1962)                                          32'
   solo pf; 3*2*3*2; 4331; timp+1, str                    ELK

Te Deum, op. 93 (1963)                                        11'
   satb cho; 2222; 4231; timp+1, str                      ELK

Introit, op. 96 (1964)                                         3'
   str                                                    BRO

Symphony No. 8, op. 106 (1967)                                30'
   3*3*3*2; 4331; timp+2, str                             ELK

The Pleiades, op. 107 (1967)                                  23'
   satb cho; solo tpt; str                                ELK

The Creation, op. 111 (1969)                                  60'
   soli s, a, t, b; satb cho; 3*3*3*2;                    ELK
   4331; timp+1, str

Symphony No. 9, op. 113 (1970)                                23'
   "Sinfonia Janiculum"                                   ELK
   4*3*4=3*; 4331; timp+3, hp, str

Night Dances, op. 114 (1970)                                  19'
   3*3*3*2; 4331; timp+3, str                             ELK

A Lincoln Address, op. 124 (1972)                        12'
   narr; 4*3*4=3*; 4331; timp+1, str                     ELK

Concerto for English Horn and Strings,
   op. 137 (1977)                                        20'
   solo eh; str                                          ELK

Flower Songs, op. 157 (1983)                             21'
   (Cantata No. 6)                                       ELK
   satb cho; str


          PETERSON, WAYNE  (1927-      )

Free Variations for Orchestra (1958)                     20'
   3*3*3*3*; 4331; timp+1, pf, str                       BH

Exaltation, Dithyramb and Caprice (1961)                 27'
   3*3*3*3*; 4331; timp+1, pf, str                       BH

Cataclysms (1968)                                        14'
   2222; 2220; 3perc, hp, pf/cel, str                    SEE

Clusters and Fragments (1969)                            12'
   str                                                   SEE

Transformations for Chamber Orchestra (1986)  18'
   1111; 2110; 2perc, hp, pf, str (2-1-1-1)              CFP

Trilogy (Evocation, Nocturne, Flight) (1987)  20'
   1111; 2110; timp+1, hp, str                           MS

The Widening Gyre (1989)                                 18'
   3*3*3*2; 4331; timp+3, hp, pf, str                    MS

The Face of the Night,
   the Heart of the Dark (1990)                          20'
   3*3*3*3*; 4331; timp+3, hp, pf, str                   MS


          PHILLIPS, BURRILL  (1907-1988)

Concerto Grosso for String Quartet and
   Small Orchestra (1950)                                14'
   solo str qt; 1111; 1000; str                          FLE

Divertimento for Strings (1950)                          14'
   str                                                   FLE

Triple Concerto for Clarinet, Viola, Piano
   and Orchestra (1953)                          25'
   soli cl, vla, pf; 1*111; 2110;               FLE
   timp+1, str

Theater Dances (1967)                            13'
   2222; 4331; timp+1, str                      FLE


          PHILLIPS, MARK   (1952-    )

Intrusus (1979)                                  18'
   1*111; 1111; timp+2, pf/cel, str             MMB

Summer Soft (1983)                               6'
   1111; 1210; 2perc, hp, pf, str (4-2-2-1)     MMB

Turning (1986)                                   12'
   4*3*3*3*; 4431; timp+4, hp, pf/cel, str      MMB


          PHILLIPS, PETER   (1930-    )

Interplays - Concerto for Jazz Drums,
   Percussion Ensemble and Orchestra (1967)     25'
   soli jazz drums, perc ens; 3*2*2*2;          AMP
   4321; 4perc, hp, pf, str

Music for a Ballet (NA)                          22'
   timp+1, hpsd, str (7-3-2-1)                  AMP

Novasonic (NA)                                   15'
   3*3*3*3*; 4331; timp+1, pf, str              AMP


          PICKER, TOBIAS   (1954-    )

Piano Concerto No. 1 (1980)                      20'
   solo pf; 2=2*2*2; 4231; timp, str            EAM

Symphony No. 1 (1982)                            28'
   3*3*3*3; 4231; timp+1, 2hp, pf, str          EAM

Violin Concerto (1982)                           28'
   solo vln; 22*3*2; 4231; timp, hp, pf, str    EAM

Encantadas (1983)                                27'
   narr; 2*2*2*2; 4231 (or 2200); timp+1,       EAM
   hp, pf, str

Keys to the City
  (Piano Concerto No. 2) (1983)                18'
  solo pf; 2*22(s sax, a sax, b cl)2*;         EAM
  4231; timp+1, str

Old and Lost Rivers (1986)                     4'
  3*23*3; 6301; timp+1, hp, pf, str            EAM

Piano Concerto No. 3 (1986)                    22'
  solo pf; 3*3*3*3*; 4331; timp+1, 2hp, str    EAM

Symphony No. 2 (1986)                          26'
  solo s; 3*3*3*3*; 4331; timp+2,              EAM
  hp, pf, str

Symphony No. 3 (1989)                          24'
  str                                          EAM

Romances and Interludes (1990)                 25'
  solo ob; 2+1*22; 4000; timp+1,               EAM
  hp, pf, str

Two Fantasies for Orchestra (1991)             11'
  2+223*; 4321; perc, hp, pf/cel, str          EAM

Seance (1991)                                  4'
  42*23; 4030; timp+3, pf,                     EAM
  str (no 2nd vln, vla)


          PIERCE, ALEXANDRA  (1934-    )

Behemoth (1976)                                15'
  2111; 2110; timp+1, hp, str                  SEE

Dances on the Face of the Deep (1988)          20'
  3*3*3*3*; 4331; timp+3, hp, str              FLE


          PIKET, FREDERICK  (1903-1974)

Curtain Raiser to an American Play (1948)      6'
  3(3picc)23*2; 4331; timp+1, str              AMP

Essays in Rhythm (1960)                        14'
  2(2picc)22*2; 2320; timp+1, str              FLE

Crossroads (1965)                              17'
  3*23*2; 4331; timp+2, str                    SEE

PINKHAM, DANIEL   (1923-      )

Concertino for Organ and
   String Orchestra (1947)            12'
   solo org; str                  ACA

Concertino in A for Small Orchestra and
   Obbligato Pianoforte (1950)      18'
   solo pf; 1200; 0200; str         ECS

Five Short Pieces (1952)           10'
   02*(opt)00; 2(opt)000; str       ACA

Concertante for Violin and
   Harpsichord (1954)             10'
   soli vln, hpsd; cel, str          ECS

Nocturne (1954)                   10'
   str                          ACA

Prothalamion (1955)              4'
   0100; 2000; str                ACA

Concerto for Violin and Orchestra (1956)  18'
   solo vln; 0200; 2000; hp, cel, str   ECS

Wedding Cantata (1956)           10'
   soli s, t; satb cho; 2hn; cel, str    CFP

Concertante No. 2 (1958)          16'
   solo vln; str                 ECS

Serenade for Violin, Harpsichord and
   Orchestra (1958)              16'
   soli vln, hpsd; 0100; 2000; str     CF

Envoi (1959)                     4'
   01*00; 2000; str               ACA

Rondo (1959)                     3'
   0100; 2000; cel, str           ACA

Scherzo (1959)                   3'
   0100; 2000; cel, str           ACA

The Reproaches (1960)          18'
   satb cho; 1111; 1100; org, str (2-1-1-1)  AMP

Symphony No. 1 (1961)          17'
   3*3*3*3*; 4331; timp+1, hp, pf, cel, str  CFP

Catacoustical Measures (1962)                          5'
    4*3*4*4*; 4441; timp+1, hp, pf, cel, str          CFP

An Emily Dickinson Mosaic (1962)                      10'
    ssaa cho; 2020; 0000; perc, cel, str              CFP

Symphony No. 2 (1963)                                 16'
    3*3*3*2; 4331; timp+3, hp, pf, str                CFP

Now the Trumpet Summons Us Again (1964)               5'
    solo s; 3*3*3*2; 4331; timp+1, hp, str            CFP

Stabat Mater (1964)                                   16'
    solo s; satb cho; 1111; 1110; timp+1,             CFP
    hp, cel, str

Signs of the Zodiac (1965)                            21'
    narr(opt); 3*3*3*2; 4331; timp+2,                 CFP
    hp, pf/cel, str

Concertante for Guitar and
    Harpsichord (1966)                                14'
    soli gtr, hpsd; perc, str                         CFP

Jonah (1967)                                          26'
    soli mez, t, b-bar; satb cho; 3*3*3*2*;           ECS
    4331; timp+6, hp, cel, str

Organ Concerto (1970)                                 21'
    solo org; 0000; 2221; timp+2, str                 CFP

To Troubled Friends (1972)                            18'
    satb cho; str, tape                               ION

Four Elegies (1975)                                   24'
    solo t; satb cho; 01*01; 1000; org, str           ION

Masks (1978)                                          14'
    11*10; 0000; perc, hpsd, str                      ECS

Hezekiah (1979)                                       10'
    soli s, t, bar; satb cho; tpt; org, str           ION

Symphony No. 3 (1985; rev 1986)                       25'
    3*3*22; 4331; timp+1, hp, cel, str                CFP

Concerto Piccolo (1989)                               9'
    solo picc; perc, str                              ECS

Symphony No. 4 (1990)                                         13'
    3*222; 3220; timp+1, hp, cel, str                        CFP

Divertimento for Oboe and
    String Orchestra (NA)                                    8'
    solo ob(rec); 2hn(opt); hp(or hpsd), str                 ECS


            PINKSTON, RUSSELL   (1949-    )

Bellwether (1984)                                            20'
    222*2; 4221; timp+2, str                                 MS


            PISK, PAUL   (1893-    )

Canzona (1955)                                               6'
    1121; 1000; str                                          ACA

Elegy (1958)                                                 6'
    str                                                      ACA

Three Ceremonial Rites (1958)                               14'
    2222; 2210; timp+1, hp, str                              ACA

Sonnet for Chamber Orchestra (1960)                          6'
    0121; 1000; str                                          ACA


            PISTON, WALTER   (1894-1976)

Suite No. 1 for Orchestra (1929)                            15'
    3*3*3*3*; 4331; timp+2, pf, str                          AMP

Concerto for Orchestra (1933)                               14'
    3*3*3*3*; 4331; timp+2, pf, str                          AMP

Prelude and Fugue (1934)                                    13'
    3*3*3*3*; 4331; timp, hp, str                            AMP

Concertino for Piano and Orchestra (1937)                   14'
    solo pf; 2222; 2000; str                                 AMP

Symphony No. 1 (1937)                                       27'
    3*3*3*3*; 4331; timp, str                                AMP

The Incredible Flutist - ballet (1938)                      25'
    3*3*3*3*; 4331; timp+2, pf, str                          AMP

The Incredible Flutist - suite (1938)                  17'
   3*3*3*3*; 4331; timp+2, pf, str                   AMP

Prelude and Fugue (1943)                               12'
   solo org; str                                     AMP

Symphony No. 2 (1943)                                  26'
   3*3*3*3*; 4431; perc, str                         AMP

Symphony No. 3 (1947)                                  31'
   3*3*3*3*; 4331; timp+2, 2hp, str                  BH

Suite No. 2 for Orchestra (1948)                       24'
   3*3*3*3*; 4331; timp+1, str                       AMP

Toccata (1948)                                          9'
   3*3*3*3*; 4331; timp+2, str                       BH

Symphony No. 4 (1950)                                  23'
   3*3*3*3*; 4331; timp+1, 2hp, str                  AMP

Fantasy for English Horn, Harp and
   Strings (1952)                                    16'
   solo eh; hp, str                                  AMP

Symphony No. 5 (1954)                                  22'
   3*3*3*3*; 4331; timp+1, 2hp, str                  AMP

Symphony No. 6 (1955)                                  25'
   3*3*3*3*; 4331; timp+1, 2hp, str                  AMP

Serenata (1956)                                        15'
   2222; 4200; timp, hp, str                         AMP

Concerto for Viola and Orchestra (1957)               19'
   solo vla; 3*3*3*3*; 4231; timp+1, hp, str  AMP

Concerto for Two Pianos and Orchestra (1959)  23'
   soli 2pf; 3*3*3*3*; 4231; timp+1, str            AMP

Three New England Sketches (1959)                     15'
   3*3*3*3*; 4331; timp+1, 2hp, str                  AMP

Concerto No. 2 for Violin and
   Orchestra (1960)                                  24'
   solo vln; 3*3*3*3*; 4231; timp+1, hp, str  AMP

Symphony No. 7 (1960)                                  19'
   3*3*3*3*; 4331; timp+1, 2hp, str                  AMP

Symphonic Prelude (1961)                                      10'
   3*3*3*3*; 4331; timp+1, hp, str                          AMP

Lincoln Center Festival Overture (1962)                      12'
   3*3*3*3*; 4331; timp+1, 2hp, str                         AMP

Capriccio for Harp and
   String Orchestra (1963)                                   8'
   solo hp; str                                             AMP

Variations on a Theme by
   Edward Burlingame Hill (1963)                            11'
   3*3*3*2; 4231; perc, str                                 AMP

Pine Tree Fantasy (1965)                                     12'
   3*3*3*3*; 4231; timp+4, str                              AMP

Symphony No. 8 (1965)                                        20'
   3*3*3*3*; 4331; timp+1, 2hp, str                         AMP

Variations for Violoncello and
   Orchestra (1967)                                         15'
   solo vc; 23*3*2; 2200; timp+1, str                       AMP

Ricercare (1967)                                             11'
   3*3*3*3*; 4331; timp+3, 2hp, str                         AMP

Fantasia for Violin and Orchestra (1970)                     16'
   solo vln; 3*3*3*3*; 4331; timp+1, str                    AMP

Concerto for Flute and Orchestra (1971)                      19'
   solo fl; 22*2*2; 4200; timp+1, hp, str                   AMP

Bi-Centennial Fanfare (1975)                                  4'
   3*333; 4331; timp+4, str                                 AMP

Concerto for String Quartet, Winds and
   Percussion (1976)                                        12'
   solo str qt; 3*3*3*2; 2220; timp+1                       AMP


      PLAIN, GERALD  (1940-    )

Facets for Orchestra (1964)                                   6'
   223*2; 3221; timp+3, pf, str                             MS

Arrows (1968)                                                16'
   3*3*3*3*; 4231; timp+3, hp, pf/cel, str                  MS

and left ol' Joe a bone, AMAZING! (1975)           17'
   3*3*3*3*; 4231; timp+4, pf, str                    MS

Violin Concerto (1979)                             12'
   solo vln; 3*3*3*3*; 4331; timp+3,               MS
   hp, pf, str

Portrait 2:  Pretty Polly (1987)                   18'
   2*112; 2110; 4perc, 2hp, pf, cel, str           MS

Portrait 1:  Sally Goodin (1989)                   12'
   3*22*2*; 4220; 3perc, 2hp, cel, str             MS

Clawhammer (1991)                                  10'
   2222; 2110; 2perc, hp, elec kybd, str           MS


      PLESKOW, RAOUL   (1931-    )

Two Movements for Orchestra (1969)                 10'
   2222; 2211; perc, hp, pf, str                   ACA

Music for Orchestra (1972)                         15'
   3*222; 2211; 2perc, pf, str                     ACA

Three Pieces for Orchestra (1974)                  7'
   2111; 1000; perc, hp, pf, str                   ACA

Suite for Orchestra (1978)                         15'
   2222; 2101; 2perc, 2pf, str                     ACA

Four Bagatelles for Orchestra (1980)               6'
   2222; 4000; str                                 ACA
   OR:   2222; 2211; str

Epitaphium (1983)                                  8'
   str                                             ACA

Three Epigrams (1984)                              8'
   str                                             ACA

Epitaphium:  Stefan Wolpe in Memoriam (1985)  7'
   2222; 3201; str                                 ACA

Paumanok:  A Long Island Cantata (1985)            12'
   solo s; satb cho; 1010; 0000;                   ACA
   timp, pf, str

Preludium (1986)                                   6'
   3*222; 2220; timp, str                          ACA

Two Preludes for Orchestra (1986)     5'
   2222; 2211; timp, str     ACA

Six Brief Verses (1987)     10'
   ssaa cho; pf, str     ACA

Consort for Strings (1988)     10'
   str     ACA

Preludium No. 2 (1988)     5'
   2222; 2220; timp, str     ACA

Six Epigrams (1988)     10'
   3*222; 4220; timp+2, pf, str     ACA

Serenade (1989)     15'
   satb cho; 2222; 2220; str     ACA

Altarpiece (1991)     10'
   satb cho; perc, pf, str     ACA


### POLAY, BRUCE

Encomium (1986)     14'
   narr; children's cho; 3*2*23*; 4331;     MMB
   timp+3, hp, pf/cel, str


### POLIN, CLAIRE (1926- )

Symphony No. 2 (Korean) (1963)     26'
   3*3*3*2; 4331; timp+1, pf, str     SEE

Journey of Owain Madok (1971)     20'
   3*3*3*2; 1211; 5perc, pf, str     SEE

Mythos - Concerto for Harp and
   String Orchestra (1983)     15'
   solo hp; str     MS


### POLSTER, IAN

Fragments from Memory: April 4, 1968 (1968)     6'
   2222; 4331; timp+2, str     MS

Textures for Orchestra (1969)     13'
   3*3*3*3*; 4331; 4perc, str     MS

Symphonic Episodes (1973)                                   14'
    22(opt ob d'am)22; 4331; 4perc, hp, str        MS

The Orchestral Punpieces (1976)                              9'
    2222; 4331; timp+2, str                        MS

Serenade for Orchestra (1980)                                9'
    23*22; 4331; 4perc, str                        MS

Humoresque for Bassoon and Orchestra (1985)     3'
    solo bsn; 2222; 4331; timp+2, str              MS

Music for a Summer Evening (1986)                            7'
    22(opt ob d'am)22; 4331; timp+2, str           MS

Something Sings (1986)                                       9'
    satb cho; 2222; 4331; timp+2, hp, str          MS


        PONÉ, GUNDARIS   (1932-     )

Concerto for Violin and Orchestra (1959)       30'
    solo vln; 2*222; 4231; timp+2, hp, str        NOR

Quattro temperamenti d'amore (1960)           18'
    solo bar; 2*22*2*; 4331; timp+2, hp, pf,     NOR
    cel, mand, str

Daniel Propheta - oratorio (1962)                           60'
    soli 3vv; satb cho; 3*3*3*3*; 6431;           NOR
    timp+2, hp, org(opt), str

Vivos voco, mortuos plango (1972)                           10'
    3*333*; 6531; 6perc, cel, str                 NOR

Avanti! (1975)                                              20'
    2*222; 4331; timp+2, str                      NOR

Five American Songs (1975)                                  10'
    solo mez (or bar); 1*111; 1210;               NOR
    2perc, str

Concerto for Horn and Orchestra (1976)         20'
    solo hn; 1*111; 0210; 2perc, pf/cel, str      NOR

La serenissima -
    Seven Venetian Portraits (1979-1981)         20'
    3*3*3*3*; 4331; timp+2, hp, cel, str          NOR

American Portraits (1984)                              20'
    2*222; 2220; timp+3, pf/elec hpsd, str            NOR

Titzarin (1984-1986)                                   22'
    3*3*3*3*; 4331; timp+4, pf, cel, str              NOR

Overture "La Bella Veneziana" (1988)                   10'
    2222; 2220; timp, str                             NOR


              PORTER, QUINCY  (1897-1966)

Poem and Dance (1932)                                  10'
    23*22; 4331; timp+3, str                          ACA

Symphony No. 1 (1934)                                  24'
    3*3*3*3*; 4331; timp+4, hp, str                   ACA

Dance in Three-Time (1937)                             9'
    1111; 2110; timp+3, str                           ACA

Two Dances for Radio (1938)                            13'
    2222; 4220; timp+2, hp, str                       ACA

Anthony and Cleopatra (1939)                           11'
    1111; 2110; timp+1, str                           ACA

Fantasy on a Pastoral Theme (1943)                     7'
    solo org; str                                     ACA

Concerto for Viola and Orchestra (1948)                20'
    solo vla; 3*3*22; 4331; perc, str                 AMP

Fantasy for Violoncello and Orchestra (1950)           9'
    solo vc; 0200; 2000; perc, str                    ACA

Concerto concertante (1953)                            18'
    soli 2pf; 2222; 4231; timp, str                   ACA

New England Episodes (1958)                            20'
    3*3*22; 4231; 3perc, str                          ACA

Concerto for Harpsichord and
    Orchestra (1959)                                   25'
    solo hpsd; 3*23*2; 4331; timp, str                ACA

Symphony No. 2 (1962)                                  25'
    3*222; 4231; timp+1, str                          CFP

POWELL, MEL    (1923-      )

Cantilena Concertante (1949)                    11'
    solo eh; 3232; 0220; perc, str              GS

Symphonic Suite (1949)                          13'
    2*3*3*2; 4231; timp+2, str                  GS

Intrada and Variants (1955)                     8'
    3*3*3*3*; 4331; timp+1, hp, pf, str         TP

Stanzas (1957)                                  7'
    2121; 2210; perc, str                       GS

Setting for Violoncello and Orchestra (1961)    7'
    solo vc; 2222; 2200; timp+2, hp, str        GS

Immobiles (1967)                                12'
    2222; 4231; timp+1, hp, str, tape           GS

Modules - An Intermezzo for
    Chamber Orchestra (1985)                    14'
    1111; 2110; 2perc, str (1-1-1-1)            GS

Duplicates:  Concerto for Two Pianos
    and Orchestra (1987-1990)                   32'
    soli 2pf; 3=3*3=3*; 4331; 3perc, 2hp, str   GS


POZDRO, JOHN    (1923-      )

Overture (1948)                                 8'
    3*2*2*2; 4231; timp+1, str                  MS

Symphony No. 1 (1949)                           19'
    3*2*2*2; 4231; timp+1, str                  MS

A Cynical Overture (1952)                       7'
    3*2*2*2*; 4231; timp+2, str                 MS

Second Symphony (1957)                          27'
    3*2*2*2; 4231; timp+1, str                  FLE

Third Symphony (1960)                           21'
    3*2*2*2*; 4231; timp+2, str                 TP

Waterlow Park:  1970  (1972)                    7'
    3*2*2*2*; 4231; timp+2, str                 MS

PRESSER, WILLIAM   (1916-   )

Concerto for Tuba and
   String Orchestra (1970)         17'
   solo tba; str                  TP


PRIMOSCH, JAMES   (1956-   )

Maranatha (1980)                 11'
   1111; 1110; 2perc, pf, str (4-2-2-1)   MS

Dappled Things (1986)           7'
   2222; 4220; 4perc, pf/cel, str     MG

The Cloud of Unknowing (1987)     37'
   solo s; 1*11*1*; 1110; 3perc,    MG
   pf/cel, str (4-2-2-1)

Chamber Symphony (1990)         18'
   112*0; 1110; 2perc, pf, str (2-1-2-1)  MER


PROCTOR, LELAND H. (1914-   )

Symphony No. 1 (1948)           30'
   2222; 4231; timp+2, str       ACA

Intimations (1952)             12'
   2222; 4241; timp, hp, str      ACA

Suite for String Orchestra (1952)   23'
   str                    ACA

Seascape (1975)                18'
   3*3*3*3*; 4231; timp+1, hp, str   ACA

Moby Dick (1979)               60'
   satb cho; 3*3*3*3*; 4231; timp+1, hp, str ACA


PTASZYNSKA, MARTA   (1943-   )

Improvisations (1968)           10'
   3*3*3*3*; 4331; perc, hp, pf, cel,  TP
   gtr, str

Spectri sonori (1973)           7'
   3*223*; 4331; 5perc, hp, pf, cel, str  TP

Concerto for Percussion and Orchestra (1974)    12'
    soli 4perc; 2222; 4331; pf, str                TP

Crystallites (1974)                                14'
    434*4*; 4441; 5perc, 2hp, pf, str              TP

Die Sonette an Orpheus (1981)                      11'
    solo mez (or bar); 1111; 2100; perc,           TP
    hp, str

Ave Maria (1982; rev 1987)                         13'
    ttbb cho; 0000; 4331; 6perc, org, str          TP

La Novella d'Inverno (1984)                        10'
    str                                            TP

Concerto for Marimba and Orchestra (1985)          31'
    solo mar; 2223*; 4331; 4perc, hp, str          TP


            PUTSCHE, THOMAS   (1929-    )

Three Bugs (1965)                                   9'
    3*23*2; 4221; 2perc, hp, cel, str              SEE

RACKLEY, LAWRENCE   (1932-    )

Symphony No. 1 in G (1957)                          17'
   3*222; 4231; timp, pf, str                       AMP

Discourse, Soliloquy and Concourse (1969)          20'
   solo vc; 3*23*2; 4231; timp+1,                   AMP
   str (4-4-4-4-2)

Confluences (1970)                                 12'
   3*23*2; 4231; timp+1, str                        AMP

The Chambered Nautilus (1991)                      11'
   222*2; 4231; timp+2, str                         MS


           RAKOWSKI, DAVID   (1958-    )

Elegy (1984)                                        5'
   str (divisi)                                     ACA

Six Bogan Poems (1989-1990)                        16'
   solo s (or mez); hp, cel, str                    CFP

Symphony No. 1
   "Scattering Dark and Bright" (1990-1991)        28'
   solo s; 2*2*3*2; 2220; 2perc, hp,                CFP
   pf/cel, str

Winged Contraption (Perpetual Motion Scherzo
   in Search of a Symphony) (1991)                  9'
   2*2*3*2; 2221; 2perc, hp, pf, str                MS


           RAKSIN, DAVID   (1912-    )

Forever Amber - suite from film
   (1948; rev 1974)                                24'
   4(2picc, 2a fl)4(3eh)4(4b cl)4*;                 MS
   444(2b tbn)1; timp+2, hp, pf/cel, str

Litany (1966)                                       8'
   33(3)3*; 4331; timp+2, hp, pf, str               MS
   N.B.  The 3 clarinet parts are written for
   3 English horns, but may be played on
   clarinets.

RAMEY, PHILLIP   (1939-    )

Concert Suite for Piano and Orchestra
  (1962; rev 1983)                                    19'
  solo pf; 2*222; 3220; timp+1, str                   GS

Seven, They Are Seven:
  Incantation for Bass-Baritone and
  Orchestra (1965)                                     12'
  solo b-bar; 2*222; 3221; timp+3, pf, str            MS

Concerto No. 1 for Piano and
  Orchestra (1969-1971)                                16'
  solo pf; 2*3*3*3*; 4331; timp+2, str                MS

Concerto No. 2 for Piano and
  Orchestra (1976)                                     21'
  solo pf; 3*3*3*3*; 4331; timp+2, str                MS

Concerto for Horn and String Orchestra
  (1987; rev 1989)                                     20'
  solo hn; str                                        MS

Cantus Arcanus
  (In Memoriam Aaron Copland) (1990)                    6'
  3*3*3*3*; 4331; timp+1, hp, str                     MS

Concerto No. 3 for Piano and
  Orchestra (1991)                                     25'
  solo pf; 2*2*22; 2221; timp+1, str                  MS


RAMSIER, PAUL   (1928-    )

Dance Variations -
  Six Dance Diversions (1960)                          13'
  2222; 4231; timp+1, hp, pf, str                     BH

Eusebius Revisited -
  Remembrances for Schumann (1978)                     17'
  solo vc (or db); pf, str                            BEL

Road to Hamelin (1978)                                 18'
  narr; solo db; 1111; 1100; 3perc,                   BH
  hp, pf, str

The Low-Note Blues (1981)                               7'
  solo db; str                                        BEL

Silent Movie (1982)                                          17'
    solo db; pf, str                                         BEL

Divertimento Concertante -
    on a theme of Couperin (NA)                              16'
    solo db; 2222; 3131; timp+1, hp, str                     GS


        RAN, SHULAMIT  (1949-    )

Concert Piece for Piano and Orchestra (1971)   12'
    solo pf; 4*24*3*; 5431; perc, str           TP
    OR:  2222; 4231; perc, str

Concerto for Orchestra (1986)                   22'
    223*2; 4331; timp+3, pf, str                TP

Symphony (1990)                                 30'
    2*2*3=3*; 4431; timp+3, str                 TP


        RANDS, BERNARD  (1934-    )

Per Esempio (1968)                              13'
    1111; 2220; 4perc, pf, str                  EAM

Wildtrack I (1969)                              14'
    3*25(a,t sax)1; 4331; 3perc, 2hp, pf,       EAM
    cel, elec org, str
    OR:  1+11*1; t sax; 0000; 3perc, hp, pf,
    cel, str

Agenda (1970)                                   13'
    2222; 2220; 2perc, str                      EAM

Formats II - Labyrinthe (1970)                  12'
    cl; tbn; 2perc, pf, cel, str                EAM

Wildtrack II (1973)                             20'
    solo s; 1+11*1; t sax; 2220; 5perc, 2hp,    EAM
    elec org, str (6-6-3-3-1)

Aum for Harp and Orchestra (1974)               20'
    solo hp; 2+300; 0220; 3perc, hp, cel,       EAM
    elec, org, str (0-4-2-1)

Wildtrack III (1975)                            20'
    soli s, mez; narr; satb cho; 1+12*1;        EAM
    t sax; 2220; 5perc, 2hp, elec org,
    str (6-6-3-3-1)

Serenade (1976) 22'
   solo fl; cl; perc, elec pf, elec org,   UE
   str (6-6-4-2-1)

Madrigali (1977) 22'
   1100; 1100; perc, str (6-6-4-2-1)   UE

Ballad 4 (1980) 22'
   soli 2s, 2a, 2t, 2b; 2030; 0330; 2perc,   UE
   hp, elec org, str (0-3-2-1)

Canti lunatici (1981) 29'
   solo s; 2222; 2220; 2perc, 2hp, pf,   UE
   cel, str

Tambourin Suites I & II (1984) 20'
   2*22*3*; 4331; timp+4, 2hp, pf, cel,   EAM
   elec org, str
   N.B. May be performed separately or together.

Canti del sole (1985) 28'
   solo t; 2=22=2; 3330; 3perc, 2hp, pf,   EAM
   cel, elec org, str (10-10-8-6-4)

Ceremonial III (1987) 13'
   3*24*2; 4331; timp+4, 2hp, pf, cel,   EAM
   elec org, str

Hiraeth (1987) 30'
   solo vc; 3=3*4*3*; 4331; timp+4, 2hp,   EAM
   pf, cel, elec org, str

...body and shadow (1989) 20'
   3*24=2; 4321; timp+4, 2hp, pf, cel,   EAM
   elec org, str

Bells (1990) 28'
   satb cho; 3*23*2; 4331; timp+4, 2hp,   EAM
   pf, cel, str


RAPCHAK, LAWRENCE (1951-    )

Chasing the Sunset (1987) 12'
   2*3*2*2; a sax; 4331; timp+4,   NOA
   hp, cel, str
   N.B. Also requires a soprano recorder in C.

RAPHLING, SAMUEL   (1910-1988)

Concerto No. 1 for Piano and Orchestra (1945) 11'
    solo pf; 1000; 1100; str                      BEL

Novelty Suite
    (from "Fugue, Blues and Workout") (1948)   5'
    2222; 4331; timp+2, hp(or pf), str            BEL

Concerto No. 3 for Piano and Orchestra (1960) 21'
    solo pf; 2222; 4221; timp, str                BEL

Dance of the Chassidim (1962)                   3'
    2222; 4331; timp+2, str                       BEL

Minstrel Rhapsody (1962)                         9'
    solo pf; 2222; 4331; timp+1, hp, str          BEL


RATHAUS, KAROL   (1895-1954)

Piano Concerto, op. 45 (1939)                   25'
    solo pf; 323*2; 4330; timp+1, str             BH

Symphony No. 3, op. 50 (1942-1943)              30'
    3*3*3*3*; 4331; timp+2, hp, cel, str          BH

Vision Dramatique, op. 55 (1945)                12'
    223*2; 4331; timp+2, pf, str                  BH

Salisbury Cove Overture, op. 65 (1949)          15'
    3*23*3*; 4331; timp+2, hp, pf, str            CF

Sinfonia Concertante, op. 68 (1951)             25'
    3*23*3*; 4331; timp+1, str                    BAR

Louisville Prelude, op. 71 (1953)                7'
    2*222; 4231; timp+1, pf, str                  BH


RAUSCH, CARLOS

Construction 3 (1971)                           15'
    1111; 1110; timp+2, pf, str (1-1-1-1)         MOB

Sonorities (1982)                                6'
    3*010; a,t sax; 1301; timp+2, str             ACA

A Legend of the Andes (1985)                    45'
    3(2picc)3*3=3*; 4431; timp+4, hp, pf, str     ACA

READ, GARDNER (1913-     )

Concerto for Violoncello and
  Orchestra, op. 55 (1945)                          25'
  solo vc; 3*23*2; 4330; timp+1, str               MS

Music for Piano and Strings, op. 47a (1946)  21'
  solo pf; str                                      MS

Quiet Music for Strings, op. 65 (1946)        9'
  str                                              SEE

Pennsylvania Suite, op. 67 (1946-1947)       16'
  3*333; 4331; timp+1, hp, pf, str               BEL

Partita for Small Orchestra, op. 70 (1946)   11'
  1111; 1110; timp, str                            MS

A Bell Overture, op. 78 (1946)                7'
  3*3*3*3*; 4331; timp+1, hp, pf, str            MS

The Temptation of St. Anthony, op. 56 (1947) 35'
  3*3*3*3*; 4331; timp+1, hp, cel, str           MS

Symphony No. 5, op. 75 (1948)                 25'
  3*3*3*3*; 4331; timp+1, pf, str               BEL

Arioso elegiaca, op. 91 (1951)                7'
  str                                             CFP

Symphony No. 4, op. 92 (1951-1959)           23'
  3*3*3*3*; 4331; timp+1, str                    MS

Toccata giocosa, op. 94 (1953)                6'
  2222; 4231; timp+1, hp, str                     TP

Vernal Equinox, op. 96 (1955)                10'
  2222; 4330; timp+1, hp, cel, str               MS

The Prophet, op. 110 (1960)                  73'
  soli 2vv; narr; satb cho; 4*3*4*3*;            MS
  4331; timp+2, 2hp, cel, str

Sonoric Fantasia No. 2, op. 123 (1965)       14'
  solo vln; 1111; 1110; 2perc, hp, str            TP

Concerto for Piano and Orchestra,
  op. 130 (1977)                                  36'
  solo pf; 2222; 4330; timp+1, str               MS

Astral Nebulae, op. 136a (1983)                    19'
   3*3*4=3*; 4431; timp+3, hp, cel, str            MS

Pan e Dafni (NA)                                   10'
   4+3*3*3*; 4031; timp+1, hp, str                 MS


     READ, THOMAS L.  (1938-    )

Isochronisms No. 2 (1975)                          10'
  str                                             ACA

Symphonic Episodes (1984)                          11'
   3*222; 4331; timp+3, str                        ACA

Adventura (1985)                                   15'
   3*222; 4331; timp+3, str                        ACA

Symphony for Orchestra with
  Piano Obbligato (1986)                          15'
  2222; 4330; timp+2, pf, str                     ACA

Sunrise Fable (1989)                               18'
   3*222; 4331; timp+2, pf, str                    CFP


     REED, ALFRED  (1921-    )

Rhapsody for Viola and Orchestra (1956)            16'
  solo vla; 3*3*3*3*; 4331; timp+4, hp, str     LML

A Festival Prelude (1968)                          12'
   3*3*5*3; 2a,t,bar sax; 4331; timp+1, str     EBM

Titania's Nocturne (1968)                          7'
  str                                             EBM

The Pledge of Allegiance (1970)                    2'
  satb cho; 23*3*2; 4331; timp+2, str          EBM

Siciliana Notturno (1977)                          5'
  solo hp; str                                    EBM

Suite Concertante (1982)                           21'
  hp, str                                         KAL

REED, HERBERT OWEN  (1910-    )

Concerto for Violoncello and
   Orchestra (1949)                                      19'
   solo vc; 3*223*; 4431; timp+3, str                    FLE

Overture for Strings (1961)                              8'
   str                                                   TP

La fiesta mexicana (1949; orch'd 1964)                   21'
   3*3*3*3*; 4331; timp+3, str                           TP

A Tabernacle for the Sun - oratorio (1963)               18'
   satb cho; male speaking cho; 2222;                    TP
   4331; timp+2, hp, pf/cel, str

The Turning Mind (1968)                                  11'
   3*222; 4231; timp+4, cel, str                         TP

Ut, Re, Mi (1979)                                        8'
   male cho (taped); 3*23*0; 4331;                       MS
   timp+3, str


         REICH, STEVE  (1936-    )

Music for Large Ensemble (1978)                          15'
   2fem vv; 1200; 2s sax; 0400; 4mar,                    BH
   3xyl, vib, 2pf, str (2-2-2-2)

Eight Lines (1979)                                       17'
   2*02*0; 0000; 2pf, str                                BH
   N.B.  This is a revision of "Octet".

Variations for Winds, Strings,
   Keyboards (1979)                                      21'
   3300; 0331; 2pf, elec org, str                        BH

Tehillim (1981)                                          30'
   soli 3s, a; 2*2*20; 0000; 6perc,                      BH
   2elec org, str
   OR:   soli 3s, a; 4*3*21; 0000; 6perc,
   str (6-6-4-2-1)

The Desert Music (1983)                                  46'
   amp satb cho; 4(3picc)4(3eh)4(3b cl)4*;               BH
   44(picc tpt)31; 2timp+7, 2pf(8-hands),
   str (12-12-9-9-6)

Three Movements (1986)                                  15'
    4(2picc)3*3*3*; 4331; perc,                         BH
    2mar, 2vib, hp, 2pf(8-hands),
    str (two groups of 7-7-4-4-4)

The Four Sections (1987)                                25'
    4*44*4*; 4441; 2vib, 2mar, 2b dr, 2pf,              BH
    2synth, str


             REIF, PAUL   (1910-1978)

Episodes for Strings (1958)                             12'
    str                                                 SEE

Accumulations (1964)                                    15'
    2222; 4231; timp+1, hp, str                         SEE

Birches (1965)                                          12'
    solo v; 2222; 4210; perc, hp, str                   BH

Portrait in Brownstone (1968)                           25'
    2222; 4231; timp+2, hp, str                         SEE

Eulogy for a Friend (1969)                              15'
    timp+2, str                                         SEE

Fanfare and Fugato (1970)                               6'
    2222; 4231; timp+1, hp, str                         SEE

America (1776-1876-1976) (1976)                         28'
    2222; 2230; timp+1, str                             SEE


             REISE, JAY   (1950-    )

Hieronymo is Mad Again (1975)                           13'
    3*3*3(E-flat alto)3*; 4331; timp+3, hp,             FLE
    pf, cel, str

Symphony No. 1 (1979)                                   16'
    3*3*22; 4221; 3perc, hp, cel, str                   TP

Poem for String Orchestra (1982)                        10'
    str                                                 TP

Symphony No. 2 (1983)                                   22'
    3*3*4=3*; 6631; timp+5, 2hp, cel, str               TP

Symphony No. 3 (1984)                                18'
   3*3*3*3*; 4331; timp+3, hp, pf, cel, str    TP

Undercurrents (1989)                                 13'
   solo bsn; str                               TP


      REYNOLDS, ROGER  (1934-    )

Graffiti (1964)                                       9'
   3*333; 4331; timp+2, 2hp, pf, str            CFP

Masks (1965)                                         25'
   ssaattbb cho; 2*22=2; 4221; timp+1,          CFP
   2pf, str

Threshold (1967)                                     19'
   4*2*33; 4442; perc, hp, pf, hpsd,            CFP
   mand, str

...Between... (1968)                                 17'
   2222; 2220; perc, pf, str,                   CFP
   function generator, ring modulator,
   sound distribution device

Fiery Wind (1978)                                    17'
   3*2*2=2*; 3331; 4perc, pf, str               CFP

Archipelago (1982)                                   32'
   2*2*2+2*; 2321; 3perc, hp, pf,               CFP
   amp hpsd, str, 4- or 8-channel tape

Transfigured Wind II (1984)                          35'
   solo fl; 2*222; 2221; 2perc, pf,             CFP
   str, tape

The Dream of the Infinite Rooms (1986)               20'
   solo vc; 2*2*2*2; 2220; 2perc, pf, str,      CFP
   4-channel tape

Symphony (Vertigo) (1987)                            22'
   3=3*3=3*; 4331; 3perc, hp, pf,               CFP
   str, computer generated 4-channel tape

Whispers Out of Time (1988)                          26'
   str (7-0-5-4-3)                              CFP

RHODES, PHILLIP (1940- )

Four Movements (1962)                                    8'
  112*0; 2221; timp+3, str                     ACA

Madrigal I (1967)                                        6'
  2*2*3*2; 4231; timp+2, str                    TP

About Faces - ballet (1970)                             23'
  1*2*11; 2110; timp+1, str                     CFP

The Lament of Michal (1970)                             17'
  solo s; 3=2*22; 4231; timp+4, hp, str         CFP

Divertimento (1971)                                     13'
  1001; 1100; str                               CFP

Three "B's" (1971)                                      13'
  2*222; 4231; timp+4, hp, str                  ACA

"Paradise Lost" - oratorio (1972)                       76'
  soli s, t, bar; narr; satb cho; 3=2*23;       CFP
  4331; timp+4, hp, str

Bluegrass Festival (1974)                               18'
  soli bj, mand, gtr, db; 2*222; 4231;          TP
  timp+2, str

A Symphony of Dances (1986)                             18'
  1212; 2100; timp+1, str                       ACA

Reels and Reveries -
  Variations for Orchestra (1991)              15'
  3*2*22; 4230; timp+3, hp, str                 MS


RICE, THOMAS (1933- )

Nocturne for String Orchestra (1958)                    5'
  str                                           MS

Concerto for Three Violins and
  Strings (1969)                                20'
  soli 3vln; str                                SEE

Overture (1970)                                         10'
  1111; 1110; timp, pf, str                     SEE

La Corona (1975)                                        37'
  solo t; narr; 1010; 0010; perc, hpsd, str     SEE

Festival Overture (1978)                              10'
    2222; 4220; timp+2, str                           SEE

Pastoral Overture (1978)                              10'
    2222; 4220; timp+2, str                           SEE

Toccata Overture (1978)                               11'
    2222; 4220; timp+2, str                           SEE

Concerto for Timpani and Orchestra (1980)             14'
    solo timp; 1111; 1111; str                        SEE

The Green Knight - ballet (1982)                      50'
    1010; 0110; perc, str                             MS

Genesis (1983)                                        20'
    2221; 2200; perc, synth, str                      SEE

Tempest! (1988)                                       12'
    str                                               SEE

Concerto for Piano and Strings (1990)                 25'
    solo pf; str                                      SEE

Two Foot Thumpers for String Orchestra (1990) 5'
    str                                               SEE


        RICHTER, MARGA   (1926-     )

Concerto for Piano (1955)                             20'
    solo pf; str (no vlns)                            CF

Lament (1956)                                         11'
    str                                               BRO

Aria and Toccata (1957)                               9'
    solo vla; str                                     BEL

Variations on a Sarabande (1959)                      8'
    2*2*22; 4221; timp+3, hp, str                     CF

Eight Pieces for Orchestra (1962)                     7'
    3*3*3*3*; 4331; timp+2, hp, pf, cel, str          CF

Abyss (1964)                                          20'
    2121; 2110; timp+1, hp, pf, cel, str              BEL

Bird of Yearning (1968)                               27'
    2222; 4220; timp+3, hp, pf, cel, str              CF

Landscapes of the Mind I -
  Piano Concerto (1968-1974)                            29'
  solo pf; 3*3*3*3*; 4400; timp+3, hp, cel,   CF
  elec gtr, b gtr, elec sitar (or synth), str

Blackberry Vines and Winter Fruit (1976)              13'
  3*222; 4321; timp+1, hp, str                          CF

Fragments (1978)                                       6'
  2222; 2111; timp+2, hp, cel, str                      CF

Music for Three Quintets and
  Orchestra (1980)                                     25'
  soli ww qnt, br qnt, str qnt; 3*3*3*3*;      CF
  4331; timp+1, hp, str
  N.B.  The solo quintets are drawn from first
  stand players in the orchestra.

Dusseldorf Concerto (1982)                             20'
  soli fl, vla, hp; timp+1, str                         CF

Out of Shadows and Solitude (1985)                     15'
  3*333; 4331; timp+1, hp, str                          CF


          RICKLEY, JAMES  (1948-    )

To Come to a Place (1983)                              15'
  1212; 2100; perc, pf, str                            SEE

Journey Through (1983)                                 10'
  2222; 4231; timp, str                                SEE

Prophecies of Zephaniah (1984)                         27'
  soli 4s; ssaattbb cho;                                MS
  4-part speaking cho; 2222; 4431;
  timp+5, handbell choir, str


          RIEGGER, WALLINGFORD  (1885-1961)

Fantasy and Fugue, op. 10 (1930-1931)                  21'
  3*3*4*3*; 4442; timp+3, hp, 2org, str                AMP

Dichotomy, op. 12 (1931-1932)                          12'
  1111; 1200; perc, pf, str                            AMP

New Dance, op. 18b (1940)                              5'
  3*3*3*3; a sax; 4331; timp+2, hp, str                AMP

Passacaglia and Fugue, op. 34a (1942)          8'
   23*3*3*; 4331; timp+1, str                  AMP

Symphony No. 3, op. 42 (1946-1947)            23'
   22*22*; 4331; timp+1, str                   AMP

Evocation for Orchestra (1948)                 4'
   3*3*3+3*; 4331; timp+2, str                 BH

Romanza, op. 56a (1948)                        5'
   str                                         AMP

Music for Orchestra, op. 50 (1952)             7'
   3*3*23*; 4331; timp+1, str                  AMP

Variations for Piano and Orchestra,
   op. 54 (1953)                              18'
   solo pf; 2222; 4231; timp+1, str            AMP

Suite for Younger Orchestras, op. 56 (1953)    7'
   various combination of ww, br, perc, str    AMP

Dance Rhythms, op. 58 (1954)                   8'
   2222; 2220; timp+2, hp, str                 AMP

The Dying of The Light, op. 59 (1955)          4'
   solo s (or t); 3*3*22; 4200; timp, str      AMP

Overture, op. 60 (1955)                       10'
   3*3*3*3*; 4331; timp+1, pf, str             AMP

Preamble and Fugue, op. 61 (1955)             10'
   3*3*3*3*; 4331; timp+1, str                 AMP

Symphony No. 4, op. 63 (1956)                 24'
   3*3*3*3*; 4331; timp+1, str                 AMP

A Shakespeare Sonnet, op. 65 (1956)            5'
   solo bar; ssab cho; 1111; 0000; timp, str   AMP

Festival Overture, op. 68 (1957)              10'
   2*222; 4331; timp+1, str                    AMP

Variations for Violin and Orchestra,
   op. 71 (1958)                              12'
   solo vln; 3*223*; 4231; timp+1, hp, str     AMP

Quintuple Jazz, op. 72 (1959)                  7'
   3*3*22; a sax; 4331; timp+3, str            AMP

Sinfonietta, op. 73 (1959)                                    24'
    3*3*3*2; 4331; timp+1, str                               AMP

Duo for Piano and Orchestra, op. 75 (1960)                   12'
    solo pf; 2*222; 2220; timp, str                          AMP


            RIETI, VITTORIO  (1898-    )

Partita (1945)                                               18'
    solo fl; ob; pf/hpsd, str                                BRO

Symphony No. 5 (1945)                                        15'
    2222; 4330; perc, str                                    AMP

Trionfo di Bacco e Arianna -
    ballet/cantata (1947)                                    25'
    satb cho; 2222; 4230; timp+1,                            ECS
    str, dancers

Concerto for Two Pianos and Orchestra (1951)                20'
    soli 2pf; 3*222; 4331; timp+1, str                       RIC

Harpsichord Concerto (1952-1955)                            15'
    solo hpsd; 3*222; 2220; timp+1, str                      ECS
    OR:  1101; 2000; timp+1, str

Cello Concerto No. 2 (1953)                                  15'
    solo vc; 2222; 4331; timp+1, str                         RIC

Introduzione e gioco delle ore (1953)                       6'
    2*222; 4231; timp, str                                   AMP

Voyage to Europe - oratorio (1954)                          60'
    soli s, mez, a, t, b; satb cho;                          ECS
    3*2*22; 4331; timp+1, hp, cel, str

Piano Concerto No. 3 (1955)                                  18'
    solo pf; 3*222; 4331; timp+1, str                        ECS

Dance Variations (1956)                                     14'
    str                                                      BRO

Conundrum - ballet (1961)                                   NA
    3*222; 4331; timp+1, hp, str                             AMP

Sylvan Dream (1965)                                         20'
    3*222; 4330; timp+1, hp, str                             ECS

La fontaine - suite (1968)                          21'
  2121; 2220; timp+1, hp, str                 ECS

Violin Concerto No. 2 (1969)                        16'
  solo vln; 2222; 2220; timp+1, str           ECS

Triple Concerto (1971)                              20'
  soli vln, vla, pf; 2222; 2220; timp, str    ECS

Missa Brevis (1973)                                 20'
  satb cho; 2222; 4200; timp, str             ECS

Symphony No. 6 (1973)                               25'
  3*2*22; 4231; timp+1, str                   ECS

Seven Sapphic Lyrics (1974)                          8'
  solo mez (or bar); 2021; 2100; hp,          ECS
  pf/cel, str

Scenes Seen - suite (1975)                          20'
  3*222; 4331; timp+1, str                    ECS

Concerto for String Quartet (1976)                  15'
  solo str qt; 3*222; 2230; timp+1, str       ECS

Symphony No. 7 (1977)                               18'
  3*222; 4331; timp+1, str                    ECS

Sinfonia Breve (1979)                               10'
  3*222; 4330; timp+1, str                    ECS

Verdiana (1983)                                     20'
  1111; 1000; pf, str                         ECS

Concertino pro San Luca (1984)                      15'
  1111; 0100; pf, str                         ECS

Indiana - suite (1984)                              15'
  2*222; 4330; timp, str                      ECS


      RILEY, DENNIS  (1943-      )

Theme and Variations (1965)                          8'
  2*122; 2220; timp+1, cel, str               CFP

Cantata No. 3
  (Whispers of Heavenly Death) (1968)          6'
  ssaa cho; 223*1; 2211; 3perc, hp, pf, str   CFP

Concertante Music III -
  Viola Concerto (1972-1974)             19'
  solo vla; 3=2*3*2; 4230; timp+5,    CFP
  hp, pf, cel, str

Elegy:  In Memoriam David Bates (1975)    4'
  solo vc; str                                CFP

Seven Songs on Poems of
  Emily Dickinson (1978-1981)         15'
  solo s; 2*22*2*; 2000; perc, hp, str    CFP

Cantata IV:  Beastly Conceits (1979-1980)   16'
  soli a, t; satb cho; 2*2*2*2; 2100;    CFP
  timp+1, pf, str

Noon Dances (1983)                    19'
  1111; 1100; perc, hp, str            CFP

Symphony (1983)                       35'
  3=3*3*3*; 4331; timp+3, hp, pf, str    CFP

Serenade (NA)                      14'
  solo vla; 1101; 2000; hp, str        CFP


RINEHART, JOHN  (1937-    )

Passages (1976)                      9'
  solo s; 3*222; 4231; timp+1, hp,    ACA
  pf, str, tape

Tombeau for Orchestra (1986)        20'
  3*223*; 4231; timp, 2hp, pf, str, tape    MS

Chaconne for Orchestra (1991)       12'
  3*223; 4231; timp, str           MS

Double Concerto (1991)             20'
  soli vln, vc; 3*222; 4231; timp, hp,    MS
  str, tape


RIVERS, JOSEPH  (1954-    )

The Exile's Return (1990)         8'
  3*222; 4331; timp+2, str          MS

ROBERTSON, LEROY   (1896-1971)

Punch and Judy Overture (1945)                    11'
  3*222; 4230; timp+1, hp, str                    GAL

Concerto for Violin and Orchestra (1948)          27'
  solo vln; 2222; 4231; timp+1, hp, str           GAL

Passacaglia (1966)                                12'
  3*3*3*3*; 4331; timp+1, hp, pf, str             GAL


ROBINSON, EARL   (1910-1991)

*The Town Crier (1947)

*Good Morning (1949)

A Country They Call Puget Sound (1957)            17'
  solo t; 3*2*3*2; 4331; 4perc, str               SHA

*Preamble to Peace (1960)

Banjo Concerto (1967)                             27'
  solo bj; 3*2*2*2*; 4320; 3perc, hp, str         MCA

*Illinois People (1968)

*Piano Concerto "The New Human" (1973)           15'
  solo pf; 4*2*2*2*; 4321; 4perc, hp, str         GS

*To the Northwest Indians (1974)                 30'
  singing narr; 4=34*2; 4321; 4perc,              GS
  hp, pf, str

*Ride the Wind (1974)                            15'
  solo bar; speakers; orch                        GS

  N.B.  The works marked with an asterisk,
  as well as other works not listed, will be
  forthcoming from G. Schirmer.  Inquiries may
  be directed to Marlies Dwyer in the Copyright
  Office.


ROCHBERG, GEORGE   (1918-    )

Night Music (1948)                               12'
  solo vc; 3*3*3*3*; 4331; timp+1, hp, str        TP

```
Symphony No. 1 (1948-1957; rev 1977)              25'
   3*3*3*3*; 4331; timp+1, str                     TP

Cantio Sacra (1954)                               12'
   02*00; 0210; str                                FLE

David, The Psalmist (1954)                        25'
   solo t; 3*3*3*3*; 4331; timp+1, str             TP

Symphony No. 2 (1956)                             26'
   3*3*3*3*; 4331; timp+1, str                     TP

Cheltenham Concerto (1958)                        15'
   1111; 1110; str                                 TP

Time-Span II (1962)                               10'
   3*3*3*2; 4331; perc, pf, cel, str               MCA

Music for the Magic Theater (1965-1969)           20'
   1111; 2110; pf, str                             TP

Zodiac (1965)                                     13'
   3*3*4=3*; 4331; timp+4, hp, pf/cel, str         TP

Symphony No. 3 (1966-1969)                        50'
   soli s, a, t, b; ssaattbb cho; satb cho;        TP
   6=5*5=6*; 6881; timp+1, cel, org, str

Tableaux (1968)                                   20'
   1=01+0; 1110; perc, pf, cel, hpsd,              TP
   str (1-1-1-1)

Sacred Song of Reconciliation (1970)              10'
   solo bar; 1111; 1010; perc, 2pf, str            TP

Phaedra: A Monodrama in Seven Scenes (1972)       32'
   solo mez; 3*3*3*3*; 4230; timp+2, str           TP

Imago Mundi (1973)                                20'
   3*3*3*3*; 4331; timp+3, hp, cel, str            TP

Concerto for Violin and Orchestra (1974)          40'
   solo vln; 3*3*3*3*; 4331; timp+2,               TP
   cel, str

Transcendental Variations (1975)                  16'
   str                                             GAL

Symphony No. 4 (1976)                             48'
   3*3*3*3*; 4331; timp+2, hp, cel, str            TP
```

Concerto for Oboe (1983)                              18'
    solo ob; 2022; 4231; timp+2, hp, cel, str        TP

Symphony No. 5 (1985)                                 25'
    4*213*; 4431; timp+3, hp, pf/cel, str            TP

Symphony No. 6 (1987)                                 33'
    4*4*4=4*; 4431; 2timp+6, 2hp, cel, str           TP


        ROCKMAKER, JODY  (1960-    )

The Secreted Peace (1987)                             10'
    solo s; 1111; 2110; perc, hp, str                NOA


        RODRIGUEZ, ROBERT XAVIER  (1946-    )

Adagio (1967)                                          5'
    1112; 2000; str                                  ECS

Lyric Variations (1970)                               6'
    0100; 2000; str                                  ECS

Canto (1973)                                          10'
    soli s, t; solo pf; 2222; 2000; timp, str        ECS

Concerto III (1974)                                   20'
    solo pf; 2222; 2210; timp, str                   ECS

Sinfonia concertante (1974)                           15'
    soli s sax, hpsd; 11*01; 2000; str               ECS

Favola concertante (1975-1977)                        20'
    soli vln, vc; str                                ECS

Concert Suite "Le Diable Amoureux" (1978)             15'
    2*2*2*2; 2210; 2perc, hp, cel, str               ECS

Frammenti musicali (1978)                             5'
    solo fl (or vln); str                            ECS

The Salvation Rag (1978)                              5'
    3*222; 4331; timp+3, str                         ECS

Favola boccacesca - tone poem (1979)                  20'
    3*3*4*3*; 4331; timp+3, hp, cel, str             ECS

Transfigurations Mysteria (1980)                12'
    soli s, a, t; satb cho; children's cho;     ECS
    21*02; 2330; perc, hp, org, str

Estampie (1981)                                 18'
    2*2*2(a sax)2; 2220; 4perc, hp, pf, str     ECS

Semi-Suite (1981)                               10'
    solo vln; 2222; 2220; 2perc, hp, pf, str    ECS

Oktoechoes (1983)                               18'
    3*3*3*3*; 4331; timp+3, hp, pf, str         ECS

Trunks (1983)                                   18'
    narr; 1*222*; 4231; timp+3, hp, pf, str     ECS

Varmi'ts! (1985)                                12'
    narr; satb cho; 2*2*2*2*; 4331; timp+3,     ECS
    pf, str

A Colorful Symphony (1987)                      20'
    narr; 3*222; 4331; timp+3, hp, pf, str      ECS

We, the People (1987)                           10'
    narr; satb cho(opt); 2*222; 4231;           ECS
    timp+3, str


        ROGERS, BERNARD   (1893-1968)

Elegy in Memory of FDR (1945)                   8'
    1000; 2000; timp, str                       ELK

Amphitryon Overture (1946)                      9'
    3*3*3*3*; 4331; timp+1, 2hp, cel, str       MG

Characters from
    Hans Christian Andersen (1946)              9'
    2222; 2210; timp+1, hp, pf, str             TP

Prelude to "The Warrior" (1946)                 5'
    2*2*2*2*; 3220; 3perc, hp, pf, str          MG

Elegy (from Symphony No. 3) (1947)              8'
    1000; 2000; timp, str                       TP

A Letter from Pete - cantata (1947)             26'
    soli s, t; satb cho; 3*2*22; 4330;          PS
    timp+4, hp, str

The Silver World (1949)                                    10'
  2*100; 0000; str                                PS

The Prophet Isaiah - cantata (1950)                        32'
  satb cho; 3*2*2*2; 4231; timp+5, pf, str         PS

The Colors of Youth (1951)                                 10'
  3*23*3*; 4331; timp+4, hp, pf, str               MG

Leaves from "The Tale of Pinocchio" (1951)                 20'
  narr; 1111; 1110; timp+5, str                    PS

Psalm LXVIII (1951)                                        13'
  solo bar; 3*222*; 4331; timp+4, str              TP

Fantasia (1952)                                           11'
  solo hn; timp, str                               TP

Portrait (1952)                                           23'
  solo vln; 3*222; 4231; timp+1, hp, str           TP

Three Dance Scenes (1953)                                  14'
  2*223*; 4231; timp+4, hp, pf, str                TP

Symphony No. 4 (1955)                                      27'
  3*22*2*; 4331; timp+2, str                       PS

Symphony No. 5 "Africa" (1959)                             14'
  3*3*3*3*; 4231; timp+1, hp, pf, str              TP

Variations on a Song by Mussorgsky (1960)                  24'
  3*3*3*3*; 4331; timp+1, hp, cel, str             TP

Allegory (1961)                                           10'
  2fl; mar, str                                    TP

Three Japanese Dances (1961)                               11'
  solo mez; 3*3*3*3*; 4231; timp+1, hp,            TP
  pf, cel, str

The Light of Man - oratorio (1964)                         13'
  soli s, a, bar; satb cho; 2222; 4231;            TP
  timp+2, pf, str

Pastorale mistico (1966)                                   9'
  solo cl; str                                     GAL

Apparitions (1967)                                        15'
  3*3*3*3*; 4331; timp+3, hp, pf, str              MCA

ROLLIN, ROBERT   (1947-     )

Concerto for Woodwind Quintet and
  Orchestra (1979)                                        45'
  solo ww qnt; 4*4*4=4*; 4541; 3perc, str                 SEE

Three Western Sound-Images (1980)                         14'
  1111; 2121; perc, pf, str                               SEE

Concerto Pastorale (1983)                                 16'
  solo hn; 2222; 2200; 2perc, str                         SEE

Song of Deborah (1985)                                    12'
  solo s; 0000; s,a sax; 0211; timp+1, str                SEE

Renaissance Suite (1987)                                  19'
  2*222*; 4341; timp+2, hp, str                           SEE

Hispanic Interchanges (1989)                              20'
  soli ob, vln, vc; perc, str                             SEE


ROLNICK, NEIL BURTON   (1947-     )

Real Time (1983)                                          14'
  112*1; 1110; perc, synth, str                           ECS

Drones and Dances (1987)                                  15'
  2222; 2220; 2perc, synth, str                           ECS


ROOSEVELT, J. WILLARD (1918-     )

Suite (1959)                                              16'
  0101; 0000; str                                         ACA

Amistad:  Danze Moderne (1960)                            14'
  2222; 4231; timp+3, pf, str                             ACA

Concerto for Cello and Orchestra (1963)                   15'
  solo vc; 2222; 4231; timp+1, str                        TP

And The Walls Came Tumbling Down (1976)                   50'
  soli 5vv; 1121; 2110; perc, pf, str                     ACA

Concerto for Piano and Orchestra (1983)                   15'
  solo pf; 2222; 2110; perc, str                          ACA

ROREM, NED   (1923-      )

A Sermon on Miracles (1947)                          6'
   solo s; unis cho; str                             BH

Concerto No. 2 for Piano and
   Orchestra (1950)                                 20'
   solo pf; 2*222; 2100; timp+4, hp, str            PS

Six Irish Poems (1950)                              18'
   solo s; 2222; 2000; 2perc, hp, str               PS

Symphony No. 1 (1950)                               18'
   2222; 4220; timp+4, hp, str                      PS

Design (1953)                                       18'
   2*222; 4220; timp+3, hp, pf, cel, str            BH

Six Songs (1953)                                    14'
   solo s; 2222; 2110; perc, hp, str                CFP

The Poet's Requiem (1954-1955)                      22'
   solo s; satb cho; 2222; 2110; timp,              BH
   hp, pf, str

Poèmes pour la paix (1956)                          13'
   solo mez (or bar); str                           BH

Symphony No. 2 (1956)                               18'
   2*2*22; 2100; timp+2, hp, pf, str                BH

Symphony No. 3 (1957-1958)                          24'
   3*3*3*3*; 4331; timp+4, hp, pf, cel, str         BH

Eagles (1958)                                        9'
   3*3*4=3*; 4331; timp+3, hp, pf/cel, str          BH

Pilgrims (1958)                                      6'
   str                                              BH

Ideas for Easy Orchestra (1961)                     13'
   1111; 2110; timp+1, hp, pf, str                  BH

Lions - A Dream (1963)                              14'
   soli a sax, pf, db, dmst; 3*3*3+2; 4331;         BH
   timp+2, str

Mourning Scene (1963)                                6'
   solo t; str                                      CFP

Laudemus Tempus Actum (1964)                                    3'
    satb cho; 2222; 2220; timp, hp, str                        BH

Letters from Paris (1966)                                      25'
    satb cho; 1111; 1110; timp+3, hp, pf,                      BH
    cel, harmonium, str

SUN - Eight Poems in One Movement (1966)                       26'
    solo s; 3*3*23*; a sax; 4321; timp+3,                      BH
    hp, pf, cel, str

Water Music (1966)                                            17'
    soli cl, vln; 1101; 1000; 3perc, hp,                       BH
    pf/cel, str

Concerto No. 3 in Six Movements for Piano
    and Orchestra (1969)                                      23'
    solo pf; 3*3*3+3*; a sax; 4331; timp+7,                    BH
    hp, cel, str

Little Prayers (1973)                                         31'
    soli s, bar; satb cho; 2222; 4220;                        BH
    timp+1, hp, pf, str

Air Music -
    Ten Variations for Orchestra (1974)                       20'
    3*3*4=3*; 4331; 3perc, hp, pf, cel, str                   BH

Assembly and Fall (1975)                                      25'
    3*3*3*3*; 4231; timp+5, hp, str                           BH
    N.B.  There are solo parts for the following
    principal players:  ob, tpt, timp, vla.

A Quaker Reader (1976)                                        20'
    2*2*22; 2110; str                                         BH

Sunday Morning (1977)                                         19'
    3*3*3*3*; 6331; timp+5, hp, pf/cel,                       BH
    mand(opt), str

Remembering Tommy (1979)                                      28'
    soli vc, pf; 2*2*22; 2220; timp+1,                        BH
    hp, str

After Long Silence (1982)                                     24'
    solo s; ob; str                                           BH

An American Oratorio (1983)                                   44'
    solo t; satb cho; 3*3*32; 4331; timp+4,                   BH
    hp, pf/cel, str

Concerto for Violin and Orchestra (1984)          22'
    solo vln; 1*121; 0100; timp, str                BH

Organ Concerto (1984)                             30'
    solo org; 0000; 2110; timp, str                 BH

String Symphony (1985)                            23'
    str                                             BH

Frolic (1986)                                      2'
    3*3*3*2; 4431; timp+3, pf, str                  BH

The Schuyler Songs (1987)                         25'
    solo s; 2*222; 1100; pf, str                    BH

Fantasy and Polka (1989)                           8'
    3*3*32; 4331; timp+5, pf, str                   BH

Goodbye My Fancy (1990)                           48'
    soli a, bar; satb cho; 3*3*32; 4331;            BH
    timp+3, hp, pf/cel, str

Swords and Plowshares (1990)                      40'
    soli 4vv; 3*3*32; 4331; timp+4, hp,             BH
    pf/cel, str

Fantasy (NA)                                       5'
    3*3*32; 4300; str                               BH


            ROSEMAN, RONALD  (1933-    )

Variations for Orchestra (1955)                   15'
    2222; 2220; str                                 MS

Fantasy for Bassoon and Strings (1980)             9'
    solo bsn; str                                   MS

Concertino for English Horn and
    Strings (1983)                                 14'
    solo eh; str                                    ACA

Psalm XXII (1989)                                 15'
    solo t; satb cho; 2222; 2230; timp, str         MS

Psalm XXVII (1991)                                12'
    solo b; solo ob; str                            ACA

ROSEN, JEROME   (1921-      )

Concerto for Alto Saxophone and
  Orchestra (1957)                                        18'
  solo a sax; 2222; 4230; timp+1, pf, str                ACA

Sounds and Movements (1963)                              12'
  3*3*3*2; 4331; timp+1, hp, pf, str                     ACA

Syn-ket Concerto (1968)                                  12'
  solo syn-ket; 1111; 1110; perc, pf, str                ACA

Five Pieces for Violin and Orchestra (1971)              12'
  solo vln; 1111; 1110; perc, pf, str                    ACA

Three Pieces   (1972)                                    10'
  soli 2rec; 1111; 1110; perc, pf, str                   ACA

Concerto for Clarinet and Orchestra (1973)               12'
  solo cl; 3*3*3*2; 4331; timp+2, pf, str                ACA

Campus Doorways (1978)                                    7'
  satb cho; 3*23*2; 4431; timp+1, pf, str                MS


        ROSENBOOM, DAVID   (1947-      )

Contrasts (1963)                                         15'
  solo vln; 2222; 4231; timp+2, hp, str                  MS

Caliban upon Sebetos (1966)                               9'
  2221; a sax; 2120; timp+1, pf, str                     SEE

Chart Piece I (1966)                                     var
  instrumentation variable                               FPM

Chart Piece II (1966)                                    var
  instrumentation variable                               FPM

How much better if Plymouth Rock had landed
  on the Pilgrims (1969-1972)                            var
  For variable ensembles, including                      FPM
  keyboards, Just-tuned instruments,
  trumpets, Neurona electronic system,
  computer assisted electronic instruments,
  winds, percussion, strings, birds, and
  outdoor environments.

In The Beginning V (The Story) (1980)              25'
    Scored for 4 quartets of instruments           FPM
    as follows:
        ww qt:   high, high, medium, low (ranges)
        br qt:   high, high, medium, low
        perc qt:   2kybd, 2perc
        str qt:   high, med, low, low (in multiples)


        ROSENMAN, LEONARD   (1924-      )

Introduction, Theme and Variations (NA)            17'
    solo cl; 1201; 2000; str                       GS

Stabat Mater (NA)                                  60'
    soli 2s, t, bar; satb cho; 2222; 4220;         GS
    timp, str

Stabat Mater:   Inflammatus (NA)                   30'
    solo t; 2222; 4220; timp, str                  GS

Threnody on a Song of
    Karol Rathaus (1971)                           23'
    3*3*3*1; a sax; 4431; 3perc, hp, pf, cel,      PS
    elec gtr, b gtr, str

Foci I (1981; rev 1983)                            22'
    2*2*2*2*; 2210; perc, str (7-7-4-4-2)          GS


        ROSKOTT, CARL   (1952-      )

Adagio (1975)                                      12'
    2223*; 4231; timp, str                         MG

Overture to a Summer Night (1980; rev 1986)        17'
    3*23*3*; 4331; timp+2, hp, cel, str            MG
    N.B.   An optional cut in a revised version
    reduces the duration to 11 minutes.


        ROSNER, ARNOLD   (1945-      )

Symphony No. 1, op. 3 (1961)                       28'
    2222; 4331; timp+2, hp, pf, str                HBM

Symphony No. 2, op. 8 (1961)                       24'
    2222; 4331; timp+2, hp, pf, str                HBM

Symphony No. 3, op. 20 (1963)                      30'
    3*3*3*3*; 4331; timp+2, hp, pf, str            HBM

Symphony No. 4, op. 29 (1964)                      30'
    3*3*3*3*; 4331; timp+2, hp, pf, str            HBM

Five Meditations, op. 36 (1967)                    18'
    solo eh; hp, str                               HBM

Six Pastorale Dances, op. 40 (1968)                12'
    1111; 0000; str                                HBM

A Gentle Musicke, op. 44 (1969)                    11'
    solo fl; str                                   HBM

A Mylai Elegy, op. 51 (1971)                       26'
    3*3*3*3*; 4431; timp+6, hp, str                HBM

Symphony No. 5, op. 57 (1973)                      34'
    2222; 4331; timp+2, hp, str                    HBM

Requiem, op. 59 (1973)                             62'
    soli s, 2t, b; satb cho; 3*3*3*3*;             HBM
    47(4 opt)31; timp+3, pf, cel, hpsd, str

Concerto Grosso No. 1, op. 60 (1974)               19'
    2202; 2200; str                                HBM

Symphony No. 6, op. 64 (1976)                      33'
    3*3*3*3*; 4331; timp+2, hp, str                HBM

Five Ko-ans, op. 65 (1976)                         31'
    3*3*3*3*; 4331; timp+1, hp, pf, str            HBM

Responses, Hosanna and Fugue, op. 67 (1977)        18'
    hp, str                                        HBM

Nocturne, op. 68 (1978)                            12'
    3*3*3*3*; 4331; timp+2, hp, pf, str            HBM

Concerto Grosso No. 2, op. 74 (1979)               21'
    2202; 2200; str                                HBM

Consort Music, op. 75 (1980)                       15'
    1222; 2230; timp, hp, str                      HBM

Tragedy of Queen Jane, op. 78 (1982)               26'
    2222; 4331; timp+2, hp, cel, str               HBM

434 ROSNER

From the Diaries of Adam Czerniakow,
  op. 82 (1986)                 22'
  narr; 3*3*3*3*; 4331; perc, str     HBM

Transformations, op. 87 (1990)       16'
  tpt; pf, str                 HBM


      ROSS, WALTER (1936- )

Concerto for Brass Quintet and
  Orchestra (1966)             20'
  solo br qnt; 3=3*1*3*; 0000; timp+2,   BH
  hp, cel, str

Concerto No. 1 for Trombone and
  Orchestra (1971)             13'
  solo tbn; 2222; 2200; timp+2, str   BH

A Jefferson Symphony (1976)         24'
  solo t; narr; satb cho; 3*3*3*3*; 4432;   MS
  timp+1, hp, str

Concerto for Woodwind Quintet and
  Strings (1977)               22'
  solo ww qnt; str             BH

Concerto No. 2 for Trombone and
  Orchestra (1981)             23'
  solo tbn; 3*3*3*3*; 4331; timp+2, hp, str  MS

Concerto for Bassoon and Strings (1983)   15'
  solo bsn; str               MS

Concerto for Oboe, String Orchestra and
  Harp (1984)                 16'
  solo ob; hp, str             MS

Overture to the Virginia Voyage (1986)   9'
  3*3*3*3*; 4331; timp+2, hp, str     MS

Concerto for Flute, Guitar and
  Orchestra (1987)             20'
  soli fl, gtr; 2222; 2220; timp+4, hp, str  MS

Concerto for Piano and Orchestra (1991)   24'
  solo pf; 2222; 2220; timp+4, hp, str   MS

ROTHKOPF, MICHAEL   (1956-    )

Cantus Sinfonia (1988)                            12'
   3*23*3*; 4221; 5perc, hp, str                  NOA


ROUSE, CHRISTOPHER   (1949-    )

Alloeidea (1978)                                  32'
   2222; 6431; 2timp+4, hp, str                   ACA

The Infernal Machine (1981)                       5'
   3(3picc)34=3*; 4331; 5perc, hp, cel, str       EAM

Gorgon (1984)                                     16'
   3(3picc)34=3*; 4331; timp+4, hp,               EAM
   pf/cel, str

Concerto for Double Bass and
   Orchestra (1985)                               18'
   solo db; 2*2*2*2*; 4331; timp+3, str           EAM

Phantasmata (1985)                                18'
   3(3picc)34=3*; 4331; 5perc, hp,                EAM
   pf/cel, str
   N.B.  Flutes and oboes also play crystal
   goblets.

Phaethon (1986)                                   6'
   3(3picc)3*3*3*; 6431; timp+3, hp, str          EAM

Symphony No. 1 (1986)                             24'
   2*2=2*2*; 4(4 Wagner tubas)331;                EAM
   timp+3, str

Jagganath (1987)                                  10'
   3*3*3*3*; 4331; timp+4, str                    EAM

Iscariot (1989)                                   12'
   12*12; 3200; 2perc, cel, str                   EAM

Concerto per corde (1990)                         22'
   str                                            EAM

Karolju (1990)                                    23'
   satb cho; 2*222; 4331; timp+4, hp, str         EAM

Trombone Concerto (1991)                          20'
   solo tbn; 0003*; 4331; timp+4, hp, str         EAM

ROUSSAKIS, NICOLAS   (1934-      )

Sinfonia (1975)                                        31'
   2222;  4220; timp+3, pf,                         ACA
   str (15-15-12-10-8)
   N.B.  The individual movements "Chromata",
   "Syrtos", "Ode & Cataclysm", and "Glendi"
   are available separately for performance.

Fire & Earth & Water & Air (1980-1983)                 21'
   3*3*3*3*; 4421; timp+3, pf, str                 ACA

God Abandons Antony - cantata (1987)                   45'
   solo s; satb cho; 2200; 2000;                   ACA
   perc, hp, str

Hymn to Apollo (1989)                                  17'
   1111; 1110; 2perc, hp, pf, str                  ACA


ROVICS, HOWARD   (1936-      )

Transformations (1968)                                  6'
   3*3*3*3*; 4331; timp+5, pf, cel, str            ACA

Three Movements (1976)                                  8'
   003*0; 0000; 2perc, hp, gtr, str                ACA

Piano Concerto (1980)                                  14'
   solo pf; 1111; 2110; 2perc, str                 ACA

Affirmation (1981)                                      8'
   0100; 2000; timp, str                           ACA

Symphony (1991)                                        13'
   3*3*2=3*; 4331; timp+2, hp, str                 ACA


ROZSA, MIKLOS   (1907-      )

Spellbound Concerto (1946)                             10'
   solo pf; 2222; 4331; timp+1, hp, str            TP

The Vintner's Daughter, op. 23 (1952)                  15'
   2*222; 4330; timp+1, hp, pf/cel, str            BRO

Concerto for Violin and Orchestra,
   op. 24 (1956)                                   28'
   solo vln; 2222; 4230; timp+1, hp,               BH
   cel, str

Concert Overture, op. 26 (1957)                                   10'
  2222; 4331; timp+1, hp, str                                    BH

Notturno Ungherese, op. 28 (1964)                                 9'
  2222; 4230; timp+1, hp, cel, str                               BH

Concerto for Piano and Orchestra,
  op. 31 (1966)                                                  30'
  solo pf; 2222; 4331; timp+1, cel, str                          BH

Sinfonia Concertante, op. 29 (1968)                              24'
  soli vln, vc; 2222; 4330; timp+4,                              BH
  hp, cel, str

Concerto for Violoncello and Orchestra,
  op. 32 (1971)                                                  30'
  solo vc; 2*2*22; 4331; timp+2, hp,                             BH
  cel, str

Tripartita, op. 33 (1972)                                        20'
  2*222; 4331; timp+5, hp, cel, str                              BH

Concerto for Viola and Orchestra,
  op. 37 (1981)                                                  28'
  solo vla; 2222; 4330; timp+1,                                  BH
  hp, cel, str


          RUBIN, ANNA  (1946-     )

Freedom, Sweet and Bitter (1987)                                 10'
  3*33*3; 434(2b tbn)1; 2perc, hp,                              NOA
  pf, cel, str, tape


          RUDHYAR, DANE  (1895-1985)

Emergence (1948)                                                 12'
  str                                                           ACA

Syntony No. 5 (1954)                                             28'
  str                                                           ACA

Thresholds (1954-1975)                                           18'
  23*3*3*; 4431; timp+1, hp, pf, str                            ACA

Threnody (1973)                                                   7'
  223*2; 4421; timp, xyl, pf, cel, str                          ACA

Dialogues:   A Cycle of Orchestral
    Trilogies (No. 3) (1977)                              25'
    1222; 2110; timp+1, pf, str                           ACA

Encounter (1977)                                          21'
    solo pf; 2222; 2221; timp+1, str                      ACA

Cosmic Cycle (1982)                                       23'
    3*3*3*2; 4331; timp+3, hp, pf, cel, str               ACA

Out of the Darkness -
    Symphonic Drama in Five Acts (1982)                   23'
    2222; 3221; timp+2, pf, str                           ACA

Sinfonietta (1982)                                        14'
    3*3*4=3*; 6432; timp, pf, str                         ACA

Three Poems of Youth (1984)                               32'
    2222; 4231; timp+4, hp, pf, str                       ACA


            RULON, C. BRYAN  (1954-    )

When Quiet Implodes (1984)                                16'
    1212; 2100; perc, pf/cel, str                         ACA

Quantum Mechanics, Lesson 1 -
    Ecstatic States (1988)                                30'
    3*3*3*3*; 4331; timp+3, hp, pf, str                   ACA


            RUSH, LOREN  (1935-    )

Nexus 16 (1964)                                           12'
    1111; 1111; timp+2, pf, cel,                          JOB
    str (2-1-1-0)

The Cloud Messenger (1966-1970)                           18'
    4*4*4*4*; 4331; 4perc, 2hp, hpsd, gtr,                JOB
    elec gtr, str

Dans le sable (1967-1968)                                 20'
    solo s, 4a; narr; 1+1*01; 1110; vib,                  JOB
    hp, pf, gtr, str

Song and Dance (1975)                                     22'
    5=4*4=2; 6421; timp+5, hp, pf, cel,                   TP
    str, tape

RUSSO, WILLIAM   (1928-      )

Music for Alto Saxophone and Strings
   (1955; rev 1985)                                         10'
   solo a sax; perc, pf, amp gtr,                           MG
   str (4-4-3-3-1)

Les Deux Errants (The Seekers) (1956)                        NA
   2*12*1; 4331; timp+1, hp, pf, str                        MG

Symphony No. 1 (1957)                                        18'
   3*23*2; 4331; timp+2, str                                MG

Symphony No. 2 "Titans" (1958)                               20'
   4*4*4*4*; 4431; timp+2, hp, pf, str                      PS

Three Pieces for Blues Band and
   Orchestra (1960)                                         24'
   soli dmst, elec pf, elec gtr, b gtr, hca;                PS
   3*3*3*3*; 4331; timp+5, hp, str

Variations on an American Theme (1960)                       14'
   2222; 4331; timp+3, pf, str                              MG

Suite for Violin and Strings (1965)                          14'
   solo vln; str (3-3-2-2-1)                                MG

Street Music - A Blues Concerto (1976)                       30'
   soli pf, hca, vln, db; 3*222; 4321;                      PS
   timp+4, str

Urban Trilogy (1981)                                         NA
   3(picc, s sax)23=2*; t sax; 4331; timp+3,                MG
   hp, pf, str

Hello (1983)                                                 15'
   1111; 2110; perc, pf, mand,                              MG
   str (3-3-2-2-1)

The Golden Bird (1984)                                       44'
   soli s, bar; narr; 1211; 211(b tbn)0;                    MG
   2perc, pf, str (6-5-4-3-2)

SACCO, P. PETER  (1928-     )

N.B.  Mr. Sacco's works are listed by opus number.

| | |
|---|---|
| Symphony No. 1, op. 11<br>3*3*3*3*; 4231; timp+2, str | 11'<br>OST |
| Meditation No. 1, op. 12<br>2222; 2210; timp+1, str | 5'<br>OST |
| Meditation No. 2, op. 13<br>2222; 2210; hp, str | 5'<br>OST |
| Meditation No. 3, op. 14<br>2122; 2210; timp+1, str | 5'<br>OST |

N.B.  The three "Meditations" may be performed collectively as a suite.

| | |
|---|---|
| Classical Overture, op. 15<br>2222; 2210; timp+1, str | 10'<br>OST |
| Sinfonietta for String Orchestra, op. 16<br>str | 10'<br>OST |
| Four Emerson Sketches, op. 17 (1970)<br>223*2; 4331; timp+2, str | 15'<br>OST |
| Symphony of Thanksgiving (No. 2), op. 18<br>3*3*4=3*; 4431; timp+3, pf, cel, str | 22'<br>OST |
| Piano Concerto No. 1, op. 19<br>solo pf; 3*3*3*2; 4231; timp+4, str | 26'<br>OST |
| Contemplation for Orchestra, op. 20<br>314*2; 4331; timp+2, str | 10'<br>OST |
| Violin Concerto No. 1, op. 21<br>solo vln; 3*3*3*2; 4231; pf, str | 24'<br>OST |
| Five Songs, op. 22<br>solo med high v; str | 14'<br>OST |

Jesu, op. 24 - oratorio                                    55'
   soli s, t; satb cho; 2222; 2210;                       OST
   timp+2, pf, str

Blessed Are The Peacemakers, op. 30                        5'
   solo s (or t); 2222; 2210; timp+1, str               OST

Take Heed That Ye Do Not Your Alms
   Before Men, op. 31                                    5'
   solo s (or t); 2222; 2210; timp+1, str               OST

The Hypocrites, op. 32                                     8'
   solo s (or t); 2222; 2210; timp+1, str               OST

Come Unto Me, op. 33                                       7'
   solo s (or t); 2222; 2210; timp+1, str               OST

All Power Is Given Unto Me, op. 34                         7'
   solo s (or t); 2222; 2210; timp+1, str               OST

Solomon, op. 162 - oratorio                                90'
   soli s, mez, t, bar; satb cho; 2222;                 OST
   2230; timp+2, hp, str


SAHL, MICHAEL  (1934-     )

Concerto for Electric Violin and
   Orchestra (1974)                                      22'
   solo elec vln; 1111; 1110; perc, hp, str             SEE


SAMUEL, GERHARD  (1924-     )

Twelve on Death and No (1968)                              10'
   soli s, t; 1*111; 1110; 2perc, cel, str              MMB

Looking At Orpheus Looking (1971)                          16'
   4*4*4*4*; 4431; 3perc, hp, elec hpsd,                TP
   elec org, str

Into Flight From (1972)                                    13'
   3*333; 4331; timp+4, elec kybd, str                  TP

To An End (1972)                                           10'
   satb cho; 2222; 2221; timp+1, hp,                    MMB
   cel, str

Requiem for Survivors (1974)                               18'
   4*4*4*4*; t sax; 0431; timp+5, hp, str               TP

Beyond McBean (1975)                                   12'
  solo vln; 1111; 1110; perc, hp,                 MMB
  hpsd, str (0-1-1-1)

Cold When The Drum Sounds For Dawn (1975)              16'
  1=2*01; 2000; 2perc, hpsd, cel, str            MMB

On A Dream (1977)                                      20'
  solo vla; 1212; 2000; perc, str               MMB

Out of Time (1978)                                     16'
  3=3*3(E-flat, b cl, a sax)3*; 4331;           MMB
  timp+4, 2hp, str

On the Beach at Night Alone (1980)                     10'
  satb cho; cl; str                             MMB

Three Minor Desperations (1980)                        17'
  solo mez; 1221; 1111; 3perc, hp, str          MMB

Chamber Concerto in the
  Shape of a Summer (1981)                       16'
  solo fl; 3perc, str                           MMB

AGAM - ballet music (1982)                             24'
  2223*; 2231; timp+2, hp, str                  MMB

Double Concerto -
  Burial Chant-Sundry Ecstasies (1983)           28'
  soli vln, vla; 3*3*3*3*; 4231;                MMB
  timp+2, str

Traumbild (1983)                                       20'
  soli s, t; 1*111; 1110; 2perc, cel,           MMB
  str (1-1-1-1)
N.B.  May be performed with multiple strings.

As Imperceptibly As Grief (1987)                       14'
  soli 3perc; 2=22*2*; 2000; timp, str          MMB

Nicholas and Concepcion (1987)                         75'
  2*2*2*2*; 2221; timp+2, hp, str               MMB

Apollo and Hyacinth (1989)                             13'
  1(picc in D)111; 1000; 2perc, hp,             MMB
  pf, str (2-1-1-1)

Lucille's Wave (NA)                                    16'
  4(2picc)44+4*; 43(picc tpt)31; timp+4,         TP
  hp, str

SAMUEL, RHIAN (1944-    )

Before Dawn (1987)                                            10'
    solo mez (or bar); 3*3*3*2; 4331; timp+2,    NOA
    hp, str


SANDERS, ROBERT (1906-1974)

Little Symphony No. 2 in B-flat (1953)                       14'
    2222; 4231; timp+1, hp, str                  TP

Symphony in A (1954-1955)                                    27'
    3*3*22; 4231; timp+1, cel, str               ECS

Little Symphony No. 3 in D (1963)                            14'
    1111; 2100; timp, str                        ECS


SANDROFF, HOWARD (1949-    )

Piano Concerto (1987)                                        19'
    solo pf; 2*3*3*1; 2230; 2perc, hp, str       MS

Concerto for Electric Wind Instrument and
    String Orchestra (1988)                                  16'
    solo Yamaha digital wind controller-WX-7;    MS
    str (all divisi)


SAPIEYEVSKI, JERZY (1945-    )

Concerto for Two Pianos and Orchestra (1974)  18'
    soli 2pf; solo s(opt); 3*3*3*2; 5331;        MRC
    timp+1, str

Summer Overture (1977)                                       10'
    3*3*3*3*; 5331; timp+4, hp, str              MRC

Concerto "Mercury" for Trumpet and
    Orchestra (1978)                                         14'
    solo tpt; 3*3*3*3*; 4331; timp+3, str        CFP

Songs of the Rose (1986)                                     30'
    solo s; synth, str                           TP

Dance of the Planets (1990)                                  30'
    solo synth; 3*24*2; 2a,t,bar sax; 4441;      TP
    timp+3, hp, str (no vlns, vlas)

SAPP, ALLEN  (1922-      )

Suite No. 1 (1949)                                    20'
  23*3*2; 4331; hp, pf, str                        ACA

Suite No. 2 (1956)                                    26'
  3*3*3*3*; 4331; hp, pf, str                      MS

The Double Image (1957)                               12'
  3*3*3*3*; 4331; timp, str                        MS

"The Women of Trachis" Overture (1960)                10'
  0200; 2000; str (4-4-3-3-1)                      MS

June (1961)                                           13'
  1111; 1000; str                                 MS

Colloquies No. 1 (1963)                               16'
  solo pf; str                                     MS

Imaginary Creatures:  A Bestiary for
  the Credulous (1980)                             17'
  solo hpsd; 2222; 2000; str (6-5-4-3-2)           MS

Xenon Ciborium (1982-1985)                            11'
  4+4*5=4*; 65(E-flat tpt)42; mar, vib,            MS
  hp, cel, str


SATUREN, DAVID  (1939-      )

Expression:
  Lyric Piece for Small Orchestra (1961)           6'
  1120; 2220; str                                  MS

Four Short Movements for Orchestra (1962)              3'
  2*222*; 2220; timp+2, hp, str                    FLE

Exposition for Sixteen (1965)                          3'
  pf(or hpsd), str (4-4-3-3-1)                      FLE
  N.B.   Each string player has a solo part.

Largo for Strings (1966)                               5'
  str                                              MS

The Love Song of
  J. Alfred Prufrock (1966-1967)                  20'
  solo bar; satb cho; 3*3*3*3*; 4320;              FLE
  timp+3, hp, cel, str

Largo and Allegro (1967)                                     5'
    soli vln, vc; str                                        MS

Ternaria (1970)                                              8'
    solo org; 2222; 4331; timp+1, str                        FLE

Dialogue Between Harpsichord and
    Strings (1972)                                           7'
    solo hpsd; str (4-3-3-2-1)                               MS

Evolution for Viola, Harpsichord and
    String Orchestra (1976-1977)                             7'
    soli vla, hpsd; str                                      MS

Variations and Fugue for Jazz Quintet and
    String Orchestra (1978-1979)                             5'
    solo jazz qnt; str                                       MS

Lyric Progression (1981)                                     5'
    solo db; str                                             MS

Symphony (1982-1990)                                         18'
    3*3*3*3*; 4331; timp+2, str                              MS


                SAUL, WALTER   (1954-    )

Metamorphosis (1974)                                         20'
    solo pf; 3*333*; 4431; timp+1, str                       MMB

From Life to Greater Life (1978)                             10'
    2*2*22*; 4331; timp, hp, str                             MMB


                SAWYER, WILSON   (1917-1979)

Symphony No. 1, "Alaskan",
    op. 19 (1974; rev 1977)                                  29'
    solo bar; 3*3*23*; 4331; timp+1, str                     MG


                SAYLOR, BRUCE   (1946-    )

Cantilena (1965)                                             5'
    str                                                      ECS

To Autumn, To Winter (1968)                                  15'
    satb cho; 2*22*2; 4231; timp+1, str                      NAU

Notturno (1969)                                    15'
    solo pf; 2*22*2; 2200; timp+1, str            NAU

Turns and Mordents (1977)                          15'
    solo fl; 2222; 2200; timp+2, pf, str          ECS

Symphony in Two Parts (1980)                       20'
    2+2*22; 2110; timp+2, hp, str                 ECS

Archangel (1990)                                    6'
    3*3*3*3*; 4341; timp+3, str                   ECS

Jubilate (1990)                                     7'
    solo s; satb cho; 2222; 4331; timp+3, str     ECS

It Had Wings (1991)                                20'
    solo mez; 1111; 1000; hp, str                 MS


          SCARMOLIN, ANTHONY LOUIS   (1890-1969)

Prelude to "The Oath" (1945)                        2'
    2222; 4331; timp+1, hp, cel, str              FLE

Symphony No. 2 (1946)                              20'
    2*222; 4331; timp+1, hp, cel, str             FLE

Invocation (1947)                                  16'
    2*222; 4331; timp+1, hp, cel, str             FLE

The Caliph - dance (1948)                           5'
    2*222; 2230; timp+1, hp, cel, str             FLE

The Sunlit Pool (1951)                              4'
    2*222; 2231; timp, hp, str                    FLE

Symphony No. 3 (Sinfonia breve) (1952)             16'
    2222; 4331; perc, hp, str                     FLE

Arioso for Strings (1953)                           8'
    str                                           FLE


          SCHELLE, MICHAEL   (1950-    )

El Medico (1977)                                    6'
    3*222; 4231; timp+3, pf, str                  MMB

Masque (1979)                                      20'
    1*212; 2000; 2perc, pf, str                   MMB

Swashbuckler! (1985)    18'
  3*222; 4431; timp+3, hp, str    MMB

Concerto for Two Pianos and Orchestra (1986)  28'
  soli 2pf; 3*222; 4221; timp+3, hp, str    MMB

Kidspeace (1987)    6'
  children's cho; 3*23*2; 4321; timp+3,    MMB
  hp, pf, str

The Big Night (1989)    15'
  3*2*3*2; 4221; timp+3, hp, pf, str    MMB

After the Meridian:
  Times of Future Passed (1990)    45'
  soli s, t, bar; satb cho; 2*2*22; 2220;    MMB
  timp+2, hp, org, str (5-4-3-3-1 minimum)

Rapscallion (1990)    14'
  1*1*11; 1110; timp+1, hp, pf,    MMB
  str (2-1-1-1 min; 5-4-3-3-1 max)


      SCHICKELE, PETER  (1935-    )

Invention for Orchestra (1958)    8'
  3*3*3*3*; 4331; timp+2, pf, str    FLE

Serenade (1959)    11'
  223*2; 4330; timp+1, str    ELK

Celebration With Bells (1960)    7'
  223*2; a,t sax; 4331; timp+3, str    BRO

The Fantastic Garden (1968)    25'
  rock group; 3 singers; 3*3*3*2; 4441;    ELK
  timp+4, hp, cel, str

Requiem Mantras (1972)    15'
  3*222; 4331; 3perc, pf, cel, str    ELK

Three Girls, Three Women (1972)    22'
  2222; 3211; perc, hp, cel, str    TP

Three Strange Cases (1972)    6'
  narr; 1111; 0000; 2perc, str    ELK

American Birthday Card (1975)    8'
  3*23*2; 4331; timp+3, str    ELK

Pentangle (1976)                                    25'
   solo hn; 3*23*2; 4221; timp+1, pf,        ELK
   cel, str

A Zoo Called Earth (1977)                           14'
   2222; 4331; 4perc, cel, str, tape          ELK

Five of a Kind (1978)                               25'
   solo br qnt; 2222; 4220; timp+3, str       ELK

The Chenoo Who Stayed To Dinner (1979)              22'
   narr; 2222; 3221; 2perc, str               ELK

Far Away From Here (1984)                           25'
   solo bluegrass band; 3*222; 3230;          TP
   3perc, str

Concerto for Flute and Orchestra (1990)             18'
   solo fl; 2222; 2210; timp+3, str           TP


       SCHIFF, DAVID  (1945-    )

Slow Dance (1989)                                   40'
   3=3*3*3*; a sax; 4331; timp+1, dmst,       MS
   pf, str

Stomp (1990)                                         7'
   2*222; 2210; dmst, pf, str                 MS


       SCHIFRIN, LALO  (1932-    )

Variations for Percussion, Strings, Harp
   and Celesta (1963)                          NA
   3perc, hp, cel, str                         MS

Dialogue for Jazz Quintet and
   Orchestra (1969)                            12'
   soli a sax, tpt, db, vib, dmst; 2212;      MJQ
   2320; timp+3, str

Variants on a Madrigal by Gesualdo (1969)           18'
   1+111; 1111; pf/cel, hpsd, str (2-1-1-1)    AMP

Double Concerto for Violin, Violoncello
   and Orchestra (1975)                        20'
   soli vln, vc; 2=2*2*2*; 4341; 3perc, hp,   AMP
   pf, cel, str

Madrigals for the Space Age (1976)                    20'
    narr; 2222; 3210; timp+1, hp, pf/cel, str       AMP

Invocations (1980)                                    25'
    3*3*3=3*; 4441; 6perc, 2hp, cel, str            AMP

Capriccio for Clarinet and Strings (1981)            10'
    solo cl; str                                     AMP

Guitar Concerto (1984)                                22'
    solo gtr; 3*3*3*2; 4330; timp+2, hp, str         TP

Concerto for Piano and Orchestra (1985)              23'
    solo pf; 3=3*3*3*; 4330; 2perc, hp, str         MJQ

    N.B.  Inquiries regarding these and other
    works by Mr. Schifrin may be directed to the
    Glendale Symphony office.


            SCHNEIDER, GARY  (1957-    )

Sheva (1977)                                           7'
    1111; 2100; timp, hp, str                       ACA

Concerto for Jazz Clarinet and
    String Orchestra (1985)                          11'
    solo cl; str                                    ACA

Nocturne (1987)                                        5'
    solo bsn; str                                   ACA

The Voice of Eternity (NA)                            25'
    soli s, mez, t, bar, b; satb cho; 3=000;         PS
    0000; timp+4, str


            SCHOBER, BRIAN  (1951-    )

Bucolics (1975)                                       23'
    2*2*2*0; s sax; 2231; 3perc, hp,                SAL
    pf, cel, str
    N.B.  Also requires 2 offstage trumpets.

Divertissements (1983)                                15'
    2020; 2200; 2perc, hp, pf, str (no db)          ACA

### SCHOENFIELD, PAUL  (1947-    )

Four Parables (1983)                                                25'
    solo pf; 3*3*3=3*; 4341; timp+1,                                GS
    synth, str


### SCHONTHAL, RUTH  (1924-    )

Concerto No. 2 for Piano and
    Orchestra (1977)                                                26'
    solo pf; 3*223*; 4221; timp, str                               FAM

Music for Horn and Chamber Orchestra (1978)                        11'
    solo hn; 1111; 0000; str                                       FAM

The Beautiful Days of Aranjuez (1981)                             12'
    solo hp; str                                                   FAM

Oceanic Poem (NA)                                                  14'
    2*223*; 4330; 2perc, hp, pf, str                               FAM


### SCHUBEL, MAX  (1932-    )

Specters and Sheldrakes - tone poem (1964)                         9'
    223*3*; 4331; timp+6, hp, str                                  MS

Linear Concentrate (1965)                                         10'
    4*34*4*; 4331; timp+3, hp, pf, str                             MS

Fracture (1969)                                                   19'
    3*3*3*3*; 4331; timp+3, hp, str                                HG

Overfeed (1973)                                                   14'
    solo fem v; satb cho; 2222; 2221;                              MS
    timp+4, 2pf, amp gtr, str, tape
    N.B.  Performers also play percussion
    instruments and transistor radios.

Spheres (1975)                                                    20'
    solo a fl; 1111; 1110; 2perc, hpsd, str                        MS

Punch and Judie (1980)                                            20'
    1111; 1110; perc, hp, pf, str                                  MS

Guale, the Golden Coast of Georgia (1984)                         18'
    3*3*3*3*; 4330; timp+3, hp, hpsd, str                          MS

Divertimento (1987)                                          14'
  soli tpt, pf; 1*1*11; t sax; 2010;               MS
  perc, hp, str

Scherzo (1987)                                               18'
  2222; 4231; timp+3, hp, str                       MS
  N.B. Requires a 5-octave bass marimba in
  the percussion section.

Superscherzo (1988-1989)                                     7'
  1*1*11; 2110; 2perc, hp, str                      MS

Lament (1990)                                                NA
  222*2*; 2220; timp, hp, pf, org(opt), str        MS


    SCHULLER, GUNTHER  (1925-    )

Concerto No. 1 for Horn and
  Orchestra (1944-1945)                             18'
  solo hn; 3*3*3*3*; 4431; timp+1,                  MG
  hp, cel, str

Concerto for Violoncello and
  Orchestra (1945; rev 1985)                        18'
  solo vc; 3*3*3*3*; 4331; timp+3, hp,              MG
  pf/cel, str

Six Early Songs (1945)                                       18'
  solo s; 3*3*4*3*; 4221; timp+1, hp,               MG
  pf, cel, str

Suite for Chamber Orchestra (1945)                           7'
  2222; 2110; str                                   MG

Vertige d'Eros (1945)                                        7'
  4(picc, b fl)3*4(2b cl)3*; 4331;                  AMP
  timp+1, 2hp, pf, cel, str

Symphonic Study (1947-1948)                                  9'
  6*5*3*2; 6441; timp+1, hp, cel, str               AMP
  OR:  3*3*3*2; 4331; timp+1, hp, cel, str

Dramatic Overture (1951)                                     11'
  3*3*23*; 4331; timp+4, 2hp, pf/cel, str           AMP

Recitative and Rondo (1953)                                  11'
  solo vln; 23*3*3*; 4331; perc,                    AMP
  hp, pf, str

Symphonic Tribute to Duke Ellington (1955)        40'
    soli db, dmst; 3*22*2*; 4331; timp+3,         MG
    hp, pf, str

Little Fantasy (1957)                              4'
    1111; 2110; timp+1, str                       MG

Contours (1958)                                   21'
    1121; 1110; perc, hp, str                     SCH

Spectra (1958)                                    23'
    4*4*4*4*; 4431; 4perc, hp, str                AMP

Concertino for Jazz Quartet and
    Orchestra (1959)                              19'
    soli vib, pf, db, dmst; 2121; 2320;           MJQ
    timp+3, str

Seven Studies on Themes of Paul Klee (1959)       23'
    3*23*2; 4331; timp+1, hp(or pf), str          UE

Capriccio (1960)                                  15'
    solo tba; 112*0; 2010; hp, str                MG

Contrasts for Wind Quintet and
    Orchestra (1960)                              15'
    solo ww qnt; 3*3*3*3*; 3331; timp+7,          AMP
    hp, pf, str

Variants (1960)                                   18'
    soli vib, pf, db, dmst; 213*3*; 4331;         MJQ
    timp+3, hp, str

Journey into Jazz (1962)                          16'
    soli a sax, t sax, tpt, db, dmst; 1111;       AMP
    1100; perc, hp, str

Journey to the Stars (1962)                       15'
    1*02*1; 2222; timp+2, hp, pf/cel, str         AMP

Movements (1962)                                  14'
    solo fl; str                                  AMP

Piano Concerto No. 1 (1962)                       24'
    solo pf; 3*3*3*3*; 4331; timp+3, hp, str      AMP

Composition in Three Parts (1963)                 20'
    3*3*4=3*; 4431; 4perc, hp, pf, str            AMP

Diptych for Brass Quintet and
  Orchestra (1963)                                8'
  solo br qnt; 3*3*3*3*; 4221; timp+1,           AMP
  hp, str

Threnos (1963)                                   18'
  solo ob; 3*3*3*3*; 4331; timp+3, hp, str       AMP

Five Bagatelles (1964)                           15'
  3*3*3*3*; 4331; timp+4, hp, pf, str            AMP

Five Shakespearean Songs (1964)                  15'
  solo bar; 3*3*3*3*; 4331; timp+1,              AMP
  hp, pf, str

American Triptych (1965)                         14'
  3*3*3*3*; 4331; timp+2, hp, str                AMP

Symphony (1965)                                  22'
  3*3*3*3*; 4431; timp+4, hp, pf, str            AMP

Concerto No. 1 "Gala Music" (1965-1966)          25'
  3*3*3*3*; 4431; timp+1, 2hp, pf,               AMP
  cel, org, str

Five Etudes (1966)                               14'
  3*3*22; 4331; timp+2, hp, pf, str              AMP

The Visitation - suite (1966)                    41'
  3*3*3=3; 4331; timp+1, hp, pf,                 AMP
  cel, hpsd, str

Triplum I (1967)                                 17'
  3*3*3*3*; 4331; timp+3, hp, pf,                AMP
  cel, org, str

Colloquy for Two Pianos and Orchestra (1968)     20'
  soli 2pf; 3*3*3*3*; 4431; timp+6,              AMP
  hp, cel, str

Concerto for Double Bass and Orchestra (1968)    16'
  solo db; 2=2*3=2*; 0220; cel, str              AMP

Shapes and Designs (1969)                        14'
  3*3*3*3*; 4331; perc, hp, pf/cel, str          AMP

Consequents (1969)                               17'
  2=2*2+2*; 4441; perc, str                      AMP

Museum Piece for Renaissance Instruments
    and Orchestra (1970)                              19'
    soli 2s rec, a rec; 2s shawms;                   AMP
    a,t,b crumhorn; 2cor; sackbut, lute,
    hpsd, 3viole da gamba, regal;
    orch:   2=2*2*2; 4231; perc, hp, pf/cel, str

Concerto da camera (1971)                            16'
    112*1; 1110; 2perc, hp, pf, cel, str             AMP

The Power Within Us - oratorio (1971)                25'
    solo bar; narr; satb cho; 3*2*2*3*; 4331;        AMP
    perc, hp, pf, cel, str

Capriccio stravagante (1972)                         19'
    3*3*4=3*; 4431; timp+1, hp, pf, cel, str         AMP

Three Nocturnes (1973)                               15'
    3*3*3*3*; 4331; timp+4, hp, pf, cel, str         AMP

Four Soundscapes
    (Hudson Valley Reminiscences) (1974)             15'
    3*3*3*3*; 4331; timp+5, hp, pf/cel, str          AMP

Triplum II (1975)                                    20'
    3*3*3*3*; 4331; 3perc, hp, pf, cel, str          AMP

Concerto for Violin and
    Orchestra (1975-1976)                            24'
    solo vln; 4*3*4(a sax, b cl)3*; 4441;            AMP
    timp+6, 2hp, pf, cel, str

Concerto No. 2 for Horn and Orchestra (1976)   24'
    solo hn; 3=3*3*3*; 4441; 7perc, hp,              AMP
    pf, cel, str

Concerto No. 2 for Orchestra (1976)                  25'
    4=4(eh, ob d'am)(5)4*; 4441; 6perc, hp,          AMP
    pf, cel, str
    N.B.   Three of the clarinets are in A.
    The doubling instruments are 3b cl, cb cl,
    E-flat cl, a sax.

Concerto for Contrabassoon and
    Orchestra (1978)                                 23'
    solo cbsn; 4*4*3*3*; 4440; timp+1, hp,           AMP
    pf/cel, str

Deai (Encounter) (1978)                              28'
  4*3(2eh)3(2b cl, cb cl)4*; 5541; 3perc,           AMP
  2hp, pf/cel, str

Concerto for Trumpet and Orchestra (1979)            15'
  solo tpt; 22*22; 4310; timp+1, hp,                AMP
  pf, str

Music for a Celebration (1980)                        6'
  satb cho; 3*3*3*3*; 4331; timp+5,                 AMP
  hp, cel, str
  N.B.  Requires offstage brass section of 2420.

Concerto No. 2 for Piano and
  Orchestra (1981)                                   30'
  solo pf; 4*3*4(b cl, cb cl)3*; 4341;              AMP
  timp+1, hp, str

Concerto for Alto Saxophone and
  Orchestra (1983)                                   29'
  solo a sax; 223*2; 4331; perc,                    AMP
  hp, cel, str

Concerto Festivo (1984)                              20'
  solo br qnt; 3*3*3*4*; 4331; perc, hp,            AMP
  pf/cel, str

Concerto Quaternio for Four Solo Instruments
  and Four Orchestral Groups (1984)                  20'
  soli fl, ob, tpt, vln;                            AMP
  group 1:  soprano v; 2+012; 0100; 8vln
  group 2:  mezzo v; 1*110; 2010; cel, 8vln
  group 3:  tenor v; 02*2=1; 1000; hp, 10vla
  group 4:  0000; 1221; euph; timp+4, hpsd,
  7vc, 5db

Jubilee Music (1984)                                 24'
  3*3*3*3*; 4331; timp+1, hp, pf/cel, str           AMP

Bassoon Concerto
  "Eine Kleine Fagottmusik" (1985)                   22'
  solo bsn; 3*3*2(s sax)3*; 4331; timp+4,           AMP
  hp, pf/cel, str

Farbenspiel (Concerto for Orchestra) (1985)          25'
  4*4*3*4*; 4441; timp+5, hp, pf, str               AMP

Concerto for Viola and Orchestra (1985)              20'
  solo vla; 3*3*3*3*; 4331; timp+1, hp,             AMP
  pf/cel, str

Concerto for Two Pianos (Three Hands)
    and Orchestra (1990)                            25'
    soli 2pf(3-hands); 2*2*2+2; 2210; timp+2,    AMP
    hp, str (6-6-4-3-2)


        SCHUMAN, WILLIAM   (1910-      )

Concerto for Piano and Orchestra (1938-1942)    21'
    solo pf; 1110; 2210; str                      GS

American Festival Overture (1939)                9'
    3*3*3*3*; 4331; timp+3, str                   GS

Prologue (1939)                                  7'
    satb cho; 3*222; 2331; timp+1, str            GS

Newsreel (1941)                                  8'
    3*3*3=3*; a,t,bar sax; 4331; timp+1,          GS
    pf, str
    OR:  2*121; 2331; timp+1, str

Symphony No. 3 (1941)                            30'
    3*2*2+2*; 4441; timp+1, str                   GS

Symphony No. 4 (1941)                            24'
    3*2*2=2*; 4331; timp+2, str                   GS

A Free Song (1942)                               22'
    satb cho; 3*4*5=4*; 4331; timp+1, str         GS

Prayer in Time of War (1943)                     14'
    3*3*3*2; 4331; timp+1, str                    GS

Symphony for Strings
    (Symphony no. 5) (1943)                       17'
    str                                           GS

Circus Overture (1944)                           7'
    3(2picc)3*4=3*; 4331; timp+1, pf, str         GS
    OR:  2230; 2331; timp+1, pf, str

Undertow - choreographic episodes (1945)        25'
    3*3*3*3*; 4231; timp+1, pf, str               GS

Concerto for Violin and Orchestra
    (1947; rev 1959)                              30'
    solo vln; 3*2*3*2*; 4330; timp+1, str        MER

Night Journey - ballet (1947)                           20'
   1111; 1000; pf, str                               MER

Symphony No. 6 (1948)                                   29'
   3*2*2*2*; 4331; timp+1, str                       GS

Judith - choreographic poem (1949)                      24'
   3*3*3*3*; 4231; timp+2, pf, str                   GS

Voyage for a Theater - ballet (1953)                    25'
   1111; 1000; pf, str                               MER

Credendum - Article of Faith (1955)                     18'
   4*3*3=3*; 6432; timp+2, pf, str                   MER

New England Triptych (1956)                             15'
   3*2*2=2; 4331; timp+1, str                        MER

Symphony No. 7 (1960)                                   28'
   4*4*5*4*; 6432; timp+1, hp, pf, cel, str    MER

A Song of Orpheus - Fantasy for Violoncello
   and Orchestra (1961)                             21'
   solo vc; 3*2*2*2; 4000; hp, str                   MER

In Praise of Shahn -
   Canticle for Orchestra (1962)                    18'
   3*3*3*3*; 4331; timp+1, pf, str                   MER

Symphony No. 8 (1962)                                   31'
   4*4*4*4*; 6441; timp+1, 2hp, pf, str        MER
   N.B.  Winds may be reduced to 3*3*3*3*.

The Orchestra Song (1963)                               4'
   2*11*1; 4331; timp+1, str                         MER

Variations on "America" (1963)                          8'
   3*2*22; 4331; timp+1, str                         MER
   N.B.  This is an arrangement of Ives'
   work for organ.

Amaryllis -
   Variations on Old English Rounds (1964)    10'
   str                                               MER

The Witch of Endor - ballet (1965)                      30'
   1111; 1111; perc, str                             MER

Symphony No. 9 "Le fosse ardeative" (1968)              30'
   3*4*4*4*; 4431; timp+4, pf, str                   MER

To Thee Old Cause (1968)                          17'
    timp, pf, str                                 MER

Voyage for Orchestra (1972)                       25'
    3*3*3*3*; 4331; timp+1, pf, str               MER

Concerto on Old English Rounds (1974)             40'
    solo vla; ssaa cho; 3*3*3*3*; 4331;           MER
    perc, str

Symphony No. 10 "American Muse" (1975)            33'
    4*4*4*4*; 6441; timp+6, hp, pf, cel, str      MER

Casey at the Bat - cantata (1976)                 40'
    soli s, t; satb cho; 3*3*3*2; 4331;           AMP
    timp+3, pf, str

The Young Dead Soldiers (1976)                    15'
    solo s; solo hn; 03*3*2; 0000;                MER
    str (0-0-4-4-1)

Three Colloquies for French Horn and
    Orchestra (1979)                              30'
    solo hn; 3*23*2; 0300; timp+4, hp,            MER
    pf/cel, str

American Hymn (1981)                              26'
    3*3*3*3*; 4331; timp+1, cel, str              MER

On Freedom's Ground - cantata (1985)              40'
    solo bar; satb cho; 3*3*3*2; 4331;            MER
    timp+4, pf/cel, str

Showcase (1986)                                    4'
    3*3*3*3*; 4331; timp+4, pf, str               MER

Let's Hear It For Lenny! (1988)                    2'
    3*3*3*2; 4331; timp+4, str                    MER


            SCHWANTNER, JOSEPH   (1943-      )

Modus caelestis (1972)                            15'
    12fl; 3perc, pf, cel, 12 strings              ACA

Aftertones of Infinity (1978)                     15'
    22*22; 4231; timp+2, hp, pf, cel, str         CFP
    N.B.  Orchestra members are required to sing.

Magabunda:
    Four Poems of Aguerdo Pizarro (1982)               29'
    solo s; 4=3*3=3*; 4331; timp+4, hp,                EAM
    amp pf/cel, str

New Morning for the World;
    Daybreak of Freedom (1982)                         23'
    narr; 4*3*3*3; 4341; timp+4, hp, amp pf,           EAM
    amp cel, str

Distant Runes and Incantations (1983)                  15'
    solo amp pf; 2*2*22*; 2200; 2perc,                 EAM
    cel, str

Dreamcaller (1984)                                     21'
    solo s; 1+2*1*2; 2100; perc, pf/cel, str           EAM

A Sudden Rainbow (1984)                                15'
    3*3*3*3*; 4331; timp+3, hp, pf, cel, str           EAM

From Afar...
    Fantasy for Guitar and Orchestra (1987)            16'
    solo amp gtr; 3*3*3*3*; 4331; timp+3, hp,          EAM
    pf/cel, str

Toward Light (1987)                                    22'
    3*333; 4331; timp+3, hp, 2pf, str                  EAM

Concerto for Piano and Orchestra (1988)                29'
    solo pf; 2*2*2*2; 2221; 2perc, cel, str            EAM

Freelight ("Fanfares and Fantasy") (1989)              6'
    3*33*3*; 4331; timp+3, hp, pf, str                 EAM

A Play of Shadows (1990)                               15'
    solo fl; 2*22*2; 2110; 3perc, hp, pf, str          EAM

Concerto for Percussion and Orchestra (1991)           20'
    solo perc; 3*3*3*3*; 4331; timp+3, hp,             EAM
    pf/cel, str

Evening Land -
    Symphony for Chorus and Orchestra (1991)           30'
    satb cho; 3*3*3*3*; 4331; timp+3, hp,              EAM
    pf/cel, str

Through Interior Worlds (1991)                         25'
    3*3*3*3*; 4331; timp+3, hp, pf/cel, str            EAM

### SCHWARTZ, CHARLES

Passacaglia for Orchestra (1948)                        9'
  4*3*3*3*; 4331; timp+4, hp, pf, cel, str    CF

Motion (1955)                                           7'
  str                                         CF

Second Symphony (1955)                                  30'
  4*3*3*3*; 4331; timp+4, hp, pf, cel, str    MS

Professor Jive (A Jazz Symphony) (1974)                39'
  4*4*4*4*; 0000; perc, str                   MS


### SCHWARTZ, ELLIOTT   (1936-      )

Music for Orchestra (1965)                             7'
  2*222; 4230; timp+2, pf, str, tape         PEM

Magic Music (1968)                                     12'
  solo pf; 2*22(b cl, a sax)2*; 4220;        CF
  timp+2, str, 2tape

Island (1970)                                          12'
  3*23*2*; 4231; timp+2, pf, str, tape       PEM

Dream Overture (1972)                                  11'
  2*22*2*; 4221; timp+1, pf, str, 2tape,     ACA
  phonodisc, lights(opt)

The Harmony of Music (1974)                            18'
  solo synth; 2*22*2*; 4221; timp+2, pf, str CF

Eclipse III (1975)                                     10'
  1111; 1110; 2perc, str                     MS

Janus (1976)                                           24'
  solo pf; 2*22*2*; 4220; timp+2, str        CF

Chamber Concerto I (1977)                              11'
  solo db; 1111; 1000; perc, pf,             MMB
  str (4-2-2-0)

Chamber Concerto III (1977)                            15'
  solo pf; 1*21*2; 2000; 2perc, str          MMB

Zebra (1981)                                           9'
  2*022; 2220; 2perc, str (no vla), tape     MMB

Celebrations/Reflections -
    A Time Warp (1984)                                        15'
    2*22*2; 4221; timp+3, pf/cel, str                         MMB

Four American Portraits (1985)                               18'
    2*1*2*1*; 2100; perc, pf, str                             MMB

Concerto for Bassoon and Strings (NA)                        14'
    solo bsn; str                                            BTN

Harupsicating on Valley View Farm (NA)                       10'
    solo bar; 1111; 1000; timp, str                          BTN

Pastorale (NA)                                                6'
    1111; 1000; str                                          BTN


            SCHWARTZ, FRANCIS  (1940-    )

Plegaria (1973)                                              12'
    2222; 4230; timp+4, str                                  PS

Yo Protesto (1974)                                          11'
    1111; 0111; timp+2, pf, str, tape                        PS

The Tropical Trek of Tristan Trimble (1975)                 10'
    1111; 0111; timp+1, str                                  PS

Un sourire festif (1981)                                     9'
    str                                                      SAL
    N.B.  Requires audience participation.

Gestos (1983)                                               20'
    3*222; 4231; timp+1, str                                 SAL
    N.B.  Requires audience participation.


            SCIANNI, JOSEPH  (1928-    )

Shiloh Overture (1956)                                       5'
    3*222; 4330; timp+1, str                                 FLE

Batik (1957)                                                 9'
    2*2*3*2; 4331; timp+1, hp, str                           FLE

Sinfonia Breve (1958)                                       12'
    2*222; 2210; timp+1, str                                 TP

SELIG, ROBERT LEIGH   (1939-1984)

Mirage (1967)                                     15'
    solo tpt; str                                MG

Islands (1968)                                    15'
    ssaattbb cho; 11*10; 1000; str               MG

Concerto for Rock Group and Orchestra (1969)  28'
    soli elec gtr, b gtr, org, dmst;             MG
    3*3*3*3*; 4331; perc, str

Symphony No. 2  "Earth Colors" (1980)             35'
    3*3*3*3*; 4331; timp+1, hp, pf, str          MG


SELLARS, JAMES   (1943-    )

Chanson Dada (1979)                               25'
    solo s; 1110; a sax; 0110; 2perc,            HRM
    pf, str (1-0-1-1)

Pianoconcert (1980)                               29'
    solo pf; 1211; 2110; str                     HRM

Concertorama (1984)                               25'
    solo pf/synth; 3*03=1; 2a,t,bar sax;         HRM
    0331; timp, elec drums, mar, gtr, b gtr, str

The Music Machine (1990)                          23'
    3*3*3*3*; 4331; timp+3, 2synth, str          HRM

Elegy (1991)                                      11'
    str                                          HRM


SEMEGEN, DARIA   (1946-    )

Triptych (1966)                                   23'
    3*23*3*; 4331; 3perc, str                    ACA

Poème 1er:  Dans la nuit (1969)                   8'
    solo bar; 2*11*0; 0100; 4perc, hp, pf,       ACA
    cel, str (5-5-3-2-1)


SEREBRIER, JOSÉ   (1938-    )

Elegia para cuerdas (1956)                        8'
    str                                          PS

Momento Psicologico (1957)                                      4'
   solo tpt; str                                 PS

Symphony No. 1 (1958)                                          18'
   3*3*3*3*; 4331; timp+2, hp, cel, org, str     PS

Partita (1959)                                                 28'
   3*3*3*3*; a sax; 4331; timp+1, pf, str        PS

Fantasia (1960)                                               12'
   str                                           PS

Poema Elegíaco (1962)                                          9'
   3*3*3*3*; a sax; 4331; timp+1, pf, str        PS

Passacaglia and Perpetuum Mobile (1965)                       12'
   solo acc; 0000; 2110; perc, str              PS

Variations on a Theme from Childhood (1965)                    5'
   solo tbn; str                                 PS

Dorothy and Carmine (1969)                                     7'
   solo fl; str                                  PS

Nueve (1969)                                                  12'
   narr; satb cho; 0020; 4231; timp+1,           PS
   pf/cel, str (no vla)

Colores Magicos:  Variations for Harp and
   Chamber Orchestra (1971)                      12'
   solo hp; 2*000; 2211; timp+1, pf/cel, str     PS

Orpheus Times Light - ballet (1972)                           24'
   solo s; 2*100; 2211; timp+1, hp,              PS
   pf/cel, str


       SERLY, TIBOR  (1901-1978)

American Elegy (1945)                                          6'
   3*222; 4331; timp+1, str                      PS

Rhapsody for Viola and Orchestra (1947)                       12'
   solo vla; 2*222; 2200; timp+4, hp, str        PS

Concerto for Trombone and
   Chamber Orchestra (1952-1954)                 15'
   solo tbn; 2*121; 1000; timp+3, str            PS

Lament (Homage to Bartok) (1955)            8'
    str                                     FLE

Symphonic Variations for Audience and
    Orchestra (1956)                        10'
    2222; 2331; timp+1, str                 GS
    N.B.  Requires audience participation.

A Little Christmas Cantata (1957)           7'
    satb cho; 1122; 2231; timp+1, str       GS

Symphony in Four Cycles (1960)              14'
    str                                     BRO

Anniversary Cantata on a Quodlibet (1966)   5'
    satb cho; 2222; 2330; timp+2, str       MCA


            SESSIONS, ROGER   (1896-1985)

Symphony No. 1 (1927)                       22'
    3*3*4=3; 4331; timp+3, pf, str          EBM

The Black Maskers - suite (1928)            23'
    3=3*4*3; 4431; timp+3, pf, str          EBM

Concerto for Violin and Orchestra (1935)    35'
    solo vln; 3=2*4=3; 4220; timp+2,        EBM
    str (no vlns)

Symphony No. 2 (1946)                       30'
    3*3*3*2; 4331; timp+1, pf, str          GS

Idyll of Theocritus (1954)                  42'
    solo s; 2222; 4231; timp+1, hp, cel, str  MER

Concerto for Piano and Orchestra (1955-1956)  18'
    solo pf; 3*3*3*3*; 4231; timp+1, str    EBM

Symphony No. 3 (1957)                       32'
    3*3*4=3*; 4231; timp+2, hp, cel, str    EBM

Symphony No. 4 (1958)                       24'
    3*3*4=3*; 4331; timp+3, hp, pf, cel, str  EBM

Divertimento (1959-1960)                    20'
    3*222; 4331; timp+1, pf, str            MER

Symphony No. 5 (1964)                       16'
    3*3*4=3*; 4231; timp+3, hp, pf, str     EBM

When Lilacs Last in the
  Dooryard Bloom'd (1964-1970)         45'
  soli s, a, bar; satb cho; 3*3*4=3*; 4231;  MER
  timp+1, hp, pf, cel, str

Psalm CXL (1966)         8'
  solo s; 3*3(hklph)3*3*; 4221; timp+3,  EBM
  hp, str

Symphony No. 6 (1966)        18'
  3*3*4=3*; 4231; timp+1, hp, pf, str  MER

Symphony No. 7 (1966-1967)        20'
  3*3*4=3*; 4331; timp+4, hp, pf, str  MER

Symphony No. 8 (1968)        14'
  3+3*4=4*; 4341; timp+5, hp, pf/cel, str  EBM

Rhapsody for Orchestra (1970)        20'
  3*3*4=3*; 4331; timp+1, hp, str  MER

Concerto for Violin, Violoncello and
  Orchestra (1971)        20'
  soli vln, vc; 3*23*2; 3120; timp+1,  MER
  pf, str

Concertino for Chamber Orchestra (1971-1972)  17'
  1=1*1=1*; 2110; timp+2, str  EBM

Three Choruses on Biblical Texts (1971-1972)  15'
  satb cho; 1122; 1110; perc, pf, str  MER

Symphony No. 9 (1975-1978)        25'
  3*3*4=3*; 4431; timp+3, hp, pf, str  MER

Concerto for Orchestra (1981)        15'
  3*3*3*3*; 4331; timp+1, hp, str  MER


      SHAPERO, HAROLD   (1920-    )

Serenade in D (1945)        28'
  str  PS

Symphony for Classical Orchestra (1947)  40'
  3*223*; 2230; timp, str  PS

Sinfonia in C minor -
  The Traveler's Overture (1948)      11'
  3*223*; 4230; timp, str  PS

Credo for Orchestra (1955)                              8'
   2021; 1211; timp, str                          PS

Partita in C (1961)                                    17'
   solo pf; 1*1*11; 1110; timp+3, hp, str         PS

Three Hebrew Songs (1973-1988)                         20'
   solo t; pf, str                                MS

On Green Mountain (1981)                               11'
   2*23(a sax, t sax)2; 2331; timp+4, hp,         PS
   pf, elec gtr, b gtr, str


      SHAPEY, RALPH   (1921-    )

Cantata (1951)                                         30'
   soli s, t, b; narr; 1111; 2111; perc, str      TP

Challenge - The Family of Man (1955)                   15'
   4*4*4*4*; 4331; timp+1, pf, str                TP

Invocation -
   Concerto for Violin and Orchestra (1958)       23'
   solo vln; 2222; 3221; 3perc, pf, gtr, str      TP

Ontogeny (1958)                                        20'
   4*2*3*2; 3211; 9perc, pf, str (9-8-4-6-2)      TP
   N.B.  The orchestra is redistributed into
   self-sufficient groups.

Rituals (1959)                                         13'
   3*3*3*3*; a,t,bar sax; 3221; 8perc,            TP
   pf, str

Chamber Symphony (1962)                                11'
   12*00; 1100; perc, pf, str (1-0-1-1)           TP

Praise - oratorio (1962-1971)                          54'
   solo b-bar; ssaattbb cho; 0200; 0230;          TP
   4perc, str (2-1-1-1)

Partita-Fantasia for Violoncello and
   Sixteen Players (1967)                         24'
   solo vc; 2222; 1110; 2perc, str (1-1-0-1)      TP

Songs of Eros (1975)                                   30'
   solo s; solo str qt; 3*3*3*3*;                 TP
   a,t,bar sax; 4221; 6perc, str, tape

The Covenant (1977) 45'
   solo s; 1111; 1111; 2perc, pf, TP
   str (2-1-1-1), 2 two-track tapes

Double Concerto for Violin, Violoncello
   and Orchestra (1983) 31'
   soli vln, vc; 2222; 2220; 5perc, TP
   hp, pf, str

Concertante No. 1 (1984) 11'
   solo tpt; 1111; 1000; perc, str TP

Symphonie Concertant (1985) 30'
   3*23*3*; 3341; 2timp+6, pf, cel, str TP

Concerto for Cello, Piano and
   String Orchestra (1986) 25'
   soli vc, pf; str TP

Concertante No. 2 (1987) 21'
   solo a sax; 1(picc, b fl)1*1=1*; TP
   11(picc tpt)10; 3perc, str (2-1-1-1)


SHAPIRO, GERALD

Mount Hope in Autumn (1989) 22'
   3*3*3*3; 4331; 4perc, hp, str MS


SHATIN, JUDITH (1949-    )

Arche (1976) 15'
   solo vla; 2111; 0121; 2perc, str ACA

Aura (1982) 17'
   2222; 4231; 3perc, str ACA

The Passion of St. Cecilia (1984) 20'
   solo pf; 2222; 4221; 2perc, str ACA

Ruah (1985) 23'
   solo fl; 0111; 1110; str (solo or section) ACA

Piping the Earth (1990) 10'
   3*3*3*3; 4321; timp+3, hp, str ACA

SHAWN, ALLEN    (1948-    )

Nocturnes (1978)                                          20'
    solo pf; 1111; 1110; perc, hp, str                   ECS

Concerto for Clarinet, Cello and
    Chamber Orchestra (1983)                             25'
    soli cl, vc; 2*2*02; t sax; 1220;                    ECS
    timp+1, pf, str

Autumnal Song (1984)                                     15'
    solo vln; 2*222; 3221; timp, str                     ECS

Concertino for Flute and Strings (1987)                  15'
    solo fl; str                                         ECS

Symphony in Three Parts (1987)                           21'
    3*3*3*2; 4231; timp+2, pf, str                       ECS


SHEINFELD, DAVID    (1906-    )

Dialogues (1966)                                         20'
    2*2*2*2; 2200; perc, str                             MS

Confrontations (1969)                                    10'
    4(4picc)23*2; 43(2cnt)31; timp+4, pf, str           MS

The Earth is a Sounding Board (1978)                     20'
    satb cho; 4(4picc)4*4=3*; 4331; timp+4,              MS
    hp, pf, str
    N.B.  Requires a small group of extra
    string players.

Dreams and Fantasies (1981)                              15'
    4(4picc)4*4=3*; 4331; timp+4, hp,                    MS
    pf/cel, str

Polarities (A Symphony) (1990)                           25'
    4(4picc)4*4=4*; 4331; timp+5, hp, pf,                MS
    cel, str


SHERE, CHARLES    (1935-    )

Small Concerto (1964)                                     6'
    solo pf; 2+2*2*2; 4(2 Wagner tba)221;                EP
    harmonium, str

Sections for Orchestra (1965)                                8'
    3*3*3*2; 4331; timp+1, pf, str                           EP

Nightmusic (1967; rev 1971, 1980)                            25'
    2020; 2002; hp, pf, cel, gtr,                            EP
    str (0-0-7-6-6)

from Calls and Singing (1968)                                9'
    2122; 2200; timp, str                                    EP

Soigneur de Gravité (1972)                                   7'
    2122; 2200; timp, str                                    EP

Music for Orchestra (Symphony) (1976)                        15'
    3*222; 4231; timp+2, hp(or mand), str                    EP

Handler of Gravity - ballet (1978)                           7'
    32*22*; 4231; timp+1, hp, pf, str                        EP

Tongues (1978)                                               28'
    poet speaking in "tongues"; 1*1*1*1;                     EP
    1(Wagner tba)110; perc, hp, pf,
    str (1-1-1-1), tape, live electronics
    N.B.  The text is improvised by the poet.

Concerto for Violin with Harp, Percussion
    and Small Orchestra (1985)                               20'
    solo vln; 2222; 2221; timp+2, hp, pf, str   EP

Symphony in Three Movements (1988)                           20'
    3*4(2eh)3(2b cl)3*; 4341; timp+3,                        EP
    hp, pf, str
    N.B.  Strings are divisi throughout.


        SHIFRIN, SEYMOUR  (1926-1979)

Chamber Symphony (1952-1953)                                 20'
    103*0; 2020; str (no db)                                 CFP

Three Pieces for Orchestra (1958)                            17'
    3*3*3*3*; 4331; timp+1, hp, cel, str                     CFP

Cantata to the Text of
    Sophoclean Choruses (1957-1958)                          35'
    satb cho; 2222; 4230; timp+1,                            CFP
    pf, cel, str

Chronicles (1970)                                    30'
    soli t, bar, b; satb cho; 2222; 2221;          CFP
    timp+1, pf, str


## SHINN, RANDALL

The Silver Whistle (1980)                            18'
  narr; 2222; 4331; timp+2, str                      MS

Reflections (1982; rev 1991)                         10'
  3*222; 4231; timp+2, hp, str                       MS

Cortège (1984)                                        9'
  2222; 4230; timp, str                              MS

Make Much Of Time (1987)                             27'
  soli s, t; satb cho; 3*3*3*3*; 4331;               MS
  timp+2, hp, pf, str

Devices and Desires (1989)                          33'
  soli s, bar; satb cho; 2222; 4231;                 MS
  timp+2, str


## SHORE, CLARE  (1954-    )

July Remembrances (1981)                             17'
  solo s; 2122; 0200; perc, str (4-4-3-2-1)          ECS

Intermezzo (1984)                                     6'
  3*23*2; 2000; timp+1, hp, str                      ECS


## SHULMAN, ALAN  (1915-    )

Concerto for Cello and Orchestra (1948)             28'
  solo vc; 2*121; 2220; timp, hp, str                TP

Waltzes for Orchestra (1949)                          9'
  2222; 4331; timp+1, hp, pf/cel, str                TP

Woodstock Waltzes (1949)                             12'
  2222; 2100; timp, str                              EBM

A Laurentian Overture (1951)                          9'
  3*3*3*2; 4331; timp+1, hp, str                     TP

Popcateptl (1955)                                    NA
  3*222; 4331; timp+1, hp, str                       SHA

Threnody (1974)                                           6'
   str                                     FLE

In Memoriam - Sophie (1916-1982) (1982)                  7'
   2222; 0000; str                         EBM

Prelude (NA)                                             5'
   2*22*2; 4220; hp, cel, str              TP

Theme and Variations for Harp and
   Orchestra (NA)                          14'
   solo hp; str                            TP


     SIEGMEISTER, ELIE   (1909-1991)

A Tooth for Paul Revere (1945)                           23'
   soli 4vv; satb cho; 1111; 1110; timp+1,  CF
   pf, str

Western Suite (1945)                                     20'
   2*2*3=2; 4331; timp+1, str               CF

Wilderness Road (1945)                                   6'
   2*2*2*2; 2220; timp+2, str               CF

Lonesome Hollow (1946)                                   7'
   2*22+2; 4220; timp+1, hp(or pf), str     CF

Sunday in Brooklyn (1946)                                15'
   3*2*3=2; a sax; 4331; timp+4, hp,        EBM
   pf, cel, str

Summer Night (1947)                                      7'
   22*3*2; 2220; timp, hp, str              CF

Symphony No. 1 (1947; rev 1972)                          27'
   3*3*3*3*; 4331; timp+4, hp, pf, str      CF

From My Window (1949)                                    9'
   2*22*2; 4321; timp+1, hp, pf, str        CF

Symphony No. 2 (1950; rev 1971)                          28'
   3*3*3*3*; 4231; timp+3, hp, pf, cel, str CF

Riversong (1951; rev 1982)                               10'
   2*2*2*2; 2211; timp+1, str               CF

Divertimento (1953)                                      14'
   2*2*22; 2220; timp+1, str                SHA

Concerto for Clarinet and Orchestra (1956)     16'
    solo cl; 111*1; 2220; 2perc, str            CF

Christmas is Coming (1957)                      24'
    narr; satb cho; 2021; 2210; timp+1, str     LG

Symphony No. 3 (1957)                           18'
    2*2*23*; 4231; timp+2, pf, str              CF

Concerto for Flute and Orchestra (1960)         21'
    solo fl; 01*21; 2110; 2perc, str            CF

Theater Set (1960)                              12'
    2*3*3*2*; 4331; 3perc, hp, pf, str          CF

In Our Time (1965)                              12'
    satb cho; 2222; 4331; timp+2, pf, str       CF

Dick Whittington and his Cat (1966)             19'
    narr; 12*11; 3110; 2perc, pf, str           CF

Five Fantasies of the Theater (1967)            12'
    2*2*3=2*; 4331; timp+4, hp, pf, str         CF

I Have A Dream - cantata (1967)                 25'
    solo bar; narr; satb cho; 2*22(a sax)2;     CF
    4231; 2perc, pf, str

The Face of War (1967-1968)                      9'
    solo bar; 2*222; 2220; timp+1,              CF
    hp, pf, str

Symphony No. 4 (1967-1970)                      34'
    2*2*3=2*; 4331; timp+1, hp, pf/cel, str     CF

Symphony No. 5 "Visions of Time" (1971-1975)    18'
    2*2*3*2*; 4331; timp+4, hp, pf, str         CF

Concerto for Piano and Orchestra
    (1974; rev 1982)                            25'
    solo pf; 2*2*23*; 4221; timp+2, str         CF

A Cycle of Cities (1974)                        23'
    soli s, t; satb cho; 2*222; 4331;           CF
    timp+2, pf, str

Shadows and Light (1975)                        18'
    2*2*2=2*; 4331; timp+3, hp, pf, cel, str    CF

Double Concerto for Violin, Piano and
   Orchestra (1976)                                 20'
   soli vln, pf; 2*2*2*2*; 4331; 4perc, str   CF

Concerto for Violin and
   Orchestra (1978-1983)                             31'
   solo vln; 2*2*2*2*; 3230; timp+3,        CF
   hp, pf, str

Fantasies in Line and Color (1981)         21'
   3*3*3=3*; 4331; timp+4, hp, pf, cel, str   CF

Symphony No. 6 (1983)                          28'
   3*3*3=2*; 4331; timp+4, hp, pf, str     CF

From These Shores (1986)                     14'
   2*22=2; 4330; timp+3, hp, pf, str       CF

Symphony No. 7 (1986)                          23'
   3*3*3=3*; 4331; timp+4, hp, pf, str     CF

Symphony No. 8 (1988)                          23'
   3*3*3*3*; 4331; timp+3, hp, pf, str     CF


SIEKMANN, FRANK (1925-    )

Concerto for Trombone and Orchestra (1977)   10'
   solo tbn; 2121; 1210; timp+1, hp, str    SEE

Music for a Poetic Reading (1977)          3'
   narr; 1111; 1110; perc, str           SEE

Scene in Monochrome (1977)                 3'
   str                                        SEE

Concerto for Bass Trombone and
   Orchestra (1983)                                15'
   solo b tbn; 2*2*2*2*; 4331; timp+1,    BRL
   hp, str

The Lower Longswamp Upper Crust Strut (1984)  3'
   1*010; 0110; dmst, pf, str           BRL

Gregarious (1984)                             4'
   solo tpt (or tbn, or mar, or vib);      BRL
   2*2*2*2*; 4331; timp+1, str

Scenes of the Mind (1987)                 NA
   2*2*2*2*; 4331; timp+3, hp, str      BRL

Triunity for Strings (1989)                      7'
    str                                          BRL


        SILSBEE, ANN L.   (1930-    )

Three Little Wind Stories (1974)                 7'
    2222; 4331; timp+2, hp, str                 ACA

Seven Rituals (1978)                            23'
    3*3*3*3*; 4331; timp+2, pf, str             ACA

Sanctuary (1991)                                 9'
    1111; 1100; timp+1, str                     ACA


        SILVER, SHEILA   (1946-    )

Galixidi (1976)                                 17'
    3*2*3+3*; 4231; 4perc, hp, str              ARG
    N.B.  The contrabassoon may be replaced
    with a contrabass clarinet.

Chariessa (1980)                                18'
    solo s; 2*2*2*2; 2220; 3perc, hp, str       ARG

Shirat Sarah - Song of Sarah (1985-1987)        24'
    str (5-4-3-2-1 minimum)                     ARG

Window Waltz (1988)                              7'
    11*1*0; 1110; perc, hp, pf, str (1-1-1-0)   ARG

Dance of Wild Angels (1990)                     15'
    1*1*1*1; 1100; 2perc, pf, str               ARG


        SILVERMAN, FAYE-ELLEN   (1947-    )

Madness (1972)                                   6'
    narr; 2222; 4220; timp+1, str               SEE

Stirrings (1979)                                14'
    1111; 2000; perc, str                       SEE

Winds and Sines (1981)                          15'
    3*3*3*3*; 4221; perc, hp, pf, str           SEE

Passing Fancies (1985)                          16'
    1111; 1110; perc, str (2-1-1-1)             SEE

Adhesions (1986)                                              12'
   3*3*3*3*; 4331; timp+2, 2hp, pf, str                      SEE

Candlelight (1988)                                           16'
   solo pf; 3*3*3*3*; 4331; timp+2, hp, str                 SEE

Free Pen (1990)                                             33'
   soli vv; narr; satb cho; 1111; 2110;                     SEE
   perc, hp, str


          SILVERMAN, STANLEY  (1938-    )


Tenso:  Afternoon Music for Orchestra (1963)  6'
   3*3*3*3*; 4331; timp+1, hp, str                          ECS


          SIMONS, NETTY  (1923-    )

Piece for Orchestra (1949)                                  10'
   1111; 2000; pf, str (4-4-4-4-2)                          MER

Lamentations I (1961)                                       9'
   4*4*3*4*; 4441; timp+1, str                              MER

Lamentations II (1966)                                      8'
   3*4*4*4*; 4441; timp+1, str                              MER

Variables (1967)                                            var
   ww, br, perc, pf, str - any five instr                  MER
   or multiple of 5

Big Sur (1981-1985)                                         30'
   3*2*2*2*; 4331; timp+1, 2hp, str                         TP

Illuminations in Space (NA)                                 15'
   solo vla; 3*3*3*3*; 4241; timp+1,                        MER
   str (no vln, vla)


          SIMS, EZRA  (1928-    )

Le Tombeau D'Albers (1959)                                  5'
   2222; 4231; timp+2, hp, str                              ACA

Three Songs (1960)                                          8'
   solo t; 222=2; 2200; vib, glock, pf, str                ACA

yr obedt servt (1977)                                       12'
   soli 2cl, vln, vc; 0020; 0110; 2mar, str                ACA

yr obedt servt II (1981)                               12'
   soli 2cl, vln, vc; 2+002; 2020; 2mar,        ACA
   str (5-2-1-1)

Pictures for an Institution (1983)                      5'
   2222; 2200; timp, str                            ACA

Night Piece (1990)                                     15'
   soli fl, cl, vla, vc; 1112; 0220; str,           ACA
   elec sounds


      SINGLETON, ALVIN  (1940-     )

Moment (1968)                                           6'
   3*3*3*3*; 4331; timp+4, pf, str                  EAM

Again (1979)                                           12'
   1*11*1; 1110; perc, pf, str (2-1-1-1)            EAM

A Yellow Rose Petal (1982)                             20'
   2=2*2*2*; 2210; 2perc, cel, str                  EAM

Shadows (1987)                                         20'
   3=3*3=3*; 4331; 2timp+4, hp, str                 EAM

After Fallen Crumbs (1988)                              7'
   3*3*3*3*; 4321; timp+1, hp, str                  EAM

An Idea is a Piece of Cloth (1988)                     10'
   str                                              EAM


      SMART, GARY  (1943-     )

Del Diario de un Papagayo (1973)                        9'
   1*212; 2000; pf, str, tape                       MG


      SMIT, LEO  (1921-     )

Symphony No. 1 in E-flat (1956)                        25'
   2*222; 4220; timp+1, str                         CF

Capriccio (1958; rev 1974)                             14'
   str                                              CF

Symphony No. 2 in Six Movements (1965)                 18'
   3*223*; 4231; timp, hp, pf, str                  TP

Concerto for Piano and Orchestra (1968)          15'
   solo pf; 3*000; 4200; timp, str              CF

Four Alchemy Marches (1972)                       8'
   2*222; 2221; timp, str, tape(opt)            CF

Caedmon (1972)                                   25'
   soli mez, t, b; ttbb cho; 3*222; 4331;       CF
   timp, hpsd, str

From Banja Luka (1987)                           17'
   solo mez; 3*222; 4231; timp+1,               TP
   hp, pf, str

Alabaster Chambers (1989)                        15'
   str                                          TP


          SMITH, HALE  (1925-    )

Orchestral Set (1952)                            15'
   3*3*3*3*; 4331; timp+3, hp, cel, str         CFP

In Memoriam:  Beryl Rubinstein (1953)            11'
   satb cho; 2*2*22; 0000; perc, str            HG

Contours (1961)                                   9'
   2222; 4431; timp+1, pf, str                  CFP

By Yearning and By Beautiful (1964)               8'
   str                                          EBM

Music for Harp and Orchestra (1967)              12'
   solo hp; 1212; 2000; str                     EBM

Concert Music (1972)                             14'
   solo pf; 2*222; 2111; 2perc, hp, cel, str    CFP

Ritual and Incantations (1974)                   16'
   2*2*2*2; 4331; timp+3, hp, pf, str           MER

Innerflexions (1977)                             12'
   2222; 2221; timp+2, hp, pf, str              MER

Symphonic Spirituals (1979)                      35'
   2222; 2221; timp+1, str                      MER

Meditations in Passage (1980)                    27'
   soli s, bar; 2222; 4230; timp+1,             MER
   hp, pf, str

SMITH, JULIA   (1911-1989)

Folksongs Symphony (1948)                          12'
  2222; 2210; perc, hp, pf(4-hands), str            CF

Our Heritage (1958)                                10'
  ssaattbb cho; 2222; 4331; timp+1, str            MWB

American Dance Suite (1963)                        20'
  2221; 2210; timp+1, str                          MWB

Remember the Alamo! (1964)                         13'
  narr(opt); satb cho; 3*3*3*2; 4431;              MWB
  timp+4, str

Concerto for Piano and Orchestra (1971)            22'
  solo pf; 23*22; 4221; timp+1, str                MWB


SMITH, LARRY ALAN   (1955-    )

Apogees (1976)                                     14'
  str                                              BOU

A New York Overture (1977)                          6'
  3*3*3*3*; 4331; timp+2, pf, str                  BOU

Crucifixus (1978)                                  16'
  solo s; 223*2; 4220; timp+3, hp, str             TP

Serenade for Marguerita (1978)                      8'
  str                                              TP

Symphony No. 1 (1980-1983)                         29'
  223*2; 4330; timp+3, str                         TP

Symphony No. 2 "Genesis/Antietam" (1984)           17'
  2222; 2220; 2perc, str                           TP

Concerto for Viola and Orchestra
  "Tableaux vivants d'Orphee" (1985)               22'
  solo vla; 3*222; 4331; timp+2, hp, str           TP

Concerto for Piano and Orchestra (1986)            17'
  solo pf; 2222; 2220; 2perc, str                  TP

Three Movements for Orchestra (1989)               13'
  3*3*3*3*; 4331; timp+3, str                      TP

A Fanfare for Wolfgang (1991)                             4'
    2222; 2200; timp, str                                 TP


            SMITH, LELAND  (1925-      )

Concerto for Orchestra (1950; rev 1961)                  22'
    3*3*4=3*; 4331; timp+1, hp, str                       MS

Symphony I for Small Orchestra (1951)                    14'
    1111; 1100; pf, str                                   MS

Divertimento No. 2 (1953-1959)                           14'
    02(hklph)01; 0000; pf, str                            MS
    N.B.  The heckelphone part may be played
    on English horn or clarinet in A.

Overture to "Santa Claus" (1962)                          7'
    3*3*3*3*; 4330; timp+1, str                           ACA

Arabesque (1969)                                          9'
     2*011; t sax; 1110; vib, str                         ACA


            SMITH, RUSSELL  (1927-      )

Tetrameron (1957)                                        15'
    2222; 3320; timp+1, hp, pf, str                       CFP

Can-Can Waltz (1962)                                      8'
    3*223*; 4331; timp+1, hp, str                         CFP

Magnificat (1978)                                        45'
    solo s; satb cho; 3*23*3*; 4331; timp+1,             TP
    hp, pf, str


            SMITH, WILLIAM O.  (1926-      )

Concerto for Trombone and
    Chamber Orchestra (1950)                             16'
    solo tbn; 1111; 1100; perc, pf, str                   MS

My Father Moved Through Domes Of Love (1955)            10'
    satb cho; 1111; 1100; perc, str                       MS

Concerto for Jazz Soloists and
    Orchestra (1962)                                     18'
    soli cl, db, dmst; 2122; 2311; timp+1,               MJQ
    cel, gtr, str

Interplay (1964)                                  14'
    soli vib, pf, db, dmst; 2122; 2311;           MJQ
    timp+1, cel, gtr, str

Tangents (1965)                                   12'
    solo cl; 3*3*3*3*; 4331; timp+3,              MS
    hp, pf, str

Quadri (1968)                                     18'
    soli vib, pf, db, dmst; 3*33*3*; 4331;        MJQ
    timp+2, hp, str

Theona (1975)                                     15'
    soli cl, tpt, pf, db dmst; 2222; 4331;        MJQ
    3perc, str

Elegia (1976)                                     15'
    solo cl; str                                  MJQ

Ecco! (1978)                                      6'
    solo elec cl; 3+3*3*3; 4331; perc,            MJQ
    hp, pf, str

Twelve (1979)                                     12'
    solo cl; str                                  MJQ


        SNYDER, RANDALL   (1944-     )

Bassoon Concerto (1971)                           13'
    solo bsn; 1100; a sax; 1000; perc, hp,        MS
    pf, cel, str (no db)

Hegemony (1973)                                   27'
    solo pf; 3*23*2; a sax; 1111; timp+5,         MS
    hp, str

Sabbatical Music (1980)                           19'
    1111; 1110; 2perc, hp, pf, str (5-4-3-2)      MS

Schubertiad (1985)                                25'
    solo a; ttbb cho; 2222; a sax; 4231;          MS
    4perc, hp, pf, str

Landscapes (1986)                                 12'
    2222; 2210; 2perc, org, str,                  MS
    slide projector

Triple Concerto (1988)                                14'
    soli vln, vla, vc; 2222; 2210; 2perc,            MS
    hp, pf, str

Fantasy Surrounding a Theme of Bartok (1990)  14'
    2222; 2210; 2perc, str                            MS

Shamanic Dances (1991)                                 9'
    3*3*3*3*; 4331; 5perc, str                        MS


            SOLLBERGER, HARVEY  (1938-    )

Persian Golf (1987)                                   16'
    str                                               ACA


            SON, YUNG WHA  (1954-    )

Distances for Composed Orchestra (1987)       12'
    2(picc, 2a fl)1*1=1; 2111; timp+1, hp,           NOA
    pf, cel, str


            SORCE, RICHARD  (1943-    )

Liberty - ballet (1987)                               30'
    3*3*22; 4321; 2perc, str                          MS

Requiem (1987)                                        40'
    soli vv; satb cho; 2222; 2221; perc, str     PLY

Piece for Orchestra (NA)                              15'
    3*223*; 4331; perc, hp, str                       MS

Semplice (NA)                                         15'
    2222; 2220; pf, str                               MS


            SOULE, EDMUND  (1923-    )

Concerto for Harp and
    Chamber Orchestra (1978)                         30'
    solo hp; 2212; 2000; timp+3, str                 MS

Concert Piece for Clarinet and
    Strings (1979)                                   17'
    solo cl; str                                      MS

Suite No. 1 for String Orchestra (1982)        15'
   str                                          MS

Suite No. 2 for String Orchestra (1984)        15'
   str                                          MS

Symphonic Piece (1984)                          15'
   223*2; 4231; timp+1, hp, str                 MS

Suite No. 3 for String Orchestra (1985)        15'
   str                                          MS


         SOWERBY, LEO   (1895-1968)

Concert Piece for Organ and Orchestra (1951)   7'
   solo org; 2222; 4231; timp+2, str            TP

The Throne of God (1956)                        33'
   satb cho; 3*3*3*2; 4331; timp+2, str         TP

Solomon's Garden (1964)                         16'
   solo t; satb cho; 1121; 2110; timp+1,        TP
   org, str

Concert Piece No. 2 in C Major (1968)          32'
   solo org; 3*3*3*2; 4331; timp+1, str         TP


         SPEARS, JARED

Voyage (1980)                                   7'
   3*23*2; 4321; timp+5, pf, str                MS


         SPIES, CLAUDIO   (1925-     )

Music for a Ballet (1955)                       15'
   3*3*22; 4220; timp, str                      TP

Il cantico de frate (1958)                      20'
   solo bar; 1111; 2220; hp, str                MS

Tempi: Music for Fourteen Instruments (1962)   18'
   03(eh, ob d'am)2*0; 1020; xyl, hp, cel,      TP
   str (1-1-1-0)

SPRATLAN, LEWIS   (1940-     )

Two Pieces for Orchestra (1971)                      NA
    2222; 2110; 2perc, str                           MS

Webs (1981)                                          NA
    solo fl; str (variable number)                   MS

Celebration (1984)                                   8'
    satb cho; 2222; 2221; perc, str                  MG

Apollo and Daphne Variations (1987)                  NA
    3*3*3*3*; 4331; perc, hp, pf, str                MS

Hung Monophonies (1990)                              NA
    solo ob; str (3-3-2-1)                           MS


STALLCOP, GLENN   (1950-     )

City Music - Song and Dance (1974)                   30'
    2222; 4331; timp+7, hp, str                      ACA

Concerto for Double Bass and
    String Orchestra (1978)                          23'
    solo db; str                                     ACA

Couplet for a Desert Summer (1980)                   14'
    1212; 2000; perc, pf, str                        ACA

In Apprehension of Spring (1986)                     4'
    2222; 4331; timp+1, str                          ACA


STALLINGS, KENDALL   (1940-     )

Confluences (1968)                                   18'
    3=3*3=3*; 4331; 6perc, hp, str                   MS
    N.B.  Requires 12 boo-bams in
    percussion section.

Antiphony (1969)                                     4'
    2222; 4220; 2perc, str                           MS


STARER, ROBERT   (1924-     )

Concerto No. 1 for Piano and
    Orchestra (1947)                                 21'
    solo pf; 2222; 2210; timp+1, str                 MCA

Symphony No. 1 (1950)                                      22'
   3*3*3*3*; 4331; timp+1, hp, cel, str          MCA

Symphony No. 2 (1951)                                      12'
   3*3*3*3*; 4331; timp+1, pf, str               IMI

Kohelet (1952)                                            24'
   soli s, bar; satb cho; 3*3*22; 2210;          MCA
   perc, str

Concerto No. 2 for Piano and
   Orchestra (1953)                              16'
   solo pf; 2222; 2210; timp+1, str              MCA

Prelude and Rondo Giocoso (1953)                          10'
   2222; 2210; timp+1, str                       MCA

Concerto a tre (1954)                                     18'
   soli cl, tpt, tbn; str                        MCA

Concerto for Viola, Strings and
   Percussion (1958)                             24'
   solo vla; timp+4, cel, str                    MCA

Ariel:  Visions of Isaiah (1959)                          27'
   soli s, bar; satb cho; 2222; 2220;            MCA
   timp+1, cel, str

A Psalm of David (1959)                                    5'
   satb cho; 2tpt; org(or pf), str               TP

Dybbuk - suite (1960)                                     26'
   2222; 2220; timp+2, cel, str                  MCA

Invocation for Trumpet and Strings (1962)                  8'
   solo tpt; str                                 TP

Phaedra - suite (1962)                                    17'
   1*111; 1110; timp+1, hp, str                  MCA

Samson Agonistes - symphonic poem (1963)                  13'
   3*3*3*3*; 4331; timp+1, pf/cel, str           MCA

Mutabili - Variants for Orchestra (1965)                  11'
   3*3*3=3*; 4331; timp+1, pf/cel, str           MCA

Joseph and his Brothers - cantata (1966)                  26'
   soli s, t, bar; narr; satb cho; 2222;         MCA
   2200; perc, hp, str

Concerto for Violin, Violoncello and
    Orchestra (1967)                                      19'
    soli vln, vc; 3*3*3*3*; 4331; timp+5,                 MCA
    hp, str

Six Variations with Twelve Notes (1967)                  5'
    3*3*3*3*; 4331; timp+3, str                          MCA

Symphony No. 3 (1969)                                    21'
    3*3*4=3; 4331; timp+4, hp, pf, str                  MCA

Concerto No. 3 for Piano and
    Orchestra (1972)                                     24'
    solo pf; 3*222; 2221; timp+3, str                   MCA

Journals of a Songmaker (1975)                           25'
    soli s, bar; 3*3*3*2; 4331; timp+1,                 MCA
    hp, pf, str

The People, Yes (1976)                                   22'
    satb cho; 2*222; 4331; timp+2, str                  MCA

Concerto for Violin and
    Orchestra (1979-1980)                                23'
    solo vln; 2222; 2220; timp+1, str                   MCA

Kli Zemer (1982)                                         24'
    solo cl/b cl; 2*2*22; 2220; timp+1, str             MMB

Concerto a quattro (1983)                                21'
    soli ob, cl, bsn, hn; 4perc, str                    MCA

Hudson Valley Suite (1984)                               20'
    2*2*22; 4221; timp+2, str                           MCA

Serenade (1984)                                          NA
    soli tbn, vib; str                                  MCA

Symphonic Prelude (1984)                                 10'
    2*2*22; 4331; timp+2, hp, str                       MCA

Elegy (1985)                                             5'
    solo cl (or vln); str                               MMB

Concerto for Violoncello and
    Orchestra (1987)                                     25'
    solo vc; 2*222; 4000; timp+1, str                   MMB

STEARNS, PETER PINDAR    (1931-    )

First Little Symphony (1951)                    14'
    solo pf; str                                ACA

Concerto in G (1956)                            16'
    solo vln; str                               ACA

Fantasy for Strings (1956)                       6'
    str                                         ACA

Third Little Symphony (1956)                    12'
    1010; 0000; hpsd, str                       ACA

Aubade and Dance No. 2 (1957)                   NA
    solo ob; str                                ACA

Two Fantasy Pieces (1958)                       13'
    2222; 4331; perc, pf, str                   ACA

Hymn (1958)                                      8'
    solo vc; 2222; 4331; timp+1, str            ACA

Passacaglia (1958)                               5'
    3*3*3*3*; 4331; perc, str                   ACA

Reminiscence (1959)                              7'
    solo pf; str                                ACA

Symphony No. 5 (1961)                           22'
    3*3*3*3*; 4341; perc, str                   ACA

Theme and Variations (1961)                     10'
    1111; 1000; str                             ACA

Six Paintings of Claude Monet (1963)            10'
    3*3*3*3*; t sax; 4341; 3perc, pf, str       ACA

Symphony No. 6 (1966)                           16'
    3*23*2; t sax; 4321; euph; str              ACA

Becoming Perfectly One (1982)                    8'
    2121; 2100; timp+1, hp, str                 ACA

Symphony No. 7 (1983)                           26'
    2222; 4331; timp+1, hp, str                 ACA

The Piper at the Gates of Dawn (1984)           18'
    223*2; 3330; 2perc, hp, str                 ACA

Interlude (NA)                                            8'
    str                                                  ACA


        STEIN, LEON  (1910-    )

Concerto for Violin and Orchestra (1939)                28'
    solo vln; 2222; 4231; timp, str                     ACA

Sailor's Hornpipe (1945)                                 4'
    223*2; 4331; timp, hp, cel, str                     ACA

A Festive Overture (1950)                               10'
    3*222; 4331; timp, str                              FLE

Symphonic Movement (1950)                               12'
    3*24=2; 4331; timp, str                             ACA

Symphony No. 3 in A (1950-1951)                         40'
    3*3*4=3*; 4331; 3perc, str                          ACA

The Lord Reigneth (Psalm XCVII) (1953)                  18'
    solo t; satb cho; 2222; 3220; timp, str             ACA

Rhapsody for Flute, Harp and Strings (1954)             23'
    soli fl, hp; str                                    ACA

Adagio and Rondo Elegiaco (1957)                        11'
    2*222; 2210; timp+1, str                            FLE

Then Shall the Dust Return (1971)                       20'
    3*3*3*3*; 4331; timp+1, hp, str                     ACA

Symphony No. 4 (1974)                                   30'
    3*3*3*3*; 4331; timp+1, str                         ACA

Concerto for Violoncello and
    Orchestra (1977)                                    30'
    solo vc; 2222; 4230; timp+1, str                    ACA

Aria Hebraique (1984)                                    4'
    solo ob; str                                        ACA
    N.B.  Solo part may also be played by
    fl, cl, vln, or vla.


        STEINER, GITTA   (1932-1989)

Music for String Orchestra (1953)                        5'
    str                                                 SEE

Suite for Orchestra (1958)                              6'
   3*3*3*2; 4331; timp+1, str                          SEE

Tetrark (1965)                                          5'
   str                                                 SEE

Concerto for Piano and Orchestra (1967)                15'
   solo pf; 2222; 2220; perc, str                      SEE


            STEINKE, GREG  (1942-    )

Threnody (1963-1964)                                    7'
   3=3*3*3*; 4331; timp+2, hp, cel, str                SEE

Music for Bassoon and Orchestra (1967)                 10'
   solo bsn; 3=2*3=0; 4331; timp+3,                    SEE
   hp, cel, str

Sound Scape for Orchestra
   (1973; rev 1979, 1991)                              20'
   3*3*3*3*; 4331; timp+3, hp, pf/cel, str             TDM

Fantasy duo concertante (1978)                         12'
   soli vln, vc; 2222; 2221; timp+2, hp, str           TDM

Northwest Sketches IIb (1982)                          20'
   soli fl, ob; 1111; 2210; 2perc,                     TDM
   hp, cel, str

Oregon Coastal Sketches (1984; rev 1991)               12'
   solo vc; perc, hp, str                              TDM


            STEINOHRT, WILLIAM J.   (1937-    )

Derivatives (1968)                                     14'
   3*222; 4331; timp+1, str                            MS

Concerto for Piano and Orchestra (1971)                26'
   solo pf; 3*222; 4331; timp+1, str                   MS

Dance (1973)                                           18'
   solo perc; 3*222; 4331; timp+1, str                 MS

Music for Strings (1975)                               16'
   str                                                 MS

The Forgotten (1977)                                   18'
   3*2*3*2; 4331; timp+4, str                          MS

Celebration Overture (1980)                           8'
  3*3*3*3*; 4331; timp+4, hp, str              MS

Miniature Suite (1982)                               25'
  3*3*3*3*; 4331; timp+5, hp, str              MS

The Remembrance (1984)                               25'
  3*3*3*3*; 4331; timp+4, hp, str              MS


## STERN, ROBERT  (1934-    )

In Memoriam Abraham (1955)                            8'
  str                                          MS

Credo for Orchestra (1956)                           15'
  3*222; 4331; timp+2, pf, str                 MS

Finale from "Fort Union" - ballet (1958)              6'
  3*222; 4331; timp+5, hp, pf, str             MS

Grant Us Peace (An Orchestra Prayer) (1959)           8'
  2*2*2*2; 4231; timp, str                     MS

Symphony in One Movement (1961)                      19'
  3*222; 4221; timp+4, pf, str                 MS

Hazkarah (1962)                                      17'
  solo vc; 3*222; 4200; timp+5, hp,            MS
  pf, cel, str

Carom (1971)                                          8'
  2020; 2210; 2perc, str, tape                 MS

Yam Hamelach - The Dead Sea (1978)                   18'
  2222; 4321; timp+3, hp, pf/cel, str          MS


## STEVENS, HALSEY  (1908-1989)

A Green Mountain Overture (1948; rev 1953)            6'
  3*3*3*3*; 4331; timp, hp, pf, str            ACA

Symphony No. 1 (1950)                                17'
  3*3*3*3*; 4331; 2perc, hp, pf, str           ACA

Triskelion (1953)                                    20'
  2222; 4231; timp+1, hp, pf, str              ACA

Four Short Pieces (1954)                          7'
    1122; 2100; timp, str                         ACA

Adagio and Allegro (1955)                        15'
    str                                           ACA

The Ballad of William Sycamore (1955)            18'
    satb cho; 3*222; 4231; timp+1, hp, str        HG

Sinfonia Breve (1957)                            15'
    3*222; 4231; timp, hp, pf, cel, str           ACA

Five Pieces for Orchestra (1958)                 11'
    2*222; 4231; timp+4, str                      PS

Symphonic Dances (1958)                          15'
    3*3*3*3*; 4331; timp+1, 2hp, pf, cel, str     CFP

Magnificat (1962)                                10'
    satb cho; solo tpt; str                       MFM

Concerto for Violoncello and
    Orchestra (1964)                             18'
    solo vc; 3*3*3*3*; 4231; timp+1, hp, str      ACA

Threnos:  In Memoriam Quincy Porter (1968)        5'
    3*222; 4230; timp+1, str                      ACA

Concerto for Clarinet and
    String Orchestra (1969)                      19'
    solo cl; str                                  PS

Concerto for Viola and Orchestra (1976)          18'
    solo vla; 2222; 2200; str                     ACA


            STEWART, ROBERT   (1918-     )

Prelude for Strings (1959)                        6'
    str                                           ACA

Two Ricercari (1962)                              6'
    solo ww qnt; str                              ACA

Fantasia for Viola and Orchestra (1964)          10'
    solo vla; 1111; 1000; pf, str                 ACA

Concerto for Horn and Orchestra (1969)           14'
    solo hn; 1111; 0000; perc, pf, str            ACA

A Requiem for a Soldier (1969)                          13'
  3*2*3*3*; 4331; timp+2, str                           ACA

Violin Concerto (1970)                                  21'
  solo vln; 3*23*3*; 2231; timp+2, str                  ACA


              STILL, WILLIAM GRANT   (1895-1978)

Darker America (1926)                                   17'
  2222; 1110; timp+1, str                               CF

From the Black Belt (1926)                              20'
  213*1; 4331; timp+2, hp, cel, str                     CF

Afro-American Symphony (1930)                           28'
  3*3*3*2; 4331; timp+3, hp, cel, str                   NOV

Dismal Swamp (1936)                                     15'
  3*3*3*2; 4331; timp+2, hp, cel, str                   TP

Symphony in G minor (1937)                              25'
  3*3*3*2; 4331; timp+3, hp, cel, str                   WGS

Can'tcha Line 'Em (1940)                                10'
  2222; 2220; timp+1, str                               WGS

Old California (1941)                                    10'
  3*3*3*2; 4331; timp+2, hp, cel, str                   WGS

In Memoriam (1943)                                       6'
  3*3*3*2; 4331; timp+3, hp, str                        MCA

Pages from Negro History (1943)                         10'
  2222; 2220; timp+1, str                               CF

Poem for Orchestra (1944)                               15'
  3*3*3*2; 4331; timp+3, hp, cel, str                   MCA

Bells (1944)                                             7'
  3*3*3*2; 4331; timp+4, hp, pf ,cel, str               MCA

Festive Overture (1944)                                 10'
  3*3*3*2; 4331; timp+3, hp, cel, str                   WGS

Symphony No. 5 "Western Hemisphere" (1945)              28'
  3*3*3*2; 4331; timp+4, hp, cel, str                   WGS
  N.B.   Originally Symphony No. 3.

Archaic Ritual (1946)                                      20'
   3*3*3*2; 4331; timp+2, hp, cel, str                  WGS

Symphony No. 4 "Autochthonous" (1947)                      29'
   3*3*3*2; 4331; timp+3, hp, cel, str                  WGS

Wood Notes (1947)                                          27'
   2222; 2320; timp+1, hp, cel, str                     TP

Danzas de Panama (1948)                                    13'
   str                                                  TP

From a Lost Continent (1948)                               15'
   satb cho; 2222; 3220; timp+1, str                    WGS

A Psalm for the Living (1954)                              10'
   satb cho; 2222; 3200; timp, str                      BOU

Rhapsody (1955)                                            15'
   solo s; 3*3*3*2; 4331; timp+3,                       WGS
   hp, cel, str

Ennanga (1956)                                             15'
   solo hp; 3*3*3*2; 4331; timp+2, cel, str             WGS
   OR:  solo hp; str

The American Scene - Five Suites (1957)                    50'
   3*3*3*2; 4331; timp+3, hp, cel, str                  WGS

Little Red Schoolhouse (1957)                              17'
   narr; 2*2*2*2; 3321; timp+2, cel, str                TP

Symphony No. 3 "The Sunday Symphony" (1958)                25'
   3*3*3*2; 4331; timp+3, hp, cel, str                  WGS
   N.B.  Originally Symphony No. 5.

Patterns (1960)                                            15'
   2*222; 3321; timp+1, str                             WGS

The Peaceful Land (1960)                                   10'
   2222; 3221; hp, str                                  TP

Los alnados de España (1962)                               12'
   3*3*3*2; 4331; timp+3, hp, cel, str                  WGS

Preludes (1962)                                            12'
   solo fl; pf, str                                     WGS

Miniature Overture (1965)                                   2'
   3*3*3*2; 4331; timp+2, hp, cel, str                  WGS

Threnody in Memory of Jean Sibelius (1965)        4'
   2*222; 3221; timp+3, hp, str                   WGS

Choreographic Prelude (1970)                      5'
   solo fl; pf, str                              WGS


      STOCK, DAVID   (1939-      )

Divertimento (1958)                               8'
   3*222; 4331; timp+3, hp, str                   ACA

Capriccio (1963)                                  7'
   1111; 1100; str                                ACA

Symphony in One Movement (1963)                   15'
   3*3*3*3*; 4431; timp+3, str                    ACA

Inner Space (1973)                                15'
   3*222; 4331; timp+3, str                       MG

Triflumena (1978)                                 9'
   3*23*2; 4331; timp, str                        MG

Zohar (1978)                                      18'
   3*3*3*3*; 4331; perc, str                      MG

A Joyful Noise (1983)                             20'
   3*3*3*3*; 4431; timp+4, 2hp, 2kybd,            ACA
   elec gtr, str

American Accents (1984)                            9'
   2222; 2200; perc, str                          ACA

Back to Bass-ics (1985)                           4'
   str                                            ACA

On the Shoulders of Giants (1986)                 24'
   4*3*3*3*; 4441; timp+4, hp, pf, str            ACA

Rockin' Rondo (1987)                              6'
   3*3*3*3*; 4331; timp+3, str                    ACA

Tekiah (1987)                                     20'
   solo tpt/flu hn/picc tpt; 1111; 1010;          ACA
   perc, hp, pf, str

Fast Break (1988)                                 6'
   3*3*3*3*; 3331; timp+3, str                    ACA

STOKES, ERIC  (1930-    )

A Center Harbor Holiday (1963)                          15'
   solo pf; 2*222; 4231; timp+4, hp, str               HOR

Sonatas (1966)                                          11'
   str                                                 HOR

On the Badlands - Parables (1972)                      13'
   1*212; 2000; 2perc, pf, str, tape                   HOR

Five Verbs of Earth Encircled (1973)                   25'
   soli 7vln, 3vla, 2vc, db; narr;                     HOR
   1211; 2000

Lampyridae (1973)                                      var*
   Indeterminate instrumentation -                     HOR
   for 14 or more players with flashlight
   assistants; a theatre piece.
   *Duration ranges from 5' to infinity.

The Spirit of Place among the People (1977)             8'
   2*000; 0300; 2perc, str, audience                   HOR
   participation

Symphony - Book I (1979)                                30'
   2*22+2*; 4331; timp+3, hp, pf/cel, str              HOR

Symphony - Book II (1981)                               17'
   1212; 2110; 3perc, pf, str                          HOR

Concert Music for Piano and Orchestra (1982)           23'
   solo pf; 2221; 2221; timp+3, hp, cel, str           HOR

The Greenhouse Effect (1983)                            8'
   1010; a sax; 1000; 3perc,                           HOR
   str (1 or more of each)
   N.B.  May be performed as part of
   "Symphony - Book II."

Cotton Candy (1986)                                      5'
   2*222; 3331; 2perc, str                             HOR

Captions on the War Against Earth
   (Symphony III) (1989)                               14'
   3*23*2; 4331; timp+3, hp, pf, str                   HOR

Smoke and Steel (1989)                                 110'
   solo t; ttbb cho; str (no vlns)                     HOR

The Ghost Bus to El Dorado (1991)                           17'
    3*23*2; 4331; timp+3, hp, pf, str                       HOR

Native Dancer (1991)                                        23'
    3*23*2; 4331; timp+3, hp, pf, str                       HOR


                STOUT, ALAN   (1932-

Symphony No. 2 (1951-1966)                                  32'
    4=4*4=4*; s,t sax; 8441; timp+6, 2hp, pf,    CFP
    cel/hpsd, str

Nune Dimittis (1953)                                         4'
    solo bar; satb cho; flute; cymbals,          ACA
    org, str

Three Hymns (1953-1954)                                     13'
    22*2*2*; 4320; timp+4, cel, str               CFP

Aria for Tranquility (1954)                                  4'
    solo fl; perc, hp, cel, str                   ACA

Intermezzo (1954)                                            7'
    solo eh; 2tom-tom, cel, str                   CFP

Serenity (1957)                                              5'
    solo bsn (or vc); tam-tam, str                CFP

Christus Factus est (1962)                                   2'
    satb cho; str                                 ACA

Ecce, Agnus Dei (1962)                                      30'
    ssatbb cho; str                               ACA

Eight Movements for Violin and Orchestra
    (1962; rev 1966)                                        12'
    solo vln; 1*1*2*1; 2110; perc, pf, str        CFP

Exspecta Dominum (1962)                                      3'
    satb cho; str                                 ACA

George Lieder (1962)                                        11'
    solo bar; 2*2*2*2*; 1210; 3perc, hp,          CFP
    pf, cel, str

Improperium (1962)                                           3'
    ttbb cho; org, str                            ACA

Pater, si non potest (1962)                      2'
  ttbb cho; tam-tam, hp, cel, str              ACA

Per lignum servi facti sumus (1962)              2'
  satb cho; hp, str                            ACA

Symphony No. 4 (1970)                           28'
  sab cho; 4=4(eh, ob d'am)4=4; a sax;         CFP
  6441; timp+6, 2hp, pf, org, str

Elegiac Suite (1973)                            11'
  solo s; str                                  CHE

Passion (1975)                                 150'
  soli s, t, bar; ssaattbb cho; 3*3*3*3*;      CFP
  a,t sax; 6341; 2timp+8, 2hp, pf, cel,
  org, str

Ricercare and Aria (NA)                          5'
  str                                          CFP


              STRANDBERG, NEWTON   (1921-    )

Elegy for String Orchestra (1950)               12'
  str                                          MS

Shades Mountain (1951)                           9'
  2222; 4000; timp, cel, str                   MS

The Legend of Emmeline Labiche (1952)            6'
  str                                          MS

Suite for Trumpet and Strings (1953)            12'
  solo tpt; str                                MS

Concerto for Pianoforte and
  Chamber Orchestra (1955)                     18'
  solo pf; 1111; 2000; str                     MS

Canticle for Chorus and Orchestra (1959)        NA
  ssaattbb cho; 3*222; 4330; timp+2,           MS
  hp, str

Delie (1960)                                     6'
  solo mez (or coloratura); 0222; 0000;        MS
  perc, cel, str

Four Preludes for Orchestra (1961)              13'
  3*222; 4331; timp+4, pf, str                 MS

Essay for Strings (1966)                        9'
   str                                          MS

Sea of Tranquility (1969)                       10'
   pf (to be played by 3 percussionists);       MS
   2 string orchestras

Amenhotep No. 3 (1971)                          12'
   3*23*2; 4331; timp+4, str                    MS

Sarx (1973)                                     9'
   ttbb cho; 002*0; 4000; timp+3, pf,           MS
   cel, str

Trinete for Orchestra (1976)                    14'
   3(3picc)23*2; 4331; timp+4, hp, pf,          MS
   cel, str

The Last Summer (1977)                          10'
   2(2picc)22*2; 2200; perc, str                MS

Mists and Exaltations (1977)                    31'
   6(2picc, a fl)4*4*4*; 4441; timp+3,          MS
   hp, pf, cel, str

Acts for Orchestra (1979)                       8'
   solo mez; 2222; a sax; 2221; 3perc,          MS
   pf, cel, str

Kludge (1982)                                   var
   timp+2, jew's harp, glass harmonica, str     MS

Three Phases of a Jock (1982)                   7'
   3*222; 4331; 3perc, pf, str                  MS

Canticle No. 2 for Chorus and
   String Orchestra (1984)                      15'
   satb cho; str                                MS

In a Lunar Cavern... (1983)                     6'
   solo vv; perc, pf(3 players), str            MS

Fiesta (1989)                                   4'
   3*222; 4231; timp+3, str                     MS


        STRANG, GERALD  (1908-1983)

Symphony No. 1 (1942)                           25'
   3*3*3*3*; 4330; timp+3, hp, str              ACA

Symphony No. 2 (1947)                          30'
    3*3*3*3*; 4331; timp+1, str               ACA


        STREET, TISON   (1943-      )

Adagio (1977)                                  15'
    solo ob; str                              AMP

Montsalvat (1980)                              10'
    2222; 2220; timp+3, hp, str               AMP

Variations on a Ground (1981)                  28'
    3*2*2*3*; 0331; timp+3, str               AMP


        STRILKO, ANTHONY   (1941-      )

...From the Pickering Manuscript of
    William Blake (1989)                       12'
    solo s; 3*2*3*2; 4331; timp+3, hp,        NOA
    pf, cel, str


        STRUNK, STEVEN   (1943-      )

Spirit Lake Suite (1965)                       15'
    223*2; 4221; perc, hp, str                MS

Geometrics for Orchestra (1971)                19'
    3*222; 4211; 3perc, str                   MS

Transformations for Thirty
    Solo Strings (1971)                         6'
    str (10-8-6-5-4)                          MS

Orpheus (1976)                                 18'
    solo s, t; satb cho; 3*222; 4231; 2perc,  MS
    hp, 2pf, str

Concerto for Chamber Orchestra (1980)          10'
    1221; 2000; perc, hpsd, str               MS


        STUCKY, STEVEN   (1949-      )

Kenningar (Symphony No. 4) (1978)              21'
    3*3*3*3*; 4431; 5perc, hp, pf, cel, str   MER

Transparent Things:   In Memoriam V.N.  (1980)   9'
    3=222; 4331; 3perc, pf, cel, str             MER

Voyages (1984)                                   26'
    solo vc; 3*3*3*3*; 4331; 3perc, hp,          MER
    pf, cel, 2-4db

Double Concerto (1985)                           18'
    soli ob/ob d'am, vln; perc, pf,              MER
    str (3-3-3-2-1)

Dreamwaltzes (1986)                              15'
    3*3*3*3*; 4431; timp+3, hp, pf/cel, str      MER

Concerto for Orchestra (1987)                    28'
    3=3*3*3*; 4431; timp+3, hp, pf/cel, str      MER

Son et Lumiere (1988)                            9'
    3=3*4=3*; 4431; timp+4, hp, pf/cel, str      MER

Angelus (1989-1990)                              12'
    4=4*4=4*; 4431; 4perc, hp, pf/cel, str       MER

Impromptus (1989-1991)                           18'
    3*3*3*3; 4431; timp+3, hp, pf, str           MER


            SUBEN, JOEL ERIC  (1947-    )

Verses of Mourning (1973)                        8'
    2222; 2211; timp+1, pf, str                  ACA

Fantasia su un soggetto cavato (1977)            4'
    1001; a sax; 1111; 2perc, hp, pf,            ACA
    str (no vln 2)

Traeume auf Dichterhoehe (1978)                  6'
    solo hn; str                                 ANM

Concerto for Piano and Orchestra (1979)          17'
    solo pf; 3=3*3*3*; a sax; 4331; 3perc,       ANM
    hp, str

Academic Overture (1986)                         5'
    3*222; 2300; timp+1, str                     ACA

SUBOTNICK, MORTON  (1933-    )

Play! No. 2 (1964)                                          12'
    223*2; 3220; timp+2, str, tape                         MCA

Lamination No. 1 (1968)                                     NA
    3*3*3*2; 4221; timp+2, mand, str, tape                 MCA

Two Butterflies (1974)                                     14'
    solo perc; 1*2*3*2*; 3301; timp+1,                     EAM
    hp, str

Before the Butterfly (1975)                                20'
    soli tpt, tbn, perc, hp, vln,                          EAM
    vla, vc (all amp); 2221*; 3211;
    timp+4, cel, str

Place (1978)                                               20'
    3*3*3*3*; 5331; timp+3, hp, cel,                       EAM
    mand, str

Axolotl (1982)                                             17'
    solo vc; 1020; 0020; 2perc, hp, pf,                    EAM
    str (0-0-0-8-4)

In Two Worlds (Saxophone Concerto) (1987)                  35'
    solo a sax/Yamaha WX-7 computerized wind               EAM
    controller; 2*22*3*; 4221; perc, xyl, hp, str

A Desert Flowers (1989)                                    25'
    1011; 1111; perc, mar, pf, str, computer               EAM


SUDERBURG, ROBERT  (1936-    )

Cantata I (1962)                                           18'
    solo s; 1111; 1110; 2perc, pf,                         TP
    str (1-1-1-1)

Orchestra Music I (1969)                                   30'
    4=4*5=4*; 6441; timp+3, 2hp, pf, str                   TP

Show (1970)                                                50'
    3*3*3*3; 4331; timp+1, hp, pf, str                     TP

Winds/Vents (1973)                                         20'
    3*3*3*3*; 4331; perc, hp, str                          TP

Concerto "Within the Mirror of Time" (1974)               26'
    solo pf; 3*3*3*3*; 4331; timp+3, hp, str               TP

Concerto for Solo Percussionist and
   Orchestra (1977)                  19'
   solo perc; 4*3*4*3*; 4331; timp+2,   TP
   hp, str

Concerto: Voyage de nuit
   d'apres Baudelaire (1978)         24'
   solo v; 1111; 2000; str        TP

Concerto for Harp and Orchestra (1981)   25'
   solo hp; 4*3*3*3*; 4331; timp+3, str   TP


      SULLIVAN, TIMOTHY  (1939-   )

Paths (1977)                   20'
   2222; 4220; timp+3, hp, pf, str   MS

In Contemplation of Endurance (1982)   21'
   1211; 2000; timp+2, hp, str      MS

Sky Wood (1989)               14'
   solo s; satb cho (opt); 1110; 0000;   MS
   perc/vib, str


      SURINACH, CARLOS  (1915-   )

Ritmo Jondo - flamenco (1953)      20'
   1*1*11; 1110; timp+2, str      AMP

Sinfonia flamenca (1953)         12'
   2*2*22; 4231; timp+1, hp, str   AMP

Fandango (1954)               8'
   3*3*3*2; 4331; timp+3, hp, str   AMP

Concertino (1956)            18'
   solo pf; perc, str          AMP

Feria magica - overture (1956)     6'
   2*222; 4231; timp+2, hp, str    AMP

Madrid 1890 (1956)           9'
   1*111; 1100; timp+1, str     BRO

Sinfonia chica (1957)          16'
   2222; 2100; timp+1, str      AMP

Tres Cantares (1958)                                        8'
    solo s; 3*3*22; 4200; timp+1, hp, str              DSH

Embattled Garden - ballet (1958)                          14'
    1*1*11; 1110; timp+2, hp, str                      AMP

Romance, Oracion y Soeta (1958)                           10'
    solo s; 2222; 4200; timp+1, hp, str                DSH

Concerto for Orchestra (1959)                             16'
    3*3*3*2; 4331; timp+1, str                         DSH

Acrobats of God - ballet (1960)                           20'
    3*3*3*3*; 4331; timp+2, hp, 3mand, str             AMP
    OR:  1*1*11; 1111; timp+1, 3mand, str

David and Bath-sheba - ballet (1960)                      23'
    2200; 2200; timp+2, pf, str                        AMP

Feast of Ashes - ballet (1962)                            35'
    soli vln, pf; 1*1*11; 1110; timp+2, str            AMP

Symphonic Variations (1962)                               15'
    3*3*3*3*; 4331; timp+3, pf, str                    CFP

Drama jondo - overture (1965)                              8'
    3*3*3*2; 4331; timp+3, hp, str                     AMP

Los Renegados - ballet (1965)                             31'
    1*1*11; 1111; timp+2, pf, str                      AMP

Melorhythmic Dramas (1966)                                20'
    3*3*3*3*; 4331; timp+3, hp, cel, str               AMP

Venta Quemada - ballet (1966)                             38'
    1*1*11; 1211; timp+2, hp, str                      AMP

Agathe's Tale - ballet (1967)                             23'
    1*1*10; 0100; perc, str                            AMP

The Missions of San Antonio (1969)                        20'
    23*3*3*; 4331; timp+3, hp, str                     AMP

Suite Espagnole - ballet (1970)                           18'
    2*111; 2111; timp+2, pf, str                       AMP

Concerto for Piano and Orchestra (1973)                   23'
    solo pf; 3*3*3*3*; 4331; timp+3, str               AMP

Las Trompetas de los Serafins -
   overture (1973)                                9'
   3*3*3*3*; 4431; timp+3, hp, str               AMP

Concerto for Harp and Orchestra (1978)         22'
   solo hp; 2*12*1; 2220; timp+1, str            AMP

Concerto for String Orchestra (1978)           25'
   str                                           AMP

The Owl and the Pussycat - ballet (1978)       23'
   narr; 2*1*21; 2220; timp+2, hp,               AMP
   clavinet, str

Bodas de Sangre (Blood Wedding) -
   ballet (1979)                                 45'
   1*1*2*1; 1210; timp+1, pf, str                AMP

Concerto for Violin and Orchestra (1980)       25'
   solo vln; 2*1*2*1; 2220; timp+4, hp, str      AMP

Symphony No. 2 (NA)                            28'
   3*3*3*2; 4331; timp+4, str                    EME


      SUSA, CONRAD (1935-      )

Pastorale (1959)                               11'
   str                                           ECS

Eulogy (1960)                                   7'
   str                                           ECS

Serenade No. 1 (1961)                           8'
   unis male cho; 6fl; str                       ECS

Symphony in One Movement (1962)                25'
   3*3*3*3*; 4431; timp+1, cel, str              ECS

Love-In (After Handel) (1967)                  38'
   2202; 2220; timp+1, hp, hpsd, 2mand,          ECS
   3gtr, str

I am the Way (1985)                             5'
   soli s, a, t, b; satb cho; 0301; 0000;        ECS
   hp, org, str

Two Motets: Sing to the Lord (1985)             6'
   soli s, a, t, b; satb cho; 0301; 0000;        ECS
   hp, org, str

Baghdad-by-the-Bay (1987)                              10'
   satb cho; 2222; 4331; timp+1, hp, str           ECS

Three Mystical Carols (1987)                           10'
   satb cho; 2222; 4331; timp+1, hp, str           ECS

A Christmas Garland (1988)                             13'
   satb cho; 1111; 2310; timp+1, hp,              ECS
   pf, org, str
   N.B.  Requires audience participation.

Even-Song (1988)                                       5'
   satb cho; org, str                             ECS

The Chanticleer's Carol (1989)                         6'
   2 ttbb cho (or ssaattbb cho); 1200;            ECS
   2100; perc, hp, str

A Christmas Garland (1991)                             13'
   satb cho; 2222; 4331; timp+1, hp, pf, str  ECS
   N.B.  Requires audience participation.


          SVOBODA, TOMAS  (1939-      )

Scherzo for Two Euphoniums and Orchestra,
   op. 8 (1955)                                        19'
   solo 2euph; 3*222; 0000; timp+1, str            STA

Symphony No. 1, op. 20 (1956-1957; rev 1984)  36'
   3*23*2; 4341; timp+3, pf, str                   STA

In a Linden's Shadow, op. 25 (1958)                    55'
   4*3*4=4*; 6331; timp+5, hp, 2pf, org, str  STA

Dramatic Overture, op. 26 (1959)                       10'
   3*23*2; 4441; timp+3, str                       STA

Suite for Mezzo-soprano and Orchestra,
   op. 30 (1961)                                       24'
   solo mez; 3*2*4*4*; 4222; timp+4, pf, str  STA

Six Variations for Violin and String
   Orchestra, op. 32 (1961)                            NA
   solo vln; str                                   STA

Christmas Concerto, op. 34 (1961)                      13'
   solo hp; 2222; 2000; str                        STA

Suite for Bassoon, Harpsichord and String
   Orchestra, op. 39 (1962)                              13'
   soli bsn, hpsd; str                                   STA

Etude, op. 40 (1963)                                     NA
   1121; s sax; 0000; 2perc, pf,                         STA
   str (2-1-0-1)

Symphony No. 2, op.41 (1963-1964)                        28'
   4*23*2; 4341; timp+4, pf, str                         STA

Symphony No. 3, op. 43 (1965)                            28'
   3*25=2; a sax; 4341; timp+6, pf, org, str             STA
   N.B. Solo parts are written for a string
   quintet.

Three Pieces for Orchestra, op. 45 (1966)                10'
   3*222; 4231; timp+2, str                             STA

Folk Dance for String Quartet and
   String Orchestra, op. 37a (1967)                      3'
   solo str qt; str                                      STA

Reflections, op. 53 (1968)                               25'
   4*3*4=3*; 4340; timp+6, pf, str                       STA

Sinfonietta, op. 60 (1972)                               20'
   3*222; 4331; timp+4, str                             STA

Child's Dream - cantata, op. 66 (1973)                   11'
   satb cho; 3*222; 4230; timp+5,                       STA
   pf, cel, str

Prelude and Fugue, op. 67 (1974)                         9'
   str                                                   STA

Piano Concerto, op. 71 (1974)                            18'
   solo pf; 1111; 1100; timp, str                       STA

Symphony No. 4, op. 69 (1975)                            27'
   3*24=2; a sax; 4341; timp+7, hp, cel, str            STA

Violin Concerto, op. 77 (1975)                           19'
   solo vln; 2222; 2230; timp, str                      STA

Overture of the Season, op. 89 (1978)                    10'
   3*222; 4331; timp+2, str                             STA

Symphony No. 5, op. 92 (1979)                            33'
   4*3*4=2; 4331; timp+5, hp, pf, str                   STA

Nocturne, op. 100 (1981)                          20'
    3*222; 4331; timp+2, hp, gtr, str            STA

Eugene Overture, op. 103 (1982)                    9'
    3*222; 4441; timp+5, str                     STA

Ex Libris, op. 113 (1983)                          8'
    3*23*3*; 4341; timp+4, str                   STA

Serenade, op. 115 (1984)                           7'
    3*222; 4331; timp+4, str                     STA

Journey - cantata, op. 127 (1984)                 24'
    soli mez, bar; satb cho; 2222; a sax;        STA
    4331; timp+5, str

Concerto for Chamber Orchestra,
    op. 125 (1986)                                23'
    solo s; 1111; 0000; perc, hp, str            STA

Dance Suite, op. 128 (1987)                        23'
    3*222; 4231; timp+2, str                     STA

Piano Concerto No. 2, op. 132 (1989)              30'
    solo pf; 3*222; 4331; timp+4, str            STA


                SWAFFORD, JAN   (1946-    )

Passage (1975)                                    11'
    solo picc; 4perc, str                        MS

After Spring Rain (1982)                          19'
    3*23*2; 4331; hp, str                        PS

Chamber Sinfonietta (1988)                        15'
    1*11*1; 1110; perc, hp, pf, str              PS

Landscape with Traveler (NA)                      17'
    2*333*; 4431; 4perc, str                     PS


            SWANSON, HOWARD   (1907-1978)

Symphony No. 1 (1945)                             25'
    2*221; 4221; perc, str                       EWM

Short Symphony (1948)                             11'
    2*222; 2210; timp, str                       EWM

Night Music (1950)                                            9'
    1111; 1000; str                                          EWM

Songs for Patricia (1951)                                   14'
    solo s; str                                              EWM

Music for Strings (1952)                                    10'
    str                                                      EWM

Concerto for Orchestra (1954)                               23'
    2202; 4231; str                                          EWM

Fantasy Piece (1969)                                         8'
    solo s sax; str                                          EWM

Symphony No. 3 (1970)                                       25'
    3*3*3*2*; 4331; perc, str                                EWM


            SWEIDEL, MARTIN

Hyperion (1980)                                             12'
    223*2; 2221; 3perc, str                                  NOR


        SWIFT, RICHARD  (1927-      )

Divertimento (1950)                                          9'
    1111; 1100; str                                          MS

A Coronal (1954)                                            11'
    2222; 2221; timp+1, pf, str                              MS

Extravaganza (1962)                                        12'
    3*3*3*2; 4231; 3perc, hp, pf/cel, str                    TP

Concerto for Violin and
    Chamber Orchestra (1968)                                16'
    solo vln; 1111; 1110; hp, cel,                           MS
    mand, str (0-0-2-1)

Symphony (1970)                                            15'
    2222; 2220; 2perc, pf/cel, str                           MS

Specimen Day (1977)                                        45'
    solo s; 2111; 2110; 2perc, hp, cel, str                  MS

Some Trees (1982)                                           9'
    2111; 1110; perc, pf, str                                MS

Roses Only (1991)                                        15'
  solo mez; 1111; 1110; perc, mar, str           MS


     SWISHER, GLORIA   (1935-    )

Two Lyric Pieces (1958)                                   8'
  2222; 4220; perc, str                          MS

Concerto for Clarinet and Orchestra (1960)               19'
  solo cl; 2203*; 4331; timp+1, str              AMC

Caneion (1964)                                            5'
  solo fl; 2222; 2220; str                       AMC

Yuki no Niigata (1968)                                    6'
  2222; 3000; timp+2, str                        AMC

Niigata no Sumie (1984)                                  12'
  2222; 2200; perc, str                          AMC

Serafina; An Orchestral Portrait (1987)                  15'
  3*3*3*2; 4341; timp+7, pf, str                 AMC


     SYDEMAN, WILLIAM   (1928-    )

Concertino for Oboe, Piano and
  String Orchestra (1956)                        10'
  soli ob, pf; str                               SEE

Orchestral Abstractions (1958)                           15'
  2222; 4331; timp+1, pf, cel, str               CFP

Concertpiece for Horn and
  String Orchestra (1959)                        10'
  solo hn; str                                   SEE

Largo for Violoncello and
  String Orchestra (1959)                         6'
  solo vc; str                                   SEE

Study No. 1 for Orchestra (1959)                         11'
  2222; 4321; timp+1, pf, str                    SEE

Concertpiece (1960)                                      25'
  1111; 2100; pf, str                            SEE

Study No. 2 for Orchestra (1963)                         10'
  2222; 4331; timp+1, pf, str                    SEE

Oecumenicus:    Concerto for Orchestra (1964)      55'
    4*4*4=3*; 8442; timp+5, str                    SEE
    N.B.  The orchestra is divided into
    two antiphonal groups; a second conductor
    is required for performance.

Study No. 3 for Orchestra (1965)                   15'
    3*3*3*3*; 6331; timp+4, str                    AMP

In Memoriam: John Fitzgerald Kennedy (1966)        27'
    narr; 3*3*3*3*; 4331; timp+4, pf,              AMP
    cel, str
    N.B.  There is a solo for the principal violist.

Concerto for Piano Four-Hands and
    Orchestra (1967)                               NA
    solo pf(4-hands); 2111; 0000; timp+1, str      ION

Texture Studies (1969)                             20'
    3*3*3*3*; 4331; timp+3, str                    SEE

Prometheus - cantata (NA)                          22'
    soli t, bar, b; ssaa cho; 2222; 2331;          CFP
    timp+1, hp, pf, str

TALMA, LOUISE   (1906-    )

Dialogues for Piano and Orchestra
    (1963-1964)                                    21'
    solo pf; 3*222; 4331; timp+2, str             CF

The Tolling Bell (1967-1969)                       18'
    solo bar; satb cho; 223*3*; 4331;             CF
    timp+2, hp, str

Celebration (1976-1977)                            10'
    ssaa cho; 2*111; 2100; perc, pf, str          CFP


TANENBAUM, ELIAS   (1924-    )

Concertante No. 1 (1954)                           14'
    2223*; 4331; timp+1, hp, str                  ACA

Symphony No. 1 in One Movement (1955)              16'
    3*222; 4011; timp+1, str                      ACA

Concertante No. 2 (1957)                           14'
    3*3*3*2; 4331; timp+1, str                    ACA

Variations for Orchestra (1958)                    23'
    23*3(a sax)3*; 4331; timp+1, hp, str          ACA

The Last of the Just (1967)                        26'
    ssaattbb cho; 23*3*3*; 4441;                  ACA
    timp+3, hp, str

Parallel Worlds (1979)                             14'
    2222; 4331; 4perc, hp, str, tape              ACA

Birthday Waves (1983)                              1'
    2222; 4331; 2perc, str                        ACA

Waves (1983)                                       20'
    solo gtr; 23*3*3; 4331; perc, hp, str         ACA

Kaleidoscope (1986)                                18'
    str; tape                                     ACA

Columbus (1991)                                    27'
    3*3*3*3*; 4331; timp+5, hp, str, tape         ACA

TANN, HILARY (1947-    )

as ferns (1977)                                    9'
  str (no db)                           OXF

The Open Field (1989)                             11'
  3*222; 4331; timp+3, str               OXF


TAUB, BRUCE J.  (1948-    )

Six Pieces for Orchestra (1971)                   25'
  3*3*3*3*; 4331; timp+5, 2hp, pf, str    ACA

Ballet (1974)                                     30'
  2022; 0221; 2perc, 2pf, str            ACA

Octet (California Music II) (1977)                19'
  str                                    ACA

Chromatic Fantasy (1983)                          11'
  4=3*4=2*; a,t,bar sax; 4431; timp+3,    CFP
  pf/cel, str

Of the Wing of Madness (1985)                     10'
  1111; 1110; 2-4perc,                   CFP
  str (solo or section)

Gridlock (1986)                                   12'
  3*3*3*3*; 4331; timp+3, hp, pf, str     ACA

An Often Fatal Malady (1990)                      18'
  1111; 1110; 2-4perc,                   CFP
  str (solo or section)


TAUTENHAHN, GUNTHER  (1938-    )

Concerto for Double Bass and
  Orchestra (1968)                        30'
  solo db; 2222; 2110; timp+1, hp, str    SEE

Prelude for Chamber Orchestra (1968)               5'
  2221; 2211; 2perc, hp, str             SEE

Symphonic Sounds No. 1 (1972)                     15'
  3*3*3*3*; 3221; timp+3, hp, pf, str     SEE

Symphonic Sounds No. 2 (1973)                     12'
  3*23*2; 3321; timp+3, hp, str          SEE

Chromatic Square (1978)                               3'
  3*3*23*; 5421; perc, hp, pf, str                   SEE

Concept, Three (1978)                                26'
  3*3*3*3*; 6331; timp+1, hp, pf, str                SEE

Concerto for Alto Saxophone and
  Orchestra (1978)                                   25'
  solo a sax; 3*3*23*; 6331; 4perc, hp,              SEE
  pf, str

Numeric Serenade (1978)                               9'
  solo pf; 2223*; 4211; timp+1, hp, str              SEE

Concerto for Violin and Orchestra (1979)             23'
  solo vln; 3*3*3*3*; 4331; timp+2, hp, str          SEE


           TAXIN, IRA   (1950-    )

Saba (1974)                                          20'
  3*3*3*3*; 4331; timp+2, hp, pf, str                MER

Fanfares and Dialogues (1976)                        14'
  3*3*3*3*; 4431; timp+3, hp, pf/cel, str            MER

Concerto for Brass Quintet and
  Orchestra (1981)                                   25'
  solo br qnt; 3*3*3*3*; 4331; timp+3, hp,            MER
  pf, str

Trumpet Concerto (1985)                              25'
  solo tpt; 4*4*4+4*; 4031; timp+3, hp,              MER
  pf, str


           TAYLOR, CLIFFORD   (1923-1987)

Introduction and Dance Fantasy (1955)                10'
  3*3*3*3; 4331; timp+2, str                         ACA

Theme and Variations (1955)                          14'
  3*3*3*3*; 4331; timp+3, pf, str                    ACA

Concerto Grosso (1957)                               13'
  str                                                ACA

Chaconne (1958)                                       9'
  3*3*3*3*; 4331; timp, str                          ACA

Symphony No. 1 (1958)                                    33'
  2222; 4230; timp+2, str                      ACA

Ballade de bon conseyl (1959)                            8'
  ssa cho (or ttb cho); 2222; 4221; timp+1,    ACA
  hp, str

Commencement Suite Processional (1959)                   15'
  str                                           ACA

Processional (1959)                                      7'
  2222; 4221; timp+1, hp, str                  ACA

Sacred Verses (1962)                                     21'
  soli 2vv; satb cho; 223*3*; 4231; timp+3,     ACA
  hp, str

Concerto for Organ (1963)                                14'
  solo org; 1210; 1111; timp+2, str            ACA

Symphony No. 2 (1965)                                    22'
  3*3*3*3*; 4331; timp+5, 2hp, str             ACA

Concerto No. 2 (1977)                                    10'
  soli vln, vla; str                           ACA

Concerto No. 3 (1978)                                    14'
  soli vln, vla; str                           ACA

Symphony No. 3 (1980)                                    23'
  3*3*4=2; 4231; 4perc, hp, cel, str           ACA

Concerto for Bass Clarinet and
  Orchestra (1983)                              15'
  solo b cl; 3*3*23; 4320; timp, hp, str       ACA


THOMAS, ANDREW   (1939-      )

Metanoia (1982)                                          28'
  1111; 1110; perc, hp, str                    ACA

Concerto for Marimba and Orchestra
  "Loving Mad Tom" (1990)                       30'
  solo mar; 2*222; 4231; timp+1, str           ACA

Four Scenes from the Summer Palace (1990)                20'
  1111; 2110; perc, str                        ACA

## THOMAS, AUGUSTA REED   (1964-     )

Glass Moon (1988)                                                11'
  3*23*2; 4331; 4perc, hp, pf, str                              TP

Echoes (1989)                                                   10'
  1111; 1110; 2perc, pf, str                                    TP

Wind Dance (1989)                                              16'
  3*3*3*3*; 4331; 4perc, 2hp, pf,                               TP
  str (16-14-12-10-8)

Haiku (1990)                                                   20'
  solo vln, vc; 1121; 1100; 2perc, str                         TP

Ritual, An Overture-Concertante (1990)                          8'
  3*3*3*2; 4331; 4perc, hp, pf, str                            TP

Vigil (1990)                                                   12'
  2222; 2210; 2perc, hp, pf, str                               TP

Cathedral Summer (1991)                                       22'
  solo vln; 2222; 2220; hp, pf, str                            TP

Trinity - Triple Concerto (1991)                              25'
  soli fl, hp, vla; 3*3*3*3*; 4331; 4perc,                     TP
  pf, str


## THOMAS, DAVID EVAN   (1958-     )

Concerto for Oboe and Chamber
  Orchestra (1988)                                             21'
  solo ob; 2*1*2*1; 121(b tbn)0;                               NOA
  timp+1, str


## THOMAS, MARILYN TAFT   (1943-     )

Concert Piece (1980)                                            9'
  1111; 1100; pf, str                                          CF

Disparities (1982)                                             14'
  1*001; 0110; pf/cel, str (1-1-1-1), tape                     MS

Soundscapes (1983)                                             12'
  2222; 4330; timp+2, hp, pf, cel, str                         CF

Nuclear Winter (1984)                                         18'
  2222; 4220; timp+2, str (6-4-4-2)                            MS

## THOME, DIANE (1942-    )

The Golden Messengers (1985)                        13'
   3*3*3*3*; 4331; timp+3, hp, pf, cel, str    MS

Lucent Flowers (1988)                               16'
   solo s; 2222; 2220; perc, hp, pf, str       MS

Indra's Net (1989)                                  18'
   3*3*3*3*; 4331; timp+3, hp, pf, str          MS

The Ruins of the Heart (1990)                       18'
   solo s; 2222; 2220; timp+2, hp, pf, str      MS


## THOMPSON, RANDALL (1899-1984)

Symphony No. 1 (1929)                               24'
   3*3*3*3*; 4331; timp+2, hp, prg, str         CF

Symphony No. 2 (1931)                               28'
   3*3*3*3*; 4331; timp+2, str                  CF

Symphony No. 3 (1947-1949)                          29'
   3*3*23*; 4331; timp+3, str                   CF

The Last Words of David (1949)                       5'
   satb cho; 3*3*3*3*; 4331; timp+3, hp, str   ECS

A Trip to Nahant - symphonic fantasy
   (1953-1954)                                  26'
   2222; 4230; 2perc, hp, cel, str              CF

Ode to the Virginia Voyage (1956-1957)              32'
   satb cho; 2*222; 4231; timp+3, hp, str      ECS

The Passion Acording to St. Luke - oratorio
   (1964-1965)                                  40'
   soli t, bar; satb cho; 2222; 4230;          ECS
   timp+2, hp, str

Frostiana (1965)                                    25'
   satb cho; 2222; 4100; perc, hp, str         ECS

A Psalm of Thanksgiving - cantata (1967)            12'
   satb cho; children's cho; 2222; 4230;       ECS
   timp, str

The Place of the Blest - cantata (1969)             10'
   ssaa cho; 2222; 2000; hp, str               ECS

A Hymn for Scholars and Pulpits (1973)                    8'
    satb cho; 2222; 2220; org, str                        ECS

A Concord Cantata (1975)                                  20'
    satb cho; 2222; 4231; timp+1, str                     ECS


            THOMSON, VIRGIL   (1896-1989)

The Plow that Broke the Plains (1937)                     15'
    11*2*2; a sax; 2220; timp+2, gtr/bj, str              GS

Eight Portraits (1940-1945)                               29'
    3*222; 4231; perc, str                                GS

Cantabile -
    Portrait of Nicolas de Chatelin (1944)                5'
    str                                                   GS

Fugue and Chorale on Yankee Doodle -
    suite (1945)                                          5'
    2131; 2320; timp+1, str                               GS

The Seine at Night (1947)                                 8'
    3*3*3*3*; 4331; timp+1, hp, cel, str                  GS

Acadian Songs and Dances (1948)                           15'
    2*2*2*2; 2220; 2perc, hp, acc, str                    GS

Louisiana Story - suite (1948)                            18'
    2222; 4231; timp+2, hp, str                           GS

Wheat Field at Noon (1948)                                6'
    3*3*3*3*; 4330; perc, hp, str                         GS

Hymns (1949)                                              5'
    22*2*2; 4210; perc, hp, pf, str                       GS

Suite from "The Mother of Us All" (1949)                  18'
    22*2*2; 4210; timp+1, hp, pf, str                     GS

Concerto for Violoncello and
    Orchestra (1950)                                      21'
    solo vc; 2223; 4200; 3perc, hp, cel, str              BEL

Tango Lullaby (1950)                                      3'
    1*111; 0000; bells, str                               MRC

Five Songs from William Blake (1951)                      18'
    solo bar; 2*222; 4231; timp+4, hp, str                PS

Sea Piece with Birds (1952)                              5'
   3*3*3*3*; 4330; perc, hp, str                      GS

Concerto for Flute, Strings, Harp
   and Percussion (1954)                              13'
   solo fl; 2perc, 2hp, cel, str                      FC

Collected Poems (1959)                                   7'
   soli s, bar; 1111; 0010; 3perc, pf, str            PS

Fugues and Cantilenas -
   suite from film "Power Among Men" (1959)           18'
   2*2*22; 4231; timp+2, hp, str                      BH

Missa pro defunctis (Requiem Mass) (1960)                45'
   satb cho; 2*3*3*3; 4331; timp+4, hp,               TP
   cel, str

Crossing Brooklyn Ferry (1961)                           8'
   ssatb cho; 22*22; 4330; timp+2, hp, str            BH

Dance in Praise (1962)                                   9'
   2222; 2000; 3perc, pf, str                         GS

Mass for Solo Voice (1962)                               14'
   solo v (or unis cho); 2*2*2*2; 2210;               GS
   perc, hp, str

A Solemn Music and a Joyful Fugue (1962)                 12'
   3*3*3*3*; 4331; timp+1, str                        GS

Autumn: Concertino for Harp, Strings
   and Percussion (1964)                              10'
   solo hp; perc, str                                 GS

The Feast of Love (1964)                                 8'
   solo bar; 1121; 0000; perc, hp, str                GS

Pilgrims and Pioneers - suite from film
   "Journey to America" (1964)                        10'
   11*2*1; 4200; perc, str                            GS

Fantasy
   (In Homage to an Earlier England) (1966)           12'
   2222; 4230; 2perc, str                             BH

The Nativity as Sung by Shepherds
   (1966-1967)                                        7'
   soli a, t, bar; satb cho; 2222; 2200;              GS
   perc, org, str

From Byron's "Don Juan" (1967)                      14'
   solo t; 4*4*4*4; 4441; 2perc, hp, pf, str       PS

Symphony No. 3 (1972)                               20'
   2222; 4231; timp+2, hp, str                      BH

Cantata on Poems of Edward Lear (1974)              21'
   soli s, bar; satb cho; 2*2*2*2; 4230;            GS
   timp+1, pf, str

Thoughts for Strings (1981)                         4'
   str                                              BH

Eleven Portraits for Orchestra (1982)              14'
   23*3*2; 4230; 2perc, hp, str                     BH

Four Saints:  An Olio for Chamber
   Orchestra (1982)                                 20'
   2*2*22; 2110; 3perc, acc, str (2-1-1-1)          GS


              THORNE, FRANCIS   (1922-    )

Symphony No. 1 (1960)                               17'
   3*3*3*3*; 4331; timp+1, str                      EBM

Fantasia (1961)                                      9'
   str                                              ACA

Elegy for Orchestra (1962)                          13'
   2*2*2*2; 4231; timp+2, hp, str                   TP

Burlesque Overture (1963-1964)                       9'
   22*22; 4331; mechanical timp+2, pf, str          TP

Symphony No. 2 (1964)                               24'
   3*3*3*3*; 4331; timp+1, hp, pf, str              ACA

Rhapsodic Variations (1964-1965)                    12'
   solo pf; 2222; 2220; timp+1, str                 ACA

Concerto for Piano and Orchestra (1965-1966)        28'
   solo pf; 3*3*3*3*; 4331; timp+2, hp, str         JC

Lyric Variations I (1966-1967)                      23'
   3*3*3*3*; 4331; perc, hp, str                    ACA

Double Concerto for Viola, Double Bass
   and Orchestra (1968)                             20'
   soli vla, db; 2222; 4220; timp+2, str            ACA

Sonar Plexus (1968)                                    6'
    2020; 4230; timp+2, elec gtr, str (no db)   ACA

Song of the Carolina Low Country (1968)        15'
    satb cho; 2121; 2220; timp+3, str           ACA

Symphony in One Movement (1968)                17'
    3*3*3*3*; 4631; timp+1, hp, pf, str         ACA

Liebesrock (1969)                              12'
    0000; 4331; timp+1, hp, pf, elec gtr,       ACA
    b gtr, str

Symphony No. 3 (1969)                          25'
    timp, hp, pf, str                           AMP

Fanfare, Fugue and Fast Four (1972)            11'
    soli 3tpt; 2222; 3030; timp+3,              ACA
    elec gtr, str

Concerto for Violin and Orchestra (1975)       23'
    solo vln; 2222; 2220; timp+2, str           ACA

Symphony No. 4 (Waterloo Bridge) (1977)        30'
    solo tpt; 2222; 4131; 2perc, hp,            ACA
    tack pf, str

Divertimento No. 1 (1979)                      17'
    solo fl; str                                AMP

The Eternal Light (1979)                       21'
    solo s (or t); 2222; 4231; timp+1,          TP
    hp, str

Gems from Spoon River (1980)                   8'
    3*222; 4231; timp+2, tack pf, bj, str       ACA

Lyric Variations V (1981)                      20'
    2222; 4231; timp+2, hp, pf, str             ACA

Divertimento No. 2 (1982)                      17'
    solo bsn; str                               AMP

Praise and Thanksgiving (1983)                 18'
    satb cho; 1*1*00; 4331; timp+1, str         AMP

Pop Partita (1984)                             17'
    2222; 4331; timp+2, pf, str                 ACA

Symphony No. 5 (1984)                               22'
    3*3*3*3*; 4331; mechanical timp, hp,            AMP
    pf, str

Concerto Concertante (1985)                         18'
    soli fl, cl, vln, vc; 0202; 2230; timp+2,       ACA
    hp, str

Humoresque (1985)                                    9'
    2222; 4231; timp+2, hp, pf, str                 ACA

Rhapsodic Variations No. 3 (1986)                   15'
    solo ob; str                                    ACA

Piano Concerto No. 3 (1989)                         23'
    solo pf; 2222; 4231; timp+1, hp, str            TP

Quartessence (NA)                                   21'
    soli vib, dmst, pf, db; 0003; 4330;             MJQ
    perc, str


            THORNE, NICHOLAS  (1953-      )

The Voices of Spring, op. 6 (1978)                   6'
    3*222; 4221; timp, pf, str                      AMP

Symphony from Silence (A Piano Symphony),
    op. 17 (1982)                                   33'
    4=3*3*3*; 4331; 2timp+2, pf, str                MG

Chaconne:   Passion of the Heart,
    op. 18 (1982)                                   17'
    1=2*12; 2100; timp, pf, str (6-6-4-4-2)         MG

Symphony No. 2:  A Symphony of Light (1984)         25'
    3*3*3*3*; 4331; timp+3, pf/cel, str             AMP

Eight Movements for Orchestra, op. 22 (1985)        14'
    2222; 4221; 2perc, pf, str                      AMP

Revelations (1987)                                  20'
    2222; 421(b tbn)0; timp+2, pf, str              AMP

Songs of Darkness, Power and Radiance (1987)        18'
    solo tbn; 2*2*22; 2200; timp+1, pf, str         AMP

TICHELI, FRANK  (1958-    )

Images of a Storm (1983)                              10'
  3*3*3*3*; a sax; 4331; timp+3, hp,                 MS
  cel, str

Concerto for Trumpet and Orchestra (1990)            17'
  solo tpt; 2222; 2210; timp+1, str                  MS


TILLIS, FREDERICK  (1930-    )

Designs for Orchestra I and II (1963)                13'
  2121; 2211; 3perc, str                             ACA

Ring Shout Concerto (1974)                           19'
  solo perc; 1111; s,a,t,bar sax; 2320;             ACA
  perc, str

Niger Symphony (1975)                                13'
  1110; 2111; timp+1, str                            ACA

Concerto for Piano (Jazz Trio) and
  Orchestra (1980)                                   18'
  soli pf, perc, db; 2222; 4331; timp+1, str ACA

Concerto for Trio Pro Viva and Chamber
  Orchestra (1980)                                   21'
  soli fl, pf, vc; 0000; 1100; perc, str            ACA

Spiritual Fantasy No. 6 (1982)                        7'
  solo tpt; 2202; 2200; perc, str                    ACA

In the Spirit and the Flesh (1985)                   21'
  soli pf, dmst, db; satb cho; 2222;                ACA
  4331; timp+1, str


TIPEI, SEVER  (1943-    )

Undulating Michigamme (1978)                         27'
  soli 5vv; 3*3*3*3*; 4332; 4perc, hp,              ACA
  pf(4-hands), org, str (18-16-12-10-8)


TIRCUIT, HEUWELL  (1931-    )

Manga (1959)                                          6'
  3*223; 4331; timp+1, hp, str                       AMP

Halcyon (1962)                                    5'
    solo fl; perc, str                           AMP
    N.B.   There are optional parts for
    harmonium, celesta, trumpet, contrabassoon,
    and antique cymbals.

Fool's Dance (1967)                               6'
    solo perc; 1111; 1110; hp(or pf), str        AMP

Concerto for Percussion and Orchestra (1969)    23'
    solo perc; 3*3*23*; 4321; timp+3, hp, str    AMP

Concerto No. 3 (1970)                            14'
    223*0; 2210; 2perc, hp, pf/cel, str          AMP

Fantasias (Concerto No. 4) (1970; rev 1975)     12'
    3*3*3*2; 4331; timp+1, pf, str               AMP

Goerdeler Triptych (1972)                        12'
    3*222; 4331; timp+3, str                     AMP

Odoru Katachi (1978)                             14'
    solo perc; 1111; 1110; hp, str               AMP

Concerto for Brass Quintet and
    Orchestra (1979)                             18'
    solo br qnt; 2222; 2000; perc, hp, pf, str AMP


          TOCH, ERNST   (1887-1964)

Hyperion, op. 71 (1947)                          12'
    3*3*3*3*; 3331; timp+1, hp, str              MCA

Symphony No. 1, op. 72 (1950)                    39'
    3*3*3*2; 3331; timp+3, hp, cel, str          SCH

Symphony No. 2, op. 73 (1951)                    31'
    3*3*3*2; 3331; timp, 2hp, pf, org, str       AMP

Circus Overture (1953)                            5'
    3*222; 3331; 3perc, pf, str                  BEL

Notturno, op. 77 (1953)                          11'
    2222; 2230; xyl, hp, str                     BEL

Symphony No. 3, op. 75 (1955)                    29'
    3*3*3*3*; 4431; timp+8, vib, org,            BEL
    glass hca, press horn, str

Peter Pan, op. 76 (1956)                                   13'
    2121; 4120; timp+1, hp, str                           SCH

Symphony No. 4, op. 80 (1957)                             24'
    narr(opt); 3*223*; 2220; timp+6,                      BEL
    1-2hp, str

Epilogue (1959)                                            3'
    3*222; 2200; timp+2, str                              BEL

Intermezzo (1959)                                          4'
    2222; 2200; timp+1, hp, str                           BRO

Short Story (1961)                                         5'
    2222; 2200; timp+1, str                               BEL

Jephta - Rhapsodic Poem (Symphony No. 5),
    op. 89 (1963)                                         21'
    3*222; 3330; timp+5, hp, str                          BEL

Capriccio, op. 91 (1963)                                   6'
    2222; 2200; timp+4, anvil, str (no db)                BEL

Puppet Show, op. 92 (1963)                                 4'
    2222; 2200; timp+4, anvil, str (no db)                BEL

Symphony No. 6, op. 93 (1963)                             23'
    3*222; 3331; timp+5, anvil, str                       BEL

The Enamoured Harlequin, op. 94 (1963)                     5'
    2222; 2200; timp+4, anvil, str (no db)                BEL

Symphony No. 7, op. 95 (1964)                             26'
    3*222; 2230; timp+4, anvil, str                       BEL

Sinfonietta for Strings, op. 96 (1964)                    17'
    str                                                   BEL


            TOENSING, RICHARD  (1940-    )

Concerto for Organ and Orchestra (1986-1987)  22'
    solo org; 2*2*2=2*; 0221; timp+2,                     MS
    pf/cel, str

Concerto for Alto Saxophone and
    Chamber Orchestra (1990)                              12'
    solo a sax; 2*2*2*2*; 2200; 2perc, hp,                MS
    pf, str

Verses (1991)                                              9'
   3*3*33; 4331; timp+3, hp, pf, str          MS

Nocturnes and Memories (NA)                               35'
   solo s; 2222; 2220; 2perc, 2hp, pf,        MS
   cel, str


## TORKE, MICHAEL   (1961-     )

Ecstatic Orange (1984)                                    12'
   3*222; 4331; timp+3, pf, str               BH

Bright Blue Music (1985)                                  12'
   3*222; 4331; timp+4, hp, pf, str           BH

Verdant Music (1986)                                      23'
   3*3*3*2; 4331; timp+3, pf, str             BH

Adjustable Wrench (1987)                                  11'
   0121; 1210; perc, pf, synth, str (1-1-1-1) BH

Ash (1988)                                                16'
   1212; 3100; timp, synth, str               BH

Black and White (1988)                                    24'
   3*3*3*3*; 4331; timp+3, hp, pf/cel,        BH
   b gtr, sampling synth, str

Copper (1988)                                             12'
   solo br qnt; 3*3*22; 4231; timp+3, hp,     BH
   pf, str

Purple (1988)                                              7'
   3*3*3*2; 4331; timp+3, hp, pf, str         BH

Slate (1989)                                              32'
   soli 3kybd, 2perc; 2222; 4310; timp, str   BH

Bronze (1990)                                             10'
   3*3*3*3*; 6331; timp, pf, str              BH

Mass (1990)                                               NA
   solo bar; satb cho; 2222; 2220; timp, str  BH


## TOWER, JOAN   (1938-     )

Composition for Orchestra (1977)                          10'
   23*20; 4331; 4perc, pf, str                ACA

Amazon II (1979)           14'
    2*222; 2211; 3perc, hp, pf/cel, str     AMP

Sequoia (1981)           16'
    2*222; 4231; 4perc, hp, pf, cel, str     AMP

Music for Violoncello and Orchestra (1984)     19'
    solo vc; 2*222; 221(b tbn)0; timp+2,     AMP
    hp, str

Concerto for Piano
    (Homage to Beethoven) (1985)     21'
    solo pf; 2*12*1; 221(b tbn)0; 2perc, str     AMP

Island Rhythms (1985)           8'
    2*222; 221(b tbn)0; timp+2, str     AMP

Silver Ladders (1986)           23'
    3*3*3*3*; 4331; timp+4, hp, pf/cel, str     AMP

Concerto for Clarinet and Orchestra (1988)     19'
    solo cl; 2*222; 4221; 2perc, hp,     AMP
    pf/cel, str

Concerto for Flute and Orchestra (1989)     15'
    solo fl; 1*11*1; 101(b tbn)0; 2perc, str     AMP

Island Preludes (NA)           10'
    solo ob; str     AMP


       TOWNSEND, DOUGLAS (1921-    )

Fantasy (1951)           8'
    2222; 2200; timp, str     FLE

Adagio (1956)           6'
    str     MS

Four Fantasies on American Folk Songs (1958)     14'
    2*2*22; 4231; timp, hp(or pf), str     CFP

Symphony for Strings No. 1 (1958)     26'
    str     MS

Chamber Concerto No. 1 for Violin and
    Strings (1959)     18'
    solo vln; str     MS

Chamber Concerto No. 2 for Trombone
    and Strings (1962)                                      13'
    solo tbn; str                                           TP

Suite No. 1 (1970)                                         17'
    str                                                     MS

Chamber Concerto No. 3 for Flute, Horn,
    Piano and Strings (1971)                                13'
    soli fl, hn, pf; str                                    MS

Suite No. 2 (1974)                                         13'
    str                                                     MS

Fantasy on Motives of Burt Bachrach (1979)                 10'
    str                                                     MS

String Symphony No. 2 (1984)                               20'
    str                                                     MS

Ridgefield Rag (1986)                                       6'
    3*222; 4331; timp+2, str                                MS

Concertino for Piano and String
    Orchestra (1990)                                        10'
    solo pf; str                                            MS


                TRAVIS, ROY  (1922-    )

Collage for Orchestra (1968)                                7'
    2222; 4231; timp+3, str                                OXF

Concerto for Piano and Orchestra (1969)                    19'
    solo pf; 2222; 2210; timp, str                         OXF

Songs and Epilogues (1975)                                 12'
    solo bar; 0100; 2000; str                              OXF


                TREFOUSSE, ROGER

Square of Sunlight (1979)                                  10'
    str                                                    ACA


            TRIMBLE, LESTER   (1923-1986)

Symphony in Two Movements (1951)                           14'
    3*3*3*2; 4331; timp+3, str                             CFP

Concerto for Woodwinds and Strings (1954)          18'
   soli fl, ob, cl, bsn; str                      CFP

Sonic Landscape (1958; rev 1968)                   10'
   3*3*3*2; 4231; timp+3, str                      DSH

Five Episodes (1961-1962)                          10'
   3*3*3*3*; 4331; timp+1, hp, str                  DSH

Notturno (1967)                                     6'
   str                                             CFP

Duo concertante (1968)                             18'
   soli 2vln; 2*2*2*2; 4230; timp+1, hp, str       CFP

Symphony No. 2 (1968; rev 1984)                    28'
   4*4*4*5*; a sax; 4331; timp+5, hp, pf,           DSH
   cel, str

Panels for Orchestra (1976; rev 1983)              19'
   3*3*3*3; 4220; 2perc, 2hp, elec gtr, str         KPP

Concerto for Violin and Orchestra
   (1976-1981)                                     27'
   solo vln; 3*3*3*3*; 4231; 4perc, hp, str         KPP

Concerto for Harpsichord and
   Orchestra (1978)                                20'
   solo hpsd; 3(2picc)2*2*2; 2110;                  KPP
   timp+1, str

Symphony No. 3:  The Tricentennial
   (1984-1985)                                     28'
   3*3*3*3*; 4331; timp+1, hp, str                  KPP


TRYTHALL, HARRY GILBERT   (1930-    )

A Solemn Chant, op. 1 (1956)                       13'
   str                                             MS

Symphony No. 1, op. 2 (1958; rev 1961)             32'
   3*3*3*3*; 4331; timp+1, 2hp, str                 MS

Concerto for Harp and Orchestra,
   op. 7 (1964)                                    18'
   solo hp; 2222; 2100; str                        MS

Dionysia, op. 11 (1967-1968)                       12'
   3*3*3*2; 4321; timp, str                        BOU

Chroma I, op. 21 (1969-1970)                    12'
    33*32; 4321; timp, str, tape,               EBM
    electronic sounds, lights

Cindy the Synth, op. 27 (1974)                  15'
    narr; 3332; 4331; timp, synth, str          BOU
    N.B.  Formerly titled "Minnie the Moog."

Sinfonia Concertante (1989)                     18'
    solo ww qnt; 1111; 2210; timp+1, str        TP


            TSONTAKIS, GEORGE  (1951-    )

Fantasía habanera (1984)                        13'
    3*3*3*3*; 4230; timp+3, pf/cel, str         ACA


            TULL, FISHER  (1934-    )

Concertino for Oboe and Strings (1970)          9'
    solo ob; str                                BH

Trumpet Concerto No. 2 (1972)                   17'
    solo tpt; 3*23*2; 4331; timp+2, str         BH

Three Episodes (1979)                           14'
    3*3*3*3*; 4331; timp+2, str                 BH

Capriccio (1980)                                9'
    2111; 2110; timp+1, pf, str                 BH

Overture to a Legacy (1981)                     11'
    2=13*1; 2100; 2perc, str                    BH

Dialogues (1988)                                17'
    solo perc; 2*222; 4331; pf, str             BH


            TURNER, CHARLES  (1921-    )

Encounter (1955)                                8'
    3*3*3*2; 4230; timp+1, hp, str              GS

Dark Pastorale (1957)                           15'
    3*3*3*2; 4331; timp+1, hp, str              GS

The Marriage of Orpheus (1963)                  12'
    4*3*4=3*; 4331; timp+1, hp, pf, gtr, str    GS

TUROK, PAUL (1929-   )

Concerto for Violin and Orchestra,
  op. 6 (1953)                      25'
  solo vln; 3*3*3*2; 4231; timp+2, hp, str   SEE

Symphony in Two Movements, op. 11 (1955)   15'
  3*3*3*2; 4231; timp+2, pf, str          SEE

Variations on an American Song,
  op. 20 (1958)                    9'
  3*3*3*3*; 4331; timp+2, hp, str         CF

Chartres West, op. 25 (1968)           8'
  3*3*3*3*; 6441; timp+4, hp, pf/cel, str  CF

Homage to Bach, op. 26 (1969)         20'
  1221; 1110; perc, str               CF

Lyric Variations, op. 32 (1971)       12'
  solo ob; str                       CF

Great Scott! - Suite after Scott Joplin,
  op. 37 (1973)                   20'
  3*3*3*2; 4331; timp+3, hp, str         GS

A Scott Joplin Overture, op. 37a (1973)   6'
  3*3*3*2; 4331; timp+1, hp, str         GS

A Sousa Overture, op. 43 (1975)       8'
  3*3*4=3*; 4331; timp+3, hp, str       GS

Ragtime Caprice (1976)             10'
  solo pf; 2*22*2; 2221; timp+1, hp, str  GS

Antoniana - ballet suite after Vivaldi,
  op. 47 (1977)                   20'
  1111; 2110; timp, pf, str             GS

Danza Viva! (1978)                 4'
  3*3*3*3*; 4331; timp+3, hp, pf, str   GS

Threnody (1979)                    10'
  str                              GS

Canzona Concertante No. 1, op. 57 (1980)  13'
  solo eh; 3*23*3*; 4331; timp+1, hp,   GS
  cel, str

Canzona Concertante No. 3, op. 64 (1980)        13'
   soli fl, ob, tpt; str                        GS

Ultima Thule, op. 60 (1981)                     13'
   3*3*3*3*; 4331; timp+1, hp, str              GS

Canzona Concertante No. 2, op. 63 (1982)        12'
   solo tbn; 2222; 4221; timp+2, str            GS

Canzone Concertante, op. 68 (1983)              15'
   solo vc; 2222; 2200; timp+2, hp, pf, str     CF

Variations on an American Song,
   op. 70 (1984)                                9'
   3*3*3*3*; 4331; timp+1, hp, str              CF

Concertino for English Horn (or Alto
   Saxophone) and Strings, op. 73 (1985)        15'
   solo eh (or a sax); str                      CF

...From Sholem Aleichem, op. 76 (1987)          NA
   3*3*3*3*; 4331; timp+3, hp, str              CF

Prelude to "Richard III" (NA)                   8'
   2223*; 4331; timp+1, hp, str                 CF


            TUTHILL, BURNET  (1888-1982)

Elegy, op. 26a (1948)                           7'
   2222; 4331; timp, str                        FLE

Rowdy Dance, op. 27a (1948)                      2'
   3*232; 4331; timp+1, str                     FLE

Concerto for Clarinet and Orchestra,
   op. 28 (1948-1949)                           16'
   solo cl; 2202; 2000; str                     FLE

Flute Song, op. 31, No. 2 (1954-1955)            6'
   solo fl; 2hn, str                            FLE

Rhapsody for Clarinet and Orchestra,
   op. 33 (1954-1956)                           9'
   solo cl; 1*101; 2110; timp+2, str            FLE

Trombone Trouble, op. 46 (1963)                  4'
   soli 3tbn; 2222; 4000; timp+2, str           FLE

ULTAN, LLOYD (1929-    )

Wakonda Sketch (1951)                               7'
  213*1; 2221; str                                 ACA

The Man With A Hoe (1956)                          40'
  soli s, a, t, b; satb cho; 4*3*3*2; 4331;        ACA
  timp+3, hp, str

Sinfonia (Second Movement of
  "Man With A Hoe") (1956)                          6'
  4*3*3*2; 4331; timp+3, hp, str                   ACA

Carlisle Concerto (1958)                           18'
  1111; 0000; pf, str (2-1-1-1)                    ACA

Symphony No. 2 (1961)                              25'
  2222; 1111; 6perc, hp, str                       ACA

Wanaki Win (1977)                                  11'
  3*23*2; 4331; timp+1, pf, str                    ACA

Concerto for Organ (1979)                          27'
  solo org; 0000; 1220; timp, str                  ACA

Concerto for Violin and Orchestra (1982)           38'
  solo vln; 3*3*3*3*; 4331; timp+1, hp,            ACA
  pf, cel, str

Pitchipoi:  The Children of Drancy (1984)          30'
  soli mez, b-bar; solo vla; 2222; 2220;           ACA
  timp+1, pf, str

Reflections on a Tradition (1989)                  11'
  2222; 2000; str                                  ACA
  OR:  1211; 2000; str

Concerto for Violoncello and
  Orchestra (1990)                                 30'
  solo vc; 2222; 2220; timp+1, hp, str             ACA

### USSACHEVSKY, VLADIMIR   (1911-      )

N.B.   For information on works which were
jointly composed by Ussachevsky and Luening,
see the complete listing under Luening.

Miniatures for a Curious Child (1950)            9'
    2222; 2222; str                                 ACA

Intermezzo (1952)                                 5'
    solo pf; 2121; 1000; str                        ACA

Colloquy (1976)                                  24'
    3*23*2; 4331; timp+2, pf, str, tape            ACA

Celebration (1980)                                8'
    str                                             ACA

Divertimento (1980-1981)                         13'
    solo EVI; 1110; 1110; timp+1, str, tape        ACA

Dances and Fanfare for a
    Festive Occasion (1981)                        9'
    3*23*2; 4331; timp+1, pf, cel, str             ACA

VAN DE VATE, NANCY  (1930-    )

Adagio (1957)                                          6'
  2222; 4231; timp, str                      ACA

Variations for Chamber Orchestra (1958)              10'
  1111; 1000; str                            ACA

Concerto for Piano and Orchestra (1968)             21'
  solo pf; 3*222; 4231; timp+1, str          ACA

Concert Piece (1978)                                  7'
  solo vc; 3perc, pf, cel, str (4-4-4-4-2)   AMC

Gema Jawa (1984)                                     10'
  str                                        ACA


VAN NOSTRAND, BURR  (1945-    )

Fragments from Symphony "Nosferatu" (1973)          18'
  3*23*3*; a,t sax; 4431; 6perc,             ACA
  elec gtr, str


VAN VACTOR, DAVID  (1906-    )

Chaconne for String Orchestra (1928)                 9'
  str                                        RRM

Five Small Pieces for Large Orchestra (1929)        17'
  2222; 4231; timp, hp, str                  RRM

Overture "Cristobal Colon" (1930)                   18'
  4*4*4=4*; 4331; timp+5, hp, str            RRM

Concerto for Flute (1932)                           20'
  solo fl; 0111; 2000; timp, hp, cel,        RRM
  str (0-6-4-2)

Masque of the Red Death (1932)                       5'
  3*3*3*3*; 4331; timp+2, str                RRM

Passacaglia and Fugue in D minor (1933)             10'
  2223*; 4331; timp, str                     RRM

Overture to a Comedy No. 1 (1934)                    10'
    3*223*; 4231; timp+1, hp, str                    RRM

Concerto a Quattro (1935)                            15'
    soli 3fl, hp; 0111; 2000; timp, str              RRM

Symphony No. 1 (1937)                                32'
    3*3*3*3*; 4331; timp+2, pf, str                  RRM

Five Bagatelles for Strings (1938)                   20'
    str                                              RRM

Symphonic Suite (1938)                               19'
    3*3*3*3*; 4331; timp+2, hp, str                  RRM

Divertimento for Small Orchestra (1939)              20'
    1111; 1110; pf, str                              RRM

Concerto for Viola (1940)                            20'
    solo vla; 2222; 2220; hp, str                    RRM

Adagio Mesto (1941)                                   7'
    str                                              RRM

Credo (1941)                                         30'
    solo mez; satb cho; 3*3*3*3*; 4331;              RRM
    timp+1, hp, org, str

Overture to a Comedy No. 2 (1941)                     6'
    3*222; 4231; timp+1, hp, str                     RRM

Variazioni Solenne (1941)                             9'
    3*3*3*3*; 4331; timp+2, hp, str                  RRM

Fanfare for Orchestra (1943)                          4'
    4*3*3*3*; 4331; timp+3, str                      RRM

Music for the Marines
    (Symphony No. 2) (1943)                          25'
    4*3*4=3*; 4431; timp+3, hp, str                  RRM

United Nations Fanfare (1944)                        10'
    223*3*; 4331; timp+3, hp, str                    RRM

Recitative and Saltarello (1946)                     16'
    2222; 2200; timp+1, hp, pf, str                  RRM

Cantata (1947)                                       21'
    ssa cho; 2222; 2200; timp+1, str                 RRM

Overture to a Cantata (1947)                                    5'
   2222; 2200; timp+1, str                              RRM

Pastorale and Dance (1947)                                      10'
   solo fl; str                                         RRM

Prelude and March (1950)                                        9'
   3*222; 4331; timp+1, str                             RRM

Armed Forces Medley (1951)                                      8'
   3*222; 4331; timp+1, str                             RRM

Concerto for Violin and Orchestra (1951)                       19'
   solo vln; 3*122; 2210; timp+1, hp, str               RRM

"The New Light" - Christmas Cantata (1954)                      32'
   soli s, bar; narr; boys vv; satb cho;               RRM
   3*222; 4331; perc, org, str

Fantasia, Chaconne and Allegro (1957)                          13'
   223*2; 4231; timp+1, str                             RRM

Symphony No. 3 in C Major (1958)                               27'
   3*3*3*3*; 4331; timp+4, hp, pf, str                  RRM

Trojan Women Suite (1959)                                      17'
   3*3*3*3*; 4331; timp+4, pf, str                      RRM

Inauguration: Fanfare and March (1960)                         6'
   3*3*3*3*; 4331; timp+4, hp, org, str                 RRM

Christmas Songs for Young People (1961)                        12'
   ssa cho; 2222; 4331; timp+1, str                     RRM

Suite for Trumpet and Small Orchestra (1962)                   11'
   solo tpt; 2*111; 3031; timp+1, pf, str              RRM

Sewanee Suite (1963)                                           11'
   3=3*3*2; 4331; timp+3, pf, str                       RRM

Suite for Orchestra on
   Chilean Folk Tunes (1963)                            13'
   3*3*3*3*; 4331; timp+4, hp, pf, cel, str             RRM

Sinfonia Breve (1964)                                          7'
   3*3*3*3*; 4331; timp+3, str                          RRM

Sarabanda With Variations (1969)                               7'
   solo br qnt; str                                     RRM

"Louise" - a Requiescat for String
   Orchestra (1970)                                        5'
   str                                                     RRM

Symphony No. 4 "Walden" (1971)                                22'
   satb cho; 3*3*3*3*; 4331; timp+2, hp, str        RRM

Andante and Allegro for Alto Saxophone
   and Strings (1972)                                     8'
   solo a sax; str                                       RRM

Suite for Three or Four Trumpets,
   One Trumpeter and Strings (1972)                       8'
   solo tpt; soli 3-4tpt(D, B-flat, E-flat,          RRM
   B-flat picc); str

"Holy Manna" - chorale prelude (1974)                        5'
   3*3*3*3*; 4331; timp+1, hp, str                    RRM

Prelude and Fugue in C (1974)                                4'
   str                                                   RRM

Veni Immanuel (1974)                                         7'
   satb cho; 2 brass cho; 3*3*3*3*; 4331;            RRM
   timp+3, hp, str

Symphony No. 5 (1975)                                        18'
   3*3*3*3*; 4331; timp+1, hp, str                    RRM

Episodes - Jesus Christ - cantata (1977)                     40'
   soli s, a, t, b; satb cho; 2*2*2*2; 2231;         RRM
   timp+1, pf, str


      VAZZANA, ANTHONY   (1922-     )

Symphonic Allegro (1958)                                     12'
   2*2*2*2*; 4331; str                                  MS

Symphony No. 1 (1964)                                        17'
   2*2*2*2; 4331; timp+2, hp, str                      MS

Trinakie (1975-1976)                                         17'
   3=3*3*3*; 4331; timp+6, pf/cel, str                MS

Concerto a Tre (1981)                                        16'
   soli cl, pf, db; 1+11(cb cl)0; 0110;               MS
   2perc, str (no vc, db)

Varianti (1982)                                              13'
  3(2picc)3*3*3*; 4331; timp+4, hp, pf,               MS
  cel, str

Odissea (1985)                                               22'
  3(2picc)3*3*3*; 4331; timp+4, 2hp, pf,              MS
  cel, str

Concerto Sapporo (1990)                                      24'
  3*3*3*3*; 4431; timp+5, str                        MS


VEGA, AURELIO DE LA   (1925-    )

Overture to a Serious Farce (1950)                           12'
  2222; 4331; timp+2, hp, str                        MS

Introduction and Episode (1952)                              16'
  34*5=4*; 6331; timp+4, hp, pf, str                 MS

Elegy (1954)                                                 12'
  str                                                MS

Divertimento (1956)                                          10'
  soli pf, vln, vc; str                              MS

Cantata (1958)                                               15'
  soli 2s, ca; 212+1; a sax; 2211; timp+1,           MS
  pf, str (2-1-1-1)

Symphony in Four Parts (1960)                                18'
  323*3*; 4331; timp+4, str                          MS

Serenade (1965)                                               8'
  23*4=3*; 4321; timp+3, hp, pf, cel, str            MS

Intrata (1972)                                               11'
  34*5=4*; 4441; timp+3, hp, pf, cel, str            MS

Olep ed Arudamot (1974)                                       8'
  213*1; 1111; 4perc, cel, str (2-2-2-1)             MS

Adios (1977)                                                 18'
  44*5=4*; 4331; timp+4, hp, pf, cel, str            MS


VERRALL, JOHN   (1908-    )

Symphony No. 2 in E minor (1943)                             22'
  3*3*23*; 4331; timp+1, hp, str                     ACA

Prelude and Allegro (1948)                        10'
    str                                           ACA

Concerto for Violin and Orchestra (1949)          21'
    solo vln; 2202; 2200; timp, str              ACA

Dark Night of St. John (1949)                     12'
    2121; 2100; str                               ACA

Portrait of St. Christopher (1956)                12'
    33*3*3; 4331; timp+3, hp, str                ACA

Concerto for Piano and Orchestra (1959)           22'
    solo pf; 2222; 2000; timp, str               ACA

Suite No. 1 (1959)                                14'
    33*3*3; 4331; timp+1, hp, str                ACA

Prelude for Orchestra
    (In Praise of Peace) (1962)                   10'
    2222; 2200; timp+1, str                      ACA

Symphony for Chamber Orchestra (1967)             15'
    1111; 1110; timp+1, str                      ACA

Concerto for Viola and Orchestra (1968)           18'
    solo vla; 2121; 1100; timp, str              ACA

Radiant Bridge (1976)                             14'
    33*3*3; 4331; timp+1, hp, str                ACA

Rhapsody (1979)                                   14'
    solo hn; str                                  ACA

Summerland Fantasy (1985)                          8'
    33*3*3; 4331; timp+1, hp, str                ACA

Legend of Chief Joseph (1988)                     17'
    solo bar; satb cho; children's cho;          ACA
    33*3*3; 4331; timp+2, str

A Lyric Symphony (1991)                           21'
    33*3*3; 4331; timp+2, str                    ACA


            VINCENT, JOHN   (1902-1977)

Soliloquy and Dance (1947)                        16'
    solo vc; str                                  TP

Suite from "Three Jacks"  (1954)                         15'
   2222; 2110; timp+3, str                              TP

Symphony in O -
   A Festival Piece in One Movement (1957)    19'
   4*2*3*2; 4331; timp+4, str                     TP

Symphonic Poem after Descartes (1958)          19'
   3*3*3*2; 4331; timp+1, hp, cel, str            TP

La Jolla Concerto (1959; rev 1966, 1973)       24'
   2222; 2110; timp, str                          TP

Overture to Lord Arling (1959)                 8'
   2222; 4331; timp+1, str                        TP

Rondo Rhapsody (1965)                          9'
   3*24=2; 4331; timp+3, hp, str                  TP

Nude Descending the Staircase (1966)           7'
   str                                            TP

Stabat Mater (1970)                            21'
   solo s; ttbb cho; 1*1*22; 2331;               TP
   timp+1, str


     VORES, ANDY  (1956-    )

Retwistification (1989)                        19'
   3=3*3=3*; 4331; timp+3, str                    NOA

WAGGONER, ANDREW (1960-    )

| | |
|---|---|
| Symphony (1984) | 17' |
| 4*23*3*; 4331; timp+2, hp, pf, str | ACA |

| | |
|---|---|
| The Train (1988) | 11' |
| 3*23*3*; 4331; timp+2, hp, pf, str | ACA |

| | |
|---|---|
| The Father and Mother Begotten - | |
| cantata (1990) | 25' |
| soli s, bar; satb cho; 2tpt; hp, | ACA |
| pf, org, str | |


WAGNER, JOSEPH   (1900-1974)

| | |
|---|---|
| Piano Concerto in G minor (1920; rev 1929) | 12' |
| solo pf; 1121; 2200; timp+1, str | FLE |

| | |
|---|---|
| Rhapsody (1928; rev 1937) | 10' |
| cl; pf, str | FLE |

| | |
|---|---|
| Sinfonietta No. 1 (1931; rev 1944) | 15' |
| 2*222; 2200; timp+1, pf, str | PS |

| | |
|---|---|
| Symphony No. 1 (1934) | 22' |
| 3*3*3*3*; 4331; timp+2, hp, pf, str | FLE |

| | |
|---|---|
| Four Miniatures (1935) | 12' |
| 2*222; 2200; timp+1, str | PS |

| | |
|---|---|
| Processions Medieval - | |
| A Choreographic Episode (1935) | 8' |
| 3*3*3*2; 4331; timp+1, pf, str | FLE |

| | |
|---|---|
| Two Moments Musical (1935) | 9' |
| str | FLE |

| | |
|---|---|
| Variations on an Old Form (1940) | 9' |
| 3*222; 4431; timp+2, org(opt), str | FLE |

| | |
|---|---|
| Sinfonietta No. 2 (1941) | 15' |
| str | PS |

| | |
|---|---|
| Hudson River Legend - suite (1941-1943) | 8' |
| 3*222; 4331; timp+2, pf, cel, str | FLE |

Dance divertissement (1942)                          14'
   2222; 2220; timp+2, str                         FLE

From the North Sea (1942)                             7'
   str                                               FLE

American Jubilee (1943)                               6'
   3*222; 4331; timp+1, hp, str                     FLE

Radio City Snapshots (1945)                           7'
   3*222; 2a,t sax; 4331; timp+1, hp,               FLE
   cel, str

Symphony No. 2 (1945; rev 1960)                       30'
   3*222; 4331; timp+1, pf, str                     FLE

Concertino for Harp and Orchestra
   (1945-1947)                                       15'
   solo hp; 2222; 2200; timp+1, cel, str            FLE

Panorama (1948-1956)                                  8'
   3*222; 4331; timp+1, pf/cel, str                 FLE

Northland Evocation - A Landscape (1949)             13'
   solo s (or tpt); 3*23*2; 4330; timp+1,           FLE
   cel, str

Introduction and Rondo (1950)                         8'
   solo tpt; 2222; 2000; timp+1, str                FLE

Symphony No. 3 (1950-1951)                            25'
   3*222; 4331; timp+2, str                         FLE

Introduction and Scherzo (1950-1954)                 10'
   solo bsn; str                                     FLE

A Fugal Triptych (1954)                               17'
   solo pf; timp+3, hp, cel, str                    FLE

Pastoral costarricense,
   un recuerdo sentimental (1955)                   10'
   1111; 2000; timp+1, pf(or cel), str              FLE


      WALDROP, GIDEON  (1919-    )

From the Southwest - suite (1949)                    11'
   3*3*22; 4231; timp+1, hp, pf, str                BH

Symphony No. 1 (1951)                              21'
   3*3*23; 4331; timp+1, hp, str                 BH

Pressures (1955)                                  9'
   str                                             BH

Prelude and Fugue (1962)                          11'
   3*222; 4331; timp+1, str                       BH

Songs of the Southwest (1982)                     15'
   solo bar; 11*11; 2110; timp+2, hp, str          BH


      WALKER, GEORGE  (1922-    )

Lyric for Strings (1947)                          9'
   str                                             MMB

Concerto for Trombone and Orchestra (1957)        18'
   solo tbn; 3*223*; 4221; timp+3, hp,             MMB
   cel, str

Address for Orchestra (1959)                      19'
   4*4*4*3*; 4231; timp+3, hp, str                 MMB

Antiphonies (1968)                                7'
   1*111; 1110; timp+2, cel, str                   MMB

Variations for Orchestra (1973)                   14'
   3+3*3*3*; 4231; timp+3, hp, pf, str             MMB

Concerto for Piano and Orchestra (1975)           25'
   solo pf; 3*23*3*; 4321; timp+1, hp,             MMB
   pf, str

Dialogus (1976)                                   13'
   solo vc; 4=3*3*3*; 4431; timp+5, hp, pf,        MMB
   cel, str

Mass (1978)                                       27'
   soli 2s, 2a, 2t, 2b; satb cho; 4=3*3*3*;        MMB
   4331; timp+1, hp, org, str

In Praise of Folly - overture (1981)              8'
   3*3*3*3*; 4431; timp+5, hp, pf/cel, str         MMB

Cantata (1982)                                    11'
   soli s, t; satb boys' cho; 1+200; 0300;         MMB
   timp+2, str

Cello Concerto (1982)                               20'
  solo vc; 4=3*3*3*; 4431; timp+4, hp, str    MMB

Eastman Overture (1983)                             8'
  3*3*3*3*; 4431; timp+4, hp, str              MMB

Serenata (1984)                                     14'
  2*222; 2210; timp+3, pf, str                 MMB

Sinfonia (1984)                                     12'
  3*3*3*3*; 4431; timp+6, hp, pf/hpsd, str     MMB

Poeme (1989)                                        18'
  solo vln; 1*211; 2111; timp+2, hp, str       MMB

Folksongs for Orchestra (1990)                      13'
  3*222; 2221; timp+2, hp, pf, str             MMB

Sinfonia II (1990)                                  18'
  3*3*3*3*; 4431; timp+2, hp, pf, gtr, str     MMB


      WALKER, GWYNETH  (1947-    )

Fanfare, Interlude and Finale (1980)                11'
  2111; 2200; timp, str                        ECS

Essay for Orchestra (1985)                          9'
  2222; 4230; 3perc, str                       ECS

Match Point
  (Tennis Match for Orchestra) (1985)          6'
  2222; 4231; perc, str                        ECS

The Light of Three Mornings (1987)                  18'
  1111; 1110; perc, str                        ECS

Three Songs in Celebration of the
  Family Farm (1988)                           13'
  satb cho; 2222; 4231; 3perc, str             ECS

Fanfare for the Family Farm (1989)                  4'
  2222; 4231; 3perc, str                       ECS
  N.B.  May be performed with brass reduced
  to 2211.

The Headless Horseman (1989)                        7'
  narr; 2*222; 4231; 3perc, str                ECS

Bicentennial Suite (1990)                        15'
  3*222; 4331; 3perc, str                        ECS

Open the Door (1990)                             4'
  2222; 4231; 3perc, str                         ECS

Roanoke Rising (1990)                            15'
  2222; 4231; timp+3, str                        ECS

Nocturne (1991)                                  NA
  solo cl; str                                   ECS


            WALLACH, JOELLE  (1946-    )

Glimpses (1981)                                  12'
  2222; 4330; timp+2, hp, str                    CF

A Prophecy and Psalm (1981)                      20'
  solo bar; satb cho; 23*3*3*; 4231;             ACA
  timp+1, hp, str

Turbulence, Stillness and Salutation (1983)      16'
  1121; 2110; timp+1, hp, str                    ACA

Columbus Prayer (1989)                           14'
  solo bar; satb cho; 3*3*3*3*; 4231;            ACA
  timp+1, hp, str

The Tiger's Tail (1990)                          10'
  2*2*22*; 4231; timp+1, hp, str                 NOA


            WARD, ROBERT  (1917-    )

Jubilation (1945)                                10'
  3*3*3*3*; 4331; timp, pf, str                  HG

Symphony No. 2 (1947)                            23'
  3*3*3*3*; 4331; timp+1, pf/cel, str            AMP

Concert Music (1948)                             8'
  3*222; 4331; timp+3, pf, str                   HG

Jonathan and the Gingery Snare (1950)            9'
  narr; 2222; 4330; timp+1, str                  HG

Symphony No. 3 (1950)                            21'
  2*2*2*2; 2100; pf, str                         HG

Sacred Songs for Pantheists (1951)                        17'
   solo s; 2*12*0; 2220; hp, str                         ECS

Euphony for Orchestra (1954)                              11'
   22*22; 4231; timp+1, str                              HG

Prairie Overture (1957)                                    7'
   3*222; 4231; timp+1, str                              HG

Symphony No. 4 (1958; rev 1959, 1977)                     26'
   22*22; 2200; timp, hp, str                            HG

Divertimento for Orchestra (1960)                         14'
   3*3*3*3*; 4331; timp+1, hp, str                       HG

Earth Shall Be Fair - cantata (1961)                      26'
   satb cho; children's cho; 2*222; 4220;                HG
   timp+1, str

Hymn and Celebration (1962; rev 1966)                     10'
   3*3*3*2; 4331; timp+1, hp, str                        HG

Let the Word Go Forth (1965)                              10'
   satb cho; 0000; 2220; hp, str                         HG

Sweet Freedom's Song - cantata (1965)                     40'
   soli s, bar; satb cho; 2*222; 2220;                   HG
   timp+1, hp, str

Festive Ode (1966)                                        11'
   3*3*3*2; 4331; timp+1, str                            HG

Hymn to the Night (1966)                                   7'
   22*22; 4331; timp+1, str                              HG

Invocation and Toccata (1966)                              9'
   3*3*3*2; 4331; timp+1, str                            HG

Concerto for Piano and Orchestra (1968)                   25'
   solo pf; 3*3*3*2; 4331; timp+1, str                   HG

Concertino for Strings (1973)                             15'
   str                                                   HG

Symphony No. 5 "Canticles of America" (1976)              40'
   soli s, bar; narr; satb cho; 2*2*2*2*;                HG
   4320; timp+1, hp, str

Sonic Structure (1980)                                    11'
   3*3*3*3*; 4331; timp+1, str                           HG

Dialogues for Violin, Cello and
    Orchestra (1983)                                          10'
    soli vln, vc; 3*3*3*2; 4331; timp+2, str      HG

Concerto for Tenor Saxophone
    and Orchestra (1984; rev 1987)                           20'
    solo t sax; 3*3*3*2; 4331; timp+1, hp, str HG

Festival Triptych (1986)                                     14'
    narr; 2*2*2*2; 4331; timp+1, hp, str          HG

Dialogue on the Tides of Time (1987)                          8'
    soli vln, vc; 2222; 4200; perc, str           HG


        WARD-STEINMAN, DAVID   (1936-     )

Concert Overture (1957)                                       7'
    3*222; 4331; timp+2, str                      EBM

Symphony (1959)                                              22'
    3*3*22; 4331; timp+3, hp, pf/cel, str         EBM

Concerto Grosso for Combo and
    Chamber Orchestra (1960)                                 17'
    soli a sax, bar sax, tpt, tbn; 0000;          MJQ
    a,t sax; 0331; dmst, pf, str

Prelude and Toccata (1962)                                   12'
    3*3*3*2; 4331; timp+3, hp, str                EBM

Concerto No. 2 for Chamber Orchestra (1963)                  17'
    1111; 1110; timp+1, str                       EBM

Western Orpheus - ballet suite (1964)                        20'
    2*2*2*2; 2220; timp+2, hp, pf/cel,            EBM
    koto(opt), str

Concerto for Violoncello and
    Orchestra (1966)                                         20'
    solo vc; 3*3*3*3*; 4331; 3perc, hp,           EBM
    pf/cel, str

These Three - ballet suite (1966)                            18'
    2*2*2*2; a sax; 4331; timp+3, pf, str         EBM

Antares (1971)                                               10'
    3*3*3*3*; 4431; perc, hp, pf/cel, synth,      EBM
    str, tape
    N.B. May also be performed with a gospel choir.

Arcturus (1972)                                          12'
    3*3*3*3*; 4331; timp+4, hp, pf/cel,                  EBM
    synth, str

Chroma (1984)                                            19'
    solo pf/cel/toy pf/synth (1 player);                 MER
    1111; 1000; 3perc, str

Olympics Overture (1984)                                 6'
    3*23*3*; 4331; 3perc, pf, str                        MER

Elegy for Astronauts (1986)                              10'
    3*3*3*3*; 4431; 4perc, hp, pf/cel,                   MER
    str, tape

Winging I (1986)                                         13'
    1110; 1000; perc, str                                MER

Season's Greetings (1987)                                2'
    3*3*3*3*; 4331; 3perc, hp, cel, str                  MER


                WARREN, ELINOR  (1900-    )

The Crystal Lake (1958)                                  9'
    2222; 4230; timp+1, hp, cel, str                     CF

Transcontinental (1958)                                  12'
    solo bar; satb cho; 2121; 2220; timp+1,              TP
    pf, str

Abram in Egypt - cantata (1960)                          24'
    solo bar; satb cho; 3*223*; 4231; timp+3,            TP
    hp, str

Along the Western Shore (1963)                           9'
    2*2*3*2*; 4231; timp+3, hp, cel, str                 CF

Sanctus (1965)                                           7'
    satb cho; timp, org, str                             LG

Requiem (1966)                                           50'
    soli a, bar; satb cho; 2222; 4231;                   LG
    timp+1, hp, cel, org, str

Four Sonnets (1968)                                      10'
    solo s; str                                          CF

Hymn of the City (1969)                                  4'
    satb cho; 1121; 2110; timp, str                      CF

Intermezzo (from "King Arthur") (1970)          6'
  223*2; 4331; timp+2, hp, str                    TP

Symphony in One Movement (1971)                 17'
  3*3*22; 4231; timp+1, hp, cel, str              CF

The Legend of King Arthur (1974)                60'
  solo t, bar; satb cho; 3*3*3*3*; 4331;          TP
  timp+1, hp, cel, str

Good Morning, America! (1976)                   16'
  narr; satb cho; 2222; 2220; timp+2,             CF
  pf/cel, str

Now Welcome Summer (1984)                        3'
  satb cho; 1121; 2100; str                       LG

Suite for Orchestra (NA)                        17'
  3*222; 4231; timp+6, hp, str                    CF


      WASHBURN, ROBERT  (1928-    )

Triplex for Orchestra (1957)                     5'
  2*222; 4231; timp+4, str                        MS

Festive Overture (1959)                          7'
  2222; 4231; timp+2, str                         OXF
  N.B.  This is the first movement of
  Symphony No. 1.

Suite for Strings (1959)                         9'
  str                                             OXF

Symphony No. 1 (1959)                           18'
  2222; 4231; timp+2, str                         OXF

Synthesis (1959)                                 7'
  2*222; 4231; timp+4, str                        SHA

Three Pieces for Orchestra (1959)                5'
  2222; 2210; timp+2, str                         OXF

St. Lawrence Overture (1962)                     5'
  2*222; 2221; timp+4, str                        BH

Passacaglia and Fugue (1963)                     7'
  str                                             MS

Sinfonietta (1963)                                            14'
   str                                         OXF

Serenade for String Orchestra (1966)                          8'
   str                                         OXF

Song and Dance (1967)                                         6'
   str                                          BH

Excursion (1970)                                              5'
   2222; 4331; timp+2, str                     OXF

Prologue and Dance (1970)                                     7'
   2222; 4331; timp+2, str                     OXF

Ode to Freedom (1973)                                         7'
   satb cho; 225=2; 4331; timp+1, str          OXF

Elegy (1974)                                                  6'
   2222; 4331; timp+2, hp, str                  BH

We Hold These Truths (1974)                                   7'
   satb cho; 2222; 4231; timp+1, str            BH

New England Holiday (1986)                                    7'
   2*222; 2331; timp+1, str                     MS

Queen Noor Suite (1986)                                       9'
   str                                          MS

Fairfax Suite (1987)                                         10'
   str                                          MS

Adirondack Sketches (1989)                                   18'
   1*111; 1110; timp+3, str                     MS

Saraswati Suite (1991)                                        9'
   tabla, str                                   MS


## WATERS, JAMES L.  (1930-    )

Three Holy Sonnets of John Donne (1966)                      20'
   solo b-bar; 2222; 4220; timp+2, str          MS

Concertino for String Quartet and
   String Orchestra (1968)                     14'
   solo str qt; str                             MS

Three Songs of Louise Bogan (1971)              17'
   solo mez; 2222; 4000; str                    MS

Overture (1974)                                  8'
   2222; 4231; timp+1, str                      MS

Concerto for Viola and
   Chamber Orchestra (1987)                    14'
   solo vla; 1111; 2000; str                    MS


      WAXMAN, DONALD   (1925-     )

Paris Overture (1965)                            6'
   2222; 2221; timp+1, str                      ECS

Overture to Serenade Concertante (1972)         10'
   1111; 1000; str                              ECS

Psalms and Supplications (1972)                 18'
   solo t; satb cho(opt); 2222; 2000; str       ECS
   N.B.  If performed without chorus,
   the duration is reduced to 13'.

A Quint of Carols (1983)                         15'
   3*23(bar sax)2; 3231; timp+3, str            ECS


      WAXMAN, FRANZ   (1906-1967)

Athaneal the Trumpeter - overture (1945)         6'
   solo tpt; 323*3*; 4431; timp+4, hp, str       TP

Sinfonietta (1955)                               14'
   timp, str                                    BH

Joshua - oratorio (1959)                         80'
   soli a, 2t, 2b; narr; satb cho;               TP
   3*3*3*3*; 4331; timp+1, hp, pf, org, str

The Song of Terezin - cantata (1965)             45'
   solo s; satb cho; children's cho; 3342;       TP
   4331; timp+3, pf/cel, str


      WEBER, BEN   (1916-1979)

Ballade (1943)                                   6'
   solo vc; 223*3*; 2200; hp, pf, str           ACA

Sinfonia, op. 21 (1945-1946)  15'
   solo vc; 2222; 4231; timp+1, hp, str  ACA

Symphony on Poems of William Blake,
   op. 33 (1950)  28'
   solo bar; solo vc; 1121; 1010; perc, cel  MOB

Two Pieces for String Orchestra,
   op. 34 (1950)  9'
   str  BOE

Concerto for Violin and Orchestra,
   op. 41 (1954)  28'
   solo vln; 3*3*3*2; 4231; timp+1, hp, str  BOE

Prelude and Passacaglia, op. 42 (1954)  12'
   2222; 4231; timp+3, hp, pf, cel, str  ACA

Rapsodie concertante, op. 47 (1957)  13'
   solo vla; 1*11*1; 1100; hp, str (6-2-2-1)  ACA

Three Songs, op. 48 (1958)  13'
   solo s; str  BOE

Concerto for Piano and Orchestra,
   op. 52 (1961)  25'
   solo pf; 3*3*3*3; 4231; timp+3, str  ACA

Dolmen, op. 58 (1964)  9'
   0201; 2000; str  EBM

The Enchanted Midnight, op. 60 (1967)  6'
   23*3*3; 4331; timp+1, hp, cel, str  ACA

Dramatic Piece, op. 61 (1970)  14'
   solo vln; 3*23*2; 4331; timp+1,  BOE
   hp, cel, str

Sinfonia Clarion, op. 62 (1973)  19'
   2222; 2210; timp, hp, str  BOE


## WEGNER, AUGUST (1941-   )

Ice-Nine (1971)  10'
   solo pf; 102*0; 1110; str  SEE

WEIGL, VALLY   (1894-1982)

Andante (1945)                                    4'
  str                                             ACA

Adagio (1951)                                     5'
  str                                             ACA

To Emily (1970)                                   5'
  str                                             ACA


WEINER, LAWRENCE   (1932-      )

Elegy (1958)                                      3'
  str                                             SMC

Quarternity (1968)                               10'
  str                                             LDW

Adagio for Horn and Strings (1982)              12'
  solo hn; str                                    MS

Capriccio for Piano and
    String Orchestra (1982)                      15'
    solo pf; str                                  MS

A Symphonic Etude (1983)                         15'
    3*23*2; 4331; timp+6, pf, str                 MS

Concerto for Piano and Orchestra (1984)         25'
    solo pf; 223*2; 4331; timp+3, str             MS

Concerto for Guitar and Orchestra (1986)        20'
    solo gtr; 223*2; 2220; timp+3, str            MS

Quest for Peace (1988)                           30'
    solo vv; satb cho; 223*2; 2221;               MS
    timp+3, str

A Symphonic Overture (1989)                      12'
    223*2; 4332; timp+3, str                      MS

Three Dance Scenes from
    "Chipita Rodriguez" (1989)                   30'
    223*2; 4331; timp+4, hp, str                  MS

Concerto for Flute and Orchestra (1991)         20'
    solo fl; 0022; 2000; timp+3, hp, str          MS

Reflections (1991)                                    12'
    solo ww qnt; str                                  MS


        WEINGARDEN, LOUIS  (1943-    )

Piano Concerto (1975)                                 29'
    solo pf; 3*3*3*3*; 4331; 5perc, 2hp,              BH
    cel, mand, gtr, str


        WEISBERG, ARTHUR  (1931-    )

Opening Statement (1985)                              19'
    223*3; 4331; 4perc, hp, pf, str                   ACA


        WEISGALL, HUGO  (1912-    )

Soldier Songs (1946; rev 1965)                        25'
    solo bar; 2222; a,t sax; 4321;                    MER
    timp+1, str

Dances from the ballet "Outpost" (1947)              17'
    3*3*22; 4332; timp+1, pf, str                     TP

A Garden Eastward - cantata (1952)                    17'
    solo s; 3*222; 4220; timp+1, hp, str              TP

A Song of Celebration (1975)                          26'
    solo s, t; satb cho; 3*222; 4331;                 TP
    timp+1, hp, str

Prospect (1983)                                       14'
    3*3*22; 4431; timp+1, pf, str                     TP

Love's Wounded (1986)                                 17'
    solo bar; 3*3*3*2; 4331; timp+2, hp,              TP
    cel, str


        WELCHER, DAN  (1948-    )

Concerto for Flute and Orchestra (1974)              20'
    solo fl; 2121; 2210; timp+1, hp,                  ELK
    pf, cel, str

Concerto da camera (1975)                             20'
    solo bsn; 1110; 1100; perc, pf, str               ELK

Dervishes (1976)                                              11'
    3*3*3*3*; 4331; timp+3, hp, pf/cel, str                  ELK

The Visions of Merlin (1980)                                  21'
    2222; 3200; timp+1, pf/cel, str                          ELK

Prairie Light:  Three Texas Watercolors of
    Georgia O'Keeffe (1985)                                   15'
    3*222; 4331; timp+3, pf/cel, hp, str                     TP

Castle Creek (1989)                                            5'
    0000; 4331; timp+1, hp, pf, str                          ELK

Concerto for Clarinet (1989)                                  19'
    solo cl; 2111; 2210; 2perc, hp, pf, str                  ELK

HALEAKLA:  How Marie Snared the Sun (1991)                    20'
    narr; 3*3*3*3*; 4331; timp+4, hp, pf, str                TP


                WERNICK, RICHARD  (1934-      )

Hexagrams (1962)                                              20'
    2222; 2000; str                                          TP

Aevia (1964)                                                  12'
    4*23*2; 4331; timp+4, str                                TP

Visions of Wonder and Terror (1976)                           28'
    solo mez; 4*4*4*4*; 4331; 2timp+5,                       TP
    hp, cel, str

Concerto for Violin and Orchestra (1984)                      25'
    solo vln; 3*3*3*3*; 4331; timp+3,                        TP
    hp, cel, str

Viola Concerto
    ("Do not go Gentle...") (1986)                            20'
    solo vla; 3*3*4=3*; 4331; timp+4,                        TP
    hp, cel, str

Symphony No. 1 (1988)                                         19'
    4*3*4=3*; 6332; timp+3, hp, pf, cel, str                 TP

Piano Concerto (1990)                                         30'
    solo pf; 3*3*3*4*; 4331; timp+3, hp, str                 TP

Chanukah Festival Overture (NA)                                3'
    satb cho(opt); 3*222; 2a,t sax; 4331;                    TP
    timp+2, str

WESTERGAARD, PETER   (1931-     )

Symphonic Movement (1954)                          NA
  3*3*3*3*; 4331; perc, hp, pf, str                MS

Five Movements for Small Orchestra (1958)          6'
  102*1; 2110; perc, hp, pf, str                   BB


WHEAR, PAUL W.   (1925-     )

Pastorale Lament (1960)                            9'
  solo hn; str                                     LDW

Olympiad (1962)                                    9'
  str                                              ELK

Catskill Legend (1963)                             6'
  2120; 2230; timp+3, str                          ELK
  OR:   2222; 4331; timp+6, str

Lancaster Overture (1963)                          6'
  2222; 4231; timp+1, str                          LDW

Psalms of Celebration (1965)                       16'
  satb cho; 3*222; 4331; timp+1, str               LDW

Quantum Suite (1965)                               9'
  2222; 4331; timp+1, str                          LDW

The Seasons - cantata (1965)                       25'
  solo bar; satb cho; 2222; 4330;                  LDW
  timp+1, str

Catharsis Suite (1967)                             15'
  3*3*3*2; 4331; timp+1, hp, str                   LDW

Decade Overture (1968)                             7'
  3*222; 4231; timp+1, str                         LDW

In Memoriam:  R.V.W.
  (from Symphony No. 2) (1970)                     8'
  3*3*3*3*; 4331; timp+1, hp, str                  LDW

Kedushah (1970)                                    23'
  satb cho; 2222; 2200; timp, hp, str              LDW

Symphony No. 2 "The Bridge" (1972)                 31'
  3*3*3*3*; 4331; timp+1, hp, str                  LDW

A Shakespeare Prelude (1974)                          6'
    2222; 2110; timp, hp, str                        LDW

The Chief Justice, John Marshall (1975)             70'
    soli s, b; 2narr; satb cho; 3*3*3*3*;           LDW
    4331; timp+1, hp, str

Symphony No. 3 "The Galleries" (1975)               35'
    2222; 3210; timp+1, hp, str                     LDW

White River Legend Overture (1976)                   8'
    3*222; 4331; timp+1, str                        LDW

Silver Celebration Overture (1977)                  10'
    2222; 3210; timp+3, str                         LDW

Mass for Today (1979)                               60'
    soli s, bar; satb cho; 1*211; 2120; timp,       LDW
    hp, org, str

Appalachian Folk Tale (1980)                        20'
    narr; 2*222; 2220; timp+1, hp(opt), str         LDW

High Flight (1984)                                  14'
    2*222; 2000; timp, hp, str                      LDW

Burberry Red (1990)                                 23'
    solo a tbn; perc, str                           LDW

Burberry Red Cabaret (1991)                          5'
    solo vc; perc, str                              LDW

Symphony No. 5 (1992)                               22'
    str                                             LDW


          WHEELOCK, DONALD  (1940-      )

Three Pieces for Orchestra (1971)                   22'
    3*3*2*1; 2211; timp+3, hp, cel, str             MS

Carnival (1975)                                     22'
    3*3*3*3*; 4331; timp+4, hp, pf/cel, str         MS

Montage (1975)                                      11'
    3*3*4=3*; 4331; timp+3, hp, pf/cel, str         MS

Diversions (1976)                                   20'
    3=3*3*3*; 4231; 4perc, hp, pf, cel, str         MS

Tesserae (1976)         10'
   3*3*3*3; 4331; 2perc, hp, cel, str     NOA

Ancient Rain (1978)         45'
   soli mez, t, bar; 2(2picc)2*2*2; 2201;    MS
   euph; 3perc, hp, pf/cel, str

Vanishing Points (1978)         6'
   2*2*2+2; 2220; timp+2, pf, str     MS

Variations for Orchestra (1978)      22'
   2*2*2*2; 2220; timp+2, hp, pf, str    MS

Dreams Before A Sacrifice (1981)      35'
   solo amp mez; 2(2picc)2*2*2; 4201;     MS
   euph; 4perc, amp hp, amp pf, str

Six Fables (1983)         13'
   ssa cho; 2122; 2200; str     MS


      WHITE, DAVID ASHLEY  (1944-   )

Ruins of Missolonghi (1980)       15'
   1*111; 1211; timp+2, pf, str     MMB


      WHITE, DONALD

Sagan:  An Overture (1946)        4'
   3*222; 4231; timp+1, str     MS

Kennecec Suite (1947)         8'
   3*222; 4231; timp+1, str     MS

Andante (1951)         7'
   solo ob; hp, str     CF

Overture for Orchestra (1951)       7'
   3*222; 4331; timp+1, str     MS

Concerto for Cello and Orchestra (1952)    23'
   solo vc; 3*222; 4331; timp+1, hp, str   MS

Serenade for Orchestra (1962)       14'
   3*222; 4331; timp+1, str     MS

Divertissement (1968)         10'
   str     LDW

Song of Mankind (NA)                                      7'
    soli s, a, t, b; satb cho; speaking cho;    MS
    3*3*4*1; 4331; timp+3, str


    WHITTENBERG, CHARLES   (1927-1984)

Event (1963)                                             8'
    2*222*; 4331; timp+3, vc, db                        ACA

Event II (1963)                                         10'
    soli fl, db; str                                    ACA

Serenade (1973)                                         12'
    str                                                 ACA


    WIDDOES, LAWRENCE   (1932-    )

The Visitors (1987)                                     17'
    3*3*3*3*; 4331; timp+3, hp, pf, str                NOA


    WIENHORST, RICHARD   (1920-    )

Te Deum (1958)                                          18'
    solo t; satb cho; 3*222; 4331;                     ACA
    timp+1, str

Three Parodies (1959)                                   6'
    solo tpt; 1111; 1100; timp+2, str                  ACA

Magnificat (1965)                                       4'
    satb cho; 3*222; 2231; timp+4, hp,                 ACA
    pf/cel, str

Canticle of the Three Children (1966)                  12'
    ttbb cho; 3*222; 2220; timp+1,                     ACA
    hp, cel, str

Canticle for Percussion and
    Chamber Orchestra (1967)                           11'
    soli 3perc; 1011; 1110; str                        ACA

Het is Goed den Herre te Loven (1984)                  11'
    satb cho; str                                      ACA

A Psalm Setting (Psalm XCII) (1984)                    11'
    satb cho; str                                      ACA

WIGGLESWORTH, FRANK   (1918-    )

| | | |
|---|---|---|
| Music for Strings (1946) | 15' | |
| str | ACA | |
| | | |
| Fantasia (1947) | 12' | |
| str | ACA | |
| | | |
| Three Movements for Strings (1949) | 15' | |
| str | ACA | |
| | | |
| Sleep Becalmed (1950) | 5' | |
| satb cho; 2220; 2210; perc, str | ACA | |
| | | |
| Summer Scenes (1951) | 12' | |
| soli fl, ob; str | ACA | |
| | | |
| Telesis (1951) | 15' | |
| 1111; 0200; str | ACA | |
| | | |
| Concertino for Piano and Strings (1953) | 14' | |
| solo pf; str | ACA | |
| | | |
| Symphony No. 1 (1953) | 23' | |
| 2222; 2221; timp+1, pf, str | ACA | |
| | | |
| Symphony No. 2 (1958) | 20' | |
| str | ACA | |
| | | |
| Symphony No. 3 (1960) | 18' | |
| str | ACA | |
| | | |
| Concertino for Viola and | | |
| Chamber Orchestra (1965) | 14' | |
| solo vla; 2011; 0110; 2perc, str | ACA | |
| | | |
| Three Portraits (1970) | 15' | |
| str | ACA | |
| | | |
| Music for Strings (1981) | 10' | |
| str | ACA | |
| | | |
| Aurora (1983) | 14' | |
| str | ACA | |
| | | |
| Sea Winds (1984) | 15' | |
| str | ACA | |
| | | |
| Janus (1988) | 10' | |
| 3*23*2; 4421; 3perc, str | ACA | |

WILDER, ALEC   (1907-1980)

Piece for Orchestra (1946)                              12'
    2223*; 4331; timp+1, hp, str                        MG

Concerto for Oboe and Strings (1950)                    24'
    solo ob; str                                        AMP

Concerto No. 1 for Horn and
    Chamber Orchestra (1954)                            15'
    solo hn; 2222; 2000; str                            MG

Carl Sandburg Suite (1960)                              16'
    2*2*22; 2220; 2perc, hp, str                        AMP

Effie Suite -
    Suite No. 1 for Tuba and Orchestra (1960)   11'
    solo tba; 2222; 4331; perc, str                     MG

Entertainment No. 2 (1960)                              13'
    2222; 2200; str                                     MG

Songs for Patricia (1964)                               NA
    solo s; 1221; 2110; perc, hp, str                   MG

Suite No. 2 for Tenor Saxophone and
    Strings (1966)                                      13'
    solo t sax; str                                     MG

Entertainment No. 4 for Horn and
    Chamber Orchestra (1972)                            15'
    solo hn; 1211; 1030; timp+1, str                    MG

Concerto for Clarinet and
    Chamber Orchestra (1974)                            17'
    solo cl; 2212; 3030; perc, str                      MG

Entertainment No. 6 (1975)                              15'
    2222; 4331; timp+1, str                             MG

Concerto for Flute and
    Chamber Orchestra (1977)                            23'
    solo fl; 0222; 3110; perc, str                      MG

Elegy for the Whale (1977)                              5'
    solo tba; 2222; 4331; perc, hp, str                 MG

Four Sentiments (and an Afterthought) (1980)   22'
    3*3*3*2; 4331; timp+1, hp, str                      MG

WILLIAMS, DAVID RUSSELL  (1932-    )

March and Fugue for String Orchestra,
     op. 17 (1956)                                    7'
     str                                              MS

In the Still of the Bayou, op. 38 (1963)             8'
     3*23*2; 2000; str                                MS

Five States of Mind, op. 42 (1964-1965)              9'
     3*23*2; 2210; perc, str                          CF

Concerto for Piano (Four Hands) and
     Orchestra, op. 39 (1964)                         19'
     solo pf (4-hands); 3*222; 2220;                  MS
     timp+2, str

Lullabye Under the Magnolias, op. 40 (1964)          6'
     2222; 0000; str                                  MS

Air for Oboe and Strings, op. 45 (1964-1965)         5'
     solo ob; str                                     MS


WILLIAMS, EDGAR  (1949-    )

Of Orpahlese (1969)                                   7'
     3*3*3*3*; 4331; 3perc, str                       MS

Fant'sy II (from "Hortus Conclusis") (1975)          10'
     1211; 0110; mar, str (2-1-1-0)                   BOE

Fant'sy III (from "Hortus Conclusis") (1975)         15'
     1211; 0110; mar, str (2-1-1-0)                   BOE

The Mystic Trumpeter (1975)                           7'
     3*3*3*2; 4331; pf, str                           MS

Landscapes with Figure (1984)                        10'
     1202; 2000; str                                  MS


WILLIAMS, JOHN  (1932-    )

Essay for Strings (1966)                             10'
     str                                              MCA

Symphony No. 1 (1966)                                24'
     3*3*3*3*; 4331; timp+6, hp, pf, str              MCA

America, the Dream Goes On (1981)                    8'
    solo bar; satb cho; 3*3*3*2; 5431;             GS
    timp+3, hp, pf, gtr, str

Olympic Fanfare and Theme (1984)                    5'
    3*033*; 6601; timp+2, hp, pf, org, str         GS

Concerto for Tuba and Orchestra (NA)                5'
    solo tba; 3223*; 4331; timp+5, pf, str         GS


          WILLIAMS, JULIUS  (1954-    )

A Norman Overture (1982)                            8'
    2222; 4331; timp+2, str                        MMB


          WILLIS, RICHARD MURAT  (1929-    )

Prelude and Dance (1956)                           15'
    1221; 2200; timp+1, pf, str                    FLE

Symphony No. 2 (1964)                              25'
    3*222; 4331; timp+1, hp, str                   FLE


          WILSON, DONALD M.  (1937-    )

Dedication (1960)                                   6'
    str (7-6-5-4-3 minimum)                        HG

Concerto for Piano and Winds (1962-1963)           18'
    solo pf; 3(2picc)3*3=3*; 4331; timp+3,         ACA
    hp, 4db

Diagon for Orchestra (1984-1986)                   14'
    3(2picc)3*3*3*; s,a sax; 2221; 4perc,          ACA
    2hp, pf, str


          WILSON, OLLY  (1937-    )

Voices (1970)                                      15'
    2*3*3*3*; 4331; timp+4, pf, str                MG

Akwan (1972)                                       16'
    solo pf/elec pf; 223*3*; 4331; 4perc, str      MG
    N.B.  Also requires an additional group of
    amplified strings (4-2-2-0).

Spiritsong (1973)                                                   21'
   solo s; satb cho; 2223*; 4331; 6perc, hp,     MG
   amp pf, str

Lumina (1981)                                                      11'
   3*222; 4330; timp+2, hp, pf, str              MG

Sinfonia (1983-1984)                                              23'
   2(2b fl)2(2eh)2*2*; 4331; timp+4,             MG
   hp, pf, str

Houston Fanfare (1986)                                             3'
   3*222; 4331; timp+4, hp, pf, str              MG


      WILSON, RICHARD  (1941-    )

Initiation (1970)                                                 14'
   3*3*3+3*; 4331; timp+3, pf, str               PS

Concerto for Violin and
   Chamber Orchestra (1979)                      26'
   solo vln; 0200; 2000; timp, str               PS

Concerto for Bassoon and
   Chamber Orchestra (1983)                      19'
   solo bsn; 1*1*1*1*; 2100; mar, hp, str        PS

Symphony No. 1 (1984)                                             24'
   3*3*3*3*; 4231; timp+2, hp, str               PS

Symphony No. 2 (1986)                                             28'
   3*222; 4200; timp+2, str                      PS

Silhouette (1988)                                                 6'
   2222; 4230; timp, str                         PS

Suite for Small Orchestra (1988)                                 12'
   11*11*; 2210; mar, hp, str                    PS

Articulations (1989)                                             20'
   3=3*3=3*; 4431; timp+4, hp, cel, str          PS

Concerto for Piano and Orchestra (1991)                          33'
   solo pf; 2*2*22*; 4210; 3perc, str            PS

WINKLER, PETER   (1943-    )

Symphony (1976-1978)                                 40'
  2*2*2*2; 2220; timp+2, str                        MS


WINSLOW, WALTER   (1947-    )

Concert Aria (1973)                                  18'
  solo s; 1010; 1000; 2perc, hp, str              ACA

Concerto for Piano and Orchestra (1974)              32'
  solo pf; 3*3*3*3*; 4221; timp+5, hp, str        ACA

Pele (1977)                                          9'
  3*24=2; 4331; 4perc, str                        ACA

Mimene (1985)                                        37'
  soli coloratura, s, a, t, b; satb cho;          MS
  3=3*3*3*; 4331; timp+3, pf, str

The Piper of the Sacred Grove (1990)                 8'
  2222; 4101; 2perc, hp, str                      ACA


WINTEREGG, STEVEN   (1952-    )

Huffman Prairie (1985)                               5'
  3*3*3*3*; 4331; timp+4, str                     MS

Only Yesterday (1987)                                15'
  3*3*3*3*; 4331; timp+4, str                     MS

Visions and Revelations (1989)                       16'
  solo hn; 1001; 0111; 2perc, pf, str             MS

Concerto for Tuba (1991)                             15'
  solo tba; 1011; 1110; 2perc, str                MS

TGV (1991)                                           3'
  2222; 4221; 3perc, str                          MS


WIRTH, CARL ANTON   (1912-    )

Rhapsody for Piano and Orchestra (1947)              10'
  solo pf; 2222; 4331; timp+1, str                FLE

Elegy on an Appalachian Folk Song (1949)             9'
  2222; 4231; timp+1, str                         FLE

Idlewood Concerto (1954)                                   20'
    solo a sax; 2*222; 4331; timp+1, str                   FLE

Diversions in Denim (1956)                                 20'
    str                                                    FLE

Jephthah:  Invocation and Dance (1959)                     10'
    soli s sax, a sax; perc, pf, str                       FLE


        WISE, BRUCE   (1929-    )

Variations (1973)                                          11'
    4*3*3*3*; 4231; 3perc, hp, cel, str                    ACA


        WITKIN, BEATRICE   (1916-    )

Reports from the Planet of Mars (1978)                     8'
    1222; 2100; perc, pf, str, tape                        BEL

Twelve Tone Variations Influenced
    by the Beatles (NA)                                    17'
    3*222; 2221; perc, prep pf, str                        MCA


        WOLFF, CHRISTIAN   (1934-    )

Burdocks (1970-1971)                                       var
    any number of players, any instruments                CFP
    or sound sources

Changing the System (1972-1973)                            var
    for 8 or more players; any instruments,                CFP
    of which some are melody and some have
    a low range
    N.B.  Duration is between 15' and 75'.

Exercise 23 (Bread and Roses) (1983)                       5'
    2222; 2220; pf, str (reduced)                          CFP

Exercise 24 (J.C.'s Bread and Roses) (1983)                5'
    1111; 2100; perc, pf, str                              CFP

Exercise 25 (Liyashiswa) (1986)                            5'
    222*2; 2221; 2perc, hp, str                            CFP

WOLPE, STEFAN   (1902-1972)

Symphony No. 1 (1955-1956)                          30'
  4*4*4*4*; 4331; timp+4, str                        PS

Piece in Three Parts for Piano and
  16 Instruments (1961)                              11'
  solo pf; 2110; bar sax; 2201; perc,                PS
  hp, elec gtr, str (1-1-1-0)

Chamber Piece No. 1 (1964)                            9'
  12*11; 1110; pf, str (2-1-1-1)                      PS

Chamber Piece No. 2 (1967)                            4'
  1111; 1110; perc, pf, str (1-1-1-1)                 PS


WOOD, JOSEPH   (1915-    )

Symphony No. 1 (1939)                                25'
  2222; 4331; timp, hp, str                          ACA

Symphony No. 2 (1949)                                10'
  2222; 4321; timp, hp, str                          ACA

Poem for Orchestra (1950)                             8'
  2222; 4331; timp+1, hp, str                        ACA

Serenade for Flute and Strings (1951)                6'
  solo fl; str                                       ACA

Symphony No. 3 (1956)                                20'
  3*3*3*3*; 4221; timp+2, hp, str                    ACA

Divertimento (1958)                                  14'
  solo pf; 1111; 2110; timp+1, str                   ACA

Concerto for Violin and Orchestra (1960)             18'
  solo vln; 2222; 4330; timp, str                    ACA

Double Concerto for Viola, Piano and
  Orchestra (1970)                                   15'
  soli vla, pf; 2222; 4230; timp+1, str              ACA

Concerto for Chamber Orchestra (1975)                20'
  1111; 2110; timp+2, hp, pf/cel, str                ACA

Symphony No. 4 (1981)                                23'
  2222; 4330; timp+3, pf, str                        ACA

WOODARD, JAMES   (1929-      )

The Dream Songs of Stephen Foster (1976)          10'
    solo s; solo vln; hp, str                     MS

American Folk Ballad (1985)                        7'
    str                                           MMB

Ballad for a Summer's Day (1988)                   8'
    str                                           MMB


WOOLLEN, RUSSELL   (1923-      )

Toccata, op. 26 (1955)                            15'
    2222; 4231; timp, str                         ACA

Symphony No. 1, op. 37 (1957-1961)                25'
    2222; 2110; timp+1, str                       ACA

Hymn on the Morning of Christ's Nativity,
    op. 33 (1958)                                 20'
    soli 2vv; satb cho; 2222; 2110; timp+1,       ACA
    hp, pf, str

Summer Jubilee Overture, op. 41 (1958)            10'
    2222; 4331; timp+2, hp, pf, str               MS

The Decorator, op. 44 (1959)                      35'
    soli 5vv; 1111; 2110; timp+1, pf,             ACA
    cel, str

Modal Offerings, op. 13 (1960)                    25'
    solo org; 1*111; 2110; str                    MS

Suite for Flute and Strings,
    op. 65 (1966; rev 1979)                       18'
    solo fl; str                                  ACA

In Martyrum Memoriam -
    cantata, op. 69 (1968-1969)                   45'
    soli 2vv; satb cho; 1111; 2110; timp+1,       ACA
    org(opt), str

Three Sacred Choruses, op. 71 (1969)              15'
    ssaa cho; 2222; 2000; 2perc, str              MS

Two Responsories, op. 76 (1971)                   10'
    ssaa cho; str                                 MS

The Pasch -
    cantata, op. 79a (1974; rev 1994)                50'
    soli 3vv; satb cho; 3*3*22; 4331; timp+3,        ACA
    hp, cel, org(opt), str

Two Pieces for Piano and Orchestra,
    op. 59a (1975-1976)                              18'
    solo pf; 3*3*3*3*; 4331; timp+2,                 MS
    hp, cel, str

Easter Sequence, from Mass for
    Easter Sunday, op. 82 (1977)                      4'
    satb cho; 2tpt; org, str                         MS

Symphony No. 2, op. 86 (1977-1978)                   30'
    3*3*3*3*; 4331; timp+3, hp, pf, str              ACA
    N.B.  The third movement, "Chaconne" is
    available separately.

Mass for a Great Space, op. 94 (1986)                15'
    satb cho; 2tpt; timp+1, hp, org, str             MS

Alexandria Suite, op. 96 (1987)                      25'
    satb cho; 1111; 1000; timp+1, str                ACA

Suite for Bassoon and Orchestra,
    op. 100 (1988-1991)                              20'
    solo bsn; 2222; 2000; 2perc, hp, pf, str         MS

Prayer and Celebration, op. 107 (1990)                9'
    2222; 2330; perc, str                            MS


            WORK, JOHN WESLEY  (1901-1968)

The Singers (1946)                                   15'
    solo bar; satb cho; 2222; 0000; timp, str        BEL

Yenvalou (1955)                                       6'
    2222; 4220; timp+1, str                          GAL


            WRIGHT, MAURICE  (1949-    )

Progression (1971)                                   10'
    2121; 2231; timp+2, pf, str                      ACA

Orchestral Composition (1974)                        22'
    3*23*3*; 4331; timp+1, str                       ACA

Music from The Fifth String (1978)                     9'
    2222; 4331; timp+1, pf, str                        ANM

Stellae (1978)                                         15'
    2222; 4231; timp+3, hp, str, tape                  MMB

Wellington's Defeat (1978)                             11'
    2222; 4431; timp+5, str                            ACA

The Times Will Change (1981)                           15'
    2222; 4331; perc, pf, str                          ANM

Night Scenes (1988-1989)                               20'
    2*2*22; 2200; timp+2, DX-7 synth, str              MS


                WUORINEN, CHARLES  (1938-      )

Music for Orchestra (1956)                             7'
    2222; 4221; timp+1, str                            ACA

Concerto No. 1 for Violin and
    Orchestra (1958)                                   21'
    solo amp vln; 3*3*3*4*; 4331; 6perc,               CFP
    hp, pf, str

Symphony No. 3 (1959)                                  17'
    3*3*3*3*; 4331; timp+3, pf, str                    ACA

Concertone for Brass Quintet and
    Orchestra (1960)                                   14'
    solo br qnt; 2222; 4231; timp+2, pf, str           ACA

Evolutio transcripta (1961)                            9'
    1111; 1110; pf, str                                ACA

Concerto No. 1 for Piano and
    Orchestra (1965)                                   18'
    solo pf; 3=3*3*3*; 4331; timp+3, hp, str           CFP

Orchestral and Electronic Exchanges (1965)             15'
    3*3*3*3*; 4331; timp+3, hp, pf, str, tape          CFP

Contrafactum (1969)                                    20'
    3*3*3*3*; 4322; timp+4, 2pf, str                   CFP

Grand Bamboula (1971)                                  6'
    str                                                CFP

Concerto No. 2 for Piano and
   Orchestra (1973)                                               25'
   solo amp pf; 3*3*3*3*; 4331; timp+6, str      CFP

Hyperion (1975)                                                     16'
   1111; 1110; pf, str (1-1-1-1)                        CFP

A Reliquary for Igor Stravinsky (1975)          17'
   4*22*3; 4231; timp+3, hp, pf, str               CFP

Tashi (1975)                                                        30'
   soli cl, pf, vln, vc; 3*23*3*; 4331;           CFP
   timp+5, hp, str

The W. of Babylon (or The Triumph of
   Love Over Moral Depravity) (1975)              120'
   soli 3s, a, 2t, bar, b; fem narr;              CFP
   2*2*2*2*; 2221; 3perc, hp, pf, str

Ancestors (1978)                                                   NA
   0101; 1000; 2perc, pf, str                         CFP

The Magic Art: An Instrumental Masque,
   after Purcell (1978)                                 80'
   1*2*1*2; 2210; timp+1, hp, str                   CFP

The Magic Art - suite (1978)                           25'
   1*2*1*2; 2210; timp+1, hp, str                   CFP

Two-Part Symphony (1978)                               21'
   3*222; 4221; timp+4, hp, pf, str               CFP

The Celestial Sphere - oratorio (1980)          60'
   satb cho; 3*333; 4331; timp+4, hp,            CFP
   pf, str, tape

Eccliastical Symphonie (1980)                         13'
   3(all picc)333; 4331; timp+4, hp, pf, str   CFP
   N.B.  Four movements taken from "The
   Celestial Sphere".

Short Suite (1981)                                             15'
   2*222; 4221; timp, xyl, str                       CFP

Bamboula Squared (1984)                                 17'
   3*23*2; 4231; timp+2, pf, str,                   CFP
   quadraphonic tape

Concertino for Orchestra (1984)                       16'
   2*24=2*; 4000; str (solo db)                      CFP

Concerto No. 3 for Piano and
  Orchestra (1984)                                  27'
  solo pf; 3*23*2; 4231; timp+3, hp, str           CFP

Crossfire (1984)                                    11'
  3*23=2; 4331; timp+2, pf, str                    CFP

Movers and Shakers (1984)                           27'
  3*3*33; 4331; timp+1, hp, pf, str                CFP

Rhapsody (1984)                                     20'
  solo vln; 3*3*3*2; 4331; timp+2,                 CFP
  hp, pf, str

Prelude to Kullervo (1985)                           6'
  solo tba; 3*222; 4330; timp+1, pf, str           CFP

Fanfare for the Houston Symphony (1986)              1'
  3*333; 4331; timp+2, str                         CFP

Golden Dance (1986)                                 21'
  3*3*3*3*; 4331; 2timp+4, pf/cel, str             CFP

Bamboula Beach (1987)                                6'
  3*33*3*; 4331; timp+4, pf, str                   CFP

Five:  Concerto for Amplified Cello and
  Orchestra (1987)                                 21'
  solo amp vc; 2*22*2*; 4231; timp+2,              CFP
  hp, str

Another Happy Birthday (1988)                        2'
  3*23*3*; 4231; timp+1, pf, str                   CFP

Machault mon chou (1988)                            11'
  22*3*3*; 4231; timp+1, hp, str                   CFP


            WYKES, ROBERT ARTHUR   (1926-     )

Divertimento (1949)                                  8'
  1211; 1110; 2perc, str                           WY

Dance Overture (1955)                                6'
  3*23*2; 4330; timp+2, hp, str                    WY

Density III (1959)                                   4'
  023*3*; 2231; timp+4, hp, str                    WY

Concertino for Flute, Oboe, Piano and
   Strings (1963)                                         12'
   soli fl, ob, pf; str                                  WY

Wave Forms and Pulses (1964)                               6'
   3*23*2; 4231; timp+1, str                            WY

The Shape of Time (1965)                                   17'
   3*3*4=3*; 4331; 2timp+6, 2bd, 2glock,                 WY
   2mar, 2xyl, hp, pf, str

Letter to an Alto-Man (1967)                               12'
   satb cho; 3*3*3*3*; 4331; timp+1,                     WY
   hp, pf, str

Resonances (1971)                                          12'
   3*3*22; 4331; timp+3, pf, str                        WY

A Shadow of Silence (1972)                                 8'
   3*222; 4330; timp+4, pf, str                         WY

Towards Times Receding (1972)                              17'
   3*222; 4231; timp+3, hp, pf, str                     WY

Adequate Earth (1976)                                      67'
   solo bar; 2narr; sssaaatttbbb cho;                   WY
   4=3*3*3*; 4031; timp+2, hp, pf, cel, str

Horizons - suite (NA)                                      3'
   2*22*1; 2221; timp+3, hp, str                        TP


      WYNER, YEHUDI   (1929-      )

Da Camera (1967)                                           8'
   solo pf; 2222; 4210; perc, str                       MS

Intermedio - Lyric Ballet (1974)                           15'
   solo s; str                                          ACA

Fragments from Antiquity (1978-1981)                       25'
   solo s; 2*22*2; 4221; 2perc, str                     ACA

YANNAY, YEHUDA   (1937-      )

Mirkamim -
    Textures of Sound for Orchestra (1968)      17'
    3*3*3*3*; 4331; timp+4, hp, pf, cel, str    IMI

Five Songs for Tenor and
    Orchestra (1976-1977)                       12'
    solo t; 2222; 2221; 3perc, hp, pf, str      ACA

Concertino (1980)                               11'
    solo vln; 1111; a sax; 2000; perc, str      ACA

Seven Late Spring Pieces
    for Orchestra (1980)                        10'
    1111; a sax; 2000; perc, str                ACA


        YARDUMIAN, RICHARD   (1917-1985)

Symphony No. 2 "Psalms" (1947-1964)             28'
    solo mez (or bar); 4*4*4*4*; 4441;          TP
    timp+1, 2hp, cel, str

Concerto for Violin and Orchestra (1949)        24'
    solo vln; 3*333; 4440; timp+1, 2hp, str     TP

Symphony No. 1 (Noah) (1950; rev 1961)          25'
    4*4*4*4*; 4441; timp+1, 2hp, cel, str       TP

Epigram: William M. Kincaid (1951)              6'
    solo fl; str                                TP

Passacaglia, Recitative and Fugue (1957)        18'
    solo pf; 3*3*3*3*; 4431; timp+1, pf, str    TP

Chorale Prelude
    "Veni Sancti Spiritus" (1958)               8'
    2322; 2220; hp, str                         TP

Mass "Come Creator Spirit" (1965-1966)          55'
    solo mez (or bar); satb cho; 2222; 2320;    TP
    timp+1, hp, str

The Story of Abraham -
 oratorio (1968-1971; rev 1973)                    68'
 soli s, a, t, b; ssaattbb cho; 3*3*3*3*;          TP
 4441; timp+3, hp, str

Two Chorale Preludes (1978)                        18'
 4*4*4*4*; 4431; perc, 2hp, str                    ELK

Chorale Fantasy
 "Ee Kerezman" (Resurrection) (1979)                9'
 3*222; 2201; timp, hp, str                        ELK

To Mary in Heaven (1979)                           14'
 solo mez (or bar); 4*4*4*4*; 4431; timp,          ELK
 hp, cel, str


                YASANITSKY, GREGORY  (1953-     )

The Great American Fairy Tale (1978)               25'
 narr; 2222; 4221; timp+2, str                     YAZ

Symphony (1981)                                    25'
 223*3*; 4221; timp+3, hp, cel, str                YAZ

Summer Music (1984)                                20'
 0000; a sax; 4321; timp+4, pf, str                YAZ

And the Sky was Cobalt Blue (1985; rev 1991)        7'
 solo tpt; timp, str                               YAZ

Magic (1985)                                       11'
 solo fl; perc, pf, str                            YAZ

The Appleville Musicians (1989-1990)               30'
 narr; 2222; 4221; timp+2, pf, str                 YAZ

Into a Star (1991)                                 12'
 3*23*2; 4331; timp+2, pf, str                     YAZ


                YASUI, BYRON  (1943-     )

Parade for Orchestra (1979)                         6'
 3*3*3*3*; 4331; 4perc, pf, str                    NOA

YAVELOW, CHRISTOPHER (1950-    )

And then we saw a sea lion (1973)                    12'
   solo mar; 2222; 2220; str                    ACA

Overture (1973)                                       1'
   1120; 0220; perc, str                        ACA

Axis (1974)                                          22'
   4=4*4=4*; 4442; timp+3, hp, pf, cel, str    ACA

The Horse with Violin in Mouth (1975)                 3'
   ssa cho; str                                 ACA

Seven Mikrophonae (1975)                              4'
   2222; 2220; 2perc, str                       ACA

Monument (1980)                                      16'
   str                                          ACA


YELLIN, VICTOR FELL   (1924-    )

Passacaglia for String Orchestra (1958)              10'
   str                                          MS


YTTREHUS, ROLV   (1926-    )

Espressioni (1962)                                   13'
   3*3*3*3*; 4231; timp+1, pf, str              ACA

Gradus ad Parnassum (1979)                           30'
   solo s; 1*1*1*1*; 1210; timp+4,              ACA
   str (solo or section)

Symphony (1991)                                      17'
   3*3*3*3*; 4331; timp+4, hp, pf, str          ACA

ZADOR, EUGENE  (1894-1977)

| | | |
|---|---|---|
| Divertimento for Strings (1955)<br>str | 13'<br>FLE | |
| Fugue-Fantasia (1958)<br>3*23*2; 4431; timp+1, str | 9'<br>SCH | |
| Christmas Overture (1961)<br>3*223*; 4331; timp+4, hp, pf, str | 8'<br>TP | |
| The Remarkable Adventure of<br>Henry Bold (1963)<br>narr; 3*3*23*; 3330; timp+5, hp,<br>pf, org(opt), acc(opt), str | 15'<br>TP | |
| Festival Overture (1964)<br>3*23*3*; 4331; timp+3, hp, pf, str | 10'<br>TP | |
| Dance Overture (1965)<br>3*23*2; 4331; timp+4, pf, str | 23'<br>SCH | |
| Five Contrasts for Orchestra (1965)<br>3*23*3*; 4431; timp+1, hp, pf/cel,<br>acc, str | 20'<br>SCH | |
| Variations on a Merry Theme (1965)<br>3*23(a sax)3; 4431; timp+5, pf, str | 18'<br>TP | |
| Aria and Allegro (1967)<br>0000; 4330; str | 9'<br>MCA | |
| Trombone Concerto (1967)<br>solo tbn; 2222; 2200; 2perc, hp, str | 14'<br>MCA | |
| Studies for Orchestra (1970)<br>3*23*2; 4331; timp+5, hp, pf, str | 22'<br>MCA | |
| Concerto for Oboe and Strings (1975)<br>solo ob; str | 12'<br>TP | |
| Hungarian Capriccio (1975)<br>3*23*2; 4230; timp+1, str | 10'<br>SCH | |

ZAIMONT, JUDITH  (1945-    )

Man's Image and His Cry (1970)                        20'
    soli a, bar; satb cho; 2222; 2220;               AMC
    perc, str

Concerto for Piano and Orchestra (1972)              32'
    solo pf; 3*3*3*3*; 4231; timp+1, str             FLE

Sacred Service for the
    Sabbath Evening (1976)                           60'
    solo a (or bar); satb cho; 2*2*2*2; 2220;        GAL
    timp+1, str

Tarantelle - overture (1985)                          7'
    3*3*22; 4231; timp+3, str                        ECS

Chroma:  Northern Lights (1986)                      11'
    1111; 1000; perc, str                            MPL

Monarchs:  Movement for Orchestra (1988)             15'
    3*3*4=2; 4331; 4perc, pf, str                    MPL


            ZAPPA, FRANK  (1940-    )

Dupree's Paradise (1969-1970)                         8'
    22(2eh)3*1*; 2221; 3perc, hp,                    BS
    pf, str (3-2-2-1)

I'm Stealing the Room (1972)                          3'
    satb cho; 5(picc, 2a fl)4*4*4*;                  BS
    2a,bar sax; 8451; timp+6, dmst, hp,
    pf, elec gtr, acc, str

Penis Dimension (1972)                                5'
    satb cho; 5(picc, 2a fl)4*4*4*;                  BS
    2a,bar sax; 8451; timp+6, dmst, hp,
    pf, acc, elec gtr, str

Strictly Genteel (1972)                              11'
    5*4*4=4*; 8451; timp+6, hp, pf/cel/hpsd,         BS
    str (divisi)

Naval Aviation in Art?  (1977)                        3'
    223*1; 2221; 3perc, hp, 2pf, str (3-2-2-1) BS

Bob in Dacron (1979)                                 12'
    5*4*4*4*; 84(flu hn)51; timp+6,                  BS
    hp, pf, str

Bogus Pomp (1979)                                    25'
  5=4*4*4(2cbsn); 84(flu hn)51; timp+6, hp,      BS
  pf/cel, str (solos for principal players)

Mo 'n' Herb's Vacation (1979)                        28'
  5(picc, 2a fl)4*4*4*; 8451; timp+6,             BS
  dmst, pf, b gtr, str (multiple divisi)

Sinister Footwear (1981)                             NA
  7(picc, 2a fl, 2b fl)4(2eh)6(E-flat picc,       BS
  2b cl)5*; 2s,2a,2t,bar sax; 8451; timp+6,
  hp, pf, moog synth, str (divisi)

Envelopes (1982)                                      4'
  2*24*3*; 4222; timp+6, str                      BS

The Perfect Stranger (1982)                          13'
  2(2a fl)2(2eh)3*1; 2221; 3perc, hp,             BS
  2pf/2cel, str (3-2-2-1)

Sad Jane (1983)                                      NA
  5*4*4=4*; 8451; timp+6, hp, pf, str             BS

Pedro's Dowry - Yes, that's right (1984)            NA
  5*4*4=4*; 8451; timp+6, dmst, hp,               BS
  pf/cel, b gtr, str (divisi)


     ZIFFRIN, MARILYN  (1926-    )

Orchestra Piece No. 1 "Colors" (1979)                9'
  2222; 2220; timp+1, str                         AMC

Symphony for Voice and Orchestra
  "Letters" (1988)                                24'
  solo v; 2222; 4231; timp+2, pf/cel, str         MS


     ZONN, PAUL  (1938-    )

Concerto for Clarinet (1966)                         13'
  solo cl; 2011; 2201; 3perc, hp, str             ACA

Interiors (1978)                                     13'
  3*3*3*3*; 4331; timp+3, hp, str                 ACA

Symphony in F (1981)                                 20'
  2(2picc)22+2; 2210; timp/perc, str              ACA

River Dawn (1990)                                          7'
  2*2*2*2*; 4331; timp+3, str                   ACA

Only the Wind (1991)                                      10'
  2*2*2*2*; 4331; timp+3, str                   ACA

Pennyrile Variations (1991)                              13'
  2*2*2*2*; 4331; timp+3, str                   ACA


    ZUPKO, RAMON  (1932-      )

Fantasia for Orchestra (1956)                            10'
  2122; 4221; 4perc, str                        ACA

Pastorale (1956)                                          8'
  solo cl; str                                  ACA

Ballade for Orchestra (1957)                              5'
  3*3*3*3*; 4231; 2perc, hp, str                ACA

Elegy (1957)                                              5'
  str                                           ACA

Prelude and Bagatelle (1961)                              5'
  str                                           ELK

Prologue, Aria and Dance (1961)                          10'
  solo hn; str                                  ACA

Variations for Orchestra (1961)                           8'
  3*222; 4331; 3perc, str                       ACA

Concerto for Violin and Orchestra (1962)                 30'
  solo vln; 3222; 4331; timp+3, hp, pf, str     SZG

This is the Garden (1962)                                10'
  soli fl, ob, cl, tpt; satb cho;              ACA
  3perc, str

Translucents (1967)                                      10'
  str                                           ACA

Radiants (1971)                                          10'
  3*3*4=2; 4431; 6perc, str                     ACA

Proud Music of the Storm (1975-1976)                     70'
  2*222; 4331; 3perc, str                       ACA
  N.B.  Also requires bands, chiors
  and dancers.

Windsongs
  (Concerto for Piano and Orchestra) (1979)  23'
  solo pf; 4*3*3*3*; 4331; timp+3, hp, str  CFP

Life Dances (1981)  17'
  4*3*3*3*; 4331; 5perc, hp, pf, str  ACA

Ritual Dances (1981)  30'
  1111; a sax; 1211; 3perc, str (2-1-1-1)  ACA

Canti terrae (1982)  13'
  4*3(2eh)3(E-flat, 2b cl)3(2cbsn); 4331;  ACA
  5perc, hp, str

Blue Roots
  (Symphony in Three Movements) (1989)  15'
  2*222; a sax; 4331; 3perc,  ACA
  pf/elec kybd, str


      ZUR, MENACHEM

Chamber Symphony (1974-1975)  19'
  1111; 1110; 3perc, hp, str  SEE


      ZWILICH, ELLEN TAAFE  (1939-    )

Symposium for Orchestra (1973)  12'
  3*3*4*3*; 4331; timp+1, 2hp, str  MER

Passages (1982)  25'
  solo s; 2=1*2*2*; 3110: perc, str  MG

Symphony No. 1:
  Three Movements for Orchestra (1982)  18'
  2*22*2*; 4231; timp+3, hp, pf, str  MG

Prologue and Variations (1983)  13'
  str  MER

Celebration for Orchestra (1984)  10'
  4*3*3*3*; 4331; timp+3, hp, pf/cel, str  MER

Concerto Grosso
  (after Handel's "Sonata in D") (1985)  15'
  solo vln; 11*01; 2000; hpsd, str  MOB

Symphony No. 2:  Cello Symphony (1985)  24'
  solo vc; 3*3*3*3*; 4331; timp+3, pf, str  MER

Concerto for Piano and Orchestra (1986)          24'
    solo pf; 3*3*4=3*; 4331; timp+1, str          MER

Images (1986)                                     18'
    soli 2pf; 2222; 2111; perc, str               MER

Concerto for Trombone and Orchestra (1988)        20'
    solo tbn; 3*3*3*3*; 6331; perc, pf, str        MER

Symbolon (1988)                                   16'
    4*3*3*3*; 4331; timp+3, hp, str               MER

Tanzspiel (1988)                                  28'
    3*3*3*4*; 4221; timp+2, pf, str               MER

Concerto for Bass Trombone, Strings,
    Timpani and Cymbals (1989)                    16'
    solo b tbn; timp+1, str                       MER

## APPENDIX A

### ORCHESTRAL WORKS LISTED BY DURATION

The works listed in Appendix A are for orchestra alone and are classified by duration. Each durational category is subdivided into sections that indicate the size of the orchestra. For exact instrumentation, please refer to the main listing in the catalog.

#### 5' OR LESS

*Large Orchestra*

J. Adams: Short Ride in a Fast Machine
Ames: Song for Orchestra
Bernstein: Overture to "Candide"
Bernstein: Slava!
Bernstein: A Musical Toast
Blank: Overture for a Happy Occasion
Bolcom: MCMXC, Tanglewood
Bond: Ringing
Cage: A Celebration of Some 100X150 Notes
Claflin: Fishhouse Punch
Cooper: Homage
Copland: Happy Anniversary
Copland: Jubilee Variations
Corigliano: Campane di Ravello
Cowell: Ancient Desert Drone
Cowell: American Pipers

Crockett: The Sun and Moon Dance and Blow Trumpets
M. Cunningham: Islands
Curtis: A Stanislaus Overture
Diamond: Overture No. 2
Ekizian: Prologue: Pulse
Farberman: The (You Name It!) March
I. Fine: Blue Towers
Fischer: A Sea Bird
Fischer: Ariadne Abandoned
Flagello: Symphonic Aria
Flagello: Overture giocosa
Floyd: Flourishes
Frankenpohl: Rondo Marziale
T.R. George: The Soul of Wit
Gould: Cheers!
Gould: Flourishes and Galop
Hailstork: Celebration
Hovhaness: Island Sunrise
Jones: Fanfare and Celebration

Kievman: Fanfare for
Everyman
Kievman:
Happybirthdaytoyou
Koykkar: Kinesis
W. Kraft: A Simple
Introduction to the
Orchestra
W. Kraft: American
Carnival Overture
W. Kraft: Fanfare
Vintage 90-91
Lang: International
Business Machine
Larsen: Collage:
Boogie
John Lewis: Fanfare -
Salute to Basie
McBride: Light
Fantastic
Milburn: The Armies of
the Night
Monello: Divertimento
Newman: Fanfare for
Orchestra
Newman: Double Piece
for Orchestra
Newman: Presto
Orrego-Salas: Fanfare
Parchman: Little Fugue
Parchman: Essay for
Orchestra
Parchman: Dramatic
Overture
Paulus: Ordway
Overture
Picker: Old and Lost
Rivers
Picker: Seance
Pinkham: Catacoustical
Measures
Piston: Bi-Centennial
Fanfare
Riegger: New Dance
Riegger: Evocation for
Orchestra
Rodriguez: The
Salvation Rag
Rorem: Frolic

Rouse: The Infernal
Machine
Schuman: Showcase
Schuman: Let's Hear It
For Lenny!
Starer: Six Variations
Stearns: Passacaglia
Still: Miniature
Overture
Tautenhahn: Chromatic
Square
Thomson: Sea Piece
with Birds
Turok: Danza Viva
Tuthill: Rowdy Dance
Van Vactor: Masque of
the Red Death
Van Vactor: Fanfare
for Orchestra
Van Vactor: Holy Manna
Ward-Steinman:
Season's Greetings
Weisgall: Love's
Wounded
John Williams: Olympic
Fanfare
D. Wilson: Houston
Fanfare
Winteregg: Huffman
Prairie
Wuorinen: Fanfare
Wuorinen: Another
Happy Birthday
Zupko: Ballade for
Orchestra

*Medium Orchestra*

J. Adams: Tromba
lontana
Adler: Summer Stock
Amram: Fox Hunt
Bach: Gala Fanfare
Bach: Alla breve
Ballard: Scenes from
Indian Life
Ballou: Beguine
Barnes: Morning Gigue
Bavicchi: Caroline's
Dance

Beck: Sinclair Listens
Beckler: Fanfare
Beeler: Homage to
   Roger Sessions
Berger: Creole
   Overture
Bernstein: Overture to
   "West Side Story"
Blank: Meditation for
   Orchestra
Blumenfeld: Miniature
   Overture
Bowman: Fantasy on a
   Carol Tune
Britain: Solar Joy
Britain: Minha Terra
Britain: This is the
   Place
Britain: Little per
   cent
J. Cohn: Variations on
   "John Henry"
Copland: Proclamation
Cordero: Momentum
   Jubilo
A. Cunningham: Night
   Lights
Daugherty: Oh Lois!
W. Davis: Festival
   Fanfare
Diemer: Youth Overture
Diemer: Rondo
   Concertante
Diemer: 1962 Overture
Ekizian: Birthday
   Chords
Flagello: Processional
Franco: Baconiana
Freund: Adagio
Gannon: Cellophane
E. George: Abraham
   Lincoln Walks At
   Midnight
E. George:
   A Thanksgiving
   Overture
T.R. George:
   Celebration Overture
T.R. George: Olympic
   Overture

Gillis: Short Overture
   to an Unwritten
   Opera
Gillis: Mandarin Dance
Gillis: Temple Dance
Gillis: Vim, Vigor and
   Velocity
Giuffre: Hex
Goeb: Gambol
Gould: Big City Blues
Gould: Celebration
   Strut
Hannay: Summer
   Festival Overture
Hartley: Festive Music
   for Orchestra
Haubiel: 1865 A.D.
Haxton: Fugue
Hazzard: Harwichport
   Interlude
Hewitt: The Wheel
Hewitt: Entering
Hewitt: Satori
Hewitt: Now That I Am
   God
Hodkinson: Dynamics
Horvit: Toccatina
Hovhaness: Monadnok
Huggler: Toccata
Hunt: Theme in Two
   Moods
Hutchison: Prologue
Janson: Skyscape
Karlins: Concert Music
   No. 4
Keller: Overture
Kirk: Intrada
Kramer: Requiem for
   the Innocent
Kubik: Bachata
LoPresti: The Masks
McBride: March of the
   Be-Bops
McBride: Stringitis
McBride: Pioneer
   Spiritual
McBride: Overture on
   Whimsical Tunes
Menotti: Lewisohn
   Stadium Fanfare

Mourant: Whistler's
Father
Muczynski: Dovetail
Overture
Musgrave: Song of the
Enchanter
Nelhybel: Slavonic
Triptych
R. Nelson: Fanfare for
a Celebration
R. Nelson: Fanfare for
the Hour of Sunrise
Orland: Initial
Orland: Epigram
Parchman: Elegy for
Orchestra
Paulus: Street Music
Pehrson: Manhattan
Plaza Painting
Raphling: Novelty
Suite
Raphling: Dance of the
Chassidim
Rorem: Fantasy
Scarmolin: Prelude to
"The Oath"
Scarmolin: The
Caliph - Dance
Scarmolin: The Sunlit
Pool
Schuman: The Orchestra
Song
Scianni: Shiloh
Overture
Shulman: Prelude
Sims: Le Tombeau
D'Albers
Stallcop:
In Apprehension of
Spring
Stallings: Antiphony
Stein: Sailor's
Hornpipe
Stevens: Threnos
Still: Threnody
Stokes: Cotton Candy
Strandberg: Fiesta
Suben: Academic
Overture

Tanenbaum: Birthday
Waves
Thomson: Fugue and
Chorale
Thomson: Hymns
Toch: Circus Overture
Gwyneth Walker:
Fanfare for the
Family Farm
Gwyneth Walker: Open
the Door
Washburn: Triplex for
Orchestra
Washburn: Excursion
Welcher: Castle Creek
Donald White: Sagan
Winteregg: TGV
Wykes: Density III
Wykes: Horizons
Zappa: Envelopes

*Small Orchestra*

Bales: Primavera
Bloch: In memoriam
Bond: Two Orchestral
Preludes
Bond: Elegy
Bond: Sonata for
Orchestra
Britain: Jewels of
Lake Tahoe
Britain: Serenata
Sorrentina
Britain: Chicken in
the Rough
Clarke: Saraband for
the Golden Goose
Copland: John Henry
Copland: Down A
Country Lane
Cowell: Polyphonica
Cowell: Saturday Night
at the Firehouse
Crawford: In Praise of
Music
Creston: A Rumor
Creston: Introit
M. Cunningham: Figg
and Bean Overture

Del Tredici: Acrostic
Song
Dembski: Refraction/
Retracja
Donato: Mission San
Jose de Aguaya
El-Dabh: Bacchanalia
Fennelly: Empirical
Rag
Foss: Elegy for Anne
Frank
Frackenpohl: Little
Suite
Franco: Prophecy
Gannon: Free From
Season's Passing
Gannon: Prickly Heat
Gerschefski: Classic
Overture
Goeb: American Dance
No. 4
Goeb: American Dance
No. 5
Goossen: Corybant
Hannay: A Farewell to
Leonard Bernstein
Hartley: Three
Patterns for Small
Orchestra
Hartley: Elizabethan
Dances
Hewitt: Scars on the
Clock's Face
Hewitt: A Tribute to
Three Masters
Hutchison: Prairie
Sketch
Ivey: Overture for
Small Orchestra
Jager: Three Pieces
Jenni: Elegy and Dance
Kirk: Divertimento
Knox: Paseos
Koch: Memorial
Koch: Dance Overture
Kremenliev: Study for
Orchestra
London: Overture to
"The Imaginary
Invalid"

Luening: Symphonic
Fantasia III
Luening: Symphonic
Fantasia VIII
MacInnes: In Memoriam
JFK
Mayer: Back Talk
McBride: Nothing Else
Matters
McBride: We are alone
Mourant: Serenade
Nelhybel: Aegean Modes
Newell: Edifice in
Memoriam
D. Ott: Wild Orchid
Overture
Parker: Revolutionary
Overture
Peaslee: Tarantella
Pinkham: Prothalamion
Pinkham: Envoi
Pinkham: Rondo
Pinkham: Scherzo
Pleskow: Two Preludes
Pleskow: Preludium
No. 2
Rodriguez: Adagio
Rogers: Prelude to
"The Warrior"
Sacco: Meditation
No. 1
Sacco: Meditation
No. 2
Sacco: Meditation
No. 3
Saturen: Four Short
Movements
Schuller: Little
Fantasy
Siekmann: The Lower
Longswamp Upper
Crust Strut
Sims: Pictures for an
Institution
L. A. Smith: A Fanfare
for Wolfgang
Suben: Fantasia su un
soggetto cavato

Tautenhahn: Prelude
for Chamber
Orchestra
Thomson: Tango Lullaby
Toch: Epilogue
Toch: Intermezzo
Toch: Short Story
Toch: Puppet Show
Toch: The Enamoured
Harlequin
Van Vactor: Overture
to a Cantata
Washburn: Three Pieces
Washburn: St. Lawrence
Overture
Wolff: Exercise 23
Wolff: Exercise 24
Wolff: Exercise 25
Yavelow: Overture
Yavelow: Seven
Mikrophonae
Zappa: Naval Aviation
in Art?

*Chamber Orchestra*

Beeler: Cinematic
Scene
Britain: Angel Chimes
Britain: Les Fameux
Douze
Hartke: Precession
Ivey: Passacaglia for
Chamber Orchestra
Wolpe: Chamber Piece
No. 2

*String Orchestra*

Ames: Prelude
Binkerd: Two
Meditations
Borishansky: In
Commemoration
Canning: Meditation
Constantinides:
Designs
Cope: Tragic Overture
(+ timp)
Cowell: Ballad

Dello Joio: Arietta
Diemente: Elegy
Dutton: Quebec, Spring
Flagello: Adoration
(+ harp)
Freund: Gold
T. R. George: Prelude
and Toccata
Gillis: From an
Evening in Autumn
Gillis: Adoration at
Eventide
Gillis: Scherzino for
Strings
Gillis: Soliloquy for
Strings
Gillis: Strictly for
Strads
Goeb: American Dance
No. 1
Goeb: American Dance
No. 2
Goeb: American Dance
No. 3
Gould: Elegy for
String Orchestra
Hagen: Adagietto for
Strings
Hartley: Elegy for
Strings
Hartley: Psalm for
Strings
Hewitt: When Spring is
Near
Hewitt: Night of
Hecate
Hewitt: Concerto
Grosso No. 3
Hewitt: The Flowers
Have No Mothers
Hewitt: The Quiet
Journey
Hewitt: Dark Journey
Hewitt: Folk Fantasia
Hodkinson: Drawings:
Set No. 7
Hodkinson: Drawings:
Set No. 8
Hoiby: Study in Design

Hovhaness: Armenian
   Rhapsody No. 1
   (+ perc)
Hovhaness: Armenian
   Rhapsody No. 2
Howe: Elegy for
   Strings
Hutchison: Lyric Piece
Kechley: The Funky
   Chicken
Kelly: Rounds for
   String Orchestra
Kohn: Interlude I
L. Kraft: Larghetto in
   Memory of Karol
   Rathaus (+ timp)
Lessard: Serenade
   No. 1
Lessard: Serenade
   No. 2
McBride: Variations on
   an Unknown Theme
McBride: Pumpkin
   Eater's Little Fugue
Mills: In a Mule Drawn
   Wagon
Mourant: Dark Forest
   (+ perc,harp)
Mourant: Valley of the
   Moon
Mourant: Pizzicato
   Polka
Mourant: Song for
   Strings
Mourant: Fantasy for
   Strings
B. Nelson: Jesus, The
   Very Thought of Thee
Newman: Hymn
Newman: Song for
   Strings and Harp
Parchman: Adagio for
   Strings
Persichetti: Introit
Rakowski: Elegy
Rice: Nocturne
Rice: Two Foot
   Thumpers
Riegger: Romanza

Saturen: Exposition
   for Sixteen
Saturen: Largo for
   Strings
Saylor: Cantilena
Siekmann: Scene in
   Monochrome
Steiner: Music for
   String Orchestra
Steiner: Tetrark
Stock: Back to
   Bass-ics
Stout: Ricercare and
   Aria
Thomson: Cantabile
Thomson: Thoughts for
   Strings
Van Vactor: Louise
Van Vactor: Prelude
   and Fugue
Weigl: Andante
Weigl: Adagio
Weigl: To Emily
Weiner: Elegy
Zupko: Prelude and
   Bagatelle

### 6' TO 10'

*Large Orchestra*

Adler: Jubilee
Adler: In Just Spring
Aitken: Happy Birthday
   Overture
Albright: Masculine/
   Feminine
Ames: Rhapsody II
Antheil: Heroes of
   Today
Antheil: Over the
   Plains
Antheil: Autumn Song
Antheil: McKonkey's
   Ferry Overture
Antoniou: Paean
J. Avshalomov: The
   Taking of T'ung Kuan
Bach: Toccata for
   Orchestra

Barber: Overture to
the School for
Scandal
Barber: Music for a
Scene from Shelley
Barber: Second Essay
Barber: Night Flight
Barber: Fadograph of a
Yestern Scene
Barnes: Solar Winds
Bassett: Colloquy
R. Bauer: Neon
Bavicchi: Sherbrook
West
Bazelon: Concert
Overture
Becker: Victory March
Beeson:
Transformations
E. Bell: Rituals for
Orchestra
Bergsma:
Documentary II
Bezanson: Rondo
Prelude
Bianchi: Rauschenberg
Variations
Binkerd: Sun Singers
Blank: Music for
Orchestra
Bloch: Scherzo
fantastique
Bolcom: Ragomania
Brehm: Hephaestus
Overture
Britain: Red Clay
Britain: Umpqua Forest
R. Brooks: Seascape
Browne: Prelude and
Scherzo
Browne: Serenade
D. Brubeck: Fugal
Fanfare
Brun: Overture
Carl: The Stars'
Harmony
D. Carlson: Twilight
Night
Carter: Holiday
Overture

Carter: Remembrance
Carter: Anniversary
Chihara: Ceremony IV
A. Cohn: Kaddish for
Orchestra
Coker: Overture
Giocoso
Coker: Lyric Statement
Coker: Declarative
Essay
Colgrass: Seventeen
Cone: Variations
Constantinides:
Dedications
Copland: Cortege
Macabre
Copland: An Outdoor
Overture
Copland: Danzon Cubano
Cordero: Obertura de
Salutacion
Corigliano: Promenade
Overture
Corigliano: Summer
Fanfare
Cowell: Some Music
Cowell: Pastorale and
Fiddler's Delight
Cowell: United Music
Cowell: Overture for
Large Orchestra
Cowell: Rondo for
Orchestra
Cowell: Music for
Orchestra
Cowell: The Tender and
the Wild
Cowell: Symphony
No. 19
Cowell: Twilight in
Texas
Creston: Frontiers
Creston: Toccata
Crockett: Wedge
Cummings: Denouement
M. Cunningham: Counter
Currents
M. Cunningham: Venus
and Adonis
Cushing: Cereus

Dahl: Quodlibet on
   American Folktunes
Davidovsky:
   Synchronisms No. 7
Dello Joio: Epigraph
Dello Joio: Five
   Images
Dello Joio: Homage to
   Haydn
Di Domenica: Dream
   Journeys
Diemente: Three Scenes
   from Pinocchio
Dollarhide: Other
   Dreams, Other
   Dreamers
Dollarhide: Pluriels
Donovan: New England
   Chronicle
Downey: La joie de la
   paix
Druckman: That
   Quickening Pulse
Dukelsky: Ode to the
   Milky Way
Dzubay: Siren Song
Dzubay: Snake Alley
Eberhard: The Bells of
   Elsinore
Ehle: Soundpiece
Ehle: Ritual Conflicts
Ehle: Biomass and
   Strange Particles
Elwell: Ode for
   Orchestra
Erb: Bakersfield
   Pieces
Erb: Treasures of the
   Snow
Erb: Music for a
   Festive Occasion
Erb: Dreamtime
Etler: Passacaglia
Felciano: Galactic
   Rounds
Feldman: In Search of
   an Orchestration
Feldman: On Time and
   the Instrumental
   Factor

Ferrito: Celebrations
I. Fine: Diversions
Fischer: Rhapsody on
   French Folk Tunes
Foss: Ode
Fuleihan: Preface to a
   Child's Storybook
Fuleihan: Invocation
   to Isis
Fuleihan: Fiesta
T. George: Bal a
   Bougival
T. George: First
   Rhapsody
T. George: Laude
Gillis: To an Unknown
   Soldier
Gillis: Intermission
Gillis: Tulsa; A
   Symphonic Portrait
   in Oil
Godfrey: Rhapsody for
   Large Orchestra
Goeb: Caprice for
   Orchestra
Goeb: Memorial
Goeb: Essay for
   Orchestra
Goossen: Hae: In
   memoriam
Gottlieb: Pieces of
   Seven
Gould: A Homespun
   Overture
Gould: Philharmonic
   Waltzes
Gould: Housewarming
P. Grant: Rhythmic
   Overture
P. Grant: Dramatic
   Overture
P. Grant: Lyrical
   Overture
Grantham: Invocation
   and Dance
Gross: Resonants for
   Divided Orchestra
Gryc: Neon Night
Gutche: Holofernes
   Overture

Gutche: Raquel
Gutche: Epimetheus USA
Hagen: Fresh Ayre
Hailstork: Epitaph
Hailstork: An American
  Port of Call
Hannay: Sonorous Image
Hannay: Listen
Hanson: Mosaics
Harbison: Remembering
  Gatsby
M. Harris: Music for
  Orchestra
Roy Harris: When
  Johnny Comes
  Marching Home
Roy Harris: Melody
Roy Harris: Kentucky
  Spring
Roy Harris: Elegy
Roy Harris: Epilogue
  to "Profiles in
  Courage"
Russell Harris:
  Minnesota Centennial
  Prelude
Haubiel: American
  Rhapsody
Heiden: Envoy
Hemmer: The Midnight
  Ride of Paul Revere
Hewitt: The Golden
  Door
Hewitt: Haven
Hoag: Symphonic
  Movement
Hodkinson: Epigrams
Hovhaness: Mountain of
  Prophecy
Iannaccone: Lysistrata
Imbrie: Ballad in D
Ince: Infrared Only
Ince: Before Infrared
Ivey: Circling
P. James: Passacaglia
Janson: Revelations
  for Orchestra
Jazwinski: Music for
  Symphony Orchestra

Jenni: Eulalia's
  Rounds
Jones: Overture for a
  City
H. Kay: Funerailles
U. Kay: Of New
  Horizons
Keats: Branchings
Kechley: Second
  Composition
Kessner: Romance
Kessner: Raging
Knehans: Passacaglia
Knight: Americana
  Overture
Knight: Canadian
  Tribute
Knight: The Great
  American Bicycle
  Race
Knox: Overture in F
Knox: Brazen
Koykkar: Evocations
Krieger: Riverside
  Variations
Kubik: Thunderbolt
  Overture
La Montaine: Jubilant
  Overture
La Montaine: Overture:
  From Sea to Shining
  Sea
La Montaine: Overture:
  An Early American
  Sampler
Lang: Eating Living
  Monkeys
Lasser: Southern
  Landscapes
Laufer: Everest
Laufer: Overture for
  Orchestra
Laufer: Prelude and
  Fugue
Laufer: Prologue and
  Epilogue
Lavenda: Affinities
Lees: Profile

Lees: Prologue,
Capriccio and
Epilogue
Leichtling: Fantasy
Piece
Lerdahl: Cross-
Currents
R. Lewis: Three Pieces
for Orchestra
Liptak: Loner
Liptak: Resoundings
Lockwood: Weekend
Prelude
Lubin: A Tragic
Overture
Luening: Two Symphonic
Interludes
Luening: Symphonic
Fantasia V
Luening: Symphonic
Interlude No. 3
Luke: Suite for
Orchestra
Luke: Concert Overture
Lybbert: Concert
Overture
Mailman: Prelude and
Fugue No. 1
Matalon: Variations
for Orchestra
Maves: Overture to an
Opera
Mayer: Overture for an
American
McBeth: Suite on a
Biblical Event
McBeth: Overture
McBeth: Grace,
Praeludium and
Response
McBeth: The Badlands
McBeth: Kaddish
McBride: Fantasy on a
Mexican Christmas
Carol
McBride: Panorama of
Mexico
McBride: Folksong
Fantasy
McKay: Dance Overture

McKay: Structure
McKay: Evocations
McKinley: Concerto for
Orchestra
McKinley: Concertino
for Orchestra
McKinley: Boston
Overture
McTee: On Wings of
Infinite Night
McTee: Circuits
Mechem: The Jayhawk
Mekeel: Vigil
Melzer: The Altered
Constellation
Mennin: Canto for
Orchestra
E. Miller: Orchestral
Changes
E. Miller: Reflections
at the Bronx Zoo
E. Miller: Anti-Heroic
Amalgam
E. Miller: Anacrusis
Mills: Toccata in C
Mills: Prelude and
Fugue
Mobberly: Aquaria
Moevs: Symphonic Piece
No. 5
Moss: Paths
Muczynski: Charade
R. Nelson: Savannah
River Holiday
R. Nelson: Jubilee
Newman: "B" for
Orchestra
Orrego-Salas: Riley's
Merriment
Ortiz: Elegia a los
Inocentes Caidos
D. Ott: Genesis II
D. Ott: The Water
Garden
D. Ott: Behold Spring
Palange: Don Juan's
Coda
Palmer: A Centennial
Overture

Parchman: Winsel
Overture
Parchman: Study for
Orchestra
Pehrson: Regions
Pellegrini: Seven
Statements in 3/4
Time
Penn: Spectrums,
Confusions and
Sometime
Perle: Six Bagatelles
Perle: Dance Fantasy
Perlongo: Myriad
Perry: A Short Piece
Perry: Hommage to
Vivaldi
Persichetti: Dance
Overture
Piket: Curtain Raiser
Piston: Toccata
Piston: Symphonic
Prelude
Pone: Vivos voco,
mortuos plango
Powell: Intrada and
Variants
Ptaszynska:
Improvisations
Ptaszynska: Spectri
sonori
Raksin: Litany
Ramey: Cantus Arcanus
G. Read: A Bell
Overture
G. Read: Pan e Dafni
Reynolds: Graffiti
Richter: Eight Pieces
Riegger: Passacaglia
and Fugue
Riegger: Music for
Orchestra
Riegger: Overture
Riegger: Preamble and
Fugue
Riegger: Quintuple
Jazz
Rochberg: Time-Span II
Rogers: Amphitryon
Overture

Rogers: The Colors of
Youth
Rorem: Eagles
Rorem: Fantasy and
Polka
Ross: Overture to the
Virginia Voyage
Rouse: Phaethon
Rouse: Jagganath
Rovics:
Transformations
Rubin: Freedom
Rudhyar: Threnody
Sacco: Contemplation
Sapieyevski: Summer
Overture
Saylor: Archangel
Schickele: Invention
for Orchestra
Schickele: Celebration
with Bells
Schickele: American
Birthday Card
Schubel: Specters and
Sheldrakes
Schubel: Linear
Concentrate
Schuller: Vertige
d'Eros
Schuller: Symphonic
Study
Schuman: American
Festival Overture
Schuman: Newsreel
Schuman: Circus
Overture
Schuman: Variations on
"America"
Schwantner: Freelight
C. Schwartz:
Passacaglia
Serebrier: Poema
Elegiaco
Shatin: Piping the
Earth
Sheinfeld:
Confrontations
Shere: Sections for
Orchestra

Shulman: A Laurentian
  Overture
S. Silverman: Tenso
Simons: Lamentations I
Simons: Lamentations
  II
Singleton: Moment
Singleton: After
  Fallen Crumbs
L.A. Smith: A New York
  Overture
L. Smith: Overture to
  "Santa Claus"
R. Smith: Can-Can
  Waltz
Snyder: Shamanic
  Dances
Spears: Voyage
Stearns: Six Paintings
Steiner: Suite for
  Orchestra
Steinke: Threnody
Steinohrt: Celebration
  Overture
Stern: Finale from
  "Fort Union"
Stevens: A Green
  Mountain Overture
Still: Old California
Still: In Memoriam
Still: Bells
Still: Festive
  Overture
Stock: Divertimento
Stock: Triflumena
Stock: Rockin' Rondo
Stock: Fast Break
Stucky: Son et Lumiere
Surinach: Fandango
Surinach: Drama jondo
Surinach: Las
  Trompetas de los
  Serafins
Svoboda: Dramatic
  Overture
Svoboda: Eugene
  Overture
Svoboda: Ex Libris
Svoboda: Serenade

Taylor: Introduction
  and Dance Fantasy
Taylor: Chaconne
Augusta Thomas: Ritual
Thomson: The Seine at
  Night
Thomson: Wheat Field
  at Noon
Ticheli: Images of a
  Storm
Tircuit: Manga
Toensing: Verses
Torke: Purple
Torke: Bronze
Tower: Composition for
  Orchestra
Trimble: Sonic
  Landscape
Trimble: Five Episodes
Turner: Encounter
Turok: Variations on
  an American Song
Turok: Chartres West
Turok: A Scott Joplin
  Overture
Turok: A Sousa
  Overture
Ultan: Sinfonia
Ussachevsky: Dances
  and Fanfare
Van Vactor: Overture
  to a Comedy
Van Vactor: Variazioni
  Solenne
Van Vactor: United
  Nations Fanfare
Van Vactor:
  Inauguration
Van Vactor: Sinfonia
  Breve
Vega: Serenade
Verrall: Summerland
  Fantasy
Vincent: Rondo
  Rhapsody
Wagner: Processions
  Medieval
Wagner: Variations on
  an Old Form

Wagner: Hudson River
Legend
Wagner: Radio City
Snapshots
Wagner: Panorama
George Walker: In
Praise of Folly
George Walker: Eastman
Overture
Ward: Jubilation
Ward: Concert Music
Ward: Hymn and
Celebration
Ward: Invocation and
Toccata
Ward-Steinman: Antares
Ward-Steinman: Olympic
Overture
Ward-Steinman: Elegy
for Astronauts
Weber: The Enchanted
Midnight
Whear: In Memoriam:
R.V.W.
Wheelock: Tesserae
E. Williams: Of
Orpahlese
E. Williams: The
Mystic Trumpeter
Winslow: Pele
Wuorinen: Bamboula
Beach
Wykes: Dance Overture
Wykes: Wave Forms and
Pulses
Wykes: A Shadow of
Silence
Yasui: Parade for
Orchestra
Zador: Fugue-Fantasia
Zador: Christmas
Overture
Zador: Festival
Overture
Zador: Hungarian
Capriccio
Zaimont: Tarantelle
Zupko: Variations for
Orchestra
Zupko: Radiants

Zwilich: Celebration
for Orchestra

*Medium Orchestra*

L. Adams: Prelude to
Blake
Adler: City by the
Lake
Adler: The Fixed
Desire of the Human
Heart
Amlin: Shadowdance
Amram: Across the Wide
Missouri
T. Anderson:
Introduction and
Allegro
T. Anderson: Squares -
An Essay
Baksa: Meditation for
Orchestra
Balada: Homage to
Casals
Balada: Homage to
Sarasate
Balazs: The Trail
Balazs: Song for
Pablito
Barati: Tribute
Barati: Vaudeville for
Orchestra
Barber: First Essay
Bavicchi: A Concert
Overture
Bavicchi: Fantasia on
Korean Folk Tunes
Bavicchi: Pyramid
Bazelon: A Quiet Piece
for a Violent Time
Becker: Prelude to
Shakespeare
Beeler: Quintessence
I & II
Beeler: A Mad Song
E. Bell: Concerto for
Orchestra
Benjamin: Invariants
Bennett: Overture to
the Mississippi

Bergsma: Music on a
  Quiet Theme
Bergsma: March with
  Trumpets
Bergsma: A Carol on
  Twelfth Night
Bernstein: On the Town
Bestor: In Memoriam
  Bill Evans
Blickhan: Dialectics
Bohrnstedt: Essay on
  an Original Air
Bohrnstedt: Romantic
  Overture
Bohrnstedt: Festival
  Overture
Bohrnstedt: Tetrachord
  Suite
Bohrnstedt: A Little
  Piece for a Great
  Hall
Bottje: Ballad Singer
Brant: Dedication in
  Memory of FDR
Britain: Paint Horse
  and Saddle
Britain: Cactus
  Rhapsody
Britain: Kambu
Britain: Anwar Sadat
H. Brubeck: The
  Devil's Disciple
H. Brubeck: Symphonic
  Movement
Cazden: Woodland
  Valley Sketches
Chenowith: Cracks/
  Reforms/Bursts
Chihara: Forest Music
Chou: And the Fallen
  Petals
Clarke: Monograph
Clarke: Variegation
Cope: Contrasts
Copland: Letter from
  Home
Cowell: Hymn and
  Fuguing Tune No. 3
Cowell: Hymn and
  Fuguing Tune No. 16

Crawford: Metracollage
Creston: Pastorale and
  Tarantella
Creston: Chant of 1942
Creston: Pre-classic
  Suite
A. Cunningham: Theatre
  Piece
M. Cunningham: Trans
  Actions
Curtis-Smith:
  Celebration
Custer: Concert Piece
Davidovsky:
  Transientes
Diamond: Timon of
  Athens
Diemer: Festival
  Overture
Diemer: Fairfax
  Festival Overture
Donato: Prairie
  Schooner Overture
Donato: The Plains
Drew: October Lights
Dutton: Songs for
  Orchestra
Eaton: Tertullian
  Overture
Eaton: The Lion and
  Androcles
Effinger: Lyric
  Overture
Effinger: Evensong
Effinger: Fanfare 1980
El-Dabh: Unity at the
  Cross Road
D. Epstein: Movement
  for Orchestra
Erb: Christmas Music
Etler: Dramatic
  Overture
Faith: Elegy
Fetler: A Comedy
  Overture
Fink: Scherzo for
  Orchestra
Fischer: Sketches from
  Childhood

Fischer: Piece
  Heroique
Fischer: Legend
Fischer: Overture on
  an Exuberant Tone
  Row
Flagello: Goldoni
  Overture
Floyd: In Celebration
Foss: Fanfare
Frackenpohl: Allegro
  Scherzando
Frackenpohl: A
  Jubilant Overture
Frackenpohl: Overture
  in D
Frederickson:
  "Illinois"
  Variations
Freed: Alleluia
Garlick: Mardi Gras
Garlick: Danza Barbara
Garlick: Pasticcio
Gelt: Tempus Fugit
E. George: Adagietto
E. George:
  Introduction and
  Allegro
T. George: Ballade for
  Orchestra
Gerschefski: Toccata
  and Fugue
Gerschefski: Nocturne
Gideon: Symphonia
  Brevis
Glass: Dance from
  "Akhnaten"
Goodenough: Choral
  Fantasy
Goossen:
  Entertainments
Gould: Minstrel Show
Gould: Notes of
  Remembrance
P. Grant: Homage Ode
P. Grant: A Mood
  Overture
Hannay: Dramatic
  Overture
Hannay: Celebration

Roy Harris: Ode to
  Consonance
Hartke: Pacific Rim
Hartley: Concert
  Overture
Hartley: Variations
  for Orchestra
Haxton: Elegy
Haxton: A Rose for
  Emily
Haxton: Involvement
Heiden: Salute for
  Orchestra
Helps: Cortege
Hennagin: A Summer
  Overture
Hennagin: Explorations
  for Orchestra
Herrmann: A Portrait
  of Hitch
Hervig: Music for a
  Concert
Hewitt: A Good-
  Natured Overture
Hewitt: Seven
Hewitt: Wizard's Eggs
Hewitt: Return of the
  White-Throat
Hewitt: Return of the
  Night-Hawk
Hill: Sangraal
Hoag: An After-
  Intermission
  Overture
Hodkinson: Caricatures
Hodkinson: Stabile
Hodkinson: Overture -
  A Little Travelin'
  Music
Hoiby: Noctambulation
Hoiby: Overture to a
  Farce
Hoiby: Music for a
  Celebration
Hopkins: Variations
  for Orchestra
Hovhaness: Storm on
  Mt. Wildcat
Hovhaness: Symphony
  No. 5

Hovhaness: Copernicus
Huggler: "D" into
  Blossom
Huggler: Desert Forms
M. Hunt: Asymptopia I
M. Hunt: Asymptopia II
Hutchison: The Desert
  Shall Bloom as the
  Rose
Ivey: Ode for
  Orchestra
Jacobi: Music Hall
  Overture
Jenni: Frescamento
Jenni: From the Top
H. Johnson: Past the
  Evening Sun
T. Johnson: The Secret
  of the River
Jones: In Retrospect
Kalbfleisch: Junctures
U. Kay: Reverie and
  Rondo
U. Kay: Of New
  Horizons
Kievman: Funeral March
Kirk: Ballet Music
Kirk: Vignettes
Kirk: Dance of the
  Border
Knox: Ballad Suite
Koblitz: Trism
Koch: Variations for
  Orchestra
Korte: Southwest
W. Kraft:
  Tintinnabulations
Kroeger: Chorale for
  Orchestra
Kroeger: Dramatic
  Overture
Kubik: Pastorale and
  Spring Valley
  Overture
Kupferman: Ostinato
  Burlesco
Kupferman: Six
  Epilogues
Kurka: Julius Caesar
La Montaine: Canons

Lange: Atoms for Peace
Lankester: Two
  Christmas Carols
Larsen: Overture
Larsen: Deep Summer
  Music
Laufer: Cry!
Laufer: In the Throes
Laufer: Resolution
Lesemann: Scherzo for
  Orchestra
Lessard: Box Hill
  Overture
James Lewis: ...the
  errant note to seize
P. Lewis: Fragments/
  Hedgehogs
D. Lieberman: June 28,
  1982
Lifchitz: Yellow
  Ribbons No. 8
Lopatnikoff: Two
  Russian Nocturnes
Luening: Short
  Symphony
Luening: Concerted
  Piece
Luening: Synthesis
Luening: Symphonic
  Interlude No. 5
MacBride: Produce
MacBride: Dance
  Interlude
MacInnes: Dialogues
  for Orchestra
MacInnes:
  Intersections
Maggio: The Hand
  Prints of Sorcerers
Mailman: Gateway City
  Overture
Mamlok: Grasshoppers
McBride: Symphonic
  Melody
McKinley: October
  Night
Mennin: Folk Overture
Mennini: Overtura
  breve
Mennini: Cantilena

Mols: Andante and
  Allegro
Monello: Country Dance
Montague: Prologue
C. Moore: Sinfonia
Mourant: Song of the
  Caribbean
Mourant: Three Acts
  from "Punch and
  Judy"
Muczynski: Symphonic
  Dialogues
Musgrave: Obliques
Musgrave: Scottish
  Dance Suite
R. Nelson: Toccata for
  Orchestra
R. Nelson: Rocky Point
  Holiday
Nin-Culmell:
  Differencias
D. Ott: Commemoration
  and Celebration
  Overture
Overton: Symphonic
  Movement
Overton: Interplay
Overton: Sonorities
Parmentier: Double
  Entendre
Paulus: Ground Breaker
Perera: The Saints
Plain: Facets for
  Orchestra
Pleskow: Six Epigrams
Polster: Fragments
  from Memory
Polster: The
  Orchestral Punpieces
Polster: Serenade for
  Orchestra
Polster: Music for a
  Summer Evening
Porter: Poem and Dance
Pozdro: Overture
Pozdro: A Cynical
  Overture
Pozdro: Waterlow Park
Primosch: Dappled
  Things

Putsche: Three Bugs
Rathaus: Louisville
  Prelude
Rausch: Sonorities
G. Read: Toccata
  giocosa
G. Read: Vernal
  Equinox
Reif: Fanfare and
  Fugato
Rhodes: Madrigal I
Rice: Festival
  Overture
Rice: Pastoral
  Overture
Richter: Variations on
  a Sarabande
Rickley: Journey
  Through
Riegger: Suite for
  Younger Orchestras
Riegger: Festival
  Overture
Rieti: Introduzione e
  gioco delle ore
Rieti: Sinfonia Breve
Rivers: The Exile's
  Return
Rozsa: Concert
  Overture
Rozsa: Notturno
  Ungherese
Saul: From Life to
  Greater Life
Schelle: El Medico
E. Schwartz: Music for
  Orchestra
Scianni: Batik
Serly: American Elegy
Serly: Symphonic
  Variations
Shere: Handler of
  Gravity
Shinn: Reflections
Shinn: Cortege
Shore: Intermezzo
Shulman: Waltzes for
  Orchestra
Siegmeister: Lonesome
  Hollow

Siegmeister: From My
  Window
Silsbee: Three Little
  Wind Stories
H. Smith: Contours
Starer: Symphonic
  Prelude
Stein: A Festive
  Overture
Stern: Grant Us Peace
Still: The Peaceful
  Land
Strandberg: Three
  Phases of a Jock
Stucky: Transparent
  Things
Surinach: Feria magica
Svoboda: Three Pieces
  for Orchestra
Svoboda: Overture of
  the Season
Swisher: Two Lyric
  Pieces
Sydeman: Study No. 2
Taylor: Processional
F. Thorne: Burlesque
  Overture
F. Thorne: Sonar
  Plexus
F. Thorne: Gems from
  Spoon River
F. Thorne: Humoresque
N. Thorne: The Voices
  of Spring
Townsend: Ridgefield
  Rag
Travis: Collage for
  Orchestra
Turok: Prelude to
  "Richard III"
Tuthill: Elegy
Van Vactor: Overture
  to a Comedy No. 2
Van Vactor:
  Passacaglia and
  Fugue in D minor
Van Vactor: Prelude
  and March
Van Vactor: Armed
  Forces Medley

Vincent: Overture to
  Lord Arling
Wagner: American
  Jubilee
Gwyneth Walker: Essay
  for Orchestra
Gwyneth Walker: Match
  Point
Wallach: The Tiger's
  Tail
Ward: Prairie Overture
Ward: Hymn to the
  Night
Ward-Steinman: Concert
  Overture
Warren: The Crystal
  Lake
Warren: Along the
  Western Shore
Warren: Intermezzo
Washburn: Festive
  Overture
Washburn: Synthesis
Washburn: Prologue and
  Dance
Washburn: Elegy
Waters: Overture
D. Waxman: Paris
  Overture
Whear: Catskill Legend
Whear: Lancaster
  Overture
Whear: Quantum Suite
Whear: Decade Overture
Whear: White River
  Legend
Whear: Silver
  Celebration
Donald White: Kennecec
  Suite
Donald White: Overture
  for Orchestra
Whittenberg: Event
Wigglesworth: Janus
D. Williams: In the
  Still of the Bayou
D. Williams: Five
  States of Mind
Julius Williams: A
  Norman Overture

R. Wilson: Silhouette
Winslow: The Piper of
the Sacred Grove
Wirth: Elegy on an
Appalachian Folk
Song
Wood: Symphony No. 2
Wood: Poem for
Orchestra
Woollen: Summer
Jubilee
Work: Yenvalou
Wright: Progression
Wright: Music from the
Fifth String
Wuorinen: Music for
Orchestra
Zonn: River Dawn
Zonn: Only the Wind
Zupko: Fantasia for
Orchestra

*Small Orchestra*

Adler: Sinfonietta for
Orchestra
Adolphus: Bitter Suite
W. Alexander: Salpinx
W. Alexander: Suite
for Small Orchestra
B. Anderson: Revel
Argento: Overture -
The Boor
Argento: From the
Album of Allegra
Harper
J. Austin: Triple Play
J. Avshalomov: Slow
Dance
Baksa: Overture to
"Aria da Capo"
Bales: St. Paul's
Communion Service
Bavicchi: Mont Blanc
Bavicchi: Music for
Small Orchestra
Bazelon: Overture to
Shakespeare's
"Taming of the
Shrew"

Beck: Innis Fodhla
Beck: Overture
Becker: Cossak
Sketches
L. Bell: Continuum
Berlin: Structures
Bernstein: Two
Meditations
Bestor: Variations for
Orchestra
Bolcom: Commedia
Bond: Concertino
Bond: Journal
Brandt: The Enchanted
Garden
Bresnick: One
Brings: Scherzi
musicale
Britain: Pyramids of
Giza
J. Brown: Fragments
J. Brown: Fixed Ideas
J. Brown: Notturno
Brunelli: Two
Gentlemen from
Verona
Carl: The Distant
Shore
Carlsen: Palette
Chou: Landscapes
Chou: All in the
Spring Wind
J. Cohn: Homage
J. Cohn: Prometheus
J. Cohn: The Little
Circus
Colgrass: Divertimento
Colgrass: Sea Shadow
Copland: Quiet City
Copland: Three Latin
American Sketches
Corigliano: Elegy
Cotel: Variations on a
Theme by Haydn
Cowell: Carol
Creston: Prelude and
Dance
Csonka: Prisma
Sinfonico
M. Cunningham: Aedon

M. Cunningham: Time
  Frame
Custer: Passacaglia
Daugherty: Flamingo
Diamond: Music for
  "Romeo and Juliet"
Dollarhide: A Fantasy
  of Ivory Thoughts
  and Shallow Whispers
Dutton: The Traveller
Effinger: Landscape I
El-Dabh: Tahmeela
Etler: Elegy
Fetler: Capriccio
Finney: Three Pieces
Foss: Symphony of
  Rossi
Franco: Sinfonia
Franco: Clodagh
Franco: Nocturne
Freund: Canzona for
  Orchestra
Fuleihan: Divertimento
Fussell: Aria of the
  Blessed Virgin
Gaburo: On a Quiet
  Theme
Gillis: Paul Bunyan
Gooch: Restless
  Landscape
Goodenough: Two Essays
Goodenough: Elegy
Goodwin: Kerr County
  Kick
Goossen: Orpheus
  Singing
Green: Passacaglia
Gross: Aria, Prelude
  and Fugue
Gutche: Rondo
  capriccioso
Gyring: Adagio for
  Orchestra
Hagen: A Stillness at
  Appomattox
Hagen: Introduction
  and Cortege
Hagen: Heliotope
Hailstork: My Lord
  what a Mourning

Haines: Informal
  Overture
Hannay: Prelude and
  Dance
Hannay: Suite
  "Billings"
Hanson: Pastorale
Russell Harris: Three
  Movements
Harrison: Seven
  Pastorales
Hartley: Sinfonia
  No. 7
Hewitt: Prelude to "A
  New Testament"
Hewitt: Taming of the
  Shrew
Hewitt: A Summer in
  Blue and Green
Hewitt: Aunt Frieda's
  Stove
Hewitt: Night Without
  Neon
Hewitt: Haunted House
Hewitt: Fantasia for
  Oboe, Two Horns and
  Strings
Hewitt: Beyond the
  Blue Mountains
Hill: Paganini Set
Hill: Secrets
Hodkinson: Laments
Hodkinson: Valence
Hoffmann: Orchestra
  Piece No. 1
Hovhaness: Kohar
Huggler: Elegy
Huggler: Continuum
Hutcheson: Transitions
  for Orchestra
Jacobi: Two Pieces in
  Sabbath Mood
P. James: Chaumont
Jazwinski: Overture in
  the Classical Style
Jenni: Inventio Super
  Nomen
Jenni: Le Kaleidoscope
  de Gide
Jenni: R-music

T. Johnson: Fission
Karpman: Six of one
  Half, a Dozen of the
  Other
Kaufman: Dance of
  Death
U. Kay: A Short
  Overture
Kelly: A Miniature
  Symphony
Kievman: Excerpts from
  Orchestra Suite
  No. 4
Kirk: Adagietto
Koblitz: Gris-Gris
Koch: Overture for
  America
Kohn: Return
L. Kraft: Overture
  in G
Krenek: Divertimento
Krenek: Static and
  Ecstatic
Krenek: Von vorn
  herein
Kubik: Folk Song Suite
Kubik: Music for
  Dancing
La Montaine: A
  Summer's Day
Larsen: Weaver's Song
  and Jig
Lazarof: Piccola
  serenata
Lazarof: Odes for
  Orchestra
Lazarof: Ritralto
Lees: Spectrum
P. Lewis: Evolution
P. Lewis: Espejo
Lifchitz: Yellow
  Ribbons No. 17
Liptak: Beginnings
Lombardo: Aphorisms
Luening: Serenade for
  Three Horns and
  Strings
Luening: Prelude to a
  Hymn Tune by William
  Billings

Luening: Wisconsin
  Suite
Luening: Symphonic
  Fantasia IV
Luening: Symphonic
  Interlude No. 4
Luening: Symphonic
  Fantasia VIII
Luening: Symphonic
  Fantasia X
Mahler: Three Pieces
Mailman: Autumn
  Landscape
Mailman: Prelude and
  Fugue No. 2
Mandelbaum:
  Convocation Overture
Matthew: Six for
  Twenty-Seven
McBeth: Quanah
McKay: Fantasy on a
  Quiet Theme
McKay: Kaleidoscope
McKay: Ritual
McKinley: Orchestral
  Study
E. McLean: Big
  Variations
McVoy: A Summer
  Overture
Menotti: Introduction,
  March and Shepherd's
  Dance
Merryman: The River
  Song
E. Miller: Images from
  the Eye of a Dolphin
Mills: Serenade
Moevs: Prometheus
Morris: Clash
Moss: Scenes
Muczynski: Serenade
  for Summer
Nelhybel: Music for
  Orchestra
Nelhybel: Movement for
  Orchestra
Nelhybel: A Mighty
  Fortress

Nelhybel: Campus
Concertante
R. Nelson: Sarabande
Newman: Divertimento
D. Ott: The Water
Garden
Paccione: Our beauties
are not ours
Perlongo: Variations
for Orchestra
Pinkham: Five Short
Pieces
Plain: Clawhammer
Pleskow: Two Movements
for Orchestra
Pleskow: Three Pieces
for Orchestra
Pleskow: Four
Bagatelles for
Orchestra
Pleskow: Epitaphium
Pleskow: Preludium
Pone: Overture "La
Bella Veneziana"
Porter: Dance in
Three-Time
Powell: Stanzas
Rakowski: Winged
Contraption
Rhodes: Four Movements
Rice: Overture
Richter: Fragments
Riegger: Dance Rhythms
Riley: Theme and
Variations
Rodriguez: Lyric
Variations
Rogers: Elegy in
Memory of FDR
Rogers: Characters
from Hans Christian
Andersen
Rogers: Elegy
Rogers: The Silver
World
Rosenboom: Caliban
upon Sebetos
Rovics: Three
Movements
Rovics: Affirmation

Sacco: Classical
Overture
Sapp: The Women of
Trachis
Saturen: Expression
Schiff: Stomp
Schneider: Sheva
Schubel: Superscherzo
Schuller: Suite for
Chamber Orchestra
E. Schwartz: Eclipse
III
E. Schwartz: Zebra
E. Schwartz: Pastorale
F. Schwartz: The
Tropical Trek of
Tristan Trimble
Shapero: Credo for
Orchestra
Shere: from Calls and
Singing
Shere: Soigneur de
Gravite
Shulman: In Memoriam
Siegmeister:
Wilderness Road
Siegmeister: Summer
Night
Siegmeister: Riversong
Silsbee: Sanctuary
Simons: Piece for
Orchestra
Smart: Del Diario de
un Papagayo
Smit: Four Alchemy
Marches
L. Smith: Arabesque
Starer: Prelude and
Rondo Giocoso
Stearns: Theme and
Variations
Stearns: Becoming
Perfectly One
Stern: Carom
Stevens: Four Short
Pieces
Still: Can'tcha Line
'Em
Still: Pages from
Negro History

Stock: Capriccio
Stock: American
  Accents
Stokes: The Spirit of
  Place among the
  People
Stokes: The Greenhouse
  Effect
Strandberg: Shades
  Mountain
Strandberg: The Last
  Summer
Street: Montsalvat
Suben: Verses of
  Mourning
Surinach: Madrid
Swanson: Night Music
Swift: Divertimento
Swift: Some Trees
Swisher: Yuki no
  Niigata
Augusta Thomas: Echoes
M. Thomas: Concert
  Piece
Thomson: Dance in
  Praise
Thomson: Pilgrims and
  Pioneers
Toch: Capriccio
Tower: Island Rhythms
Townsend: Fantasy
Tull: Capriccio
Ultan: Wakonda Sketch
Ussachevsky:
  Miniatures for a
  Curious Child
Van de Vate: Adagio
Verrall: Prelude for
  Orchestra
Wagner: Pastoral
  costarricense
George Walker:
  Antiphonies
Washburn: New England
  Holiday
D. Waxman: Overture to
  Serenade Concertante
Weber: Dolmen
Westergaard: Five
  Movements

Whear: A Shakespeare
  Prelude
Wheelock: Vanishing
  Points
D. Williams: Lullabye
  Under the Magnolias
E. Williams:
  Landscapes with
  Figure
Witkin: Reports from
  the Planet of Mars
Woollen: Prayer and
  Celebration
Wuorinen: Evolutio
  transcripta
Wykes: Divertimento
Yannay: Seven Late
  Spring Pieces
Yardumian: Chorale
  Prelude
Yardumian: Chorale
  Fantasy
Zador: Aria and
  Allegro
Zappa: Dupree's
  Paradise
Ziffrin: Orchestra
  Piece No. 1

*Chamber Orchestra*

Amram: Three Songs for
  America
Babbitt: Composition
  for Twelve
  Instruments
Babbitt: The Crowded
  Air
Berlin: Menagerie
D. Carlson: Variations
Cummings: Morning
  Music
Daugherty: Snap!
Davidovsky: Inflexions
Eaton: Adagio and
  Allegro
Hannay: Abstraction
Hass: City Life
Heussenstamm: Scherzo

Jazwinski: Music for
  Chamber Orchestra
Kennedy: Two Sonnets
Krenek: Ausgerechnet
  und verspielt
Kupferman: Sound
  Objects
D. Lee: Overture for
  Chamber Orchestra
D. Lewin: Essay on a
  Subject by Webern
Lifchitz: Tiempos
Lifchitz: Yellow
  Ribbons No. 12
M. Phillips: Summer
  Soft
Pisk: Canzona
Pisk: Sonnet
Silver: Window Waltz
Strunk: Concerto for
  Chamber Orchestra
Taub: Of the Wing of
  Madness
Van de Vate:
  Variations
Vega: Olep ed Arudamot
Wagner: Rhapsody
E. Williams: Fant'sy
  II
Wolpe: Chamber Piece
  No. 1

*String Orchestra*

Adler: Elegy
Amram: Autobiography
R. Anderson: Fugue
R. Anderson: Two
  Pieces
R. Anderson: Two
  Movements
E. Applebaum: The
  Princess in the
  Garden
Balada: Musica
  Tranquila
Ballou: Prelude and
  Allegro (+ piano)
R. Bauer: Sospenso
Beeler: Sinfonia

A. Berger: Three
  Pieces
J. Berger: Short
  Overture
Blank: Concertino
Bohrnstedt: Idyll
  (+ harp)
Bond: Four Fragments
  (+ perc, pf)
Brant: Stresses
  (+ hp, pf/cel)
Britain: Earth of God
E. Brown: For P.B.
  (+ pf)
J. Brown: Intermezzo
Browne: Concerto for
  Strings
Brunswick: Air with
  Toccata
Calabro: Ten Short
  Pieces
D. Carlson: Lilacs
Chance: Elegy
Cheetham: Three
  Binghams
Cone: Music for
  Strings
Constantinides:
  Composition
Constantinides: China
  II
Cordero: Adagio
  Tragico
Cordero: Elegy
Corigliano: Voyage
Cowell: Ensemble
Cowell: Hymn and
  Fuguing Tune No. 2
Cowell: Hymn and
  Fuguing Tune No. 5
Cowell: Hymn, Chorale
  and Fuguing Tune
  No. 8
Creston: Homage
Daugherty: Strut
Dello Joio: Air
Dello Joio:
  Choreography
Dello Joio: East
  Hampton Sketches

Diemente: Italian
  Serenade
Diemer: Pavane
Diemer: Serenade
Dzubay: Tantalus
Effinger: Quiet
  Evening (+ mar, fl)
Ehle: Folk Song Suite
El-Dabh: Fantasia
  (+ timp)
I. Fine: Serious Song
Fredrickson:
  Reflections
Gaburo: Three
  Interludes
Gelt: Lamento
Ghezzo: Echoes of
  Romania
Giannini: Prelude and
  Fugue
Gideon: Lyric Piece
Gillis: Three Sketches
Glass: Company
Goeb: Divertissement
J. Grant: Lament
P. Grant: Instrumental
  Motet
P. Grant: Suite No. 2
P. Grant: A Quiet
  Piece
Hailstork: Sport of
  Strings
Hailstork: Essay for
  Strings
Hannay: Music for
  Strings
M. Harris: Invitation
  to the Waltz
Hartke: The Bull
  Transcended
Haxton: Largo
Hewitt: Ode
Hewitt: Concerto
  Grosso No. 4
Hewitt: Fantasia on
  Old Welsh Airs
Hewitt: Sinfonia on
  Expanding Matrices
Hovhaness: Psalm and
  Fugue

Hovhaness: Celestial
  Fantasy
Hovhaness: Alleluia
  and Fugue
Hovhaness: In Memory
  of an Artist
M. Hunt: Con Cordes
M. Hunt: Lento
Husa: Pastorale
Hutchison: Tombeau
  (+ cl, 2perc)
Jenni: In Memoriam
H. Johnson: Music for
  String Orchestra
Jones: Elegy
Kelly: Garden of Peace
Kelly: Shenandoah
  Variations
Kennedy: Lyric Ode
Kirk: Hemis Dance
  (+ timp)
Kirk: Latham Suite
Krenek: Five Short
  Pieces
Krenek: Seven Easy
  Pieces
Lange: Divertimento
T. Lee: Morango
Lombardo: Threnody
Luening: Elegy for the
  Lonesome Ones
Luening: Fantasia for
  String Orchestra
MacBride: Once Removed
MacInnes: Four
  Miniatures
Mailman: Partita
Mailman: Generations
Mailman: Elegy
Mandelbaum: Memorial
Mayer: Andante for
  Strings
McVoy: Elegy
Mennin: Fantasia
Mennini: Arioso
Mills: Prologue and
  Dithyramb
Mills: Symphonic Ode
L. Mitchell: Melody
  for Strings

Mourant: Prelude and
  Rondo (+ cl, hp)
Murray: Epitaph
R. Nelson: Elegy for
  Strings
Nixon: Air for Strings
Parchman: Petit
  Symphony
Park: Out Island
Parsi: Rapsodia
  elegiaca
Pinkham: Nocturne
Pisk: Elegy
Pleskow: Epitaphium
Pleskow: Three
  Epigrams
Pleskow: Consort for
  Strings
Ptaszynska: La Novella
  d'Inverno
G. Read: Quiet Music
G. Read: Arioso
  elegiaca
T. Read: Isochronisms
  No. 2
A. Reed: Titania's
  Nocturne
H. Reed: Overture for
  Strings
Reise: Poem for String
  Orchestra
Rogers: Allegory
  (+ 2fl, mar)
Rorem: Pilgrims
Sacco: Sinfonietta
Scarmolin: Arioso for
  Strings
Schuman: Amaryllis
C. Schwartz: Motion
F. Schwartz: Un
  sourire festif
Serebrier: Elegia para
  cuerdas
Serly: Lament
Shulman: Threnody
Siekmann: Triunity for
  Strings
Singleton: An Idea is
  a Piece of Cloth

H. Smith: By Yearning
  and By Beautiful
L.A. Smith: Serenade
  for Marguerita
Stearns: Fantasy for
  Strings
Stearns: Interlude
Stern: In Memoriam
  Abraham
Stewart: Prelude for
  Strings
Strandberg: The Legend
  of Emmeline Labiche
Strandberg: Essay for
  Strings
Strandberg: Sea of
  Tranquility (+ pf)
Strunk:
  Transformations
Susa: Eulogy
Svoboda: Prelude and
  Fugue
Swanson: Music for
  Strings
Tann: as ferns
F. Thorne: Fantasia
Townsend: Adagio
Townsend: Fantasy on
  Motives of Burt
  Bachrach
Trefousse: Square of
  Sunlight
Trimble: Notturno
Turok: Threnody
Ussachevsky:
  Celebration
Van de Vate: Gema Jawa
Van Vactor: Chaconne
Van Vactor: Adagio
  Mesto
Verrall: Prelude and
  Allegro
Vincent: Nude
  Descending the
  Staircase
Wagner: Two Moments
  Musical
Wagner: From the North
  Sea
Waldrop: Pressures

George Walker: Lyric
   for Strings
Washburn: Suite for
   Strings
Washburn: Passacaglia
   and Fugue
Washburn: Serenade
Washburn: Song and
   Dance
Washburn: Queen Noor
   Suite
Washburn: Fairfax
   Suite
Washburn: Saraswati
   Suite (+ tabla)
Weber: Two Pieces
Weiner: Quarternity
Whear: Olympiad
Donald White:
   Divertissement
Wigglesworth: Music
   for Strings
D. Williams: March and
   Fugue
John Williams: Essay
   for Strings
D. Wilson: Dedication
Woodard: American Folk
   Ballad
Woodard: Ballad for a
   Summer's Day
Wuorinen: Grand
   Bamboula
Yellin: Passacaglia
Zupko: Translucents

**11' TO 15'**

*Large Orchestra*

Adler: Toccata for
   Orchestra
Adler: Requiescat in
   Pace
Albright: Chasm
W. Alexander: Episodes
T.J. Anderson:
   Messages
Antoniou:
   Micrographies

Antoniou: Events II
Antoniou: Skolion
E. Applebaum: Symphony
   No. 1
Babin: Capriccio
Bach: Sprint
Bach: Escapade
Bach: Estampie
D. Baker: Kosbro
Balada: Auroris
Balada: Sardana
Balada: Quasi un
   pasodoble
Balada: Fantasias
   Sonoras
Balazs: Passacaglia
Balazs: Two Pieces
Ballard: Devil's
   Promenade
Ballard: Fantasy
   Aborigine No. 5
Barati: Configuration
Barati: Confluence
Barber: Medea's
   Meditation and Dance
   of Vengeance
Barber: Toccata
   festiva
Barber: Third Essay
Bassett: Echoes from
   an Invisible World
Bassett: From a Source
   Evolving
Bazelon: Short
   Symphony
Bazelon: Dramatic
   Movement
Bazelon: Excursion
Beck: State of the
   Union
Beckler: Concerto for
   Orchestra
Beeson: Hymns and
   Dances
Bennett: Suite of Old
   American Dances
Bergsma: Chameleon
   Variations
Bergsma: In
   Celebration

Bernstein:
  Divertimento
Bestor: Overture to a
  Romantic Comedy
Blackwood: Symphonic
  Fantasy
Blank: Six Miniatures
Bohrnstedt: Dance
  Suite
Bohrnstedt: Variations
  for a Celebration
Boone: First Landscape
Borishansky: Music for
  Orchestra
Bottje: Symphony No. 5
Bottje: Chiaroscuros
Brant: Antiphony I
Brant: Desert Forests/
  Spatial Panoramas
Bresnick: Ocean of
  Storms
Brings: Two Pieces
Britain: Cowboy
  Rhapsody
E. Brown: Time Spans
E. Brown: Sounder
  Rounds
Bubalo: Spacescape
Bubalo: Concertino for
  Orchestra
S. Burton: Dithyramb
S. Burton: Fanfare for
  Peace
S. Burton: Pied Piper
  Overture
Caltabiano: Poplars
Campo: Alpine Holiday
  Overture
Cheetham: Amalgam
Cheetham: Variations
  on a Gregorian Theme
Çlarke: Points West
Colgrass: As Quiet As
Constantinides:
  Symphony No. 1
Coolidge: Spirituals
  in Sunshine and
  Shadow
Coolidge: Pioneer
  Dances

Coolidge: The Voice
Cooper: Variants
Copland: Short
  Symphony
Copland: El Salon
  Mexico
Copland: Inscape
Corbett: Ghost
  Reveille
Cordero: Panamanian
  Overture No. 2
Cordero: Five Brief
  Messages
Corigliano:
  Tournaments Overture
Corigliano: Three
  Hallucinations
Corigliano: Fantasia
  on an Ostinato
Cortes: Yerma
Cory: Tapestry
Cotton: Fantasia
Cowell: Synchrony
Cowell: Big Sing
Cowell: Symphony
  No. 12
Cowell: Chiascuro
Creston: Walt Whitman
Creston: Invocation
  and Dance
Creston: Dance
  Overture
Creston: Janus
Creston: Corinthians
  XIII
Creston: Pavane
  Variations
Crockett: Melting
  Voices
Cummings: Composition
  for Orchestra
Curtis-Smith: Chaconne
  à son goût
Custer: Found Objects
  II
Davidovsky: Planos
C. Davis:
  Recollections
Del Tredici: The Last
  Gospel

De Mars: Ventura and
Clemente
Diamond: The Enormous
Room
Diamond: The World of
Paul Klee
Diemer: Symphony No. 2
Dodge: Rota
Dollarhide: Movements
Donato: Episode for
Orchestra
Donovan: Epos
Downey: Chant to
Michelangelo
Druckman: Aureole
Dutton: Black Moon
Effinger: Tone Poem on
a Square Dance
Effinger: Capriccio
Effinger: Landscape II
Ekizian: The Exiled
Heart
Ekizian: Saber Dance
El-Dabh: Symphony
No. 1
Elisha: Ten Variations
D. Epstein: Sonority
Variations
D. Epstein: Ventures
Erb: Sonnaries for
Orchestra
Erb: Prismatic
Variations
Erickson: Variations
Etler: Concerto in One
Movement
Etler: Convivialities
Evett: Concertino
Felciano: Mutations
Feldman: Structures
Ferneyhough: La Terre
est un Homme
Ferrito: Omaggio a
Berio e Fellini
Ferrito: Variations
Fetler: Cantus Tristis
I. Fine: Toccata
concertante
I. Fine: Partita for
Orchestra

Fink: Suite from
"Chinchilla"
Finney: Variations for
Orchestra
Fischer: Marco Polo
Foss: The Prairie
Foss: Recordare
Foss: Folksong for
Orchestra
Fountain:
Manifestation
Fountain: Exiled
Franco: Peripetie
Fuleihan:
Mediterranean
Fuleihan: Three Cyprus
Serenades
Giannini:
Frescobaldiana
Giuffre: Symphonic
Movement
Glass: Music in
Similar Motion
Godfrey: Mestengo
Goeb: Fantasia for
Orchestra
Goossen: Music for
Orchestra
Goossen: Prospero's
Spell
Gottlieb: Articles of
Faith
Gottschalk: Communique
Gould: Festive Music
Gould: Columbia
P. Grant: A Musical
Tribute
Gruenberg: Jazz Suite
Gryc: Three Fantasias
Gutche: Symphony No. 4
Gutche: Bi-Centurion
Hagen: Lyric
Variations
Hagen: Common Ground
Hanson: Lux aeterna
Hanson: Pan and the
Priest
Hanson: Dies Natalis I
M. Harris:
Illuminations

Roy Harris: Farewell
  to Pioneers
Roy Harris: Three
  Symphonic Essays
Roy Harris: Memories
  of a Child's Sunday
Roy Harris:
  Celebration:
  Variations on a
  Timpani Theme
Roy Harris: The Quest
Roy Harris: Symphonic
  Epigram
Hartley: Symphony
  No. 3
Hass: Chimera
Haubiel: Heroic Elegy
Haufrecht: When Dad
  was a Fireman
Haufrecht: Suite for
  Orchestra
Heiden: Euphorion
Helm: Brasiliana
Herman: Interludes
Hervig: In those Days
Hewitt: In the Sun
Hiller: A Preview of
  Coming Attractions
Hoag: Cloud Tango
Hoag: A Vinland
  Narrative
Hodkinson: Bumberboom
Hodkinson: Epitaphium
Hoffmann: Stouffler
Hopkins: Symphony
  No. 1
Hopkins: Three Pieces
Horvit: The Gardens of
  Hieronymus B.
Hovhaness: Concerto
  No. 4
Hovhaness: Meditations
  on Orpheus
Hovhaness: Variations
  and Fugue
Hovhaness: Floating
  World
Hovhaness: Ode to the
  Temple of Sound

Hovhaness: And God
  Created Great Whales
Hovhaness: Greek
  Rhapsody No. 2
Hovhaness: Symphony
  No. 61
Huggler: Ecce homo
Huggler: Music in Two
  Parts
Husa: Fresco
Hutcheson: Metaphors
Iannaccone:
  Divertimento
Iannaccone: Night
  Rivers
Imbrie: Legend
Ince: Ebullient
  Shadows
Ivey: Little Symphony
Ivey: Short Symphony
P. James: Overture to
  a Greek Play
H. Johnson: North
  State Suite
Jones: Chaconne and
  Burlesque
Jones: Listen Now, My
  Children
Karlins: Concert Music
  No. 1
Karlins: Concert Music
  No. 5
H. Kay: Suite
U. Kay: Trigon
U. Kay: Theater Set
U. Kay: Chariots
Keller: Sonorities
Kelly: The Legend of
  the Maize
Kennedy: Symphonic
  Fantasy
Kernis: Invisible
  Mosaic III
Kessner: Strata
Kessner: Mobile
Kirchner: Music for
  Orchestra
Knight: Three Musical
  Elements for
  Orchestra

Koch: River Journey
Kohn: Three Scenes for
  Orchestra
Kolb: Grisaille
Koykkar: Composite
L. Kraft: Symphony in
  One Movement
W. Kraft: Vintage
  Renaissance
W. Kraft:
  Of Ceremonies,
  Pageants and
  Celebrations
Kremenliev: Bulgarian
  Rhapsody
Krenek: Scenes from
  the West
Krenek: Fivefold
  Enfoldment
Krenek: Six Profiles
Krieger: Remnants
Kriesberg: Short
  Symphony
Kubik: Symphony No. 3
Kupferman: Sound
  Phantoms No. 8
Kupferman: Savage
  Landscape
Kupferman: Markings
  for Orchestra
Kurek: Chimera
Lange: American
  Pastorale No. 1
Lange: American
  Pastorale No. 2
Larsen: Coriolis
Layton: An American
  Portrait
Lazarof: Mutazione
Lazarof: Poema
Le Baron: Strange
  Attractors
D. Lee: Tea House of
  the August Moon
D. Lee: Polynesian
  Suite
T. Lee: Jana
Lees: Passacaglia
Lerdahl: Chords
Le Siege: Montage

Le Siege: Sapphire
  Seesaw
R. Lewis: Designs
R. Lewis: Moto
Lopatnikoff: Festival
  Overture
Lovendusky: Metathesis
Luening: Sonority
  Forms No. 1
Luening: Symphonic
  Fantasia VI
Luke: Second Suite
Luke: Quartz Mountain
Lundborg: Scherzo
MacBride: Measuring
  the Future
Mailman: Suite in
  Three Movements
Mailman: Sinfonietta
Martino: Mosaic for
  Grand Orchestra
Martino: Ritorno
Maves: Symphony No. 3
May: Orpheus
Mayer: Two Pastels
Mayer: Of Rivers and
  Trains
McBeth: Symphony No. 4
McCulloh: Two Pieces
  for Orchestra
McDermott: Siftings
  upon Siftings
McDonald: Overture for
  Children
McKay: Fantasy on Sea
  Things
McKay: Jubilee
McKinley: Symphony
  No. 1
McLennan: Celebration
McLennan: Triptych
McPhee: Transitions
Mechem: Haydn's Return
Mennin: Symphony No. 2
Mennin: Sinfonia
Mennin: Concerto "Moby
  Dick"
Meyer: Festival
  Overture

Meyerowitz: Flemish
  Overture
Meyerowitz: Sinfonia
  brevissima
Milburn: Voussoirs
Milburn: Salus...Esto
Mills: Theme and
  Variations
Mobberly: Synthesis
Moevs: Overture
Moevs: Main-travelled
  Roads
Moevs: Symphonic Piece
  No. 6
Morris: Syzygy
Moryl: The Untuning of
  the Skies
Mourant: Aria for
  Orchestra
Neikrug: Fantasy for
  Orchestra
Neikrug: Eternity's
  Sunrise
Nelhybel: Etude
  Symphonique
Newell: Four-fold
  World View
Newman: Toccata for
  Orchestra
O'Brien: Symphony
O'Brien: Rites of
  Passage
Ogden: Five Comments
  and Capriccio
Ortiz: Kantuta, Ritual
  para Orquesta
D. Ott: From Darkness
  Shines
D. Ott: Celebration at
  Vanderberg
J. Ott: Premise for
  Orchestra
Packales: Ciudad del
  Sol
Parchman: Violin
  Overture
Paulus: Seven Short
  Pieces
Paulus: Concertante
Paulus: Sinfonietta

Perera: Chanteys
Perle: A Short
  Symphony
Perlongo: Ephemeron
M. Phillips: Turning
P. Phillips: Novasonic
Piston: Suite No. 1
Piston: Concerto for
  Orchestra
Piston: Prelude and
  Fugue
Piston: Three New
  England Sketches
Piston: Lincoln Center
  Festival Overture
Piston: Variations on
  a Theme of Edward B.
  Hill
Piston: Pine Tree
  Fantasy
Piston: Ricercare
Polster: Textures for
  Orchestra
Powell: Symphonic
  Suite
Ptaszynska:
  Crystallites
Rackley: Confluences
Rands: Wildtrack I
Rands: Ceremonial III
Rapchak: Chasing the
  Sunset
Rathaus: Salisbury
  Cove Overture
Rathaus: Vision
  Dramatique
T. Read: Symphonic
  Episodes
T. Read: Adventura
A. Reed: A Festival
  Prelude
H. Reed: The Turning
  Mind
Reich: Three Movements
Reise: Hieronymo is
  Mad Again
Richter: Out of
  Shadows and Solitude
Robertson: Passacaglia
Rochberg: Zodiac

Rogers: Symphony No. 5
Rogers: Three Dance
  Scenes
Rogers: Apparitions
Rosen: Sounds and
  Movements
Rosner: Nocturne
Rothkopf: Cantus
  Sinfonia
Rovics: Symphony
Rudhyar: Sinfonietta
Sacco: Symphony No. 1
G. Samuel: Into Flight
  From
Sapp: The Double Image
Sapp: Xenon Ciborium
Schickele: Requiem
  Mantras
Schickele: A Zoo
  Called Earth
Schuller: Dramatic
  Overture
Schuller: Five
  Bagatelles
Schuller: American
  Triptych
Schuller: Five Etudes
Schuller: Shapes and
  Designs
Schuller: Three
  Nocturnes
Schuller: Four
  Soundscapes
Schuman: Prayer in
  Time of War
Schuman: New England
  Triptych
Schwantner: A Sudden
  Rainbow
E. Schwartz: Island
Sessions: Symphony
  No. 8
Sessions: Concerto for
  Orchestra
Shapero: Sinfonia in
  C minor
Shapero: On Green
  Mountain
Shapey: Challenge
Shapey: Rituals

Sheinfeld: Dreams and
  Fantasies
Siegmeister: Sunday in
  Brooklyn
Siegmeister: Theater
  Set
Siegmeister: Five
  Fantasies
Siegmeister: From
  These Shores
F. Silverman: Winds
  and Sines
F. Silverman:
  Adhesions
H. Smith: Orchestral
  Set
L.A. Smith: Three
  Movements for
  Orchestra
Sorce: Piece for
  Orchestra
Soule: Symphonic Piece
Starer: Symphony No. 2
Starer: Samson
  Agonistes
Starer: Mutabili
Stein: Symphonic
  Movement
Steinohrt: Derivatives
Stern: Credo for
  Orchestra
Stevens: Sinfonia
  Breve
Stevens: Symphonic
  Dances
Stewart: A Requiem for
  a Soldier
Still: Dismal Swamp
Still: Poem for
  Orchestra
Still: Los alnados de
  Espana
Stock: Symphony in One
  Movement
Stock: Inner Space
Stokes: Captions on
  the War Against
  Earth
Strandberg: Four
  Preludes

Strandberg: Amenhotep
Strandberg: Trinete
Stucky: Dreamwaltzes
Stucky: Angelus
Surinach: Symphonic
  Variations
Swift: Extravaganza
Swisher: Serafina
Sydeman: Study No. 3
Tanenbaum: Concertante
  No. 1
Tanenbaum: Concertante
  No. 2
Tann: The Open Field
Taub: Chromatic
  Fantasy
Taub: Gridlock
Tautenhahn: Symphonic
  Sounds No. 1
Tautenhahn: Symphonic
  Sounds No. 2
Taxin: Fanfares and
  Dialogues
Taylor: Theme and
  Variations
Augusta Thomas: Glass
  Moon
Thome: The Golden
  Messengers
Thomson: A Solemn
  Music and a Joyful
  Fugue
Thomson: Eleven
  Portraits
Tircuit: Fantasias
Tircuit: Goerdeler
  Triptych
Toch: Hyperion
Torke: Ecstatic Orange
Torke: Bright Blue
  Music
Trimble: Symphony in
  Two Movements
Trythall: Dionysia
Trythall: Chroma I
Tsontakis: Fantasia
  habanera
Tull: Three Episodes
Turner: Dark Pastorale

Turner: The Marriage
  of Orpheus
Turok: Symphony in Two
  Movements
Turok: Ultima Thule
Ultan: Wanaki Win
Van Vactor: Sewanee
  Suite
Van Vactor: Suite for
  Orchestra on Chilean
  Folk Tunes
Vazzana: Varianti
Vega: Intrata
Verrall: Portrait of
  St. Christopher
Verrall: Suite No. 1
Verrall: Radiant
  Bridge
Waggoner: The Train
Waldrop: From the
  Southwest
Waldrop: Prelude and
  Fugue
George Walker:
  Variations for
  Orchestra
George Walker:
  Sinfonia
Gwyneth Walker:
  Bicentennial Suite
Ward: Divertimento for
  Orchestra
Ward: Festive Ode
Ward: Sonic Structure
Ward-Steinman: Prelude
  and Toccata
Ward-Steinman:
  Arcturus
D. Waxman: A Quint of
  Carols
Weber: Prelude and
  Passacaglia
Weiner: A Symphonic
  Etude
Weiner: A Symphonic
  Overture
Weisgall: Prospect
Welcher: Dervishes
Welcher: Prairie Light
Wernick: Aevia

Whear: Catharsis Suite
Wheelock: Montage
Wilder: Piece for
  Orchestra
D. Wilson: Diagon
O. Wilson: Voices
O. Wilson: Lumina
R. Wilson: Initiation
Winteregg: Only
  Yesterday
Wise: Variations
Wright: Stellae
Wright: Wellington's
  Defeat
Wuorinen: Orchestral
  and Electronic
Exchanges
Wuorinen: Eccliastical
  Symphonie
Wuorinen: Crossfire
Wykes: Resonances
Yasanitsky: Into a
  Star
Yttrehus: Espressioni
Zaimont: Monarchs
Zappa: Strictly
  Genteel
Zappa: Bob in Dacron
Zonn: Interiors
Zupko: Canti terrae
Zwilich: Symposium for
  Orchestra

*Medium Orchestra*

J. Adams: The Chairman
  Dances
L. Adams: Ode to Life
Adolphe: Night Journey
T.J. Anderson:
  Classical Symphony
T.J. Anderson:
  Symphony in Three
  Movements
Antheil: Capitol of
  the World
Appleton: After "Nude
  Descending a
  Staircase"

Appleton: The American
  Songs
Armer: Pearl
J. Austin: Prelude,
  Fugue and Chorale
Averitt: Gentle, Into
  That Night
Averitt: Palmer House
  Dream Dances
Bacon: From These
  States
Bacon: Erie Waters
Balada: Guernica
Balazs: Statement of
  Faith
Ballard: Fantasy
  Aborigine No. 1
Ballard: Ishi
Barati: The Dragon and
  the Phoenix
Barati: Festival Hula
Bassett: Forces
Bavicchi: Tobal
Bazelon: Symphony
  No. 8½
Beale: Divertimento
Beckler: Playing in
  the Paintbox
Beckler: Symphony
  No. 3
Beckler: Varied
  Distortions
Beckler: Festival
  Overture
Beckler: Symphony
  No. 5
Benson: The Man with
  the Blue Guitar
A. Berger: Ideas of
  Order
A. Berger: Polyphony
J. Berger: Short
  Symphony
Berlin: Variants for
  Orchestra
Binkerd: Symphony
  No. 3
Biscardi: At the Still
  Point
Bloch: Suite hebraique

Boone: The Edge of the Land
Brun: Mobile for Orchestra
E. Burton: Ballade
Caltabiano: Northwest!
Cone: Elegy for Orchestra
Constantinides: Suite No. 2
Cope: Streams
Copland: Prairie Journal
Copland: Our Town
Copland: Orchestral Variations
Cortes: The Eternal Return
Cowell: Antiphony for Divided Orchestra
Creston: Two Choric Dances
Creston: Lydian Ode
M. Cunningham: Free Designs
Danielpour: First Light
Dello Joio: To a Lone Sentry
Dello Joio: On Stage
Diamond: Concert Piece
Diemente: Murmurs
Diemer: Symphony No. 1
Diemer: Symphony No. 3
Donovan: Passacaglia on Vermont Folk Tunes
Downey: Jingalodeon
Duckworth: When in Eternal Lines to Time Thou Grow'st
Effinger: Landscape III
Farberman: Suite from "The Great American Cowboy"
Fetler: Gothic Variations
Fischer: Variations on an Original Theme

Fischer: Mountain Tune Trilogy
Fischer: Short Symphony
Fischer: Passacaglia and Fugue
Foley: Glasperlenspiel
Franco: Symphony No. 3
Franco: Supplication, Revelation and Triumph
Frazelle: Playing the "Miraculous Game"
Fredrickson: Sinfonia Concertante
Gannon: On the Surface
Garlick: Canto
E. George: Introduction, Variations and Finale
Gillis: Symphony No. 5½
Gillis: The Alamo
Gimbel: The Four Temperaments
Goeb: Concertino II
Goeb: Sinfonia I
Goeb: Sinfonia II
Gould: Family Outing
Gould: Classical Variations on Colonial Themes
Gould: Cinerama Holiday
Green: Prologue and Fugue
Haines: Rondino and Variations
Haines: Three Dances
Hannay: The Age of Innocence
Hanson: Elegy in Memory of Serge Koussevitsky
Hanson: Suite
Hartley: Ballet Music for Orchestra
Hartley: Sinfonietta

Hartley: Scenes from
  Lorca's "Blood
  Wedding"
Hartley: Sinfonia
  No. 2
Haxton: Chorale
  Prelude and Fugue
Heiden: Memorial
Hellermann: Time and
  Again
Hellermann: Anyway
Hennagin: Passacaglia
  for Orchestra
Hibbard: Processionals
Hill: Variations for
  Orchestra
Hill: Mosaics
Hoag: Fantasy on a
  Bach Chorale
Hoag: Encounter for
  Orchestra
Hoiby: Rock Valley
  Narrative
Hollingsworth:
  Divertimento
H. Howe: Scherzo
Huggler: Variations
  for Orchestra
Hunt: Emerald
  Reflection
Ivey: Festive Symphony
T. Johnson: Five
  Americans
U. Kay: Danse Calinda
U. Kay: Fantasy
  Variations
U. Kay: Umbrian Scene
U. Kay: Presidential
  Suite
Keats: Concert Piece
Kelly: Emancipation
  Symphony
Kirk: Concerto for
  Orchestra
Kohn: Castles and
  Kings
Kohn: Interludes
Kohs: Concerto in One
  Movement
Kolb: Cross Winds

Krenek: From Three
  Make Seven
Kroeger: Sinfonietta
  No. 1
Kroeger: Concert
  Overture
Kupferman: Variations
  for Orchestra
Kupferman: Festivals
Kupferman: Sculptures
Kupferman: Sinfonia
  Brevis
Kupferman: Wings of
  the Highest Tower
Lange: American
  Pastorale No. 3
Laufer: Festival and
  Frolic
D. Lee: Waltzing
  Matilda
Le Siege: Star Gazers
Lessard: Little
  Concert
Lessard: Suite
Levi: Symphonic
  Movement
M. Levy: Caramoor
  Festival Overture
M. Levy: Pascua
  Florida
R. Lewis: Destini
Lifchitz: Yellow
  Ribbons No. 9
Lopatnikoff: Music for
  Orchestra
Lubet: La Armonia del
  Mundo
Luening: Music for
  Orchestra
Luening: Poem in
  Cycles and Bells
Mayer: Scenes from
  "The Snow Queen"
McBeth: Symphony No. 2
McKinley: The Mountain
McVoy: Reflections
McVoy: Spring Fancies
Merryman: In the
  Dreamtime

E. Miller: Music for
  Orchestra
L. Mitchell: Kentucky
  Mountain
C. Moore: Catwalk
Mourant: Flea Dance
Musgrave: Peripeteia
Musgrave: Rainbow
Nabokov: Studies in
  Solitude
Nin-Culmell: Tres
  Piezas
J. Ott: Matrix IX
Overton: Symphony
  No. 2
Park: Gawain's Passage
Pasatieri: Three
  Sisters
Persichetti: Serenade
  No. 5
Persichetti: Fairy
  Tale
Peterson: Cataclysms
B. Phillips: Theater
  Dances
Picker: Two Fantasies
Piket: Essays in
  Rhythm
Pinkham: Symphony
  No. 4
Piston: Serenata
Plain: Portrait One
Polster: Symphonic
  Episodes
Porter: Two Dances for
  Radio
Powell: Immobiles
Proctor: Intimations
Rackley: The Chambered
  Nautilus
Ramsier: Dance
  Variations
T. Read: Symphony for
  Orchestra
Reif: Accumulations
Rhodes: Three "B's"
Rhodes: Reels and
  Reveries
Rice: Toccata Overture

Richter: Blackberry
  Vines and Winter
  Fruit
Rieti: Symphony No. 5
Rieti: Indiana
Rinehart: Chaconne for
  Orchestra
Robertson: Punch and
  Judy Overture
Roosevelt: Amistad
Roskott: Adagio
Rozsa: The Vintner's
  Daughter
Russo: Variations on
  an American Theme
Sacco: Four Emerson
  Sketches
Sanders: Little
  Symphony No. 2
Schelle: The Big Night
Schickele: Serenade
Schonthal: Oceanic
  Poem
E. Schwartz: Dream
  Overture
E. Schwartz:
  Celebrations/
  Reflections
F. Schwartz: Plegaria
Shere: Music for
  Orchestra
R. Smith: Tetrameron
Spies: Music for a
  Ballet
Stearns: Two Fantasy
  Pieces
Stevens: Five Pieces
  for Orchestra
Still: Patterns
Stout: Three Hymns
Strunk: Spirit Lake
  Suite
Subotnick: Play! No. 2
Surinach: Sinfonia
  flamenca
Sydeman: Orchestral
  Abstractions
Sydeman: Study No. 1
Tanenbaum: Parallel
  Worlds

M. Thomas: Soundscapes
Thomson: Fantasy
F. Thorne: Elegy for
Orchestra
F. Thorne: Liebesrock
N. Thorne: Eight
Movements
Toch: Notturno
Toch: Peter Pan
Townsend: Four
Fantasies
Van Vactor: Fantasia,
Chaconne and Allegro
Vazzana: Symphonic
Allegro
Vega: Overture to a
Serious Farce
George Walker:
Folksongs for
Orchestra
Gwyneth Walker:
Roanoke Rising
Wallach: Glimpses
Ward: Euphony for
Orchestra
Ward-Steinman: Concert
Overture
Donald White: Serenade
for Orchestra
Wilder: Entertainment
No. 6
Woollen: Toccata
Wright: The Times Will
Change
Wuorinen: Short Suite
Wuorinen: Machault mon
chou
Zonn: Pennyrile
Variations
Zupko: Blue Roots

*Small Orchestra*

Adolphe: A Dream of My
Parents Dancing
Albright: Night
Procession
Ames: High Mountain
Lake
Ames: Excursion II

B. Anderson:
Revelation
T.J. Anderson: Chamber
Symphony
T.J. Anderson: Chamber
Concerto
Antoniou: Op Overture
Antoniou: Events III
J. Avshalamov: Cues
from the Little Clay
Cart
Bavicchi: Concertante
Becker: Symphony No. 5
Beerman: Mourning
Songs
A. Berger: Chamber
Concerto
Bergsma: Serenade "To
Await the Moon"
Berlin: Metamorphism
Bezanson: Sinfonia
concertante
Binkerd: Movement for
Orchestra
Blackwood: Symphony
No. 3
Brant: On the Nature
of Things
Brant: Curriculum II
E. Brown: Available
Forms I
D. Brubeck:
Brandenburg Gate:
Revisited
Bubalo: Strata
Cage: The Seasons
Caldwell: Sinfonia
Concertate in Stilo
Moderno
D. Carlson: Rhapsodies
Cazden: Three Ballads
Chance: Planesthai
Chihara: Ceremony III
J. Cohn: Sinfonietta
in F
J. Cohn: Variations on
"The Wayfaring
Stranger"
J. Cohn: Nine
Miniatures

Hewitt: At the Gate of
the Kingdom of Fools
Hill: Chambers
Hill: Toccata
Nipponica
Hoag: When the Yellow
(Dream) Leaves Fell
Holt: Symphony
Concertante
Hopkins: Revelations
and Transformations
Hopkins: Fantasy on
Cortege a Litanie'
Hovhaness: Anahid
Hovhaness: Zartik
Parkim
Hovhaness: Concerto
No. 1
Hovhaness: Vision from
High Rock
Hovhaness: Symphony
No. 21
Hovhaness: Symphony
No. 40
Hovhaness: Symphony
No. 41
Husa: Musique
d'amateurs
Husa: Mosaiques
Hutchison: Varied
Carols
Ince: Deep Flight
Jaffe: The Rhythm of
the Running Plough
Jager: A Child's
Garden of Verses
P. James: Miniver
Cheever and Richard
Cory
Janson: Nocturne
Kallman: Spring Flings
U. Kay: Danse Calinda
Kelly: Colloquy
Kelly: Concertino
Kievman: Prologue
Kievman: Suite No. 2
Kirchner: Toccata
Kitzke: The Snow Crazy
Copybook

Kolb: Yet that things
go round
Koutzen: Divertimento
Koutzen: Elegiac
Rhapsody
Koutzen: Fanfare,
Prayer and March
Koykkar: Chamber
Symphony
W. Kraft: Settlers
Suite
Krenek: In the Valley
of Time
Kroeger: Suite for
Chamber Orchestra
Larsen: What the
Monster Saw
Laufer: Small Concerto
Lavenda: Free Fall
Lees: Silhouettes
Leichtling: Capriccio
Lennon: Metapictures
Lentz: Apache Wine
Leon: Bata
Lerdahl: Waves
Lessard: Sinfonietta
concertante
Lessard: Pastimes and
an Alleluia
Levi: Transformations
of the Heart
M. Levy: Trialogus II
G. Lieberman: Beards
of a Father
Luening: Prelude:
World Without People
Luening: Symphonic
Fantasia IX
MacBride: 1010
Mackey: Square Holes,
Round Pegs
McBeth: Pastorale and
Allegro
McBeth: Allegro
agitato
McKinley: New York
Overture
P. McLean: A Magic
Dwells

Mekeel: Obscurities of
  Order
Milburn: Chiaroscuro
D. Miller: Piece in
  Three Parts
Moevs: Pandora
D. Moore: Farm Journal
Morris: Interiors
Moryl: Total
Mourant: Four Garden
  Scenes
Muczynski: Dance
  Movements
Musgrave: Theme and
  Interludes
Neikrug: Chetro Ketl
Newlin: Triple Play
Newman: Discourse for
  Orchestra
Newman: Overture-
  Fantasy
Ortiz: Antillas
Palmer: Memorial Music
Parchman: Symphony
  No. 5
Paulus: Spectra
Perle: Sinfonietta I
Perle: Sinfonietta II
Perlongo: Voyage for
  Orchestra
Perlongo: Concertino
Pierce: Behemoth
Pinkham: Masks
Pisk: Three Ceremonial
  Rites
Pleskow: Music for
  Orchestra
Pleskow: Suite for
  Orchestra
Porter: Anthony and
  Cleopatra
Rands: Per Esempio
Rands: Agenda
Rands: Formats II
G. Read: Partita
Rhodes: Divertimento
Rickley: To Come to a
  Place
Riegger: Dichotomy

Rochberg: Cheltenham
  Concerto
Rodriguez: Concert
  Suite "Le Diable
  Amoureux"
Rollin: Three Western
  Sound-Images
Rolnick: Real Time
Rolnick: Drones and
  Dances
Rorem: Ideas for Easy
  Orchestra
Roseman: Variations
  for Orchestra
Rosner: Six Pastorale
  Dances
Rosner: Consort Music
Rouse: Iscariot
Sanders: Little
  Symphony No. 3
Schober:
  Divertissements
Schuller: Journey to
  the Stars
F. Schwartz: Yo
  Protesto
Scianni: Sinfonia
  Breve
Shulman: Woodstock
  Waltzes
Siegmeister:
  Divertimento
Silver: Dance of the
  Wild Angels
F. Silverman:
  Stirrings
H. Smith:
  Innerflexions
J. Smith: Folksongs
  Symphony
Leland Smith:
  Symphony I
Leland Smith:
  Divertimento No. 2
Snyder: Landscapes
Snyder: Fantasy
  Surrounding a Theme
  of Bartok
Son: Distances
Sorce: Semplice

Stallcop: Couplet for
a Desert Summer
Stein: Adagio and
Rondo
Stokes: On the
Badlands
Surinach: Embattled
Garden
Swanson: Short
Symphony
Sweidel: Hyperion
Swift: A Coronal
Swift: Symphony
Swisher: Niigata no
Sumie
Augusta Thomas: Vigil
M. Thomas: Nuclear
Winter
Thomson: The Plow that
Broke the Plains
Thomson: Acadian Songs
and Dances
Tillis: Designs for
Orchestra
Tillis: Niger Symphony
Tircuit: Concerto
No. 3
Tower: Amazon II
Tull: Overture to a
Legacy
Ultan: Reflections on
a Tradition
Verrall: Dark Night of
St.John
Vincent: Suite from
"Three Jacks"
Wagner: Sinfonietta
No. 1
Wagner: Four
Miniatures
Wagner: Dance
divertissement
George Walker:
Serenata
Gwyneth Walker:
Fanfare, Interlude
and Finale
Whear: High Flight
David White: Ruins of
Missolonghi

Wigglesworth: Telesis
Wilder: Entertainment
No. 2
Willis: Prelude and
Dance
R. Wilson: Suite for
Small Orchestra
Zappa: The Perfect
Stranger

*Chamber Orchestra*

Antoniou: Protest II
Bezanson: Songs of
Innocence
Boone: Second
Landscape
E. Brown: Novara
Campo: Alba
Consoli: Music for
Chambers
Cowell: Sinfonietta
Crockett: Still Life
With Bell
Davidovsky: Pennplay
Diemente: Wheels
Eaton: Ajax
Ghezzo: Seven Short
Pieces
Heussenstamm: Chamber
Symphony
R. Lewis: Prelude and
Finale
R. Lewis: Concerto for
Chamber Orchestra
Lifchitz: Roberta
Lifchitz: Suenos
London: In Memoriam
Loos: Percepts
Moryl: Multiples
Moryl: Chroma
Overton: Nonage
Powell: Modules
Primosch: Maranatha
Rausch: Construction 3
Rieti: Concertino pro
San Luca
Rochberg: Cantio Sacra
Rush: Nexus 16
Russo: Hello

G. Samuel: Apollo and
  Hyacinth
Sapp: June
Schelle: Rapscallion
Schwantner: Modus
  caelestis
Shapey: Chamber
  Symphony
Singleton: Again
Stearns: Third Little
  Symphony
Swafford: Chamber
  Sinfonietta
M. Thomas: Disparities
Torke: Adjustable
  Wrench
Verrall: Symphony for
  Chamber Orchestra
Ward-Steinman:
  Winging I
E. Williams:
  Fant'sy III
Zaimont: Chroma

*String Orchestra*

Adler: Concertino
  No. 2
R. Anderson: Prelude
  and Rondo (+ fl)
Antheil: Serenade
Antoniou: Kinesis ABCD
Babbitt:
  Correspondences
  (+ tape)
Baksa: Sonnet for
  Strings
Balada: Divertimentos
Balazs: Kentuckia
Ballard: Fantasy
  Aborigine No. 2
Barber: Adagio for
  Strings
Barkin: Plus ca change
  (+ 3perc)
Bavicchi: Canto I
Beglarian: Sinfonia
  for Strings
Benson: Beyond Winter

J. Berger:
  Divertissement
J. Berger: Diversion
  for Strings
Bingham: Connecticut
  Suite
  (+ tpt, tbn, org)
Bond: C-A-G-E-D
Boone: String Piece
Castaldo: Lacrimosa I
Clarke: Lyric Sonata
J. Cohn: Music for
  Strings
Copland: Two Pieces
Cotel: Harmony of the
  World
M. Cunningham: Irish
  Symphony
Cushing: Divertimento
Dahl: Variations on a
  Theme by C.P.E. Bach
Davidovsky: Contrastes
  (+ elec sounds)
De Mars: Spirit Horses
  (+ navajo flute,
  perc)
Donato: Suite for
  Strings
Dutton: Images for
  Strings
Dutton: Krakow, Summer
Eberhard: Marginals
  (+ 4tbn)
Entsminger: Suite
  No. 1
P. Epstein: Variations
Falaro: Cosmoi
Falaro: Suite for
  Strings
Ferneyhough: Epicycle
I. Fine: Notturno
  (+ harp)
Franco: Suite
Frank: Symphony for
  Full String
  Orchestra
Frazelle: Elegy for
  Strings
E. George: Concerto
  for Strings

T. George: Suite for
Strings
Goeb: Romanza
Gould: Harvest
(+ vib, hp)
P. Grant: Suite No. 1
Haimo: Symphony for
Strings
Harbison: The Merchant
of Venice
Roy Harris: Prelude
and Fugue
Hewitt: Concerto
Grosso No. 2
Hewitt: Divertimento
No. 1 (+ 2hn)
Hewitt: The Sad
Snowman
Hewitt: Fantasia on
Old British Airs
Hodkinson: Celestial
Calendar
Hovhaness: Vibration
Painting
Husa: Divertimento
Husa: Portrait
Husa: Four Little
Pieces
Kolb: Sequela
Krenek: Symphonic
Elegy
Krenek: Brazilian
Sinfonietta
Kroeger: Sinfonietta
for String Orchestra
La Montaine: Colloquy
Lazarof: Konkordia
Lees: Interlude
Lesemann: Seven Pieces
(+ tape)
R. Lewis: Atto
Lifchitz: Expressions
Liptak: Ellipses
Lockwood: Symphony for
String Orchestra
London: Aquaries
D. Moore: Cotillion
Suite
Mourant: Sleepy Hollow
Suite

Moylan: Two Movements
Orrego-Salas:
Variaciones Serenas
D. Ott: String
Symphony
Park: Second Fantasy
Peterson: Clusters and
Fragments
B. Phillips:
Divertimento
Reif: Episodes
Reif: Eulogy for a
Friend
(+ timp, perc)
Rice: Tempest!
Richter: Lament
Rieti: Dance
Variations
Rudhyar: Emergence
Sellars: Elegy
Serebrier: Fantasia
Serly: Symphony in
Four Cycles
Smit: Capriccio
Smit: Alabaster
Chambers
L.A. Smith: Apogees
Soule: Suite No. 1
Soule: Suite No. 2
Soule: Suite No. 3
Stevens: Adagio and
Allegro
Still: Danzas de
Panama
Stokes: Sonatas
Strandberg: Elegy
Susa: Pastorale
Taylor: Concerto
Grosso
Taylor: Commencement
Suite
Townsend: Suite No. 2
Trythall: A Solemn
Chant
Vega: Elegy
Wagner: Sinfonietta
No. 2
Ward: Concertino for
Strings
Washburn: Sinfonietta

F. Waxman: Sinfonietta
(+ timp)
Whittenberg: Serenade
Wigglesworth: Music
for Strings
Wigglesworth: Fantasia
Wigglesworth: Three
Movements
Wigglesworth: Three
Portraits
Wigglesworth: Aurora
Wigglesworth: Sea
Winds
Zador: Divertimento
Zwilich: Prologue and
Variations

## 16' TO 20'

### Large Orchestra

Adler: Concerto for
Orchestra
Albert: Voices Within
Albert: Anthem of
Processionals
J. Alexander:
Dithyrambe
Ames: Night Voices
Antheil: Symphony
No. 6
Antoniou: Fluxus I
Antoniou: The GBYSO
Music
E. Applebaum: Symphony
No. 2
E. Applebaum: Symphony
No. 3
E. Applebaum:
Variations for
Orchestra
Argento: Fire
Variations
Atkinson: A Musical
Trick or Treat
Babbitt: Relata I
Babbitt: Relata II
Bach: Burgundy
Variations
Bacon: Ford's Theater

C. Baker: Shadows
Balada: Steel Symphony
Balazs: Symphony on a
Plain-Chant Fragment
Balazs: Variations on
Five Notes
Barber: Symphony in
One Movement
Barber: Die Natali
Bassett: Concerto for
Orchestra
M. Bauer: Symphony
No. 1
Bazelon: Spirits of
the Night
Bazelon: Symphony
No. 7
Bazelon: Memories of a
Winter Childhood
Becker: Symphony No. 1
Beckler: The Seven
Ages of Man
Beeson: Symphony No. 1
E. Bell: Symphony
No. 1
Bernstein: Dybbuk -
Suite No. 2
Biggs: Concerto for
Orchestra
Bloch: Sinfonia breve
Blumenfeld: Scenes
from Rimbaud
Bond: Great Galloping
Gottschalk
Bottje: Tangents
E. Brown: Available
Forms II
E. Brown: Cross
Sections and Color
Fields
Bubalo: Seven Rays
Bubalo: Trajectories
S. Burton: Sinfonia
S. Burton: Variations
on a Theme of Mahler
Cage: Dance Four
Orchestras
Calabro: Symphony
No. 1

Calabro: Symphony
No. 3
Campo: Variations for
Orchestra
Campo: Luce bianca
Carter: A Symphony of
Three Orchestras
Carter: Three
Occasions
Chance: Liturgy
Chihara: Symphony
No. 1
Chihara: Symphony
No. 2
Cohen: Symphony in One
Movement
Coker: Symphony No. 1
Consoli: Profiles
Consoli: The Last
Unicorn
Constantinides: Diukos
Suite
Constantinides:
Concerto for
Orchestra
Coolidge: An Evening
in New Orleans
Cooper: Symphony No. 5
Copland: Dance
Symphony
Copland: Symphony
No. 1
Copland: Symphonic Ode
Copland: Statements
for Orchestra
Copland: Four Dance
Episodes
Copland: The Tender
Land -suite
Copland: Connotations
Cordero: Introduccion
y Allegro Burlesco
Cordero: Symphony
No. 3
Cordero: Six Mobiles
Cowell: Symphony No. 4
Creston: Chthonic Ode
Crumb: Echoes of Time
and the River

Crumb: A Haunted
Landscape
Csonka: Fantastic
Variations
Csonka: Santa Lucia
Variations
Csonka: Ten Symphonic
Etudes
Curtis-Smith: Float
wild birds
Dahl: Aria sinfonica
W. Mac Davis: Symphony
in Three Movements
Dello Joio: Serenade
Diamond: Symphony
No. 4
Diamond: Symphony
No. 5
Downey: Declamations
Drew: Donaldson
Druckman: Chiaroscuro
Druckman: Brangle
Druckman: Shog
Effinger: Symphony
No. 2
Effinger: Symphony
No. 1
Effinger: Symphony
No. 5
Ehle: Earth Garden
Symphony
El-Dabh: Symphony
No. 2
El-Dabh: Ramesses the
Great
Elisha: Dance Suite
Ellington: Harlem
Ellington: Night
Creature
Erb: Symphony of
Overtures
Erb: The Seventh
Trumpet
Erb: Autumn Music
Erb: Concerto for
Orchestra
Erb: Concerto for
Brass and Orchestra
Felciano: Orchestra
Feldman: Orchestra

630

Fennelly: In
Wilderness is the
Preservation of the
World
Fennelly: Thoreau
Fantasy No. 2
Fetler: Symphony No. 3
Finney: Spaces
Flagello: Symphony
No. 2
Flanagan: A Concert
Ode
Floyd: Introduction,
Aria and Dance
Foss: Pantomime
Foss: Quintets for
Orchestra
Foss: Exeunt
Fox: Variables No. 5
Fox: Beyond Winterlock
Frank: Brightness
Falls from the Air
Fredrickson:
Sinfonia II
Freund: Sinfonietta
Frohne: Antimony
T.R. George:
Sinfonietta
Giannini: Psalm CXXX
Glass: The Canyon
Gould: Foster Gallery
Suite
Gould: Lincoln Legend
Gould: Concerto for
Orchestra
Gould: Showpiece
Gould: Declaration
Suite
Gould: Soundings
Gould: Holiday Music
Grofe: Death Valley
Suite
Gruenberg: The
Enchanted Isle
Gruenberg: Americana
Gutche: Aesop Fabler
Suite
Gutche: Helios Kinetic
Hagen: A Handful of
Days

Hanson: Symphony No. 5
Hanson: Symphony No. 6
Hanson: Symphony No. 7
Hanson: The Mystic
Trumpeter
Harbison: Diotima
Harbison: Symphony
No. 2
D. Harris: Symphony in
Two Movements
Roy Harris: Symphony
No. 3
Roy Harris: Cumberland
Concerto
Roy Harris: Symphony
No. 7
Roy Harris: Symphony
No. 11
Hartke: Maltese Cat
Blues
Haubiel: Pioneers
Heiden: Variations for
Orchestra
Heiden: Partita
Hewitt: Symphony
No. 25
Hewitt: Moonscapes
Hill: Ceremonies of
Spheres
Hilliard: Symphony of
Nocturnes
Hodkinson: Fresco
Hoiby: Second Suite
for Orchestra
Hoiby: After Eden
Hoiby: Landscape
Hopkins: Elegy and
Dithyramb
Hopkins: Symphony
No. 5
Hovhaness: Symphony
No. 2
Hovhaness: Meditation
on Zeami
Hovhaness: Fra
Angelico
Hovhaness: Symphony
No. 55
Husa: Music for Prague

Matthews: Larchwood
Maves: Symphony No. 2
McCulloh: Concerto for
  Orchestra
McKay: Symphony No. 1
McKinley: Symphony
  No. 5
P. McLean: Variations
  and Mosaics
Mekeel: Quilt
Mennin: Symphony No. 3
Mennin: Symphony No. 9
Mennini: Andante and
  Allegro energico
E. Miller: Orchestral
  Fantasies
Mills: Symphony No. 4
Moevs: Fourteen
  Variations
Mollicone: Suite from
  "Young Goodman
  Brown"
Mols: Symphony No. 2
Montague: Sound Round
Morris: Continua
Moryl: Strobe
Muczynski: Symphonic
  Memoir
Musgrave: Concerto for
  Orchestra
Musgrave: Moving into
  Aquarius
Nabokov: Symphony
  No. 3
Nelhybel: Polyphonies
L. Nelson: Variations
  for Orchestra
Newell: Modular
  Melliphony
D. Ott: Music of the
  Canvas
Penn: Symphony
Perle: Three Movements
Persichetti: Night
  Dances
Peterson: Free
  Variations
Peterson: The Widening
  Gyre

Peterson: The Face of
  the Night, the Heart
  of the Dark
Pierce: Dances on the
  Face of the Deep
Pinkham: Symphony
  No. 1
Piston: The Incredible
  Flutist
Piston: Symphony No. 7
Piston: Symphony No. 8
Plain: Arrows
Plain: and left ol'
  Joe a bone, AMAZING!
Pone: La serenissima
Proctor: Seascape
Rands: Tambourin
  Suites I & II
Rands: ...body and
  shadow
G. Read: Pennsylvania
  Suite
G. Read: Astral
  Nebulae
Reise: Symphony No. 3
Reynolds: Threshold
Rinehart: Tombeau for
  Orchestra
Rochberg: Imago Mundi
Rodriguez: Favola
  boccacesca
Rodriguez: Oktoechoes
Rollin: Renaissance
  Suite
Rorem: Design
Rorem: Air Music
Rorem: Sunday Morning
Roskott: Overture to a
  Summer Night
Rouse: Gorgon
Rouse: Phantasmata
Rozsa: Tripartita
Rudhyar: Thresholds
Rush: The Cloud
  Messenger
Russo: Symphony No. 1
Russo: Symphony No. 2
G. Samuel: Looking at
  Orpheus Looking

G. Samuel: Requiem for
  Survivors
G. Samuel: Out of Time
G. Samuel: Lucille's
  Wave
Sapp: Suite No. 1
Saturen: Symphony
Schelle: Swashbuckler!
Schubel: Fracture
Schubel: Guale, the
  Golden Coast of
  Georgia
Schuller: Composition
  in Three Parts
Schuller: Triplum I
Schuller: Capriccio
  stravagante
Schuller: Triplum II
Schuman: Credendum
Schuman: In Praise of
  Shahn
Serebrier: Symphony
  No. 1
Sessions: Symphony
  No. 5
Sessions: Symphony
  No. 6
Sessions: Symphony
  No. 7
Sessions: Rhapsody for
  Orchestra
Shapey: Ontogeny
Shere: Symphony in
  Three Movements
Shifrin: Three Pieces
  for Orchestra
Siegmeister: Symphony
  No. 5
Siegmeister: Shadows
  and Light
Silver: Galixidi
Singleton: Shadows
Smit: Symphony No. 2
H. Smith: Ritual and
  Incantations
Stallings: Confluences
Stearns: Symphony
  No. 6
Stein: Then Shall the
  Dust Return

Steinke: Sound Scape
Steinohrt: The
  Forgotten
Stevens: Symphony
  No. 1
Still: Archaic Ritual
Stock: Zohar
Stock: A Joyful Noise
Stokes: The Ghost Bus
  to El Dorado
Stucky: Impromptus
Subotnick: Place
Suderburg: Winds/Vents
Surinach: Concerto for
  Orchestra
Surinach: Acrobats of
  God
Surinach: Melorhythmic
  Dramas
Surinach: The Missions
  of San Antonio
Svoboda: Sinfonietta
Svoboda: Nocturne
Swafford: Landscape
  with Traveler
Sydeman: Texture
  Studies
Taxin: Saba
Augusta Thomas: Wind
  Dance
Thome: Indra's Net
F. Thorne: Symphony
  No. 1
F. Thorne: Symphony in
  One Movement
Trimble: Panels for
  Orchestra
Turok: Great Scott!
Van Nostrand:
  Fragments from
  Symphony "Nosferatu"
Van Vactor: Overture
  "Cristobal Colon"
Van Vactor: Symphonic
  Suite
Van Vactor: Trojan
  Women Suite
Van Vactor: Symphony
  No. 5
Vazzana: Trinakie

Vega: Introduction and
  Episode
Vega: Symphony in Four
  Parts
Vega: Adios
Vincent: Symphony in O
Vincent: Symphonic
  Poem after Descartes
Vores:
  Retwistification
Waggoner: Symphony
George Walker: Address
  for Orchestra
George Walker:
  Sinfonia II
Warren: Symphony in
  One Movement
Warren: Suite for
  Large Orchestra
Weisgall: Dances from
  "Outpost"
Wernick: Symphony
  No. 1
Wheelock: Diversions
Widdoes: The Visitors
R. Wilson:
  Articulations
Wood: Symphony No. 3
Wuorinen: Symphony
  No. 3
Wuorinen: Contrafactum
Wuorinen: A Reliquary
  for I.S.
Wuorinen: Bamboula
  Squared
Wykes: The Shape of
  Time
Wykes: Towards Times
  Receding
Yannay: Mirkamim
Yardumian: Two Chorale
  Preludes
Yttrehus: Symphony
Zador: Five Contrasts
  for Orchestra
Zador: Variations on a
  Merry Theme
Zupko: Life Dances
Zwilich: Symbolon

*Medium Orchestra*

J. Adams: Common Tones
  in Simple Time
W. Alexander:
  Discourses
Ames: Morning
T.J. Anderson: New
  Dances
Antheil: Spectre of
  the Rose Waltz
Averitt: Inventions
J. Avshalomov: Phases
  of the Great Land
J. Avshalomov: Open
  Sesame!
Balada: Sinfonia en
  Negro
Balada: Zapata
Balada: Columbus
Barati: Polarization
Barber: Souvenirs
Beckler: Dirge
Beglarian: Sinfonia
  for Orchestra
Beglarian: Partita for
  Orchestra
Beglarian:
  Divertimento
Bergsma: Documentary I
Bezanson: Capriccio
  concertante
Blitzstein: The Guests
Bolcom: Symphony No. 2
Bottje: Sounds from
  the West Shore
Brandt: Sinfonietta II
Britain: Sam Houston
Britain: Texas
R. Brooks: Symphony
Carl: Images of Birth
Childs: Second
  Symphony
Colgrass: Letter from
  Mozart
Consoli: Naked Masks
Corigliano: Gazebo
  Dances
Creston: Symphony
  No. 1

Mailman: Mirror Music
Mandelbaum: Sursum
  corda
Meyerowitz: Six Pieces
  for Orchestra
Meyerowitz: Cinque
  Pezzi da Machaut
Moevs: Introduction
  and Fugue
Montague: From the
  White Edge of
  Phrygia
Musgrave: Memento
  Vitae
Nixon: Mooney's Grove
  Suite
Oliveros: Tashi gomang
Orland: Symphony No. 3
Orrego-Salas:
  Resonancia Esfercia
Peaslee: Afterlight
Piket: Crossroads
Pinkston: Bellwether
Plain: Portrait 2
Pone: Avanti!
Porter: New England
  Episodes
Pozdro: Symphony No. 1
Rackley: Symphony
  No. 1 in G
T. Read: Sunrise Fable
Reise: Symphony No. 1
Reynolds: Fiery Wind
Rieti: Sylvan Dreams
Rieti: Scenes Seen
Rieti: Symphony No. 7
Rodriguez: Estampie
Rorem: Symphony No. 1
Scarmolin: Symphony
  No. 2
Scarmolin: Invocation
Scarmolin: Symphony
  No. 3
Schubel: Scherzo
Schuller: Consequents
F. Schwartz: Gestos
Sessions: Divertimento
Shatin: Aura
Siegmeister: Western
  Suite

Siegmeister: Symphony
  No. 3
Starer: Hudson Valley
  Suite
Stearns: The Piper at
  the Gates of Dawn
Stern: Symphony in One
  Movement
Stern: Yam Hamelach
Stevens: Triskelion
Still: From the Black
  Belt
Strunk: Geometrics
Sullivan: Paths
Swafford: After Spring
  Rain
Tanenbaum: Symphony
  No. 1
Thomson: Louisiana
  Story
Thomson: Suite - "The
  Mother of Us All"
Thomson: Fugues and
  Cantilenas
Thomson: Symphony
  No. 3
F. Thorne: Lyric
  Variations V
F. Thorne: Pop Partita
N. Thorne: Revelations
Tower: Sequoia
Van Vactor: Five Small
  Pieces
Vazzana: Symphony
  No. 1
Ward-Steinman: These
  Three
Washburn: Symphony
  No. 1
Weisberg: Opening
  Statement
Witkin: Twelve Tone
  Variations
Wuorinen: Concertino
  for Orchestra
Yasanitsky: Summer
  Music
Zwilich: Symphony
  No. 1

*Small Orchestra*

Adler: Joi, Amor and
Cortezia
W. Alexander:
Portraits of Friends
Ames: Symphony No. 1
Ames: Excursion
Amram: American Dance
Suite
Antheil: Serenade II
L. Austin: Sinfonia
Concertante
J. Avshalomov:
Sinfonietta
Babbitt: Ars
Combinatoria
D. Baker: Homage
Ballard: Incident at
Wounded Knee
Barber: Medea
Benjamin: Symphony
No. 2
Bolcom: Symphony No. 1
Bottje: Mutations
Brings: Concerto for
Orchestra
J.E. Brown: Symphony
H. Brubeck: The
Gardens of
Versailles
Brunswick: Symphony in
B-flat
Bubalo: Offset I
Bubalo: The Sound of
Isness
Caltabiano: Concertini
Campo: Serenade
J. Cohn: Symphony
No. 1
J. Cohn: Symphony
No. 4
J. Cohn: Enchanted
Journey
J. Cohn: Symphony
No. 6
J. Cohn: Symphony
No. 7
J. Cohn: Symphony
No. 8

J. Cohn: Mount Gretna
Suite
Colgrass: The Schubert
Birds
Copland: Music from
the Movies
Cowell: Symphony
No. 13
Cowell: Symphony
No. 16
Anthony Davis: Still
Waters
Dello Joio: New York
Profiles
Dello Joio: Antiphonal
Fantasy
Diamond: Music for
Chamber Orchestra
Dresher: Cornucopia
El-Dabh: Clytemnestra
Etler: Triptych
Evett: Concerto for
Small Orchestra
Farberman: Symphony
for Percussion and
Strings
Feldman: The Turfan
Fragments
Fenner: Chamber
Symphony
Flagello: Serenata
Flanagan: Divertimento
Fox: Nightscenes for
Strings and
Percussion
T.R. George: Four
Games
T.R. George: Erica
T.R. George: Third
Suite
Gillis: Four Scenes
from Yesterday
Glanville-Hicks:
Masque of the Wild
Man
Goeb: Iowa Concerto
Goldstein: Pond
Gooch: Ontogeny
Gutche: Concertino for
Orchestra

Gutche: Rites in
  Tenochtitlan
Hailstork: Symphony
  No. 1
Hannay: Symphony No. 1
Hanson: For the First
  Time
Heiden: Concerto for
  Small Orchestra
Hewitt: Anglesley
  Abbey
Hodkinson: Sinfonia
  concertante
Hopkins: Dance Suite
Hopkins:
  Theatrikomelos
Hovhaness: Symphony
  No. 13
Hovhaness: Concerto
  No. 8
Hovhaness: Symphony
  No. 6
Hovhaness: Symphony
  No. 10
Hovhaness: Symphony
  No. 16
Hovhaness: Symphony
  No. 30
Hovhaness: Symphony
  No. 42
Hovhaness: Symphony
  No. 43
Hovhaness: Symphony
  No. 44
Husa: Fantasies
Husa: Serenade
Husa: Symphony No. 2
Janson: Variations for
  Orchestra
Jenni: Divertimento
Karlins: Symphony
  No. 1
Kaufman: When the
  Twain Meet
U. Kay: The Quiet One
U. Kay: Scherzi
  musicali
Kievman: Overture from
  "Hamlet"
King: Sinfonietta

Kohs: Symphony No. 1
Koutzen: Sinfonietta
Kramer: Musica pro
  Musica
Krenek: Circle, Chain
  and Mirror
Krenek: Exercises of a
  Late Hour
Krenek: The Arc of
  Life
Kubik: Divertimento
  No. 1
Kurka: Serenade
Laderman: Concerto for
  Chamber Orchestra
Lankester: Seven
  Nursery Rhymes
Lazarof: Sinfonietta
Le Baron: Three
  Movements for
  Orchestra
Lees: Concerto for
  Chamber Orchestra
F. Levy: Symphony
  No. 1
M. Levy: Trialogous I
Lockwood: Prayers and
  Fanfares
Lopatnikoff:
  Sinfonietta
Lopatnikoff:
  Divertimento
Luedeke: Chamber
  Symphony No. 1
Luening: Potawatomi
  Legends
MacBride: Four Sonnets
Marshall: Spiritus
Marshall: A Peaceable
  Kingdom
Menotti: Sebastian
Menotti: Errand into
  the Maze
Meyerowitz: Tre Pezzi
  Romantici
Mols: Symphony No. 1
Mols: Concerto for
  Orchestra
Montague: At the White
  Edge of Phrygia

Musgrave: Night Music
Newman: Cain
Nowak: Blend
D. Ott: Short Symphony
Parchman: Sonata for
  Little Symphony
Paulus: Translucent
  Landscapes
Perlongo: Lake Breezes
Peterson: Trilogy
M. Phillips: Intrusus
Pone: American
  Portraits
Reich: Eight Lines
Reynolds:
  ...Between...
Rhodes: A Symphony of
  Dances
Rice: Genesis
Richter: Abyss
Rieti: Verdiana
Riley: Noon Dances
Rochberg: Music for
  the Magic Theater
Rorem: Symphony No. 2
Rorem: A Quaker Reader
Rosner: Concerto
  Grosso No. 1
Rosner:
  Transformations
Roussakis: Hymn to
  Apollo
Rulon: When Quiet
  Implodes
G. Samuel: Cold When
  The Drum Sounds For
  Dawn
Saylor: Symphony
Schelle: Masque
Schubel: Punch and
  Judie
Schuller: Concerto da
  camera
Schuman: Night Journey
Schuman: To Thee Old
  Cause
E. Schwartz: Four
  American Portraits

Sessions: Concertino
  for Chamber
  Orchestra
Sheinfeld: Dialogues
Singleton: A Yellow
  Rose Petal
J. Smith: American
  Dance Suite
L.A. Smith: Symphony
  No. 2
Starer: Phaedra
Still: Darker America
Stokes: Symphony -
  Book II
Surinach: Ritmo Jondo
Surinach: Sinfonia
  chica
Surinach: Suite
  Espagnole
Andrew Thomas: Four
  Scenes from the
  Summer Palace
N. Thorne: Chaconne
Torke: Ash
Turok: Homage to Bach
Turok: Antoniana
Van Vactor:
  Divertimento
Van Vactor: Recitative
  and Saltarello
Gwyneth Walker: The
  Light of Three
  Mornings
Wallach: Turbulence,
  Stillness and
  Salutation
Ward-Steinman:
  Concerto No. 2
Ward-Steinman: Western
  Orpheus
Washburn: Adirondack
  Sketches
Weber: Sinfonia
  Clarion
Wernick: Hexagrams
Wilder: Carl Sandburg
  Suite
Wood: Concerto for
  Chamber Orchestra
Wright: Night Scenes

Zonn: Symphony in F
Zur: Chamber Symphony

*Chamber Orchestra*

Ames: Prologue
Baksa: Chamber
  Concerto No. 1
Blank: Six Significant
  Landscapes
Brings: Sinfonia da
  Camera
W. Brooks: Dancing on
  Your Grave
E. Brown: Sign Sounds
Carter: Penthode
Castaldo: Askesis
Erickson: Chamber
  Concerto
Feldman: First
  Principles
Fox: Now and Then
Frank: Paraphonia
Hartley: Partita
Heussenstamm: Das
  Dreieck
Heussenstamm:
  Seventeen
  Impressions
Imbrie: Chamber
  Symphony
L. Kraft: Chamber
  Symphony
Krenek: A Question of
  Time
Lazarof: Omaggio
Lazarof: Chamber
  Symphony
Lees: Concertante
  breve
Leichtling: Concerto
  for Chamber
  Orchestra
McKinley: Symphony for
  Thirteen Players
McKinley: Chamber
  Symphony No. 2
Neikrug: Mobile
O'Brien: Mysteries of
  the Horizon

Overton: Pulsations
Park: Rondo con
  Fantasia Concertante
Peterson:
  Transformations
Primosch: Chamber
  Symphony
Rochberg: Tableaux
Roosevelt: Suite
Schifrin: Variants on
  a Madrigal by
  Gesualdo
Shifrin: Chamber
  Symphony
F. Silverman: Passing
  Fancies
Snyder: Sabbatical
  Music
Spies: Tempi
Taub: An Often Fatal
  Malady
Thomson: Four Saints -
  An Olio
Ultan: Carlisle
  Concerto
Wuorinen: Hyperion

*String Orchestra*

Aitken: In Praise of
  Ockeghem
Albright: Gothic Suite
  (+ org, 2perc)
J. Alexander: Quiet
  Music
Babbitt: Transfigured
  Notes
Bacon: Concerto Grosso
Baksa: Sinfonia for
  Strings
Barab: Concerto Grosso
Beale: Suite for
  Strings
Bergsma: The Fortunate
  Islands
Binkerd: Five
  Transcriptions
Binney: Chorale
  (+ 5hn)

Calabro: Symphony
No. 2
Castaldo: Lacrimosa II
Cooper: Symphony No. 3
Cordero: Movimiento
Sinfonico
Csonka: Symphonietta
Davidovsky: Concertino
(+ perc)
Eaton: Remembering
Rome
Finney: Concerto for
Strings
Gerschefski: Classic
Symphony
Hagen: Prayer for
Piece
Hailstork: Sonata da
chiesa
Hannay: Symphony No. 6
Harrison: Suite No. 1
Harrison: Suite No. 2
Harrison: Suite for
Symphonic Strings
Hartke: Alvorada
Heiden: Concertino for
String Orchestra
Hewitt: Under the
Birches
Hovhaness: Symphony
No. 51 (+ tpt)
Jacobs: Caravans
(+ tape)
U. Kay: Six Dances
Krenek: Symphonic
Piece
Lentz: 10 Minus 30
Minutes
Luening: Suite for
String Orchestra
McKinley: SinfoNova
Meyerowitz: Silesian
Symphony
Mills: Symphony No. 5
Parchman: Symphony
No. 1
Rice: Tempest!
Rochberg:
Transcendental
Variations

Rosner: Responses,
Hosanna and Fugue
(+ hp)
Schuman: Symphony for
Strings
Sollberger: Persian
Golf
Steinohrt: Music for
Strings
Tanenbaum:
Kaleidoscope
(+ tape)
Taub: Octet
Toch: Sinfonietta
Townsend: Suite No. 1
Townsend: String
Symphony No. 2
Van Vactor: Five
Bagatelles
Wigglesworth: Symphony
No. 2
Wigglesworth: Symphony
No. 3
Wirth: Diversions in
Denim
Yavelow: Monument

21' TO 25'

*Large Orchestra*

Adler: Symphony No. 6
J. Alexander: Symphony
No. 1
J. Alexander: Epitaphs
J. Alexander: Symphony
No. 2
J. Alexander: Symphony
No. 3
Allanbrook:
Four Orchestral
Landscapes
Ames: Equinox
Antheil: Symphony
No. 4 "Tragic"
Antheil: Symphony
No. 5 "Joyous"
A. Applebaum: Symphony
in Two Movements

Etler: Symphony No. 1
Evett: Anniversary
  Concerto
Fennelly: Fantasy
  Variations
Fetler: Contrasts
Fetler: Soundings
Fetler: Symphony No. 4
Fetler: Celebration
I. Fine: Symphony
Finney: Symphony No. 2
Finney: Symphony No. 3
Finney: Symphony No. 4
Foss: Baroque
  Variations
Fountain: Ritual Dance
  of the Amaks
Fox: Night Ceremonies
Fox: Tracings
Fox: Januaries
Fuleihan: Symphony
  No. 1
Fuleihan: Symphony
  No. 2
Gelt: Symphony No. 1
Giannini: Symphony
  No. 1
Giannini: Symphony
  No. 5
Gillis: Symphony No. 3
Glass: The Light
Goeb: Symphony No. 3
Goeb: Symphony No. 4
Goeb: Symphony No. 5
Goeb: Symphony No. 6
Gottschalk: Infinity
Gould: Jekyll and Hyde
  Variations
P. Grant: Symphony
  No. 3
Grofe: Niagara Falls
  Suite
Grofe: Hollywood Suite
Gutche: Perseus and
  Andromeda
Hagen: Symphony No. 1
Hannay: Symphony No. 2
Hanson: Symphony No. 4
Harbison: Symphony
  No. 1

Roy Harris: Symphony
  No. 8
Hartke: Symphony No. 1
Helps: Symphony No. 1
Hennagin: Symphonic
  Essay
Herman: Hawthorne
  Symphony
Hewitt: Symphony No. 4
Hewitt: Symphony
  No. 11
Hewitt: Symphony
  No. 18
Hewitt: Symphony
  No. 22
Hewitt: The Triumph of
  Flora
Hilliard: Symphony in
  Two Movements
Hopkins: Visions of
  Hell
Hovhaness: Symphony
  No. 3
Hovhaness: Symphony
  No. 22
Hovhaness: Symphony
  No. 50
Husa: Monodrama
Iannaccone: Symphony
  No. 2
Imbrie: Symphony No. 2
Ivey: Forms in Motion
Jacobi: Symphony No. 2
Jaffe: Four Images
Jones: A Symphonic
  Requiem
Jones: Palo Duro
  Canyon
Kaufman: American
  Symphony No. 5
Keats: Symphony No. 1
Kechley: Four Horsemen
  of the Apocalypse
Keller: Symphony No. 3
Kennedy: Symphony in
  Two Movements
Knight: Kidnapped
Kubik: Scenario for
  Orchestra

Kupferman: Symphonic
  Odyssey
Kurka: Symphony No. 2
Laderman: Symphony
  No. 2
Laderman: Concerto for
  Orchestra
Laderman: Sonore
Lange: Symphony No. 1
Lazarof: Concerto for
  Orchestra
Lazarof: Symphony
Lazarof:
  Second Concerto
  for Orchestra
Lees: Concerto for
  Orchestra
Leichtling: Symphony
  No. 2
Lennon: Spectra
Lesemann: Symphony in
  Three Movements
Lesemann: Legends
M. Levy: Symphony
  No. 1
R. Lewis: Symphony
  No. 2
R. Lewis: Nuances II
R. Lewis:
  Three Movements of
  Hieronymous Bosch
Mailman: Symphony
  No. 2
Mailman: Symphony
  No. 3
Marshall: Sinfonia
  Dolce far Niente
McCulloh: Symphony
  No. 1
McKay: Parables of
  Kyai Gandrung
McKay: Concerto for
  Orchestra
Mechem: Symphony No. 1
Mennin: Symphony No. 5
Mennin: Symphony No. 7
Menotti: Apocalypse
Menotti: "Goya" Suite
Meyer: Three American
  Visions

Mills: Symphony No. 1
Mills: Symphony No. 3
C. Moore: Wildfires
  and Field Songs
C. Moore: Hit
Musgrave: Nocturnes
  and Arias
Nabokov: The Hunter's
  Picnic
Nanes: Symphony No. 1
R. Nelson: Five Pieces
  for Orchestra
Orrego-Salas: Symphony
  No. 3
Orrego-Salas: Symphony
  No. 4
Packales: Five
  Anagogic Dances
Parris: Angels
Parris: Chamber Music
  for Orchestra
Parris: Symphonic
  Variations
Paulus: Concerto for
  Orchestra
Paulus: Suite from
  "The Postman Always
  Rings Twice"
Persichetti: Symphony
  No. 4
Persichetti: Symphony
  No. 9
Pinkham: Symphony
  No. 3
Piston: The Incredible
  Flutist
Piston: Suite No. 2
  for Orchestra
Piston: Symphony No. 4
Piston: Symphony No. 5
Piston: Symphony No. 6
Pone: Titzarin
Porter: Symphony No. 1
Raksin: Forever Amber
Ran: Concerto for
  Orchestra
Rathaus: Sinfonia
  Concertante
G. Read: Symphony
  No. 5

G. Read: Symphony
No. 4
H. Reed: La fiesta
Mexicana
Reich: The Four
Sections
Reise: Symphony No. 2
Reynolds: Symphony
(Vertigo)
Riegger: Fantasy and
Fugue
Riegger: Symphony
No. 4
Riegger: Sinfonietta
Rochberg: Symphony
No. 1
Rochberg: Symphony
No. 5
Rogers: Variations on
a Song by Mussorgsky
Rorem: Symphony No. 3
Rorem: Assembly and
Fall
Rosenman: Threnody on
a Song of K.R.
Rouse: Symphony No. 1
Roussakis: Fire &
Earth & Water & Air
Rudhyar: Cosmic Cycle
Rush: Song and Dance
Sacco: Symphony of
Thanksgiving
Schifrin: Invocations
Schuller: Spectra
Schuller:
Seven Studies on
Themes of Paul Klee
Schuller: Symphony
Schuller: Concerto
No. 1
Schuller: Concerto
No. 2 for Orchestra
Schuller: Jubilee
Music
Schuller: Farbenspiel
Schuman: Symphony
No. 4
Schuman: Undertow
Schuman: Judith

Schuman: Voyage for
Orchestra
Schwantner: Toward
Light
Schwantner: Through
Interior Worlds
Sellars: The Music
Machine
Semegen: Triptych
Sessions: Symphony
No. 1
Sessions: The Black
Maskers
Sessions: Symphony
No. 4
Sessions: Symphony
No. 9
Shapiro: Mount Hope in
Autumn
Shawn: Symphony in
Three Parts
Sheinfeld: Polarities
Siegmeister: Fantasies
in Line and Color
Siegmeister: Symphony
No. 7
Siegmeister: Symphony
No. 8
Silsbee: Seven Rituals
Leland Smith: Concerto
for Orchestra
Starer: Symphony No. 1
Starer: Symphony No. 3
Stearns: Symphony
No. 5
Steinohrt: Miniature
Suite
Steinohrt: The
Remembrance
Still: Symphony in
G minor
Still: Symphony No. 3
Stock: On the
Shoulders of Giants
Stokes: Native Dancer
Strang: Symphony No. 1
Stucky: Kenningar
Susa: Symphony in One
Movement
Svoboda: Reflections

Swanson: Symphony
No. 3
Tanenbaum: Variations
for Orchestra
Taub: Six Pieces for
Orchestra
Taylor: Symphony No. 2
Taylor: Symphony No. 3
Thomson: Symphony
No. 1
F. Thorne: Symphony
No. 2
F. Thorne: Lyric
Variations I
F. Thorne: Symphony
No. 5
N. Thorne: Symphony
No. 2
Toch: Jephta
Toch: Symphony No. 4
Toch: Symphony No. 6
Torke: Black and White
Torke: Verdant Music
Tower: Silver Ladders
Ussachevsky: Colloquy
Van Vactor: Music for
. the Marines
Vazzana: Odissea
Vazzana: Concerto
Sapporo
Verrall: Symphony
No. 2
Verrall: A Lyric
Symphony
Wagner: Symphony No. 1
Waldrop: Symphony
No. 1
Ward: Symphony No. 2
Ward-Steinman:
Symphony
Wheelock: Carnival
Wilder: Four
Sentiments
John Williams:
Symphony No. 1
O. Wilson: Sinfonia
R. Wilson: Symphony
No. 1
Wood: Symphony No. 1

Wright: Orchestral
Composition
Wuorinen: Two-Part
Symphony
Wuorinen: Golden Dance
Yardumian: Symphony
No. 1
Yasanitsky: Symphony
Yavelow: Axis
Zador: Dance Overture
Zador: Studies for
Orchestra
Zappa: Bogus Pomp

*Medium Orchestra*

Argento:
The Resurrection
of Don Juan
Ballard: Fantasy
Aborigine No. 4
Barati: Symphony
Bassett: Variations
for Orchestra
Beckler: Symphony
No. 4
Bernstein: Fancy Free
Bernstein: Facsimile
Biggs: Symphony No. 2
Boda: Sinfonia
Brandt: Symphony No. 1
Carter: Suite -
The Minotaur
Carter: Variations for
Orchestra
Cazden: The Tempest
Cowell: Symphony
No. 11
Cowell: Symphony
No. 17
Creston: Symphony
No. 4
Dahl: The Tower of
St. Barbara
Diamond: Sinfonia
concertante
Drew: Symphonies
Dutton: Symphony No. 2
Dutton: Symphony No. 4
Evett: Symphony No. 1

Willis: Symphony No. 2
Wood: Symphony No. 4

*Small Orchestra*

Adam: Concerto
  Variations
Adolphus: United
  Nations Suite
Amram: Shakespearean
  Concerto
Antoniou: Circle of
  Accusation
Argento: Royal
  Invitation Suite
Bales: National
  Gallery Suite No. 4
Beale: Symphony for
  Chamber Orchestra
Beerman: Moments
Beglarian: To Manitou
L. Bell: Sacred
  Symphonies
Bolcom: Summer
  Divertimento
Carter: Symphony No. 1
J. Cohn: Symphony
  No. 2
J. Cohn: Symphony
  No. 3
J. Cohn: Symphony
  No. 5
Consoli: Odefonia
Constantinides: New
  Orleans Divertimento
Copland: Music for the
  Theatre
Cowell: Symphony No. 7
Cowell: Symphony No. 9
Cowell: Symphony
  No. 10
Creston: Choreografic
  Suite
Allan Davis:
  Divertimento
Anthony Davis:
  Wayang V
Anthony Davis: Notes
  from the Underground

Diemente: Scenes from
  Miro
Dlugoszewski: Strange
  Tenderness of Naked
  Leaping
Douglas: Pachyderm
Fletcher: Symphony
  No. 1
Foss: Griffelkin Suite
Franco: Symphony No. 5
Giannini: Suite
  "Love's Labour Lost"
Goossen: Stanzas and
  Refrains
Harrison: The Marriage
  at the Eiffel Tower
Hartke: Symphony No. 2
Hewitt: In Other
  Gardens
Hovhaness: Symphony
  No. 8
H. Johnson: Letter to
  the World
Kievman: Suite,
  Intelligent Systems
Kupferman: Little
  Symphony
Laderman: Stanzas
Lees: Divertimento
  Burlesca
Lees: Scarlatti
  Portfolio
John Lewis: Original
  Sin
McKinley: Symphony
  No. 3
McKinley: Symphony
  No. 4
Morris: Tapestries
Musgrave: The Seasons
D. Ott: Visions
Parris: Symphony No. 1
Paulus: Reflections
Rands: Madrigali
Reich: Variations for
  Winds, Strings,
  Keyboards
Rhodes: About Faces
Rieti: La fontaine

Rosenboom: In The
  Beginning V
Rosenman: Foci I
Rosner: Concerto
  Grosso No. 2
Rudhyar: Dialogues
Schuller: Contours
Schuman: Voyage for a
  Theater
Shere: Nightmusic
Subotnick: A Desert
  Flowers
Sullivan: In
  Contemplation of
  Endurance
Surinach: David and
  Bath-sheba
Surinach: Agathe's
  Tale
Sydeman: Concertpiece
Vincent: La Jolla
  Concerto
Ward: Symphony No. 3
Wigglesworth: Symphony
  No. 1
Woollen: Symphony
  No. 1
Wuorinen: The Magic
  Art

*Chamber Orchestra*

Boykan: Concerto for
  Thirteen Players
Ghezzo: Celebrations

*String Orchestra*

Bach: Dompes and
  Jompes
Bazelon: Symphony
  No. 8
Bresnick: Wir weben,
  wir weben
Cage: Twenty-Three
Claflin: Teen Scenes
Dello Joio:
  Meditations on
  Ecclesiastes

Fenner: Suite for
  Strings
Flagello: Concerto for
  String Orchestra
Frackenpohl: Symphony
  No. 2
P. Grant: Suite No. 3
Gutche: Symphony No. 5
La Montaine: Concerto
  for String Orchestra
Luedeke: The Moon in
  the Labyrinth
McKinley: Adagio for
  Strings
Overton: Symphony for
  Strings
Paulus: Symphony for
  Strings
Persichetti: Symphony
  for Strings
P. Phillips: Music for
  a Ballet
  (+ perc, hpsd)
Picker: Symphony No. 3
Proctor: Suite for
  String Orchestra
A. Reed: Suite
  Concertante (+ hp)
Rorem: String Symphony
Rouse: Concerto per
  corde
Silver: Shirat Sarah
Surinach: Concerto for
  String Orchestra
F. Thorne: Symphony
  No. 3
  (+ timp, hp, pf)
Whear: Symphony No. 5

**26' TO 35'**

*Large Orchestra*

Adler: Symphony No. 1
Adler: Symphony No. 2
Adler: Symphony No. 4
Adler: Beyond the Land
Albright: Alliance
J. Alexander: Symphony
  No. 4

Ames: Symphony II
Argento: A Ring of
  Time
Argento: In Praise of
  Music
A. Avshalomov:
  Symphony No. 2
A. Avshalomov:
  Symphony No. 3
J. Avshalomov:
  Symphony
  "The Oregon"
Balazs: An American
  Symphony
Barber: Symphony No. 2
Bazelon: Symphony
  No. 1
Bazelon: Symphony
  No. 4
Bazelon: Symphony
  No. 5
Binkerd: Symphony
  No. 2
Blackwood: Symphony
  No. 1
Blackwood: Symphony
  No. 4
Blitzstein: Lear; A
  Study
Bradshaw: Five
  Movements for
  Orchestra
Bradshaw: Symphony in
  Three Movements
Brant: Prisoners of
  the Mind
Cage: Renga
Cage: Thirty Pieces
  for Five Orchestras
Cage: Et cetera 2/4
  Orchestras
Castaldo: Flight
Cazden: Symphony
Chihara: Mistletoe
  Bride
A. Cohn: Four
  Symphonic Documents
Cooper: Symphony No. 6
Copland: Billy the Kid

Cordero: Symphony
  No. 4
Corigliano: Symphony
  No. 1
Cowell: Symphony No. 5
Cowell: Symphony
  No. 18
Creston: Symphony
  No. 3
Creston: Symphony
  No. 5
Dello Joio: Colonial
  Variants
Del Tredici: Steps
Diamond: Symphony
  No. 2
Diamond: Symphony
  No. 3
Diamond: Symphony
  No. 8
Ehle: A Space Symphony
Erb: Ritual
  Observances
Feldman: Coptic Light
Finney: Symphonie
  concertante
Flagello: Theme,
  Variations and Fugue
Flagello: Symphony
  No. 1
Foss: Symphony No. 1
Foss: Symphony of
  Chorales
Fox: In the Elsewhere
Gaburo: Antiphony IX
Giannini: Symphony
  No. 4
Gillis: Symphony No. 4
Gould: Symphony No. 1
Gould: Symphony No. 2
Gould: Venice for
  Double Orchestra
Gould: American
  Ballads
Gould: Symphony of
  Spirituals
Gould: Burchfield
  Gallery
Grofe: Grand Canyon
  Suite

Gruenberg: Symphony
  No. 2
Gruenberg: Symphony
  No. 3
Gruenberg: White
  Lilacs
Gutche: Symphony No. 6
Gutche: Icarus
Hagen: Symphony No. 2
Hannay: Symphony No. 5
Hanson: Symphony No. 1
Hanson: Symphony No. 2
Hanson: Symphony No. 3
Hanson: Bold Island
  Suite
Harbison: Ulysses' Bow
Roy Harris: Symphony
  No. 9
Harrison: Symphony
  No. 3
Harrison: Elegiac
  Symphony
Hewitt: Symphony
  No. 14
Hewitt: Symphony
  No. 15
Hewitt: Symphony
  No. 24
Hewitt: Symphony
  No. 27
Hewitt: Symphony
  No. 31
Hovhaness: Symphony
  No. 11
Hovhaness: Symphony
  No. 19
Hovhaness: Symphony
  No. 26
Hovhaness: Symphony
  No. 35
Hovhaness: Symphony
  No. 48
Hovhaness: Symphony
  No. 60
Husa: Symphony No. 1
Imbrie: Symphony No. 1
Ince: Symphony No. 1
P. James: Symphony
  No. 2
Jazwinski: Stryga

Jones: Symphony No. 1
H. Kay: Stars and
  Stripes
Kechley: Pathways
Kelly: Symphony No. 2
Kelly: Symphony No. 3
Kohn: Centone per
  Orchestra
Korf: Symphony in the
  Twilight
Kramer: Moments in and
  out of time
Krenek: Symphony No. 4
Kroeger: Suite No. 1
Laderman: Symphony
  No. 1
Laderman: Symphony
  No. 4
Laderman: Pentimento
Laderman: Symphony
  No. 6
Laderman: Concerto for
  Double Orchestra
Layton: Dance Fantasy
Lazarof: Structures
  sonores
Lees: Symphony No. 3
Lees: Symphony No. 5
Luening: A Wisconsin
  Symphony
McKinley: Symphony
  No. 6
Mechem: Symphony No. 2
Mennin: Symphony No. 6
Mennin: Symphony No. 8
Menotti: Symphony
  No. 1
Meyerowitz: Esther
  Midrash
Meyerowitz: Seven
  Pieces for Orchestra
Mills: Symphony No. 2
Moevs: Three Symphonic
  Pieces
Montague: Voussoirs
Musgrave: The Five
  Ages of Man
Nabokov: Don Quichotte
Nanes: Symphony No. 2

Oliveros: To Valerie
  Solanas and Marilyn
  Monroe
D. Ott: Vertical
  Shrines
D. Ott: Symphony No. 2
Parchman: Symphony
  No. 3
Paulus: Symphony in
  Three Movements
Perry: Symphony No. 4
Persichetti: Symphony
  No. 3
Persichetti: Symphony
  No. 7
Persichetti: Symphony
  No. 8
Peterson: Exaltation,
  Dithyramb and
  Caprice
Picker: Symphony No. 1
Piston: Symphony No. 1
Piston: Symphony No. 2
Piston: Symphony No. 3
Polin: Symphony No. 2
G. Read:
  The Temptation
  of St. Anthony
Riley: Symphony
Rochberg: Symphony
  No. 2
Rochberg: Symphony
  No. 6
Rosner: Symphony No. 3
Rosner: Symphony No. 4
Rosner: A Mylai Elegy
Rosner: Symphony No. 6
Rosner: Five Ko-ans
Rouse: Alloeidea
Roussakis: Sinfonia
Rulon: Quantum
  Mechanics
Sapp: Suite No. 2
Schuller: Deai
  (Encounter)
Schuman: Symphony
  No. 3
Schuman: Symphony
  No. 7

Schuman: Symphony
  No. 8
Schuman: Symphony
  No. 9
Schuman: Symphony
  No. 10
Schuman: American Hymn
C. Schwartz: Second
  Symphony
Selig: Symphony No. 2
Serebrier: Partita
Sessions: Symphony
  No. 2
Sessions: Symphony
  No. 3
Shapey: Symphonie
  Concertant
Siegmeister: Symphony
  No. 1
Siegmeister: Symphony
  No. 2
Siegmeister: Symphony
  No. 6
Stein: Symphony No. 4
Still: Afro-American
  Symphony
Still: Symphony No. 5
Still: Symphony No. 4
Stokes: Symphony -
  Book I
Stout: Symphony No. 2
Strandberg: Mists and
  Exaltations
Strang: Symphony No. 2
Street: Variations on
  a Ground
Stucky: Concerto for
  Orchestra
Suderburg: Orchestra
  Music I
Surinach: Symphony
  No. 2
Svoboda: Symphony
  No. 2
Svoboda: Symphony
  No. 3
Svoboda: Symphony
  No. 4
Svoboda: Symphony
  No. 5

Tanenbaum: Columbus
Tautenhahn: Concept,
  Three
Thompson: Symphony
  No. 2
Thompson: Symphony
  No. 3
N. Thorne: Symphony
  from Silence
Toch: Symphony No. 2
Toch: Symphony No. 3
Toch: Symphony No. 7
Trimble: Symphony
  No. 2
Trimble: Symphony
  No. 3
Trythall: Symphony
  No. 1
Van Vactor: Symphony
  No. 1
Van Vactor: Symphony
  No. 3
Wagner: Symphony No. 2
Weiner: Three Dance
  Scenes
Whear: Symphony No. 2
Wolpe: Symphony No. 1
Woollen: Symphony
  No. 2
Wuorinen: Movers and
  Shakers
Zappa: Mo 'n' Herb's
  Vacation
Zwilich: Tanzspiel

*Medium Orchestra*

J. Adams: Fearful
  Symmetries
Albert: Into Eclipse
Allanbrook: Serenade
Bacon: Symphony No. 1
Ballard: Koshare
Ballard: The Four
  Moons
Benjamin: Sinfonia
Biggs: Symphony No. 1
Cope: Afterlife
Copland: Appalachian
  Spring

Cordero: Symphony
  No. 1
A. Cunningham:
  Concentric
Dello Joio: The
  Triumph of St. Joan
D. Epstein: Symphony
  No. 1
Fink: Symphony No. 2
Garlick: Symphony
  No. 5
Garlick: Symphony
  No. 6
Gillis: Symphony No. 1
Gillis: Symphony No. 5
Gimbel: Symphony
Hansen: Symphony No. 1
Harrison:
  Symphony on G
Hewitt: Symphony No. 7
Hewitt: Symphony No. 8
Hewitt: The Magic
  Fountain
Hovhaness: Symphony
  No. 37
H. Kay: The Clowns
Kievman: Aspen
  Symphony
Kubik: Symphony No. 2
Kupferman: Symphony
  No. 4
Lees: Concerto for
  Brass Choir and
  Orchestra
Loos: Symphony
Lopatnikoff: Symphony
  No. 3
Moevs: Endymion
Palmer: Variations,
  Chorale and Fugue
Parmentier:
  Symphony III
Pozdro: Second
  Symphony
Proctor: Symphony
  No. 1
Ran: Symphony
Reynolds: Archipelago
Richter: Bird of
  Yearning

Roger: Symphony No. 4
Rosner: Symphony No. 1
Rosner: Symphony No. 5
Rosner: Tragedy of
  Queen Jane
Rudhyar: Three Poems
  of Youth
Sanders: Symphony in A
Schuman: Symphony
  No. 6
Siegmeister: Symphony
  No. 4
Simons: Big Sur
L.A. Smith: Symphony
  No. 1
Sorce: Liberty
Stallcop: City Music
Stearns: Symphony
  No. 7
Still: Wood Notes
Taylor: Symphony No. 1
Thompson: A Trip to
  Nahant
Thomson: Eight
  Portraits
R. Wilson: Symphony
  No. 2

*Small Orchestra*

Albert: Into Eclipse
Argento: Bravo Mozart!
Ballard: Newakis
Barab: Child's Garden
  of Verses
Becker: Rain Down
  Death
Bond: Equinox
Brandt: Suite for
  Small Orchestra
Cope: Threshold and
  Visions
Copland: Dance Panels
Curtis-Smith: Xanthie
Custer: Petrouchka '65
Dresher: Reaction
El-Dabh: Lucifer
Haubiel: Portals
Hewitt: Symphony No. 5

Hewitt: Symphony
  No. 13
Hewitt: Beautiful
  Morris
Hill: Symphony No. 1
Hovhaness: A Rose for
  Miss Emily
Hovhaness: Symphony
  No. 27
Hovhaness: Symphony
  No. 28
Hovhaness: Symphony
  No. 32
Hovhaness: Symphony
  No. 33
Janson: Symphonia
Kernis: Symphony in
  Waves
Korf: Symphony No. 2
Leon: The Golden
  Windows
R. Lewis: Concerto
London: In Heinrich's
  Shoes
North: A Streetcar
  Named Desire
J. Ott: Music for
  Chamber Orchestra
Parwez: Punjab - Land
  of Five Rivers
Reif: America
Schuman: The Witch of
  Endor
H. Smith: Symphonic
  Spirituals
Starer: Dybbuk
Surinach:
  Los Renegados
Taub: Ballet
Andrew Thomas:
  Metanoia
Ward: Symphony No. 4
Whear: Symphony No. 3

*Chamber Orchestra*

Blitzstein: Native
  Land
Bolcom: Symphony No. 3
E. Brown: Indices

Cage: Et cetera
Cage: Score and 23
  Parts
Hovhaness: Symphony
  No. 52
Kupferman: Symphony
  for Twelve
Zupko: Ritual Dances

*Strings*

J. Adams: Shaker Loops
A. Cohn: Histrionics
Fitelberg: Symphony
  for Strings
Hewitt: Morning of the
  Moss Roses
Hovhaness: Symphony
  No. 31
M. Hunt: Hidden Walls
  of Time (+ 3perc)
Mamlok: Concerto for
  String Orchestra
Monello: Symphony
  No. 1
Reynolds: Whispers Out
  of Time
Rudhyar: Syntony No. 5
Shapero: Serenade in D
Townsend: Symphony for
  Strings No. 1

**36' TO 45'**

*Large Orchestra*

J. Adams:
  Harmonielehre
Albert: Riverrun
T.J. Anderson:
  Intervals - Set VIII
A. Avshalomov:
  Symphony No. 1
Bacon: Symphony No. 1
Bloch: Concerto
  symphonique
Cage: Quartets I-VIII
Cone: Symphony
Copland: Symphony
  No. 3

Davidovsky: Suite
  Sinfonica Para El
  Payaso
Dukelsky: Symphony
  No. 3
Ehle: Rebus for
  Orchestra
Ellington: Black,
  Brown and Beige
Gillis: Symphony No. 2
Gillis: Atlanta Suite
Gould: Symphony No. 3
Grofe: World's Fair
  Suite
Harris: Folksong
  Symphony
Hewitt: Symphony
  No. 10
Hovhaness: Symphony
  No. 59
Husa: Concerto for
  Orchestra
A.P. Johnson: Cento
Kievman: Hollowangels
Kubik: Symphony No. 1
Kupferman: Yin-Yang
  Symphony
Laderman: Symphony
  No. 3
Laderman: Symphony
  No. 5
Laderman: Symphony
  No. 7
Larsen: Symphony No. 3
McKinley: Symphony
  No. 2
Nabokov: Symphonic
  Variations
Rausch: A Legend of
  the Andes
Schiff: Slow Dance
Schuller: The
  Visitation
C. Schwartz: Professor
  Jive
Stein: Symphony No. 3
Svoboda: Symphony
  No. 1
Toch: Symphony No. 1

### Medium Orchestra

L. Adams: A Kiss in
  Xanadu
Cage: Quartets I-VIII
Chihara: Shinju
Dello Joio: Air Power
Goossen: Grimmtales
Haxton: Welty Women
Hewitt: Symphony
  No. 16
Hewitt: The Loveliness
  of Longwood
Hill: Symphony No. 2
Hiller: A Triptych for
  Hieronymous
H. Howe: Symphony
Kupferman: Symphony
  No. 10
Larsen: Coming Forth
  Into Day
McVoy: Orion
Monello: Symphony
  No. 1
Shapero: Symphony for
  Classical Orchestra
Susa: Love-In

### Small Orchestra

Cage: Quartets I-VIII
Claflin: Seven
  Meditations for
  Holy Week
Hiller: Divertimento
  for Chamber Ensemble
Hovhaness: Symphony
  No. 9
Hovhaness: Symphony
  No. 25
Kievman: Overture,
  Prologue and
  Prelude, C.M.P.
Surinach: Venta
  Quemada
Surinach: Bodas de
  Sangre
Winkler: Symphony

### String Orchestra

Hewitt: Earth Songs

### OVER 45'

### Large Orchestra

L. Adams: Symphony
  No. 1
Brant: Secret Calendar
Downey: Symphonic
  Modules V
Fink: Symphony No. 1
Gould: Audobon
Harbison: Ulysses'
  Raft
Hewitt: Symphony No. 9
Iannaccone: Symphony
  No. 1
Leichtling: Symphony
  No. 1
Newman: Symphony No. 1
Rochberg: Symphony
  No. 4
Still: The American
  Scene
Suderburg: Show
Svoboda: In a Linden's
  Shadow
Sydeman: Oecumenicus

### Medium Orchestra

Chihara: The Tempest
Dutton: Symphony No. 6
McBeth: Symphony No. 1

### Small Orchestra

Rice: The Green Knight
G. Samuel: Nicholas
  and Concepcion
Wuorinen: The Magic
  Art

**VARIABLE DURATION**

*Large Orchestra*

Cage: Atlas
  Eclipticalis
Cage: Cheap Imitation
Cage: 101
A.P. Johnson: Be Well
  Mov'd
Moryl: Loops

*Medium Orchestra*

Cage: Cheap Imitation
Fenner: Untitled
Foss: Geod
Hewitt: Yugen

*Small Orchestra*

E. Brown: Modules I
E. Brown: Modules II
E. Brown: Modules III
Cage: Cheap Imitation
Moryl: Particles
Strandberg: Kludge

*Chamber Orchestra*

E. Brown: Pentathis
E. Brown: Event:
  Synergy II
E. Brown: Hear We Go
  Again
Cage: Ryonji
Cage: Europeras I/II
  (+ soloists)

*String Orchestra*

Childs: Music for
  Piano and Strings
Kievman: String Rumble

*Unspecified*

E. Brown: Folio
E. Brown: Four Systems
E. Brown: One to Five
E. Brown: New Piece
Feldman:
  Intersection I
Feldman: Marginal
  Intersection
Moryl: Meta
Oliveros: The Well and
  the Gentile
Oliveros: The New
  Sound Meditation
Rosenboom:
  Chart Piece I
Rosenboom:
  Chart Piece II
Rosenboom: How much
  better if Plymouth
  Rock had landed on
  the Pilgrims
Simons: Variables
Stokes: Lampyridae
Wolff: Burdocks
Wolff: Changing the
  System

## APPENDIX B

## SOLO INSTRUMENTS AND ORCHESTRA

Piano
  2 or more pianos

Violin
  2 or more violins
Viola
  2 violas
Violoncello
  2 violoncellos
Double Bass
Multiple strings
  2 string soloists
  3 string soloists
  String quartet
  Other combinations

Flute
  2 flutes
Piccolo
Alto flute
Oboe
English horn
Clarinet
  2 clarinets
Bass clarinet
Bassoon
  3 bassoons
Contrabassoon
Multiple wind soloists

Soprano saxophone
Alto saxophone
Tenor saxophone
  2 or more saxophones

Horn
  2 horns
Trumpet
  2 or more trumpets
Trombone
Bass trombone
Alto trombone
  2 or more trombones
Euphonium
Tuba
Multiple brass

Timpani
Percussion
Marimba
Multiple percussion

Harp
  2 harps
Organ
Celeste
Harpsichord
Accordion
Guitar
  4 guitars
Other plucked
  instruments

Synthesizer

Multiple diverse
  instruments
    2 soloists
    3 soloists
    4 or more soloists

Jazz group
Rock group

The works listed in Appendix B are for orchestra with instrumental soloist(s). The larger listings have been subdivided into durational categories and, if necessary, by size of accompanying ensemble. If a work requires only a string orchestra, this is indicated in parentheses after the title of the work. Complete information on any of these works may be obtained by referring to the main listing in the catalog.

## PIANO

### 10' or less

*Large Orchestra*

L. Austin: Open Style
Csonka: Cuban Concerto No. 1
Ellington: New World A Comin'
Knox: Concert Piece

*Medium Orchestra*

Creston: Fantasy for Piano
A. Cunningham: Pataditas
Dello Joio: A Ballad of the Seven Lively Arts
Kirk: Fantasy and Frolic
Leon: Kabiosile
McBride: Ill Tempered
Raphling: Minstrel Rhapsody
Rozsa: Spellbound Concerto
Shere: Small Concerto
Tautenhahn: Numeric Serenade
Wirth: Rhapsody for Piano
Wyner: Da Camera

*Small Orchestra*

Beck: Ballade
A. Cunningham: Dialogue
Goeb: Fantasy for Piano
Roy Harris: Radio Piece
H. Howe: Concerto for Piano
Jenni: Chopiniana
U. Kay: Ancient Saga
Kohn: Interlude II
Lees: Declamations
Mollicone: Fantasy
Nelhybel: Two Movements
Persichetti: Concerto for Piano
Stearns: Reminiscence
Townsend: Concertino
Turok: Ragtime Caprice
Ussachevsky: Intermezzo
Wegner: Ice-Nine

### 11' to 20'

*Large Orchestra*

E. Applebaum: Piano Concerto
Barnes: Concerto for Piano
Bazelon: Trajectories
Beaser: Piano Concerto
Bond: Black Light
Claflin: Concerto Giocoso

Claflin: Pop Concert
  Concerto
Colgrass: Demon
Copland: Piano
  Concerto
Cowell: Four Irish
  Tales
Cowell: Little
  Concerto
M. Cunningham: Piano
  Concerto
Curtis-Smith: Bells
Erb: Concerto for
  Keyboards
Farberman: Paramount
  Concerto
Finney: Concerto No. 2
Hanson: Concerto for
  Piano
Hartley: Concerto for
  Piano
Helps: Concerto for
  Piano
Helps: Concerto No. 2
Hoag: Pianoplay II
Hoffmann: Piano
  Concerto
Ince: Concerto for
  Piano
Kohs: Concerto for
  Piano
Kupferman: Concerto
  for Piano
La Montaine: Birds of
  Paradise
Leon: Concerto criollo
Lifchitz: Piano
  Concerto
Luke: Concerto for
  Piano
Lundborg: Concerto for
  Piano
McKinley: Concerto
  No. 1
McKinley: Concerto
  No. 2
Moevs: Concerto Grosso
C. Moore: Concerto for
  Blues Piano
Moryl: Volumes

Packales: Concerto for
  Piano
Ramey: Concerto No. 1
Ran: Concert Piece
Rieti: Concerto No. 3
Robinson: Piano
  Concerto
Saul: Metamorphosis
Sessions: Concerto for
  Piano
F.E. Silverman:
  Candlelight
Stokes: A Center
  Harbor Holiday
Suben: Concerto for
  Piano
Woollen: Two Pieces
  for Piano
Wuorinen: Concerto
  No. 1
Yardumian:
  Passacaglia,
  Recitative and Fugue

*Medium Orchestra*

Babbitt: Concerto for
  Piano
Becker: Satirico
Biscardi: Concerto for
  Piano
Bohrnstedt: Concerto
  for Piano
Bottje: Concerto for
  Piano
Bubalo: Symmetricality
Cone: Nocturne and
  Rondo
Creston: Concerto for
  Piano
Dello Joio: Ricercari
Diamond: Concertino
  for Piano
Diemer: Concerto for
  Piano
Finney: Concerto No. 1
Fischer: Piano
  Concerto
E. George: Concerto
  for Piano

Gillis: Concerto No. 1
Harbison: Concerto for
  Piano
Roy Harris: Fantasy
  for Piano
Koch: Concerto for
  Acoustic/Electric
  Piano
Kohn: Sinfonia
  concertante
Kohn: Episodes
Krenek: Concerto No. 3
Krenek: Concerto No. 4
La Montaine: Symphonic
  Variations
La Montaine: Concerto
  III
Mandelbaum: Concerto
  for Piano
Muczynski: Concerto
  for Piano
Nin-Culmell: Concerto
  for Piano
Picker: Concerto No. 1
Picker: Keys to the
  City
Ramey: Concert Suite
Riegger: Variations
Sandroff: Piano
  Concerto
E. Schwartz: Magic
  Music
Shatin: The Passion of
  St. Cecilia
Smit: Concerto for
  Piano
H. Smith: Concert
  Music
D. Wilson: Concerto
  for Piano and Winds

*Small Orchestra*

J. Adams: Eros Piano
Antoniou: Piano
  Concerto
Antoniou: Fluxus I
Argento: Divertimento
  for Piano

Beck: Piano Concerto
  No. 1
Becker: Concerto
  Arabesque
Becker: Soundpiece
  No. 1
Benjamin: Concerto for
  Piano
Brings: Concerto da
  Camera No. 1
Cage: Concerto for
  Prepared Piano
Campo: Concerto for
  Piano
J. Cohn: Concertino
Cotel: Concerto for
  Piano
Doppmann:
  Counterpoints
Effinger: Concerto for
  Piano
Erb: Chamber Concerto
Evett: Concerto for
  Piano
Franco: Serenade
  Concertante
Franco: Concerto
  Lirico No. 3
Ghezzo: Thalla
Glanville-Hicks:
  Etruscan Concerto
Goeb: Concerto for
  Piano
Gould: Concerto for
  Piano
Hanson: Fantasy-
  Variations
Helm: Concerto No. 2
Hollingsworth:
  Concerto for Piano
Hovhaness: Lousadzak
Hovhaness: Partita
Husa: Concertino
Imbrie: Concerto No. 1
Jacobi: Concerto for
  Piano
Jenni: Concertino
Karpman: Theme and
  Variations

Keller: Concerto for
Piano
Kirk: Concerto Grosso
Kohn: Concerto
mutabile
Koutzen: Concertino
for Piano
L. Kraft: Concerto
No. 4
Kroeger: Five
Bagatelles
Lazarof: Concerto for
Piano
Monello: Concerto
Grosso
Newell: Concerto for
Piano
Palmer: Concerto for
Piano
Parmentier: Concerto
for Piano
Parris: Concerto for
Piano
Pinkham:
Concertino in A
Piston: Concertino for
Piano
Raphling: Concerto
No. 1
Richter: Concerto for
Piano
Riegger: Duo for Piano
Rodriguez:
Concerto III
Roosevelt: Concerto
for Piano
Rorem: Concerto No. 2
Rovics: Piano Concerto
Sapp: Colloquies No. 1
Saylor: Notturno
Schwantner:
Distant Runes and
Incantations
E. Schwartz: Chamber
Concerto III
Shapero: Partita in C
Shawn: Nocturnes
L.A. Smith: Concerto
for Piano
Starer: Concerto No. 2

Stearns: First Little
Symphony
Steiner: Concerto for
Piano
Strandberg: Concerto
for Pianoforte
Surinach: Concertino
Svoboda: Piano
Concerto
F. Thorne: Rhapsodic
Variations
Travis: Concerto for
Piano
Wagner: Piano Concerto
Wagner: A Fugal
Triptych
Ward-Steinman: Chroma
Weiner: Capriccio
Wigglesworth:
Concertino
O. Wilson: Akwan
Wolpe: Piece in Three
Parts
Wood: Divertimento

21' to 30'

*Large Orchestra*

Ames: Concerto for
Piano
Barber: Concerto for
Piano
Bernstein: Symphony
No. 2
Bolcom: Concerto for
Piano
Brant: Spatial
Concerto
Carter: Concerto for
Piano
Corigliano: Concerto
for Piano
Cowell: Concerto for
Piano
Danielpour: Concerto
for Piano
Dello Joio: Fantasy
and Variations

Diamond: Concerto for
  Piano
Dickerson: New Orleans
  Concerto
Feldman: Piano and
  Orchestra
Freund: Piano Concerto
Gaburo: Concertante
T. George: Concerto
  No. 2
Hemmer: The Voice of
  the Grand Piano
Imbrie: Concerto No. 2
Kirchner: Concerto
  No. 1
Kirchner: Concerto
  No. 2
W. Kraft: Concerto for
  Piano
Laderman: Concerto for
  Piano
Laderman: Concerto
  No. 2
La Montaine: Concerto
  for Piano
La Montaine:
  Concerto IV
Lazarof: Tableaux
Lees: Concerto No. 1
Lees: Concerto No. 2
Lees: Variations
M. Levy: Concerto
  No. 1
Martino: Concerto for
  Piano
Mennin: Concerto for
  Piano
Menotti: Piano
  Concerto in F
Mills: Concerto for
  Piano
Orrego-Salas: Concerto
  No. 2
Perle: Concerto for
  Piano
Perry: Concerto No. 2
Perry: Concerto in Two
  Uninterrupted Speeds
Picker: Concerto No. 3
Ramey: Concerto No. 2

Richter: Landscapes of
  the Mind
Rorem: Concerto No. 3
Rozsa: Concerto for
  Piano
Sacco: Concerto No. 1
Schifrin: Concerto for
  Piano
Schoenfield: Four
  Parables
Schonthal: Concerto
  No. 2
Schuller: Concerto
  No. 1
Schuller: Concerto
  No. 2
Sellars: Concertorama
Steinohrt: Concerto
  for Piano
Suderburg: Concerto
  "Within the Mirror
  of Time"
Surinach: Concerto for
  Piano
Svoboda: Concerto
  No. 2
Talma: Dialogues for
  Piano
F. Thorne: Concerto
  for Piano
Van de Vate: Concerto
Waldrop: Concerto for
  Piano
Ward: Concerto for
  Piano
Weber: Concerto for
  Piano
Weiner: Concerto for
  Piano
Weingarden: Piano
  Concerto
Wernick: Piano
  Concerto
Wuorinen: Concerto
  No. 2
Wuorinen: Concerto
  No. 3
Zupko: Windsongs
Zwilich: Concerto for
  Piano

*Medium Orchestra*

L. Adams: Piano
    Concerto
Adler: Concerto for
    Piano
Bacon: Riolama
Balada: Piano Concerto
Barati: Piano Concerto
Biggs: Variations on a
    Theme of
    Shostakovich
Blackwood: Concerto
    for Piano
Danielpour:
    Metamorphosis
Di Domenica: Concerto
    No. 2
Fink: Concerto No. 1
Flagello: Concerto
    No. 1
Flagello: Concerto
    No. 2
Foss: Concerto for
    Piano
Helm: Concerto No. 1
Kievman: Prisoners of
    Conscience
Lazarof: Textures
Mayer: Octagon
Palange: Concerto for
    Piano
Ramey: Concerto No. 3
Raphling: Concerto
    No. 3
Ross: Concerto for
    Piano
E. Schwartz: Janus
Siegmeister: Concerto
    for Piano
J. Smith: Concerto for
    Piano
Snyder: Hegemony
Starer: Concerto No. 3
Stokes: Concert Music
F. Thorne: Concerto
    No. 3

*Small Orchestra*

L. Bell: Concerto for
    Piano
Cope: Concert for
    Piano
Fetler: Concerto No. 1
Fink: Concerto No. 2
Gould: Dialogues
Hoiby: Concerto No. 2
Lieberman: Lighted
    Stones
Lockwood: Concerto for
    Piano
Montague: Piano
    Concerto
Neikrug: Concerto for
    Piano
G. Read: Music for
    Piano & Strings
Rice: Concerto for
    Piano & Strings
Rudhyar: Encounter
Schuman: Concerto for
    Piano
Schwantner: Concerto
    for Piano
Sellars: Pianoconcert
Starer: Concerto No. 1
Tower: Concerto for
    Piano
Verrall: Concerto for
    Piano

**Over 30'**

*Large Orchestra*

A. Avshalomov:
    Concerto in G
Bach: Piano Concerto
Foss: Concerto No. 2
Gillis: Concerto No. 2
Gruenberg: Piano
    Concerto No. 2
Haxton: Concerto No. 1
Keats: Concerto for
    Piano
La Montaine:
    Concerto II

Lieberson: Piano
  Concerto
D. Ott: Concerto No. 1
Persichetti: Concerto
  for Piano
Winslow: Concerto for
  Piano
Zaimont: Concerto for
  Piano

  *Medium Orchestra*

Ballou: Concerto for
  Piano
Hewitt: Concerto for
  Piano
Kessner: Piano
  Concerto
Pellegrini: Piano
  Concerto
G. Read: Concerto for
  Piano
R. Wilson: Concerto
  for Piano

  *Variable Duration*

Cage: Concerto for
  Piano

  TWO PIANOS

J. Adams: Grand
  Pianola Music
Ames: Nocturne and
  Scherzo
Babin: Concerto No. 2
D. Baker: Concerto for
  Two Pianos, Jazz
  Band, Percussion and
  Strings
Barati: Branches of
  Time
Bassett: Concerto for
  Two Pianos
Colgrass: Memento
Creston: Concerto for
  Two Pianos
Gould: Dance
  Variations

Gutche: Gemini
  (1 pf, 4-hands)
Roy Harris: Concerto
  for Two Pianos
Hopkins: Concerto for
  Two Pianos
Imbrie: Little
  Concerto
  (1 pf, 4-hands)
Koch: Concerto sonica
Krenek: Concerto for
  Two Pianos
Kurka: Concertino
Lopatnikoff: Concerto
Maves: Concerto
Parchman: Twelve
  Variations
Parchman: Concerto for
  Piano (4-hands)
Parchman: Concerto
  No. 2
Piston: Concerto for
  Two Pianos
Porter: Concerto
  concertante
Powell: Duplicates
Rieti: Concerto for
  Two Pianos
Sapieyevski: Concerto
  for Two Pianos
Schelle: Concerto for
  Two Pianos
Schuller: Colloquy for
  Two Pianos
Schuller: Concerto for
  Two Pianos (3-hands)
D. Williams: Concerto
  for Piano (4-hands)
Zwilich: Images

  VIOLIN

  10' or less

Aitken: Aspen Concerto
Brant: Saraband
Clarke: Gloria
  (+ satb cho)
Constantinides:
  Mountains of Epirus

Constantinides:
  Patterns
Cowell: Air for Violin
Cowell: Fiddler's Jig
Daugherty: Lex
Fischer: Fantasie with
  Fugue
Fischer: Poem
Gillis: Retrospection
Harbison: Sinfonia for
  Violin
D. Harris: Fantasy
Hewitt: The Stars Will
  Heal Us
Hovhaness: Sosi
Lazarof: Rhapsody
Mitchell: Toccata
Ogdon: Five Preludes
Parris: The Unquiet
  Heart
Rodriguez: Frammenti
  musicali
Rodriguez: Semi-Suite
Starer: Elegy
Woodard: The Dream
  Songs of Stephen
  Foster (+ solo s)

          11' to 20'

Adler: Rhapsody for
  Violin
Albert: In Concordiam
Ames: Rhapsody
Amram: Elegy
Antoniou: Violin
  Concerto
E. Applebaum:
  Landscape of Dreams
Balada: Concerto for
  Violin
Balazs: Kentuckia
Becker: Violin
  Concerto
Benjamin: Unto the
  Hills (+ satb cho)
Binkerd: A Part of
  Heaven
Binney: Sonnet for
  Violin

Blackwood: Concerto
  for Violin
Bolcom: Concerto
  Serenade
Bolcom: Concerto in D
E. Brown: Centering
Cooper: Concerto No. 1
Csonka: Cuban Concerto
  No. 2
Custer: Doubles
Dahl: Elegy Concerto
Di Domenica: Concerto
  for Violin
Diemer: Concerto for
  Violin
Farberman: Concerto
  for Violin
Finko: Violin Concerto
Finney: Concerto No. 2
Fischer: Idyll
Foss: Three American
  Pieces
Franco: Concerto
  Lirico No. 1
Fuleihan: Concerto for
  Violin
Gerschefski:
  Celebration
Goeb: Concerto for
  Violin
Goldstein: Cascades of
  the Brook
Gottschalk: Blue
  Fantasy
Gutche: Concerto for
  Violin
Hagen: Concerto for
  Violin
Haubiel: Gothic
  Variations
Heilner: Concerto in
  Memory of Dvorak
Hoffmann: Violin
  Concerto
Hoiby: Serenade
Hollingsworth:
  Concerto for Violin
Hovhaness: Concerto
  No. 2

Hovhaness: Ode to
  Freedom
Huggler: Concerto for
  Violin
Hutcheson: Concerto
  for Violin
Iannaccone: Concertino
  for Violin
Kurka: Concerto for
  Violin
Larsen: Pinions
D. Lewin: Fantasy
Lifchitz: Night Voices
  No. 10
Mailman: Concerto for
  Violin
McBride: Variety Day
McKinley: Summer
  Dances
C. Moore: Concerto for
  Jazz Violin
Orrego-Salas: Violin
  Concerto
Overton: Rhythms
Parris: Concerto for
  Violin
Pinkham: Concerto for
  Violin
Pinkham: Concertante
  No. 2
Piston: Fantasia for
  Violin
Plain: Violin Concerto
G. Read: Sonoric
  Fantasia No. 2
Riegger: Variations
  for Violin
Rieti: Concerto No. 2
Rosen: Five Pieces
Rosenboom: Contrasts
Russo: Suite for
  Violin
G. Samuel: Beyond
  McBean
Schuller: Recitative
  and Rondo
Shawn: Autumnal Song
Shere: Concerto for
  Violin
Stearns: Concerto in G

Stout: Eight Movements
Svoboda: Violin
  Concerto
Swift: Concerto for
  Violin
Townsend: Chamber
  Concerto No. 1
Van Vactor: Concerto
  for Violin
George Walker: Poeme
Weber: Dramatic Piece
Wood: Concerto for
  Violin
Wuorinen: Rhapsody
Yannay: Concertino
Zwilich: Concerto
  Grosso

**21' to 30'**

Aitken: Concerto for
  Violin
Amram: Concerto for
  Violin
Antheil: Concerto for
  Violin
A. Avshalomov:
  Concerto in D
Barati: Violin
  Concerto
Barber: Concerto for
  Violin
L.T. Bell: The Idea of
  Order at Key West
  (+ solo s)
Benjamin: Violin
  Concerto
Benjamin: Unto the
  Hills (+ satb cho)
Bergsma: Concerto for
  Violin
Biggs: Concerto for
  Violin
Brant: Litany of Tides
  (+ 4s soli)
D. Carlson: Violin
  Concerto
Carter: Violin
  Concerto

Cone: Concerto for
  Violin
Cooper: Concerto No. 2
Cordero: Concerto for
  Violin
Creston: Concerto
  No. 1
Creston: Concerto
  No. 2
Anthony Davis: Maps
Diamond: Concerto
  No. 3
Diemente: Violin
  Concerto
Effinger: Concerto for
  Violin
Farberman: Reflected
  Realities
Fetler: Concerto for
  Violin
Fink: Concerto for
  Violin
Fox: Concerto for
  Violin
E. George: Concerto
  for Violin
Glass: Concerto for
  Violin
Harbison: Concerto for
  Violin
Roy Harris: Concerto
  for Violin
Hodkinson: Symphony
  No. 6
Hoffmann: Music for
  Strings
Kechley: Concerto for
  Violin
Kelly: Concerto for
  Violin
Kohs: Concerto for
  Violin
Koutzen: Concerto for
  Violin
Krenek: Concerto No. 2
Laderman: Concerto for
  Violin
Lazarof: Concerto for
  Violin

D. Lee: Concerto for
  Violin
Lees: Violin Concerto
Levi: Songs for the
  Synagogue
Lifchitz: Intervencion
Lopatnikoff: Concerto
  for Violin
Menotti: Concerto for
  Violin
Nanes: Rhapsody
  pathetique
Neikrug: Concerto for
  Violin
Nielson: Concerto for
  Violin
Paulus: Violin
  Concerto
Perry: Concerto for
  Violin
Picker: Violin
  Concerto
Piston: Concerto No. 2
Pone: Concerto for
  Violin
Robertson: Concerto
  for Violin
Rogers: Portrait
Rorem: Concerto for
  Violin
Rozsa: Concerto for
  Violin
Sacco: Concerto No. 1
Sahl: Concerto for
  Electric Violin
Schuller: Concerto for
  Violin
Schuman: Concerto for
  Violin
Shapey: Invocation
Starer: Concerto for
  Violin
Stein: Concerto for
  Violin
Stewart: Violin
  Concerto
Surinach: Concerto for
  Violin
Tautenhahn: Concerto
  for Violin

Augusta Thomas:
Cathedral Summer
F. Thorne: Concerto
for Violin
Trimble: Concerto for
Violin
Turok: Concerto for
Violin
Verrall: Concerto for
Violin
Weber: Concerto for
Violin
Wernick: Concerto for
Violin
R. Wilson: Concerto
for Violin
Wuorinen: Concerto
No. 1
Yardumian: Concerto
for Violin
Zupko: Concerto for
Violin

**Over 30'**

Bernstein: Serenade
Feldman: Violin and
Orchestra
Fetler: Concerto No. 2
Finney: Concerto No. 1
Gerschefski: Concerto
Imbrie: Concerto for
Violin
Lees: Symphony No. 4
(+ solo mez)
Pellegrini: Violin
Concerto
Rochberg: Concerto for
Violin
Sessions: Concerto for
Violin
Siegmeister: Concerto
for Violin
Ultan: Concerto for
Violin

**2 OR MORE VIOLINS**

Colgrass:
Concertmasters
(2vln)
Foss: Orpheus and
Euridice (2vln)
Fussell: Northern
Lights (4vln)
Rice: Concerto for
Three Violins
Trimble: Duo
concertante

**VIOLA**

**15' or less**

Adler: Song and Dance
E. Applebaum: Concerto
for Viola
Ballou: Konzertstuck
Beale: Ballade
Bottje: Rhapsodic
Variations
Brant: Saraband
Clarke: Encounter
Cooper: Descants
Hanson: Summer
Seascape II
Harbison: Concerto for
Viola
Hovhaness: Talin
Huggler: Divertimento
Husa: Three Fresques
Husa: Poem for Viola
Koutzen: Viola
Concerto
LoPresti: Nocturne
Musgrave: From One to
Another
Newell: Viola-Mobile
Richter: Aria and
Toccata
Riley: Serenade
Serly: Rhapsody
Shatin: Arche
Simons: Illuminations
in Space
Stewart: Fantasia

Waters: Concerto for
  Viola
Weber: Rapsodie
  concertante
Wigglesworth:
  Concertino

### 16' to 30'

D. Baker: Concert
  Piece
Becker: Concerto for
  Viola
Benjamin: Viola
  Concerto
Bergsma: Sweet was the
  Song the Virgin Sang
Biggs: Concerto for
  Viola
Bohrnstedt: Concerto
  for Viola
Castaldo: Concerto for
  Viola
Cazden: Concerto for
  Viola
Colgrass: Chaconne
Constantinides:
  Grecian Variations
Dello Joio: Lyric
  Fantasies
Druckman: Concerto for
  Viola
Feldman: The Viola in
  My Life IV
Friedman: Concerto
Glanville-Hicks:
  Concerto Romantico
Goossen: Concerto for
  Viola
Hibbard: Concerto for
  Viola
Kelly: Concerto for
  Viola
Kohs: Chamber Concerto
Laderman: Concerto for
  Viola
Lazarof: Viola
  Concerto
Lazarof: Volo
F. Lewin: Concerto

McKinley: Concerto
  No. 1
Musgrave: Viola
  Concerto
Nelhybel: Viola
  Concerto
Nielson: Concerto for
  Viola
Nixon: Concerto for
  Viola
D. Ott: Viola Concerto
Parris: Concerto for
  Viola
Piston: Concerto for
  Viola
Porter: Concerto for
  Viola
A. Reed: Rhapsody
Riley: Concertante
  Music III
Rozsa: Concerto for
  Viola
G. Samuel: On a Dream
Schuller: Concerto for
  Viola
L.A. Smith: Concerto
  for Viola
Starer: Concerto for
  Viola
Stevens: Concerto for
  Viola
Van Vactor: Concerto
  for Viola
Verrall: Concerto for
  Viola
Wernick: Viola
  Concerto

### Over 30'

Leichtling: Concerto
  for Viola
McKinley: Concerto
  No. 2
Schuman: Concerto on
  Old English Rounds
  (+ ssaa cho)

## TWO VIOLAS

Cowell: Variations on
  Thirds

## VIOLONCELLO

### 15' or less

Adolphus: Interlude
Antoniou: Jeux
E. Applebaum: Concert
  Aria
D. Baker: Concerto for
  Cello
Balazs: Kentuckia
Beale: Concerto for
  Violoncello
Carl: A Wide Open
  Field
Csonka: Serenata
Diamond: Kaddish
Effinger: Suite
Erb: Concerto for
  Violoncello
Erickson: Fantasy
Fennelly: Scintilla
  Prisca
Finney: Narrative
Fischer: Lament
Fox: Matrix
Franco: Fantasy
Gerschefski: Nocturne
Hagen: Stanzas
Jenni: Romanza
Kaufman: Kaddish
  Concerto
Kohs: Concerto for
  Violoncello
Koutzen: Concert Piece
Krenek: Capriccio for
  Cello
Mandelbaum: Creations
Piston: Variations for
  Violoncello
Porter: Fantasy for
  Violoncello
Powell: Setting for
  Violoncello
Rieti: Concerto No. 2

Riley: Elegy
Rochberg: Night Music
Roosevelt: Concerto
  for Cello
Rozsa: Concerto for
  Violoncello
Stearns: Hymn
Steinke: Oregon
  Coastal Sketches
Stout: Serenity
Sydeman: Largo for
  Violoncello
Turok: Canzone
  Concertante
Van de Vate: Concert
  Piece
George Walker:
  Dialogus
Weber: Ballade
Weber: Sinfonia
Whear: Burberry Red
  Cabaret

### 16' to 30'

Adam: Concerto for
  Cello
Albert: Concerto for
  Cello
Amram: Honor Song
Balazs: Concerto
Barati: Concerto for
  Cello
Barber: Concerto for
  Cello
Bernstein: Three
  Meditations
Bubalo: Concerto for
  Cello
D. Carlson: Cello
  Concerto
Castaldo: Cello
  Concerto
Chihara: Windsong
Consoli: Cello
  Concerto
Cooper: Concerto for
  Violoncello
Creston: Sadhana
Custer: Five Dialogues

Davidovsky:
  Divertimento
Dukelsky: Concerto for
  Violoncello
Evett: Concerto No. 1
Evett: Concerto No. 2
Feldman: Cello and
  Orchestra
Ferrito: Concerto for
  Violoncello
Flagello: Capriccio
Foss: Cello Concerto
Franco: Concerto
  Lirico No. 2
Freund: Cello Concerto
Fuleihan: Rhapsody
Heiden: Concerto for
  Cello
Hoffmann: Cello
  Concerto
Hovhaness: Concerto
  for Cello
Husa: Concerto for
  Violoncello
Imbrie: Concerto for
  Cello
Ivey: Voyager
Jazwinski: Concerto
Kelly: Concerto for
  Violoncello
Kessner: Breath
Krenek: Concerto No. 1
Krenek: Concerto No. 2
Kupferman: Concerto
  for Violoncello
Laderman: Concerto for
  Violoncello
Lazarof: Concerto for
  Cello
Lubin: Variations and
  Epilogue
Martino: Concerto for
  Violoncello
McCulloh: Concerto for
  Cello
Mennin: Concerto for
  Violoncello
Menotti: Fantasia
Nabokov: Les hommages

Nabokov: Prelude,
  Variations and
  Finale
Nin-Culmell: Concerto
  for Cello
O'Brien: Concerto for
  Violoncello
D. Ott: Cello Concerto
Perle: Concerto for
  Cello
Rackley: Discourse,
  Soliloquy and
  Concourse
Ramsier: Eusebius
  Revisited
Rands: Hiraeth
G. Read: Concerto for
  Violoncello
H. Reed: Concerto for
  Violoncello
Reynolds: The Dream of
  the Infinite Rooms
Schuller: Concerto for
  Violoncello
Schuman: A Song of
  Orpheus
Shapey: Partita-
  Fantasia
Shulman: Concerto for
  Cello
Starer: Concerto for
  Violoncello
Stein: Concerto for
  Violoncello
Stern: Hazkarah
Stevens: Concerto for
  Violoncello
Stucky: Voyages
Subotnick: Axolotl
Thomson: Concerto for
  Violoncello
Tower: Music for
  Violoncello
Ultan: Concerto for
  Violoncello
Vincent: Soliloquy and
  Dance
George Walker: Cello
  Concerto

Ward-Steinman:
Concerto for
Violoncello
Weber: Symphony on
Poems of William
Blake (+ solo bar)
Donald White: Concerto
for Cello
Wuorinen: Five
Zwilich: Symphony
No. 2

**Over 30'**

McKinley: Concerto for
Violoncello

**TWO VIOLONCELLOS**

D. Ott: Concerto for
Two Violoncellos

**DOUBLE BASS**

**15' or less**

A. Cunningham: The
Walton Statement
Fennelly: Lunar Halos
Hodkinson: Tango,
Boogie and Grand
Tarantella
Ramsier: The Low-Note
Blues
Saturen: Lyric
Progression
E. Schwartz: Chamber
Concerto I

**16' to 30'**

Chihara: Grass
Douglas: Concerto
Downey: Concerto for
Double Bass
Harbison: Concerto for
Double Bass
Hewitt: Concertino for
String Bass

Hoag: Concerto for
Double Bass
Hopkins: Concerto for
Contrabass
Menotti: Concerto for
Double Bass
Ramsier: Eusebius
Revisited
Ramsier: Road to
Hamelin
Ramsier: Silent Movie
Ramsier: Divertimento
Concertante
Rouse: Concerto for
Double Bass
Schuller: Concerto for
Double Bass
Stallcop: Concerto for
Double Bass
Tautenhahn: Concerto
for Double Bass

**MULTIPLE STRINGS**

*2 String Soloists*

Beglarian: Diversions
(vla, vc)
Bolcom: Fantasia
Concertante
(vla, vc)
Cooper: Double
Concerto (vln, vla)
Finko: Concerto
(vla, db)
Frank: Sinfonia
Concertante
(vln, vla)
Kelly: Concerto
(vln, vc)
Kelly: Concerto
(vln, vla)
Laderman: Concerto
(vln, vc)
Lifchitz: Yellow
Ribbons No. 18
(vln, db)
Rinehart: Double
Concerto (vln, vc)

Rodriguez: Favola
  Concertante
  (vln, vc)
Rozsa: Sinfonia
  Concertante
  (vln, vc)
G. Samuel: Double
  Concerto (vln, vla)
Saturen: Largo and
  Allegro (vln, vc)
Schifrin: Double
  Concerto (vln, vc)
Sessions: Concerto
  (vln, vc)
Shapey: Double
  Concerto (vln, vc)
Starer: Concerto
  (vln, vc)
Steinke: Fantasy duo
  concertante
  (vln, vc)
Taylor: Concerto No. 2
  (vln, vla)
Taylor: Concerto No. 3
  (vln, vla)
Augusta Thomas: Haiku
  (vln, vc)
F. Thorne: Double
  Concerto (vla, db)
Ward: Dialogues
  (vln, vc)
Ward: Dialogue on the
  Tides of Time
  (vln, vc)

3 String Soloists

V. Fine: Romantic Ode
  (vln, vla, vc)
Fussell: Sweelinck
  Liedvariationen
  (vln, vla, vc)
Snyder: Triple
  Concerto
  (vln, vla, vc)

String Quartet

Antoniou: Antithesis

Balazs: Concerto for
  String Quartet
Bloch: Concerto Grosso
  No. 2
Chihara: Concerto for
  String Quartet
Cooper: Symphony No. 1
Davidovsky:
  Concertante
Edwards: Heraclitean
  Fire
Etler: Concerto for
  String Quartet
Feldman:
  String Quartet
  and Orchestra
Fenner: Variations for
  String Quartet
Fuleihan: Symphonie
  Concertante
Giannini: Concerto
  Grosso
Gould: Vivaldi Gallery
Laderman: Concerto for
  String Quartet
Lees: Concerto for
  String Quartet
Luening: Fantasia
Mayer: Inner and Outer
  Strings
Neikrug: Concerto for
  String Quartet
Nelhybel: Houston
  Concerto
Nelhybel: Concerto
  Spiritoso No. 4
  (+ solo med v)
B. Phillips: Concerto
  Grosso
Piston: Concerto for
  String Quartet,
  Winds and Percussion
Rieti: Concerto for
  String Quartet
Shapey: Songs of Eros
  (+ solo s)
Svoboda: Folk Dance
Waters: Concertino

*Other Combinations*

Canning: Fantasy on a
Hymn by Justin
Morgan (2str qt)
A. Cohn: Quintuple
Concerto for Five
Ancient Instruments
Hewitt: Concerto
Grosso No. 1
(str qnt)
Keyes: Concerto Grosso
(str qt, db)
Stokes: Five Verbs of
Earth Encircled
(7vln, 3vla, 2vc,
db)

## FLUTE

### 15' or less

Averitt: Elegy for
Flute, Percussion
and Strings
A. Avshalomov:
Concerto for Flute
Balada: Alegrias
Balazs: Two Dances
after David
Beaser: Song of the
Bells
Binney: Haiku Cycle
Blackwood: Concerto
for Flute
Bloch: Suite modale
Bloch: Two Last Poems
Brings: Concerto da
Camera No. 3
Constantinides: Homage
Di Domenica: Music for
Flute (str)
Ferneyhough: Carceri
d'Invenzione II
Foss: Three American
Pieces
Frackenpohl: Arioso
(str)
Fuleihan: Suite
Concertante

T. George: Concerto
for Flute
Goldstein: "a breaking
of vessels, becoming
song"
P. Grant: Scherzo for
Flute
Horban: Australis
Hovhaness: Elibris
U. Kay: Aulos
Kirchner: Music for
Flute
Krenek: Suite (str)
La Montaine: Two
Scenes from the Song
of Solomon
Lifchitz: Night Voices
No. 5
Lubin: Pavane
Luening: Concertino
for Flute
Luening: Serenade
(str)
Luening: Lyric Scene
Moryl: The Pond
Mourant: Idyl
Mourant: Mountain Air
Mourant: Spring Idyll
Musgrave: Orfeo 11
Parris: Concerto for
Flute
Rodriguez: Frammenti
musicali
Rosner: A Gentle
Musicke
Saylor: Turns and
Mordents
Schuller: Movements
Schwantner: A Play of
Shadows
Serebrier: Dorothy and
Carmine
Shawn: Concertino
(str)
Still: Preludes
Still: Choreographic
Prelude
Stout: Aria for
Tranquility
Swisher: Caneion

Thomson: Concerto for
　Flute
Tircuit: Halcyon
Tower: Concerto for
　Flute
Tuthill: Flute Song
Van Vactor: Pastorale
　and Dance
Wood: Serenade (str)
Yardumian: Epigram
Yasanitsky: Magic

### Over 15'

Adler: Concerto for
　Flute
Aitken: Rameau
　Remembered
Benson: Concertino for
　Flute, Percussion
　and Strings
Bohmler: Celebre
Brant: Odyssey - Why
　Not?
S. Burton:
　Stravinskiana
Cooper: Concerto for
　Flute
Corigliano: Concerto
　for Flute
Diemer: Concerto for
　Flute
Elisha: Concerto for
　Flute
Feldman: Flute and
　Orchestra
Flagello: Concerto
　Antoniano
Flaherty: Flute
　Concerto
Foss: Renaissance
　Concerto
Franco: Concerto
　Lirico No. 6
Frazelle: Blue Ridge
　Airs II
Gould: Concerto for
　Flute
Gryc: The Moon's
　Mirror

Hovhaness: Symphony
　No. 36
Imbrie: Concerto for
　Flute
Laderman: Celestial
　Bodies
Laderman: Concerto for
　Flute
La Montaine: Concerto
　for Flute
Lazarof: Concerto for
　Flute
McKinley: Concerto for
　Flute
Mennin: Concerto for
　Flute
Meyerowitz: Flute
　Concerto
Morris: Streams and
　Willows
Neikrug: Concerto for
　Flute
Pellegrini: Memorie
　for Alto/C Flute
Piston: Concerto for
　Flute
Rands: Serenade
Reynolds: Transfigured
　Wind II
Rieti: Partita
G. Samuel: Chamber
　Concerto in the
　Shape of a Summer
Schickele: Concerto
　for Flute
Shatin: Ruah
Siegmeister: Concerto
　for Flute
F. Thorne:
　Divertimento No. 1
Van Vactor: Concerto
　for Flute
Weiner: Concerto for
　Flute
Welcher: Concerto for
　Flute
Wilder: Concerto for
　Flute and Chamber
　Orchestra

Woollen: Suite for
Flute and Strings

TWO FLUTES

J. Berger: Concert
Piece
Bottje: Concerto for
Two Flutes
Daugherty: Mxyzptlk

PICCOLO

Bottje: Concertino for
Piccolo
Kechley: Silver Tears
Pinkham: Concerto
Piccolo
Swafford: Passage

ALTO FLUTE

D. Ott: Concerto for
Alto Flute
Schubel: Spheres

OBOE

15' or less

Bacon: Elegy
Ballou: Concertino
(str)
Ballou: In Memoriam
Barber: Canzonetta
Benjamin: Epode
Bezanson: Concertino
(str)
Blackwood: Concerto
for Oboe (str)
Bolcom: Spring
Concertino
Canning: Meditation on
"Hyfrydol"
Constantinides:
Transformations
(str)
Corigliano: Aria

Cowell: Hymn and
Fuguing Tune No. 10
A. Cunningham: Adagio
Daugherty: Firecracker
Dukelsky: Variations
on an Old Russian
Chant
Effinger: Pastorale
Farberman: Impressions
for Oboe
Foss: Concerto for
Oboe
Fox: Ternion
Goeb: Fantasy (str)
Hannay: Lament
Harbison: Snow Country
Hemmer: Idyll for Oboe
Hoag: November 22,
1963
U. Kay: Brief Elegy
Koch: Veltin Fantasy
Kohs: Legend
Kroeger: Concerto da
Camera
Laderman: A Single
Voice
Lessard: Cantilena
Luening: Legend (str)
Mamlok: Oboe Concerto
Mills: Concertino
(str)
Mols: Cantilena
Mourant: Air and
Scherzo
Mourant: Remembrance
of Things Past
Mourant: The Marble
Faun
Pinkham: Divertimento
Stein: Aria Hebraique
Street: Adagio
F. Thorne: Rhapsodic
Variations No. 3
Tower: Island Preludes
Tull: Concertino (str)
Turok: Lyric
Variations
Donald White: Andante
D. Williams: Air (str)

Zador: Concerto for
Oboe (str)

Over 15'

Amram: The Trail of
Beauty (+ solo mez)
Baksa: Chamber
Concerto (str)
Bergsma: In Campo
Aperto
Biggs: Concerto for
Oboe (str)
Carter: Oboe Concerto
Corigliano: Concerto
for Oboe
Donovan: Suite
Downey: Discourse
Feldman: Oboe and
Orchestra
Krenek: Kitharaulos
Lees: Oboe Concerto
Lockwood: Concerto for
Oboe
Meyerowitz: Oboe
Concerto
Orrego-Salas: Concerto
for Oboe (str)
Picker: Romances and
Interludes
Rochberg: Concerto for
Oboe
Ross: Concerto for
Oboe, String
Orchestra and Harp
Schuller: Threnos
D. Thomas: Concerto
for Oboe
Wilder: Concerto for
Oboe (str)

ENGLISH HORN

Binney: Three Poems
(str)
Bond: Recitative (str)
Childs: Concerto for
English Horn
A. Cunningham: Dim du
mim

Farberman: Shapings
Hansen: Contrasts
Haxton: Music (str)
Hodkinson: Edge of the
Olden One
U. Kay: Pieta
Mourant: Elm Street
Persichetti: Concerto
for English Horn
(str)
Piston: Fantasy
(hp, str)
Powell: Cantilena
Concertante
Roseman: Concertino
(str)
Rosner: Five
Meditations
Stout: Intermezzo
Turok: Canzona
Concertante No. 1
Turok: Concertino
(str)

CLARINET

15' or less

T.J. Anderson:
Six Pieces for
Clarinet and Chamber
Orchestra
Blackwood: Concerto
for Clarinet
Blank: Concerto for
Clarinet (str)
Bourland: Clarinet
Rhapsody
Brant: Concerto for
Clarinet
Bubalo: Adagio and
Allegro
Cazden: Chamber
Concerto (str)
J. Cohn: Concerto for
Clarinet (str)
Cordero: Funeral
Message
Corigliano: Soliloquy
Eberhard: Berceuse

Erb: Concerto for
Clarinet
Fennelly: Tropes and
Echoes
Foss: Elegy for
Clarinet
Goode: Phrases of the
Hermit Thrush
Gould: Guajira
Gryc: A Dance Concerto
Karlins: Catena No. 1
Kaufman: Concerto for
Clarinet (str)
L. Kraft: Clarinet
Concerto
Krenek: Suite for
Clarinet (str)
McKinley: Rhapsody for
Clarinet
McKinley: Blues Lament
Mourant: Burlesque
Mourant: Blue Haze
Mourant: The Pied
Piper
Mourant: Concertino
for Clarinet
Mourant: Ecstasy
Rogers: Pastorale
mistico
Rosen: Concerto for
Clarinet
Schifrin: Capriccio
(str)
Schneider: Concerto
for Jazz Clarinet
and String Orchestra
W. Smith: Tangents
W. Smith: Elegia
W. Smith: Ecco!
W. Smith: Twelve
Starer: Elegy
Tuthill: Rhapsody for
Clarinet
Zonn: Concerto for
Clarinet
Zupko: Pastorale

## Over 15'

Ames: Concerto for
Clarinet
Argento: Capriccio for
Clarinet
J. Avshalomov:
Evocations
D. Baker: Concerto for
Clarinet
Balazs: Symphonic
Metamorphosis
Bavicchi: Concerto for
Clarinet (str)
Bazelon: Tides
Bolcom: Concerto for
Clarinet
Childs: Concerto for
Clarinet
Copland: Concerto for
Clarinet
Corigliano: Concerto
for Clarinet
Allan Davis: Festival
Concerto
Dello Joio:
Concertante
Fischer: Concerto
giocoso
Foss: Concerto No. 2
Frackenpohl:
Concertino for
Clarinet
Giuffre: Mobiles
Giuffre: Piece for
Clarinet (str)
Goeb: Concertant IV
Knehans: Hell's
Response
Kohn: Waldmusik
Kupferman: Concerto
for Clarinet
Lazarof: Clarinet
Concerto
McKinley: Concerto
No. 1
McKinley: Concerto
No. 2
Musgrave: Concerto for
Clarinet

Neikrug: Concerto for
  Clarinet
North: Revue
Rosenman:
  Introduction, Theme
  and Variations
Siegmeister: Concerto
  for Clarinet
Soule: Concert Piece
  (str)
Starer: Kli Zemer
Stevens: Concerto for
  Clarinet (str)
Swisher: Concerto for
  Clarinet
Tower: Concerto for
  Clarinet
Tuthill: Concerto for
  Clarinet
Welcher: Concerto for
  Clarinet
Wilder: Concerto for
  Clarinet

### TWO CLARINETS

Dahl: Symphony
  Concertante
Kupferman: Double
  Concerto

### BASS CLARINET

Callaway: Concerto for
  Bass Clarinet
Taylor: Concerto for
  Bass Clarinet

### BASSOON

Amram: Concerto for
  Bassoon
Ballou: Adagio
Blank: Concertino
Campo: Concerto for
  Bassoon (str)
J. Cohn: March-Caprice
Downey: The Edge of
  Space
Evett: The Windhover

Farberman: Concerto
  for Bassoon (str)
Fuleihan: Concertino
Goeb: Concertant II
Hoag: Ephemeral
  Gestures
Knox: Concert Music
Lifchitz: Night Voices
  No. 6
Lombardo: Mesto
Luke: Concerto for
  Bassoon
Orland: Concerto for
  Bassoon (str)
Polster: Humoresque
Reise: Undercurrents
Roseman: Fantasy for
  Bassoon (str)
Ross: Concerto for
  Bassoon (str)
Schneider: Nocturne
Schuller: Bassoon
  Concerto
E. Schwartz: Concerto
  for Bassoon (str)
Snyder: Bassoon
  Concerto
Steinke: Music for
  Bassoon
Stout: Serenity
F. Thorne:
  Divertimento No. 2
Wagner: Introduction
  and Scherzo
Welcher: Concerto da
  camera
R. Wilson: Concerto
  for Bassoon
Woollen: Suite for
  Bassoon

### THREE BASSOONS

Brant: Antiphonal
  Responses

## CONTRABASSOON

Erb: Concerto for
   Contrabassoon
Schuller: Concerto for
   Contrabassoon

## MULTIPLE WIND SOLOISTS

Barati: Chamber
   Concerto
   (fl, ob, cl)
Bergsma: Changes
   (ww qnt)
Bottje: Concerto for
   Oboe and Bassoon
E. Burton: Nocturne
   (ww qnt)
Csonka: Concertino
   (ob, bsn)
M. Cunningham:
   Dialogue
   (fl, cl, bsn)
Diamond: Elegies
   (fl, eh)
Di Domenica: Concerto
   for Woodwind Quintet
Etler: Concerto for
   Wind Quintet
Goeb: Concertant I
   (fl, ob, cl)
Harbison: Concerto for
   Oboe, Clarinet (str)
Helm: Serenade
   (eh, cl, bsn)
Karpman: Duets, Trios,
   Quintets
   (fl, ob, cl, bsn)
Laderman: Concerto
   (fl, bsn)
Laderman: Double Helix
   (fl, ob)
Lees: Concerto for
   Woodwind Quintet
Martino: Triple
   Concerto
   (cl, b cl, cb cl)
McBride: Concerto for
   Doubles (cl, a sax)

Orland: Double
   Concerto (fl, eh)
Parsi: Divertimento
   del Sur (fl, cl)
Rollin: Concerto for
   Woodwind Quintet
Rosen: Three Pieces
   (2 rec)
Ross: Concerto for
   Woodwind Quintet
Schuller: Contrasts
   for Wind Quintet
Steinke: Northwest
   Sketches IIb
   (fl, ob)
Stewart: Two Ricercari
   (ww qnt)
Trimble: Concerto for
   Woodwinds and
   Strings
   (fl, ob, cl, bsn)
Trythall: Sinfonia
   Concertante (ww qnt)
Weiner: Reflections
   (ww qnt)
Wigglesworth: Summer
   Scenes (fl, ob)

## SOPRANO SAXOPHONE

Hovhaness:
   Concerto for Soprano
   Saxophone
Mamlok: Concerto for
   Soprano Saxophone
   and Chamber
   Orchestra
Swanson: Fantasy Piece

## ALTO SAXOPHONE

Amram: Ode to Lord
   Buckley
Benson: Aeolian Song
Caltabiano: Concerto
   for Alto Saxophone
Chihara: Saxophone
   Concerto

Cohen: Adagio for Alto
  Saxophone and
  Chamber Orchestra
Cowell: Air and
  Scherzo
Creston: Concerto for
  Alto Saxophone
Fennelly: Concerto for
  Alto Saxophone
Hansen: Contrasts
Hartley: Concerto
  No. 2
Huggler: Elaborations
Husa: Elegie et
  Rondeau
Karlins: Concerto for
  Alto Saxophone
Kechley: Concerto for
  Alto Saxophone
Koch: Concertino for
  Alto Saxophone
Kupferman: Jazz
  Symphony
  (+ solo mez)
Leichtling: Symphonic
  Rhapsody
Martino: Concerto for
  Alto Saxophone
Mols: Serenade (str)
Muczynski: Concerto
  for Alto Saxophone
R. Nelson: Danza
  Capriccio
O'Brien: Concerto for
  Alto Saxophone
D. Ott: Saxophone
  Concerto
Rosen: Concerto for
  Alto Saxophone
Russo: Music for Alto
  Saxophone and
  Strings
Schuller: Concerto for
  Alto Saxophone
Shapey: Concertante
  No. 2
Subotnick: In Two
  Worlds
Tautenhahn: Concerto
  for Alto Saxophone

Toensing: Concerto for
  Alto Saxophone
Van Vactor: Andante
  and Allegro
Wirth: Idlewood
  Concerto

TENOR SAXOPHONE

Cope: Concerto for
  Tenor Saxophone
Hartley: Rhapsody
  (str)
McKinley: Tenor
  Rhapsody
D. Ott: Concerto for
  Tenor Saxophone
Ward: Concerto for
  Tenor Saxophone
Wilder: Suite No. 2

TWO OR MORE SAXOPHONES

Adler: Concerto for
  Saxophone Quartet
Luedeke: Concerto for
  Saxophone Quartet
E. McLean: Big City
  Ballads (sax trio)
Wirth: Jephthah
  (s sax, a sax)

HORN

Amram: Concerto for
  Horn
Bach: Concerto for
  Horn
D. Baker: Life Cycles
  (+ solo t)
Ballou: Concerto for
  Horn (str)
Becker: Concerto for
  Horn
Benson: Concerto for
  Horn
Bowman: Ballad
Frackenpohl: Largo and
  Allegro (str)

Heiden: Concerto for
  Horn
Hovhaness: Artik (str)
Huggler: Concerto for
  Horn
Karlins: Catena III
Kohn: Concerto for
  Horn and Small
  Orchestra
W. Kraft: Veils and
  Variations
Kurka: Ballad (str)
Lockwood: Panegyric
  (str)
London: Be Bop Dreams
McKinley: Concerto for
  Horn
D. Mitchell: And
  still...
Musgrave: Concerto for
  Horn
Pone: Concerto for
  Horn
Ramey: Concerto for
  Horn (str)
Rogers: Fantasia
  (timp, str)
Rollin: Concerto
  Pastorale
Schickele: Pentangle
Schonthal: Music for
  Horn and Chamber
  Orchestra
Schuller: Concerto
  No. 1
Schuller: Concerto
  No. 2
Schuman: Three
  Colloquies
Stewart: Concerto for
  Horn
Suben: Traeume auf
  Dichterhoehe
Sydeman: Concertpiece
  (str)
Verrall: Rhapsody
  (str)
Weiner: Adagio (str)
Whear: Pastorale
  Lament (str)

Wilder: Concerto No. 1
Wilder: Entertainment
  No. 4
Winteregg: Visions and
  Revelations
Zupko: Prologue, Aria
  and Dance (str)

TWO HORNS

Bohrnstedt: Concerto
  for Two Horns

TRUMPET

J. Alexander:
  Concertino for
  Trumpet (str)
Amram: Travels
D. Baker: Concerto for
  Trumpet, Jazz Band
  (str)
Bazelon: Spires
Bloch: Proclamation
Bohrnstedt: Concerto
  for Trumpet
Campo: Concerto for
  Trumpet
A. Cunningham: Lullaby
  for a Jazz Baby
M. Cunningham:
  Concerto for Trumpet
Diemer: Concerto for
  Trumpet
Dlugoszewski: Abyss
  and Caress
Erb: Concerto for
  Trumpet
Farberman: Double
  Concerto for Single
  Trumpet
Fennelly: Concert
  Piece
Frackenpohl:
  Concertino (str)
Giannini: Concerto for
  Trumpet
Gillis: Rhapsody
Roy Harris: Horn of
  Plenty

Hartley: Sonatina for
 Trumpet
Hilliard: The Grand
 Traverse
Hovhaness: Khrimian
 Hairig (str)
Hovhaness: Prayer of
 St. Gregory
Hovhaness: Haroutiun
Hovhaness: The Holy
 City
Husa: Concerto for
 Trumpet
Jenni: Canticum beatae
 virginis
Kupferman: Concerto
 for Trumpet
Larsen: Concerto for
 Trumpet
Lazarof: Spectrum
T. Lee: Concertino
 (timp, str)
Mandelbaum: Concerto
 for Trumpet
Mayer: Concert Piece
 (perc, str)
McCulloh: Concerto
 No. 1
Mourant: Blue Horizons
 (str)
Mourant: Fantasia
Paulus: Trumpet
 Concerto
Sapieyevski: Concerto
 "Mercury"
Schuller: Concerto for
 Trumpet
Selig: Mirage (str)
Serebrier: Momento
 Psicologico (str)
Shapey: Concertante
 No. 1
Siekmann: Gregarious
Starer: Invocation
 (str)
Stock: Tekiah
Strandberg: Suite
 (str)
Taxin: Trumpet
 Concerto

F. Thorne: Symphony
 No. 4
Ticheli: Concerto for
 Trumpet
Tillis: Spiritual
 Fantasy
Tull: Concerto No. 2
Van Vactor: Suite
Wagner: Introduction
 and Rondo
F. Waxman: Athaneal
Wienhorst: Three
 Parodies
Yasanitsky: And the
 Sky was Cobalt Blue
 (timp, str)

TWO OR MORE TRUMPETS

W. Alexander: Music
 for Two Trumpets and
 Strings
F. Thorne: Fanfare,
 Fugue and Fast Four
 (3tpt)
Van Vactor: Suite for
 Three or Four
 Trumpets, One
 Trumpeter and
 Strings

TROMBONE

D. Baker: Concert
 Piece (str)
Bassett: Concerto
 Lyrico
Bavicchi: Fusions
Bazelon: Motivations
Bloch: Symphony for
 Trombone
Bohrnstedt: Concertino
 (str)
Bowman: Commentary
 (str)
Creston: Fantasy
Dubensky: Trombone
 Concerto
Erb: Concerto for
 Trombone

Hogg: Concerto for
  Trombone
Holt: Songs of Love
Hovhaness: Concerto
  No. 3
McCulloh: Concerto for
  Trombone
McCulloh: Concerto for
  Large Trombone
Parris: Concerto for
  Trombone
Ross: Concerto No. 1
Ross: Concerto No. 2
Rouse: Trombone
  Concerto
Serebrier: Variations
  on a Theme from
  Childhood
Serly: Concerto for
  Trombone
Siekmann: Concerto for
  Trombone
W. Smith: Concerto for
  Trombone
N. Thorne: Songs of
  Darkness, Power and
  Radiance
Townsend: Chamber
  Concerto No. 1 (str)
Turok: Canzona
  Concertante No. 2
George Walker:
  Concerto for
  Trombone
Zador: Trombone
  Concerto
Zwilich: Concerto for
  Trombone

### BASS TROMBONE

T. George: Concerto
  for Bass Trombone
Hovhaness: Symphony
  No. 34
Moylan: Concerto for
  Bass Trombone
Siekmann: Concerto for
  Bass Trombone

Zwilich: Concerto for
  Bass Trombone

### ALTO TROMBONE

Whear: Burberry Red
  (perc, str)

### TWO OR MORE TROMBONES

L. Mitchell: Concerto
  Grosso (3tbn)
Tuthill: Trombone
  Trouble

### EUPHONIUM

Bach: Euphonium
  Concerto
Constantinides:
  Concerto for
  Euphonium
Hartley: Euphonium
  Concerto
Hovhaness: Symphony
  No. 29
Svoboda: Scherzo for
  Two Euphoniums

### TUBA

Bazelon: For Tuba With
  Strings Attached
  (str)
Bottje: Concerto for
  Tuba
Brehm: Concerto for
  Tuba
T. George: Concertino
  (str)
Hartley: Fantasia
Heiden: Concerto for
  Tuba
Jager: Concerto for
  Tuba
W. Kraft: Concerto for
  Tuba
Kupferman: Concerto
  for Tuba

Presser: Concerto for
  Tuba (str)
Schuller: Capriccio
Wilder: Effie Suite
Wilder: Elegy for the
  Whale
John Williams:
  Concerto for Tuba
Winteregg: Concerto
  for Tuba
Wuorinen: Prelude to
  Kullervo

MULTIPLE BRASS SOLOISTS

Allanbrook: Symphony
  No. 5 (br qnt)
Bazelon: De-tonations
  (br qnt)
Biggs: Triple Concerto
  (hn, tpt, tbn)
Druckman: Incenters
  (hn, tpt, tbn)
Dubensky: Concerto
  Grosso (3tbn, tba)
Effinger: Trio
  Concertante
  (hn, tpt, tbn)
Etler: Concerto for
  Brass Quintet
  (perc, str)
Fennelly: Quintuplo
  (br qnt)
Foss: Night Music for
  John Lennon (br qnt)
Husa: Concerto for
  Brass Quintet
U. Kay: Quintet
  Concerto (br qnt)
Lifchitz: Globos
  (hn, tpt, tbn)
McKay: Jubilee
  Concerto (br qnt)
Moss: Symphonies
  (br qnt)
Nanes: Concerto Grosso
  (hn, tpt, tbn)
D. Ott: Concerto for
  Three Brass
  (hn, tpt, tbn)

Ross: Concerto for
  Brass Quintet
Schickele: Five of a
  Kind (br qnt)
Schuller: Diptych
  (br qnt)
Schuller: Concerto
  Festivo (br qnt)
Taxin: Concerto for
  Brass Quintet
Tircuit: Concerto for
  Brass Quintet
Torke: Copper (br qnt)
Van Vactor: Sarabanda
  (br qnt)
Wuorinen: Concertone
  (br qnt)

TIMPANI

Ames: Prologue (str)
Ames: Suite (str)
C. Baker: Three Pieces
  for Five Timpani and
  Five Roto-Toms
Childs: Concerto for
  Timpani
Elisha: Concerto for
  Timpani
Farberman: Concerto
  for Timpani
Gutche: Timpani
  Concertante
Hartley: Concertante
  for Timpani
W. Kraft: Concerto for
  Timpani
Levi: Stringalevio
  (str)
Nielson: Timpani
  Concerto
Parchman: Concerto for
  Timpani
Parris: Concerto for
  Five Kettledrums
Parris: The Phoenix
Rice: Concerto for
  Timpani

## PERCUSSION

Balada: Three
  Anecdotes
Chadabe: Many
  Mornings, Many Moods
Colgrass: Rhapsodic
  Fantasy
Cowell: Persian Set
Erb: Concerto for
  Percussionist
Foss: Concerto for
  Solo Percussion
Franco: Concerto
  Lirico No. 4
J. Grant: Concerto
  Fantasy
Gutche: Bongo
  Divertimento
Hovhaness: Fantasy on
  Japan Woodprints
  (xyl)
Kaufman: Symphony
  No. 3
Maves: Concerto for
  Percussion
McCulloh: Symphony
  Concertante
Nielson: Concerto for
  Percussion
Nielson: Fantasia
D. Ott: Percussion
  Concerto
Schwantner: Concerto
  for Percussion
Steinohrt: Dance
Subotnick: Two
  Butterflies
Suderburg: Concerto
  for Solo
  Percussionist
Tillis: Ring Shout
  Concerto
Tircuit: Fool's Dance
Tircuit: Concerto for
  Percussion
Tircuit: Odoru Katachi
Tull: Dialogues

## MARIMBA

Borroff: Concerto for
  Marimba
Creston: Concertino
Diemer: Concerto in
  One Movement
Kurka: Concerto for
  Marimba
Parchman: Concerto for
  Marimba
Ptaszynska: Concerto
  for Marimba
Andrew Thomas:
  Concerto for Marimba
Yavelow: And then we
  saw a sea lion

## MULTIPLE PERCUSSION

Antoniou: Double
  Concerto
Bazelon:
  Fourscore and 2
  (4perc)
Bohrnstedt: Concertino
  for Timpani,
  Xylophone
Colgrass: Déjà Vu
  (perc qt)
Cowell: Concerto for
  Percussion (timp+4)
Eberhard: Ephrata
  (4perc)
Finney: Concerto for
  Percussion (4perc)
Kogan: Gemini
  (vib, mar)
W. Kraft: Three
  Miniatures (timp+3)
W. Kraft: Concerto for
  Four Percussion
  Soloists
M. Levy: Arrows of
  Time (4perc)
Lombardo: Sicilian
  Lyric (timp+3)
Moryl: Balloons
  (2perc)

Parchman: Concerto for
  Percussion Ensemble
Parchman: Concerto for
  Percussion No. 2
  (7perc)
Parchman: Concerto for
  Five Percussion
P. Phillips:
  Interplays
  (perc ens, jazz
  drums)
Ptaszynska: Concerto
  for Percussion
  (4perc)
G. Samuel:
  As Imperceptibly As
  Grief (3perc)
Wienhorst: Canticle
  for Percussion
  (3perc)

### HARP

Bach: Harp Concerto
Bavicchi: Fantasy
Colgrass: Auras
Coolidge: Rhapsody
Creston: Poem
Dello Joio: Concerto
  for Harp
Downey: Concerto for
  Harp
Gillis: Rhapsody for
  Harp
Heilner: Suite for
  Harp
Hovhaness: Concerto
  for Harp (str)
Kelly: Fantasia (str)
Krenek: Concerto for
  Harp
Kurek: Concerto for
  Harp
Lange: Arabesque
T. Lee: Harp Concerto
Lessard: Concerto for
  Harp
MacBride: Elegies
  (str)
Mourant: Blue Horizons

Paulus: Divertimento
Piston: Capriccio
  (str)
Polin: Mythos (str)
Rands: Aum
A. Reed: Siciliana
  Notturno
Schonthal:
  The Beautiful Days
  of Aranjuez (str)
Serebrier: Colores
  Magicos
Shulman: Theme and
  Variations (str)
H. Smith: Music for
  Harp
Soule: Concerto for
  Harp
Still: Ennanga
Suderburg: Concerto
  for Harp
Surinach: Concerto for
  Harp
Svoboda: Christmas
  Concerto
Thomson: Autumn
Trythall: Concerto for
  Harp
Wagner: Concertino for
  Harp

### TWO HARPS

Lockwood: Concerto for
  Two Harps

### ORGAN

Adler: Concerto for
  Organ
Albright: Bacchanal
Bingham: Concerto for
  Organ
Bolcom: Humoresk
Colgrass: Snow Walker
Cooper: Concerto for
  Organ
Copland: Symphony for
  Organ

Creston: Symphony
   No. 6
Diemer: Concert Piece
Felciano: Concerto for
   Organ
Fischer: Chorale
   Fantasy
Hannay: Concertino
   (str)
Hopkins: Voces Organi
   (4-hands)
Husa: Concerto for
   Organ
Janson: Concerto for
   Organ
Kohs: Passacaglia
   (str)
Krenek: Concerto for
   Organ (str)
Krenek: Organ Concerto
Lockwood: Concerto for
   Organ
Lubet: Concerto for
   Organ (str)
Maves: Concerto for
   Organ
Pinkham: Concertino
   (str)
Pinkham: Organ
   Concerto
Piston: Prelude and
   Fugue (str)
Porter: Fantasy on a
   Pastoral Theme (str)
Rorem: Organ Concerto
Saturen: Ternaria
Sowerby: Concert Piece
Sowerby: Concert Piece
   No. 2
Taylor: Concerto for
   Organ
Toensing: Concerto for
   Organ
Ultan: Concerto for
   Organ
Woollen: Modal
   Offerings

CELESTE

Fischer: The Pearly
   Bouquet (str)
Mourant: Three New
   Hampshire Idylls
   (str)

HARPSICHORD

Albright: Concerto
   (str)
Baksa: Concerto (str)
Diemer: Concerto
Evett: Concerto
Porter: Concerto
Rieti: Harpsichord
   Concerto
Sapp: Imaginary
   Creatures
Saturen: Dialogue
   Between Harpsichord
   and Strings
Trimble: Concerto

ACCORDION

Cowell: Concerto
   Brevis
Creston: Concerto
Creston: Fantasy
Roy Harris: Theme and
   Variations
Hovhaness: Concerto
Serebrier: Passacaglia
   and Perpetuum Mobile

CONCERTINA

J. Cohn: Concerto in A
   (str)

GUITAR

E. Applebaum: Night
   Waltz
Balada: Guitar
   Concerto
Balada: Sinfonia
   Concertanta

Ballou: Concerto for
  Guitar
Barati: Concerto for
  Guitar
Bottje: Commentaries
Chihara: Concerto for
  Guitar
Constantinides:
  Anniversary
  Celebration (str)
A. Cunningham: Sun
  Bird (+ solo ca)
Curtis-Smith: Songs
  and Cantillations
Fetler: Three
  Impressions
Foss: Guitar Concerto
Franco: Concerto
  Lirico No. 5
Haufrecht:
  Divertimento
Hewitt: Concerto for
  Guitar
Hovhaness: Symphony
  No. 39
Hovhaness: Concerto
  for Guitar
Hovhaness: Concerto
  No. 2
Kupferman: Rhapsody
Lennon: Zingari
Peaslee: Suite (str)
Schifrin: Guitar
  Concerto
Schwantner: From
  Afar...
Tanenbaum: Waves
Weiner: Concerto for
  Guitar

FOUR GUITARS

Balada: Concerto
Gould: Troubador Music

OTHER PLUCKED INSTRUMENTS

Cowell: Concerto No. 1
  (koto)
Cowell: Concerto No. 2
  (koto)
Hovhaness: Khorhoort
  Nahadagats (oud)
McKay: Voice of the
  Phoenix (koto)
Robinson: Banjo
  Concerto

HARMONICA

Cowell: Concerto for
  Harmonica
Hovhaness: Concerto
  No. 6

SYNTHESIZER

Rosen: Syn-ket
  Concerto
Sandroff: Concerto for
  Electric Wind
  Instrument
Sapieyevski: Dance of
  the Planets
E. Schwartz: The
  Harmony of Music

MULTIPLE DIVERSE INSTRUMENTS

*Two Soloists*

J. Alexander: Duo
  concertante
  (tbn, perc)
Antoniou: Events I
  (vln, pf)
Bennett: Concerto for
  Violin and Piano
Berlin: Concerto for
  Clarinet
Bloch: Concertino
  (fl, vla)
Bottje: Concerto for
  Flute, Trumpet and
  Strings

Bottje: Concerto for
Oboe, Violin and
Small Orchestra
Brant: Nomads/Triple
Concerto (babone,
steel drums, solo
bar)
Carter: Double
Concerto (hpsd, pf)
Cone: Cadenzas
(ob, vln)
Cowell:
Duo Concertante for
Flute, Harp and
Orchestra
Effinger: Sinfonie
concertante (hp, pf)
Fitelberg: Concertino
for Trombone, Piano
and Strings
Hanson: Concerto for
Organ, Harp and
Strings
Hanson: Serenade
(fl, hp)
Hopkins: Concert
Variations (vln, pf)
Hovhaness: Janabar
(tpt, pf)
Hovhaness: Shambala
(vln, sitar)
Kievman: Concerto for
Percussion, Piano
and Small Orchestra
Knehans: Concerto for
Guitar, Orchestra
and Concertante
(gtr, hpsd)
W. Kraft: Double Play
(vln, pf)
Krenek: Little
Concerto (pf,org)
Krenek: Double
Concerto (vln, pf)
Larsen: Concerto: Cold
Silent Snow (fl, hp)
Lees: Double Concerto
(vc, pf)
Luke: Symphonic
Dialogues (ob, vln)

McKinley: "Lucy"
Variations (cl, vln)
McKinley: Miniature
Portraits (tpt, bsn)
Nabokov: Concerto
corale (fl, pf)
Palmer: Chamber
Concerto (ob, vln)
Peaslee: Nightsongs
(flu hn, hp)
Pinkham: Concertante
for Violin and
Harpsichord
Pinkham: Serenade
(vln, hpsd)
Pinkham: Concertante
for Guitar and
Harpsichord
Rodriguez: Sinfonia
Concertante
(s sax, hpsd)
Rorem: Water Music
(cl, vln)
Rorem: Remembering
Tommy (vc, pf)
Ross: Concerto for
Flute, Guitar and
Orchestra
Saturen: Evolution
(vla, hpsd)
Schubel: Divertimento
(tpt, pf)
Shapey: Concerto for
Cello, Piano and
String Orchestra
Shawn: Concerto for
Clarinet, Cello and
Chamber Orchestra
Siegmeister: Double
Concerto (vln, pf)
Stein: Rhapsody for
Flute, Harp and
Strings
Stucky: Double
Concerto (ob, vln)
Surinach: Feast of
Ashes (vln, pf)
Svoboda: Suite for
Bassoon, Harpsichord
and String Orchestra

Sydeman: Concertino
  for Oboe, Piano and
  String Orchestra
Whittenberg: Event II
  (fl, db)
Wood: Double Concerto
  (vla, pf)

*Three Soloists*

Barber: Capricorn
  Concerto (fl,ob,tpt)
Bazelon: Symphony
  concertante
  (cl, tpt, mar)
Bolcom: Concertante
  for Violin, Flute,
  Oboe and Orchestra
Colgrass: Delta
  (vln, cl, perc)
Constantinides:
  Concerto for Violin,
  Cello, Piano and
  Orchestra
Cooper: Symphony No. 4
  (fl, tpt, vla)
Cooper: A Shenandoah
  for Ives' Birthday
  (fl, tpt, vla)
Heiden: Triple
  Concerto
  (pf, vln, vc)
Hervig: Trio
  Concertino
  (cl, pf, vln)
Hovhaness: Tzaikerk
  (fl, timp, vln)
L. Kraft: Concerto
  No. 1
  (fl, cl, tpt)
Kubik: Symphonic
  concertante
  (vla, tpt, pf)
Laufer: Concerto for
  Flute, Oboe, Trumpet
  and Strings
Leichtling: Concerto
  for Violin, Cello,
  Piano and Orchestra

Luke: Symphonic
  Dialogues II
  (vln, ob, hpsd;
  solo s)
Newell: Solo Suite II
  (fl, timp, vln)
Orrego-Salas: Concerto
  a tre (vln, vc, pf)
B. Phillips: Triple
  Concerto
  (cl, vla, pf)
Richter: Dusseldorf
  Concerto
  (fl, vla, hp)
Rieti: Triple Concerto
  (vln, vla, pf)
Rollin: Hispanic
  Interchanges
  (ob, vln, vc)
Starer: Concerto a tre
  (cl, tpt, tbn)
Augusta Thomas:
  Trinity
  (fl, hp, vla)
Tillis: Concerto for
  Trio Pro Viva and
  Chamber Orchestra
  (fl, pf, vc)
Townsend: Chamber
  Concerto No. 3
  (fl, hn, pf)
Turok:
  Canzona Concertante
  No. 3 (fl, ob, tpt)
Vazzana: Concerto a
  Tre (cl, pf, db)
Vega: Divertimento
  (pf, vln, vc)
Wykes: Concertino for
  Flute, Oboe, Piano
  and Strings

*Four or More Soloists*

Amram: Triple Concerto
  (fl, ob, cl, bsn, a
  sax, bar sax, 2hn,
  2tpt, tbn, tba,
  perc, pf, db)

Barati: Baroque
Quartet Concerto
(fl, ob, db, hpsd)
A. Berger: Serenade
concertante
(fl, ob, cl, bsn,
vln)
R. Brooks: Chorale
Variations
(2hn, str qnt)
Cazden: Adventure
(2fl, 2cl, 2vln)
Cowell: Concerto
Grosso
(fl, ob, cl, hp, vc)
Del Tredici: An Alice
Symphony
(s sax/a sax,
s sax/t sax, mand,
t bj, acc; solo s)
Del Tredici:
The Lobster
Quadrille (2s sax,
mand, t bj, acc;
solo s or t)
Del Tredici:
Adventures
Underground (2s sax,
mand, t bj, acc;
solo s)
Del Tredici:
Vintage Alice
(2s sax, mand, t bj,
acc; + rock group)
Del Tredici:
Final Alice
(2s sax, mand, t bj,
acc; + narr)
Fetler: "Three
Excursions"
(timp+3, pf)
Helm: Concerto for
Five Solo
Instruments and
Strings (fl, ob,
bsn, tpt, vln)
Hovhaness: Agori
(fl, eh, bsn, tpt)
Kalbfleisch: Eruptions
(3perc, db)

W. Kraft: Concerto
Grosso
(fl, bsn, vln, vc)
Laderman: Sinfonia
Concertante
(picc, eh, b cl,
tpt, b tbn)
Luke: Cantata
Concertante
(ww qnt, br qnt, str
qt; + 3 satb cho)
Mandelbaum: Sinfonia
concertante
(ob, hn, vln, vc)
McKinley: Sinfonia
Concertante
(perc, pf, vln, vc)
Menotti: Triplo
Concerto a Tre
(ob, cl, bsn, perc,
hp, pf, vln, vla,
vc)
Rhodes: Bluegrass
Festival
(bj, mand, gtr, db)
Richter: Music for
Three Quintets and
Orchestra (ww qnt,
br qnt, str qnt)
Russo: Three Pieces
for Blues Band and
Orchestra
(dmst, elec pf, elec
gtr, b gtr, hca)
Schickele: Far Away
From Here
(bluegrass band)
Schuller: Museum Piece
for Renaissance
Instruments and
Orchestra
(17 soloists)
Schuller: Concerto
Quaternio
(fl, ob, tpt, vln)
Sims: yr obedt servt
(2 cl, vln, vc)
Sims: yr obedt servt
II (2 cl, vln, vc)

Sims: Night Piece
  (fl, cl, vla, vc)
Starer: Concerto a
  quattro
  (ob, cl, bsn, hn)
Subotnick: Before the
  Butterfly (tpt, tbn,
  perc, hp, vln, vla,
  vc)
F. Thorne: Concerto
  Concertante
  (fl, cl, vln, vc)
Torke: Slate
  (3kybd, 2perc)
Van Vactor: Concerto a
  Quattro (3fl,hp)
Wuorinen: Tashi
  (cl, pf, vln, vc)
Zupko: This is the
  Garden
  (fl, ob, cl, tpt)

JAZZ GROUP

Amram: En Memoria de
  Chano Pozo
T.J. Anderson:
  Spirituals
L. Austin:
  Improvisations
D. Baker: Concerto for
  Trumpet, Jazz Band
  and String Orchestra
D. Baker: Le Chat qui
  pêche
D. Baker: Two
Improvisations
Brant: Western Springs
  (+ satb cho)
D. Brubeck: Cathy's
  Waltz
D. Brubeck: In Your
  Own Sweet Way
D. Brubeck: Truth is
  Fallen
D. Brubeck: Out of the
  Way of People
D. Brubeck: Summersong
H. Brubeck: Four
  Dialogues

A. Cunningham: Night
  Bird
Farberman: Initiation
  Ballet
Farberman: There's Us,
  There's Them...
  Together?
Giuffre: Threshold
Giuffre: Mirrors for
  Jazz Trio
Jager: Concerto Grosso
W. Kraft: Contextures:
  Riots
J. Lewis: England's
  Carol
J. Lewis: Concert
  Piece
J. Lewis: Jazz
  Ostinato
J. Lewis: Na
  Dubrovacki
J. Lewis: The Queen's
  Fancy
J. Lewis:
  The Spiritual
McKinley: Triple
  Concerto
McKinley: American
  Blues
McKinley: Can You Sing
  Me A Song
  (+ fem cho)
C. Moore: Tone Roads
  to HK
Rorem: Lions
Russo: Street Music
Saturen: Variations
  and Fugue
Schifrin: Dialogue for
  Jazz Quintet
Schuller: Symphonic
  Tribute to Duke
  Ellington
Schuller: Concertino
  for Jazz Quartet
Schuller: Variants
Schuller: Journey into
  Jazz
W. Smith: Concerto for
  Jazz Soloists

W. Smith: Interplay
W. Smith: Quadri
W. Smith: Theona
F. Thorne:
  Quartessence
Tillis: Concerto for
  Piano (jazz trio)
Tillis: In the Spirit
  and the Flesh
Ward-Steinman:
  Concerto Grosso for
  Combo and Chamber
  Orchestra

## ROCK GROUP

A. Cunningham: Rooster
  Rhapsody (+ narr)
Del Tredici: The Last
  Gospel (+ solo s)
Del Tredici:
  Pop-pourri
  (+ soli s, mez)
Del Tredici:
  Vintage Alice
  (+ folk group)
Erb: Klangfarbenfunk I
Farberman: If Music
  Be...
Peaslee: October Piece
Schickele:
  The Fantastic Garden
Selig: Concerto for
  Rock Group

APPENDIX C

VOCAL SOLOISTS AND ORCHESTRA

Soprano
Alto or Mezzo-soprano
Contralto
Tenor
Baritone
Bass
High Voice
Medium Voice
Multiple Vocal Soloists
    2 vocalists
    3 vocalists
    4 vocalists
    5 or more vocalists
Narrator

The works listed in Appendix C are for orchestra with vocal soloist(s). Within each main category are subdivisions by duration. Works in which a composer has indicated only a general registral preference (e.g., soprano *or* tenor, mezzo *or* baritone) are listed under High Voice and Medium Voice, respectively. Complete information regarding any of these works may be obtained by referring to the main listing in the catalog.

SOPRANO

15' or less

J. Adams: This is prophetic! from "Nixon in China"
Aitken: Cantata IX
E. Alexander: So Many Corners
Amlin: Quotations
Argento: Songs About Spring
Barab: Six Tennyson Songs
Barber: Do Not Utter A Word from "Vanessa"

Barber: Andromache's Farewell
Bavicchi: Farewell and Hail
Bavicchi: There is Sweet Music Here
Beale: Music for Soprano and Orchestra
Beeson: Two Concert Arias
Berg: Four Songs
Bernstein: Glitter and Be Gay from "Candide"
Blickhan: Five Songs
Boone: Chinese Texts

J.E. Brown: Fontaine,
Je ne boirai pas de
ton eau
Calabro: Cantilena
Constantinides:
Midnight Song
Constantinides:
China I
Creston: Dance
Variations
C. Davis: Four Sonnets
De Mars: Two World
Overture
Dembski: Of Mere Being
Druckman: The Sound of
Time
Eaton: Aria from "The
Reverend Jim Jones"
D. Epstein: Four Songs
Flanagan: Another
August
Floyd: The Trees on
the Mountains from
"Susannah"
Gibbons: Stories of
Passion
Grantham: Kyng
Celestial
Hoiby: Where The Music
Comes From
Hoiby: The Serpent
Hovhaness: As on the
Night
Hovhaness: Canticle
Huggler: Sculptures
Hutchison: Psalm CXLII
Hutchison: The Prairie
Grass Dividing
Imbrie: Three Songs
Jazwinski: Essay for
Soprano
Karchin: Songs of John
Keats
Kernis: Barbara Allen
La Montaine: Songs of
the Rose of Sharon
Lerdahl: Beyond the
Realm of the Bird
Lieberson: Three Songs
Luening: Three Songs

McDonald: Song of a
Free Nation
Menotti: Monica's
Waltz from
"The Medium"
Menotti: Lucy's Aria
from "The Telephone"
Menotti: Lullaby from
"The Consul"
Menotti: Magda's Aria
from "The Consul"
Moss: Ariel
Nabokov: Six Lyric
Songs
O'Brien: Dedales
O'Brien: Dreams and
Secrets of Origin
Packales: Cassandra's
Monologue
Parchman: Concerto for
Soprano
Pinkham: Now the
Trumpet Summons Us
Again
Riley: Seven Songs on
Poems of Emily
Dickinson
Rinehart: Passages
Rockmaker: The
Secreted Peace
Rollin: Song of
Deborah
Rorem: A Sermon on
Miracles
Rorem: Six Songs
Schuman: The Young
Dead Soldiers
Sessions: Psalm CXL
Still: Rhapsody
Stout: Elegiac Suite
Strilko: ...From the
Pickering Manuscript
of William Blake
Surinach: Tres
Cantares
Surinach: Romance,
Oracion y Soeta
Swanson: Songs for
Patricia

Wagner: Northland
  Evocation
Warren: Four Sonnets
Weber: Three Songs
Woodard: The Dream
  Songs of Stephen
  Foster
Wyner: Intermedio

16' to 30'

Albert: Wolf Time
Albert: Flower of the
  Mountain
Argento: Ode to the
  West Wind
Argento: Variations
  for Orchestra
Barber: Knoxville:
  Summer of 1915
Barber: Two Scenes
  from "Antony and
  Cleopatra"
Bazelon: Junctures
Beaser: Symphony
Bergsma: In Space:
  Four Play
S. Burton: Ode to the
  Nightingale
Caltabiano: Medea
Carlsen: Four Journeys
Cortese: Canso D'Amare
Cotel: Symphonic
  Pentad
Crockett: The Tenth
  Muse
Custer: Songs of the
  Seasons
Del Tredici: Szygy
Del Tredici:
  Illustrated Alice
  from "An Alice
  Symphony"
Del Tredici: In
  Wonderland from "An
  Alice Symphony"
Del Tredici:
  Adventures
  Underground

Del Tredici: Quaint
  Events from "Child
  Alice"
De Mars: Two World
  Symphony
Druckman: Lamia
Eaton: Song Cycle on
  "Holy Sonnets" of
  John Donne
El-Dabh: The Ghost
Fink: Ann Rutledge
Floyd: The Mystery
Foss: Song of Songs
Foss: Time Cycle
Frohne: Adam's Chains
Giannini: Antigone
Hartke: Two Songs for
  an Uncertain Age
Hays: Southern Voices
Helps: Gossamer Noons
Herman: Scripts for a
  Pageant
Hopkins: Phantasms
Hovhaness: Avak the
  Healer
Huggler: Seven Songs
Hutchison: Death-Words
  from the Cherokee
Karchin: Five
  Orchestral Songs
Kechley: Five Ancient
  Lyrics
Kernis: Dream of the
  Morning Sky
Kirk: Carol Service
Knehans: Five
  Orchestral Songs
L. Kraft: Silent
  Boughs
La Montaine: Fragments
  from the Song of
  Songs
T. Lee: Phantasia for
  Elvira Shatayev
M. Levy: Canto de los
  Marranos
Luke: Symphonic
  Dialogues II
Mailman: Love Letters
  from Margaret

Murray: Evocations
Murray: City of Cities
Musgrave: Monologues
of Mary
Neikrug: Nachtlieder
R. Nelson: Trilogy-
JFK-MLK-RFK
Picker: Symphony No. 2
Rakowski: Symphony
No. 1
Rands: Wildtrack II
Rands: Canti lunatici
Rhodes: The Lament of
Michal
Rorem: After Long
Silence
Rorem: Six Irish Poems
Rorem: SUN
Rorem: The Schuyler
Songs
Sapieyevski: Songs of
the Rose
Schuller: Six Early
Songs
Schwantner: Magabunda
Schwantner:
Dreamcaller
Sellars: Chanson Dada
Serebrier: Orpheus
Times Light
Shapey: Songs of Eros
Shore: July
Remembrances
Silver: Chariessa
L.A. Smith: Crucifixus
Suderburg: Cantata I
Svoboda: Concerto for
Chamber Orchestra
Ward: Sacred Songs for
Pantheists
Weisgall: A Garden
Eastward
Winslow: Concert Aria
Wyner: Fragments from
Antiquity
Yttrehus: Gradus ad
Parnassum
Zwilich: Passages

Over 30'

T.J. Anderson:
Horizons `76
D. Baker: Le Chat qui
pêche
Brant: Voyage Four
D. Brubeck: Truth is
Fallen
Del Tredici: In Memory
of a Summer Day from
"Child Alice"
Del Tredici: All in
the Golden Afternoon
from "Child Alice"
Fussell: Symphony
No. 2
Giannini: The Medead
Hovhaness: Symphony
No. 38
Jacobs: "Gestures in
the Face of Time"
Primosch: The Cloud of
Unknowing
Sessions: Idyll of
Theocritus
Shapey: The Covenant
Swift: Specimen Day
Toensing: Nocturnes
and Memories

ALTO OR MEZZO-SOPRANO

15' or less

T.J. Anderson: In
Memoriam-Malcolm X
Bales: Ozymandia
Barber: Must Winter
Come So Soon from
"Vanessa"
Brant: Mythical Beasts
Corigliano: The
Cloister
Eaton: Aria from
"Herakles"
Eaton: Songs of Ariel
from "The Tempest"
Ekizian: Two Roethke
Songs

Jenni: Canticum beatae
  virginis
Luke: Symphonic Songs
Mamlock: Four German
  Songs
Orrego-Salas: Ash
  Wednesday
Rogers: Three Japanese
  Dances
Strandberg: Delie
Strandberg: Acts for
  Orchestra
Swift: Roses Only

### 16' to 30'

Adler: Symphony No. 5
Amram: The Trail of
  Beauty
Argento: Casa Guidi
Berg: Not waving but
  drowning
Bernstein: Jeremiah
  Symphony
Cooper: Coram Morte
Eaton: Songs of
  Despair
Eaton: The Cry of
  Clytaemnestra
Ekizian: Morning of
  Light
Ekizian: Beyond the
  Reach of Wind and
  Fire
Handel: Acquainted
  with the Night
Harbison: Elegiac
  Songs
Ivey: Testament of Eve
Jaffe: Three Yiddish
  Songs
Krenek: Medea
Kriesberg: Parte sin
  Novedad
Kupferman: Jazz
  Symphony
Rakowski: Six Bogan
  Poems
G. Samuel: Three Minor
  Desperations

Smit: From Banja Luka
Svoboda: Suite for
  Mezzo-soprano and
  Orchestra
Waters: Three Songs of
  Louise Bogan
Wernick: Visions of
  Wonder and Terror

### Over 30'

Floyd: Citizen of
  Paradise
Lees: Symphony No. 4
R. Nelson: Vox Aeterna
  Amoris
Rochberg: Phaedra
Wheelock: Dreams
  Before A Sacrifice

### CONTRALTO

Bavicchi: Four Songs
  for Contralto and
  Chamber Orchestra
A. Cunningham: Sun
  Bird
M. Levy: One Person
Menotti: Baba's Aria
  from "The Medium"
Menotti: The Black
  Swan

### TENOR

### 15' or less

Barber: Anatol's Aria
  from "Vanessa"
J. Cohn: Israfel
Constantinides:
  Antithesis
Constantinides: Hymn
  to the Human Spirit
Floyd: It's about the
  way people is made
  from "Susannah"
Foss: Measure for
  Measure

Hovhaness: Shepherd of
Israel
Jenni: Get Hence,
Foule Griefe
Musgrave: Triptych
Rorem: Mourning Scene
Sims: Three Songs
Thomson: From Byron's
"Don Juan"
Yannay: Five Songs

16' to 30'

D. Baker: Life Cycles
Beaser: The Seven
Deadly Sins
Biggs: Songs of
Laughter, Love and
Tears
Carlsen: Fair Seed-
Time
Carter: In Sleep, In
Thunder
Crockett: Lyrikos
Glanville-Hicks:
Letters from Morocco
Larocca: The Pure Fury
M. Levy: In Memoriam:
W.H. Auden
London: Peter Quince
at the Clavier
Rands: Canti del sole
Robinson: A Country
they call Puget
Sound
Rochberg: David, The
Psalmist
Rosenman: Stabat
Mater: Inflammatus
Shapero: Three Hebrew
Songs

Over 30'

T.J. Anderson:
Spirituals
Bolcom: Open House
S. Burton: Song of the
Tulpehocken

Roy Harris: Pere
Marquette Symphony
Harrison: Symphony
No. 4
Kessner: The Telltale
Heart

BARITONE

15' or less

J. Adams: News is a
kind of mystery from
"Nixon in China"
J. Adams: Mr. Premier,
Distinguished Guests
from "Nixon in
China"
J. Adams: I am old and
I cannot sleep from
"Nixon in China"
Adler: Lament
Anthony Davis:
Malcolm's "Prison
Aria"
Eaton: Mad Scene from
"The Reverend Jim
Jones"
Eaton: Prospero Arias
from "The Tempest"
Flagello: L'Infinito
Floyd: Blitch's Prayer
from "Susannah"
Floyd: I'm a lonely
man, Susannah from
"Susannah"
Roy Harris: Give Me
the Splendid Silent
Sun
Heiden: Triptych
Hoiby: The Tides of
Sleep
Hoiby: I Have A Dream
Kernis: Morning Songs
Mechem: Speech to a
Crowd
Meyerowitz: Funf
Geistliche Lieder
Nabokov: Quatre Poemes

Rochberg: Sacred Song
  of Reconciliation
Rogers: Psalm LXVIII
Schuller: Five
  Shakespearean Songs
E. Schwartz:
  Harupsicating on
  Valley View Farm
Semegen: Poeme ler
Siegmeister: The Face
  of War
Stout: George Lieder
Thomson: The Feast of
  Love
Travis: Songs and
  Epilogues
Waldrop: Songs of the
  Southwest

### 16' to 30'

J. Adams: The Wound
  Dresser
Aitken: Cantata VI
D. Baker: Alabama
  Landscape
Bernstein: Concerto
  for Orchestra
Boykan: Symphony
Brant: Nomads/Triple
  Concerto
Brant: Homage to Ives
Chance: Odysseus
Dello Joio:
  Lamentation of Saul
Dello Joio: Songs of
  Remembrance
Flagello: The Land
Flanagan: The Weeping
  Pleiades
Floyd: Pilgrimmage
Foss: Song of Anguish
Geller: Where Silence
  Reigns
Hutchison: The
  Sacrilege of
  Alan Kent
Ivey: Tribute
Krenek: The Dissembler
McCulloh: Six Songs

Nabokov: Symboli
  Chrestiani
Paulus: Night Speech
Perera: The White
  Whale
Pone: Quattro
  temperamenti d'amore
Sawyer: Symphony No. 1
Spies: Il cantico de
  frate
Thomson: Five Songs
  from William Blake
Weber: Symphony on
  Poems of William
  Blake
Weisgall: Soldier
  Songs

### Over 30'

S. Burton: Symphony
  No. 2
Leichtling: Eleven
  Songs "Shropshire"

### BASS

A. Cunningham: The
  Prince
Downey: Meni Odnakoro
Laderman: "Visions-
  Columbus"
La Montaine:
  Wilderness Journal
London: Two A'
  Marvells for Words
Ramey: Seven, they are
  Seven
Roseman: Psalm XXVII
Waters: Three Holy
  Sonnets

### HIGH VOICE

L. Adams: Meadow Lark
L. Adams: Dunbar Songs
Argento: Le Tombeau
  D'Edgar Allan Poe
Constantinides:
  Kaleidoscope

Creston: Nocturne
Del Tredici: The
Lobster Quadrille
Diemer: Four Poems by
Alice Meynell
Flagello:
Contemplazioni
Flagello: Island in
the Moon
Gideon: Songs of Youth
and Madness
Hodkinson: Chansons de
Jadis
Hovhaness: Angelic
Song
Hovhaness: Adoration
Hovhaness: Symphony
No. 57
Hutchison: Three Love
Songs
Kernis: Simple Songs
La Montaine: Sonnets
for Orchestra
Nabokov: The Return of
Pushkin
Nabokov: La vita nuova
Riegger: The Dying of
the Light
Sacco: Blessed Are The
Peacemakers
Sacco: Take Heed That
Ye Do Not Your Alms
Before Men
Sacco: The Hypocrites
Sacco: Come Unto Me
Sacco: All Power Is
Given Unto Me
F. Thorne: The Eternal
Light

MEDIUM VOICE

L. Adams: Five Millay
Songs
L. Adams: Six Songs on
Texts of African-
American Poets
J. Alexander: Canticle
of the Night
Antoniou: Meli

Antoniou: Stimmung Der
Abwesenheit
Bolcom: Fourth
Symphony
Brings: A Cradle Song
Brings: Never Seek To
Tell Thy Love
Brings: Song
Brings: Three Songs
Bucci: Little Bird
Carter: Voyage
Copland: Old American
Songs Sets 1 and 2
Copland: Eight Poems
of Emily Dickinson
Kirk: Prayers from the
Ark: Five Songs
Koch: Symphonic Suite
Mayer: The Greatest
Sound Around
Pasatieri: Three Poems
of James Agee
Pasatieri: Rites de
Passage
Pasatieri: Three
Sonnets from the
Portuguese
Patterson: The Five
Degrees
Pone: Five American
Songs
Ptaszynska: Die
Sonette an Orpheus
Rieti: Seven Sapphic
Lyrics
Rorem: Poemes pour la
paix
Sacco: Five Songs
R. Samuel: Before Dawn
Yardumian: Symphony
No. 2
Yardumian: To Mary in
Heaven

LOW VOICE

A. Cunningham:
Prometheus

## MULTIPLE VOCAL SOLOISTS

### Two vocalists

Adolphe: Out of the
  Whirlwind (mez,t)
Albert: Treestone (st)
Albert: Distant Hills
  Coming Nigh (st)
Antoniou: Chorochronos
  II (bar,narr)
Balazs: Angels
  (boy s,narr)
Bernstein: Dybbuk:
  Suite No. 1 (bar,b)
Bernstein: Arias and
  Barcarolles
  (mez,bar)
Blumenfeld: Starfires
  (mez,t)
Danielpour: Symphony
  No. 2 (st)
Eaton: Aria and Scena
  from "Herakles"
  (mez,t)
Farberman: War Cry on
  a Prayer Feather
  (s,bar)
Finney: Bleheris (at)
Floyd: Jay-Bird Song
  from "Susannah" (st)
Hailstork: Four
  Spirituals (2s)
Hodkinson: Burning
  Bell (2narr)
Hovhaness: Symphony
  No. 58 (s,bar)
Kohs: Four Orchestral
  Songs (s,b-bar)
Krenek: Nach wie vor
  der Reihe nach
  (2narr)
Krenek: Instant
  Remembered (s,narr)
Mandelbaum: Song Cycle
  (s,bar)
Orland: Symphony No. 4
  (male reciter,
  high fem v)

Reich: Music for Large
  Ensemble (2 fem vv)
Rice: La Corona
  (t,narr)
Rodriguez: Canto (st)
G. Samuel: Twelve on
  Death and No (st)
G. Samuel: Traumbild
  (st)
H. Smith: Meditations
  in Passage (s,bar)
Starer: Journals of a
  Songmaker (s,bar)
Thomson: Collected
  Poems (s,bar)
Ultan: Pitchipoi
  (mez,b-bar)

### Three vocalists

L. Adams: Hymn to
  Freedom (st,bar)
Eaton: Three Arias
  from "Herakles"
  (st,bar)
Hodkinson: November
  Voices (st,narr)
Kirk: Prayers from the
  Ark (st,bar)
Laderman: And David
  Wept (mez,t,b-bar)
Lerdahl: Aftermath
  (s,mez,bar)
Perera: Mass (stb)
Russo: The Golden Bird
  (s,bar,narr)
Vega: Cantata (2s,ca)
Wheelock: Ancient Rain
  (mez,t,bar)

### Four vocalists

Amirkhanian: Egusquiza
  to Falsetto (4vv)
J. Austin: Requiem
  (satb)
Blank: Utterances
  (satb)
Brant: Labyrinth I
  (2s,2a)

Brant: Litany of Tides
(4s)
Cage: Apartment House
(4vv)
Druckman: Vox Humana
(s,mez,t,bar)
Gould: American Sing
(s,mez,t,bar)
Handel: Low Country
Hauntings (satb)
Hannay: Symphony No. 4
(satb)
Heath: Afro-American
Suite of Evolution
(st,bar,b)
Mechem: The King's
Contest
(mez,t,bar,b)
C. Moore: Gospel Fuse
(2s,2a)
Nelhybel: Fables for
All Time (satb)
Nelhybel: Let There Be
Music (satb)
Reich: Tehillim (3s,a)
Rorem: Swords and
Plowshares (4vv)
Shapey: Cantata
(stb,narr)

*Five or more vocalists*

Antoniou: Kontakion
(2s,2a,tb)
Bernstein: Songfest
(s,mez,at,bar,b)
Binkerd: Tight-Rope
(9vv)
Fussell: Poems for
Chamber Orchestra
and Voices
(2s,2a,2t,2b)
Harrison: Four Strict
Songs (8bar)
Musgrave: Cantata for
a Summer Day
(satb,narr)
Rands: Ballad 4
(2s,2a,2t,2b)

Rush: Dans le sable
(s,4a,narr)
Wuorinen: The W. of
Babylon (3s,a,2t,
bar,b,fem narr)

## NARRATOR

### 15' or less

J. Adams: Christian
Zeal and Activity
E. Applebaum: Waltz in
Two
Atkinson: Alexander
Evergreen
Bales: Episode from a
Lincoln Ballet
Copland: Lincoln
Portrait
Copland: Preamble for
a Solemn Occasion
A. Cunningham: Rooster
Rhapsody
Fischer: Orchestral
Adventures of a
Little Tune
Freund: A Sermon of
Jonne Donne
Gillis: The Man Who
Invented Music
Haufrecht: The Little
Red Hen
Haufrecht: A Walk in
the Forest
Hollingsworth: Three
Ladies by the Sea
Jager: The War Prayer
Kechley: Clocks and
More Clocks
Kirk: An Orchestra
Primer
W. Kraft: Dream Tunnel
Lankester: The Time
Machine
Larsen: Tom Twist
D. Lee: Peter and his
Magic Flute
Lennon: Suite of
Fables

P. Lewis: Images
R. Nelson: Meditation
and Dance
Paulus: Suite from
"Harmoonia"
Persichetti: A Lincoln
Address
Schickele: Three
Strange Cases
Siekmann: Music for a
Poetic Reading
F. Silverman: Madness
Trythall: Cindy the
Synth
Gwyneth Walker: The
Headless Horseman
Ward: Jonathan and the
Gingery Snare
Ward: Festival
Triptych
Zador: The Remarkable
Adventure of Henry
Bold

### 16' to 30'

J. Alexander: Salute
to the Whole World
Armer: The Great
Instrument of the
Geggerets
Atkinson: A Musical
Trip to the Zoo
Atkinson: A Dinosaur's
Tale
L. Austin:
Phantasmagoria
J. Avshalomov:
Thirteen Clocks
Bacon: Fables
Bacon: Great River
Balada: Ponce de León
Bales: National
Gallery Suite No. 3
Ballard: Why the Duck
has a Short Tail
Barab: G.A.G.E., A
Christmas Story
Barati: The Ugly
Duckling

Bond: The Frog Prince
Bond: What's the Point
of Counterpoint?
Brandt: Music for the
Decalogue
Brant: The Old
Italian's Dying
Dickerson: Orpheus an'
his Slide Trombone
Donato: Solitude in
the City
Fetler: Three Poems by
Walt Whitman
Gillis: Alice in
Orchestralia
Gould: Rhythm Gallery
Herman: ...from The
River Why
Husa: The Steadfast
Tin Soldier
Kechley: Alexander and
the Wind-Up Mouse
W. Kraft: A Kennedy
Portrait
Laderman: Magic Prison
Lees: The Trumpet of
the Swan
Mayer: Hello World
P. McLean: Everything
Awakening Alert and
Joyful
Nabokov: The Last
Flower
R. Nelson: This is the
Orchestra
Paulus: Voices from
the Gallery
Persichetti: Fables
for Narrator and
Orchestra
Picker: Encantadas
Pinkham: Signs of the
Zodiac
Ramsier: Road to
Hamelin
Robinson: To the
Northwest Indians
Rodriguez: Trunks
Rodriguez: A Colorful
Symphony

Rogers: Leaves from
  "The Tale of
  Pinocchio"
Rosner: From the
  Diaries of Adam
  Czerniakow
Schickele: The Chenoo
  Who Stayed To Dinner
Schifrin: Madrigals
  for the Space Age
Schwantner: New
  Morning for the
  World
Shere: Tongues
Shinn: The Silver
  Whistle
Siegmeister: Dick
  Whittington and
  his Cat
Still: Little Red
  Schoolhouse
Surinach: The Owl and
  the Pussycat
Sydeman: In Memoriam
Thome: Lucent Flowers
Thome: The Ruins of
  the Heart
Welcher: HALEAKLA
Whear: Appalachian
  Folk Tale
Yasanitsky: The Great
  American Fairy Tale
Yasanitsky: The
  Appleville Musicians

Over 30'

Amram: The American
  Bell
Bach: The Happy Prince
Barab: Tales of Rhyme
  and Reason
Del Tredici: Final
  Alice
Fischer: Symphonic
  Adventures of a
  Little Tune
Luedeke: Tales of the
  Netsilik

APPENDIX D

CHORUS AND ORCHESTRA

Mixed chorus
Double chorus
Triple chorus
Male chorus
Female chorus
Children's chorus

The works listed in Appendix C are for orchestra with chorus. The main categories are grouped according to size of orchestra and then by duration. Solo vocalists are indicated in parentheses after the title of the work. Complete information regarding any of these works may be obtained by referring to the main listing in the catalog.

## MIXED CHORUS

*Large Orchestra*

### 15' or less

J. Alexander:
  Dialogues Spirituels
J. Austin: The Moon
  Wears a Wax
  Moustache (s)
Ballard: The Gods Will
  Hear
Barati: The Waters of
  Kane Bassett:
  Celebration (narr)
Bennett: Carol Cantata
Blumenfeld: Elegy for
  the Nightingale
  (bar)
Brant: Fire in Cities
Chance: In Paradisum
  (s)
Clarke: Gloria
Coker: Paean

Colgrass: The Earth's
  A Baked Apple
Copland: Canticle of
  Freedom
Creston: Psalm XXIII
  (s)
A. Cunningham: Sun
  Catcher (satb)
Curtis: Testament
  (narr)
Dello Joio: Three
  Hymns Without Words
Del Tredici: The Last
  Gospel (s)
Dickerson: A Musical
  Service for Louis
Diemer: To Him All
  Glory Give
Diemer: Anniversary
  Choruses
Diemer: Invocation
Eaton: Danton and
  Robespierre
  (s,mez,bar,b)

Effinger: Let Your
Mind Wander Over
America
Erb: Cummings Cycle
Felciano: The Captives
Feldman: Chorus and
Orchestra I (s)
Flagello: Tristis est
anima mea
Flagello: Te Deum For
All Mankind
Gerschefski: There is
a Man on the Cross
(ca)
Gerschefski:
Salutation of the
Dawn
Hannay: Sayings for
Our Time
Hanson: Cherubic Hymn
Hanson: Song of
Democracy
Hanson: Song of Human
Rights
Hanson: Two Psalms
(bar)
Hanson: Streams in the
Desert
Hoiby: Hymn to the New
Age
Huchison: Let Us Be
Grateful
Huggler: Cantata
Husa: Festive Ode
Jenni: This is the
Year
Kirk: King David's
Deliverance
D. Lee: Canticle of
the Pacific
Lindenfeld: And the
Eagles
Lockwood: The Closing
Doxology
Lo Presti: Elegy
Lo Presti: Tribute
Luke: Plaintes and
Dirges
Mailman: Alleluia

Mandelbaum: A
Mourner's Kaddish
(s)
McDonald: God Give Us
Men
Menotti: A Song of
Hope (bar)
Menotti: For the Death
of Orpheus (t)
Menotti: Llama de Amor
Viva (bar)
Nelhybel: Sine nomine
(satb)
R. Nelson: Fanfare for
a Festival
D. Ott: The Twelve
Days of Christmas
Palmer: Abraham
Lincoln Walks at
Midnight
Parmentier: Eclipse
(bar)
Persichetti: Te Deum
Polster: Something
Sings
A. Reed: The Pledge of
Allegiance
Rodriguez: Varmi'ts!
(narr)
Rodriguez: We, the
People (narr)
Rogers: The Light of
Man (sa,bar)
Rosen: Campus Doorways
Saylor: To Autumn, To
Winter
Saylor: Jubilate
Schuller: Music for a
Celebration
Siegmeister: In Our
Time
J. Smith: Remember the
Alamo! (narr)
Susa: Baghdad-by-
the-Bay
Susa: Three Mystical
Carols
Susa: Christmas
Garland
Svoboda: Child's Dream

Thompson: The Last
  Words of David
Thompson: A Psalm of
  Thanksgiving
Thomson: Crossing
  Brooklyn Ferry
Van Vactor: Veni
  Immanuel
Gwyneth Walker: Three
  Songs in Celebration
Wallach: Columbus
  Prayer (bar)
Washburn: Ode to
  Freedom
Washburn: We Hold
  These Truths
Wernick: Chanukah
  Festival Overture
Donald White: Song of
  Mankind (satb)
Wienhorst: Magnificat
John Williams:
  America, the Dream
  Goes On (bar)
Wykes: Letter to an
  Alto-Man
Zappa: I'm Stealing
  the Room
Zappa: Penis Dimension

### 16' to 30'

Adler: A Whole Bunch
  of Fun (mez)
Adler: A Falling of
  Saints (t,bar)
Albert: Bacchae (b)
Ames: Granite and
  Cypress
Antoniou: Circle of
  Thanatos and Genesis
  (t,narr)
Antoniou: Prometheus
  (bar,narr)
J. Avshalomov: City
  Upon a Hill (narr)
Bach: The Oregon Trail
  (t,bar)
Ballard: Portrait of
  Will Rogers (narr)

Barber: Prayers of
  Kierkegaard (s)
Beck: Requiem for the
  Twentieth Century
Beglarian: Twelve
  Hungarian Songs
Bennett: A
  Commemoration
  Symphony
Bennett: The Easter
  Story
Bergsma: Symphony
  No. 2 (vv)
Brant: Atlantis
  (mez,narr)
S. Burton: I Have A
  Dream (s,narr)
D. Carlson: Notturno
Cheetham: Propheta
  Lucis
Colgrass: Image of Man
  (vv)
Colgrass: Theatre of
  the Universe
  (s,mez,t,bar,b)
Cooper: Refrains
  (s,bar)
Cooper: Voyagers
Cowell: The Creator
  (satb)
M. Cunningham:
  Symphonic Arias
  (s,ca,tb)
Danielpour: Journey
  Without Distance
W. Davis: The City of
  Light (st,bar,narr)
Del Tredici:
  Pop-pourri (s)
Del Tredici: Tattoo
Di Domenica: The Holy
  Colophon
Effinger: Symphony
  No. 4
Ehle: Bay Psaulmes
El-Dabh: Music of the
  Pharaohs
Entsminger: The Happy
  Prince (sab)

Feldman: Elemental
Procedures (s)
Fetler: Of Earth's
Image (s)
Fetler: This Was the
Way (s)
Finney: Earthrise
Trilogy (sat,narr)
Foss: With Music
Strong
Fussell: Landscapes
Giannini: Canticle of
Christmas (bar)
Giannini: Canticle of
the Martyrs
Gillis: This is Our
America (bar)
Glass: Music from the
"Civil Wars"
Grantham: Fiddler's
Fancy (bar)
Grofe: Atlantic
Crossing (narr)
Hanson: Lament for
Beowulf
Hewitt: Symphony
No. 26
Hovhaness: Blue Flame
(stb)
Hovhaness: Praise the
Lord With Psaltery
Husa: Apotheosis of
this Earth
Iannaccone: Magnificat
(4vv)
Imbrie: Requiem (s)
A.P. Johnson: Noche
oscura del Alma
Jones: The Trumpet of
the Swan
Jones: Canticles of
Time
U. Kay: Inscriptions
from Whitman
U. Kay: Once there was
a man (narr)
Korf: Requiem (narr)
Krenek: To believe and
to know (4narr)

Kubik: Magic, Magic,
Magic! (at,narr)
Lockwood: Prairie
London: The Iron Hand
(mez,bar)
MacBride: Four Sonnets
of Feng Zhi (2vv)
Mandelbaum: Sea
Surface Full of
Clouds (satb)
Mechem: Songs of the
Slave (bar)
Mekeel: Toward the
Source...
Mennin: Symphony No. 4
Menotti: The Death of
Bishop Brindisi
Meyerowitz: The Glory
Around His Head
Moevs: Et occidentum
illustra
Musgrave: The Phoenix
and the Turtle
Nelhybel: Dies Ultima
(st,bar)
Newell: Visions and
Dreams (bar)
Orrego-Salas: Bolivar
Parker: Gaudete
Parmentier: From the
Diary of a Northern
Window
Pasatieri: Permit Me
Voyage (s)
Pinkham: Jonah
(mez,t,bar)
Rands: Bells
H. Reed: A Tabernacle
for the Sun
Rieti: Trionfo di
Bacco e Arianna
Rogers: A Letter from
Pete (st)
Ross: A Jefferson
Symphony (t,narr)
Rouse: Karolju
Saturen: The Love Song
of J. Alfred
Prufrock (bar)

Schuller: The Power
Within Us (bar,narr)
Schuman: Free Song
Schwantner: Evening
Land
Sheinfeld: The Earth
is a Sounding Board
Shinn: Make Much of
Time (st)
Siegmeister: I Have A
Dream (bar,narr)
Siegmeister: A Cycle
of Cities
Starer: The People,
Yes
Stevens: The Ballad of
William Sycamore
Stout: Symphony No. 4
Strunk: Orpheus (st)
Svoboda: Journey
(mez,bar)
Talma: The Tolling
Bell (bar)
Taylor: Sacred Verses
(2vv)
Thompson: A Concord
Cantata
Thomson: Cantata on
Poems of Edward Lear
(s,bar)
Van Vactor: Credo
(mez)
Van Vactor: Symphony
No. 4
Wallach: A Prophesy
and Psalm (bar)
Warren: Abram in Egypt
(bar)
Weisgall: A Song of
Celebration (st)
Whear: Psalms of
Celebration
Whear: The Seasons
Wienhorst: Te Deum (t)
O. Wilson: Spiritsong
(s)

31' to 45'

J. Adams: Harmonium
Adler: Choose Life
(mez,t)
Antoniou: Nenikakamen
(mez,bar,narr)
Argento: Te Deum
J. Avshalomov:
Glorious Th'
Assembled Fires
(boy s)
Balada: No-Res (narr)
Barber: The Lovers
(bar)
Benjamin: The
Righteous Nation
(s,t)
Bernstein: Symphony
No. 3 (s,narr)
Bottje: Songs from the
Land Between Rivers
Brunswick: Eros and
Death
Cordero: Cantata para
la Paz (bar)
Dello Joio: Song of
Affirmation (s,narr)
Dello Joio: Evocations
Diamond: To Music
(t,bar)
Diemente: Credo (s)
Flagello: Passion of
Martin Luther King
(bar)
Freed: The Zodiac
(narr)
Freund: Passion Music
(s,mez,t,b)
Glass: Itaipu
Hailstork: Done Made
My Vow
Hannay: Requiem (s)
Hannay: Symphony No. 3
Roy Harris: Folksong
Symphony
Haxton: A Psalm Cycle
(st)
Hennagin: A Song of
Songs (s,bar)

Husa: An American Te
Deum (bar)
Iannaccone: The Prince
of Peace (4vv)
Imbrie: Prometheus
Bound (st,bar)
Kievman: Symphony
No. 2
La Montaine: Novellis,
Novellis (8vv)
Lees: Vision of Poets
(st)
Lockwood: Light Out of
Darkness (bar)
Mailman: Requiem,
Requiem (sat,narr)
Martino: Portraits
(mez,bar)
Menotti: Landscapes
and Remembrances
(satb)
Menotti: Missa O
Pulchritudo
(s,mez,t,bar)
C. Moore: The American
Nebula
R. Nelson: The
Christmas Story
(bar,narr)
Parker: The World's
One Song (s)
Paulus: Voices (s)
Rogers: The Prophet
Isaiah
Rorem: An American
Oratorio (t)
Schuman: Casey at the
Bat (st)
Schuman: On Freedom's
Ground (bar)
Sessions: When Lilacs
Last In The Dooryard
Bloom'd (sa,bar)
Shifrin: Cantata to
the Text of
Sophoclean Choruses
Shinn: Devices and
Desires (s,bar)
R. Smith: Magnificat

Sowerby: The Throne of
God
Thompson: Ode to the
Virginia Voyage
Thompson: The Passion
According to St.
Luke (t,bar)
Thomson: Missa pro
defunctis
Ultan: The Man With A
Hoe (satb)
Van Vactor: The New
Light (s,bar,narr)
Van Vactor: Episodes
(satb)
Ward: Symphony No. 5
(s,bar,narr)
Winslow: Mimene
(2s,atb)

**Over 45'**

Adler: B'Shaaray -
Tefilah (b)
Adler: The Binding
(ssatb)
Bach: Spectra (s,bar)
Bavicchi: Songs of
Remembrance (satb)
Bernstein: West Side
Story (sat,bar)
Bolcom: Songs of
Innocence and
Experience
(s,mez,ca,t,bar)
Corigliano: A Dylan
Thomas Trilogy
(t,bar)
Effinger: The
Invisible Fire
(satb)
Freund: Passion With
Tropes
T.R. George: The
People, Yes
(mez,t,bar)
Glass: Civil Wars
(sat,bar,b)

Hanson: New Land,
New Covenant
(s,bar,narr)
Haxton: Moses
(satb,narr)
Hoiby: Galileo Galilei
(7vv)
Hovhaness: The Way of
Jesus (stb)
Hovhaness: Revelation
of St. Paul (st,bar)
Kitzke: The Rime of
the Ancient Mariner
(t,bar)
Kohs: Lord of the
Ascendant (7vv)
La Montaine: Be Glad
Then America (4vv)
M. Levy: For the Time
Being
(2s,mez,t,bar,b)
M. Levy: Masada
(t,narr)
Lockwood: Children of
God (5vv)
Moevs: Attis Catulis
(st)
B. Nelson: The Feast
of Lights (s)
R. Nelson: What is
Man? (s,bar,narr)
Orrego-Salas: Missa
"In tempore
Discordiae" (t)
Orrego-Salas: The Days
of God (satb)
D. Ott: Cornerstone of
Loveliness (s,mez,t)
Parker: Journeys
(s,bar)
Persichetti: The
Creation (satb)
Pone: Daniel Propheta
(3vv)
Proctor: Moby Dick
G. Read: The Prophet
(2vv,narr)
Reich: The Desert
Music

Rhodes: Paradise Lost
(st,bar,narr)
Rieti: Voyage to
Europe (s,mez,atb)
Rorem: Goodbye My
Fancy (a,bar)
Rosner: Requiem
(s,2t,b)
Sacco: Solomon
(s,mez,t,bar)
Warren: Requiem
(a,bar)
Warren: The Legend of
King Arthur (t,bar)
F. Waxman: Joshua
(a,2t,2b,narr)
Whear: The Chief
Justice, John
Marshall (sb,2narr)
Woollen: The Pasch
(3vv)
Wuorinen: The
Celestial Sphere
Zupko: Proud Music of
the Storm

*Medium Orchestra*

15' or less

Adler: The Feast of
Lights
Adler: Vision of
Isaiah
Adler: A Song of
Hanukkah
Adler: Wisdom Cometh
With the Years
J. Austin: Eight
Changes on "Amazing
Grace"
J. Avshalomov: How
Long, O Lord (a)
Bohrnstedt: Ballad for
LaCrosse
Brings: Three Holy
Sonnets
Britain: The Earth
Does Not Wish For
Beauty

Copland: The Promise
of Living
Copland: Stomp Your
Foot
Cowell: Edson Hymns
and Fuguing Tunes
A. Cunningham: Litany
for the Flower
Children
Evett: Monadnock
Foss: Psalms
Glass: Hymn to the Sun
(countertenor)
Gooch: One Star, Ours
Hailstork: Songs of
Isaiah
Hannay: Cantata (t)
Hanson: Lumen in
Christo
Roy Harris: Blow the
Man Down (ca,bar)
Haubiel: Father
Abraham (2a,tb)
Hoiby: A Christmas
Carol
Hollingsworth: Stabat
Mater
Jazwinski: Cantique de
Saint-Jean
Karlins: Concert Music
No. 2
U. Kay: Song of
Jeremiah (bar)
Kohs: Psalm XXV
L. Kraft: A Proverb of
Solomon
Kramer: No Beginning,
No End
Kroeger: Moravian
Praise
Lockwood: Give Me The
Splendid Silent Sun
Mayer: Letters Home
(vv,narr)
Mayer: Eve of St.
Agnes (s,mez,bar)
Menotti: Muero, Porque
no Muero (s)
Milburn: Prologue:
Venosa

Orland: Christmas
Candlelight
Orland: Christmas
Legend
Parker: Our Native
Land
Parris: Alas For The
New Day (t)
Pleskow: Serenade
Rorem: Laudemus Tempus
Actum
Roseman: Psalm XXII
(t)
G. Samuel: To An End
Schubel: Overfeed
(fem v)
Schuman: Prologue
Serebrier: Nueve
(narr)
Serly: Anniversary
Cantata
Spratlan: Celebration
Still: From a Lost
Continent
Still: A Psalm for the
Living
Susa: A Christmas
Garland
Thompson: A Hymn for
Scholars and Pulpits
Thomson: The Nativity
As Sung By Sheperds
(at,bar)
F. Thorne: Song of the
Carolina Low Country
Warren:
Transcontinental
(bar)
Wigglesworth: Sleep
Becalmed

**16' to 30'**

Amram: A Year in Our
Land (sat,bar)
Amram: Let Us Remember
(vv)
J. Avshalomov:
Raptures for
Orchestra

Becker: Out of the
  Cradle Endlessly
  Rocking (vv,narr)
Becker: Symphony No. 6
  (narr)
Berg: Mass (s)
Blumenfeld: Dramatic
  Symphony (mez,bar)
Blumenfeld: Song of
  Innocence (mez, t)
E. Brown: New Piece:
  Loops
Creston: Missa
  Solemnis
Creston: Isaiah's
  Prophecy (satb)
Crockett: Vox in Rama
  (satb)
Dello Joio: A Psalm of
  David
Drew: Symphony No. 2
Effinger: The Long
  Dimension (bar)
Elwell: Lincoln:
  Requiem Aeternam
  (bar)
Feldman: Chorus and
  Orchestra II
Foss: A Parable of
  Death (t,narr)
Gillis: The Coming of
  the King (narr)
Hodkinson: Missa
  Brevis
Hoiby: A Hymn of the
  Nativity (s,bar)
U. Kay: Phoebus Arise
  (s,bar)
Kohs: Symphony No. 2
Korte: Mass for Youth
Kubik: Choral Suite
  No. 1 (narr)
Kubik: Choral Suite
  No. 2 (narr)
La Montaine: The
  Whittier Service
Lockwood: Magnificat
  (s)
Lockwood: Thought of
  Him I Love

Mayer: Spring Came On
  Forever (mez,t,bar)
McCulloh: Vox Humana
  (s)
Montague: Varshavian
  Spring
Parker: Seven Carols
  for Christmas (s)
Rieti: Missa Brevis
Riley: Cantata IV (at)
Rorem: The Poet's
  Requiem (s)
Shifrin: Chronicles
  (t,bar,b)
Siegmeister: Christmas
  is Coming (narr)
Starer: Kohelet
  (s,bar)
Starer: Ariel (s,bar)
Starer: Joseph and His
  Brothers
  (st,bar,narr)
Stein: The Lord
  Reigneth (t)
Thompson: Frostiana
F. Thorne: Praise and
  Thanksgiving
Warren: Good Morning,
  America (narr)
Weiner: Quest for
  Peace (vv)
Whear: Kedushah
Woollen: Hymn on the
  Morning of Christ's
  Nativity (2vv)
Zaimont: Man's Image
  and His Cry (a,bar)

### 31' to 45'

Balada: Maria Sabina
  (narr)
Bales: The Confederacy
  (s,bar,narr)
Hodkinson: Cantata
  Appalachia (s,bar)
Kroeger: Pax vobis
  (s,bar)
Parker: That Sturdy
  Vine (s)

Paulus: So Hallow'd is
the Time (st,bar)
Rorem: Little Prayers
(s,bar)
Sorce: Requiem (vv)
Ward: Sweet Freedom's
Song

Over 45'

Antheil: Cabeza de
Vaca
Bacon: Requiem "The
Last Invocation"
(sb)
Bottje: Wayward
Pilgrim (s)
A. Cunningham: Night
Song
Franco: The Stars Look
Down (5vv)
Parker: Songs from the
Dragon Quilt
(s,narr)
Rosenman: Stabat Mater
(2s,t,bar)
Sacco: Jesu (st)
Yardumian: Mass "Come
Creator Spirit"
(mez/bar)
Zaimont: Sacred
Service for the
Sabbath Evening
(a/bar)

*Small Orchestra*

15' or less

Adler: Judah's Song of
Praise
Antoniou: Klima tis
apoussias
Balazs: An Evening
Song
Bavicchi: Three Psalms
(satb)
Benjamin: Unto the
Hills
Bezanson: Memory

Blank: American Folio
Brings: A Herrick
Suite
Britain: The Builders
E. Brown: From Here
Canning: O God, Our
Lord, Thy Holy Word
Canning: Anthem (s)
Carlsen: Polter te
Creso
M. Carlson: Mass
Carter: Musicians
Wrestle Everywhere
Consoli: Greek Lyrics
Crawford: Magnificat
Effinger: Sonnet at
Dusk
Fischer: Statement (s)
Gerschefski: Letter
from BMI
Gideon: Adon Olom
Harbison: The Flight
Into Egypt (s,bar)
Harrison: Easter
Cantata
Hennagin: A Meditation
Hovhaness: Missa
Brevis (b)
Hovhaness: The Stars
(s)
Hovhaness: The
Beatitudes
Imbrie: On the Beach
at Night
U. Kay: Choral
Triptych
Keller: Magnificat
Krenek: Ich singe
wieder, wenn es tagt
London: Hast Thou Not?
Loos: Psalm CXX
Luening: Pilgrim's
Hymn
Paulus: Letters for
the Times (st,bar)
Paulus: Christmas
Tidings
Perry: Frammenti dalle
lettere de Santa
Caterina (s)

Pinkham: Wedding
Cantata (st)
Pinkham: Hezekiah
(st,bar)
Pleskow: Paumanok (s)
Pleskow: Altarpiece
Riegger: A Shakespeare
Sonnet (bar)
G. Samuel: On the
Beach at Night Alone
Sessions: Three
Choruses on
Biblical Texts
H. Smith: In Memoriam
W. Smith: My Father
Moved Through Domes
Of Love
Starer: A Psalm of
David
Stevens: Magnificat
Stout: Nune Dimittis
(bar)
Stout: Christus Factus
est
Stout: Exspecta
Dominum
Stout: Per lignum
servi facti sumus
Strandberg: Canticle
No. 2
Sullivan: Sky Wood (s)
Susa: I am the way
(satb)
Susa: Two Motets
(satb)
Susa: Even-Song
Ward: Let the Word Go
Forth
Warren: Sanctus
Warren: Hymn of the
City
Warren: Now Welcome
Summer
Wienhorst: Het is Goed
den Herre te Loven
Wienhorst: A Psalm
Setting
Woollen: Easter
Sequence

Woollen: Mass for a
Great Space
Work: The Singers
(bar)

## 16' to 30'

Adler: Any Human to
Another
L. Austin: The
Ordinary of the Mass
Balazs: Pueblo Bonito
(narr)
Ballard: Live On,
Heart of My Nation
(satb,narr)
Bergsma: Confrontation
Bernstein: Chichester
Psalms (boy s)
M. Carlson: A Wreath
of Anthems
Danielpour: Prologue
and Prayer
Dello Joio: Mass in
Honor of the
Eucharist (cantor)
Dello Joio: As of a
Dream! (sat)
De Mars: The Prophet
De Mars: Tito's Say
Effinger: Cantata for
Easter
Evett: Vespers
Hagen: A Walt Whitman
Requiem (s)
Hailstork: I Will Lift
Up Mine Eyes (t)
Harrison: Mass to
St. Anthony
Herman: Canticle for
the Sacred Heart
Hovhaness: 30th Ode of
Solomon (bar)
Hovhaness: Easter
Cantata (s)
Hovhaness: Magnificat
(satb)
Hovhaness: Symphony
No. 12

Hovhaness: In the
Beginning was the
Word (ab)
Jaffe: Three Images
(vv,narr)
Kechley: Faint Hearts
and Silver Voices
(sb)
Kirk: Night of Wonder
Krenek: Mass "Give Us
Peace" (satb)
Krenek: Anniversary
Cantata
(mez,bar,narr)
Kubik: A Christmas Set
La Montaine: The
Marshes of Glynn (b)
Levi: The Natural
History of the Water
Closet
Martino: The White
Island
McKay: Lamentations of
Joseph
Mechem: Singing is so
Good a Thing
Mennin: The Christmas
Story (st)
Moryl: Illuminations
Persichetti: The
Pleiades
Persichetti: Flower
Songs
Pinkham: The
Reproaches
Pinkham: Stabat Mater
(s)
Pinkham: To Troubled
Friends
Pinkham: Four Elegies
(t)
Rands: Wildtrack III
(s,mez,narr)
Rorem: Letters from
Paris
Schneider: The Voice
of Eternity
(s,mez,t,bar,b)

Siegmeister: A Tooth
for Paul Revere
(4vv)
Sowerby: Solomon's
Garden (t)
Stout: Ecce, Agnus Dei
Waggoner: The Father
and Mother Begotten
(s,bar)
D. Waxman: Psalms and
Supplications (t)
Woollen: Alexandria
Suite

### 31' to 45'

Castaldo: Ancient
Liturgy (narr)
Cooper: Cantigas
Diamond: A Secular
Cantata (t,bar)
Effinger: The St. Luke
Christmas Story
(satb)
Effinger: Paul of
Tarsus (bar)
Finney: Nun's Priest's
Tale (s,bar,b,narr,
folk singer)
Gooch: Wisdom
(mez,bar)
Heussenstamm: Litany
of L.H.
Hovhaness: Anabasis
(s,bar)
Hovhaness: Lady of
Light (s,bar)
Hovhaness: Symphony
No. 24 (t)
Larsen: In a Winter
Garden (mez,t)
Lesemann: The Garden
of the Prosperine
(mez,bar)
Paulus: Canticles
(s,mez,narr)
Paulus: North Shore
(mez,bar)
Roussakis: God
Abandons Antony (s)

Schelle: After the
Meridian (st,bar)
Silver: Free Pen
(vv,narr)
Woollen: In Martyrum
Memoriam (2vv)

**Over 45'**

E. Applebaum: The
Frieze of Life
(satb)
A. Avshalomov: Feng-
Huang (3vv)
Bales: The Republic
(s,bar,narr)
Bales: The Union
(s,bar,narr)
Bernstein: Suite from
"Candide" (vv)
Foss: The Prairie
(satb)
Whear: Mass for Today
(s,bar)

**Variable Duration**

London: Moon Sound
Zone

**DOUBLE CHORUS**

L. Adams: Righteous
Man
Brant: Meteor Farm
(2s)
Brant: Western Springs
D. Brubeck: The Light
in the Wilderness
(bar)
D. Brubeck: Beloved
Son (bar)
Cage: A Collection of
Rocks
Colgrass: Best Wishes
USA (s,mez,t,bar)
Constantinides: Walls
of Time (sa)
Cooper: Credo

Foss: American Cantata
(st,2narr)
Gould: Quotations
Hennagin: Variations
on an Oh So Familiar
Tune
Hewitt: The Good
Samaritan
Hoffmann:
Lacrymosa `91
Hovhaness: Ad Lyram
(satb)
Laufer: And Thomas
Jefferson... (bar)
London: According to
the Number
Mennin: Cantata de
Virtue (t,bar,narr)
Perle: Songs of Praise
and Lamentation
(satb)
Reynolds: Masks
Rickley: Prophecies of
Zephaniah (4s)
Selig: Islands
Shapey: Praise (bar)
J. Smith: Our Heritage
Stout: Passion
(st,bar)
Tanenbaum: The Last of
the Just
George Walker: Mass
Yardumian: The Story
of Abraham (satb)

**TRIPLE CHORUS**

Erb: New England's
Prospect (narr)
Rochberg: Symphony
No. 3 (satb)
Wykes: Adequate Earth
(bar,2narr)

**MALE CHORUS**

Blitzstein: The
Airborne Symphony
(t,bar,narr)

Britain: Brothers of
the Clouds
Carter: Tarantella
Conte: Invocation and
Dance
Conte: Hymn to the
Nativity (s)
Cowell: Lines from the
Dead Sea Scrolls
Diamond: The Martyr
Eaton: Opening Storm
from "The Tempest"
Evett: Lauds
Gottschalk: Beati
Omnes
Gould: Declaration
(2narr)
Hemmer: A Festival of
Spirituals (bar)
Hoffmann: Memento Mori
Hovhaness: Wind Drum
Orrego-Salas: America,
No en vano Invocamus
Tu Nombre (s,bar)
Ptaszynska: Ave Maria
H. Reed: Ut, Re, Mi
Smit: Caedmon (mez,tb)
Snyder: Schubertiad
(a)
Stokes: Smoke and
Steel
Stout: Improperium
Stout: Pater, si non
potest
Strandberg: Sarx
Susa: Serenade No. 1
Susa: The
Chanticleer's Carol
Vincent: Stabat Mater
(s)
Wienhorst: Canticle of
the Three Children

FEMALE CHORUS

Bacon: From Emily's
Diary
Balazs: Concerto for
Orchestra and Voices
(4vv)

Beglarian: Nurse's
Song
Benson: Psalm XXIV
Biscardi: Eurydice
Brant: Spatial
Concerto
(+ solo pf)
Britain: Nisan
Carter: The Harmony of
the Morning
Clarke: Primavera
Consoli: Musiculi
Frackenpohl: The
Natural Superiority
of Men
Gerschefski: Half Moon
Mountain (bar)
Gerschefski: The
Lord's Controversy
With His People
(bar)
Hoiby: The Nations
Echo Round
Hovhaness: Fuji
Kitzke: And Miles to
Go Before I Sleep
(s)
Krenek: Cantata for
Wartime
Menotti: Miracles
Musgrave: Echoes
Through Time
Parker: Commentaries
Pinkham: An Emily
Dickinson Mosaic
Pleskow: Six Brief
Verses
Riley: Cantata No. 3
Sydeman: Prometheus
(t,bar,b)
Talma: Celebration
Taylor: Ballade de bon
conseyl
Thompson: The Place of
the Blest
Van Vactor: Cantata
Van Vactor: Christmas
Songs for Young
People
Wheelock: Six Fables

Woollen: Three Sacred
  Choruses
Woollen: Two
  Responsories
Yavelow: The Horse
  With Violin in Mouth

CHILDREN'S CHORUS

Adolphe: Three Pieces
  for Kids and
  Orchestra
Antoniou: Die Weisse
  Rose (bar,2narr)
E. Applebaum: The Song
  of the Sparrows
  (stb,narr)
Binkerd: On the King's
  Highway
D. Brubeck: La Fiesta
  de la Posada (satb)
Cowell: ...if He
  please
Crumb: Star Child (s)
Diamond: This Sacred
  Ground
D. Epstein: Night
  Voices (narr)
W. Kraft:
  Contextures II (st)
Lockwood: Mass for
  Children and
  Orchestra
Martino: Paradiso
  Choruses
  (3s,4mez,3t,2bar)
Mennin: Cantata de
  Virtue (t,bar,narr)
Parker: Earth, Sky and
  Spirit
Polay: Encomium (narr)
Rodriguez:
  Transfiguration
  Mysteria (sat)
Schelle: Kidspeace
Verrall: Legend of
  Chief Joseph (bar)
George Walker: Cantata
Ward: Earth Shall Be
  Fair

F. Waxman: The Song of
  Terezin (s)

APPENDIX E

LIST OF PUBLISHERS

AA          Accord Associates
            4500 Lee Road   Suite 227
            Cleveland, OH    44128
            (216) 799-6328

ACA         American Composers Alliance
            170 West 74th Street
            New York, NY    10023
            (212) 362-8900

ACC         Accura Music
            P.O. Box 887
            Athens, OH    45701

AMC         American Music Center
            30 West 26th Street
            Suite 1001
            New York, NY    10010-2011
            (212) 366-5260

AME         American Music Editions
            AGENT:   Carl Fischer

AMG         Ashmere Music Group
            154 Bradley Street
            New Haven, CT    06511
            (203) 497-9798

AMP         Associated Music Publishers
            AGENT:   G. Schirmer

ANM         Association for the Promotion of
            New Music
            2002 Central Avenue
            Ship Bottom, NJ    08008
            (609) 494-8513
            (718) 499-0019

AP              Antheil Press
                7722 Lynn Avenue
                El Cerrito, CA    94530
                (510) 527-4942

APP             Arts Plural Publishing
                7722 Lynn Avenue
                El Cerrito, CA    94530
                (510) 527-4942

ARC             American Music Research Center
                College of Music
                University of Colorado
                Boulder, CO    80309

ARG             Argenta Music
                68-37 Dartmouth Street
                Forest Hills, NY    11375
                (718) 520-8673

AUS             Australian Music Center
                3 Smail Street
                Broadway, N.S.W.    2007
                Australia
                (61) 2 212 1611

BAR             Barenreiter
                AGENT:   European American Music

BB              Bote and Bock
                AGENT:   G. Schirmer

BE              Blackwood Enterprises
                5300 South Shore Drive
                Chicago, IL    60615
                (312) 324-0219

BEL             Belwin-Mills
                AGENT:   Theodore Presser

BG              Barbara Gillis
                165 Valley Wood Drive
                Athens, GA    30306
                (404) 546-5123

BH              Boosey and Hawkes Music Publishers
                Rental Department
                200 Smith Street
                Farmingdale, NY    11735
                (516) 752-1122

BKJ     BKJ Publications
Box 377
Newton, MA   02161

BOE     Boelke-Bomart, Inc.
Hillsdale, NY   12529

BOU     Bourne Music Publishers
5 West 37th Street
New York, NY   10018
(212) 391-4300

BRL     Brelmat Music
241 Kohler's Hill Road
Kutztown, PA   19530
(215) 756-6324

BRO     Broude Brothers Ltd.
170 Varick Street
New York, NY   10013
(800) 225-3197

BS     Barfko-Swill
Box 5418
North Hollywood, CA   91616-5418
(818) 786-7546

BTA     Barta Music Company
AGENT:   Jerona Music Corporation

BTM     Beteca Music, Inc.
P.O. Box 8106
Pittsburgh, PA   15217

BTN     Boston Music Corporation
Airport Drive
Hopedale, MA   01747
(617) 478-4813

CBM     Cambium Music
AGENT:   Theodore Presser

CBP     Claude Benny Press
2445 First Avenue South
Minneapolis, MN   55404

CCM     Cornucopia Music Publications
3025 Broadmoor
Las Cruces, NM   88001
(505) 524-2748

CCP        Conneauttee Composers Press
           116 Terrace Drive
           Edinboro, PA  16412

CF         Carl Fischer, Inc.
           62 Cooper Square
           New York, NY  10003
           (800) 762-2328

CFP        Edition Peters
           C. F. Peters Corporation
           373 Park Avenue South
           New York, NY  10016
           (212) 686-4147

CHE        Chester Music Limited
           AGENT:  G. Schirmer

CLE        Composers Library Editions
           P.O. Box 2580
           Park West Finance Station
           New York, NY  10025-1514

CMP        CMP, Inc.
           307 Southwood Drive
           Columbia, SC  29205

CRE        Crescendo Music Sales
           P.O. Box 395
           Naperville, IL  60540

CRP        Casa Rustica Publications
           255 Massachusetts Avenue  No. 305
           Boston, MA  02115
           (617) 262-1775

CST        Consort Music Press
           P.O. Box 50413
           Santa Barbara, CA  93150

CUM        Cummings Music
           415 West 23rd Street #11-D
           New York, NY  10011
           (212) 741-1559

DAN        Dantalian, Inc.
           11 Pembroke Street
           Newton, MA  02159

| | |
|---|---|
| DFM | Departed Feathers Music<br>19 Ware Street  No. 5<br>Cambridge, MA  02138 |
| DLF | Delfon Recording and Publishing<br>305 Third Avenue West<br>Newark, NJ  07107<br>(201) 484-6438 |
| DLP | Deep Listening Publications<br>The Pauline Oliveros Foundation<br>156 Hunter Street<br>Kingston, NY  12401 |
| DRN | Dorn Publications<br>P.O. Box 206<br>Medfield, MA  02052<br>(508) 359-4417 |
| DRY | Derry Music<br>240 Stockton Street<br>San Francisco, CA  94108 |
| DSH | Deshon Music, Inc.<br>AGENT:  Theodore Presser |
| DVG | Dunvagen Music Publishers<br>AGENT:  G. Schirmer |
| DYD | Dryad Music<br>801 South Pitt Street  Apt. 418<br>Alexandria, VA  22314 |
| EAM | European American Music Corporation<br>P.O. Box 850<br>Valley Forge, PA  19482<br>(215) 648-0506 |
| EBM | E. B. Marks<br>AGENT:  Theodore Presser |
| ECK | E. C. Kerby, Ltd.<br>198 Davenport Road<br>Toronto, Ontario M5R 1J2<br>Canada |
| ECS | E. C. Schirmer<br>138 Ipswich Street<br>Boston, MA  02215<br>(617) 236-1935 |

EDB          Editions Billaudot
             AGENT:   Theodore Presser

ELK          Elkan-Vogel
             AGENT:   Theodore Presser

EM           Edition Modern
             AGENT:   Theodore Presser

EME          Editions Max Eschig
             AGENT:   G. Schirmer

EP           Ear Press
             1824 Curtis Street
             Berkeley, CA   94702
             (510) 841-3254

EWM          E. Weintraub Music
             AGENT:   G. Schirmer

FAM          Fine Arts Music
             P.O. Box 311
             Wykagyl, NY   10804

FB           Fine Books
             12 East Vine Street
             Redlands, CA   92373
             (714) 792-7299

FBE          Freddy Bienstock Enterprises
             1619 Broadway
             New York, NY   10019
             (212) 489-8170

FC           Franco Colombo, Inc.
             AGENT:   Theodore Presser

FEM          Fema Music Publications
             P.O. Box 395
             Naperville, IL   69540

FLE          The Edwin A. Fleisher Collection
             Free Library of Philadelphia
             Logan Square
             Philadelphia, PA   19103

FPM          Frog Peak Music
             Box A-36
             Hanover, NH   03755

FRE      Fredonia Press
3947 Fredonia Drive
Hollywood, CA   90068
(213) 851-3043

FUJ      Fujihara Music Publishers
18206 51st Avenue South
Seattle, WA   98188

GAL      Galaxy Music
AGENT:   E. C. Schirmer

GS      G. Schirmer
Rental Department
P.O. Box 572
5 Bellvale Road
Chester, NY   10918
(914) 469-2271

HAR      Hargail Music
28 West 38th Street
New York, NY   10018

HBM      Horizon Bay Music
3311 Shore Parkway   No. 2A
Brooklyn, NY   11235
(718) 743-3839

HC      Edition Wilhelm Hansen/Chester Music
AGENT:   G. Schirmer

HG      Highgate Press
AGENT:   E. C. Schirmer

HMI      Hinshaw Music, Inc.
P.O. Box 470
Chapel Hill, NC   27514

HMP      Heroico Music Publications
1945 North Curson Avenue
Hollywood, CA   90046

HNS      Edition Wilhelm Hansen
AGENT:   G. Schirmer

HOR      Horspfal Music Concern
1611 West 32nd Street
Minneapolis, MN   55408
(612) 825-2922

HRM          Hog River Music
             1800 Albany Avenue
             Hartford, CT   06105-1005
             (203) 523-1820

IBU          Ibu Music
             17 Rolfe Road
             Hamden, CT   06517

ICP          Intelligent Company Publishers
             7323 SW 113 Circle Place
             Miami, FL   33173
             (305) 271-9138

IMI          Israeli Music Institute
             AGENT:  Boosey and Hawkes

ION          Ione Press, Inc.
             112 South Street
             Boston, MA   02111
             AGENT:  E. C. Schirmer

IR           Ivan Romanenko
             12 Webster Drive
             Greenville, PA   16125
             (412) 588-9505

JC           Joshua Corporation
             AGENT:  Boston Music Company
             Screen Gems - EMI

JER          Jerona Music Corporation
             81 Trinity Place
             Hackensack, NJ   07601

JMC          Joshua Music Corporation
             P.O. Box 267
             Hastings-on-Hudson
             New York, NY   10706

KAL          Edwin F. Kalmus Music
             Miami-Dade Industrial Park
             P.O. Box 1007
             Opa Locka, FL   33054

KPP          King Philip Press
             98 Riverside Drive
             New York, NY   10024
             (212) 799-6328

LDW  Ludwig Music Publishing
   557-59 East 140th Street
   Cleveland, OH  44110

LED  Alphonse Leduc
   AGENT:  Theodore Presser

LEE  Leeds Music
   AGENT:  Theodore Presser

LG   Lawson Gould
   AGENT:  G. Schirmer

LML  Luck's Music Library
   P.O. Box 71397
   Madison Heights, MI  48071
   (800) 348-8749

LTZ  Lentz Music
   13599 North 92nd Way
   Scottsdale, AZ  85260
   (602) 860-6910

MCA  MCA Music
   AGENT:  Theodore Presser

MER  Merion Music, Inc.
   AGENT:  Theodore Presser

MF   Mark Foster Music
   28 East Springfield Avenue
   Champaign, IL  61820
   (217) 398-2760

MG   Margun Music, Inc.
   167 Dudley Road
   Newton Centre, MA  02159
   (617) 332-6398

MGP  Music Graphics Press
   121 Washington Street
   San Diego, CA  92103
   (619) 298-3629

MJQ  MJQ Music, Inc.
   1697 Broadway
   New York, NY  10019
   (212) 582-6667

MLC          MLC Publishers
             R.D. 2  Box 33
             Petersburg, NY  12138
             (518) 658-3595

MMA          Mira Music Associates
             199 Mountain Road
             Wilton, CT  06897

MMB          Magnamusic Baton
             10370 Page Industrial Boulevard
             St. Louis, MO  63132
             (314) 427-5660

MMC          Master Musicians Collective
             240 West Street
             Reading, MA  01867-2847
             (617) 944-0959

MMP          Midbar Music Press
             AGENT: ASCAP

MMX          Minmax Music
             1937 Carleton Street
             Berkeley, CA  94704

MOB          Mobart Music
             AGENT:  Boelke-Bomart

MOL          Mols Publications
             37 Rockford Place
             Buffalo, NY  14221

MPB          M. P. Belaieff
             AGENT:  C. F. Peters

MPL          MPL Productions
             Attn:  Michael Leavitt
             170 West 74th Street
             New York, NY  10023
             (212) 874-3990
             (212) 874-4513
             (516) 487-3216

MRC          Mercury Music Corporation
             AGENT:  Theodore Presser

MSM            Morris Music
               Eastman School of Music
               26 Gibbs Street
               Rochester, NY   14604

MWB            Mowbray Publications
               AGENT:  Theodore Presser

NAU            Nautilus Press
               318 West 85th Street
               New York, NY   10024
               (212) 724-7495

NMW            New Music West
               P.O. Box 7434
               Van Nuys, CA   91409-7434
               (818) 363-6913

NOA            The National Orchestral Association
               475 Riverside Drive, Suite 249
               New York, NY   10115
               (212) 870-2009

NOR            Norruth Music
               10370 Page Industrial Boulevard
               St. Louis, MO   63132
               (314) 427-5660

NSE            North South Editions
               P.O. Box 698
               Cathedral Station
               New York, NY   10025-0698

NSW            The New Southwest Music Publications
               P.O. Box 4552
               Santa Fe, NM   87502

OST            Ostara Press
               c/o Music & Church Discount Suppliers
               P.O. Box 7634
               Ventura, CA   93006-7634
               (805) 642-6165

OXF            Oxford University Press
               AGENT:  G. Schirmer

PAP            Pro Art Publications
               AGENT:  Theodore Presser

PEM         Pembroke Music
            AGENT:  Carl Fischer

PLY         Plymouth Music Company, Inc.
            170 N.E. 33rd Street
            Fort Lauderdale, FL  33334
            (305) 563-1844

PM          Panmanok Music
            9 Dunster Road
            Great Neck, NY  11021

PS          Peer-Southern Concert Music
            810 Seventh Avenue
            New York, NY  10019
            (212) 265-3910

PTP         Pomona Thatcher Prints
            College & Fourth
            Claremont, CA  91711
            (714) 621-8155

PVP         Pine Valley Press
            P.O. Box 582
            Williamstown, MA  01267

REG         Regus Publications
            10 Birchwood Lane
            White Bear Lake, MN  55110

RIC         G. Ricordi and Company
            AGENT:  G. Schirmer

RIN         Rinaldo Music Press
            95-27 239th Street
            Floral Park, NY  11001

RKI         Robert King Music Company
            7 Canton Street
            North Easton, MA  02356

RMP         Rochester Music Publications
            AGENT:  Accura Music

RRM         Roger Rhodes Music, Ltd.
            P.O. Box 1550
            Radio City Station
            New York, NY  10101

RVM         Rock Valley Music
            71 Rock Valley Road
            Long Eddy, NY  12760

SAL         Editions Salabert
            AGENT:  G. Schirmer

SCH         Schott Music Corporation
            AGENT:  European American Music

SEE         Seesaw Music Corporation
            2067 Broadway
            New York, NY  10023
            (212) 874-1200

SG          Screen Gems - EMI Music, Inc.
            6920 Sunset Boulevard
            Hollywood, CA  90028
            (213) 469-8371

SHA         Shawnee Press, Inc.
            AGENT:  G. Schirmer

SIK         Hans Sikorski Musikverlag
            AGENT:  G. Schirmer

SJM         Sweet Jams Music
            148 Columbus Avenue
            Apartment 4-R
            New York, NY  10023
            (212) 580-0825

SMC         Southern Music Company
            1100 Broadway
            P.O. Box 329
            San Antonio, TX  78292
            (512) 226-8167

SMI         Smith Publications
            2617 Gwynndale Avenue
            Baltimore, MD  21207
            (301) 298-6509

SP          Soundings Press
            P.O. Box 8319
            Santa Fe, NM  86504
            (505) 983-5405

SS          Soundspells Productions
            86 Livingston Street
            Rhinebeck, NY   12572
            (914) 876-6295

SSM         Sheldon Soffer Management
            130 West 56th Street
            New York, NY   10019
            (212) 757-8060

STA         Thomas C. Stangland Company
            P.O. Box 19263
            Portland, OR   97219

SWP         Southwest Publishers
            309 East Broadway
            Tempe, AZ   85282
            (602) 966-0778

SZG         Casa Musicale Sonzogno
            AGENT:   G. Schirmer

TCM         Transcontinental Music Publications
            838 5th Avenue
            New York, NY   10021

TCP         The Composers Press
            AGENT:   Seesaw Music Corp.

TDM         Tierra del Mar Music
            5112 West Canterbury Drive
            Muncie, IN   47304
            (317) 282-5296

TJP         Tajilor Press
            1501 SE Holly Street
            Portland, OR   97214

TMP         Tamar Music Publishers
            Box 379
            North Amherst, MA   01059

TP          Theodore Presser Company
            Presser Place
            Bryn Mawr, PA   19010
            (215) 525-3636

UE          Universal Edition
            AGENT:   European American
            Music Distributors

UMP      United Music Publishers
           AGENT:   Theodore Presser

VPF       VPF Music
           78 North Route 303
           Congers, NY  10920

WGS       William Grant Still Music
           26892 Preciados Drive
           Mission Viejo, CA  92691
           (714) 830-7697

WJ        Wingert-Jones Music Inc.
           2026 Broadway
           P.O. Box 1878
           Kansas City, MO  64141

WMB       Wimbledon Music Inc.
           1888 Century Park East  Suite 10
           Century City, CA  90067

WY        Wylyn Associates
           6963 Amherst
           St. Louis, MO  63130

XLNT      X.L.N.T. Music
           38-62 240th Street
           Little Neck, NY  11363

YAZ       Yazz Music
           NW 1800 Hall Drive
           Pullman, WA  99163

## APPENDIX F

### LIST OF COMPOSER ADDRESSES

| | |
|---|---|
| Adler, Samuel | 54 Railroad Mills Road<br>Pittsford, NY 14534<br>(716) 381-5924 |
| Albright, William | 2555 Roseland<br>Ann Arbor, MI 48103<br>(313) 995-2449 |
| Alexander, Josef | New York, NY<br>(212) 362-0771 |
| Alexander, William | 116 Terrace Drive<br>Edinboro, PA 16412<br>(814) 734-1818 |
| Amlin, Martin | Boston University<br>School of Music<br>855 Commonwealth Avenue<br>Boston, MA 02215<br>(617) 353-3341 |
| Appleton, Jon | Dartmouth College<br>Department of Music<br>Hopkins Center<br>Hanover, NH 03755<br>(603) 646-2530 |
| Armer, Elinor | 821 Creston Road<br>Berkeley, CA 94708<br>(415) 526-5030 |
| Averitt, William | Shenandoah College<br>Conservatory of Music<br>Winchester, VA 22601<br>(703) 667-8714 |
| Avshalomov, Jacob | Portland Junior Symphony<br>2741 SW Fairview Boulevard<br>Portland, OR 97201<br>(503) 223-5939 |

Bach, Jan

Northern Illinois University
School of Music
Music Building 140
Dekalb, IL   60115
(815) 753-1551

Barnes, Larry

Transylvania University
Department of Music
Lexington, KY   40508
(606) 233-8141

Bazelon, Irwin

142 East 71st Street
New York, NY   10021
(212) 988-0877

Beckler, S. R.

645 West Rose
Stockton, CA   95203
(209) 464-5496

Beeler, C. Alan

Eastern Kentucky University
College of Arts and
Humanities
Department of Music
Richmond, KY   40475-0944

Beeson, Jack

Columbia University
Department of Music
New York, NY   10027
(212) 280-3825

Beglarian, Grant

1865 Brickwell Avenue
Apt. A-2001
Miami, FL   33129
(305) 573-0490

Benjamin, Thomas

6305 Blackburn Court
Baltimore, MD   21212
(301) 377-4910

Berg, Christopher

158 West 81st Street
No. 105
New York, NY   10024

Blickhan, Timothy

Northern Illinois University
School of Music
Music Building 140
Dekalb, IL   60115-2889
(815) 753-1551

Bohrnstedt, Wayne     University of Redlands
1200 East Colton Avenue
P.O. Box 3080
Redlands, CA   92373-0999

Bolcom, William     University of Michigan
School of Music
Ann Arbor, MI   48109
(313) 764-1817

Bond, Victoria     Roanoke Symphony Orchestra
111 West Campbell Avenue
Roanoke, VA   24014
(212) 691-6858

Brandt, William E.     NW 413 Sunset Drive
Pullman, WA   99163

Brown, Earle     52 Brevoort Lane
Rye, NY   10580
(914) 698-4114

Brown, J. E.     R.D. No. 9
Box 384 Creek Road
Bethlehem, PA   18015
(215) 691-6579

Browne, Philip     1900 Nicollet Avenue
Minneapolis, MN   55403
(612) 870-0943

Bubalo, Rudolph     Cleveland State University
Department of Music
1983 East 24th
Cleveland, OH   44115
(216) 687-2033

Burton, Stephen     George Mason University
Department of Music
4400 University Drive
Fairfax, VA   22030-4444
(703) 764-6200

Caldwell, James     Western Illinois University
Department of Music
Macomb, IL   61455
(309) 298-1240

Campo, Frank                12336 Milbank Street
                            Studio City, CA  91604
                            (213) 985-3062

Castaldo, Joseph            736 Christian Street
                            Philadelphia, PA  19147
                            (215) 829-9112

Chadabe, Joel               P.O. Box 8748
                            Albany, NY  12208

Cheetham, John              408 Woodridge Drive
                            Columbia, MO  65201

Childs, Barney              University of Redlands
                            1200 East Colton Avenue
                            P.O. Box 3080
                            Redlands, CA  92373-0999

Cohen, Steve                333 West 52nd Street
                            Suite 1410
                            New York, NY  10019
                            (212) 763-5828

Cone, Edward                18 College Road West
                            Princeton, NJ  08540-5050
                            (609) 921-2609

Constantinides, D.          Louisiana State University
                            School of Music
                            Baton Rouge, LA  70803
                            (504) 766-3487

Cope, David                 University of California
                            Department of Music
                            Santa Cruz, CA  95064
                            (408) 429-2292

Cordero, Roque              Illinois State University
                            Music Department
                            Normal, IL  61761
                            (309) 438-5362

Crawford, John              703 11th Street
                            Santa Monica, CA  90402
                            (213) 394-5770

Cunningham, Arthur          Box 614
                            Nyack, NY  10960
                            (914) 358-4625

Cunningham, Michael — University of Wisconsin
Department of Music
Eau Claire, WI   54701
(715) 836-4954

Curtis, Marvin — 1120 Hutchinson Avenue
Stockton, CA   95201
(209) 473-0817

Curtis-Smith, Curtis — 2412 Crest Drive
Kalamazoo, MI   49008
(616) 382-4645

Davidovsky, Mario — Columbia University
Department of Music
New York, NY   10027
(212) 854-3825

Davis, William Mac — Southwestern Baptist
Theological Seminary
P.O. Box 2200
Fort Worth, TX   76122

DeMars, James — Arizona State University
School of Music
Tempe, AZ   85287
(602) 965-3371

Diemente, Edward — 72 Montclair Drive
West Hartford, CT   06107
(203) 233-4869

Diemer, Emma Lou — 2249 Vista del Campo
Santa Barbara, CA   93101
(805) 687-2457

Douglas, Samuel — University of South Carolina
School of Music
Columbia, SC   29208

Downey, John — University of Wisconsin
School of Fine Arts
Department of Music
P.O. Box 413
Milwaukee, WI   53201
(414) 964-8158

Dutton, Brent

San Diego State University
Department of Music
San Diego, CA  92182-0217
(619) 594-4760

Ehle, Robert C.

University of Northern
Colorado
School of Music
Greeley, CO  80639
(303) 351-2678

Elisha, Haim

120 West 86th Street
Apt. 7-B
New York, NY  10024
(212) 724-6934

Entsminger, Deen

142 Sheila Drive
Antioch, TN  37013

Felciano, Richard

1326 Masonic Avenue
San Francisco, CA  94117
(415) 863-3337

Fennelly, Brian

2 Schryver Court
Kingston, NY  12401
(914) 331-3228

Fenner, Burt

201 Music Building
University Park, PA  16802
(814) 863-4409

Fetler, Paul

University of Minnesota
2106 4th Street
200 Ferguson
Minneapolis, MN  55455
(612) 624-5093

Fine, Vivian

R.R. 2  Box 630
Hoosic Falls, NY  12090
(518) 686-5591

Fink, Myron

10836 Charbono Point
San Diego, CA  92131

Frank, Andrew

2901 Buena Vista Way
Berkeley, CA  94708
(415) 841-5319

| | |
|---|---|
| Frazelle, Kenneth | 155 Piedmont Avenue<br>Winston-Salem, NC  27101<br>(919) 723-6867 |
| Fredrickson, Thomas | University of Illinois<br>School of Music<br>1114 West Nevada Street<br>Urbana, IL  61801<br>(217) 333-2620 |
| Freund, Don | 5295 Keatswood Circle<br>Memphis, TN  38119<br>(901) 685-7448 |
| Fussell, Charles | 1530 Beacon Street<br>Apt. 302<br>Brookline, MA  02146<br>(617) 396-6223 |
| Gaburo, Kenneth | 648 South Lucas<br>Iowa City, IA  52240<br>(319) 338-9908 |
| Gannon, Lee | 628 Fatherland Street<br>Nashville, TN  37206<br>(615) 255-4151 |
| Gelt, Andrew | 1935 Rodman Street<br>Apt. Rear West<br>Hollywood, FL  33020-6039<br>(305) 922-4358 |
| George, Thom Ritter | Idaho State University<br>Department of Music<br>Campus Box 8099<br>Pocatello, ID  83209-8099<br>(208) 234-4922 |
| Gimbel, Allen | Lawrence University<br>Department of Music<br>Appleton, WI  54912 |
| Goldstein, Malcolm | P.O. Box 134<br>Sheffield, VT  05866 |
| Gooch, Warren | 56 Doyle Way<br>Kirksville, MO  63501<br>(816) 627-0215 |

| | |
|---|---|
| Gottschalk, Arthur | Rice University<br>School of Music<br>Houston, TX  77251-1892<br>(713) 527-4854 |
| Grant, James | Middlebury College<br>Department of Music<br>Middlebury, VT  05753 |
| Grantham, Donald | 2700 Clarkdale Lane<br>Austin, TX  78758<br>(512) 451-0779 |
| Gryc, Stephen | 19 Tanglewood Road<br>Farmington, CT  06032<br>(203) 674-1168 |
| Hailstork, Adolphus | 521 Berry Pick Lane<br>Virginia Beach, VA<br>(804) 499-6709 |
| Haimo, Ethan | University of Notre Dame<br>Department of Music<br>Notre Dame, IN  46556 |
| Handel, Darrell | 431 Wood Avenue<br>Cincinnati, OH  45220<br>(513) 221-8160 |
| Hannay, Roger | 609 Morgan Creek Road<br>Chapel Hill, NC  27514<br>(919) 929-2718 |
| Harrison, Lou | 7121 Viewpoint Road<br>Aptos, CA  95003<br>(408) 688-5005 |
| Hennagin, Michael | P.O. Box 2844<br>Norman, OK  73070<br>(405) 360-5911 |
| Herman, Martin | 3231 Gondar Avenue<br>Long Beach, CA  90808 |
| Hervig, Richard | The Juilliard School<br>Lincoln Center<br>New York, NY  10023<br>(212) 799-5000 |

Hill, Jackson

Bucknell University
College of Arts and Sciences
Lewisburg, PA  17837
(717) 524-1216

Hoag, Charles

511 Boulder Street
Lawrence, KS  66049
(913) 842-9914

Hoffman, Richard

Oberlin College
Conservatory of Music
Department of Music Theory
Oberlin, OH  44074-1588
(216) 775-8200

Holt, Darrell

Stephen F. Austin
State University
Department of Music
P.O. Box 13043, SFA Station
Nacogdoches, TX  75962
(409) 568-4602

Hopkins, James

165 Linda Vista Avenue
Pasadena, CA  91105-1231
(818) 792-8414

Huggler, John

2199 South Broadway
Grand Junction, CO  81503
(303) 245-5462

Husa, Karel

1032 Hanshaw Road
Ithaca, NY  14850
(607) 257-7018

Iannaccone, Anthony

521 Kewanee
Ypsilanti, MI  48197
(313) 482-2394

Imbrie, Andrew

2625 Rose Street
Berkeley, CA  94708

Jager, Robert

615 Laurel Circle
Cookeville, TN  38501
(615) 528-3161

Janson, Thomas

Kent State University
School of Music
Kent, OH  44242-0001
(216) 672-2172

Jenni, Donald Martin   University of Iowa
School of Music
Iowa City, IA 52242
(319) 335-1603

Keats, Donald   9261 East Berry Avenue
Englewood, CO 80111
(303) 779-1297

Kechley, David   69 Lindley Terrace
Williamstown, MA 01267
(413) 458-2431

Kessner, Daniel   10955 Cozycroft Avenue
Chatsworth, CA 91311
(818) 709-8534

Kirk, Theron   2502 Old Brook Lane
San Antonio, TX 78230
(512) 344-2507

Knox, Charles   482 Page Avenue NE
Atlanta, GA 30307
(404) 658-3676

Koch, Frederick   38 Barrow Street
Apt. 4-F
New York, NY 10014
(212) 989-2156

Kogan, Robert   2784 Bedford Avenue
Brooklyn, NY 11210
(718) 434-3043

Korte, Karl   1401 The High Road
Austin, TX 78746
(512) 327-0970

Krenek, Ernst   c/o European American Music

Kroeger, Karl   9260 Newton Street
Westminster, CO 80030
(303) 428-5683

Kurek, Michael   Vanderbilt University
Blair School of Music
Nashville, TN 37212
(615) 322-7311

Larocca, Frank              409 De Leon Avenue
                            Fremont, CA   94539
                            (415) 657-2138

Laufer, Beatrice            P.O. Box 3
                            Lenox Hill Station
                            New York, NY   10021
                            (212) 988-1378

Lavenda, Richard            4706 Kingfisher
                            Houston, TX   77035
                            (713) 728-8528

Lesemann, Frederick         2342 Panorama Drive
                            La Crescenta, CA   91214
                            (818) 957-2061

Lewin, David                Harvard University
                            Department of Music
                            Cambridge, MA   02138
                            (617) 495-2791

Lockwood, Normand           P.O. Box 10053
                            University Park Station
                            Denver, CO   80250

London, Edwin               Cleveland State University
                            Department of Music
                            1983 East 24th Street
                            Cleveland, OH   44115
                            (216) 687-2033

Lubet, Alex                 University of Minnesota
                            Twin Cities Campus
                            School of Music
                            100 Ferguson Hall
                            2106 4th Street South
                            Minneapolis, MN   55455
                            (612) 624-5093

Luke, Ray                   6017 Glencove Place
                            Oklahoma City, OK   73132
                            (405) 721-5586

Mailman, Martin             University of North Texas
                            School of Music
                            Denton, TX   76203-3887
                            (817) 565-2791

| | |
|---|---|
| Mandelbaum, Joel | 39-49 46th Street<br>Sunnyside, NY  11104<br>(718) 361-8154 |
| Mayer, William | 15 Gramercy Park South<br>New York, NY  10003<br>(212) 533-7974 |
| McBeth, William F. | Ouachita University<br>Box 3665<br>Arkadelphia, AR  71923 |
| McCulloh, Byron | 1306 Penn Avenue<br>Pittsburgh, PA  15221<br>(412) 371-3880 |
| McKay, Neil | 3310 Keahi Street<br>Honolulu, HI  96822<br>(808) 988-3700 |
| McVoy, James | West Chester<br>State University<br>Department of Music Theory<br>West Chester, PA  19383 |
| Mekeel, Joyce | 29 Aldrich Road<br>Watertown, MA  02172<br>(617) 923-9281 |
| Miller, Dennis | Northeastern University<br>Department of Music<br>Boston, MA  02115<br>(617) 437-2440 |
| Moevs, Robert | Blackwell's Mills<br>Belle Mead, NJ  08502<br>(908) 359-6776 |
| Moryl, Richard | Route 67<br>Roxbury, CT  06783 |
| Murray, J.D. Bain | 2371 Edgerton Road<br>University Hts., OH  44118<br>(216) 321-5821 |
| Nelhybel, Vaclav | 21 Hi Barlow Road<br>Newton, CT  06470 |
| Nelson, Bradley | 1321 Pillsbury Lane<br>El Cajon, CA  92020-1726 |

Nelson, Ron

Brown University
Music Box 1924
Orwig Building
One Young Orchard Avenue
Providence, RI   02912-1924
(401) 863-3234

Nixon, Roger

2090 New Brunswick Drive
San Mateo, CA  94402
(415) 341-8145

O'Brien, Eugene

3424 Ashwood Drive
Bloomington, IN  47401
(812) 336-4904

Packales, Joseph

University of Texas
Department of Music
El Paso, TX  79968
(915) 747-5606

Palmer, Robert

108 Valley Road
Ithaca, NY  14850
(607) 272-7248

Panerio, Robert, Sr.

Central Washington
University
Department of Music
Ellensburg, WA  98926

Parker, Alice Stuart

801 West End Avenue
No. 9-D
New York, NY  10025
(212) 663-1165

Patterson, David

University of Massachusetts
Harbor Campus
Boston, MA  02125-3393

Peaslee, Richard

90 Riverside Drive
New York, NY  10024
(212) 724-9278

Pellegrini, Ernesto

603 Alden Road
Muncie, IN  47304
(317) 288-3166

Penn, William

114 Dunham Pond Road
Storrs, CT  06268
(203) 429-7009

Perera, Ronald

30 Lyman Road
Northampton, MA   01060
(413) 586-2970

Peterson, Wayne

810 Gonzalez Drive
No. 12-L
San Francisco, CA   94132
(415) 587-4326

Pinkston, Russell

University of Texas
Department of Music
Austin, TX   78712
(512) 471-7764

Plain, Gerald

30 Doncaster Road
Rochester, NY   14623
(716) 475-1453

Polin, Claire

Rutgers University
Department of Music
Camden College of Arts
and Sciences
Camden, NJ   08102

Polster, Ian

2003 Timberline Trail
Springfield, OH   45503
(513) 399-6775

Pozdro, John

University of Kansas
School of Fine Arts
Department of Music
and Dance
452 Murphy Hall
Lawrence, KS   66045-2279
(913) 864-3436

Primosch, James

7710 Penrose Avenue
Elkins Park, PA   19117
(215) 887-4255

Rackley, Lawrence

440 North Arlington
Kalamazoo, MI   49007
(616) 381-4648

Rakowski, David

2 Shore Drive
Spencer, MA   01562
(508) 885-7434

Raksin, David                    University of
                                 Southern California
                                 School of Music
                                 Los Angeles, CA   90089-0851
                                 (213) 740-3123

Ramey, Phillip                   825 West End Avenue
                                 New York, NY   10025

Read, Gardner                    47 Forster Road
                                 Manchester, MA   01944

Reed, Herbert Owen               7805 West Lake Drive
                                 Stanwood, MI   49346
                                 (616) 972-8765

Rhodes, Phillip                  32925 Ensley Avenue
                                 Northfield, MN   55057

Rice, Thomas                     2352 Windway Lane   No. 102
                                 Virginia Beach, VA   23455
                                 (804) 464-0996

Rickley, James                   (215) 635-5945

Rinehart, John                   405 West South College
                                 Yellow Springs, OH   45387
                                 (513) 767-2364

Rivers, Joseph                   University of Tulsa
                                 College of Arts and Sciences
                                 Department of Music
                                 600 South College Avenue
                                 Tulsa, OK   74104-3189
                                 (918) 592-6000

Roseman, Ronald                  156 West 86th Street
                                 New York, NY   10024
                                 (212) 724-0072

Rosen, Jerome                    502 12th Street
                                 Davis, CA   95616
                                 (916) 753-3786

Rosenboom, David                 California Institute
                                 of the Arts
                                 School of Music
                                 24700 McBean Parkway
                                 Valencia, CA   91355
                                 (805) 253-7818

| | |
|---|---|
| Ross, Walter | Route 6  Box 301<br>Charlottesville, VA  22901<br>(804) 293-9617 |
| Sandroff, Howard | 1008 Greenleaf Avenue<br>Wilmette, IL  60091<br>(312) 256-2787 |
| Sapp, Allen | 6871 Ken Arbre Drive<br>Cincinnati, OH  45236 |
| Saturen, David | 4283 Hilltop Place<br>Bethlehem, PA  18017<br>(215) 974-9385 |
| Saylor, Bruce | 318 West 85th Street<br>New York, NY  10024 |
| Schiff, David | Reed College<br>Department of Music<br>Portland, OR  97202<br>(503) 771-1112 |
| Schifrin, Lalo | Glendale Symphony Orchestra<br>401 North Brand Boulevard<br>Suite 520<br>Glendale, CA  91203<br>(213) 278-0733 |
| Schubel, Max | Box 604<br>Greenville, ME  04441 |
| Schwartz, Charles | 463 West Street<br>No. G 219<br>New York, NY  10014<br>(212) 691-1793 |
| Schwartz, Elliott | 5 Atwood Lane<br>Brunswick, ME  04011<br>(217) 725-2621 |
| Shapero, Harold | Brandeis University<br>Department of Music<br>Waltham, MA  02254<br>(617) 736-3311 |

Shapiro, Gerald            Brown University
                          Music Box 1924
                          Orwig Building
                          One Young Orchard Avenue
                          Providence, RI    02912-1924
                          (401) 863-3234

Sheinfeld, David          1458 24th Avenue
                          San Francisco, CA    94122
                          (415) 566-2902

Shinn, Randall            2105 West De Palma
                          Mesa, AZ    85202
                          (602) 834-6279

Smith, William O.         5607 16th Street NE
                          Seattle, WA    98105

Snyder, Randall           3140 Calvert
                          Lincoln, NE    68502

Sorce, Richard            297 Franklin Turnpike
                          Mahwah, NJ    07430
                          (201) 529-5057

Soule, Edmund             85897 Bailey Hill Road
                          Eugene, OR    97405

Spears, Jared             Arkansas State University
                          Department of Music
                          Box 2259
                          State Univ., AR    72467-0779

Spies, Claudio            Princeton University
                          Department of Music
                          Woolworth Center of
                          Musical Studies
                          Princeton, NJ    08544-1007
                          (609) 258-4241

Spratlan, Lewis           Amherst College
                          Department of Music
                          Amherst, MA    01002
                          (413) 542-2364

Stallings, Kendall        Webster University
                          Department of Music
                          470 East Lockwood
                          St. Louis, MO    63119
                          (314) 968-6900

Steinberg, Paul

State University of New York
Crane School of Music
Potsdam, NY   13676
(315) 265-4396

Steinohrt, William

Wright State University
Department of Music
Dayton, OH   45435
(513) 873-2346

Stern, Robert

University of Massachusetts
Fine Arts Center
Amherst, MA   01003
(413) 545-2227

Strandberg, Newton

Sam Houston State University
Music Department
Huntsville, TX   77341
(409) 295-2887

Strunk, Steven

1545 18th Street NW
No. 322
Washington, DC   20036
(202) 797-3666

Sullivan, Timothy

4245 East Avenue
Rochester, NY   14610
(716) 663-3678

Swafford, Jan

37 Magnolia Avenue
No. 1
Cambridge, MA   02138
(617) 876-8660

Swift, Richard

University of California
Department of Music
Davis, CA   95616
(916) 753-5719

Swisher, Gloria

7228 6th Avenue NW
Seattle, WA   98117
(206) 782-0549

Thomas, Marilyn Taft

913 Golfview Drive
McKeesport, PA   15135

Thome, Diane

3514 Northeast 187th Street
Seattle, WA   98155
(206) 365-2386

Ticheli, Frank            12474 Starcrest
                          No. 1315
                          San Antonio, TX    78216
                          (512) 496-3906

Toensing, Richard         2155 Topaz Drive
                          Boulder, CO    80304
                          (303) 449-1838

Townsend, Douglas         72-28 153rd Street
                          Flushing, NY    11367
                          (718) 793-9146

Trythall, Harry G.        41 West Main
                          Morgantown, WV    26505
                          (304) 292-6447

Vazzana, Anthony          1228 21st Street
                          Manhattan Beach, CA    90266
                          (213) 546-1816

Vega, Aurelio de la       California State University
                          Department of Music
                          18111 Nordhoff Street
                          Northridge, CA    91330
                          (818) 885-1200

Washburn, Robert          Route 4   Box 538
                          Parishville Road
                          Potsdam, NY    13676
                          (315) 265-6293

Waters, James L.          Kent State University
                          School of Music
                          Kent, OH    44242
                          (216) 672-2172

Weiner, Lawrence          Corpus Christi
                          State University
                          Department of Music
                          6300 Ocean Drive
                          Corpus Christi, TX    78412
                          (512) 994-2314

Westergaard, Peter        40 Pine Street
                          Princeton, NJ    08542

Wheelock, Donald          66 North Street
                          Whately, MA    01093
                          (413) 665-7632

White, Donald

312 Lookout Mountain Drive
Ellensburg, WA   98926
(509) 925-3734

Williams, David R.

273 Central Park West
Apt. 1
Memphis, TN   38111
(901) 323-8318

Williams, Edgar

The College of William
and Mary
Department of Music
Williamsburg, VA   23185
(804) 221-4000

Winkler, Peter

15 Bayview Avenue
East Setauket, NY   11733

Winslow, Walter

54 Humbert Street
Princeton, NJ   08542

Winteregg, Steven

117 Walden Farm Circle
Union, OH   45322
(513) 836-8593

Woodard, James

818 Randle Street
Edwardsville, IL   62025

Wright, Maurice

302 Hillside Avenue
Jenkintown, PA   19046
(215) 576-6363

Wyner, Yehudi

State University College
Department of Music
Purchase, NY   10577
(914) 253-5031

Yellin, Victor Fell

New York University
Department of Music
268 Waverly Building
New York, NY   10003
(212) 598-3431

Ziffrin, Marilyn

P.O. Box 179
Bradford, NH   03221
(603) 927-4994

BIBLIOGRAPHY

Ahouse, John B. and Kee DeBoer, ed. *Daniel Pinkham; A Bio-Bibliography*. Westport, CT: Greenwood Press, 1988.

*American Composers Alliance Catalogue of Contemporary Music; Choral and Stage Works.* New York: American Composers Edition, Inc., 1989.

*American Composers Alliance Catalogue of Contemporary Music; Orchestra, Band, and Electronic Music.* New York: American Composers Edition, Inc., 1989.

*The American Music Center Membership Directory, October 1990.* New York: The American Music Center, 1990.

Anderson, Ruth E., ed. *Contemporary American Composers; A Biographical Dictionary.* 2nd edition. Boston: G.K. Hall, 1982.

*ASCAP Symphonic Catalog.* 3rd edition. New York: R.R. Bowker, 1977.

*Association for the Promotion of New Music Catalog* New York: Gutenberg Printing, 1986.

Bailey, Nancy Gisbrecht and Walter B. Bailey. *Radie Britain; A Bio-Bibliography.* Westport, CT: Greenwood Press, 1990.

*BMI Symphonic Catalog.* New York: Broadcast Music, Inc., 1971.

*Bourne Music Catalog 1989.* New York: Bourne Music Publishers, 1989.

Bowles, Garrett H. *Ernst Krenek; A Bio-Bibliography.* Westport, CT: Greenwood Press, 1989.

*Carl Fischer Rental Catalogue of Standard and Contemporary Works.* New York: Carl Fischer, Inc., 1978.

Carnovale, Norbert. *Gunther Schuller;
A Bio-Bibliography.* Westport, CT:
Greenwood Press, 1987.

*Catalog of the American Music Center Library;
Music for Orchestra, Band, and Large Ensemble,
vol. 3.* New York: The American Music Center,
1982. *Supplement Number One, 1990.*

*Contemporary Music Catalogue 1990.* New York:
C.F. Peters Corporation, 1990.

*Directory of Music Faculties in Colleges and
Universities, United States and Canada,
1990-1992.* Boulder, CO: The College Music
Society, 1991.

*The Edwin A. Fleisher Collection of Orchestral
Music in the Free Library of Philadelphia; a
cumulative catalog, 1929-1977.* Boston: G.K.
Hall, 1979.

*European American Music Corporation Performance
Catalog.* Valley Forge, PA: European American
Music Corp., 1988.

Farish, Margaret K., ed. *Orchestral Music in
Print.* Philadelphia: Musicdata, Inc., 1979.

Ferencz, George J. *Robert Russell Bennett;
A Bio-Bibliography.* Westport, CT:
Greenwood Press, 1990.

*Galaxy-Highgate Orchestral Catalog.*
New York: Galaxy Music Corporation, 1987.

Henessee, Don A. *Samuel Barber;
A Bio-Bibliography.* Westport, CT:
Greenwood Press, 1985.

Hitchcock, H. Wiley and Stanley Sadie, eds.
*The New Grove Dictionary of American Music,
vols. I-IV.* New York: Macmillan Press Limited,
1986.

Hitchens, Susan Hayes. *Karel Husa;
A Bio-Bibliography.* Westport, CT:
Greenwood Press, 1991.

Howard, Richard.   *The Works of Alan Hovhaness;*
*A Catalog:  Opus 1 - Opus 360.*   White Plains, NY:
Music Resources, Inc., 1983.

*Jerona Music Corporation Master Catalogue,*
*A complete listing of all music published or*
*distributed by Jerona Music Corporation.*
Hackensack, NJ:   Jerona Music Corporation, 1987.

Kreitner, Kenneth.   *Robert Ward;*
*A Bio-Bibliography.*   Westport, CT:
Greenwood Press, 1988.

Lichtenwanger, William.   *The Music of Henry*
*Cowell; A Descriptive Catalogue.*   Brooklyn, NY:
Institute for Studies in American Music, 1986.

*Margun Music Complete Catalog.*   Newton Centre, MA:
Margun Music, Inc., 1990.

*MCA Symphonic/Rental Catalog.*   New York:
MCA Music, 1982.

McDonald, Arlys L.   *Ned Rorem; A Bio-Bibliography.*
Westport, CT:   Greenwood Press, 1989.

Meckna, Michael.   *Virgil Thomson;*
*A Bio-Bibliography.*   Westport, CT:
Greenwood Press, 1986.

*MJQ Catalog of Music.*
New York:   MJQ Music, Inc., 1983.

*Music for Hire; A catalog of publications*
*available on hire from Chester Music, G. Schirmer,*
*Associated Music Publishers, Edition Wilhelm*
*Hansen, Union Musical Ediciones, and Associated*
*Music Sales companies.*   Compiled by Joan Redding.
Tiptree, England:   Courier International Limited,
1990.

*Music for Orchestra; A Reference Catalog.*
New York:   Broude Brothers Limited, 1986.

*The Music of David Van Vactor; A Catalog.*
New York:   Roger Rhodes Music, Ltd., 1977.

Patterson, Donald L. and Janet L. Patterson.
*Vincent Persichetti; A Bio-Bibliography.*
Westport, CT:   Greenwood Press, 1988.

*Peer-Southern Concert Music; Rental Catalog.*
New York:   Peer International Corporation, 1989.

Perone, Karen L.   *Lukas Foss; A Bio-Bibliography.*
Westport, CT:   Greenwood Press, 1991.

*Rental Library of Orchestral and Instrumental
Music held by Theodore Presser, Elkan-Vogel,
and their affiliated agencies.*   Bryn Mawr, PA:
Theodore Presser, 1984.

*Repertoire Guide of the National Orchestral
Association's New Music Orchestral Project.*
New York:   National Orchestral Association, 1991.

*G. Schirmer and Associated Music Publishers;
Rental and Performance Catalog,* prepared by
Margaret Ross Griffel.   New York:
G. Schirmer, 1987.

*Schott Orchesterkatalog '83.*   Mainz, Germany:
B. Schott's Sohne, 1983.

*Smith Publications 1992 Catalog of Music.*
Baltimore, MD:   Smith Publications, 1991.

*Universal Edition Concert Catalog.*
Vienna:   Universal Edition A.G., 1985.

## ABOUT THE AUTHOR

Richard Koshgarian is a graduate of Rhode Island College. He earned two Master of Music degrees from the University of Michigan and the Doctor of Musical Arts degree from the University of Iowa. He has held conducting positions with the National Orchestral Association of New York, the University of Michigan, Western Carolina University, Rhode Island College, and Fort Hays State University in Kansas. He has studied conducting with Gustav Meier at the University of Michigan and James Dixon at the University of Iowa. He is currently Director of Development for the Salina Symphony in Salina, Kansas and teaches music at Sacred Heart Junior/Senior High School.